Top CAT

15 $\frac{1}{4}$ 2 $\frac{1}{2}$+

SHAPING SURF HISTORY

SHAPING SURF HISTORY

TOM CURREN AL MERRICK CALIFORNIA 1980–1983

JIMMY METYKO

RIZZOLI NEW YORK

New York · Paris · London · Milan

This book is dedicated to my friend Willy Morris and to all who appear in this book who have passed before us.

Willy was such a big part of this time period for me. The entire Morris family treated me as one of their own.

Countless days of great surf together, from Malibu to Rincon.

No one was better to chase waves and shoot with because Willy loved surfing—the sport and the culture—more than anyone.

You are missed, old friend.

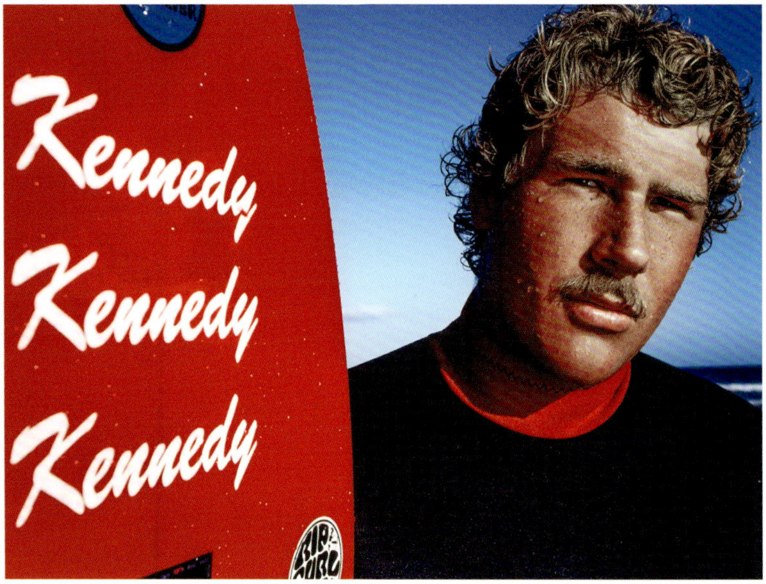

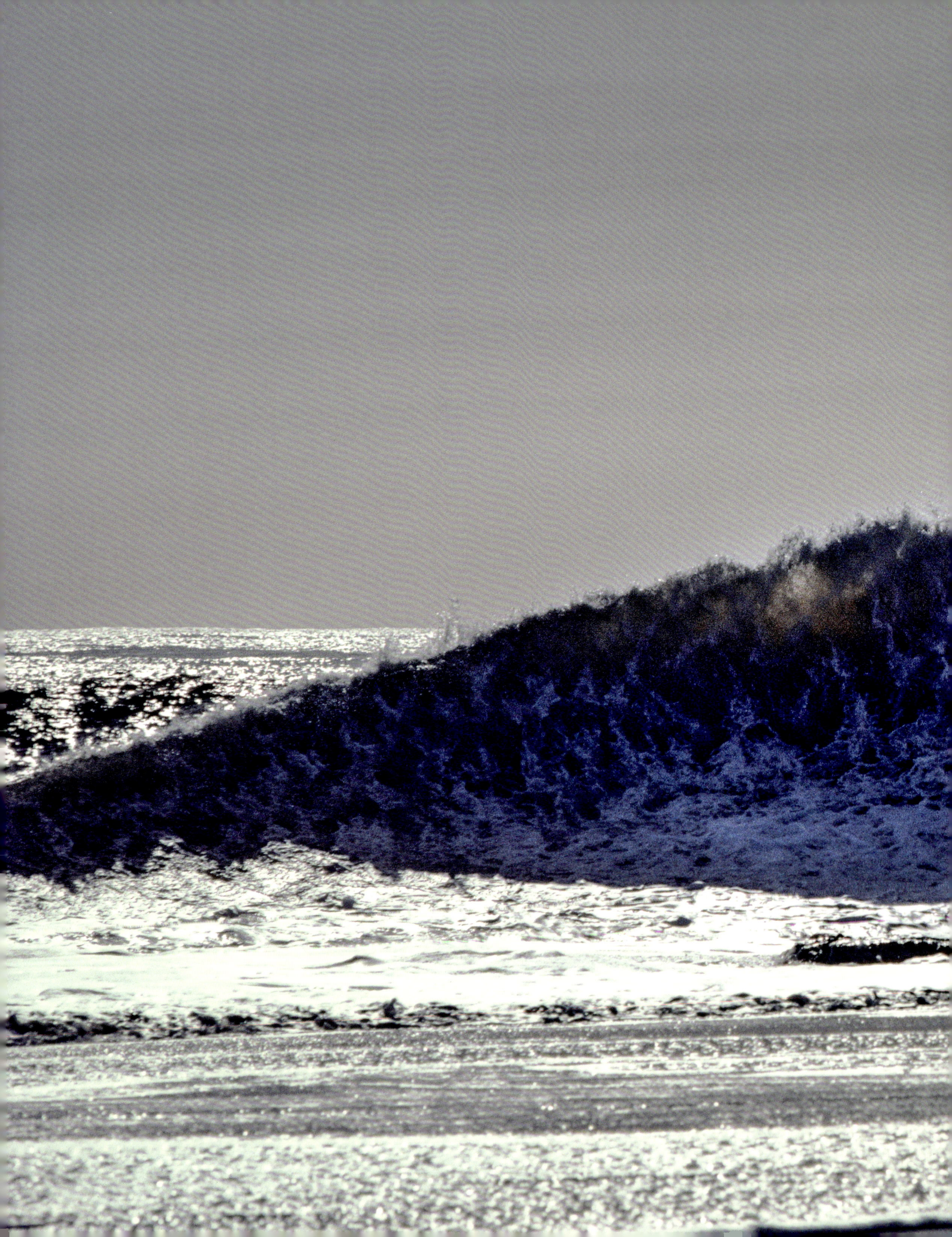

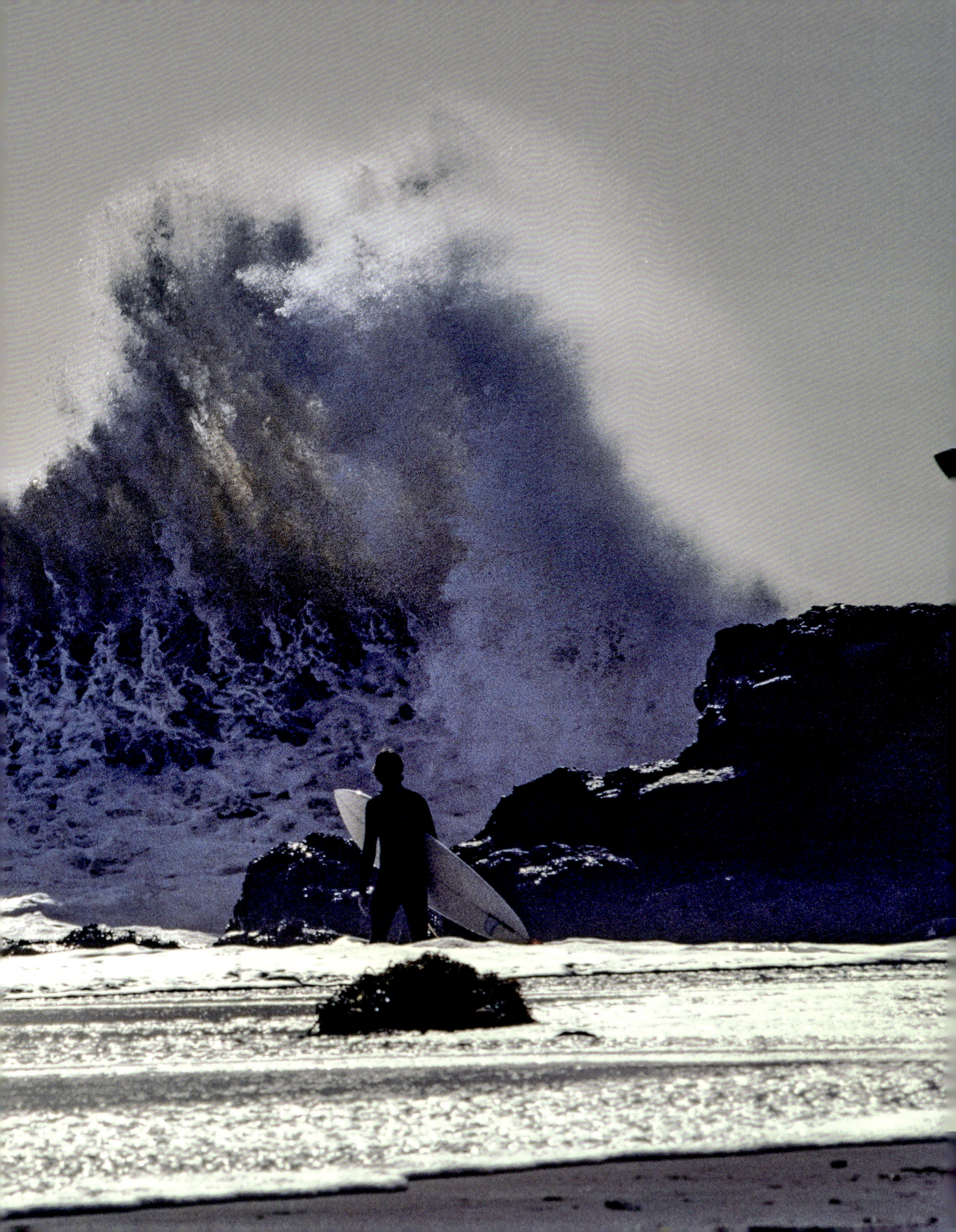

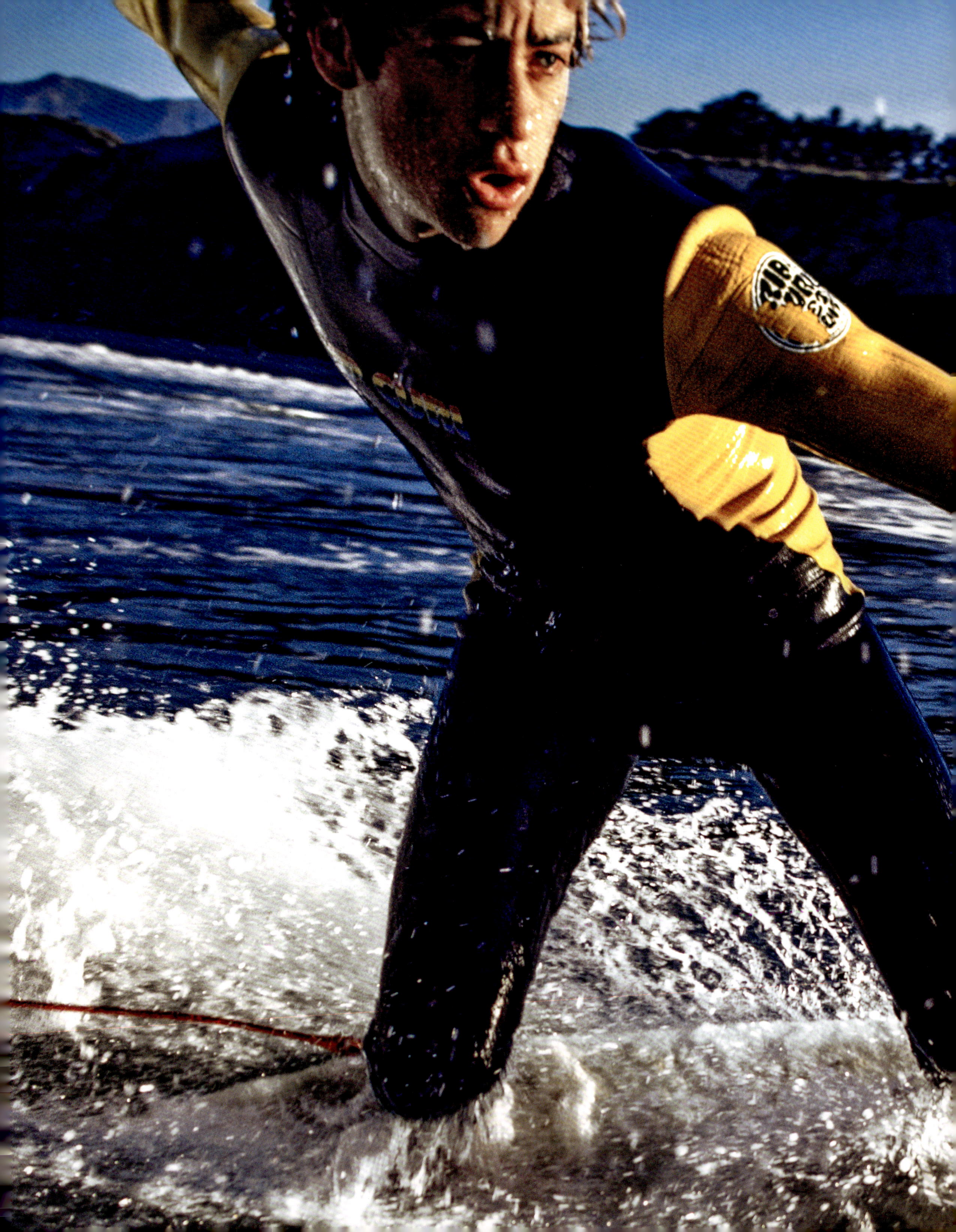

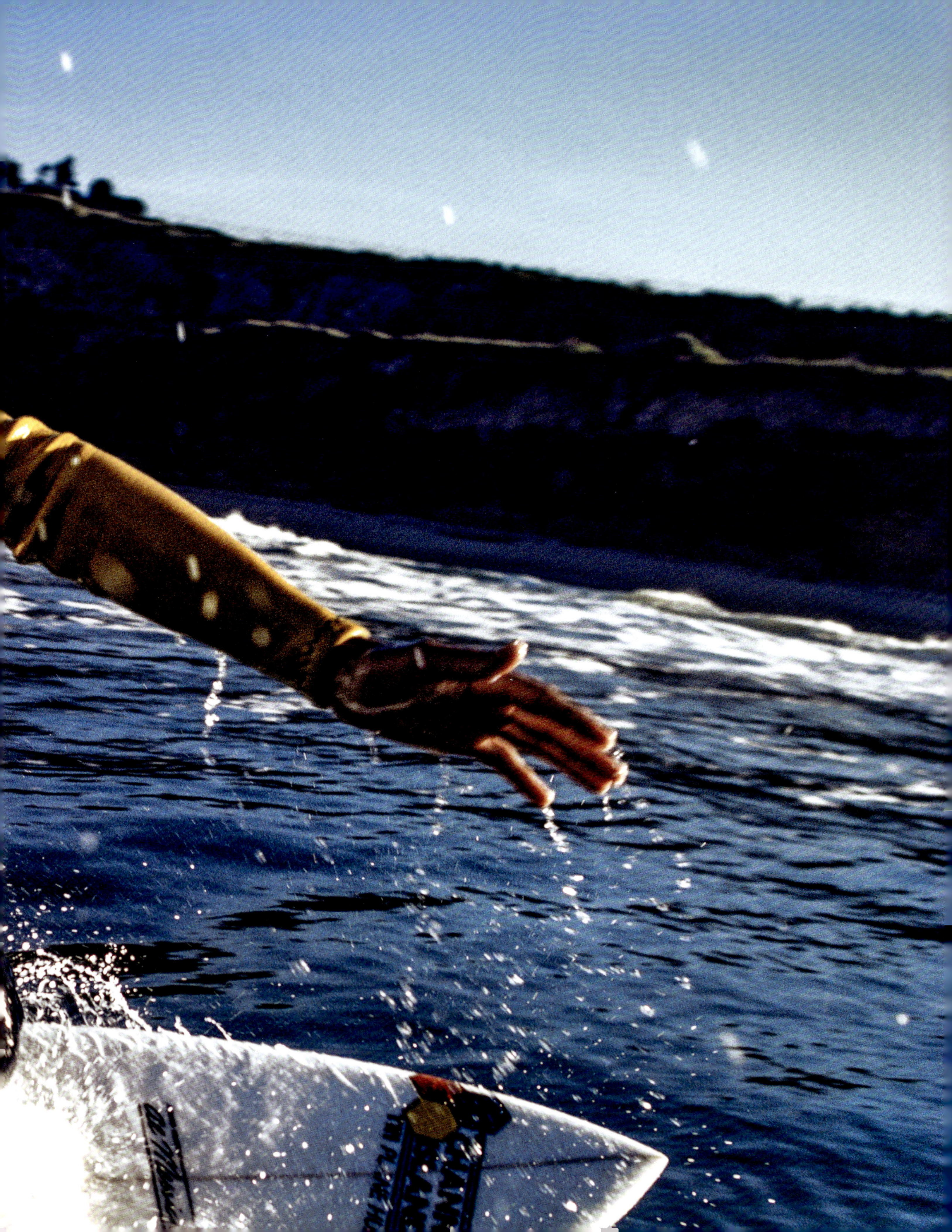

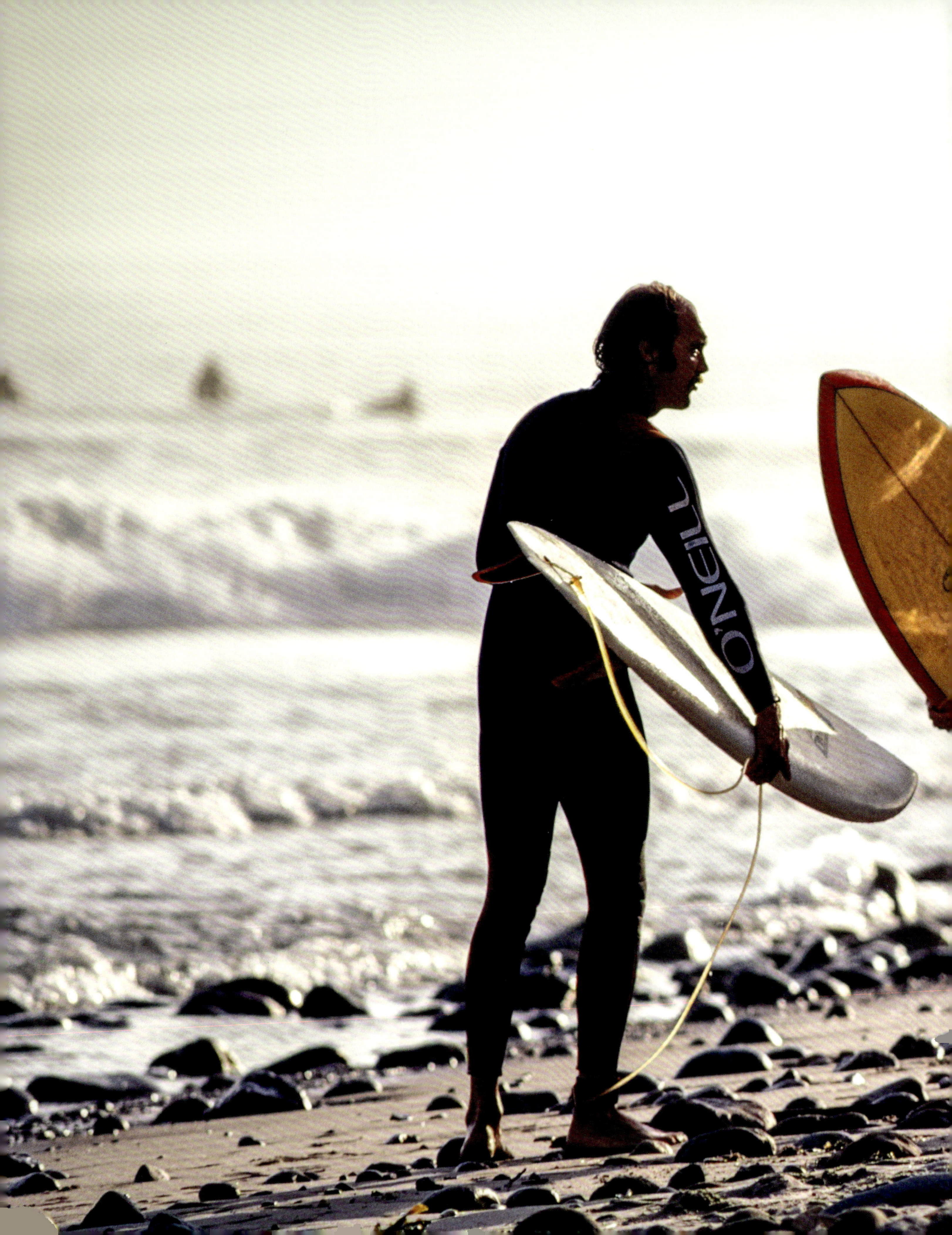
O'NEILL

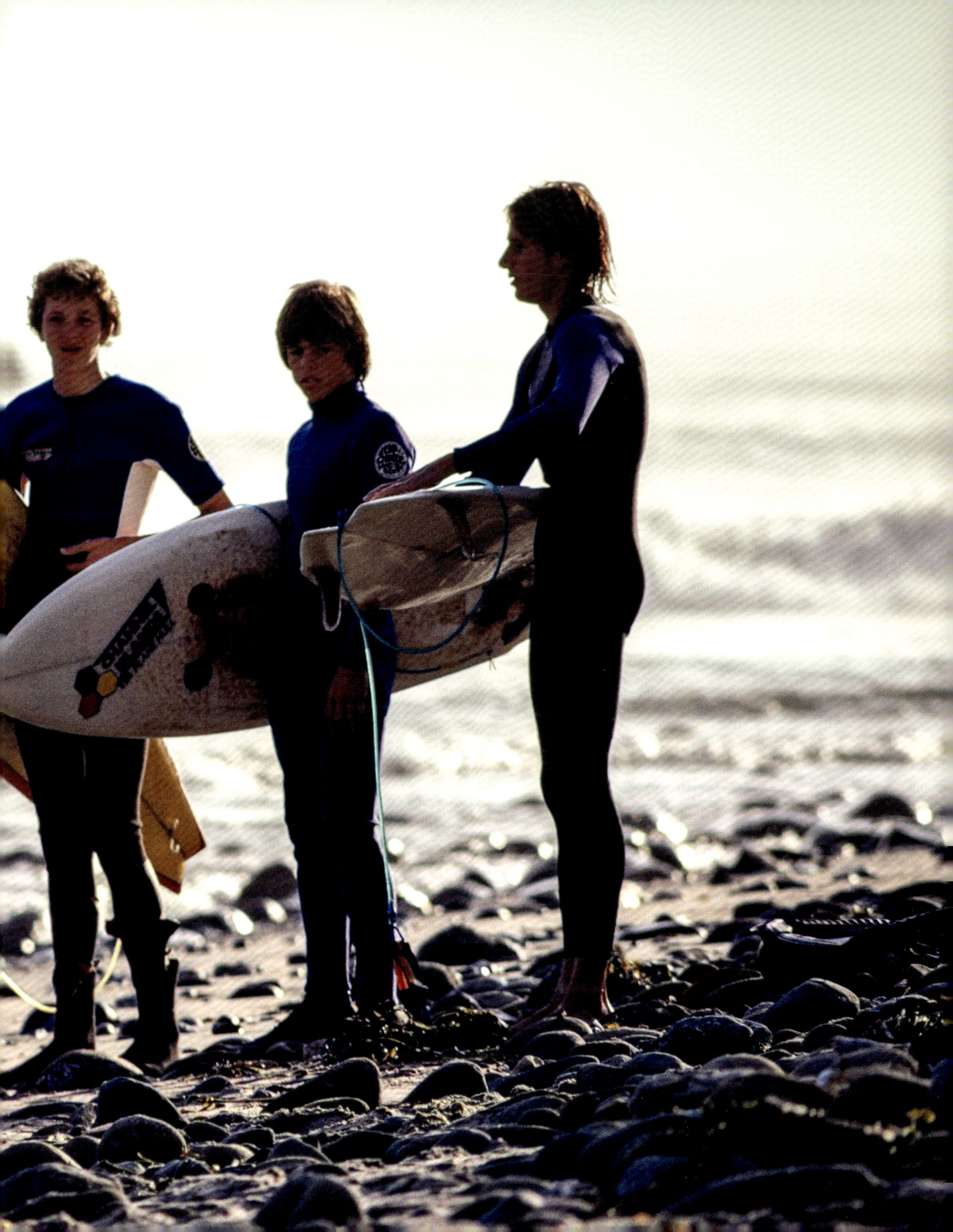

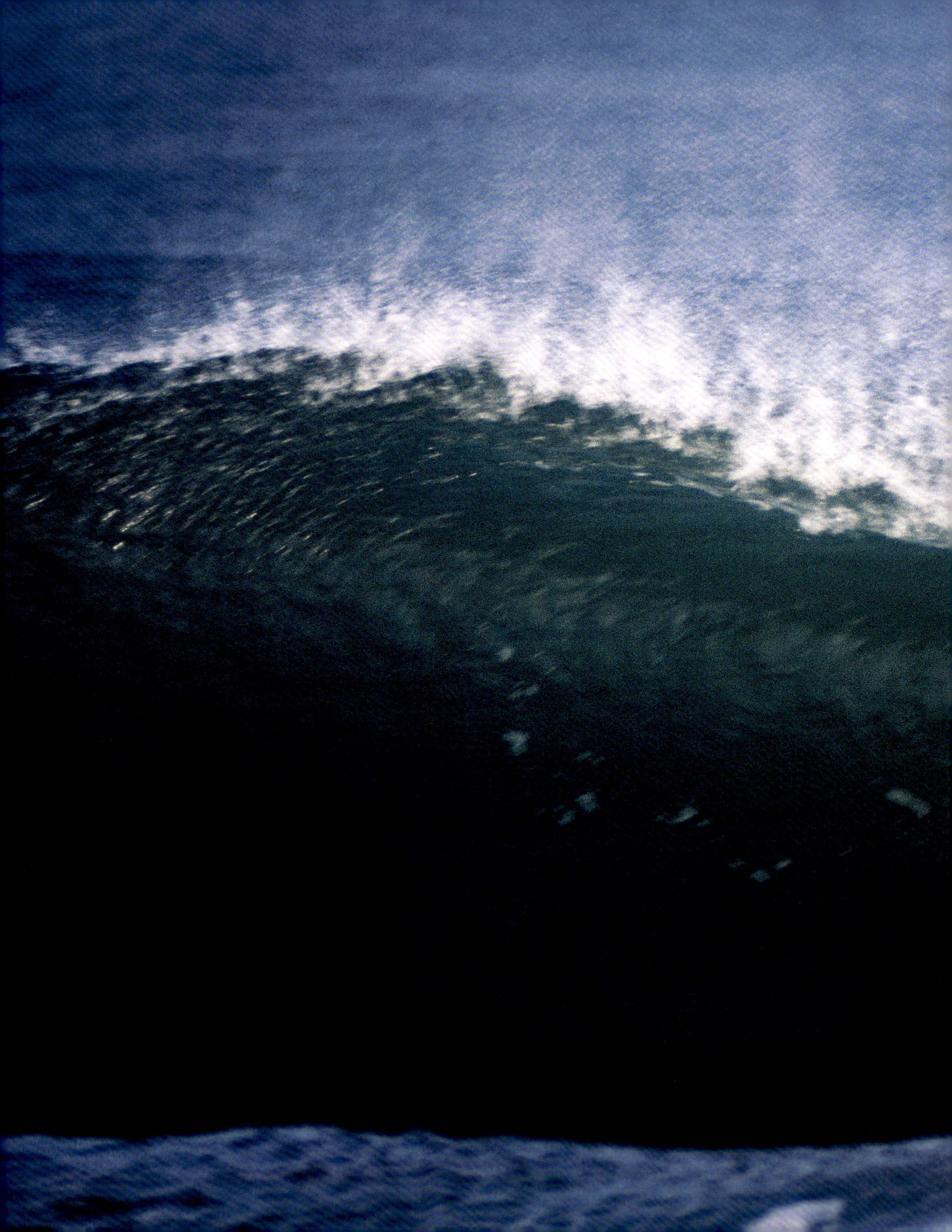

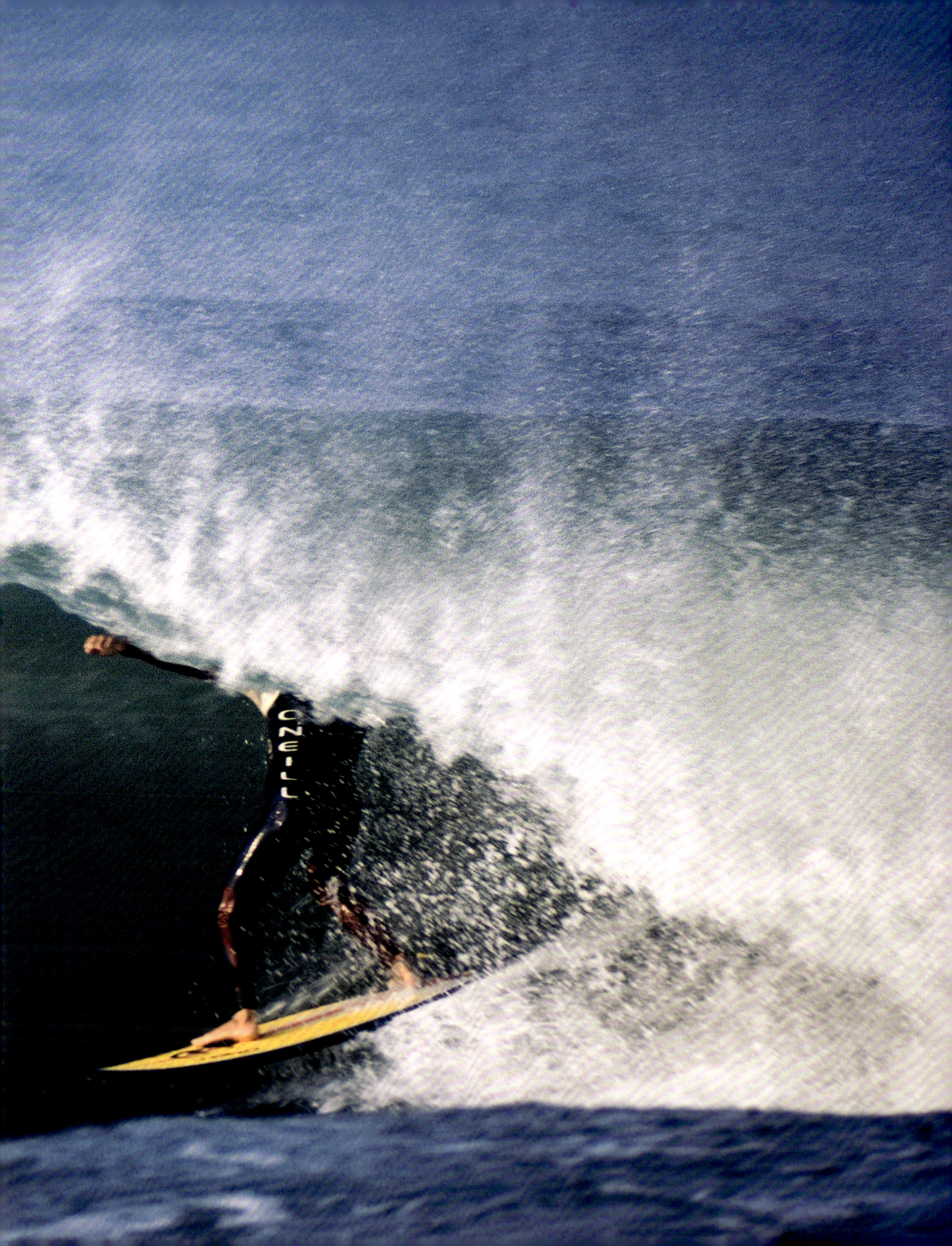
ONEILL

First published in the United States of America
in 2023
by Rizzoli International Publications, Inc.
300 Park Avenue South
New York, NY 10010
www.rizzoliusa.com

Publisher: Charles Miers
Author: Jimmy Metyko
Editorial Direction: Martynka Wawrzyniak
Writers: Sam George, Jamie Brisick,
Tom Curren
Designer: Jim Newitt
Copy Editor: Kim Stravers
Proofreader: Sarah Stump
Production Manager: Colin Hough Trapp
Managing Editor: Lynn Scrabis

2023 2024 2025 2026/ 10 9 8 7 6 5 4 3 2 1

Distributed in the U.S. trade by Random House,
New York

Printed in China

ISBN: 9780847873562

Library of Congress Control Number:
2023934200

Visit us online:
Facebook.com/RizzoliNewYork
Twitter: @Rizzoli_Books
Instagram.com/RizzoliBooks
Pinterest.com/RizzoliBooks
Youtube.com/user/RizzoliNY
Issuu.com/Rizzoli

Pages 6–7: Sandspit, Santa Barbara Harbor break wall, El Niño 1983. Lone surfer frozen in time.

Pages 8–9: A young Tommy Curren, 1981, up close. It was the twin-fin, specifically the Channel Islands Tri-Plane Hull Twin, that Tommy was riding when we first started shooting.

Pages 10–11: Al Merrick, "The Professor" with his students in 1980, a time of radical transition. Three Tri-Plane Hull Twins and one 1979 Al Merrick winged swallow tail. *(Left to right)* Al Merrick, Tommy Hassenbien, Billy Deardorff, and Alexis Usher.

Pages 12–13: Shaun Tomson, 1983. I could not believe my luck to have a surfer of Shaun's caliber in Santa Barbara through the early '80s.

Page 303: Leaving the past behind, Al Merrick, Davey Smith, and Matt George head back up Rincon Point for one more.

Page 304: Heading out to shoot. Photo by Sam George.

FOREWORD

SAM GEORGE

It could have happened somewhere else, at some other time, in some other waves, and have been chronicled by some other photographer. But it didn't. And it wasn't. When in late December 1979 nineteen-year-old Jimmy Metyko walked into the venerable Santa Barbara surf shop where my brother Matt and I happened to be employed, we weren't quite sure what to make of him. Modest and almost excessively polite by the standards of more typical surf-shop customers, in a soft drawl he introduced himself as a friend of a group of Texas surfers we'd encountered on a recent trip to the British Virgin Islands, subtly dropping their names as if to establish his bona fides. He might have needed to: upon first glance, Jimmy, wearing tassel loafers and pants with an actual belt, didn't look much like a surfer to us, at least not of the sort we appeared to be, with our sun-bleached hair, scruffy flip-flops, and weird wetsuit tans. How could we have known, on that first day, that not only was he a lifelong, very accomplished surfer, but also a gifted photographer, and that with this combination of attributes he was destined to change our two lives as well as to have a direct hand in shaping one of the most fertile, influential periods in modern surf history?

If Jimmy was an unlikely disrupter, then Santa Barbara, California, was just as unlikely a place for a major paradigm shift to occur. With the exception of a brief period of influence during the late 1960s—when, during the surfboard-design tumult known as "The Shortboard Revolution," Santa Barbara's fabulous winter waves provided the medium necessary to validate innovation that saw board lengths drop from nine feet to seven virtually overnight—the region's relatively inconsistent surf kept it from maintaining a progressive aesthetic. By the 1980s, in comparison to hotbeds like Santa Cruz to the north and LA's South Bay, Orange County, and San Diego to the south, Santa Barbara was considered a backwater, populated by reactionary surfers who assiduously eschewed current trends of design and technique in favor of a rigidly self-imposed pause on the timeline, dismissing any more contemporary, demonstrative display of expertise as vanity—even worse, uncool.

This, then, was the scene that Jimmy Metyko stepped into soon after his arrival in Santa Barbara, when between (and often during) classes at the prestigious Brooks Institute of Photography he found himself drawn into a tight circle of ambitious surfers who sought to flow against the region's aesthetic tide. Most prominently there was young Tommy Curren, a preternaturally talented US amateur champion in the Under-14 Boys division. Tommy, unlike so many of his older friends, with their old-fashioned beaver-tail wetsuits and circa-'72 surfboard designs, looked to the nascent professional-surfing competition scene and, most notably, what was happening in Australia for inspiration. Tommy had recently begun riding boards designed and shaped by Al Merrick, a thirty-six-year-old board builder who previously had been a paragon of Santa Barbara soul surfing, crafting sleek sleds for fellow Rincon riders under his Channel Islands label. To accommodate Tommy's competitive ascent, however, Al began adapting the highly maneuverable boards being ridden by top Australian and Hawaiian pros to fit Tommy's innate ability to seamlessly link maneuvers at high speed, the result being a much more refined version of the contemporary performance

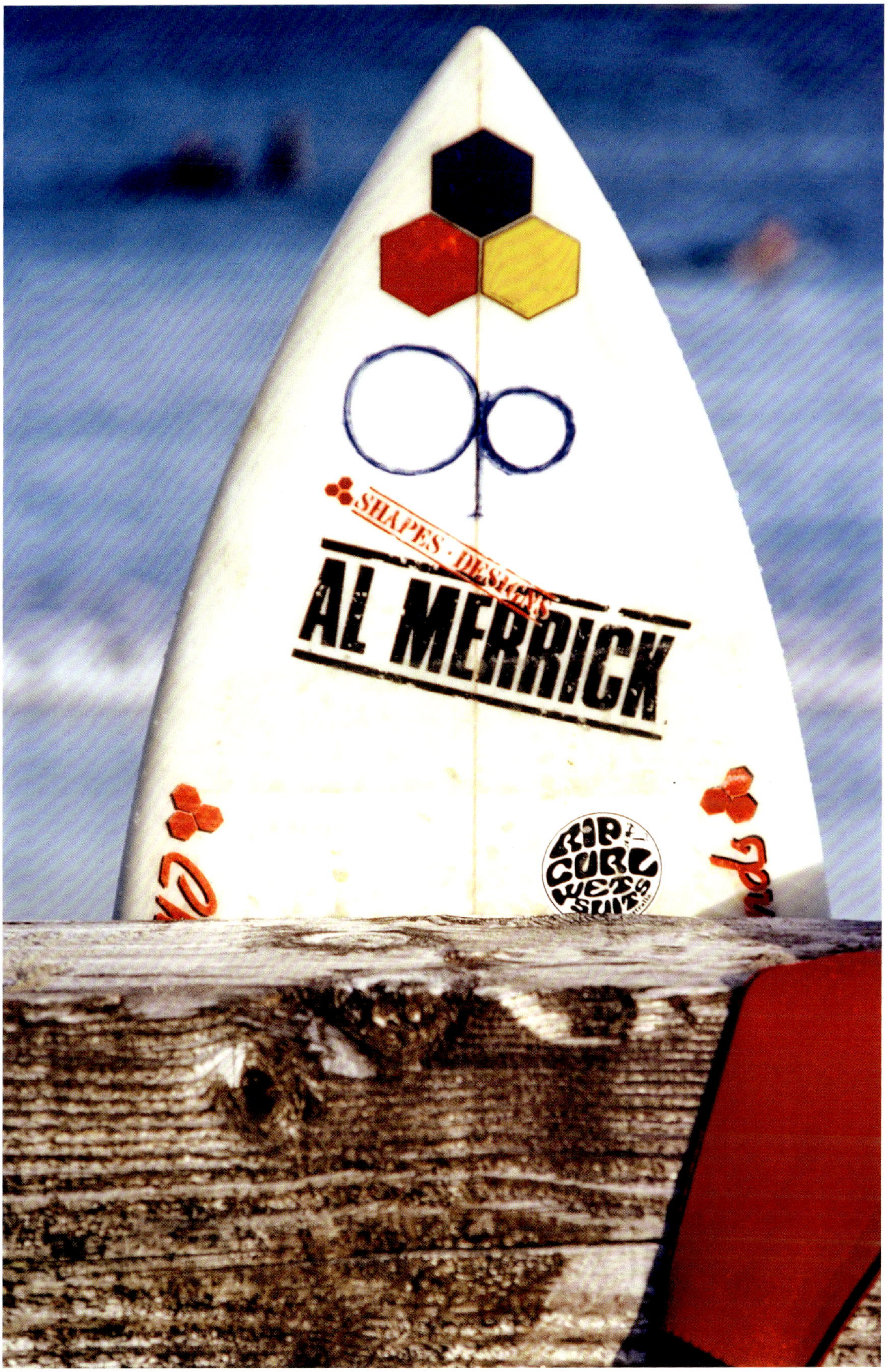
SHAPES · DESIGNS
AL MERRICK

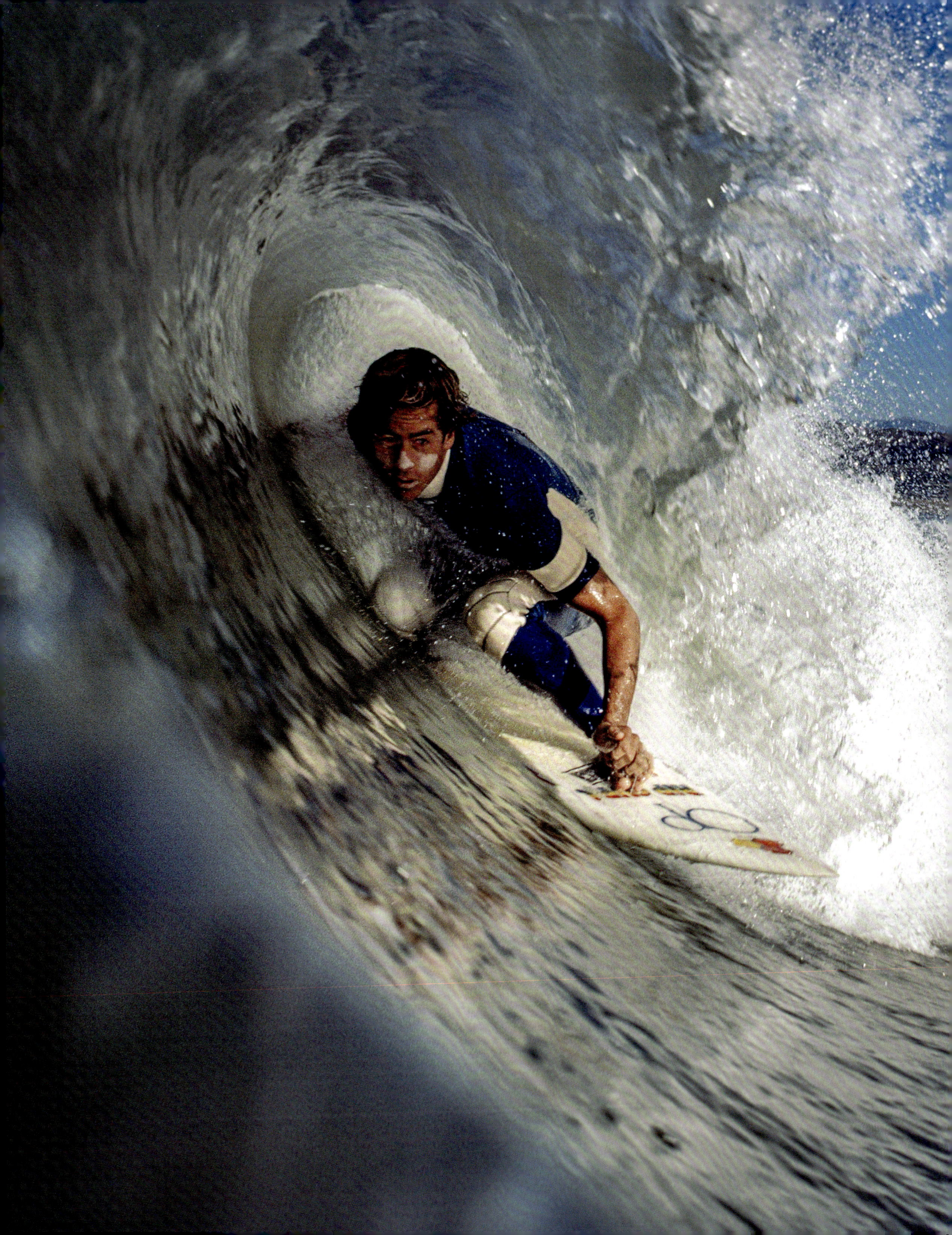

surfboard. These caught the eye of 1977 world champion Shaun Tomson, who, having recently moved to Santa Barbara from South Africa, and no doubt having noted Curren's progress through the amateur ranks, turned to Al for equipment—a big deal, considering Shaun's surf-star status. Meanwhile, my brother Matt and I, both of us also riding Merrick's boards, were fledgling competitors on the international pro tour, while red-hot CI team rider Davey Smith lit up every local lineup he graced with his aggressive flair. Underneath this action was a lively strata of middle school and high school freshmen grommets, including future women's world champion Kim Mearig, who, with Tommy as role model (and with typical contrarian teen spirit), longed to push against the Santa Barbara surfing establishment. The stage was set for this small subset of local surfers to make a big statement on the state of the art. And we might have, except for one missing detail: nobody in the wider surfing world had any idea what was happening in Santa Barbara. In fact, without context, neither did we.

Jimmy Metyko changed all that. Not merely by photographing Santa Barbara surfing—local lensmen Steve Bissell and Don Balch had been providing beautiful images of the area's elusive waves for years. But by focusing his lens almost exclusively on this New Thing, Jimmy not only presented the rest of the world with its first look, but also, by holding up a mirror to our involvement, helped define it, and in doing so articulated the identity of so many of us determined to make names for ourselves outside the 805 area code.

Now if these were the only ripples caused when Jimmy dropped into our pond—like a talented wedding photographer, capable with lenses, filters, and forced perspectives that made his subjects look fantastic on their special days—well, that probably would've been good enough. Yet Jimmy's chronicling of what he saw happening with the Channel Islands crew had a much farther-reaching impact. Consider how provincial California surfing was in 1980, with factions defined not only by regions, but by distinct beaches, and sometimes even blocks; a Hermosa Beach Pier local would no doubt give the stink eye to a Manhattan Beach Pier local who happened to drift down the several hundred yards that separated the two surf spots. Surfboard alliances were even more rigidly maintained: a surfer from the Westside of Santa Cruz wouldn't dream of riding a board with an Eastside label. Yet when a junior champion from Malibu named Willy Morris began riding Al Merrick's boards, and in turn was photographed riding them, it validated the concept of not simply getting one's equipment from the board builder down the street, but riding surfboards that maximized your surfing potential, regardless of where they were shaped. Following the example of standouts like Tommy, Shaun, and Willy, all of whom were appearing on boards sporting the Channel Islands logo in photos taken by Jimmy, fellow top surfers from all over the state began making the pilgrimage to Al's modest Anacapa Street shaping room, looking to tap into the energy emanating from within. This tactile interaction, bringing with it the mix of previously isolated surf cultures and ideals, would eventually provide to a surfing world dominated by Hawaiian and Australian influencers a new archetype: the Modern California Surfer.

From 1980 through 1983, Jimmy Metyko was there at the epicenter, capturing it all on film: Tommy Curren's first tracks on the path that would one day lead to three professional world titles; Al Merrick, on his way to being recognized as the sport's preeminent surfboard shaper; Kim Mearig, winning both the 1981 US championship and 1983 world title; Channel Islands Surfboards establishing itself as a major international brand, its tri-hex logo absolutely ubiquitous in surf media. With his work being published in the period's two most significant surf publications, *Surfer* and *Surfing* magazines, these more quantifiable developments played a major role in the sport's progression. Just ask Kelly Slater, who would win all eleven of his world titles on a board designed by Al Merrick. Yet the most indelible mark made during Jimmy Metyko's time in Santa Barbara had nothing to do with world titles or board sales or surfing celebrity, these aspects of his sphere of influence being mere offshoots of the greater gift he provided to those of us lucky enough to have his lens pointed our way. By affording equal attention to us all—world champs and up-and-comers, legends and legends-to-be, local heroes and local kids, parents and friends—Jimmy, through his imagery, inspired a sense of community seldom seen in modern surfing's decidedly insular culture. Quite simply, by reflecting back at us his vision of what we were experiencing, he made us feel like we were doing something truly special. Which, of course, is exactly what he was doing during the time he shared with us. Four short years—but his photos are forever.

NOTE

TOM CURREN

I remember Jimmy as always being very laid-back, very cool, just real Texas. Meaning that wherever he went, he'd have his iced tea with him, a big one, very large. And we'd just go wherever the waves were, putting so many miles on that green Honda of his.

With Jimmy, it wasn't so much about the session, but more about working with him to get the shots, and that was a new thing for me. Like when he'd shoot from the water, his lens was a 35 millimeter, so you'd have to try to stay in close, almost running him over. We were stoked to have him, stoked to have this documentation. It could have been like, "Oh, here comes Mr. Camera," but he was one of the gang. He was mellow, never like, "Hey, I got these really good photos." Even when we had a good photo session, it seemed like he was always humble.

Looking back at those days, we had no idea at the time that we were experiencing something special. We were just surfing. But when I look at these photos of that exciting period in board design, and of being on the Channel Islands team, testing boards out at Rincon and Santa Clara Rivermouth and everywhere else during a great run of surf, I realize not only that it was a special time, but also that Jimmy was there to document it all. Back then, it was just fun. Now, I'm really grateful to have been a part of it.

Central Coast, 2022
(as told to Jamie Brisick)

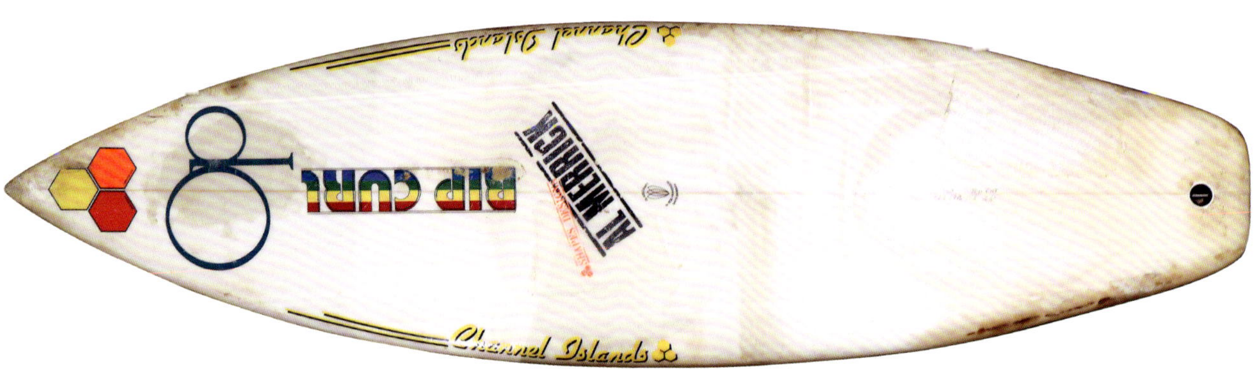

Above
The board everyone wanted, One of many that Al shaped and Tommy rode in 1983, fully logoed, squash tail thruster. This board is on display in the Santa Barbara Harbor Channel Islands surf shop on Anacapa Street.

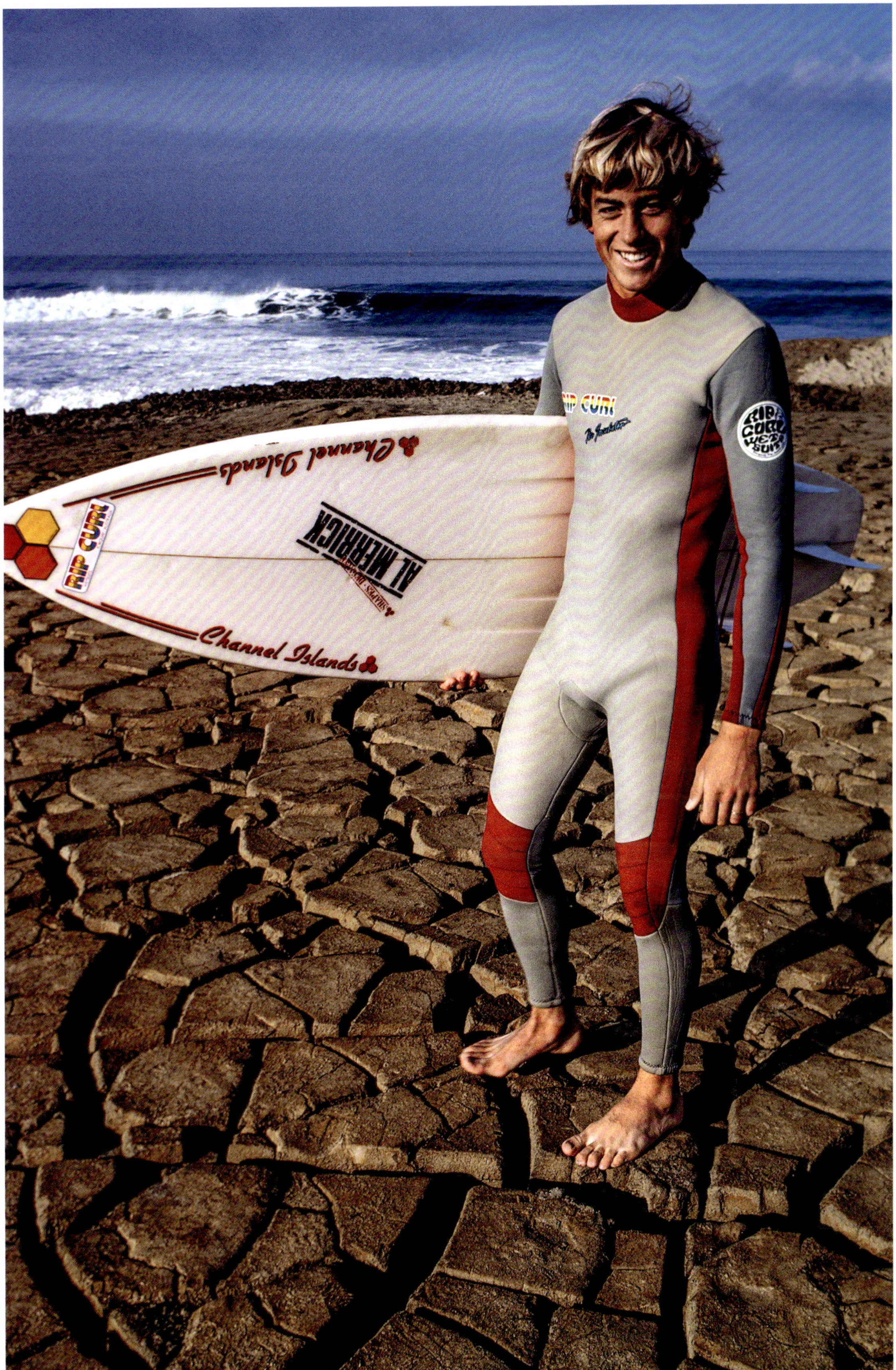
Channel Islands
AL MERRICK
RIP CURL
Channel Islands

THE METYKO DAYS HELD ME TOGETHER

JAMIE BRISICK

I first saw Tom Curren surf in 1980. His reputation preceded him: my brother Steven and I had pored over his picture in *Surfer*. We knew that he was a US junior champion, and that he rode Channel Islands surfboards.

Steven was fifteen. I was fourteen. We lived in LA. Dad let us take the day off school so we could accompany him up to Santa Barbara, where he'd drop us off to surf Hammond's Reef while he worked at UCSB.

Steven and I were between surf sessions, wetsuits peeled halfway down, wet, shivering hands bringing Mom's PB&J sandwiches to mouth, when an older surfer walked up. We got to talking. He said his name was Kim, that he worked with Channel Islands surfboards.

"Those are the boards Tom Curren rides," Steven and I said in unison.

"That's right," said Kim. "Tom surfs here every day after school. He'll show up around three fifteen."

Like clockwork, at three fifteen we watched a guy zip-zap across a bottle-green, now backlit, wall. He was fifty yards away, and we couldn't distinguish wetsuit or board in the glare, but we knew in our guts that it was Tom. I'm tempted to call it a clinic, but it was more like a concerto. He carved, hooked, banked, bounced. His style was fluid, nimble, jaunty. His surfing had a way of putting you in a good mood. And it was much more than just what he did on the wave—he was on every good wave, which is to say that he had a preternatural connection with the sea. He seemed to be always in the right place at the right time.

The next morning, we went to Rincon. We saw Tom again, doing those same beautiful carves across the winding walls of California's finest pointbreak. After a series of conveyor-belt-like waves to the inside, he'd prone to shore, loop his leash in his fingers, and, with board under arm, jog back up to the top of the point. His artistry was in full effect. Hopscotching mossy cobblestones, sidestepping clumps of seaweed, he moved with balletic grace. You needn't know a thing about surfing to know that you were watching a great surfer. Tom's surfing resonated, played back, appeared in those light, liminal moments between wakefulness and sleep.

My brother and I started competing, got sponsored, made friends with a tribe of surfers who chased contests up and down the California coast. Santa Cruz one weekend, La Jolla the next. We were all praying to the same god. We wanted to score good waves and, along the way, earn respect and take home trophies. Pro surfing was not a viable career at that time, but we liked the sound of it. It hung out there, slightly blurred.

It was right around this time that we met Jimmy Metyko.

Jimmy was a student at Brooks Institute, one of the most respected photography schools in the country. We were introduced to him by our friend Jeff Novak, who arranged our first photo session.

We met at first light at Santa Clara Rivermouth in Ventura. The waves were head-high. The wind was offshore, carrying agricultural smells that seemed more Midwest than SoCal. The sun hung low, the sky cloudless—or, as Jimmy put it, "good lighting."

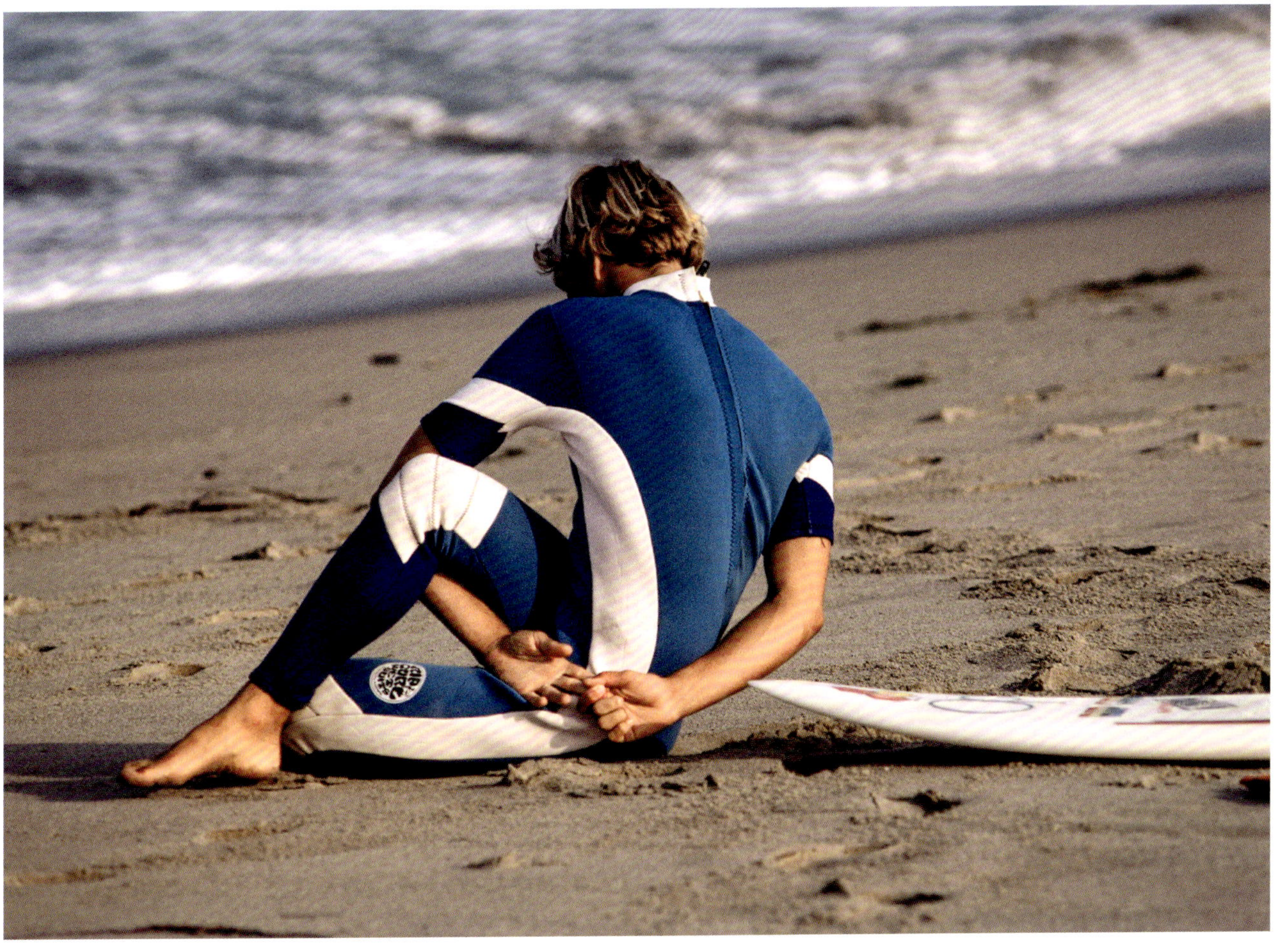

Jimmy was fresh-faced, polite, earnest. He spoke with a Texan accent that seemed at odds with the cockiness of your typical California surfer. He said "y'all." What surfer said "y'all"?

Jeff explained that it was not about stringing a long ride together, but the big "kill move." You take off, gather speed, aim for that G-spot, and lay into the hardest carve or the most vicious lip bang, holding your arms just so, hurling as much spray as possible. The term was not yet popular in 1980, but it was all about the "money shot."

Jimmy shot from the beach. These were manual-focus days. Standing behind his 650-millimeter lens mounted on a tripod, he thanked us for our bright wetsuits and boards, said they helped him nail "tack-sharp" focus. He was humble about what he got, and he was still humble when he shared the slides with us the following weekend. In the dirt parking lot at Santa Clara Rivermouth, huddled around the hood of Jimmy's forest-green Honda Accord, we looked at sheets of slides through a loupe. For some of us, this was the first time we'd ever seen ourselves in action. I liked my hands, liked the way I wrapped my arms around the wave.

That first photo session led to many more—a quid pro quo. Jimmy was a Brooks student; he needed subjects. We were thrilled to rip, shred, and tear for him. There was a sense of collaboration. The stakes were upped. Shooting with Jimmy made us feel important. On Monday morning, in earth science, I'd look around the classroom and think, *What did you guys do this weekend?*

Later that year, my friend and mentor Willy Morris got me on the Channel Islands team, and I fell in with a new crew of pro-surfing aspirants—Tommy, Davey, Tim, Dana, Kim, Sam, Matt. We shared notes. "Quiksilver's looking for team riders in the LA area." "Might want to check out *Creative Visualization* by Shakti Gawain." "*Surfer*'s doing a Hot 100 article; maybe you can get in it." Competitive surfing consumed us, insulated us.

Al Merrick was the father figure. Mustachioed, deep-voiced, baseball-capped, he spoke slowly and carefully. "I believe the boards should have drive, should always be driving forward," he explained to me at a Western Surfing Association contest at C Street. "There are a lot of fads and gimmicks out there. I'm interested in the elements of board design that have been proven over time."

Al's boards were an extension of himself. He was a no-nonsense, walk-the-talk, Bible-studying man. His shaping room was adjacent to the Lobster House and across the street from Stearns Wharf. Seafood smells commingled with a creosote stench. Watching him trace a template onto a raw blank, saw out the plan shape, glide up and down it with a planer, surform, screens, sandpaper—it was beautiful, sculptural. Every dozen or so strokes he'd stop, examine the board, raise it up with his foam-dusted fingertips. Like many of Bob Dylan's great lyrics, Al's pearls of wisdom came out muffled. He'd pull his mask to the side and say, "We must always remain humble" or "Just focus on your surfing and the rest will take care of itself."

Muzz and Fran arranged for Steven and me to get on the Rip Curl team. They picked us up in Fran's bone-white Valiant, patchouli incense burning in the ashtray. We stuffed our boards alongside theirs and squeezed in. On the ride down, they talked about girls. At Rip Curl, amid floor-to-ceiling racks of brightly colored wetsuits, team manager Don Craig let us trade our old suits in for new ones. Handing us a stack of stickers, he said, "It's important to be a good person. All we have is our reputations." On the ride back, Steven and I finding it most comfortable to lie beneath the boards, Muzz and Fran shared a joint and talked more about girls. Somebody got herpes; somebody slept with their boyfriend's best friend. On an exhale, Fran turned back to us and said, "Whatever you guys do, never tell a girl you love her."

Willy and Steve Morris invited us to a punk show in the Valley. We drank beer and pogoed to the Dickies, spent the night at their house, got up early, loaded Steve's Gray Ghost with the boards, and beelined north to Ventura. Along the way, they told us about the Day of Dreams, on which swell, tide, and howling Santa Ana winds conspired to transform Santa Clara Rivermouth into a world-class break. They vividly described late drops, screaming cutbacks, guillotine lips slamming heads, the euphoric feeling of standing inside a swirling tube, the way the spit gathers from way back and whooshes you forward—a birthing of sorts. But there was a larger lesson: good waves are fleeting. To be a serious surfer is to align nervous system to sea, to be at the whim of swell/tide/wind.

Jeff Novak's VW bus had a distinct advantage. The side door slid open, making it easier to land, say, a burrito or a large chocolate shake or both on Jimmy's or Willy's or Sam's windshield as we convoyed along the coast. Food fights were an essential part of those long, wave-chasing drives, much like podcasts are today. They entertained. They engaged our imaginations. And they never really ended. We each carried our own mental scorecard. Retaliations sometimes happened months or even years later.

Breakfasts were a thing. When one of us got up to use the toilet, the rest informed the server that it was our friend's birthday. Halfway through our pancakes, out would walk the entire waitstaff, a plate of something sweet with a lit candle atop it, "Happy Birthday" sung in heartwarming chorus, our fellow diners joining in. We learned how not to be surprised. During Jimmy's four years in California, I must have had at least a dozen birthdays.

Jimmy's photos started appearing regularly in *Surfing* and *Surfer*, and so did the guys we surfed with, laughed with, competed against. The gap between us bumbling mortals and those godlike figures in the mags narrowed. Willy Morris scored a cover. Tom Curren bagged a center spread. Davey Smith got the first documented sequence of a landed frontside aerial.

Tom raised the bar. He employed Olympian training techniques, something called "plyometrics," which Al demonstrated for me, a way to build what we now call "fast-twitch" muscles. You stepped off a platform a foot or so high. The moment you landed, you bent your knees and sprang as high as you could. I did them in my backyard, along with push-ups and sit-ups. When Tom's famous spinal-twist shot appeared in *Surfing*, it was a rallying cry. It demanded that we all step up our acts.

Al brought in the team workout. We'd meet at Backside Rincon or La Conchita, some subpar beachbreak that demanded our bounce and exuberance. With a flag planted several yards up from the mean high-tide line, we'd hold a contest, the caveat being that if you wanted your ride to count, you had to round the flag. This did a couple of things. It built our leg power and cardio. It also encouraged us to ride every wave to shore. (Length of ride carried big weight in the amateur leagues.)

Team workouts were followed by team BBQs at Al's house. Tri-tip, or whatever fish Al had recently caught, wafted from the backyard grill. Al's daughter, Heidi, was witty, son Britt was curious, wife Terry was beautiful and mother to us all. We were there under the guise of improving our surf game. Really he was showing us what the good life looks like.

After dinner, we squeezed into the den and watched video from the contest, had what in art school would be called a crit. "See, you needed to keep racing down the line rather than stomp that cutback." "Look at the wave out the back—gotta read the sets for patterns. Swells have patterns, moods, personalities." "Relax that front hand. It looks mannered." This was new ground. The 1970s ethos was about insouciance, never looking like you were trying. We were unapologetic about wanting it.

There was a sweet, G-rated wholesomeness to the Channel Islands team gatherings. There were many bad influences and wrong turns. Al was trying to keep us on the straight and narrow.

I knew this firsthand. My brother Kevin was plunging into drugs. My parents would soon divorce.

During the El Niño winter of 1982–83, the waves got bigger, the tide got higher, and the rain dumped more torrentially. The swollen creek and incessant runoff transformed Steven's and my beloved Malibu into a new break. What had been a fairly gentle, playful wave turned hollow and hard-slamming. The rock bottom was covered in shallow sand. The water went chocolate brown. Things were changing on land as well. Barron Burns got arrested. Glenny B.'s older brother died in a car accident on Kanan Road.

The Jimmy Metyko world, the Al Merrick world, the Tom Curren world—it was the opposite of an undertow, of a nihilism that I was beginning to feel. Surf contests were a buttress. Shooting with Jimmy was a buttress. Watching Al pour every cell of himself into a surfboard was a buttress.

I turned pro in 1986. A year later, Kevin fatally overdosed. I continued on the Tour, racked with grief but trying to summon the Rocky Balboa within. I felt dueling forces riding on my shoulders. One wanted to give up, to fall to the floor in the fetal position; the other saw a way forward. Much of the latter was cultivated during those Metyko years.

I did five years on the World Tour, then started writing for surf magazines. Part of my job was to obsess over surfing, to make sense of, to contextualize. Looking back at the early '80s, we were part of something truly special and resonant. Tom Curren would go on to win three world titles and become one of the most influential surfers of all time. Al Merrick's Channel Islands would become the most popular surfboard brand in the world. The El Niño winter of 1982–83—have the waves in Santa Barbara and Ventura ever been that consistently excellent? In the rearview, we can see the aligning of stars: ace board designer, prodigious test pilot, the great incubators that are those waves.

Jimmy should have gone on to a big career as a surf photographer, but he didn't. Upon graduating from Brooks, his father got sick, and he went back to Texas to be with him.

I see it as a film. We open on a closeup tracking shot of a pair of legs trotting along the shoreline. A wetsuit cuffs the ankles, along with a surfboard leash, as the nimble feet dance over mossy cobblestones and clumps of seaweed.

INTRODUCTION

JIMMY METYKO

It was a sunny Saturday in January 1980 when, camera in hand, I made my way down the well-worn trail from the parking lot to the beach at Rincon del Mar, the world-renowned surf break located some fifteen miles south of Santa Barbara, California. I had traveled a long way to get there, both literally and figuratively. Nineteen years old at the time, I had grown up chasing waves along the Texas coast; calling yourself a surfer in those swell-challenged barrier islands meant that you spent a lot more time dreaming about surfing than actually surfing. We craved imagery especially, poring over and memorizing the period's surf magazines until their pages grew thin and tattered. Unlike a lot of my friends, however, I not only studied the pictures of famous surfers like Jeff Hakman, Gerry Lopez, and Shaun Tomson, but also followed the exploits of the era's best surf photographers, with top lensmen like Art Brewer, Jeff Divine, Larry Moore, and Aaron Chang firing my imagination as much as their star subjects did.

I had been around cameras almost my entire life. The sons of world travelers, my brothers and I often were pulled from school for months at a time in order to accompany our parents on their far-flung voyages. By age nine, I had graduated from holding my father's camera bag to taking charge of shooting the family's travel images, mastering on the go many of the important basics of photography. With all that exposure, my passion for making photographs grew more personal, to be taken much more seriously at home between trips abroad. I even began to bring my camera along to the beach, fostering the unlikely notion that a guy from Texas could someday become a successful surf photographer. It was a crazy idea, but one that I pursued over the years with all my youthful optimism. It led to me applying to and being accepted at the Brooks Institute of Photography in Santa Barbara—and eventually finding myself walking down the trail to the waves of Rincon.

I distinctly remember it being one of those beautiful, sunny winter afternoons, the waves clean and green and folding uniformly around this "corner of the sea"—nothing exceptional for this stretch of coast, but for a surfer/photographer from Texas, like something out of a dream...or maybe like going back in time. The first wave I saw was being ridden by a surfer on a longboard, in a manner reminiscent of stylists Reynolds Yater and Kemp Aaberg, both of whom were standouts at Rincon in the 1960s. The next wave had two riders jockeying

Facing

Metyko, in the foreground, suited for immersion, alongside friend and fellow photographer/surfer Simone Reddingius and visiting South African Jimmy "China" Smith. November 1983.
Photo: Sam George

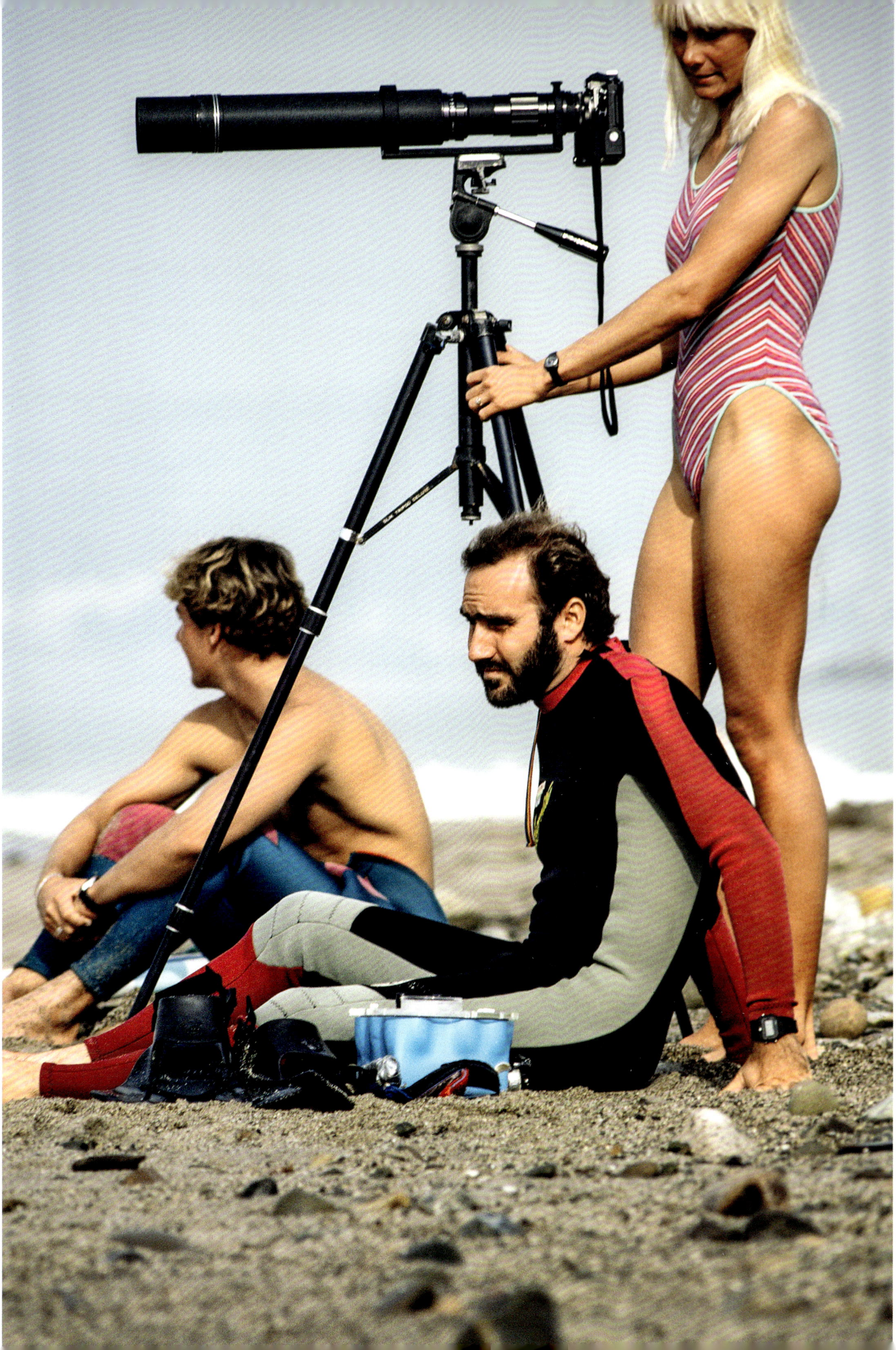

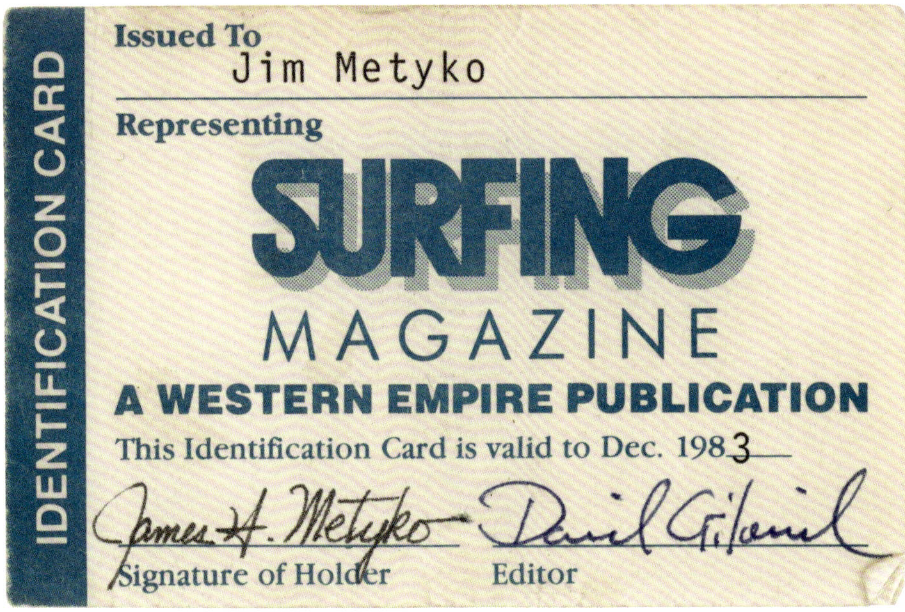
IDENTIFICATION CARD

Issued To
Jim Metyko

Representing
SURFING
MAGAZINE
A WESTERN EMPIRE PUBLICATION

This Identification Card is valid to Dec. 1983

Signature of Holder
Editor

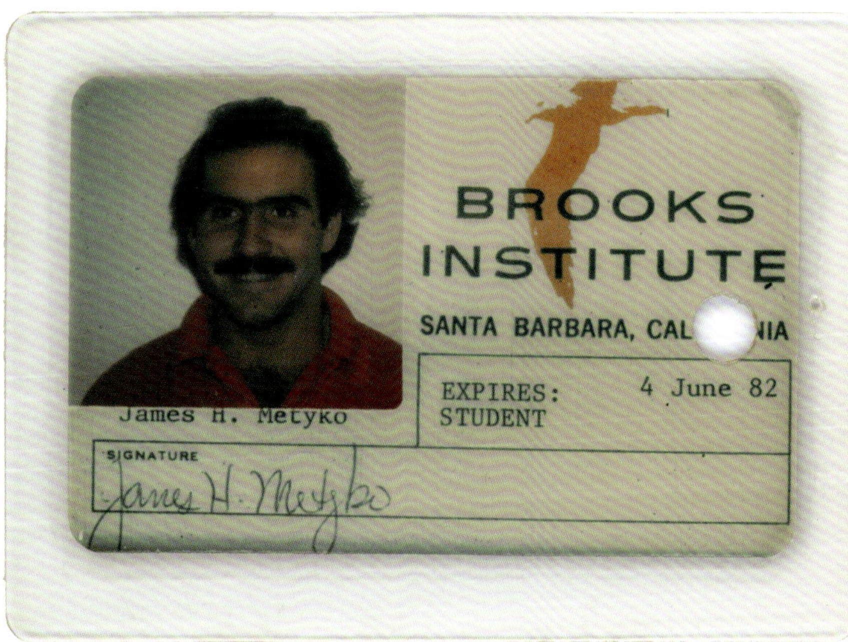
BROOKS
INSTITUTE
SANTA BARBARA, CALIFORNIA

EXPIRES: 4 June 82
STUDENT

James H. Metyko

SIGNATURE

with each other for dominance in the pocket, both riding early 1970s surfboard shapes and sporting "soulful" all-black wetsuits, outdated beaver-tail jackets flapping. The surfer on the third wave, however, was something else entirely, something completely of this time—or, more accurately, of the future. Clad in red-and-blue neoprene, riding a short twin-fin surfboard, this diminutive young performer already stood out from the crowd of older surfers. But it was the manner in which he rode across a clean set wave that commanded the most attention, gliding from turn to turn so precisely, so smoothly, with effortlessness beyond his years. Watching him, you almost felt as if you were riding along with him, anticipating and experiencing every crisp maneuver as he carved his way through the crowd, from the top of the point all the way to the inside shorebreak at the base of Highway 101.

The young surfer was fifteen-year-old Tommy Curren, son of legendary big-wave pioneer Pat Curren, US Boys Amateur Champion, and Santa Barbara High sophomore. He was also the surfer I had come to Santa Barbara—and, more specifically, Rincon—to photograph. And here he was, on the very first set of waves I saw that day. Yet this wasn't the first time I had seen Tommy surf. Nor was this the first time I'd wished to point a camera at him.

It was six months earlier, the summer when the United States Surfing Championships were held on South Padre Island, Texas. I was eighteen years old and competing in the junior division, but all the talk was about a skinny young Californian who was turning the modest Texas waves into something beautiful, eventual victory in his division a foregone conclusion. I remember sitting on the beach watching Tommy Curren surf and realizing two things: First, I would never achieve the level of performance on display, and therefore my days of competitive surfing were over. Second, even sitting there without a camera, I was already becoming a surf photographer.

The transition was made clear the next day, sharing the surf with Tommy between his competitive heats. I had just finished riding a wave of my own and was standing on an inside sandbar, waist deep. Tommy, farther outside, took off on a glassy two-foot wave and headed straight for me. Without losing any speed or composure, he set his edge and whipped a perfectly timed slashing cutback right in front of me, his tiny Channel Islands single-fin completing a full 180-degree arc, showering me with spray. Just like on the beach the day before, I found I was mentally snapping images, frame by frame, as he deftly reengaged his rail and passed me by. From that unique perspective, I couldn't help but feel that I was seeing something no one else was seeing, but that every surfer would want to: images of a future world champion in the making. Standing there in the Texas shorebreak, I knew I wanted to share my perspective, my imagery, in the same way as did all those legendary photographers who filled my surf magazines. My path was now clear. I would become a surf photographer.

So there I was, standing on the beach at Rincon, and there was Tommy Curren, masterfully leaving his mark on a glassy wall, six months later but seeming to me only moments after the spray from his Texas turn had settled. This time I did have a camera in my hands, ready to capture my first photo of the young phenom. But, as the shutter clicked, how could I ever have imagined the adventure I was about to embark upon? That I was, in fact, standing at the beginning of an entirely new, vastly influential era of surfing, its epicenter this previously quiet corner of the surfing world, where I would meet and be embraced by some remarkable agents of change—future champions and local heroes, a little-known surfboard builder and his family and friends, a pair of talented surfers/writers—many of whom would go on to define this profound shift in the sport's direction? I hardly knew then, on that very first day, with that very first photo, that a kid from Texas would be the one, over the next four years, to document it all.

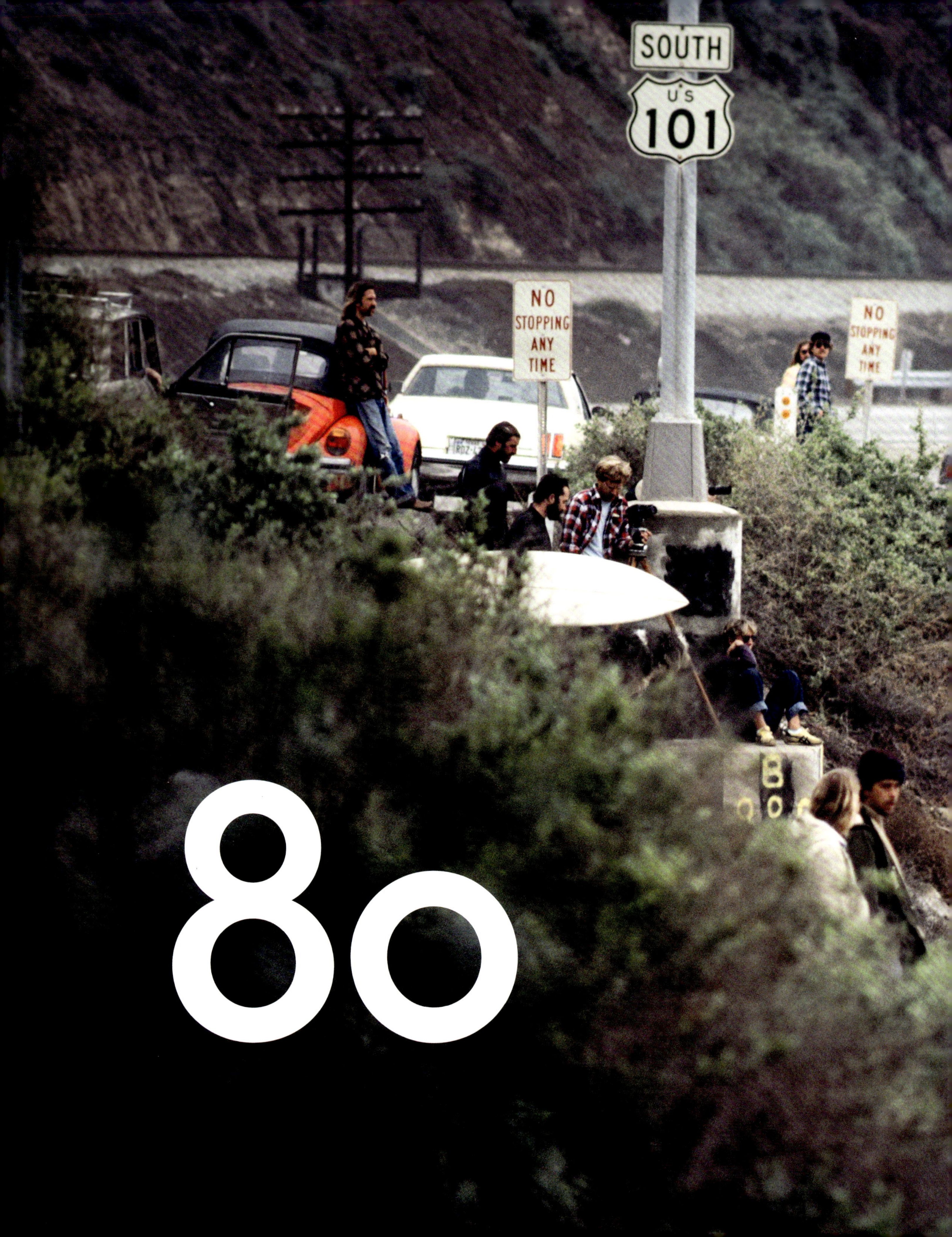

80

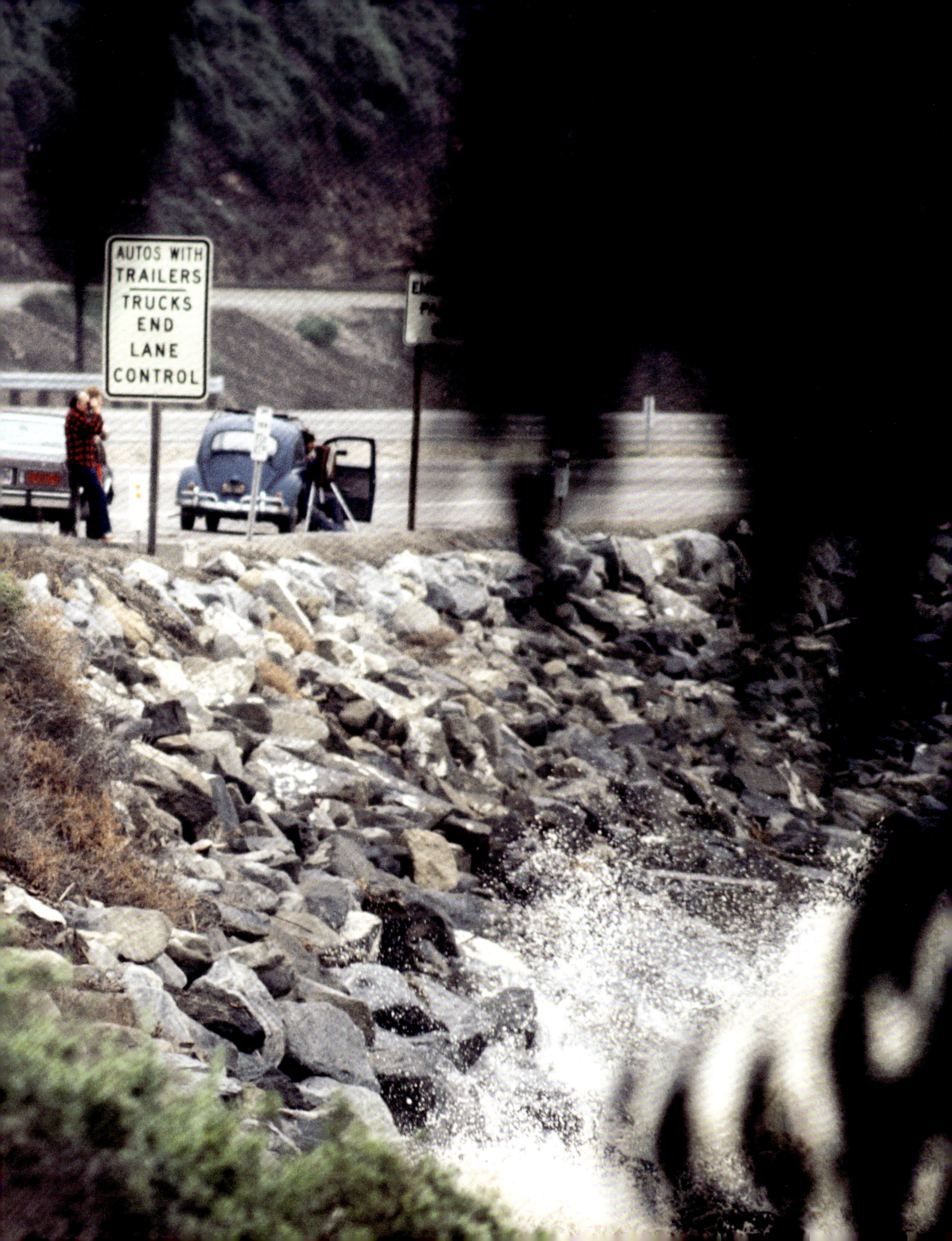
AUTOS WITH
TRAILERS
TRUCKS
END
LANE
CONTROL

1980

Finding Home

Upon first arriving in Santa Barbara, I quickly discovered that it was not the typical California beach town that I had experienced during my previous summers spent surfing in Malibu, San Diego, Los Angeles's South Bay, Orange County, or La Jolla. Though filled with beautiful, scenic shorelines, it featured little of the broad expanses of sand found in these other seaside communities farther south, and as a result it seemed to offer very little in the way of a well-developed beach culture. In Santa Barbara, I found, you mostly had to park your car and then make a long walk in to reach the coast. It was all extremely beautiful, but I found it strangely different. Every break seemed isolated and with its own culture. By comparison, Texas spots had a much beachier vibe.

This could help explain the insular nature of Santa Barbara's surfing scene in 1980. Unlike in Hermosa or Newport Beach, for example, here surfing seemed to be more low-key, trying not to demand too much attention—in fact, not wanting any attention. The region's historically inconsistent surf contributed to this attitude, it being seen by local surfers as hard enough to get their share of waves without promoting the place as some sort of hot spot. Santa Barbara surfers pretty much just went about their business. This isn't to say they lacked passion; in the city harbor, you'd see plenty of surfboards lashed to fishing-boat wheelhouses, hardworking deckhands enjoying plenty of lonely surf sessions between diving for abalone in the offshore Channel Islands. Surfing found a home in the sea along the Santa Barbara coastline, but maintained a more hidden presence on land.

That's why one of the first things I did when moving to Santa Barbara was to make the rounds of the local surf shops. Rather than the beach, it was the area's small-time retail outlets/surfboard factories that served as the surf community's cultural centers, each one having established its own sub-group of devoted customers. In most cases, each surfboard brand was associated with a particular surf spot. Even for someone who grew up there, it could be a tricky thing figuring out into which camp you fit. For an outsider? Good luck. But I knew that if I wanted to find out anything about the new surf scene I'd stepped into, I'd find it in one of these shops. Thing was, I didn't necessarily want to be found out myself.

Standing in front of the Channel Islands shop on Helena Street, I was understandably nervous. Like all non-local surfers entering a very local surf shop, I wanted to be seen as cool, and not come across like a guy who'd just moved there from Texas, of all places. As I walked through the door, however, I felt strangely at home in the quiet, earthy atmosphere, surrounded by all the standard elements of a soulful 1970s surf shop: surf movie posters and faded surf prints on the walls, circular racks of Ocean Pacific trunks and Eenie Meenie crocheted bikinis, screen-printed T-shirts folded on shelves, and fins, surf stickers, wax, and tide charts laid out underneath a glass counter. And beautiful, perfectly buffed surfboards, mostly sleek, racy looking single-fins, many with three stringers.

The place appeared empty, but nevertheless I instinctively followed the safe, tried-and-true surfer protocol of going straight to the surfboards, pulling a few out of the rack, checking things like rocker and rail contour, making sure to give the impression that I was a real surfer and knew what I was doing. Just in case anyone was watching—just in case I had "Texas" stamped across my forehead.

I had eventually worked my way over to the counter when a guy stepped out from a back room. Tall, a bit older than me, with long, straight blond hair and an Errol Flynn mustache, he eyed me closely as I pulled the latest copy of *Surfer* from the magazine rack and asked for a bar of wax. I made doubly sure not to say "y'all" when inquiring if he'd accept a check (luckily, from my new local bank account) and was relieved when he agreed, so long as I provided identification. Without much thought, I handed him my driver's license.

"Texas, huh?" he said, his voice dripping with California cool.

Oh, shit, I thought. *My license. I forgot about my Texas license*. I hadn't yet interacted with many surfers in Santa Barbara, but having since the age of fourteen spent my summers along the San Diego area beaches, I was very used to catching crap for being from Texas, and so I readied myself for the inevitable ridicule. Instead, after peering at my license again for effect, the shop guy just smiled.

"I'm from Texas!" he said.

Turned out that Kim Robinson, Santa Barbara's widely respected Channel Islands shop manager, was, in fact, originally from Houston, and before we knew it we were enthusiastically trading names of places and acquaintances. The sense of relief I felt is hard to explain to anyone who's never been a surfer transplanted to a new shore, to a new scene. All I knew was that my initial impression when walking into Channel Islands was the right one. I had found my surf shop. A home.

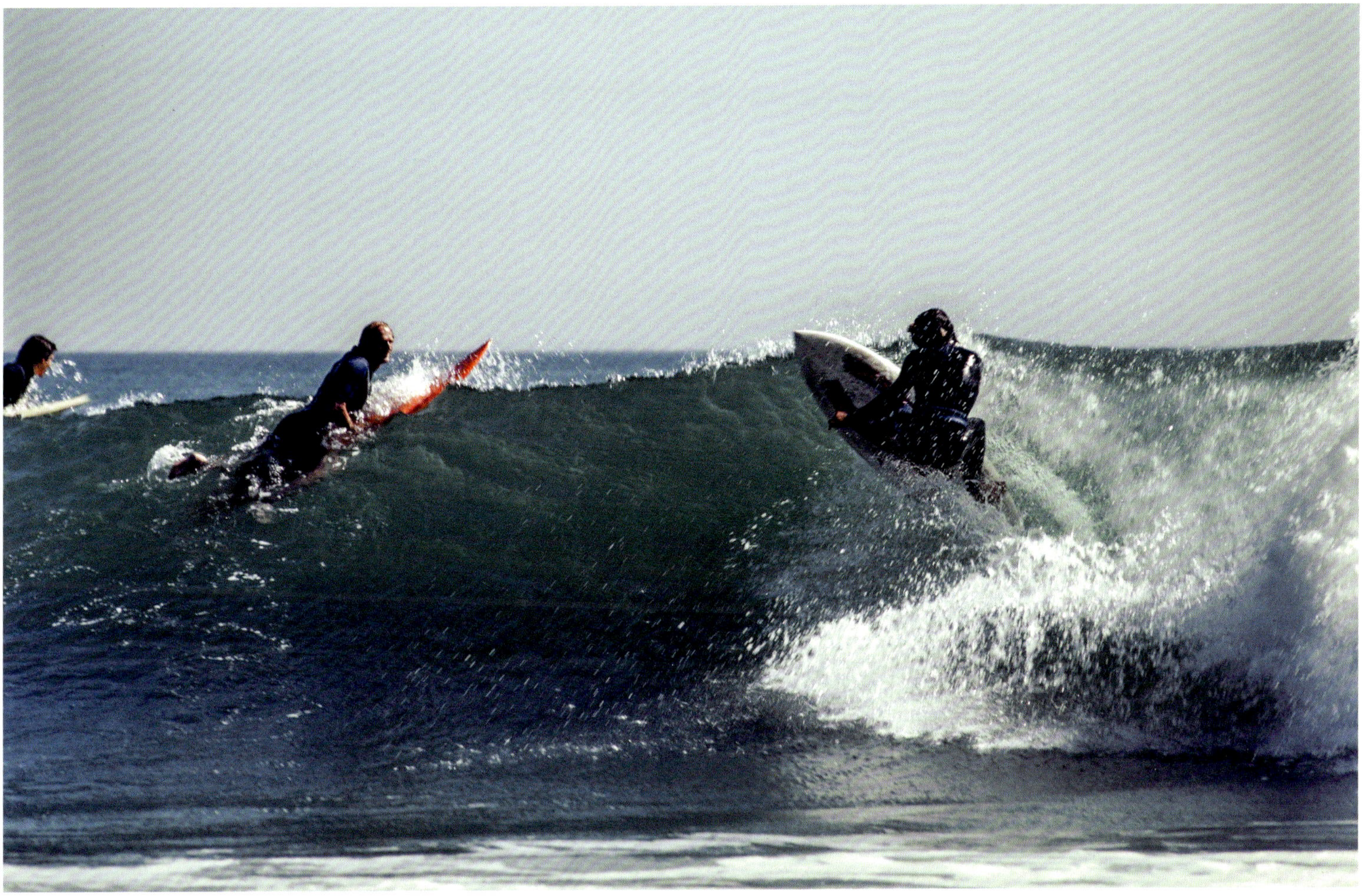

Back when I was just pointing and shooting at anyone on a good wave, I unwittingly managed to capture an impressive array of some of Rincon's most respected locals—sometimes more than one in the same shot. Here, Bill "Pugsley" Bernhardt's top turn earns a grin from Stu Fredericks, one of the original members of the venerable Santa Barbara County Surf Club.

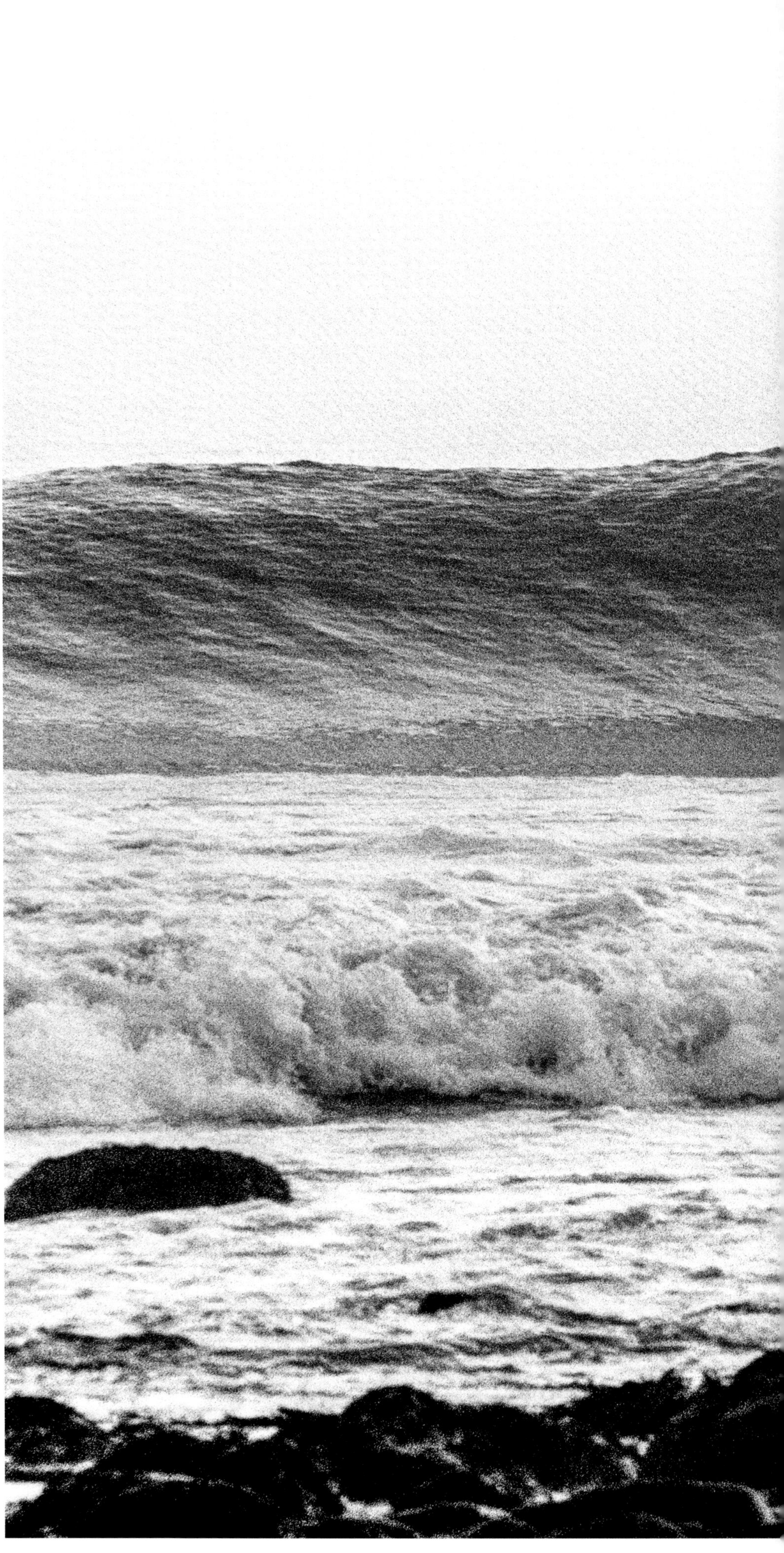

Spread

While my early use of black-and-white film might appear to be a deliberate attempt to capture a past era, the truth was I couldn't afford color film and development every time I shot, and so I used what I could develop and print myself in the Brooks darkrooms. An unidentified surfer achieves perfect trim through the very identifiable Rincon Rivermouth section, on perhaps some of the best Rivermouth I would ever shoot.

Overleaf, left to right

Channel Islands team rider Soren Hansen enjoying a nice low-tide Rincon Cove runner. Ventura's Ross Keck, drawing out his backside bottom turn. Stan Cowan, perfect Rincon Rivermouth. Again, Stan Cowan on the kind of Rincon wave surfers dream about.

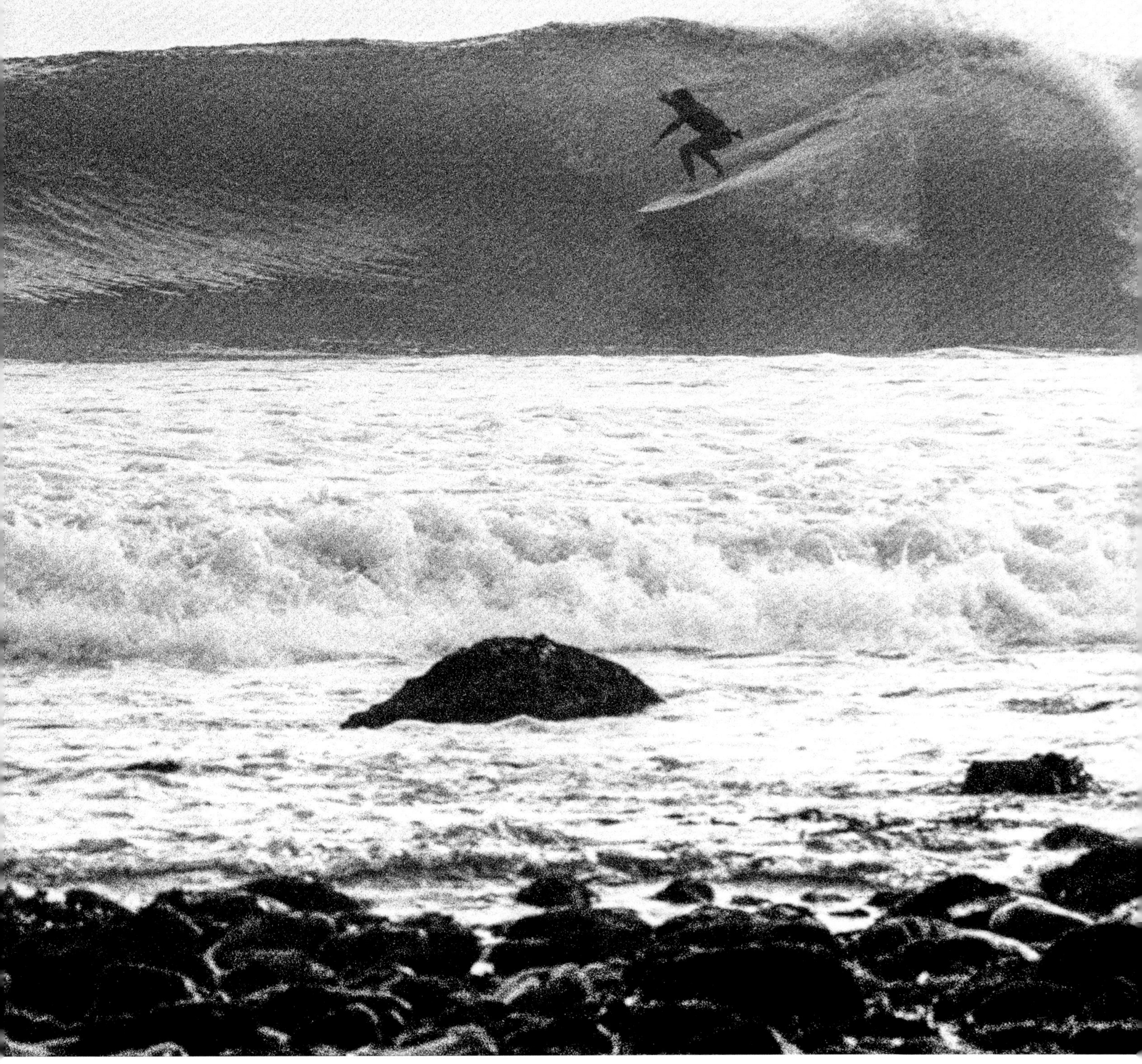

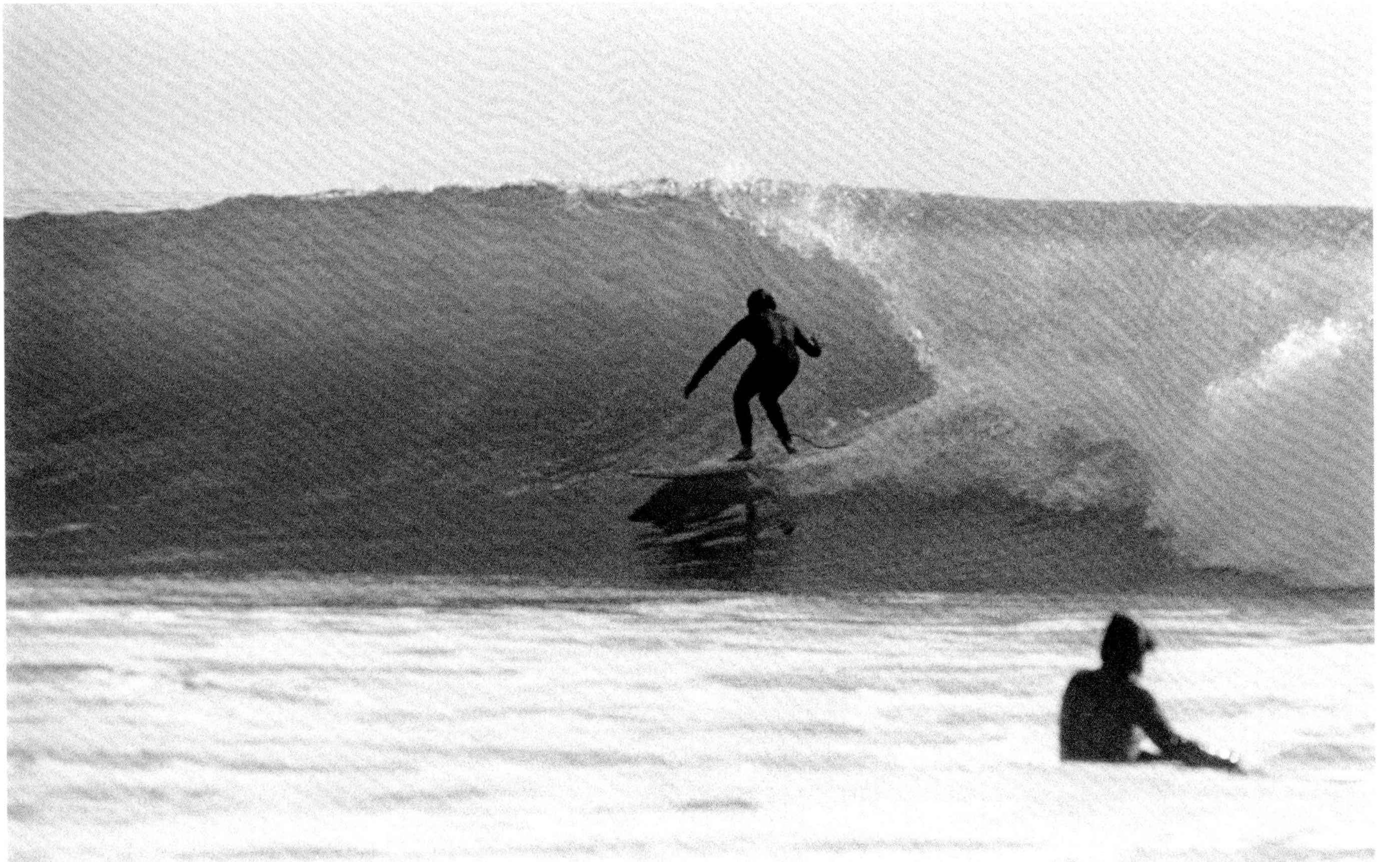

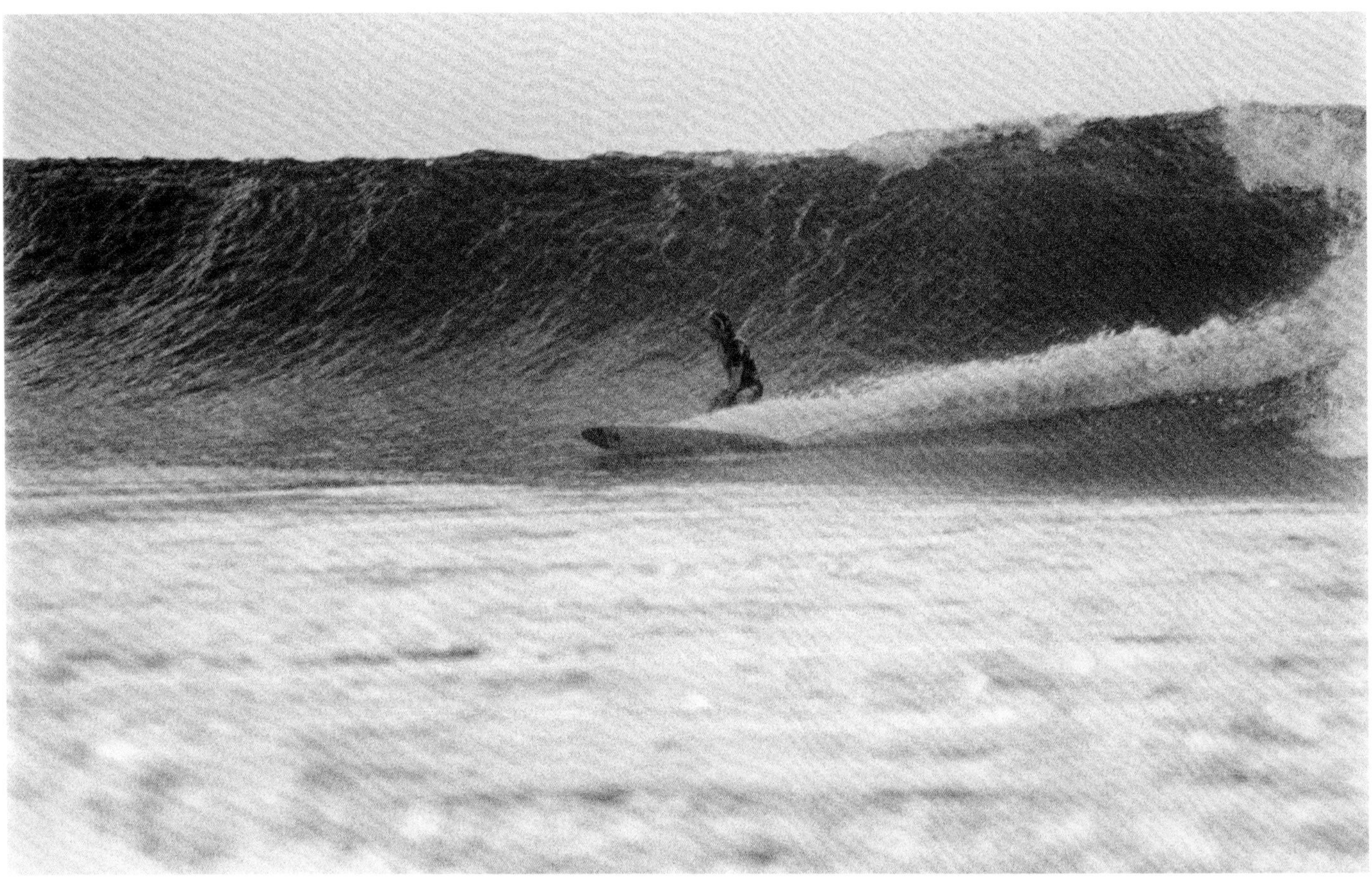

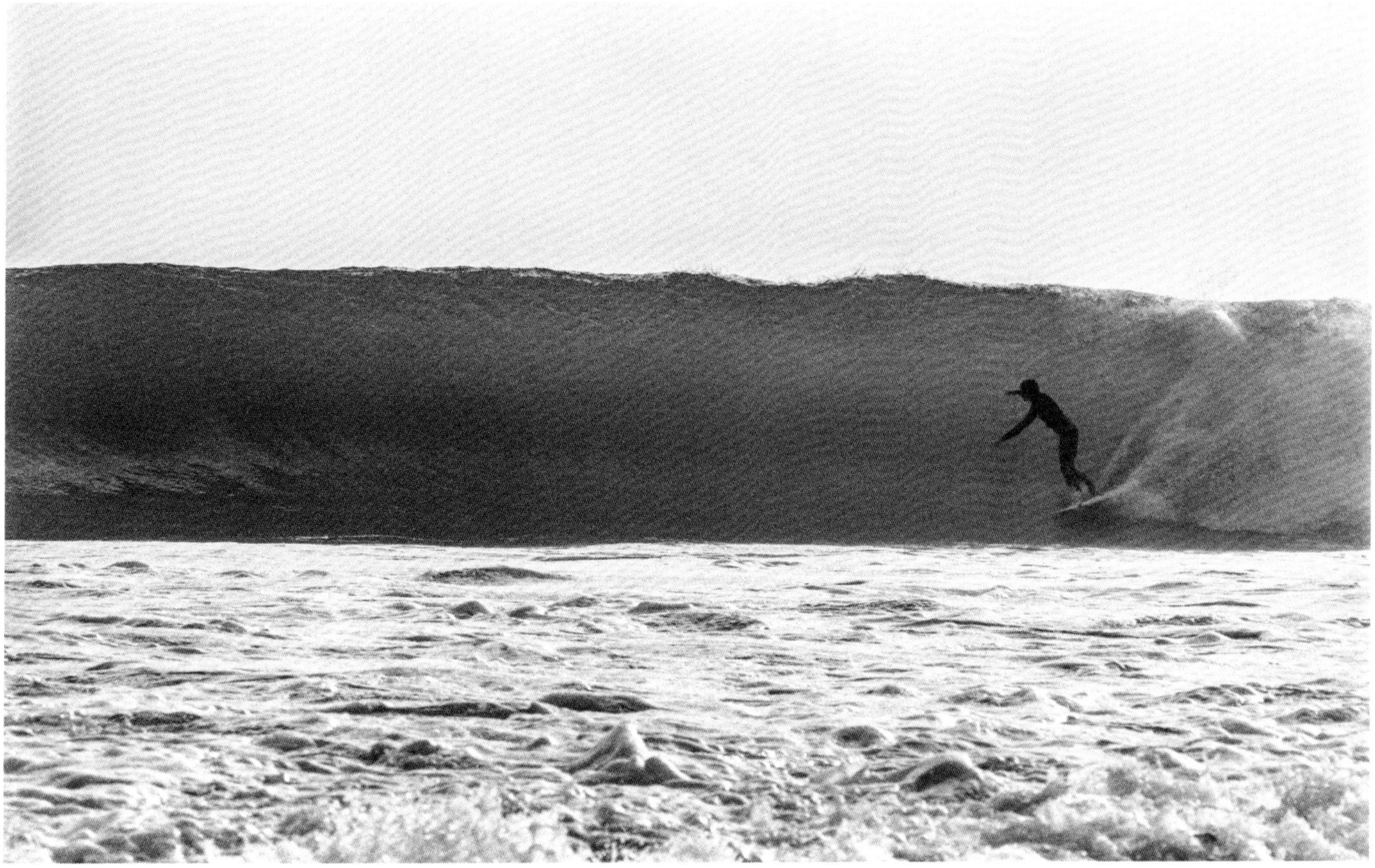

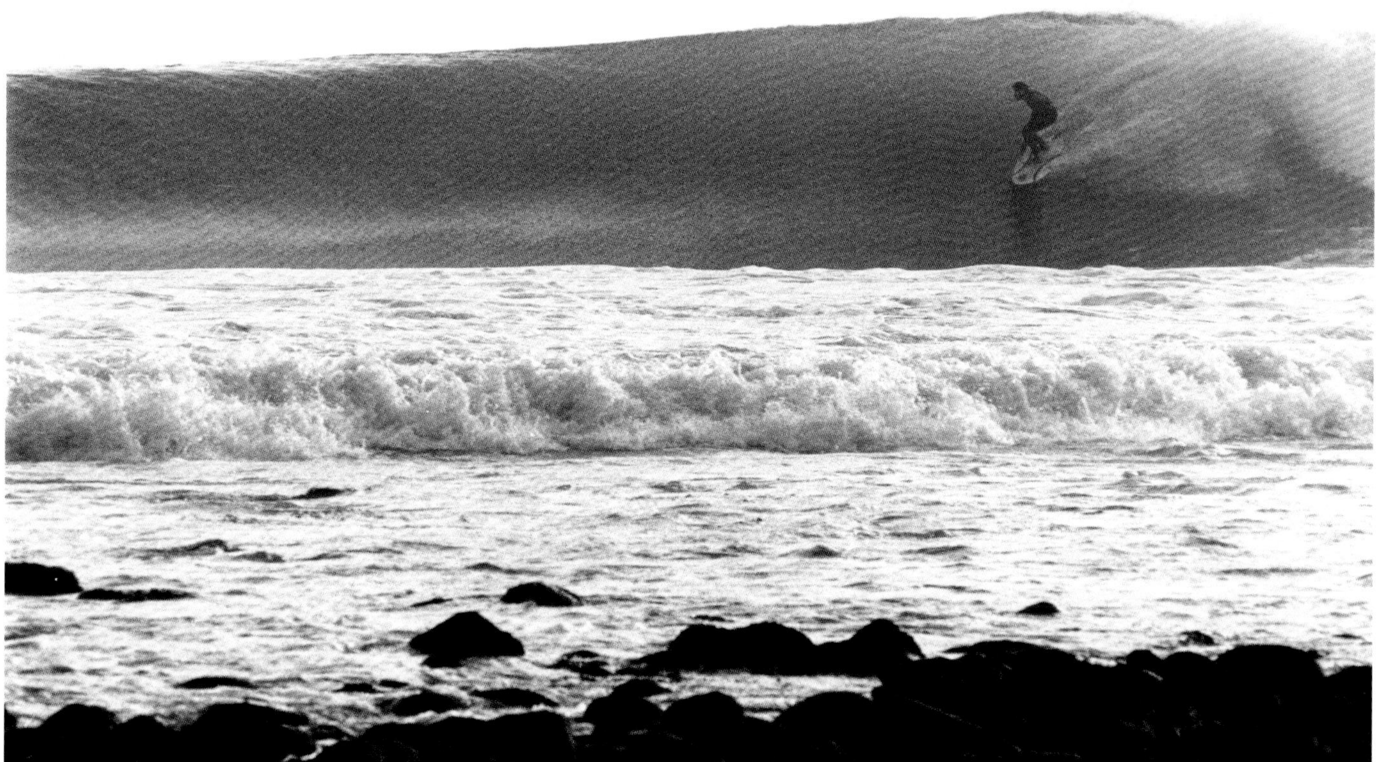

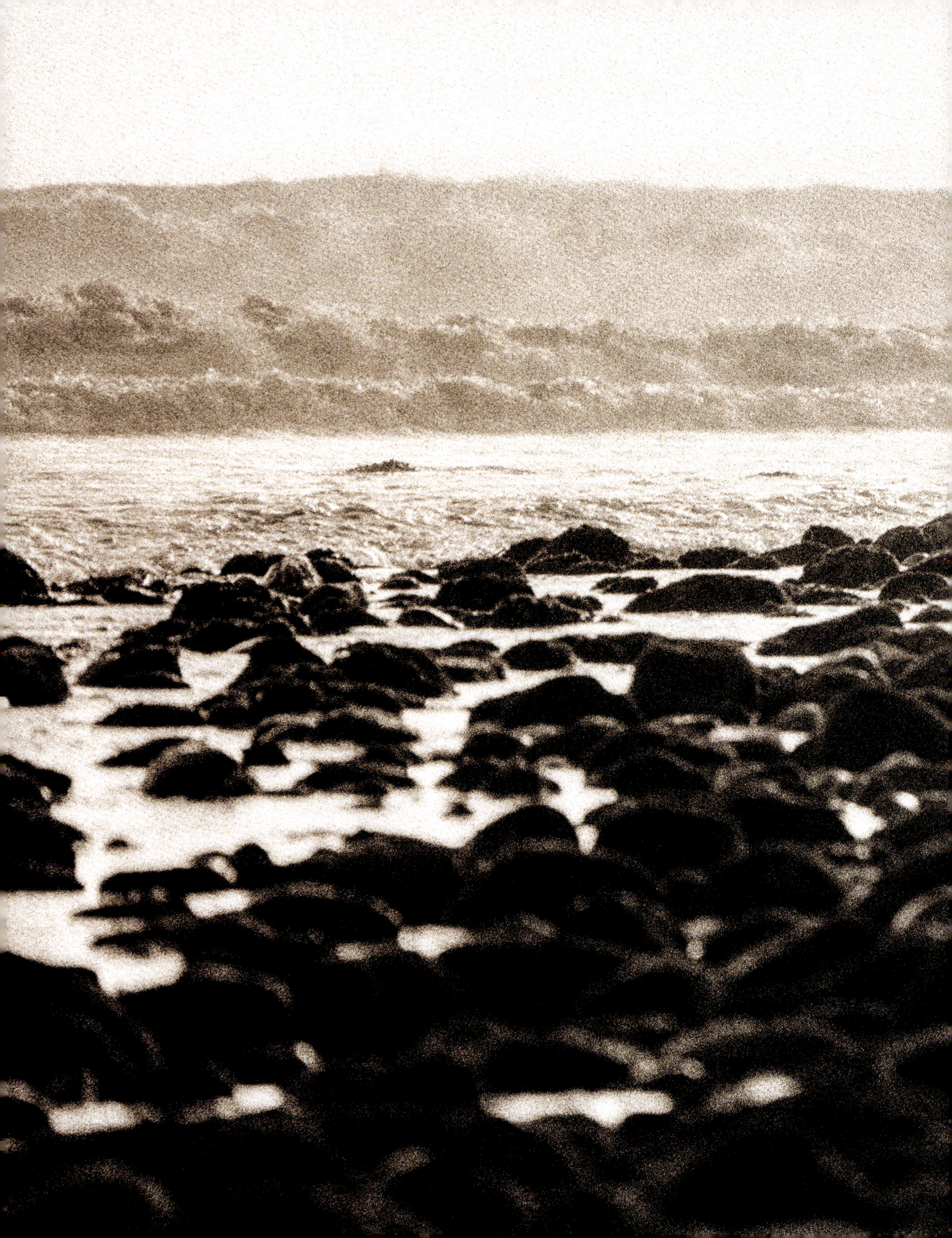

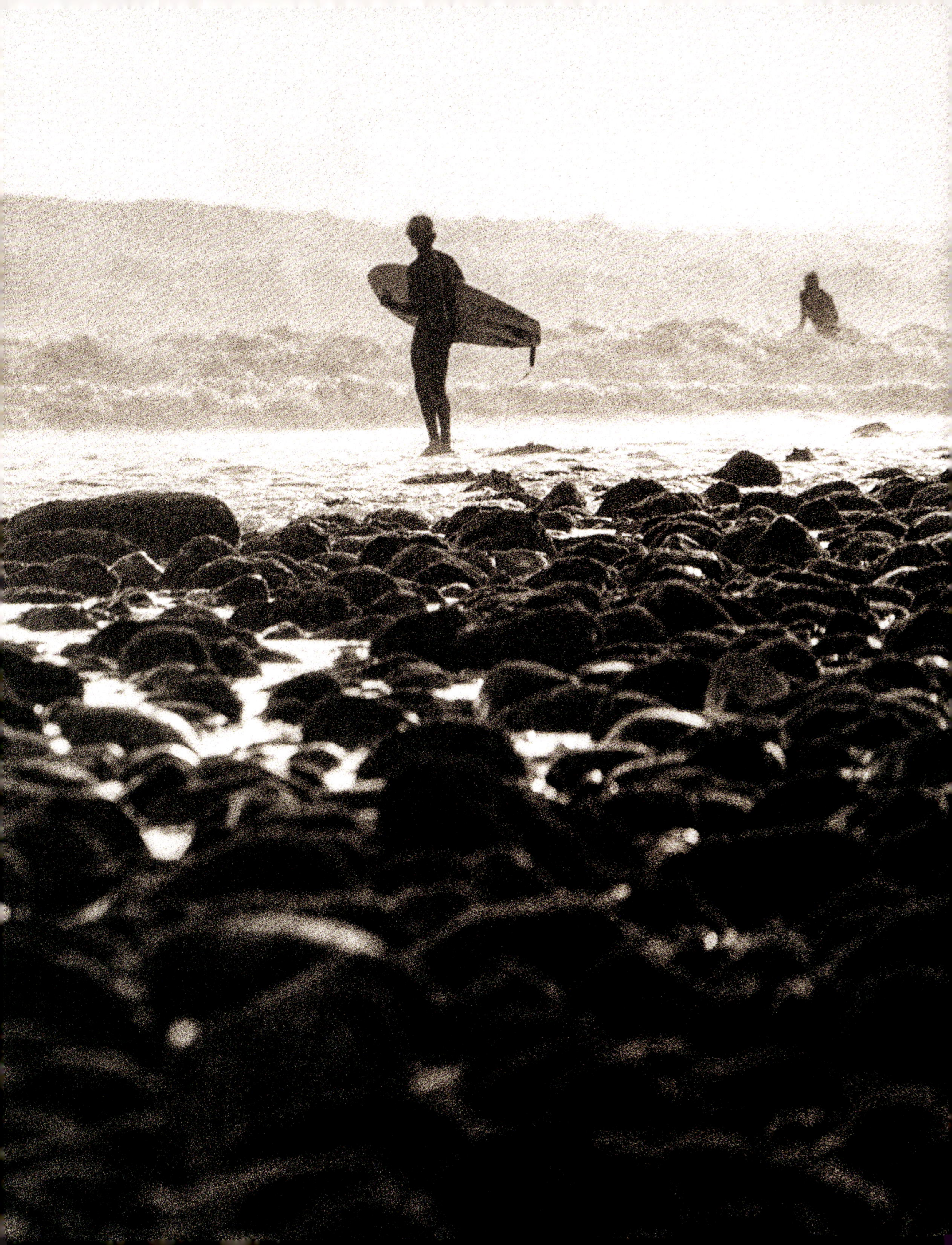

Previous

The sea spray created as a big set pours through Rincon Cove produces a dramatic mood as Oxnard's Russ Short contemplates his paddle out. Russ, one of California's best surfers at the time, was laying down heavy three-fin bonzer tracks years before the thruster appeared.

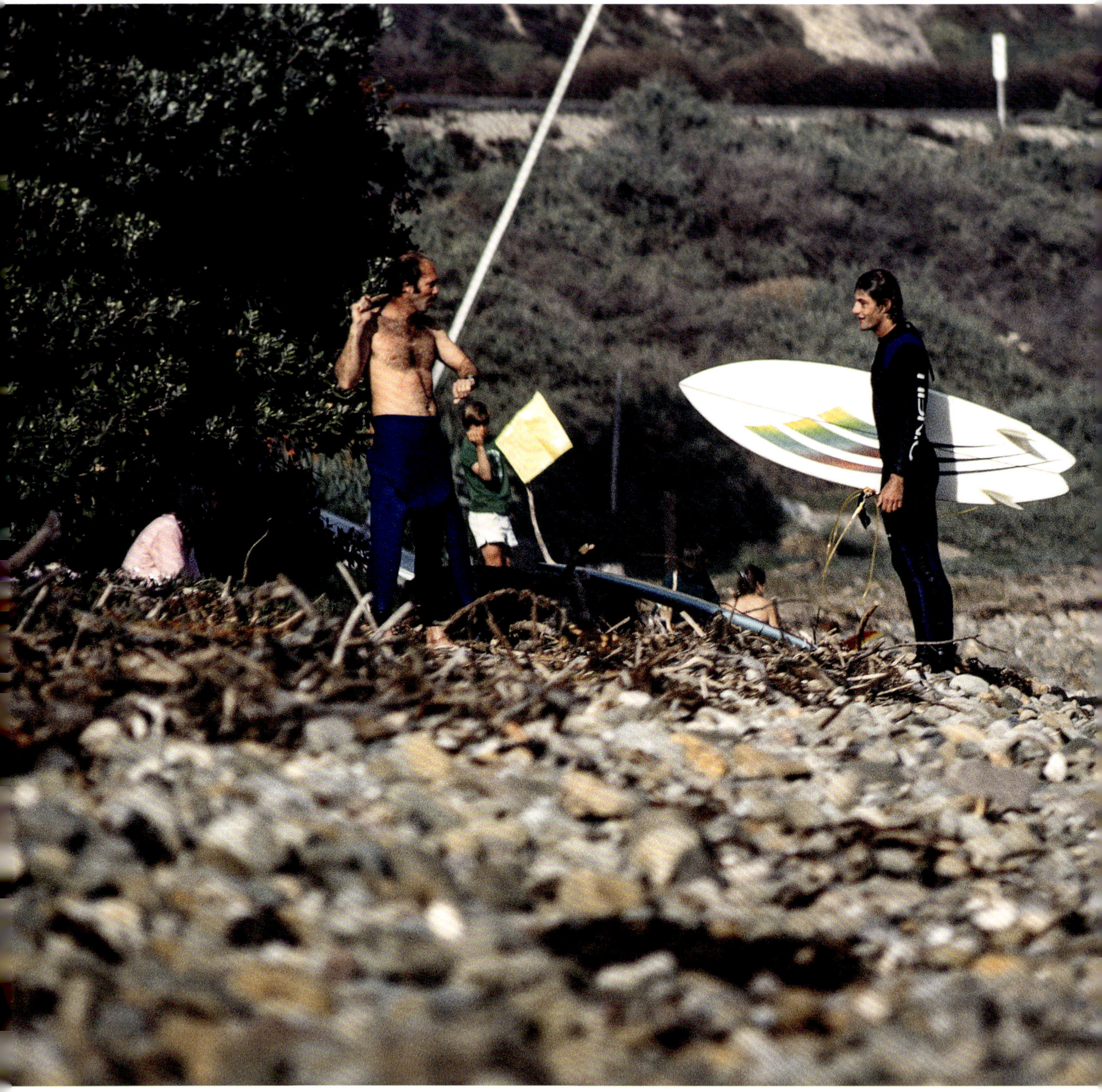

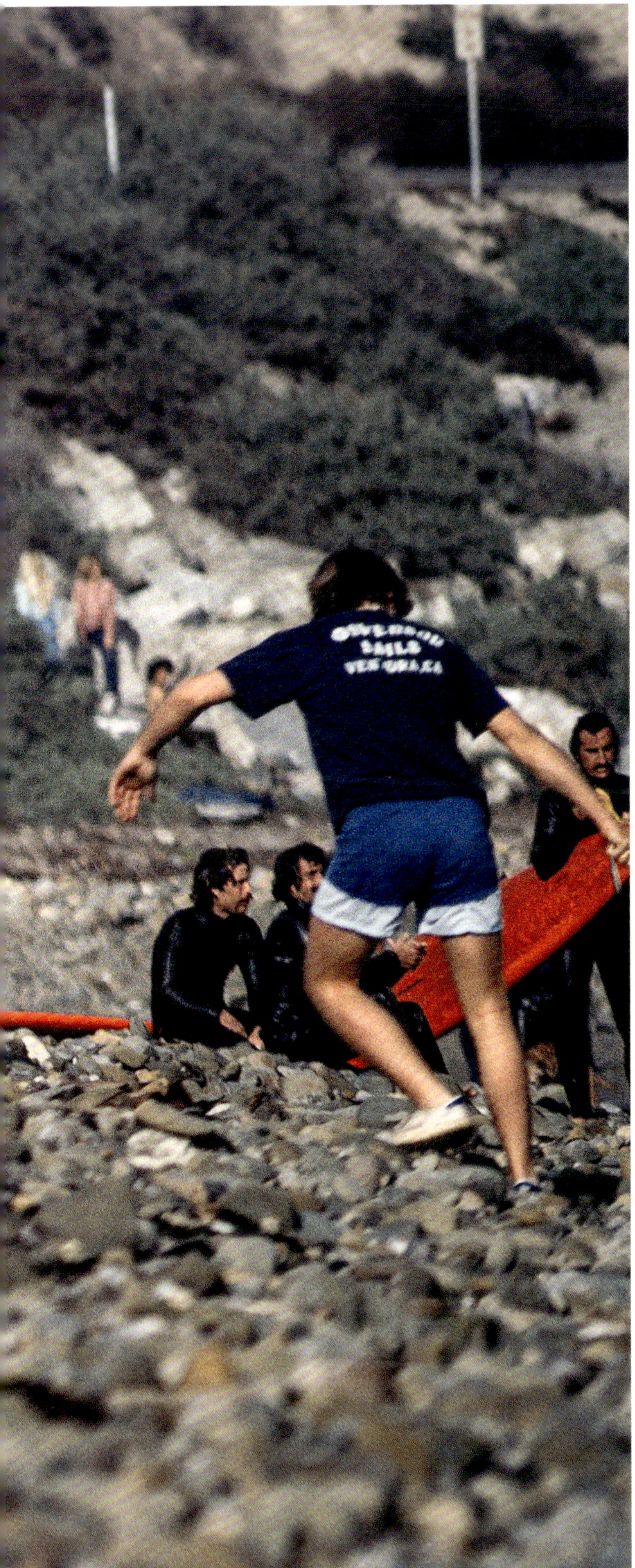

Flash Point

When color came to Rincon. Shaun Tomson's wetsuit, airbrushed design, and style of surfing contrasted sharply with the local crew's all-black rubber and solid-tone boards. The presence of a bona fide world champion surfer like Shaun, although not always welcome in Santa Barbara's conservative lineups, was nevertheless disruptive, providing the area's more open-minded surfers an example of how progressively Rincon could be surfed. One of those was Al Merrick, whose relationship with Shaun carried from Rincon Cove to the shaping room, where Al fine-tuned the twin-fin designs that Shaun would eventually take out on the pro tour. But it was those early days at Rincon that Al would later point to as some of his most cherished memories, the dynamic obvious in this photo as Shaun encourages "The Professor" (his affectionate nickname for Al) to pull his wetsuit up and get back out there. I hadn't met either of these two legendary figures yet, and I'm so glad I was there to capture moments like this one.

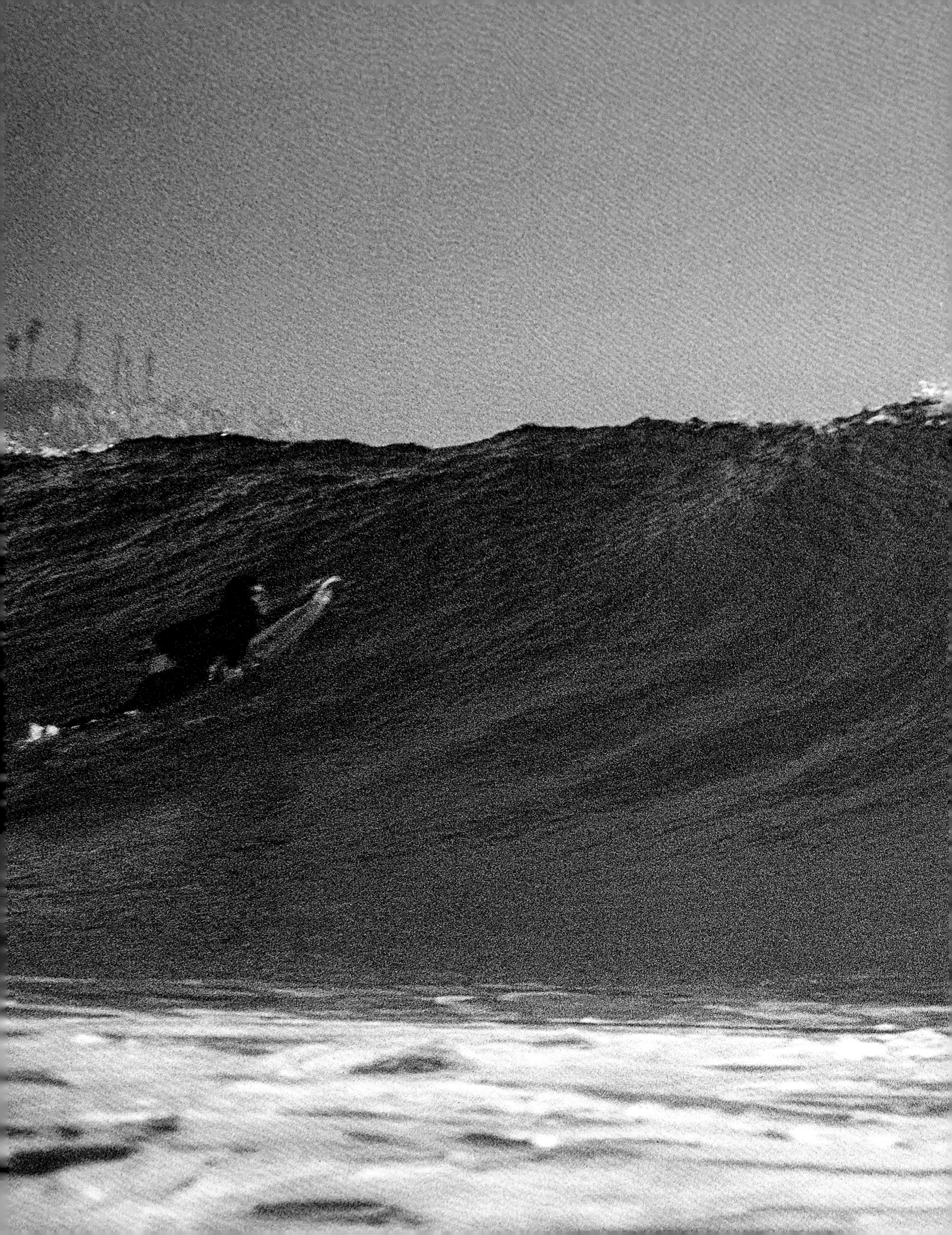

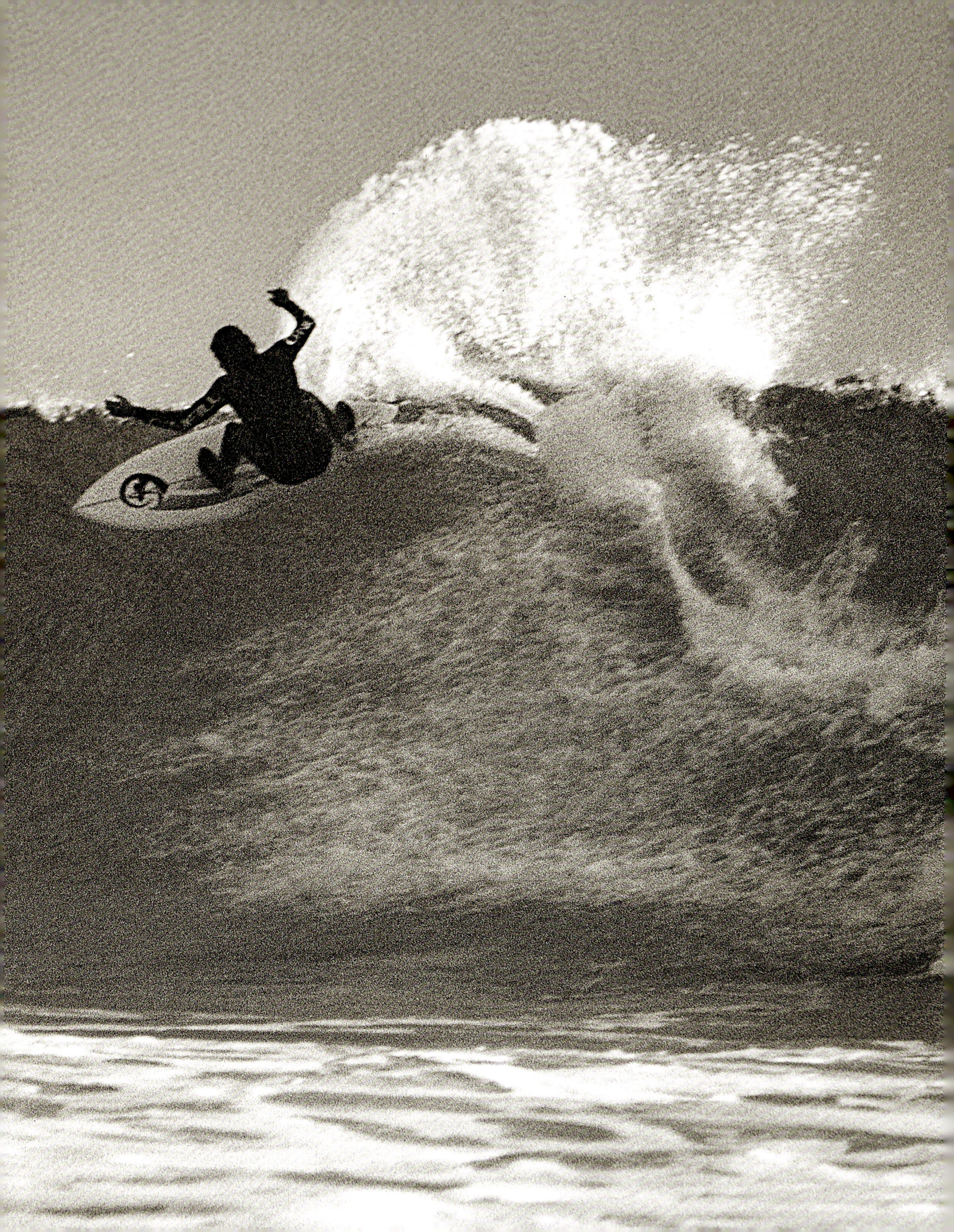

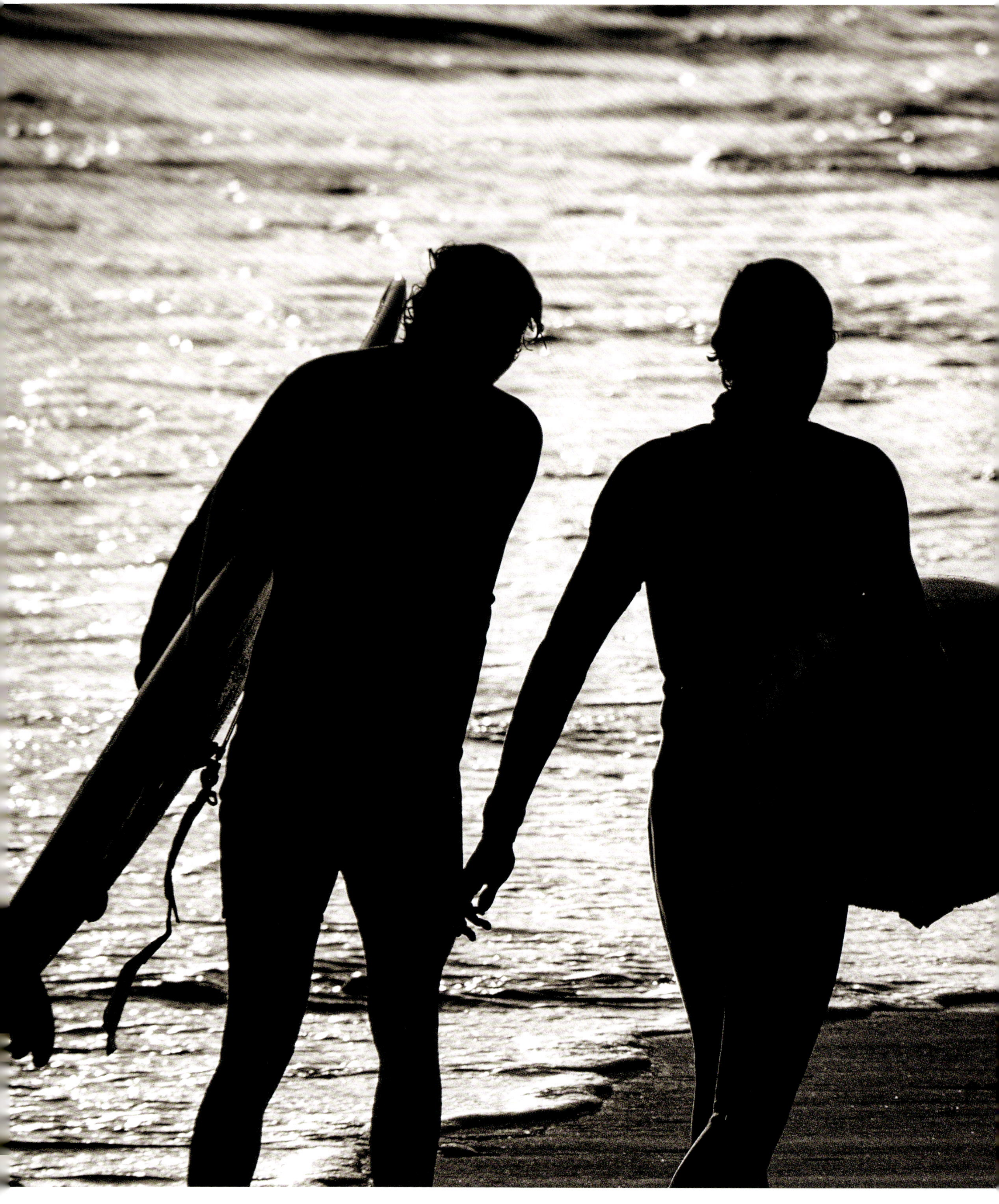

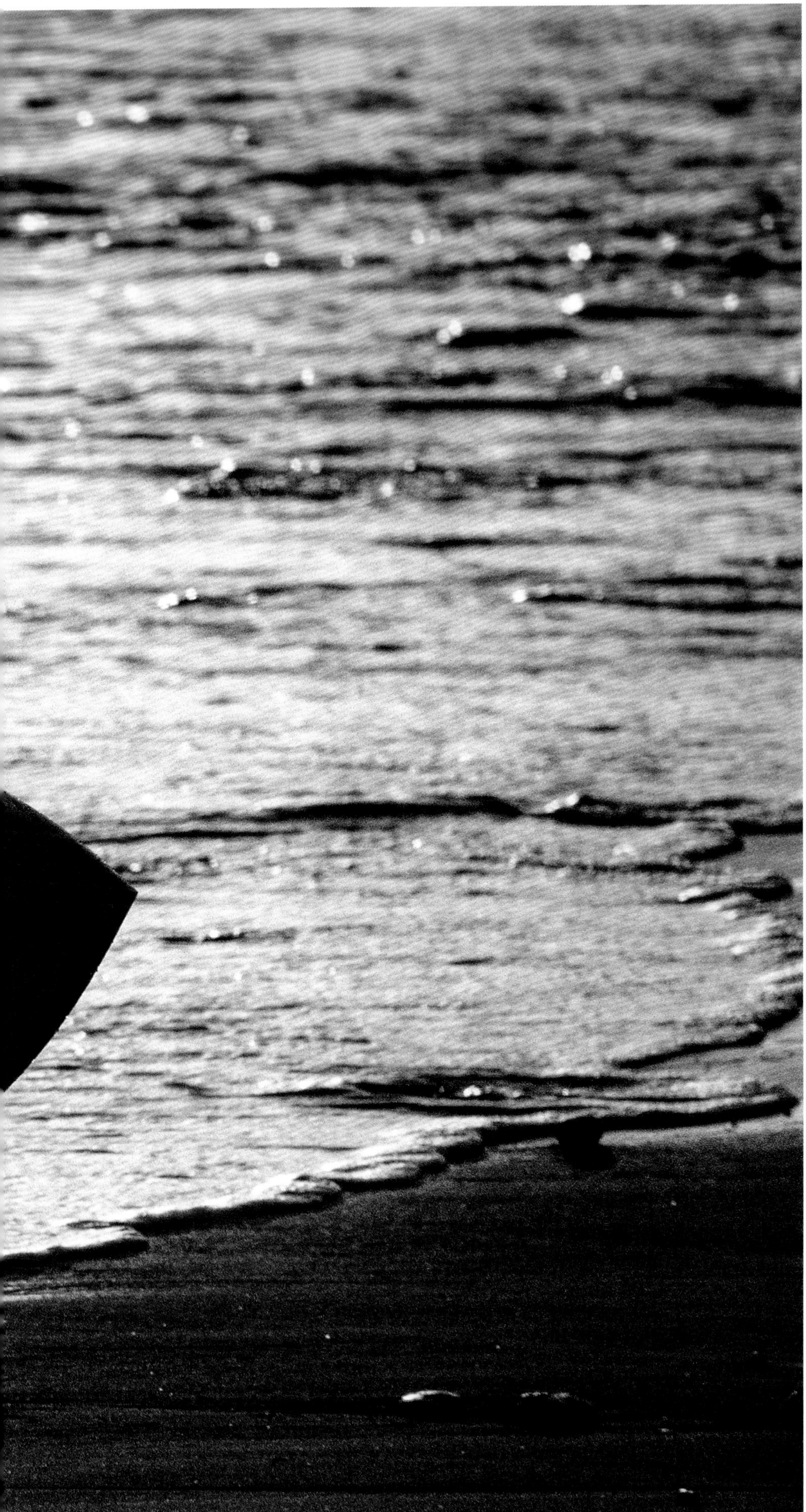

Previous

Shot on the same day as the previous spread of Russ Short, this was the first time I saw Shaun surfing Rincon. On days that followed, I would hang at Rincon, pretending to be seriously shooting, trying to conserve my film, hoping Shaun would show. It would just kill me to hear, "Yeah, Shaun was here, but he just left. You really missed it; he was ripping!"

Spread

Bridging the eras at Rincon, Stu Fredericks and Shaun Tomson head back up to the top of the point for "just one more." I didn't know Stu well, but he would always smile and say "Hi!" as he passed. I always admired how gracious he was in the midst of the Rincon crowd, even though he'd been surfing there long before most of the others had even picked up a board.

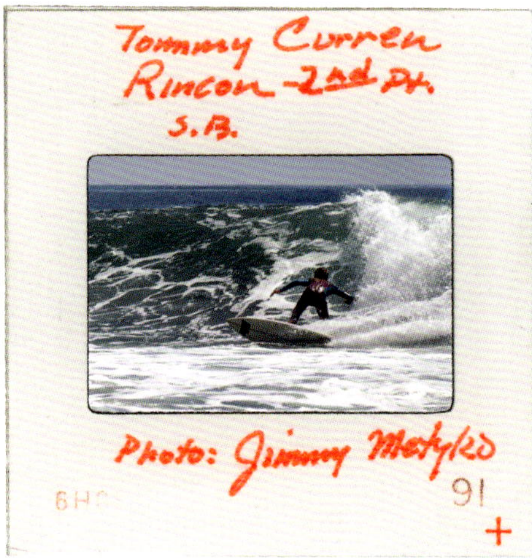
Tommy Curren
Rincon - 2nd Pt.
S.B.
Photo: Jimmy Metyko

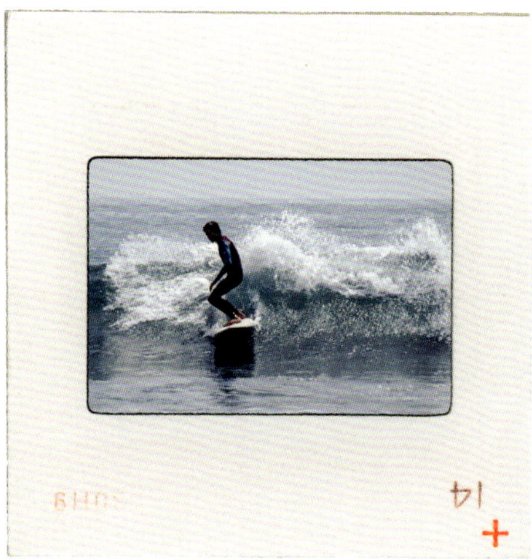

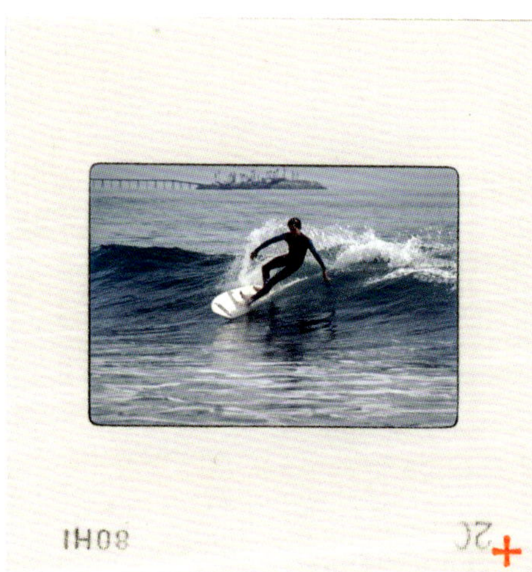

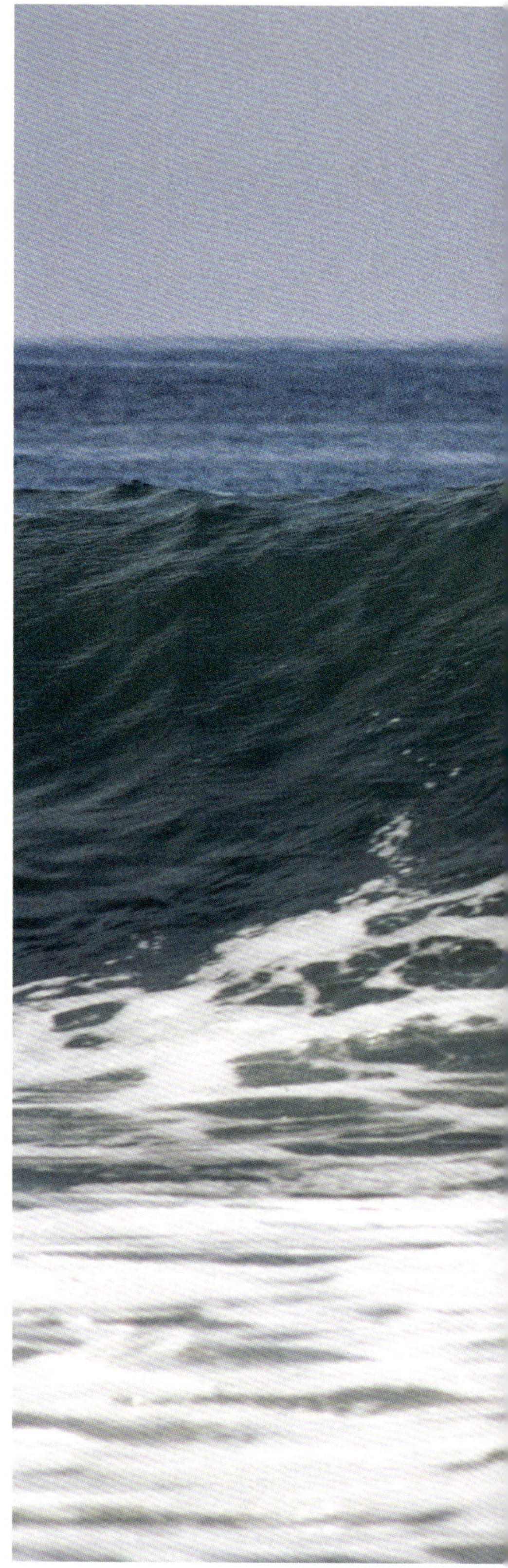

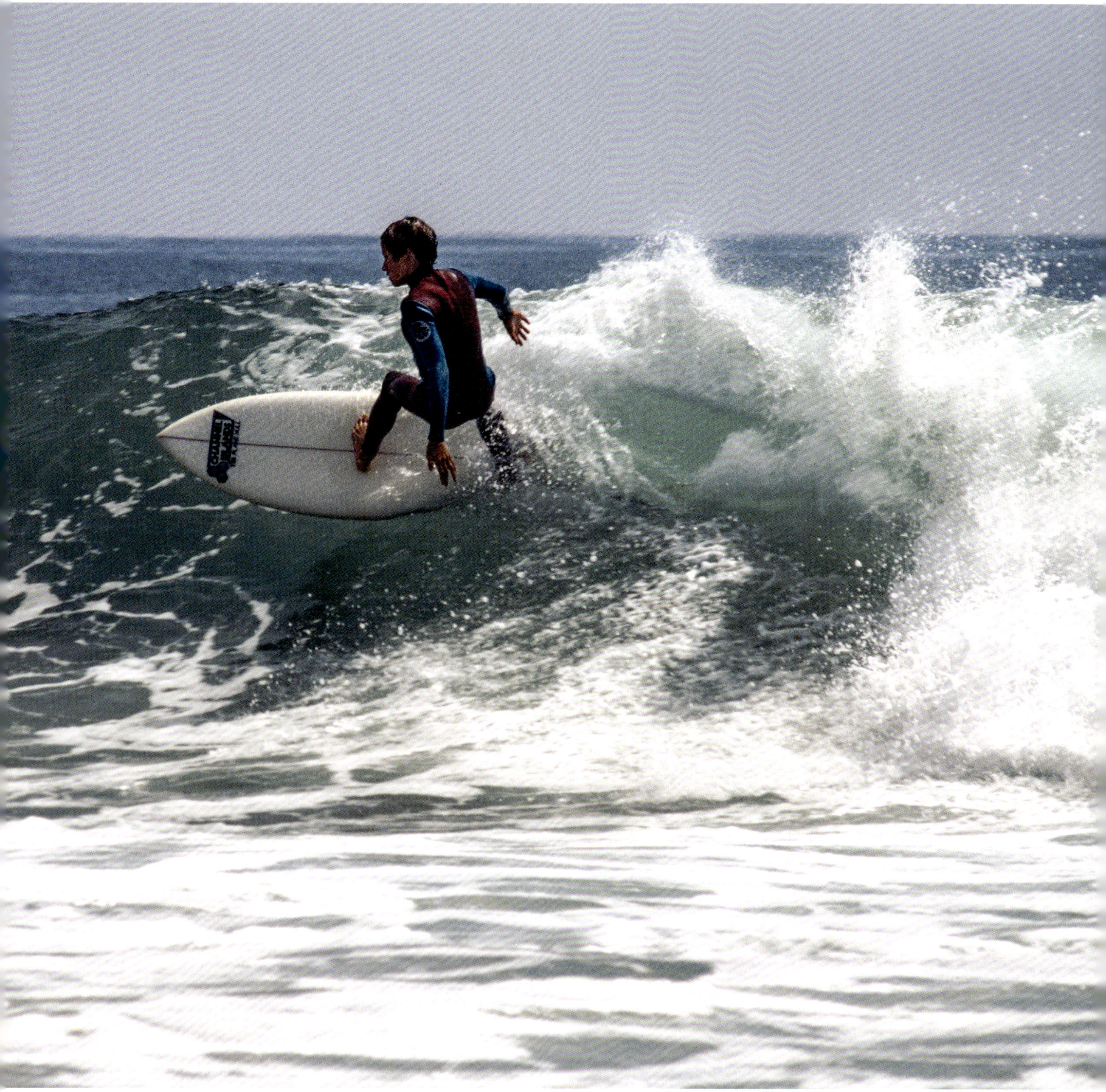

These are my first photos of Tommy Curren at Rincon. Just fifteen years old, he was already a two-time US Boys champion, but watching him riding his Al Merrick tri-plane-hull twin-fin this day, it was clear that even bigger things were in store.

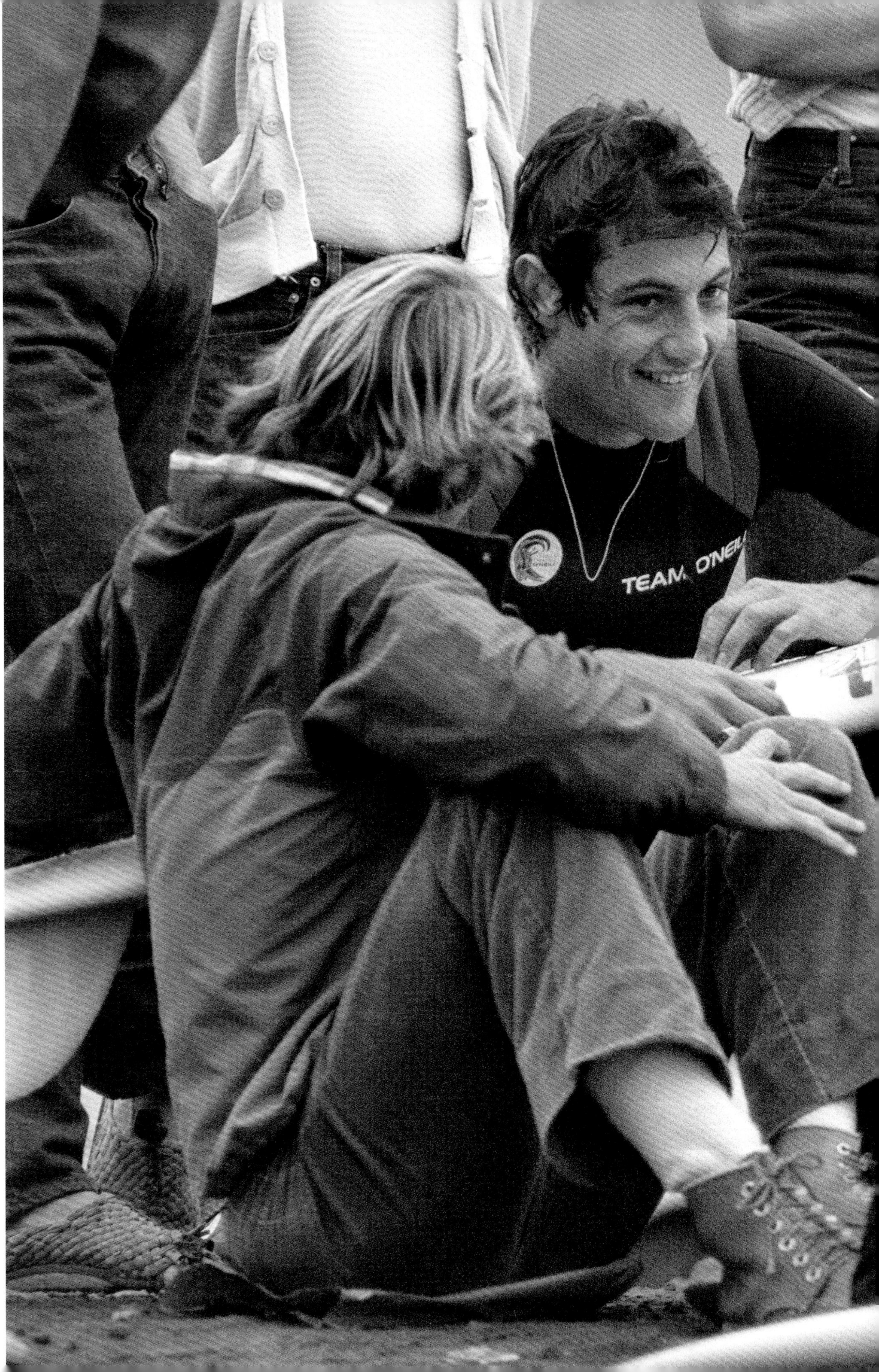
TEAM

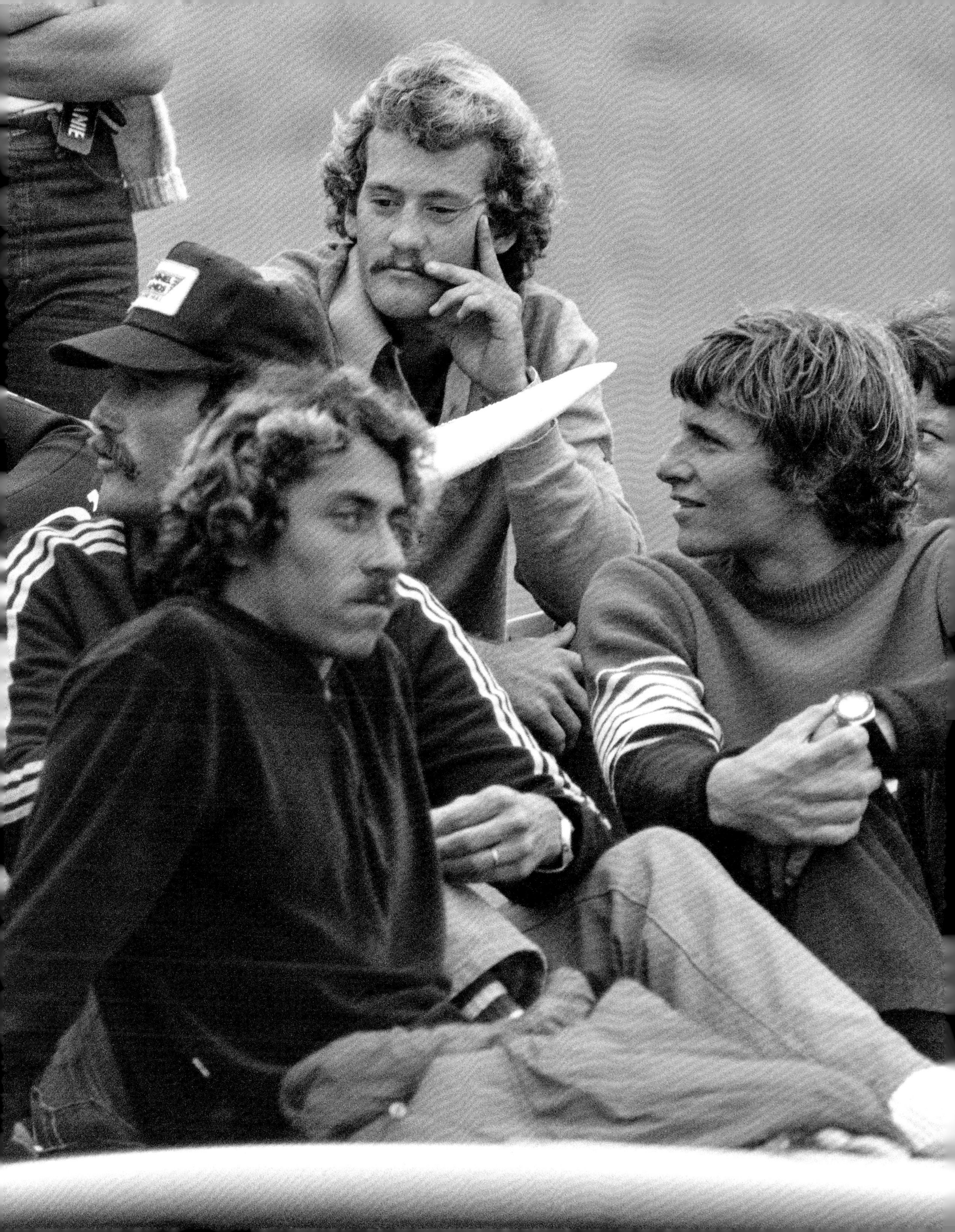

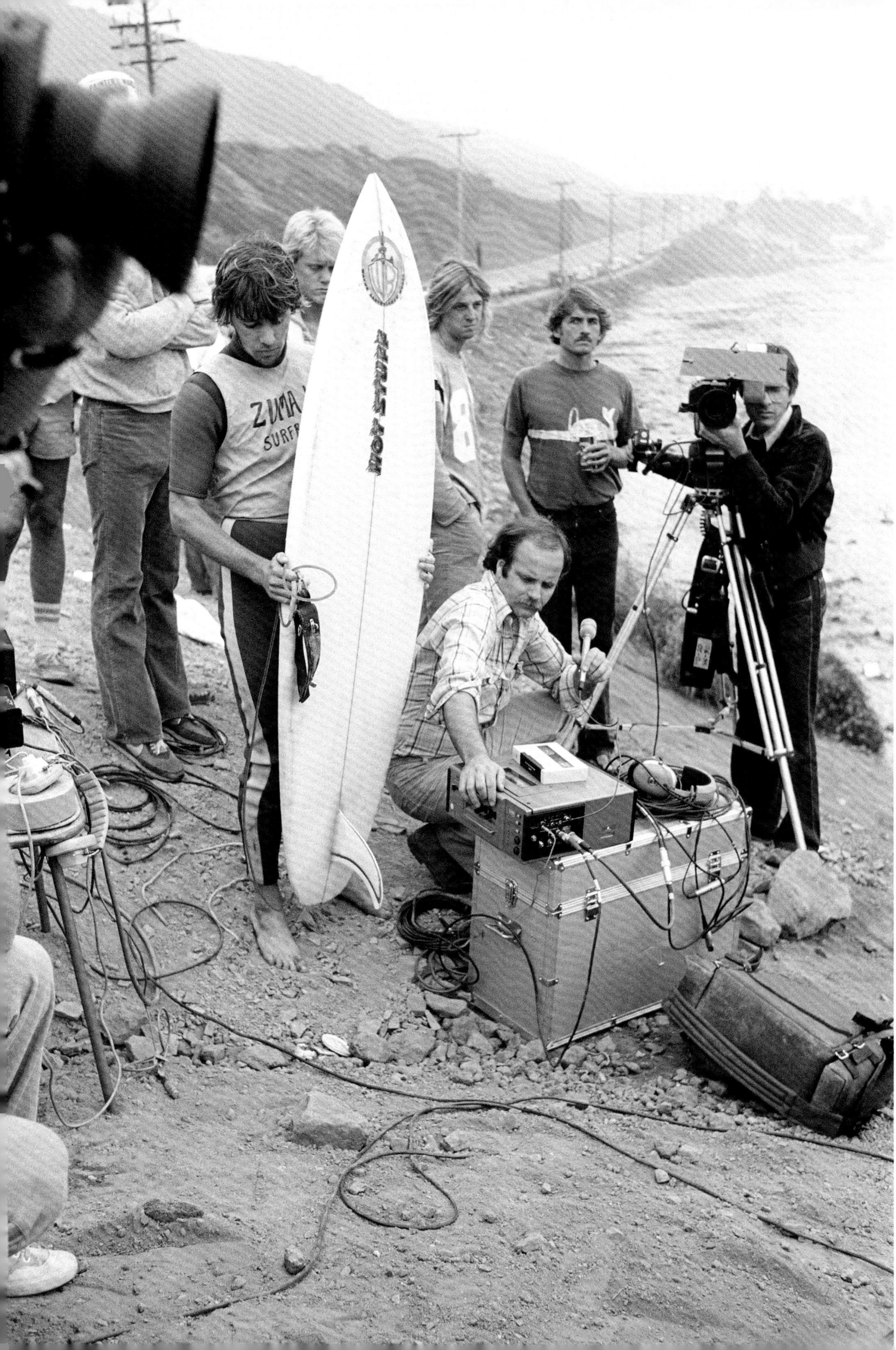

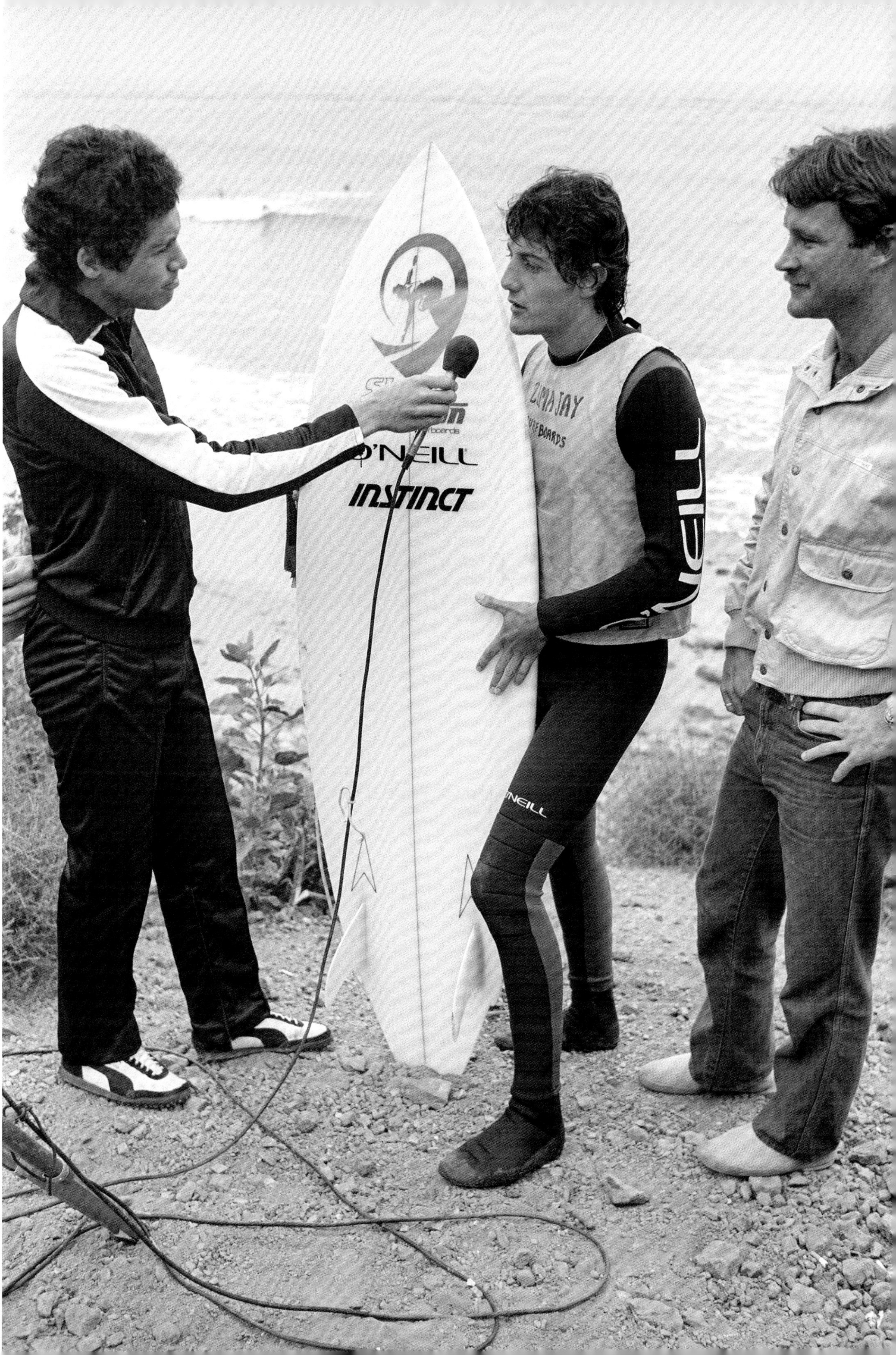
O'NEILL
INSTINCT
ZUMA JAY
O'NEILL
O'NEILL

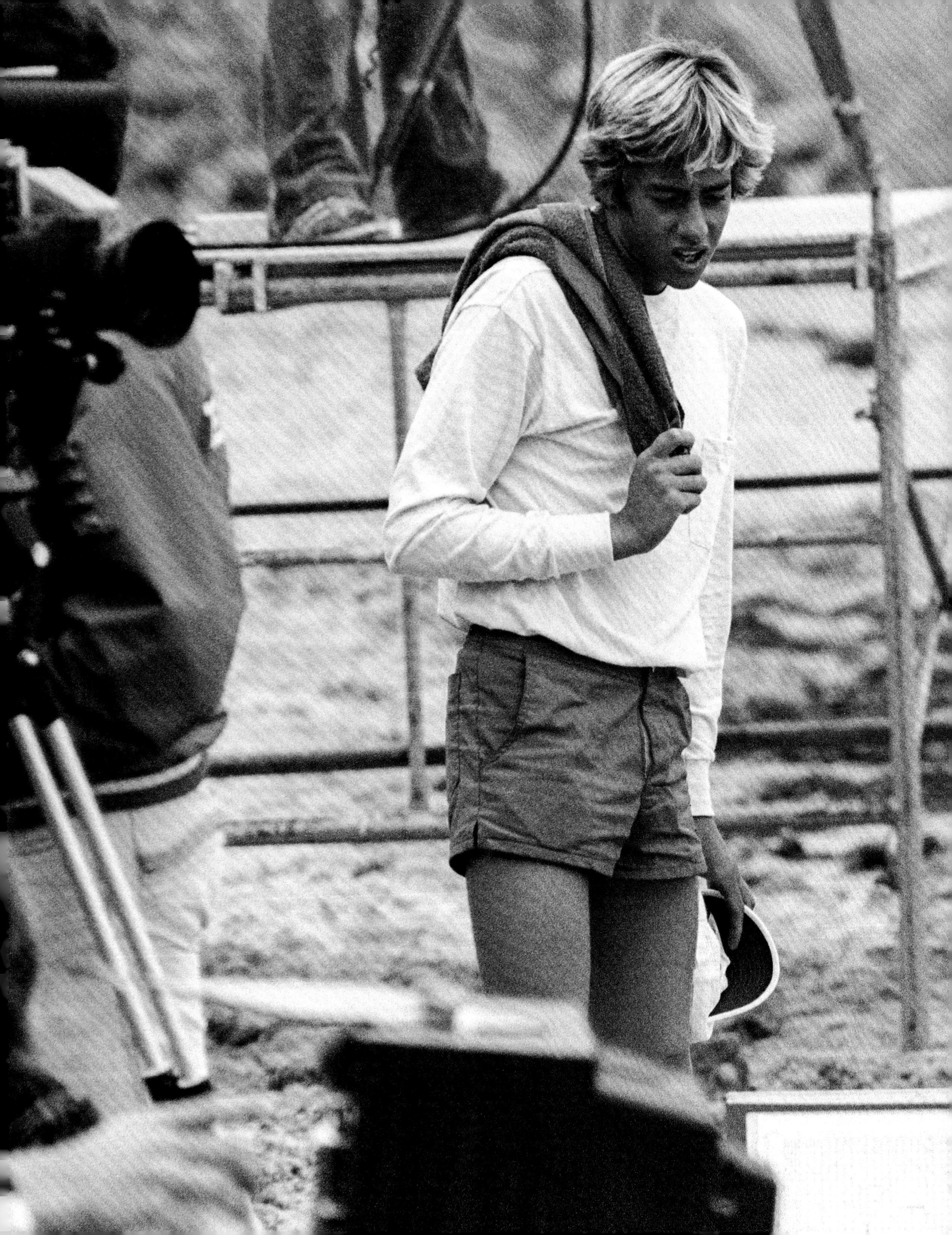

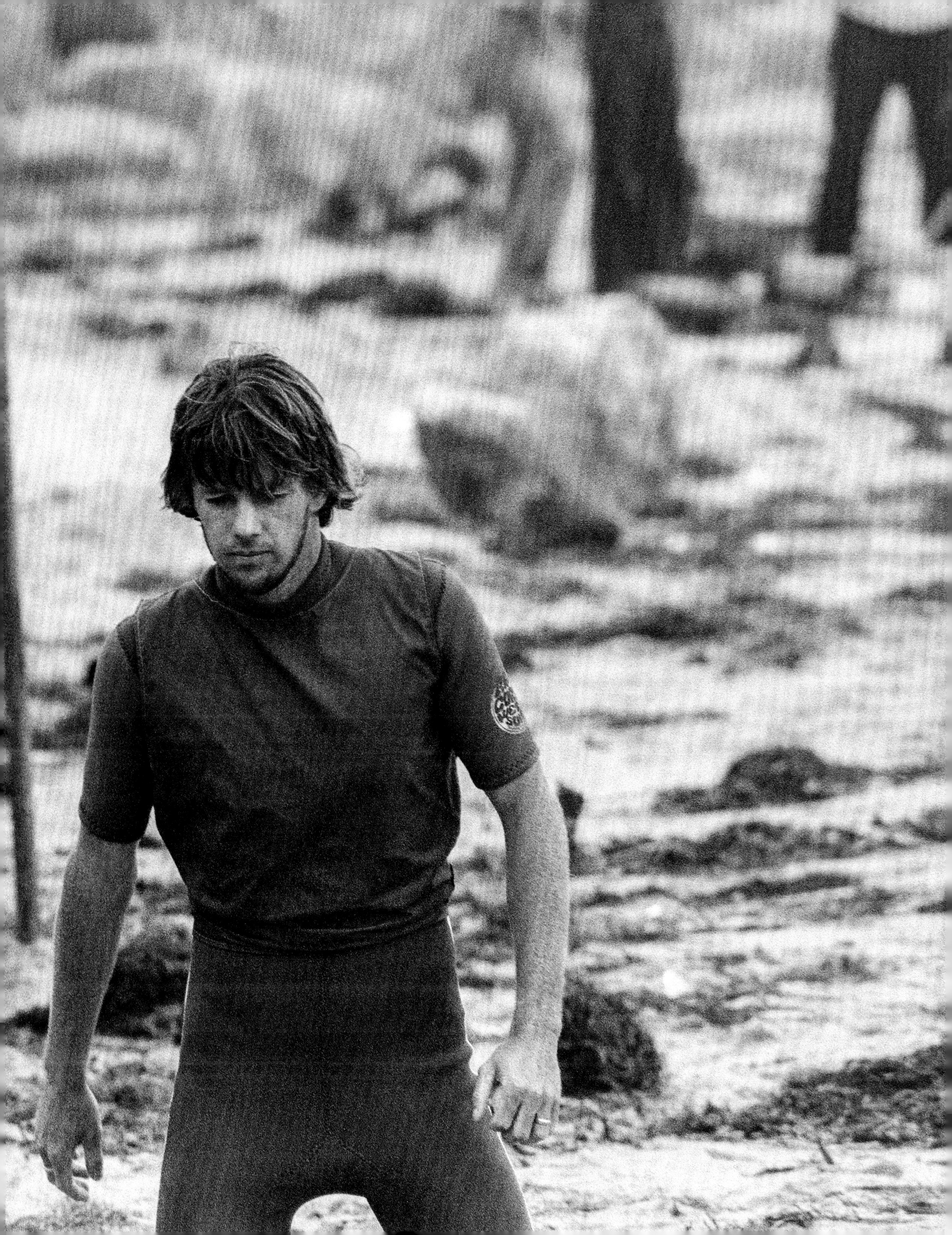

Pages 48–49

Back before there were "contestants only" areas at surf contests, everyone just found a spot on the beach and grouped together by surfboard label or surf shop team. The Malibu Pro was no exception, as evidenced by this shot of the Channel Islands camp, assembled to watch Tommy Curren's heat. *(Left to right)* Matt George, Shaun Tomson, Al Merrick, Soren Hansen, Sam George, Jeanine Curren *(partially obscured)*, and David Pu'u *(foreground)*.

Page 50

Wayne "Rabbit" Bartholomew, surfing's version of Mick Jagger, preparing for the final pre-heat interview. Rabbit would go on to win this event on his Hot Stuff single-fin.

Page 51

Shaun Tomson, flanked by International Professional Surfers pro-tour founder Randy Rarick while being interviewed by sports commentator Roy Firestone. Firestone would later play himself in the famous "Show me the money!" scene from the 1996 film *Jerry Maguire*, while pro-surfing advocates Shaun and Randy would spend the next decade making the same fervent request of the surf industry.

Pages 52–53

Matt George and I were in line at Neptune's Net café, across the highway from the contest site, when we found ourselves chatting with Wayne "Rabbit" Bartholomew. Matt had just suggested introducing Rabbit to Tommy Curren, who considered the 1979 world champion his favorite surfer, when we looked across the street and saw Tommy take off on a wave and pull a stylish twin-fin swoop before disappearing from view behind traffic. Rabbit must've seen something he liked, because I later noticed the two checking out each other's boards.

Facing

Pre-heat strategy talk, with Tommy's hair still wet from his warm-up surf. Note Tommy's mismatched Kanvas by Katin contest jersey.

Pages 56–57

Giving notice: Tommy's surfing in the Malibu Pro was more than just a top performance. It was a glimpse of surfing's future.

Off Broadway

Preston Murray and Craig Brazda, up from Newport Beach, were crashing at Sam George's place in Santa Barbara and offered me a ride down to the contest. Early the next morning, I found myself crammed like a sardine in the back seat of Preston's VW Squareback for the trip down the coast to a spot called County Line. As we pulled into the dirt parking lot, the George Benson song "On Broadway" playing at full volume, I tumbled out of the car into what appeared to be a decidedly off-Broadway scene: folding chairs and tables, and milk crates full of soggy, mismatched competitor jerseys. Apparently the Malibu Pro's contest organizers had at the last minute lost their permit to hold the event at the more prestigious Surfrider Beach and had scrambled to set up on the bluff at County Line, some fifteen miles and a world away from the fabled pointbreak. But if the contest site looked like a typical amateur event, the competitors were anything but: here was a collection of the world's best surfers—top pros from Australia, South Africa, Hawaii, and California, so many of whom I'd seen only in magazines and surf movies. It might have been easy to get star-struck had our Channel Islands crew not represented so well, with Sam George reaching the quarterfinals before losing to 1976 World Champion Peter Townend, and Tommy Curren placing in the money round (later forfeiting the prize to retain amateur status). This was the first time many of the pros had the chance to watch Tommy surf, and it was obvious to all that they'd be seeing a lot more of him.

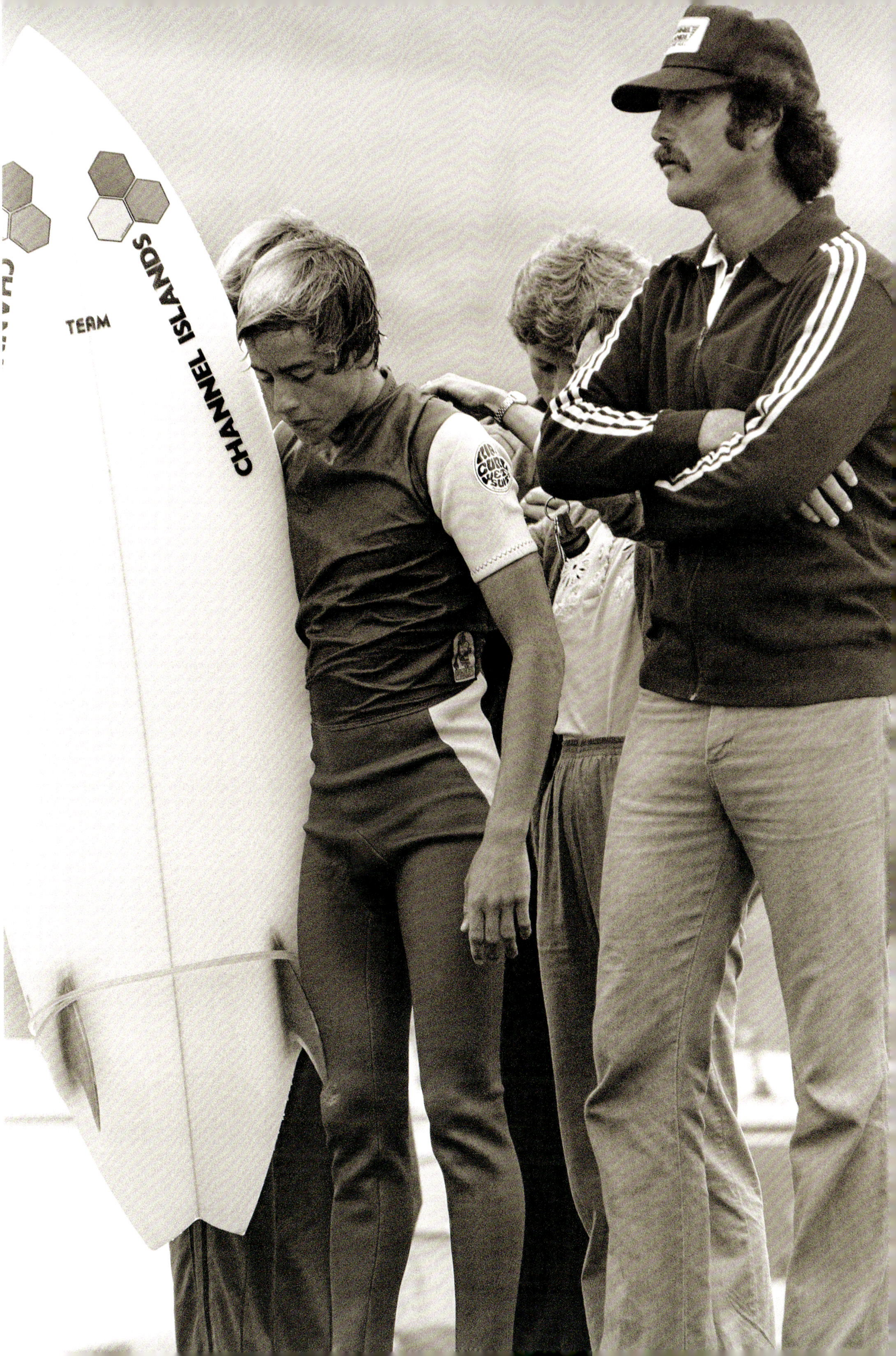
TEAM
CHANNEL ISLANDS

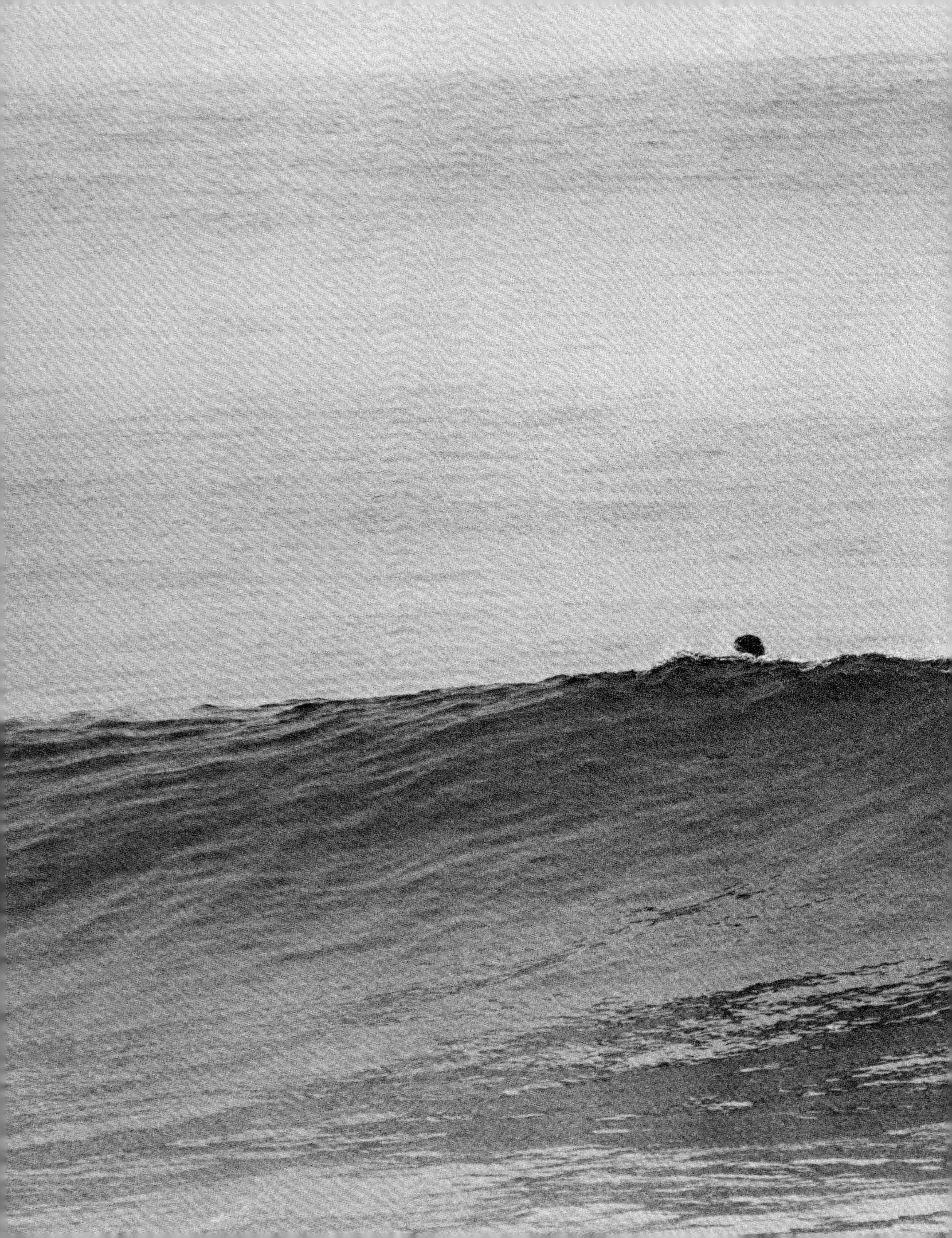

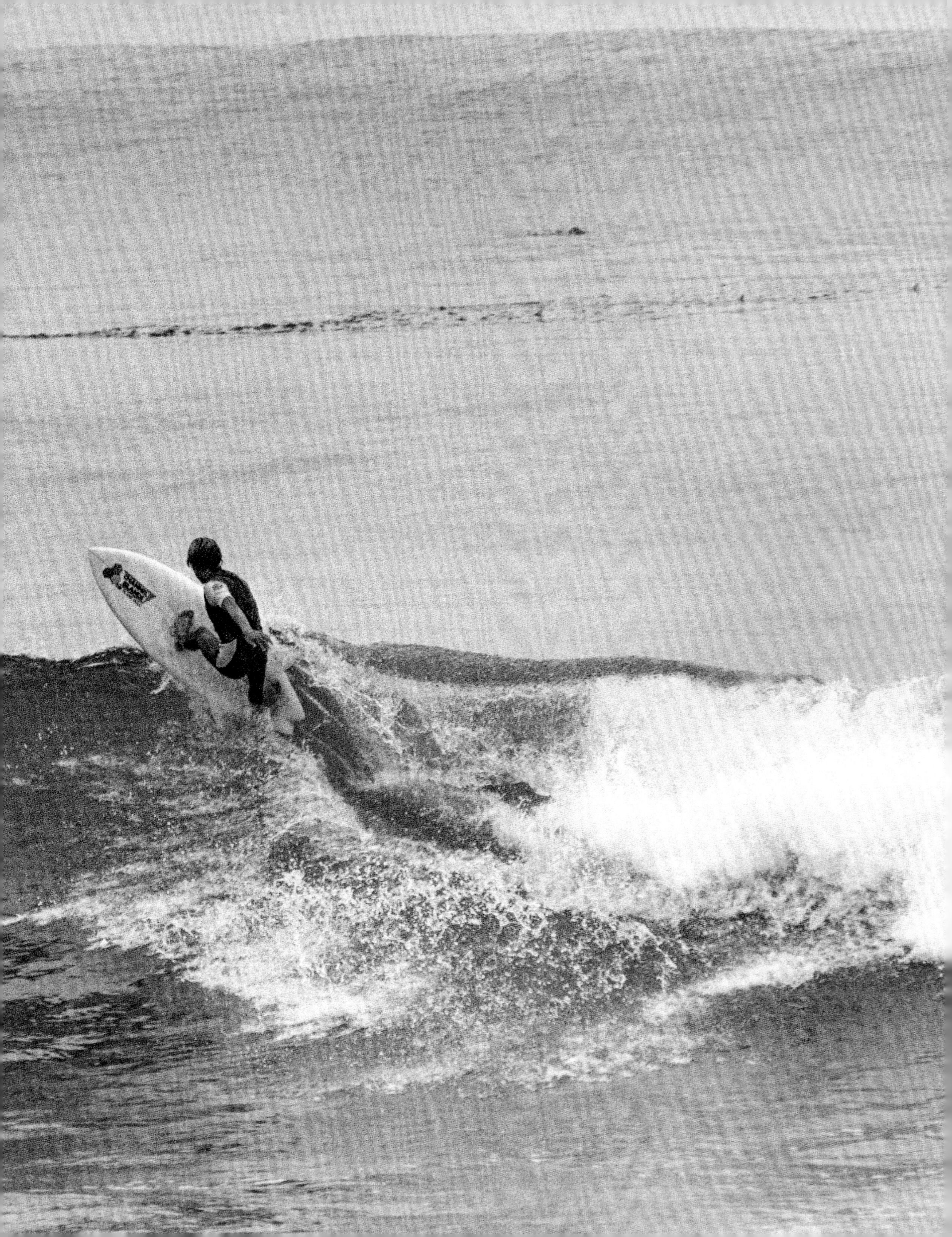

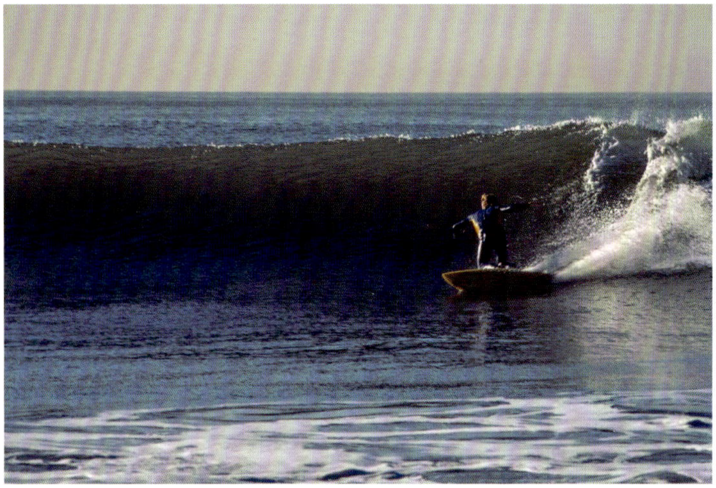

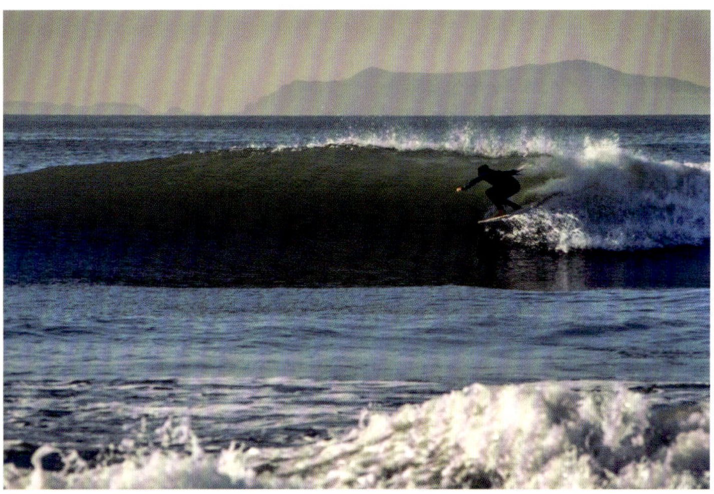

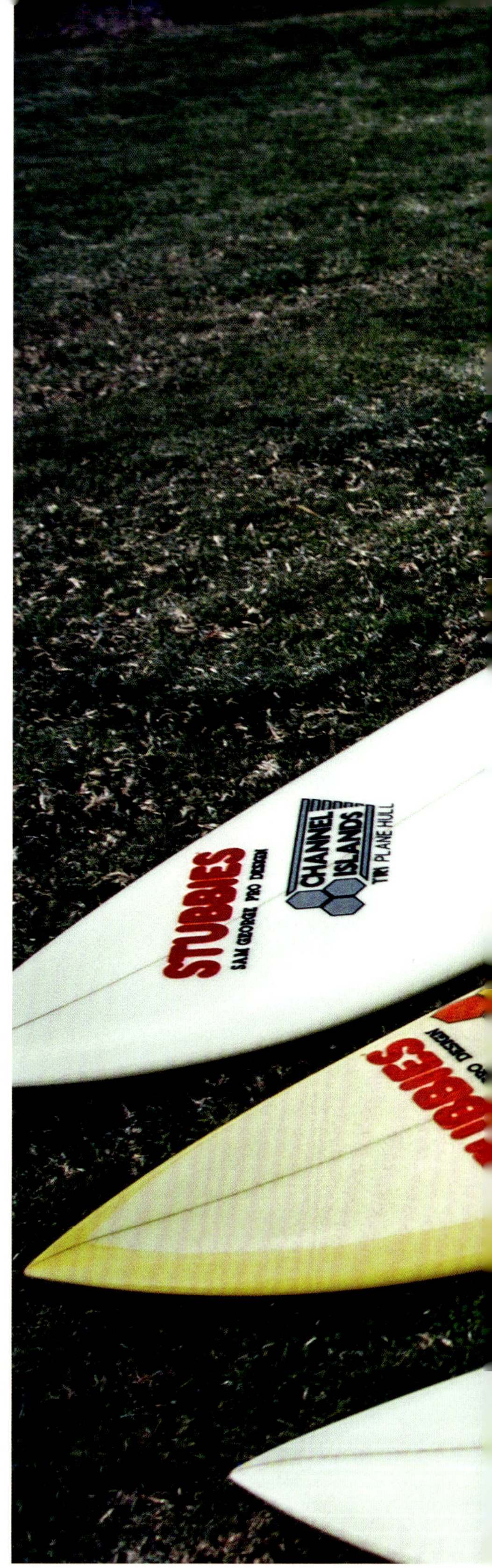

Top

Matt George, driving straight into an early morning sunrise, C Street, Ventura.

Bottom

Sam George, tucked tight on takeoff at C Street.

Main

(Left to right) Sam and Matt George, fully sponsored and appropriately equipped with Al Merrick pintails before heading to Hawaii for the winter season.

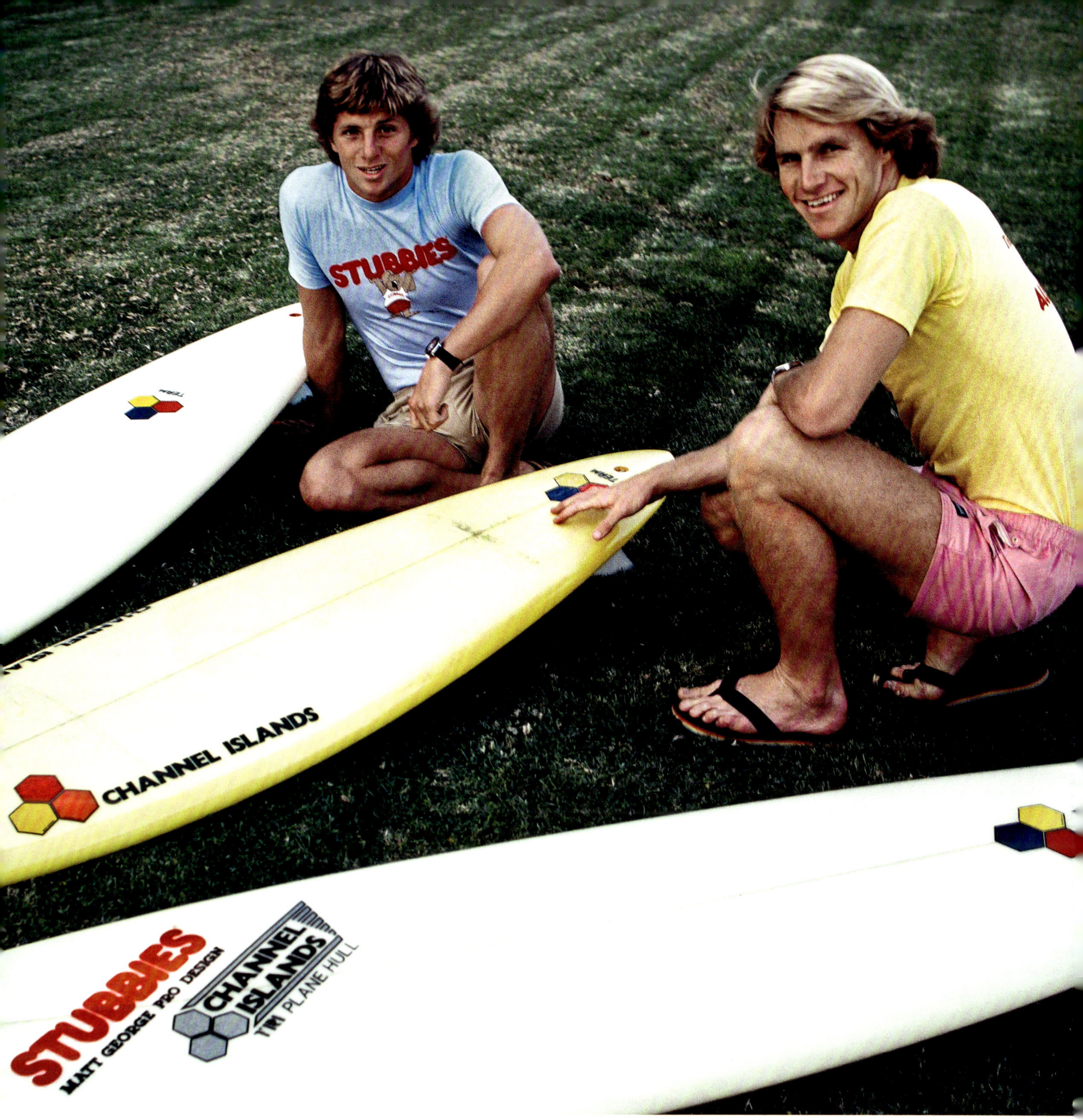
STUBBIES
CHANNEL ISLANDS
STUBBIES
MATT GEORGE PRO DESIGN
CHANNEL ISLANDS
TM PLANE HULL

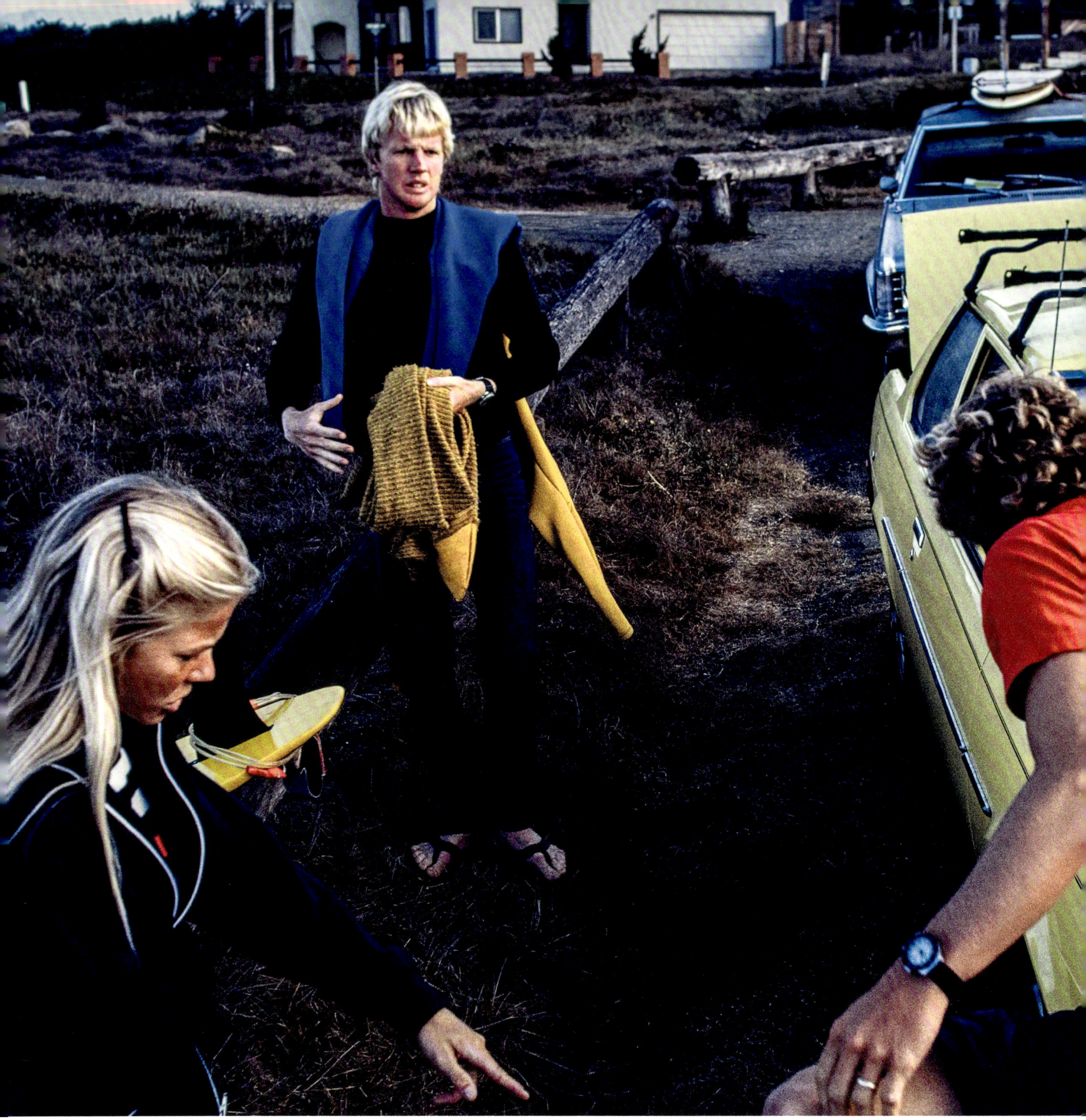

Australian pro Jim Banks, Sam George, and Galveston, Texas's Pat Leva chasing waves on the Central Coast. While visiting Southern California, Banks had driven up to Rincon, where his car promptly died in the parking lot. He ended up staying for a year, infusing the area with his positive energy and progressive surfing.

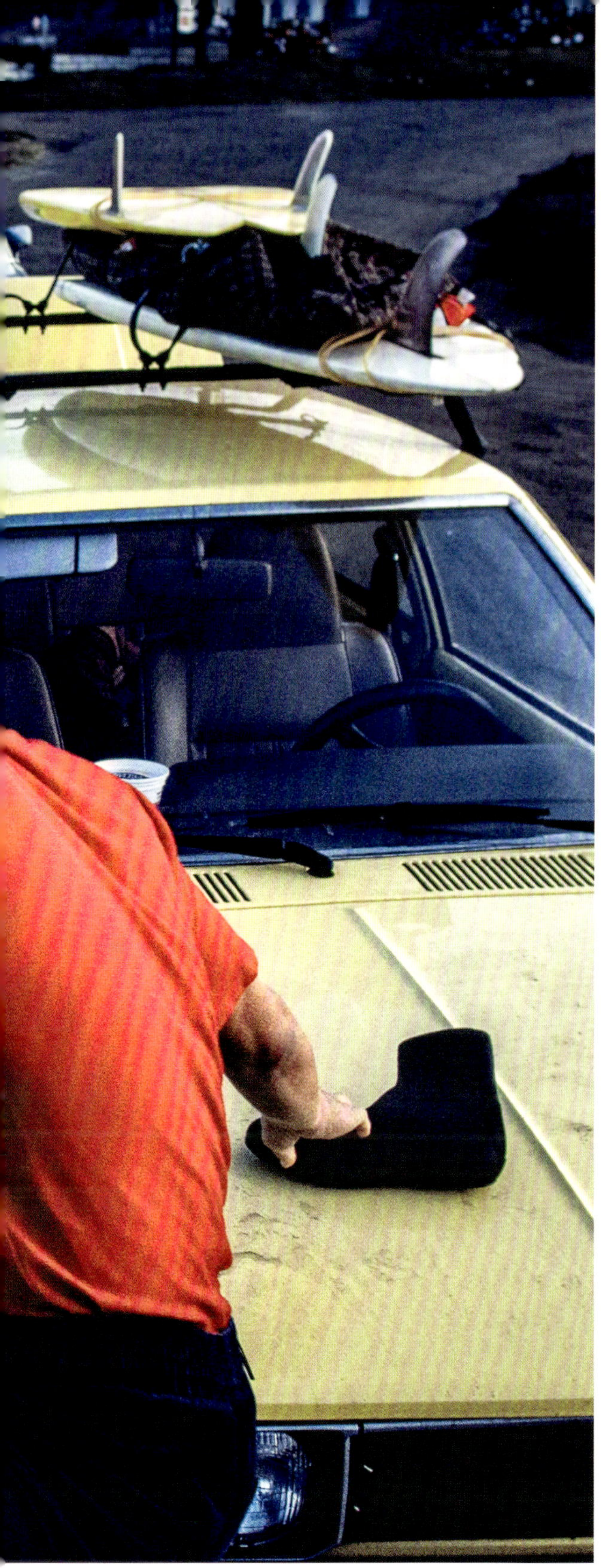

Sam & Matt

Sam and Matt George and I have shared more surf adventure over the years than can be chronicled. Starting back on that fateful day, coming straight from a Brooks new-student event, dressed nothing like a surfer, I walked through the Surf N Wear surf shop doors, introduced myself, and proclaimed straight up that I was here to be a surf photographer.

Even though the George brothers were from California, they were from the Central Coast, specifically San Luis Obispo by way of the San Francisco Bay Area—at the time, regions of California that were almost as isolated as Texas from the mainstream surf world of Southern California.

We were all bonded by our mutual early influence by the surf magazines, by dreaming the same dream—feeling a little like outsiders, wanting to participate and to contribute to all those glossy *Surfer* magazine pages, each in our own way.

As much as I knew about surfing, I knew very little about how the business side worked. It would be from both Sam and Matt that I would begin to understand the surf industry behind those very same pages.

During my years at Brooks, I watched firsthand as Sam and Matt pursued sponsorships with Stubbies and Rip Curl and made a go at the world tour as pro surfers in the early days of professional surfing, all the while capturing our adventures on film.

Ultimately it would be Sam and Matt who would give not just me, but all of us, a better understanding (both in real time and in hindsight), so beautifully with their words, of what was being accomplished by our loose-knit Santa Barbara group within the larger surf world.

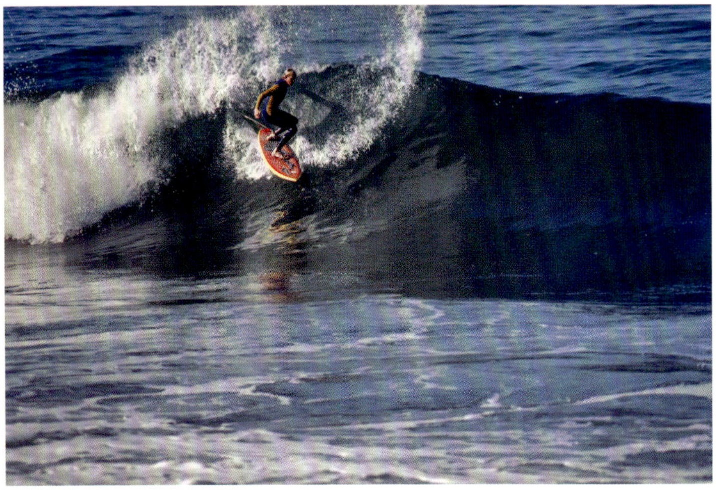 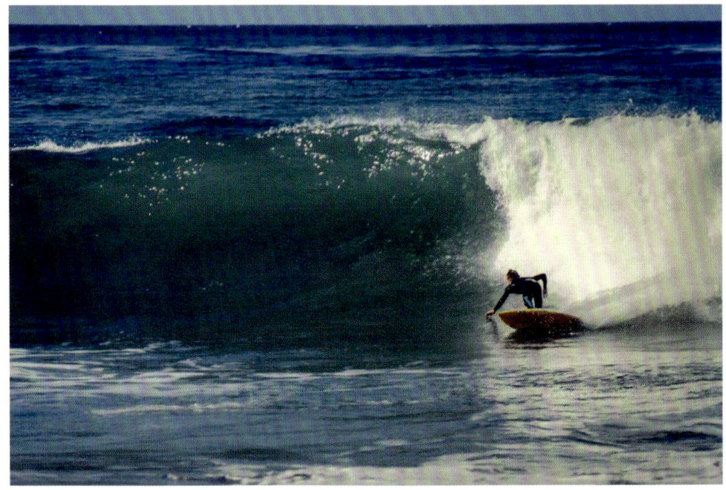

Those Waffles

We left early from Santa Barbara—Sam and Matt George, Jim Banks, and me—on a Central Coast strike mission, hoping to catch better waves than what our area had to offer at the time. Arriving in Morro Bay several hours later, we found the surf poorly shaped and not much bigger than what we'd left at home. Undeterred, we continued north, picking up local California pro Dave Parmenter on our way to Cambria's Moonstone Beach, where we were again met with dismal conditions. In an attempt to salvage something from what was now obviously a lost cause, Sam and Matt enthusiastically declared that the breakfast café across the street from the beach had the best waffles in California and marched off to get some. I was just about to follow when Banks and Parmenter tugged on their wetsuits and paddled out into the cold waist-high slop. I had a decision to make: delicious waffles or terrible surf—but terrible surf with two of the sport's hottest young surfers paddling out.

I set up my tripod and waited for something to happen. Incredibly, it did. Within minutes, a set of bigger waves approached, then another, bigger still, and, just like that, the session was on. For the next half-hour, the pair shared relatively clean, well-shaped overhead waves, Banks riding the lefts and Parmenter the rights, as I clicked away on shore, hardly believing my luck. Then, as suddenly as they appeared, the big sets died down, the wave shape deteriorated, and the conditions returned to their earlier state of awfulness, driving Banks and Parmenter back to shore. Just then, Sam and Matt strolled back from their breakfast and, regarding the empty lineup, said, "Boy, you guys really missed it. Those waffles were great." We just looked at them and smiled. There was no point in saying anything until I'd get the film back a week later.

Top

Jim Banks *(left)* and Dave Parmenter *(right)*, missing out on some great waffles.

Facing

Banks, showing some leg after the Cambria session.

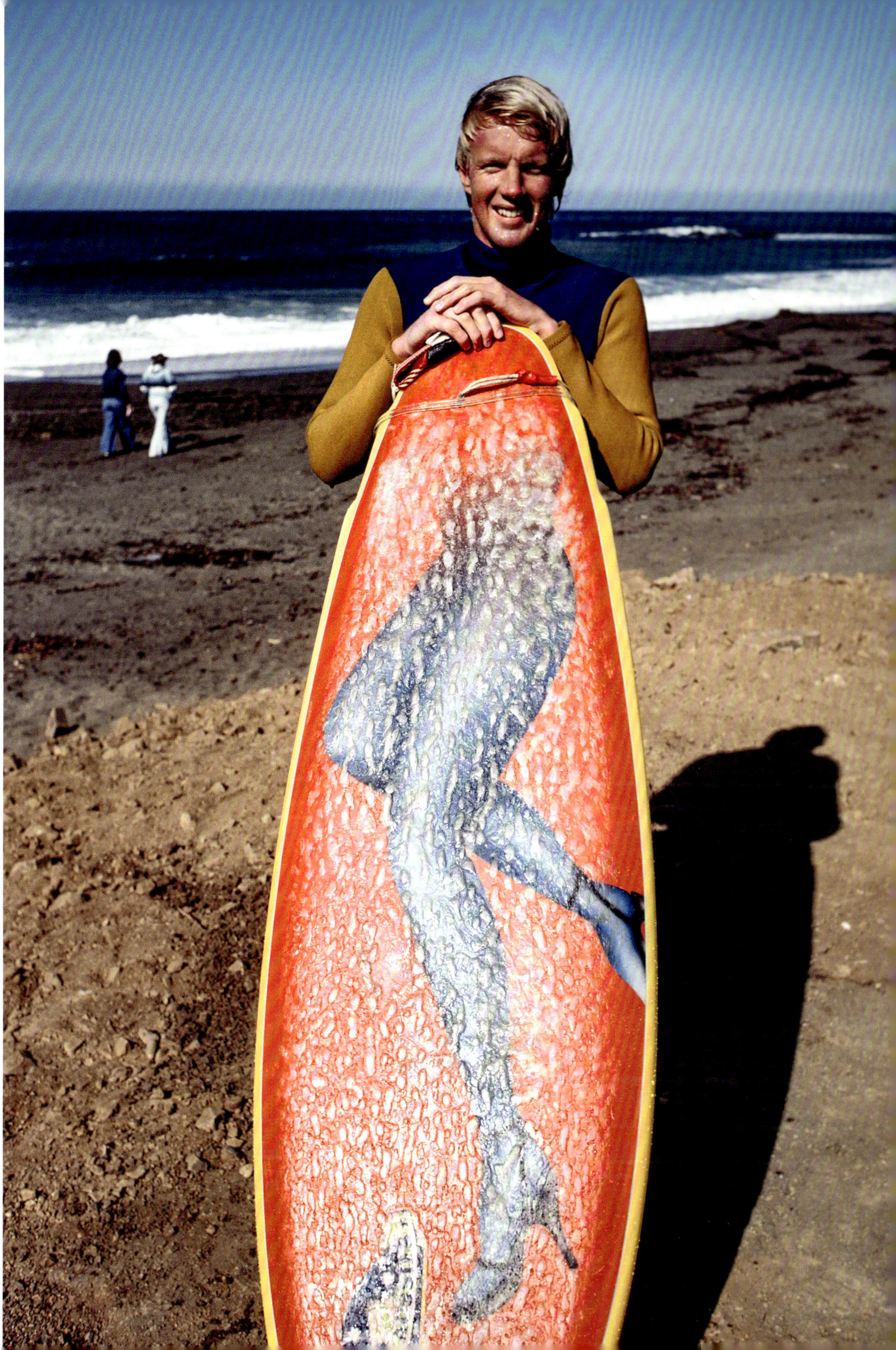

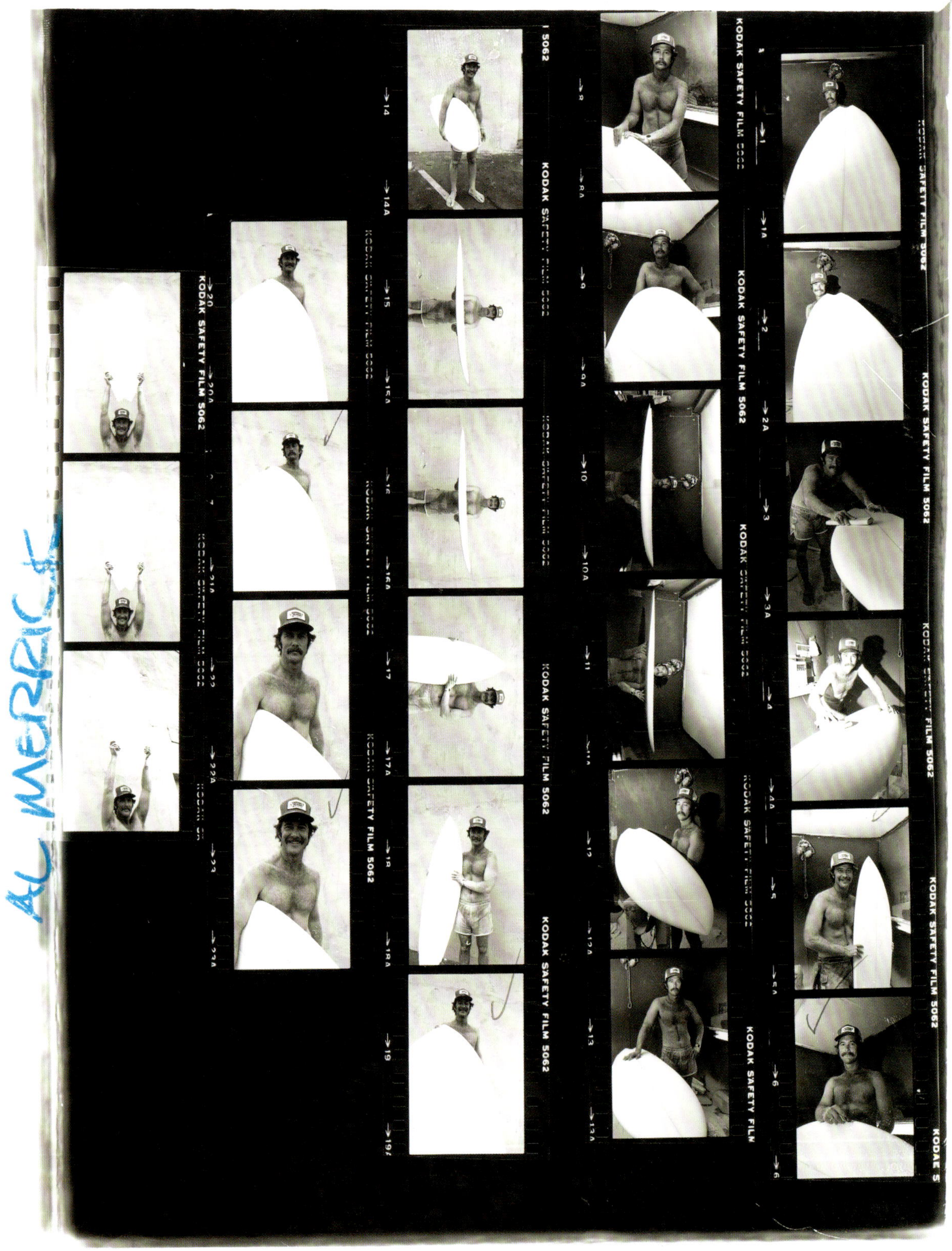

Above

Contact sheet from my first photo shoot with Al Merrick.

Facing

I wish I would've shot more of Al Merrick actually shaping back then. Shooting in a shaping room is difficult, being by design built to absorb light, not bounce it, and so it takes a lot of time to set up proper lighting. As this meant stopping production, I always gave myself a thirty-minute disruption limit. Merrick was always great about it, though, and never pressured me to hurry.

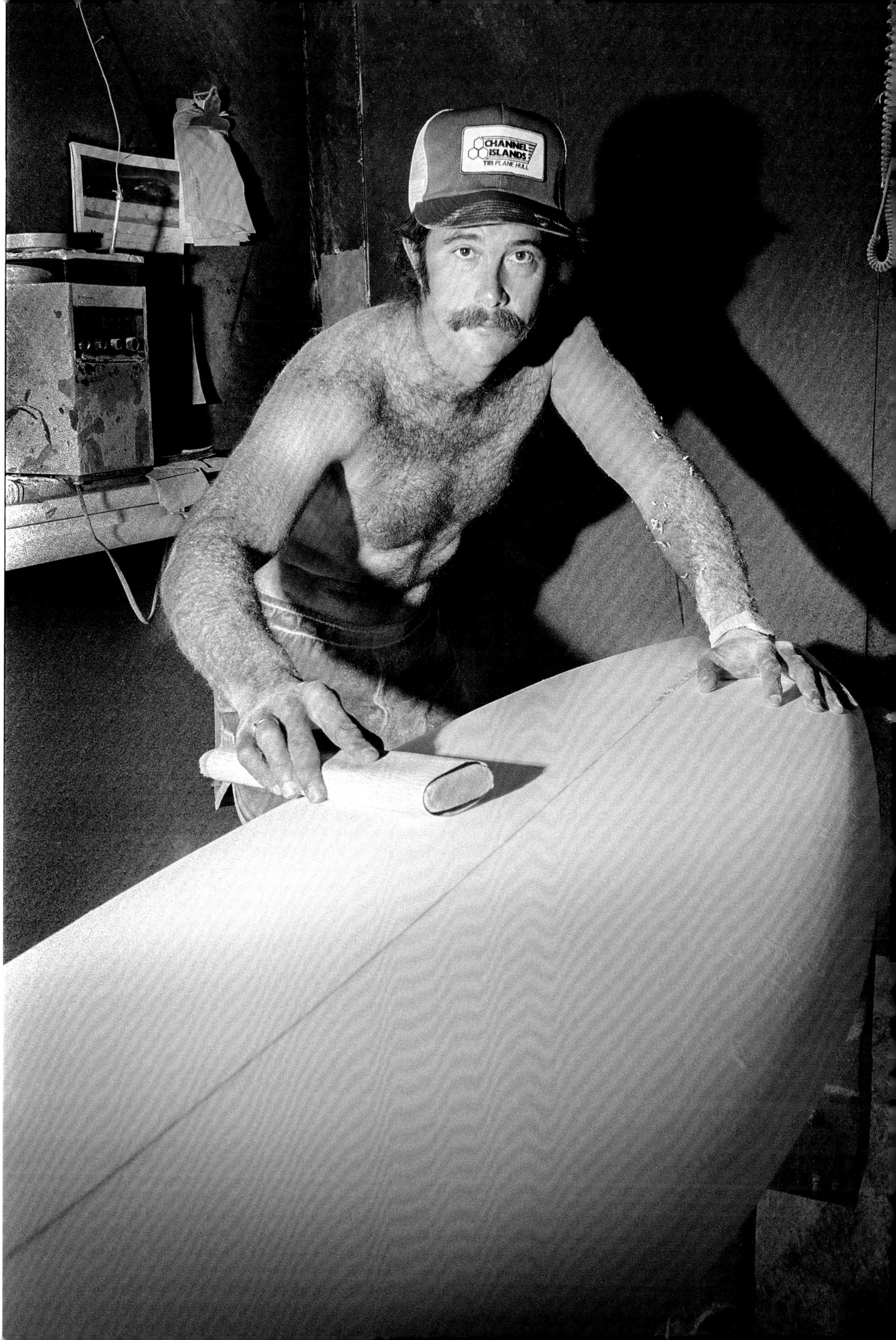
CHANNEL ISLANDS
TRI PLANE HULL

ASAP

When I first started submitting my photos to *Surfer* magazine, the results were pretty discouraging. I can still recite the wording of the many rejection letters I received: "Thank you for your submission, but we are unable to use any of your photos at this time. Please find enclosed all of your photos." Rumor had it that the publication's legendary photo editor, Art Brewer, had in his office a knee-high pile of submissions never to be opened, let alone reviewed. I didn't lose hope, however, and faithfully kept submitting my images despite never receiving a direct response.

One day, completely out of the blue, I was delivered a postcard, handwritten by Brewer himself, informing me that they needed black-and-white images of Al Merrick ASAP. I could hardly believe it: Art Brewer, who, more than any other surf photographer, I wanted to impress, needed my photos—and ASAP, whatever that meant. Kim Robinson, Channel Islands shop manager, would explain that acronym to me when setting up the shoot with Merrick, the results of which I had to submit undeveloped "as soon as possible." A single image later ran in the magazine, and it was years before I came across the whole contact sheet in my own "Metyko" file at *Surfer*. But it was that first postcard from Art Brewer that let me know I had almost arrived.

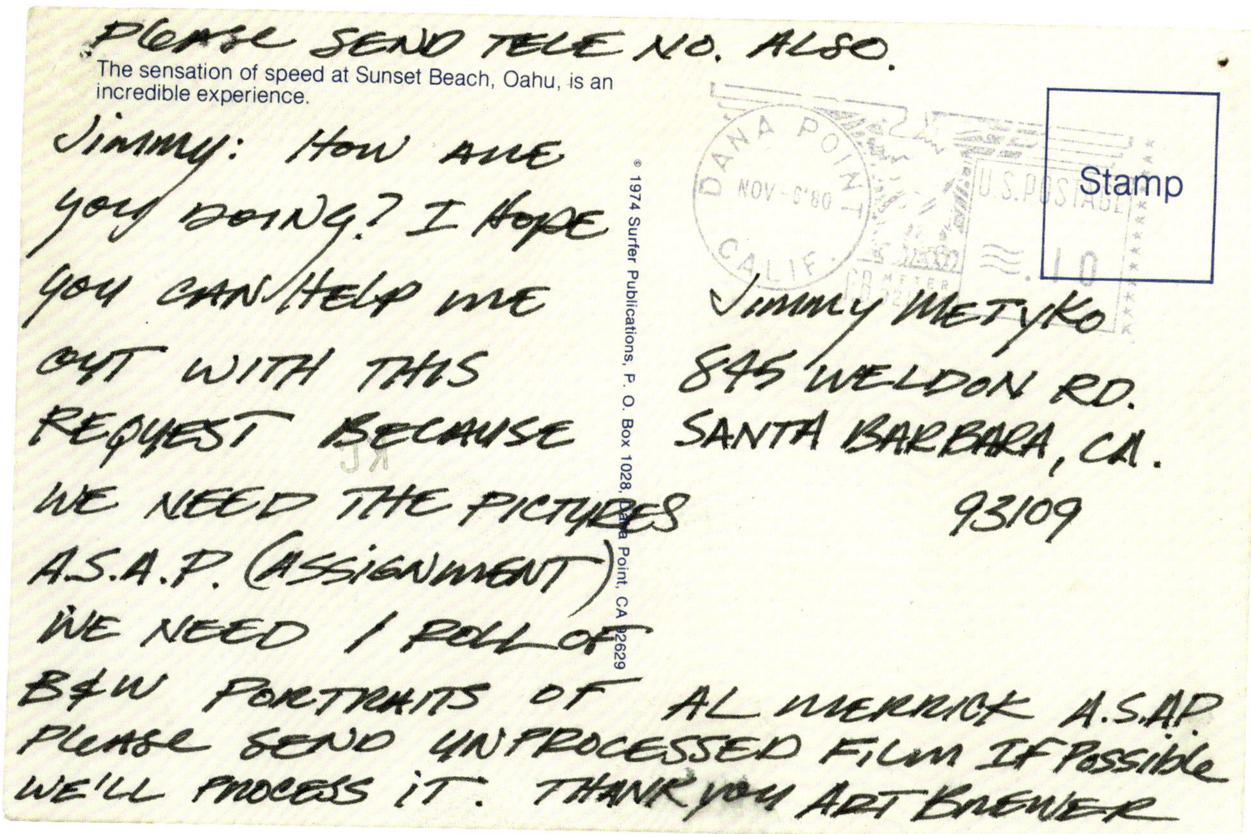
PLEASE SEND TELE NO. ALSO.

The sensation of speed at Sunset Beach, Oahu, is an incredible experience.

JIMMY: HOW ARE YOU DOING? I HOPE YOU CAN HELP ME OUT WITH THIS REQUEST BECAUSE WE NEED THE PICTURES A.S.A.P. (ASSIGNMENT) WE NEED 1 ROLL OF B&W PORTRAITS OF AL MERRICK A.S.A.P. PLEASE SEND UNPROCESSED FILM IF POSSIBLE WE'LL PROCESS IT. THANK YOU ART BREWER

© 1974 Surfer Publications, P. O. Box 1028, Dana Point, CA 92629

DANA POINT NOV-6 '80 CALIF.

U.S. POSTAGE .10

Stamp

JIMMY METYKO
845 WELDON RD.
SANTA BARBARA, CA.
93109

Overleaf

Al Merrick, presenting for examination one of his innovative twin-fin shapes.

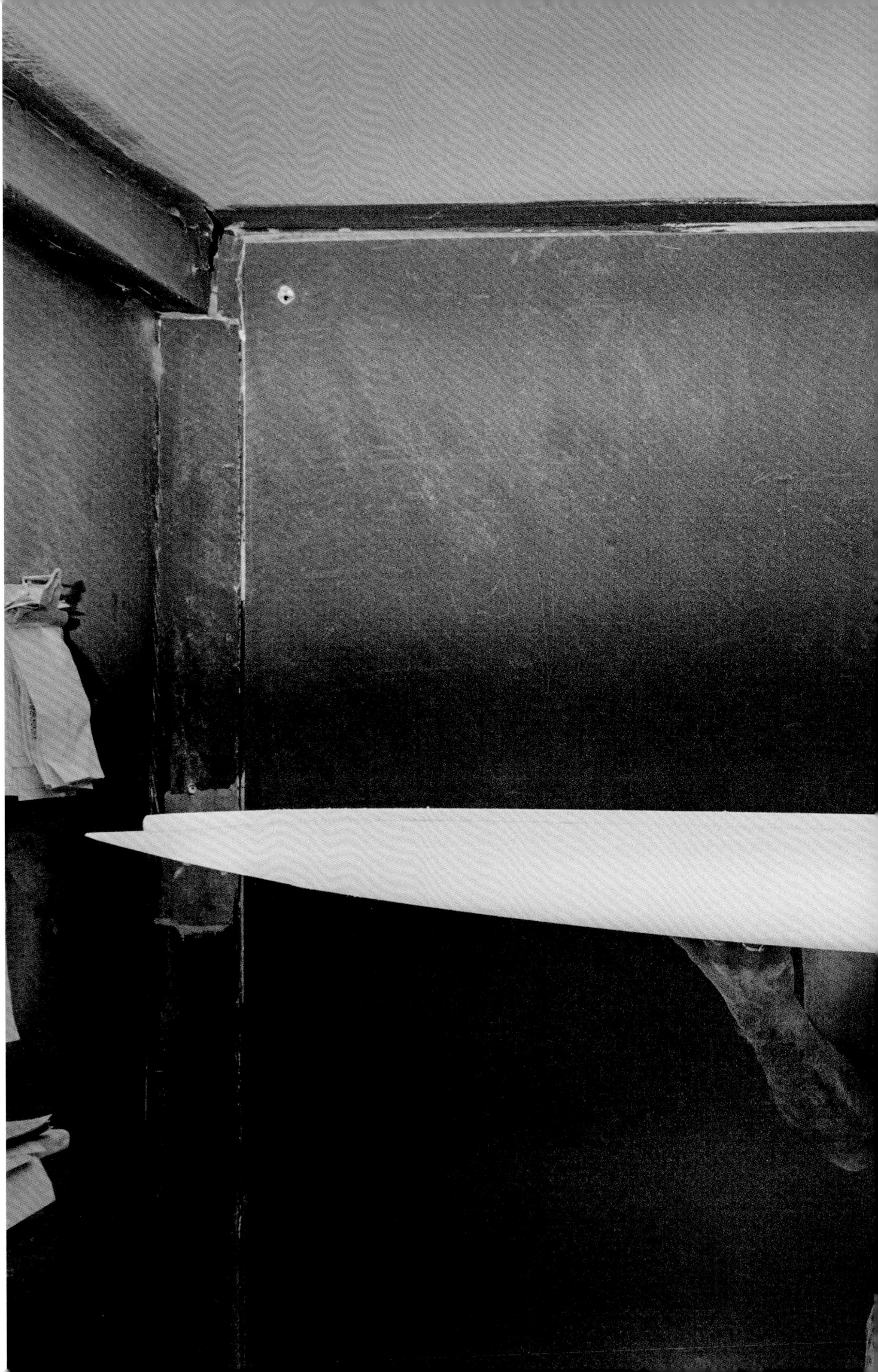

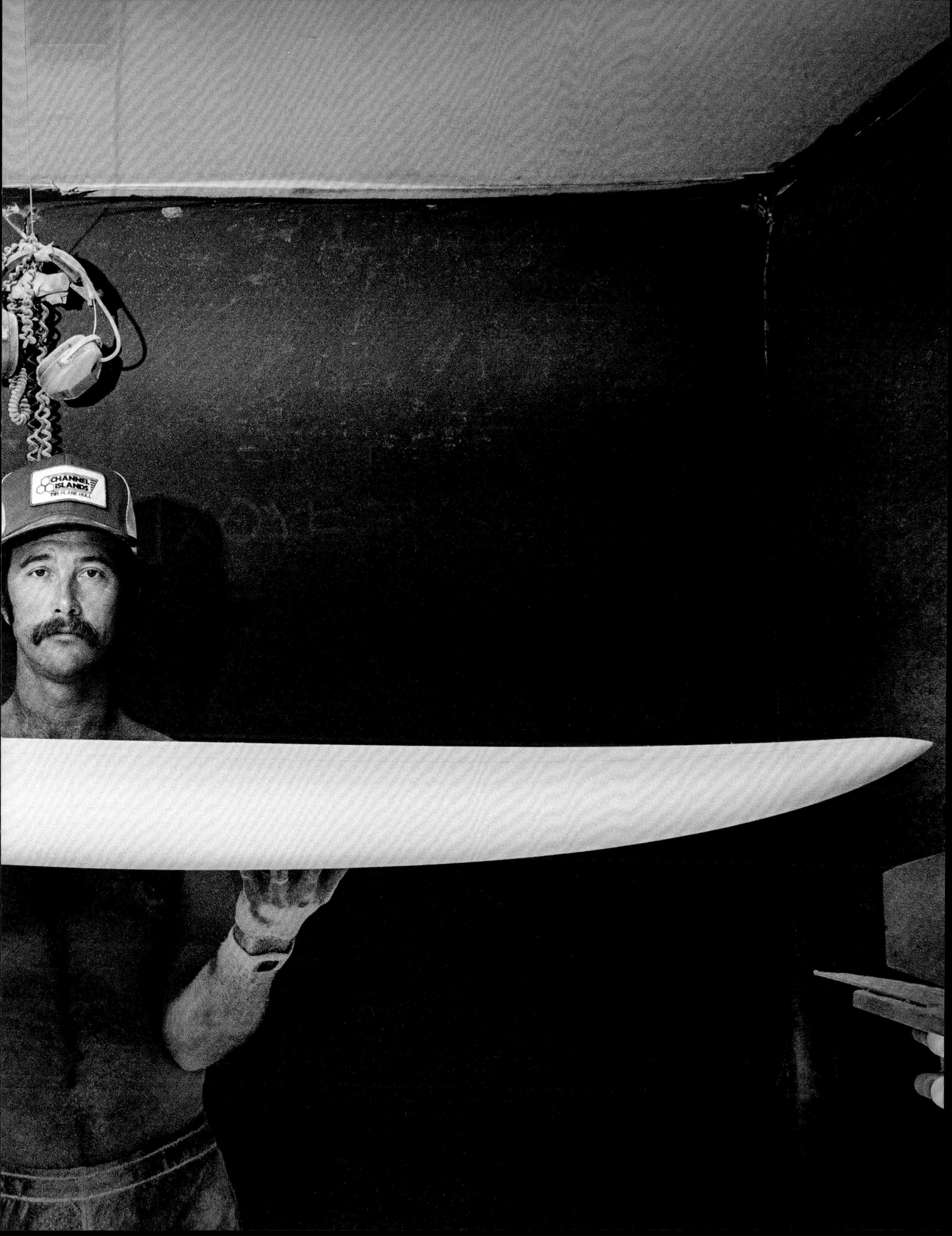
CHANNEL ISLANDS
TRI PLANE HULL

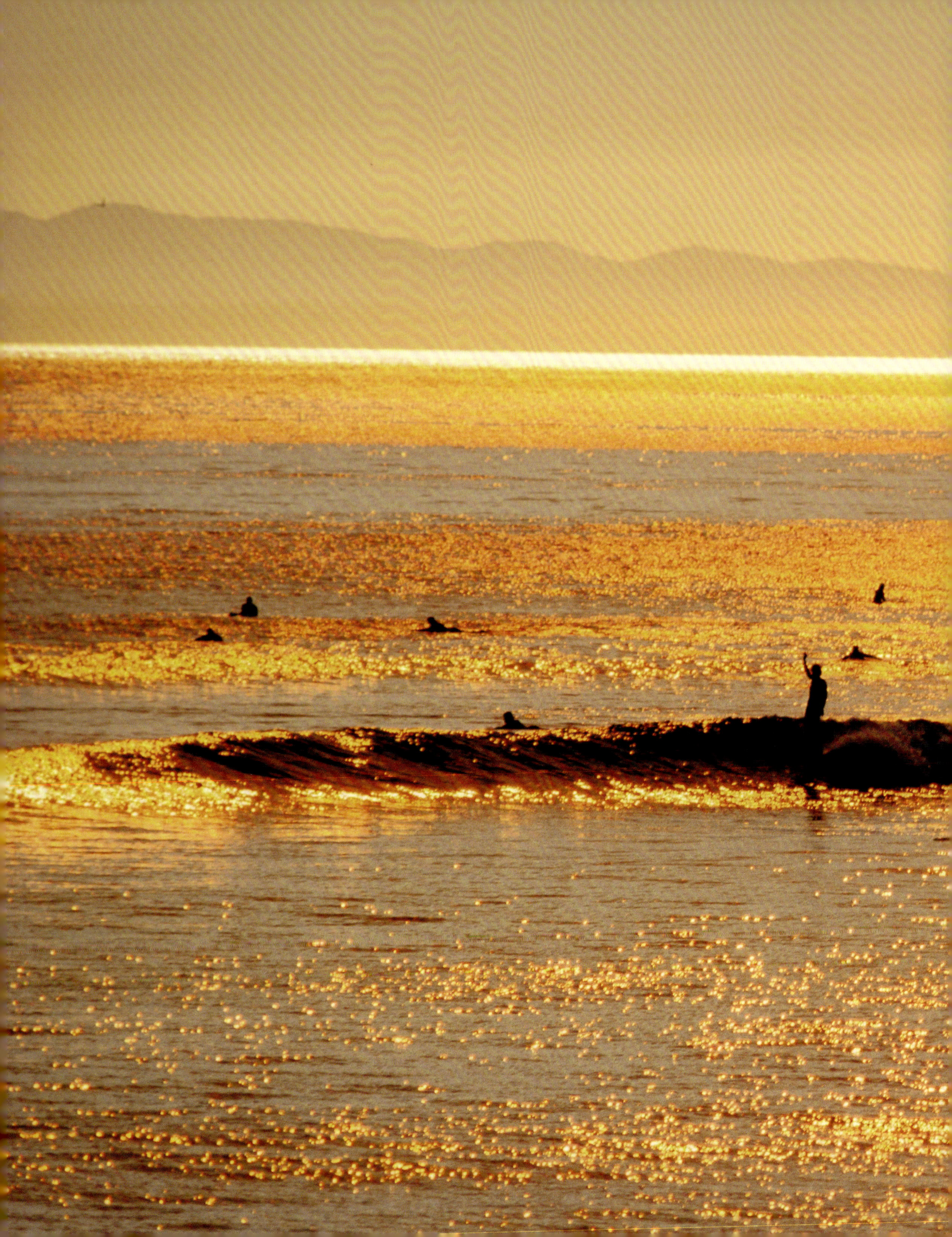

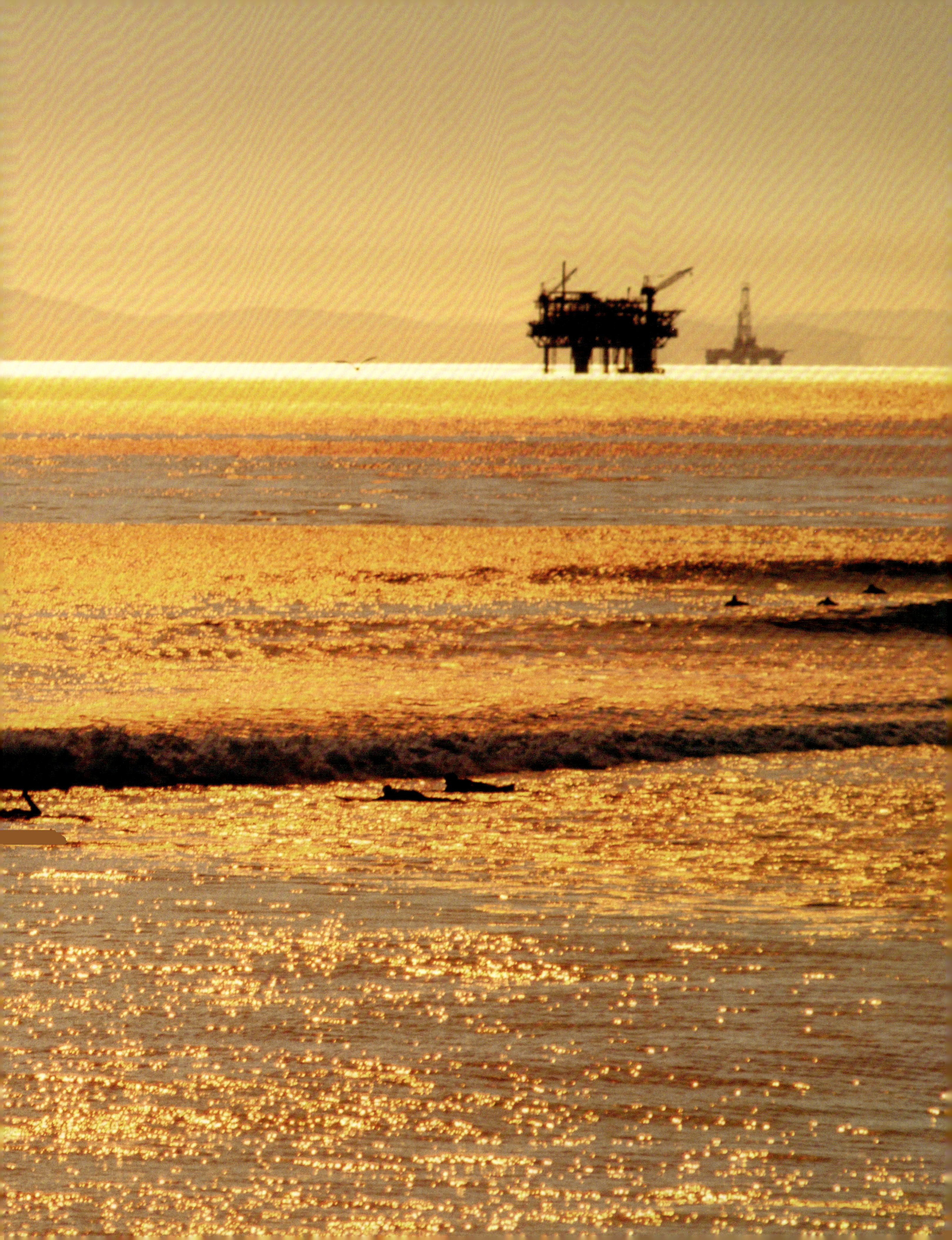

Previous

This photo was taken as smoke from a wildfire in nearby Ojai filtered out the blue light, casting an otherwise unremarkable afternoon at Rincon in an eerie glow.

Spread

A quarter mile west of Rincon is another point of interest, at least to the elite group of Carpinteria locals who claim to have ridden waves along its rocky shore. Known as Holly's, it was one those rarely breaking waves that required the perfect alignment of swell direction, tide, and wind to show itself, and even then only once every few years. I was standing on the bluff behind Rincon this particular afternoon, planning to carry my gear down to the Indicator section, when I happened to look in the other direction and for the very first time saw that there was a lone surfer out at Holly's. Once he was up and riding, I immediately recognized him as Jupe Risque, a talented transplant from San Diego, a Rincon local we'd dubbed "Section Maker" due to his ability to make magic in long, lined-up point surf. This afternoon was no different, so I aimed my lens in a completely different direction and spent a beautiful hour shooting one of the area's classic locals doing his thing at the area's ultimate secret spot. I'd never again see Holly's break like this.

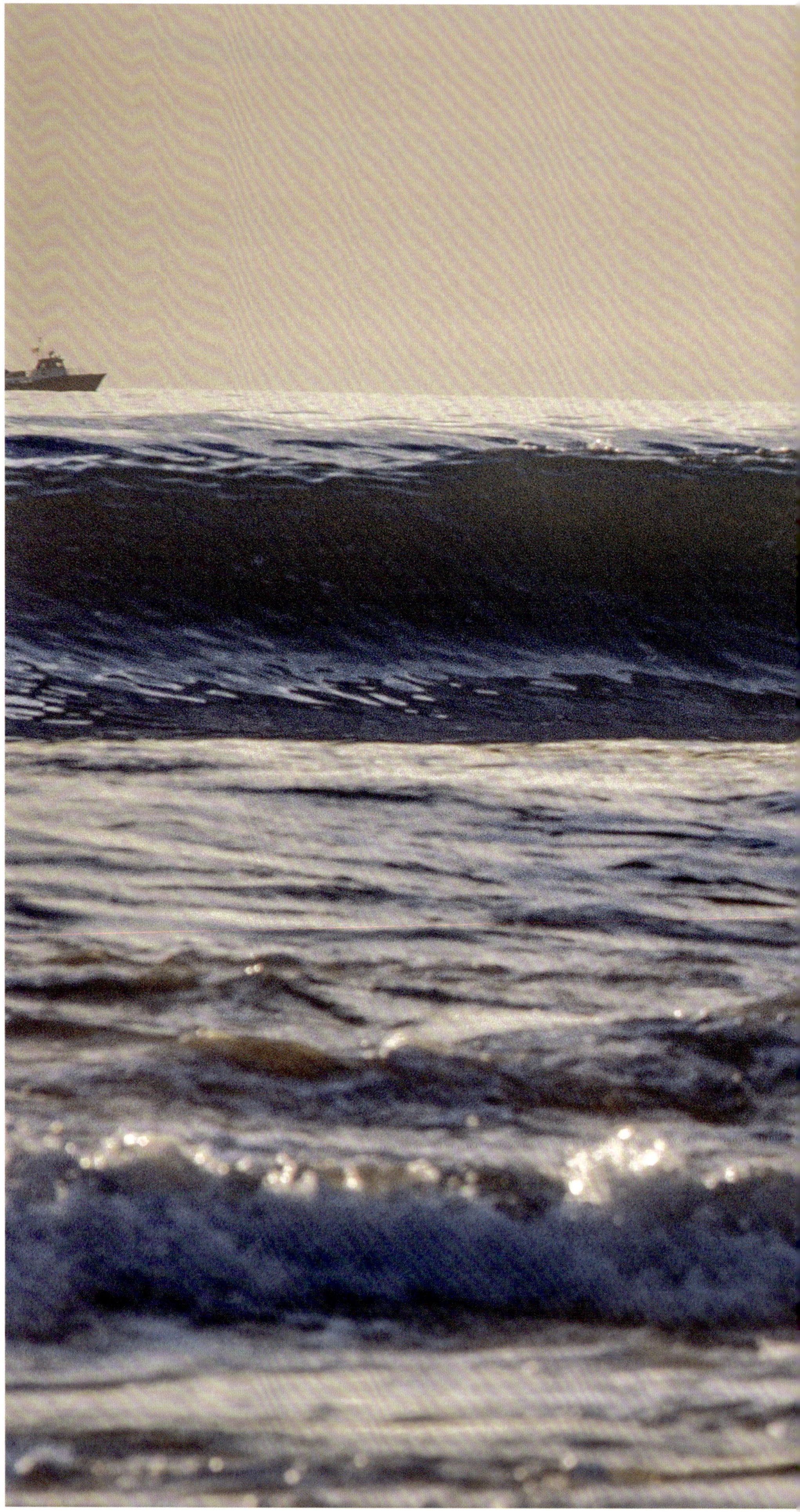

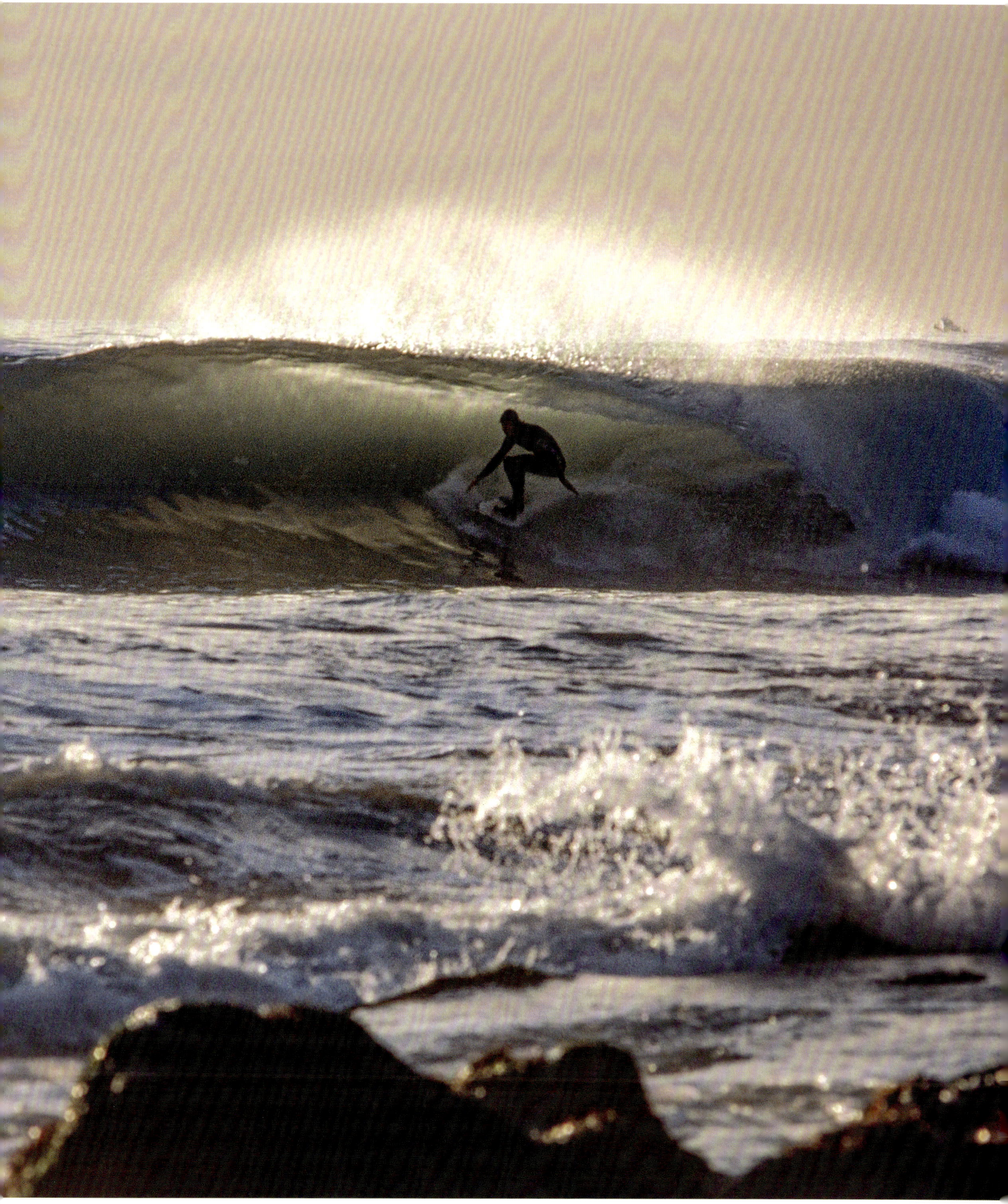

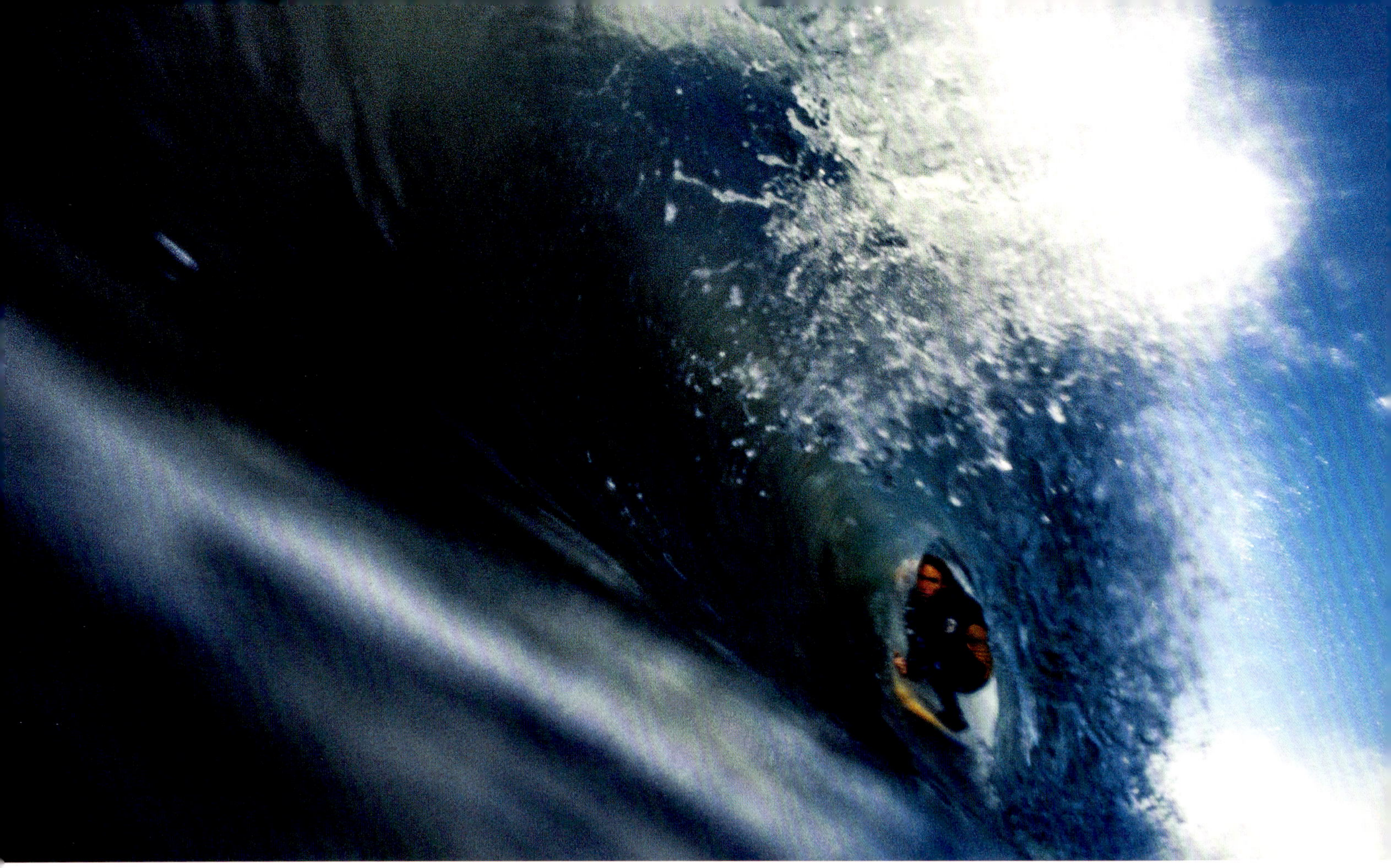

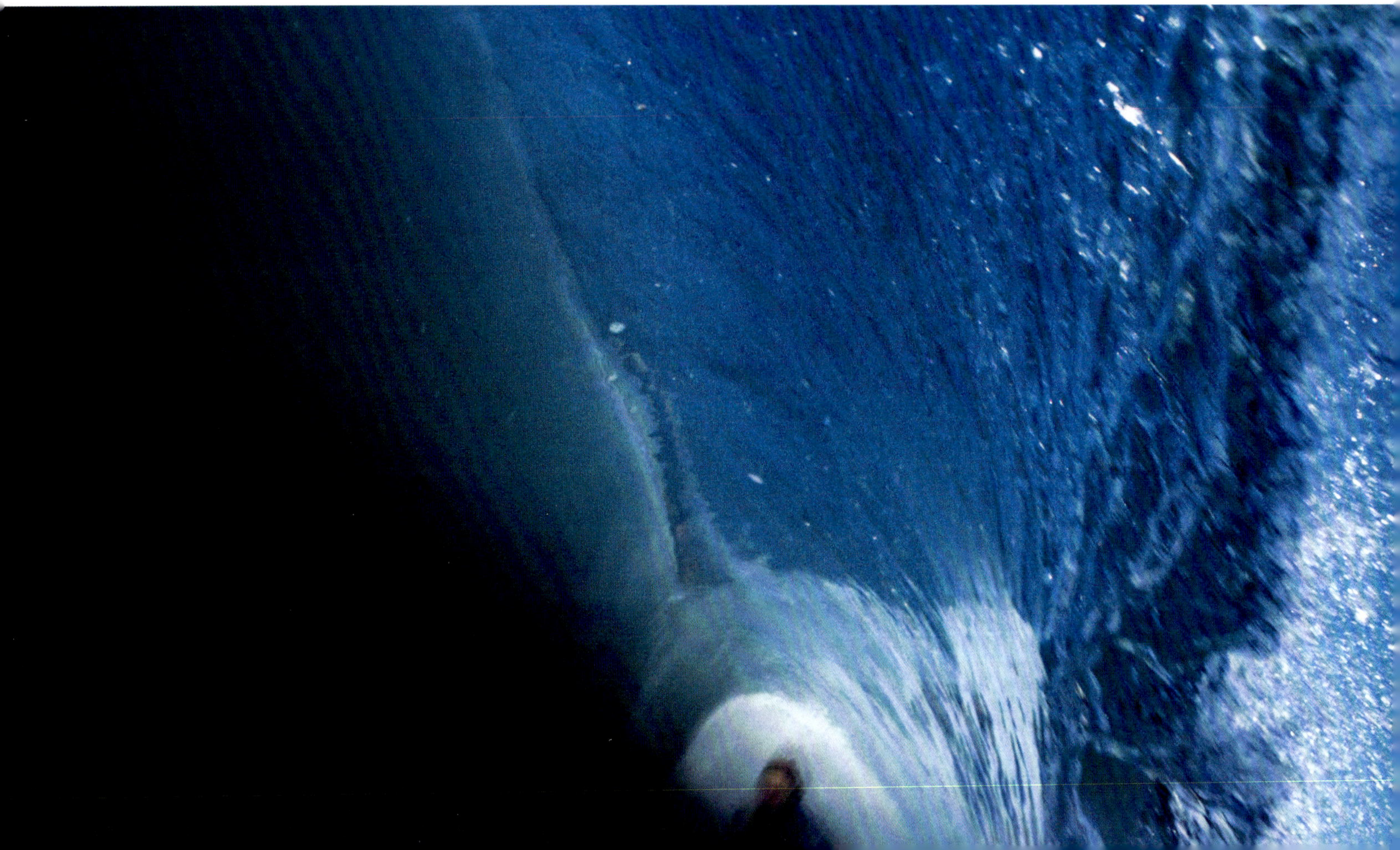

Avant-Garde

Matt George and I had been talking about shooting at Backside Rincon ever since I got my first water housing with a 35-millimeter port from Scott Preiss. With epic, in-the-tube water shots dancing in our heads, we would check the totally closed-out, totally empty beachbreak waves pounding the shallow sandbars to the west of Rincon's point, hoping for just the right combination of swell and light. On the day it all came together, the crew was startled when, instead of heading down to Rincon proper, Matt and I chose to battle our way through the Backside closeouts. Swimming out, cradling my precious water housing, I envisioned myself to be following the flippers of guys like Aaron Chang and Don King, two of the sport's best water photographers—and rough-water swimmers. I also knew that I had a good subject in Matt, who had this incredible knack for traveling long distances in otherwise un-makeable tubes. What I didn't know, however, was that Chang and King didn't shoot in the tube with a 35-millimeter lens, as I was attempting to do, but used 16-millimeter or 10-millimeter fisheye lenses. With much wider focal lengths, this allowed them to hold their cameras with arm extended, essentially sticking it in the surfer's face and firing off a shot before slipping through the back of the wave at the last second. I, on the other hand, was trying to look through my camera's viewfinder as Matt hurtled by, totally locked into gnarly eight-foot cylinders that regularly pounded me onto the shallow sandbar, then rag-dolled me all the way to the beach. The result was not a single image with Matt, who took his share of beatings, properly framed or in focus. I took a lot of abuse from the boys, but Matt, while disappointed, was kind, even referring to the one shot in which he could be seen tucked way back inside the tube as "avant-garde." It's framed and hanging on my office wall today, a reminder of my first attempt at water photography, and the only photo of mine ever described as "avant-garde."

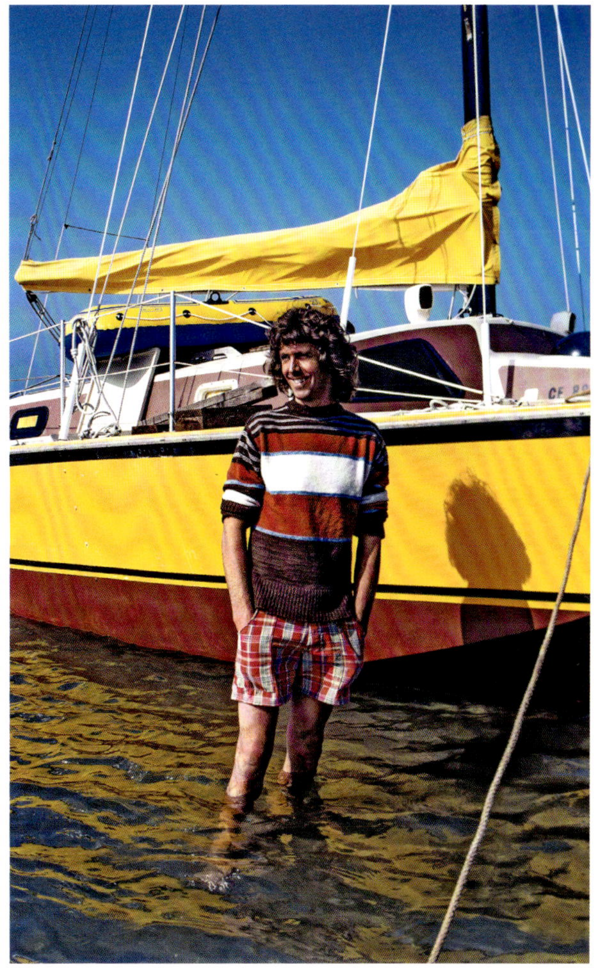

Opposite
My first water shots. Matt George in deep.

Above
Scott Preiss was a premier water photographer who, along with his self-made cruising trimaran, built the best waterproof camera housings in the business. Taking delivery of mine signaled a major step up in my photography "career."

Overleaf
The Day of Dreams, Ventura, California, December 19, 1980.

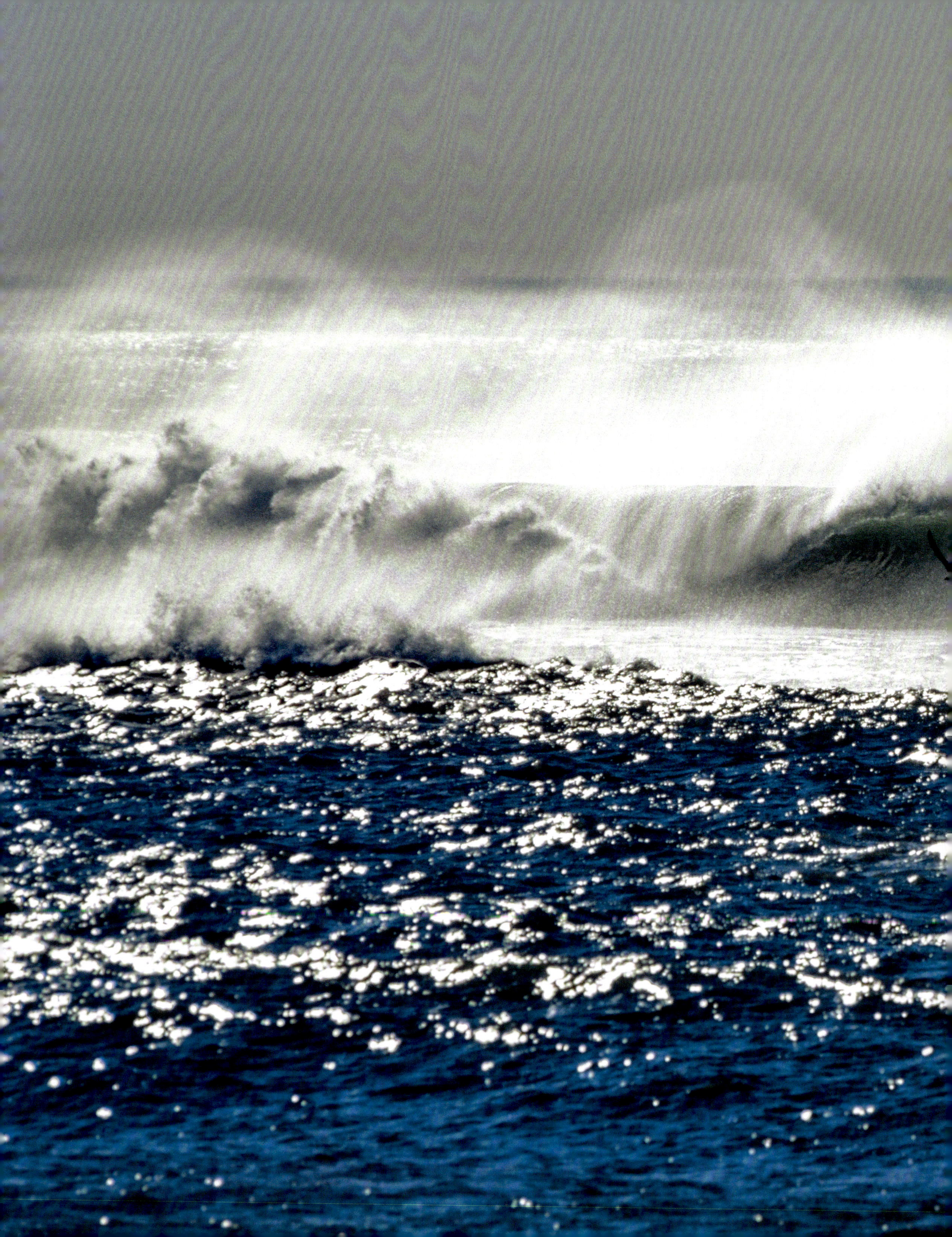

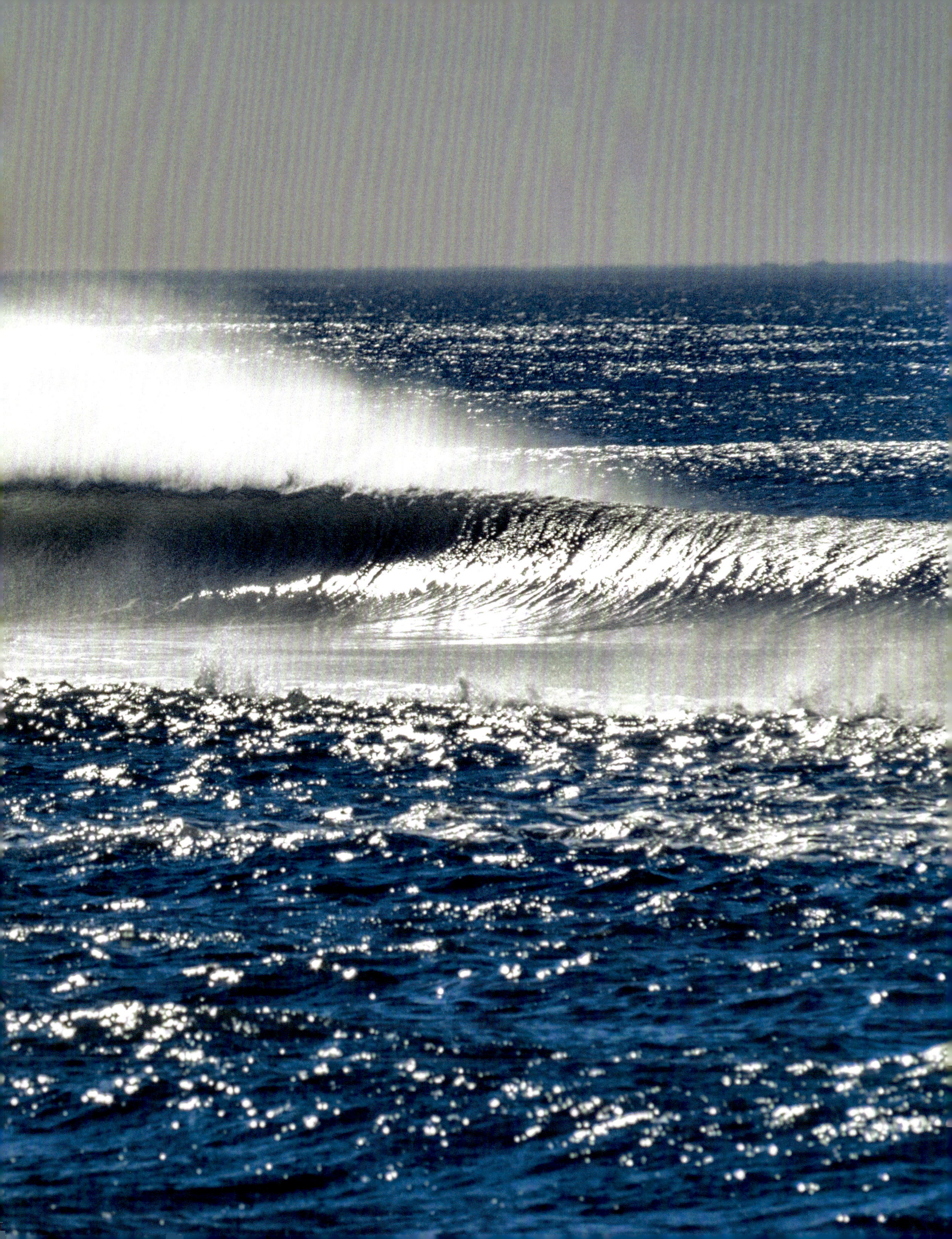

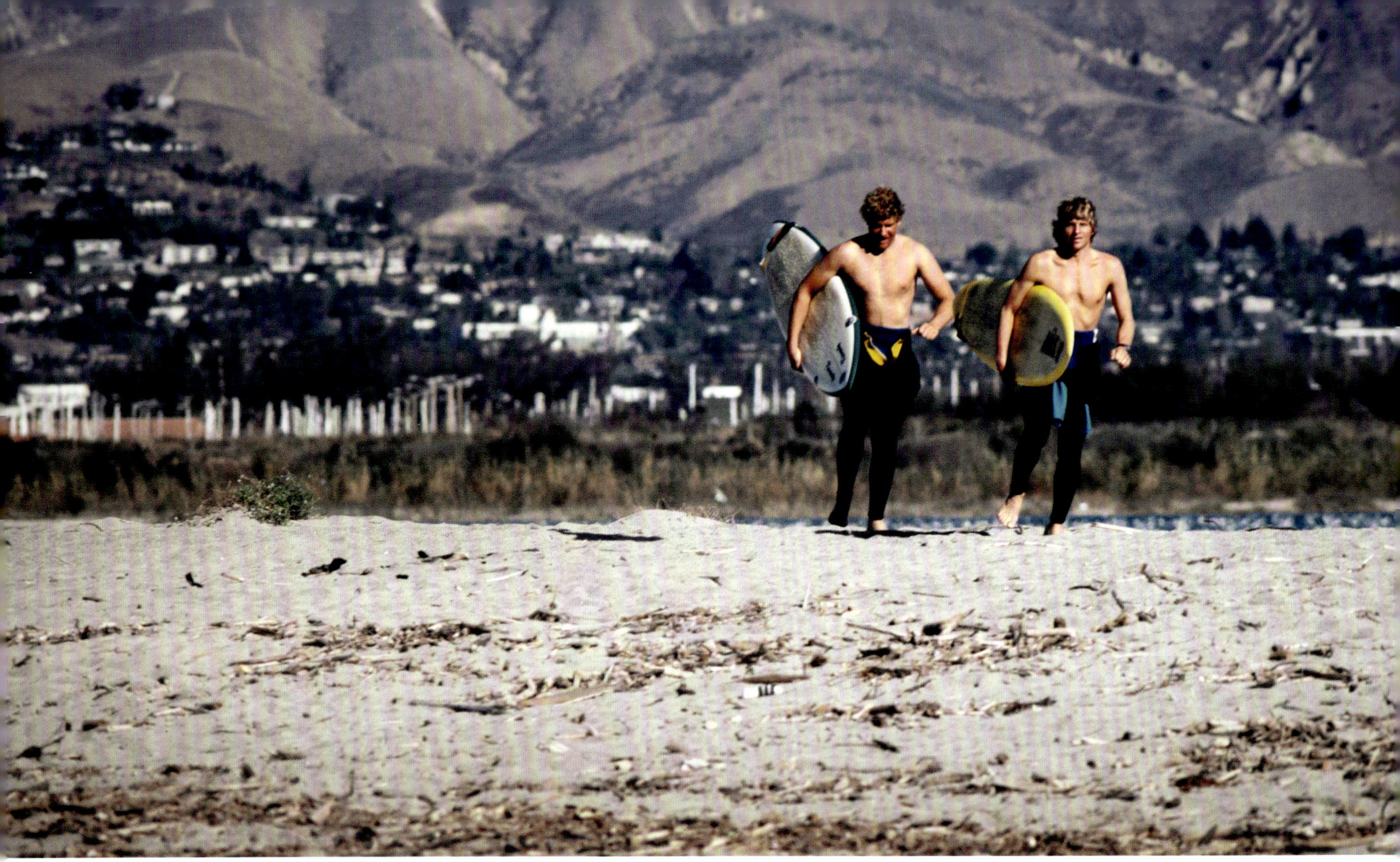

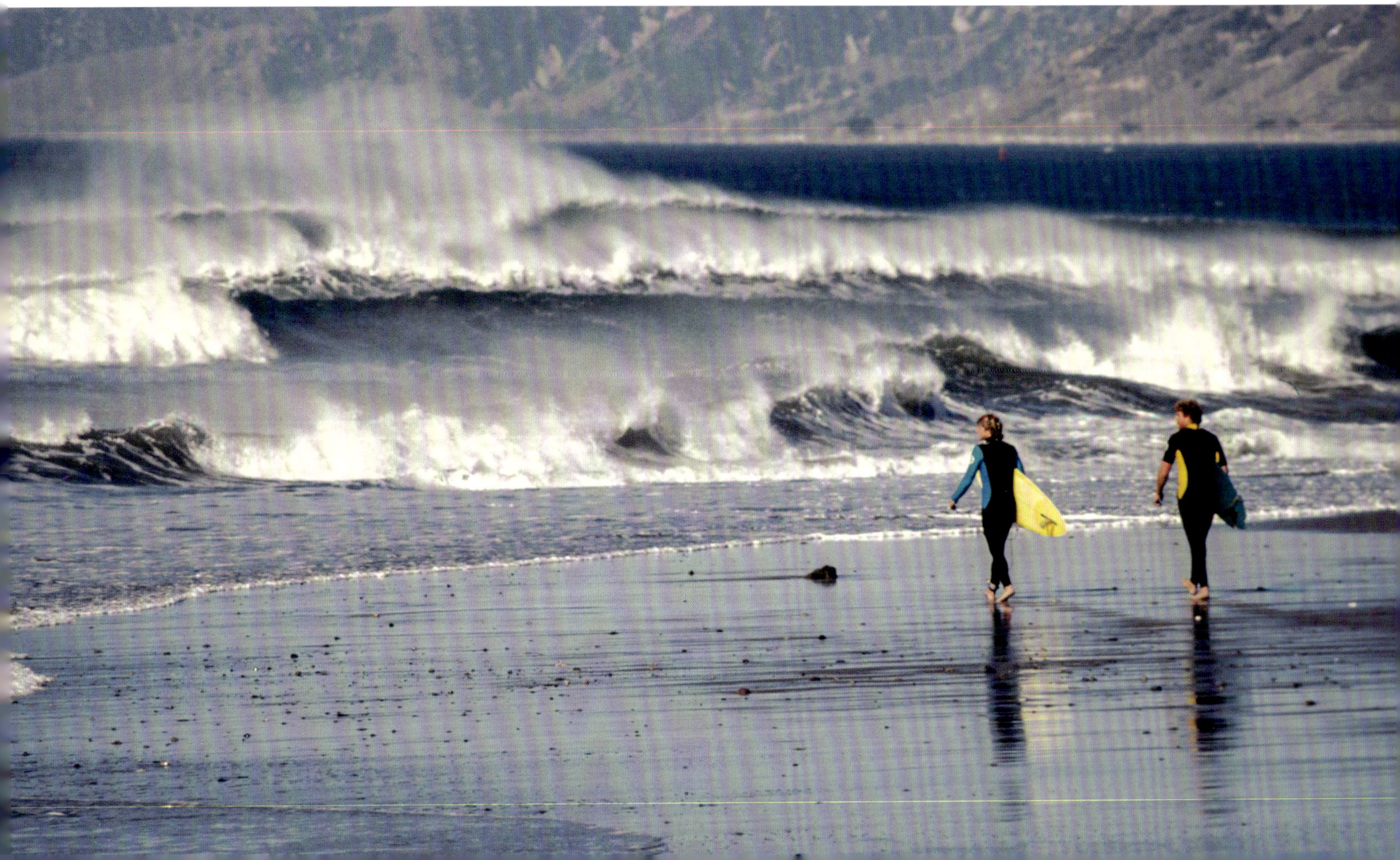

Day of Dreams

On this particular morning, our strike team fragmented before the day had barely begun, two carloads setting off from Santa Barbara with different destinations in mind, the pretense being to meet up somewhere later in the day.

Rincon was showing two-foot dribble with an evil, onshore southeast wind, so with Matt George at the wheel and Jimmy Redmon, my high school surf buddy from Texas, riding shotgun, we headed back into Santa Barbara and Esau's Café on Lower State Street—the classic surfer's breakfast spot. Mornings where you didn't have to worry about the surf and could enjoy a good breakfast bloat at Esau's were special.

Little did we know that even as we downed our massive omelets, a long-interval northwest swell was running straight down the Santa Barbara Channel, completely missing Rincon on its way to Ventura's beachbreaks, where the southeast wind would be blowing right into the wave faces, grooming them to perfection. Nor did we know that, only the day before, county workers had bulldozed the mouth of the estuary building up at the mouth of the Santa Clara River, allowing untold metric tons of sand to flow freely into the sea, forming a perfectly shaped sandbar where none previously existed. Exactly why, with our bellies full and not much else to do, we decided to drive back to Ventura and check this stretch of beach—a place none of us had ever surfed before—I honestly can't recall. But head south we did.

At the same time, while waiting for the tide to drop or the wind to switch, Sandra Morris sat watching her youngest son, Willy, playing Ping-Pong with Sam George at an outdoor table at the beautiful old Miramar Beach Hotel, where she and Willy had spent the night. The table was set directly beside the Amtrak railway tracks that run the length of this coast—a bizarre scenario in its own right, yet made even more so when, following one of Willy's wicked slices, their only ball was caught in the slipstream of the passing Coastal Starlight and sucked under its grinding wheels. Incredibly, it was found on the opposite side of the tracks, marked by grease yet unscathed. It's fascinating to observe the small flutters that sometimes precede great events. Sam, cupping the greasy little ball in his hand, sensed that there was something very special about this day, and suggested they should immediately go look for surf.

Farther south, we were greeted by the typical seasonal pattern of land breezes funneling out of Camarillo Valley, which, as the day heated up, would switch direction to an onshore sea breeze around 11 a.m., generally ruining the surf. We were already perilously late by the time we pulled up to McGrath State Beach, the spot from which to check this stretch of shoreline, but no one really questioned the decision; Matt, Jimmy, and I simply unloaded our gear and, staggering a bit under the weight of our breakfasts, traipsed over the dunes, following the bulldozer tracks to see what the day might have in store for us.

It was actually surf-savvy Mrs. Morris who'd suggested that Sam and Willy go check the waves at McGrath, a spot she and the Morris family had camped at in the past, but never surfed. Passing small, choppy Rincon, they headed south and eventually found themselves in the state-park lot, pulling up right next to our car and following the same bulldozer's path along the river and out to the top of the dunes.

Do I even have to tell you what they found? Nothing less than a perfectly formed sandbar where the day before there had been no sandbar, so ideally set up that you could paddle out to the takeoff point without even getting your head wet. Totally makeable, riffling barrels that sped down the bar at just under closeout speed. Offshore wind that, for some reason, forgot it was supposed to reverse direction at eleven, and would instead hold up the wave faces from dawn to dusk. And only our crew (joined later by Steve Mendelson, Willy's brother Steve, and kneeboarder Rick Burger) there to experience it. Perfect tubes, offshore wind, nobody else out. All day. A dreamy day. A day of dreams.

And so that's what we called it.

Willy Morris and Sam George would be the last ones in the water and last ones out on this amazing day of surf.

Facing

Matt George, three phases of total involvement on the Day of Dreams.

Pages 82–83

Willy Morris Water Shot Spread

After shooting for hours on land, I eventually swam out with my new Scott Preiss water housing, only the second time I had used it. These two sequences of Willy Morris, wrapped up in perfect tube after perfect tube, more than justified the effort.

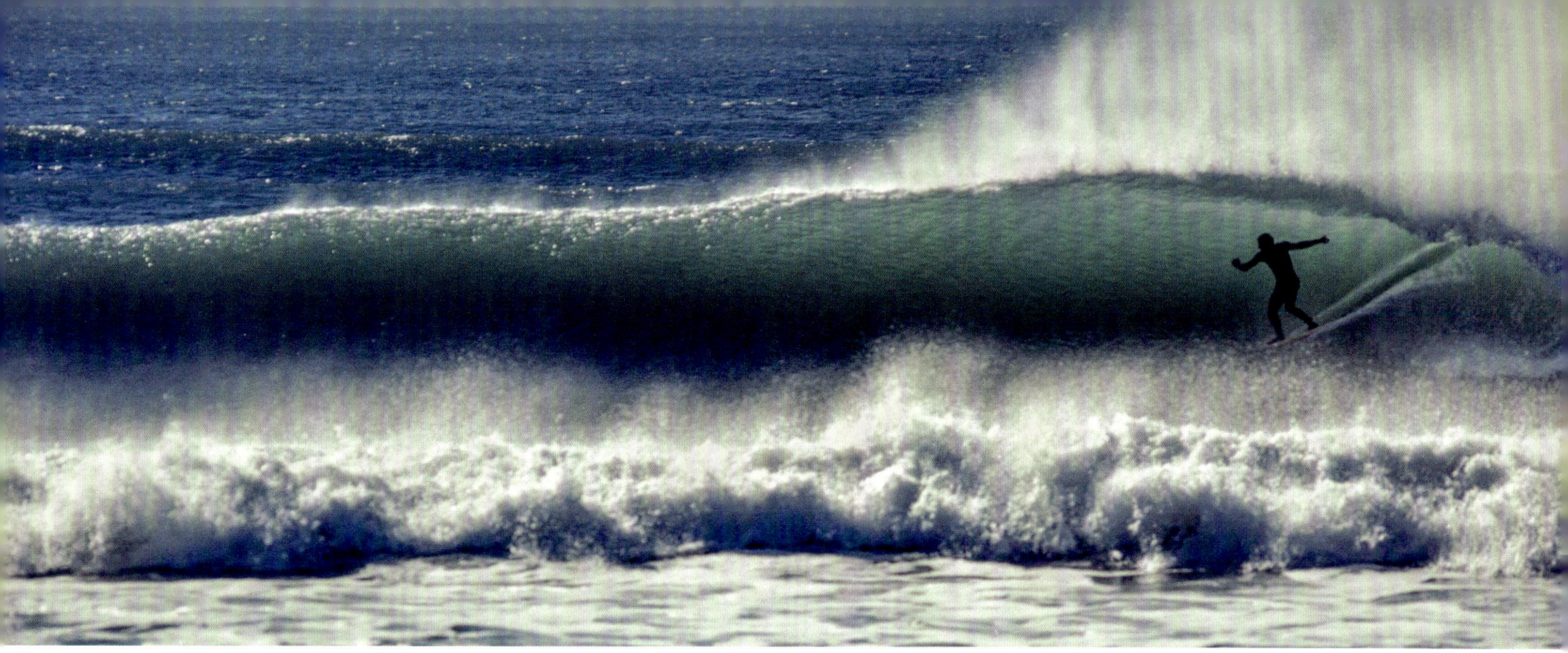
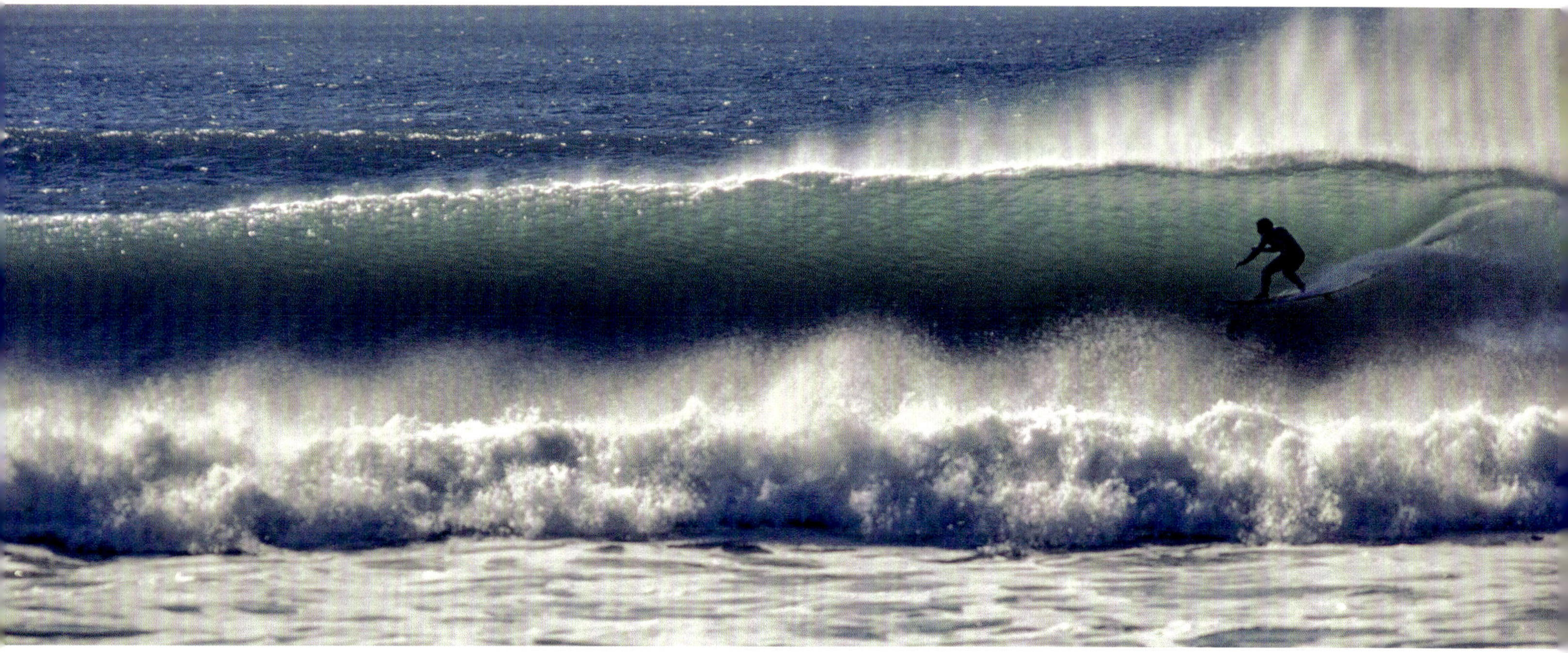
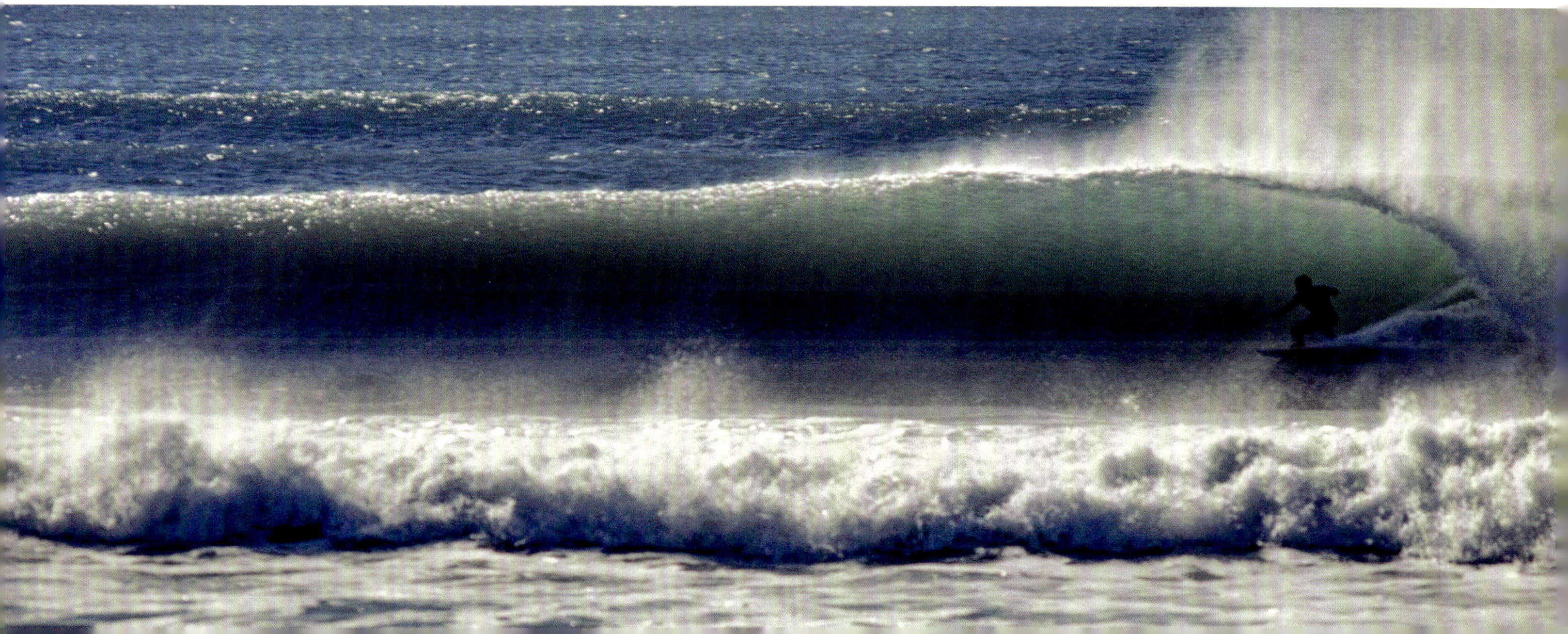

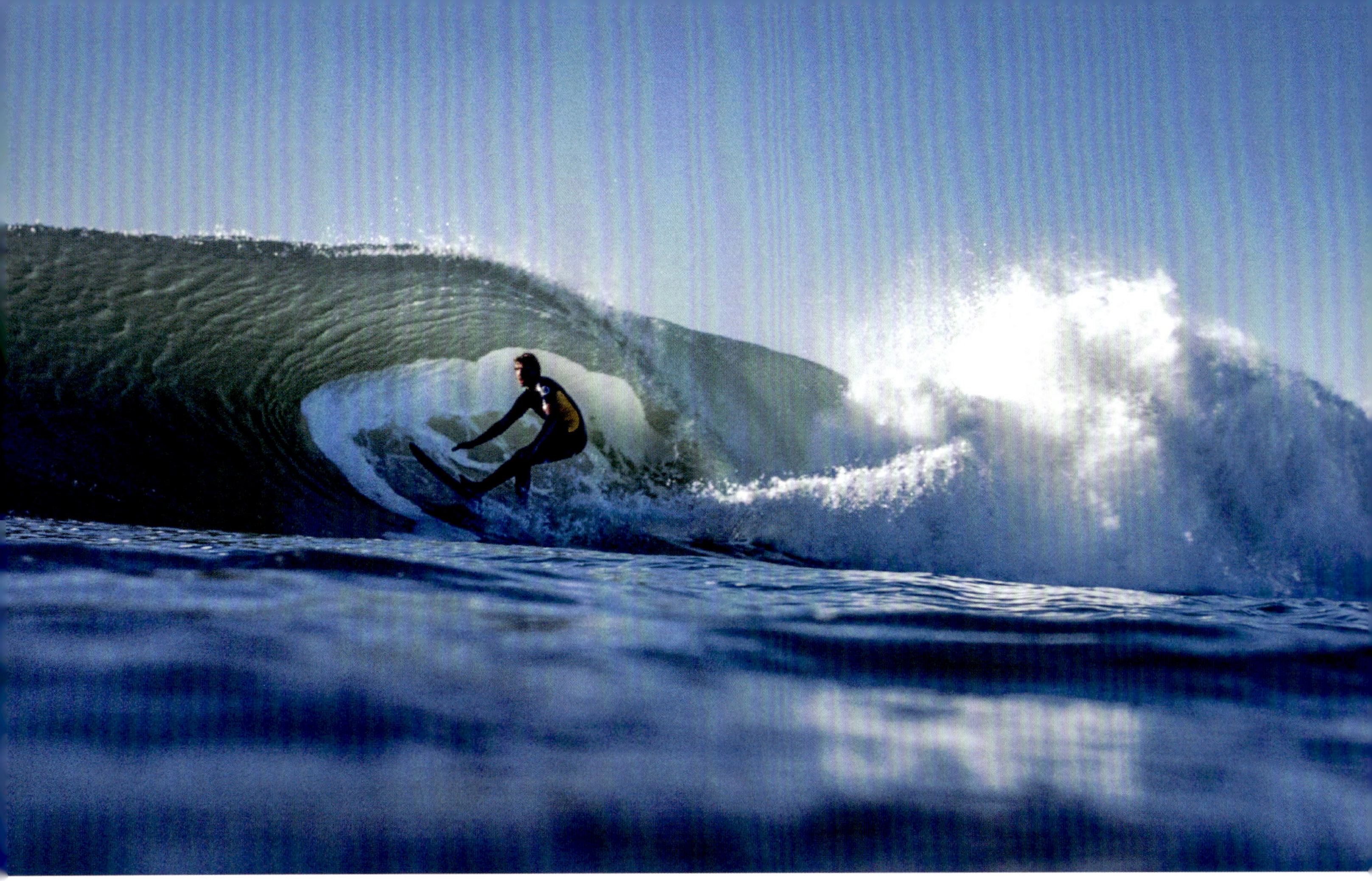

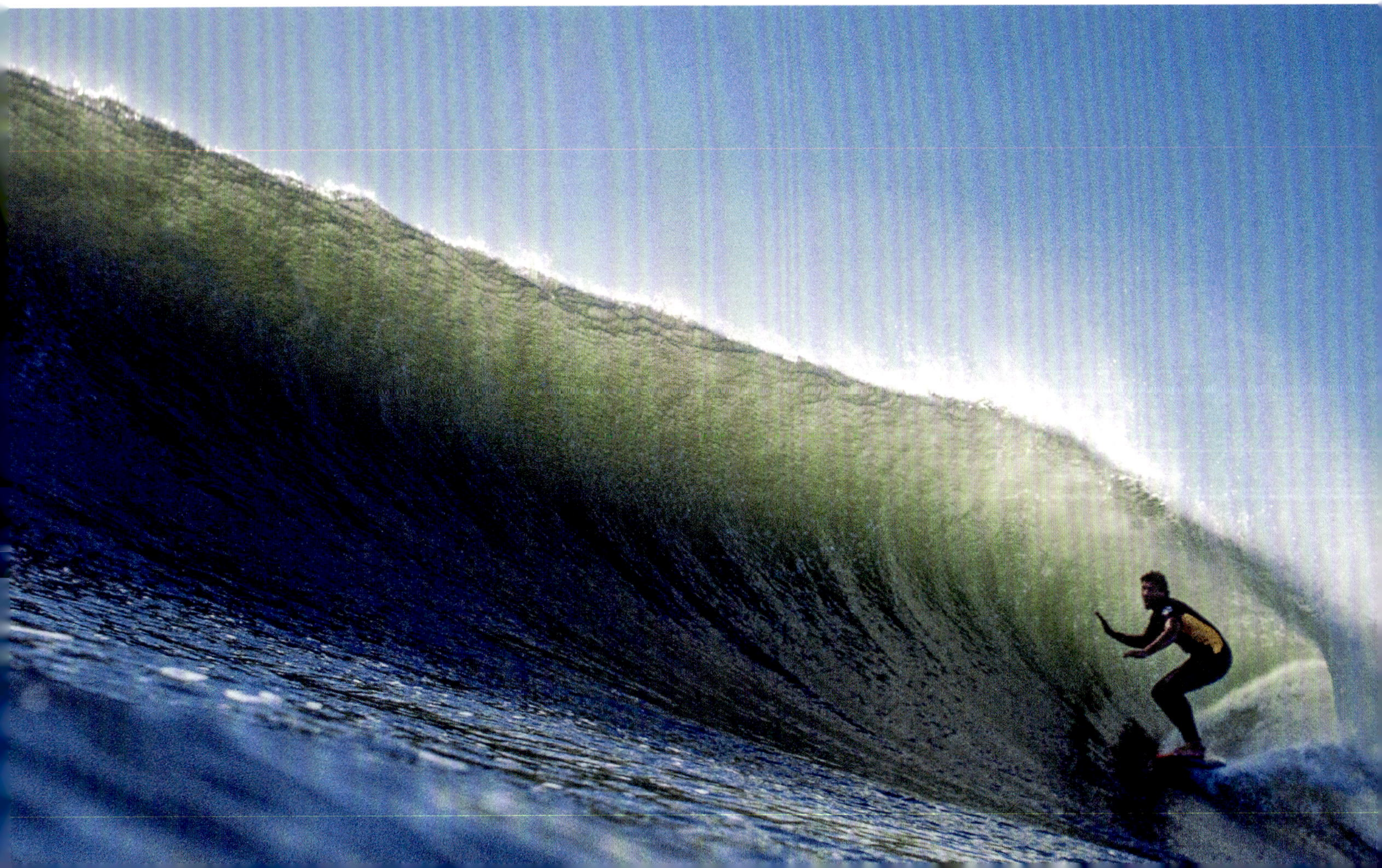

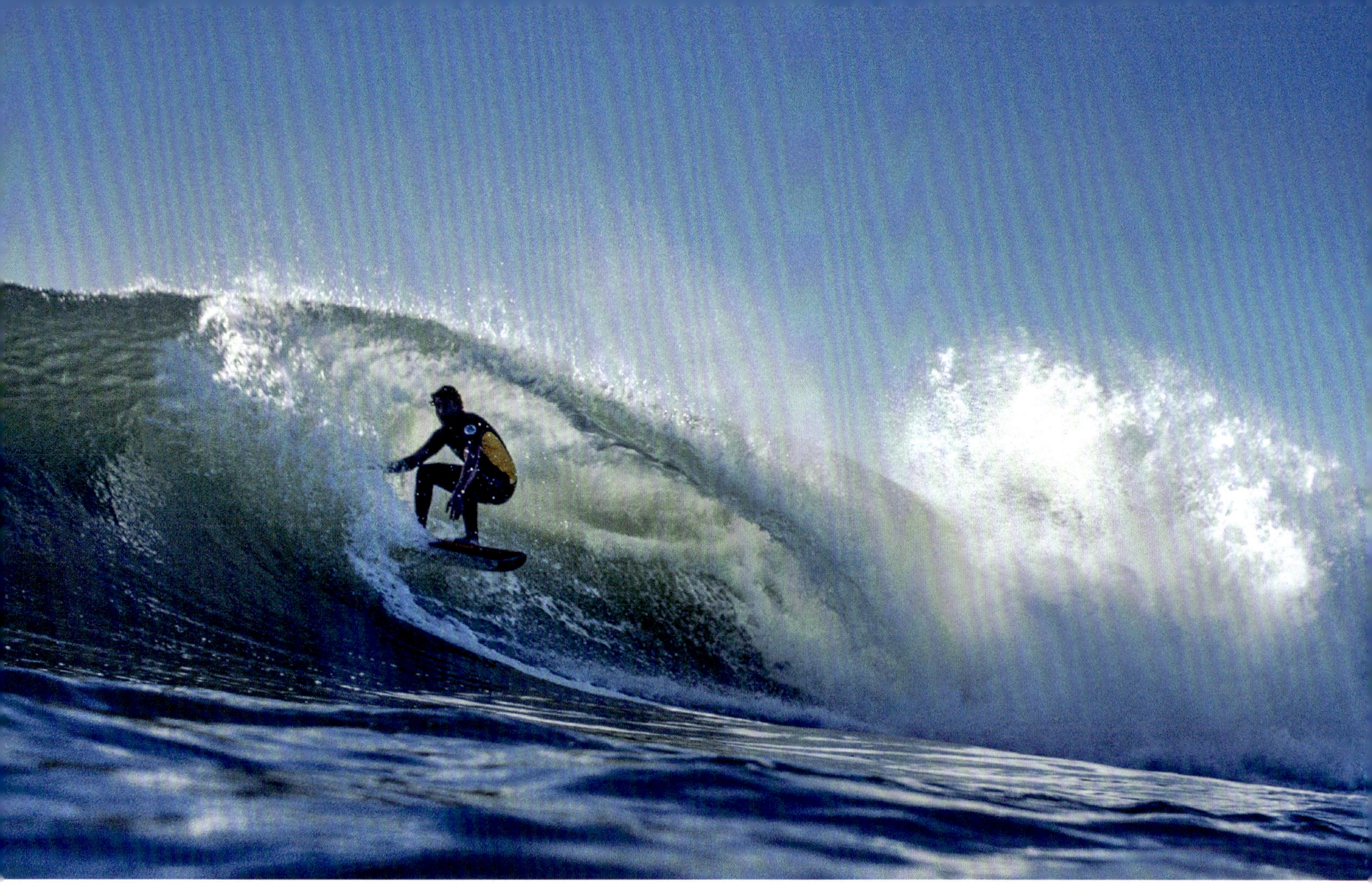

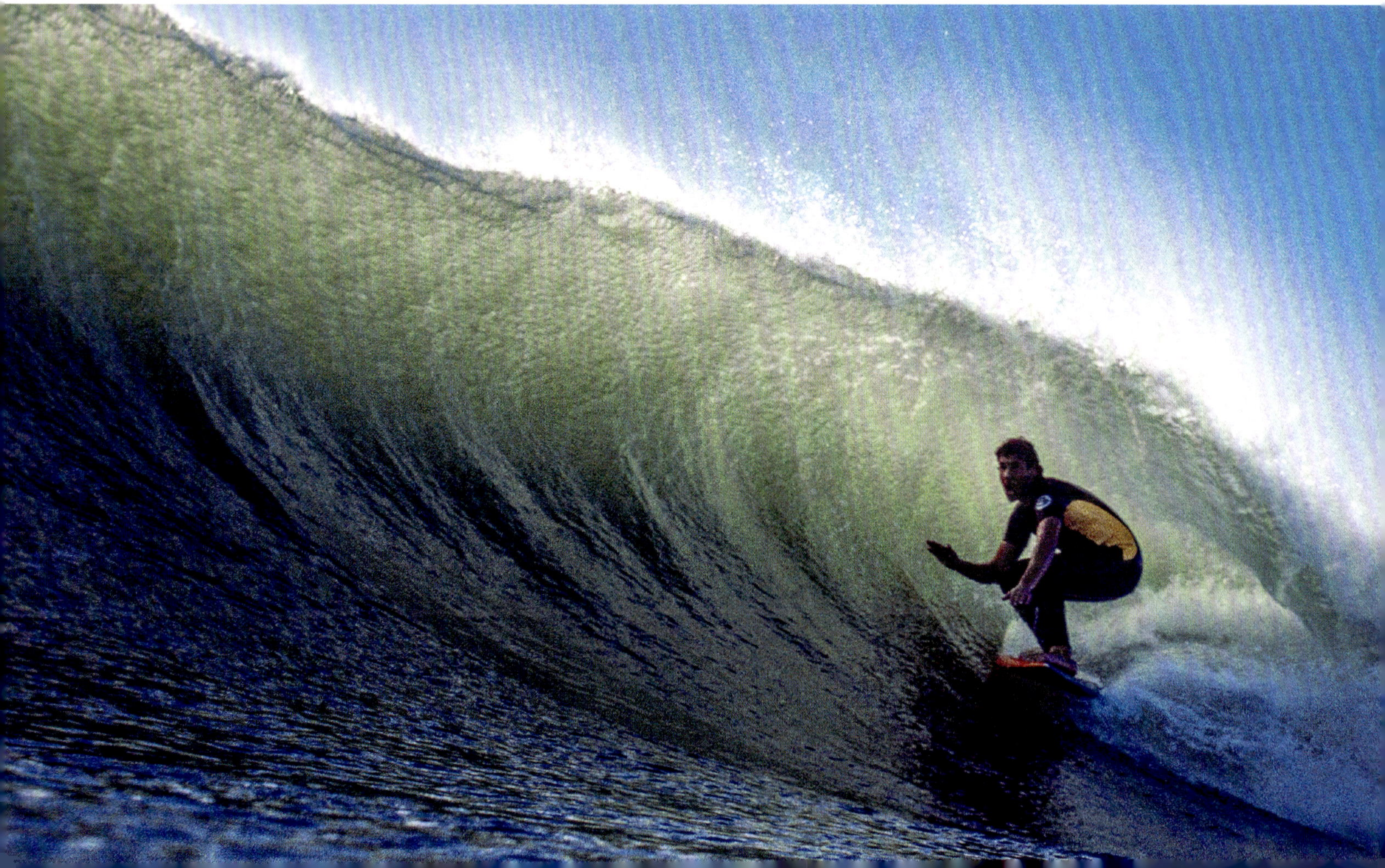

Totally surfed out, but unable to turn away, our lucky crew basking in the warm evening light—and the loving gaze of Mrs. Morris, who sat and watched the entire remarkable session with attention undimmed.

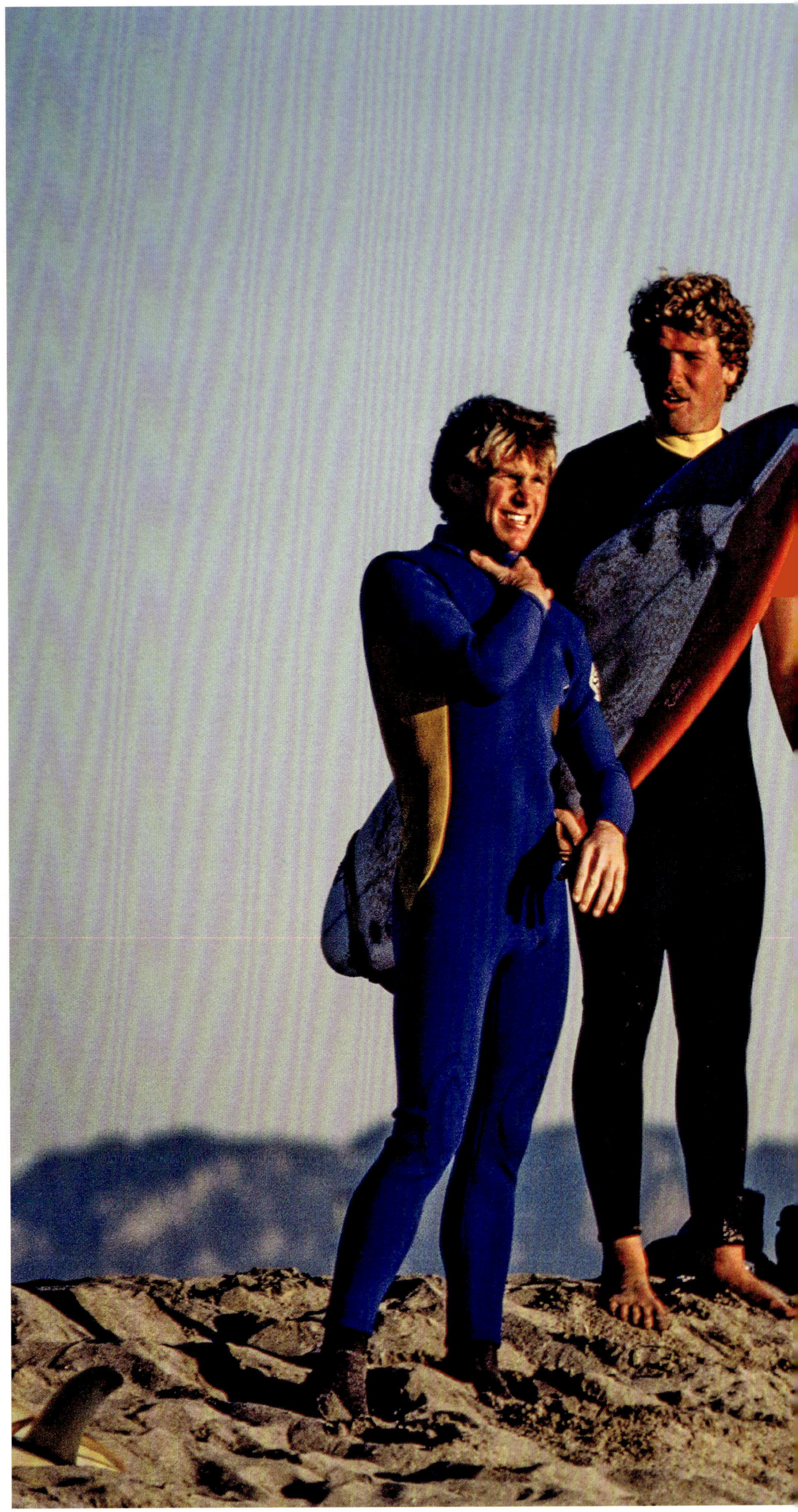

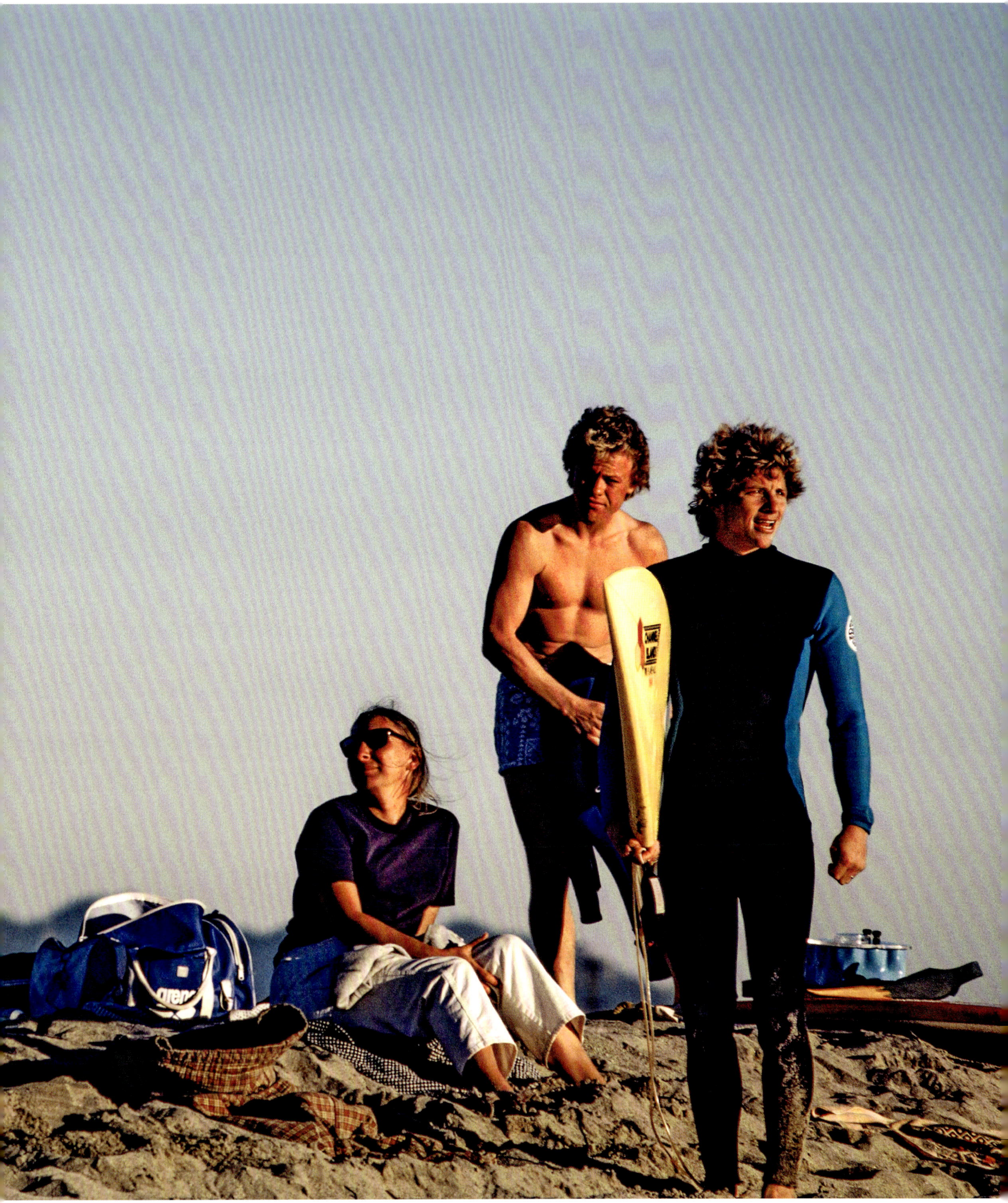

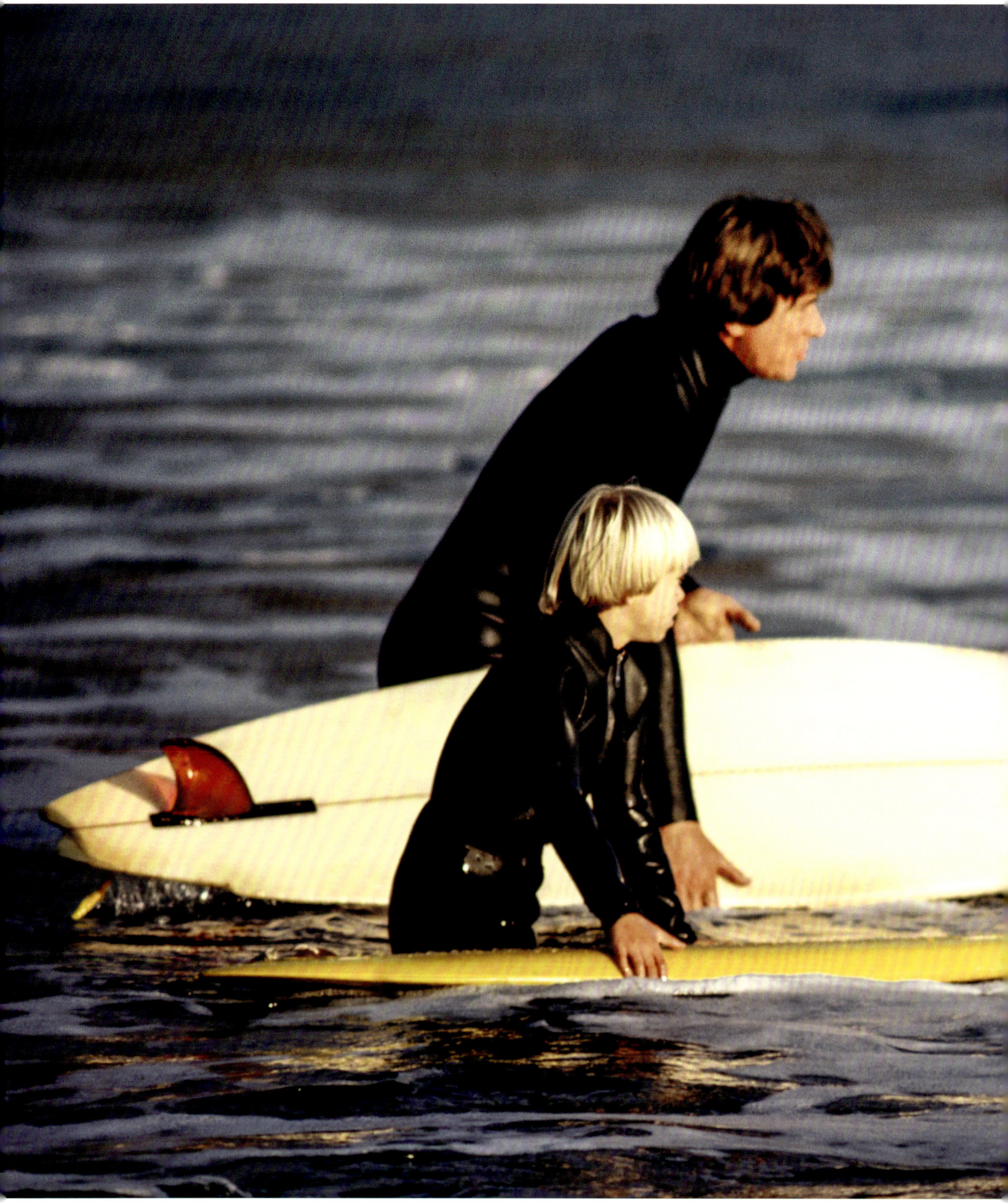

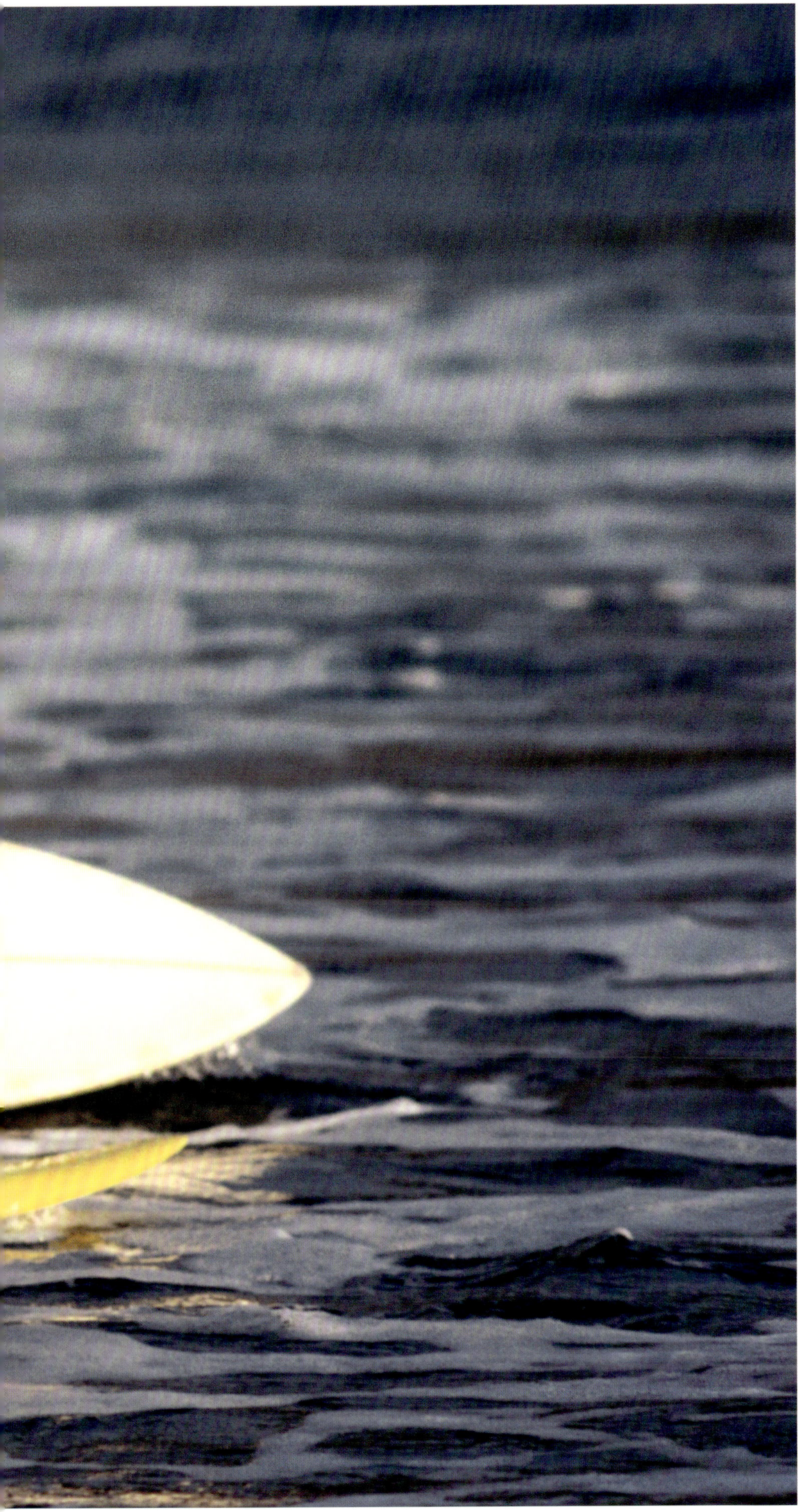

Spread

Ten-year-old Chris Brown and his father, Dave Brown, wading out into the Cove. Chris was one of the first young Santa Barbara surfers to grow up on a steady diet of Tom Curren shredding Rincon on finely tuned Al Merrick surfboards and, perhaps more importantly, the full support of a dad who enthusiastically encouraged him to follow Curren's path to the pros.

Overleaf

Tommy Curren trots up the point at Rincon for one last ride before dark, his mom, Jeanine, no doubt tapping her foot up in the parking lot while waiting to drive him home to family dinner.

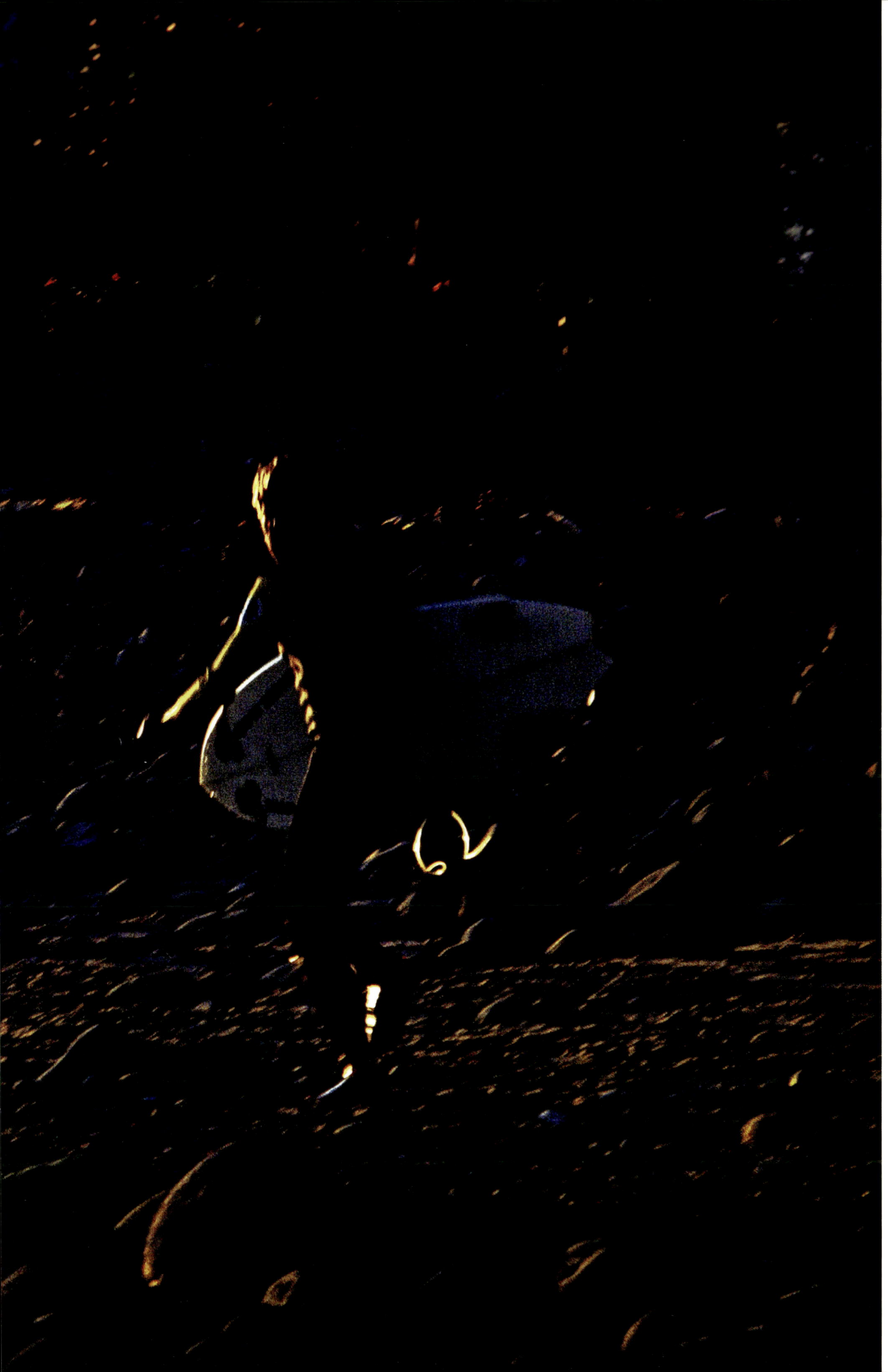

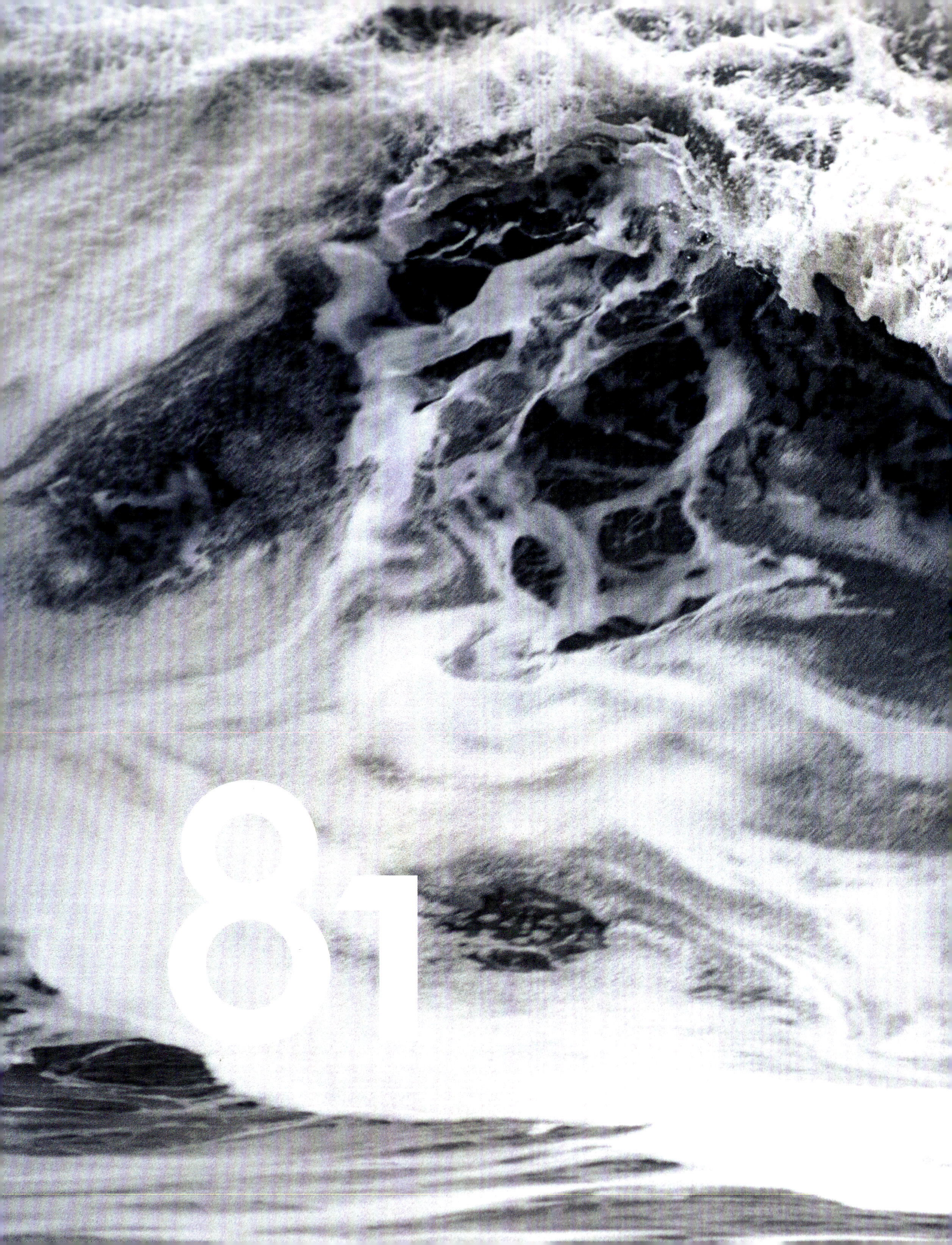
01

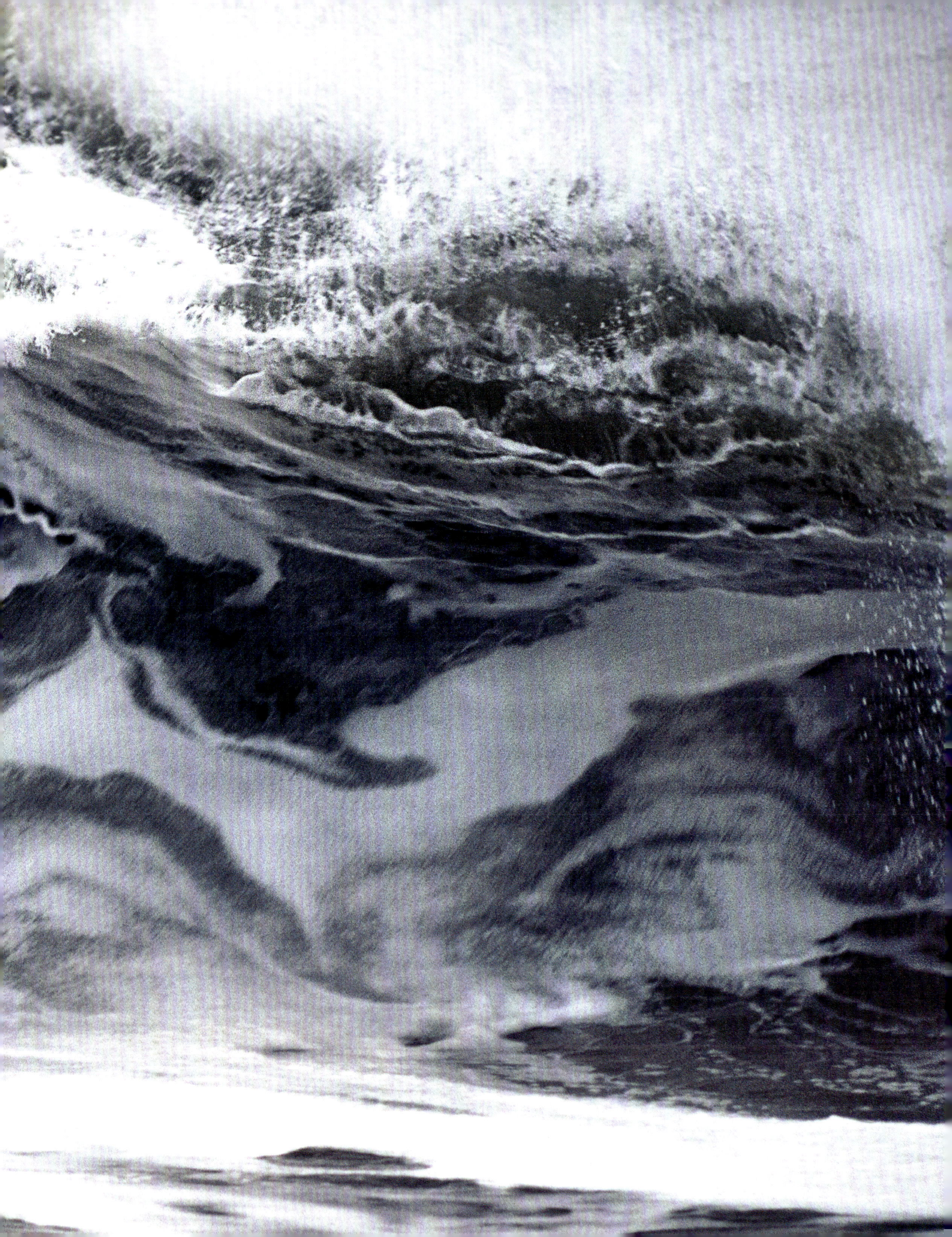

1981

Mag Trip

In March 1981, word got to me that *Surfer* magazine photo editor Art Brewer, with whom I was just beginning to establish a working relationship, was leaving his position, to be replaced by the equally legendary Jeff Divine. This was hardly good news: getting anything across Brewer's light table was a huge accomplishment, and now I'd have to begin the whole process over again, starting from scratch with Divine, whom I'd heard of, of course, but never met.

Back then, this presented a much bigger challenge than one might think. While only a 156-mile, three-hour drive south, the *Surfer* offices in Orange County's Capistrano Beach seemed a world away from Santa Barbara. After all, along with neighboring beach towns Dana Point and San Clemente, this was the place where the modern surfing industry was born: the first surf magazine, the first modern surfboard factory, the first retail surf shop. This is where Hobie Alter and Gordon Clark perfected the first polyurethane surfboard, where in his beachside studio Bruce Brown edited his classic documentary *The Endless Summer*, home to spots like San Onofre, Trestles, and Doheny, where so much of California surf culture took shape. And it wasn't all just history: legends of the sport still walked the sands here, as well as the surfboard factories, the surf shops—and the halls of *Surfer* magazine.

Considering that the era's biggest technological breakthrough in communications was the home answering machine—no email or cell phones, let alone Zoom calls—presenting my work, and my legitimacy as a *Surfer* contributor, still involved the licking of stamps. So, after receiving back a batch of new images of a recent swell, I resolved to take charge of my destiny, recruiting Sam George and Willy Morris for what we would later call a "mag trip," driving down to the surf magazine offices to submit my photos in person.

Sam and I left Santa Barbara in the morning, swinging by Willy's house in Woodland Hills along the way. After a welcome home-cooked breakfast from Willy's classic "surf mom," Sandra, we three crammed in the front bench seat of Sam's Datsun pickup and headed south.

Maybe it was because Willy, though years younger than Sam and me, was bigger than us, or maybe it was just his natural ease and confidence, but we seemed to have no problem assigning him the leadership role on this mission. After all, he was the only one of us who had actually met Jeff Divine, and I was looking to him to provide an introduction. I had also assumed Willy had notified Jeff to let him know that we were coming by that day; though building up my own confidence as a surf photographer, I could never have found the nerve to cold call someone like Jeff Divine. Meanwhile, Sam, ordinarily displaying no shortage of confidence, was also a bit apprehensive, having never met Divine either. Approaching the *Surfer* offices, he directed his question to me.

"We're not just showing up, right?" he asked. "You did call to let him know we were coming."

"No," I said, startled. "Willy did."

"I didn't call him," said Willy. "I thought you did."

Volatile recriminations flew fast and furious as we pulled off the I-5 freeway onto Capistrano Road, the three of us mortified at the idea of showing up at *Surfer* unannounced and being refused an audience. All back to normal and calm by the time we pulled into the parking lot, I walked bravely into the magazine's front office with what I felt was a reasonable plan. I told the receptionist that, rather than having driven all the way from Santa Barbara without an appointment, we just happened to be passing by on our way to San Diego and wanted to take the opportunity to drop off my latest submission. Oh, and if Jeff had a few spare minutes, we might just want to duck in and say hello. It worked: after a brief phone exchange, she led us through the hallowed "employees only" door and nonchalantly pointed to Jeff Divine's office down the hall.

In the early 1980s, just being in the *Surfer* building, let alone the photo editor's office, was a big deal. When we stepped into his modest work space, Jeff was gracious and welcoming, stoked to personally take my submission. He immediately opened up the envelope, pulled out the slide pages, grabbed his loupe, and turned to his task. I watched expectantly as he hunched over his giant light table, one practiced eye peering into the loupe. Dead silence—until, without looking up, he said, "Jimmy, you send slides to Flame at *Surfing*, too."

Larry "Flame" Moore was rival *Surfing* magazine's photo editor. I froze. The truth was, if you weren't locked into an arrangement with one of the two major surf magazines, you submitted your work to both. It was always an exercise in finesse, dividing your best slides, trying to guess which photo editor would like which slide and of which surfer. It was a familiar topic of discussion among photographers, the choice of one mag over another being viewed by some as an act of betrayal. Being relatively new to the game, I felt as if every relationship I was forming, and especially this new one with Jeff Divine, was on the line with every word that I spoke. Was my entire future here at *Surfer*, and as a surf photographer, wrapped up in this one response?

"*Surfing* magazine thinks I send them my best images," I said, stridently explaining how I'd bought my first *Surfer* at age seven and never missed an issue, memorizing all the photos, the captions, all the photographers' names—even his. I spoke of my years of dreaming of shooting for *Surfer*, and what it meant to me to finally be here in this office, working with him. "Jeff, I'm a *Surfer* mag guy through and through," I said. "Even though I do occasionally send images to *Surfing*, I only send my very best images to you!"

The entire time I was speaking, Jeff remained slumped over the light table, not saying a word. He finally lifted up, removing a single slide from the plastic sheet.

"Sorry, Jimmy," he said. "I wasn't listening. Were you just saying something?"

If I managed to stammer a response, I can't remember it.

"But this shot of Tommy is cool," Jeff continued. "This will definitely get run. Keep sending me images like this, Jimmy. I'm stoked."

Over the course of the next few years, I would make many more "mag trips" to both *Surfer* and *Surfing*, but I never forgot that first one. And even though my relationships with both Jeff Divine and Larry Moore would eventually develop into real friendships, from that day on I continued to maintain the fiction that I was only passing through on my way down to San Diego.

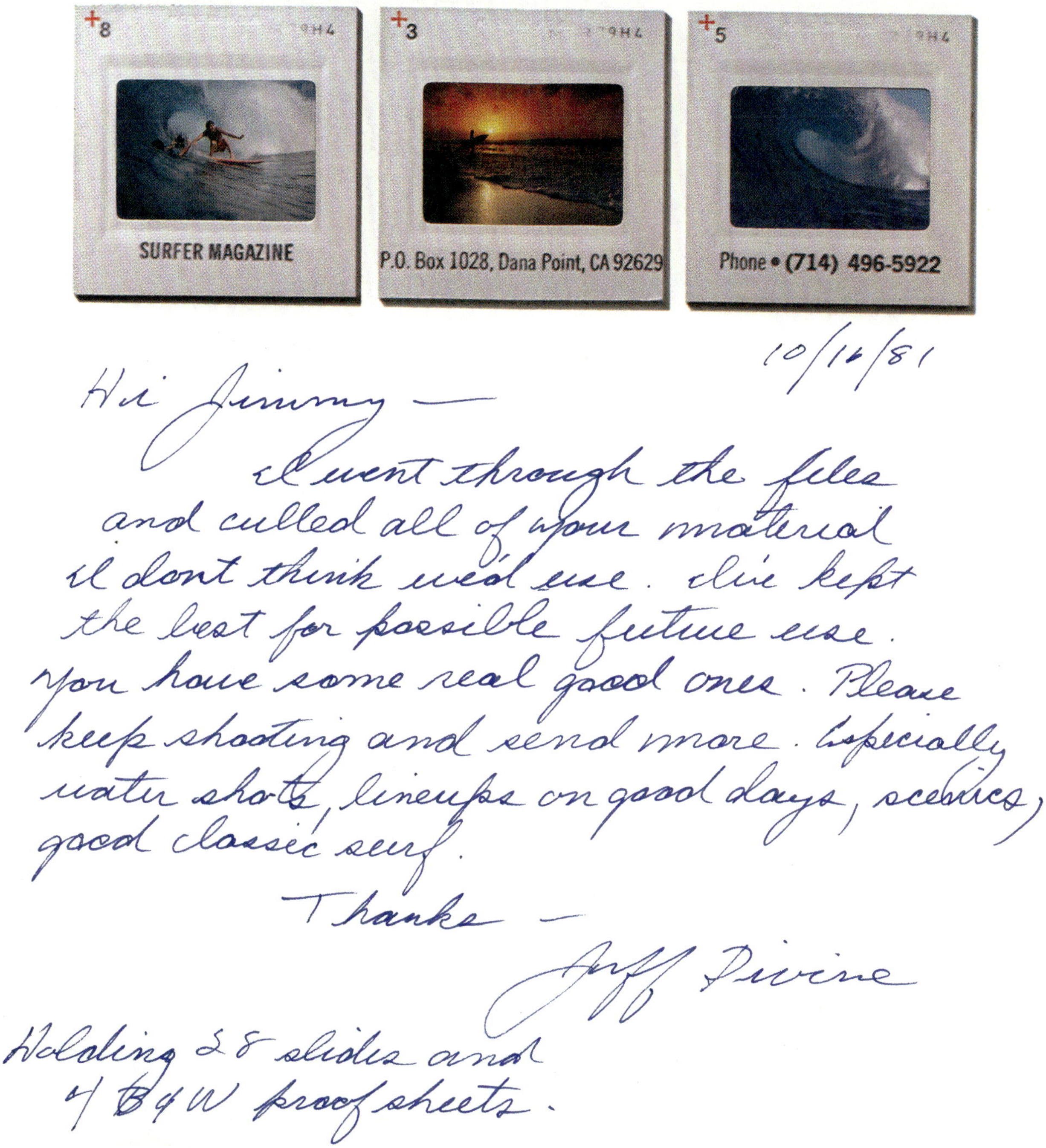

SURFER MAGAZINE
P.O. Box 1028, Dana Point, CA 92629
Phone • (714) 496-5922

10/16/81

Hi Jimmy —

I went through the files and culled all of your material I dont think we'd use. I've kept the best for possible future use. You have some real good ones. Please keep shooting and send more. Especially water shots, lineups on good days, scenics, good classic surf.

Thanks —

Jeff Divine

Holding 28 slides and 4 B&W proof sheets.

Back when penmanship mattered: first letter and words of encouragement from Jeff Divine, the new photo editor at *Surfer* magazine.

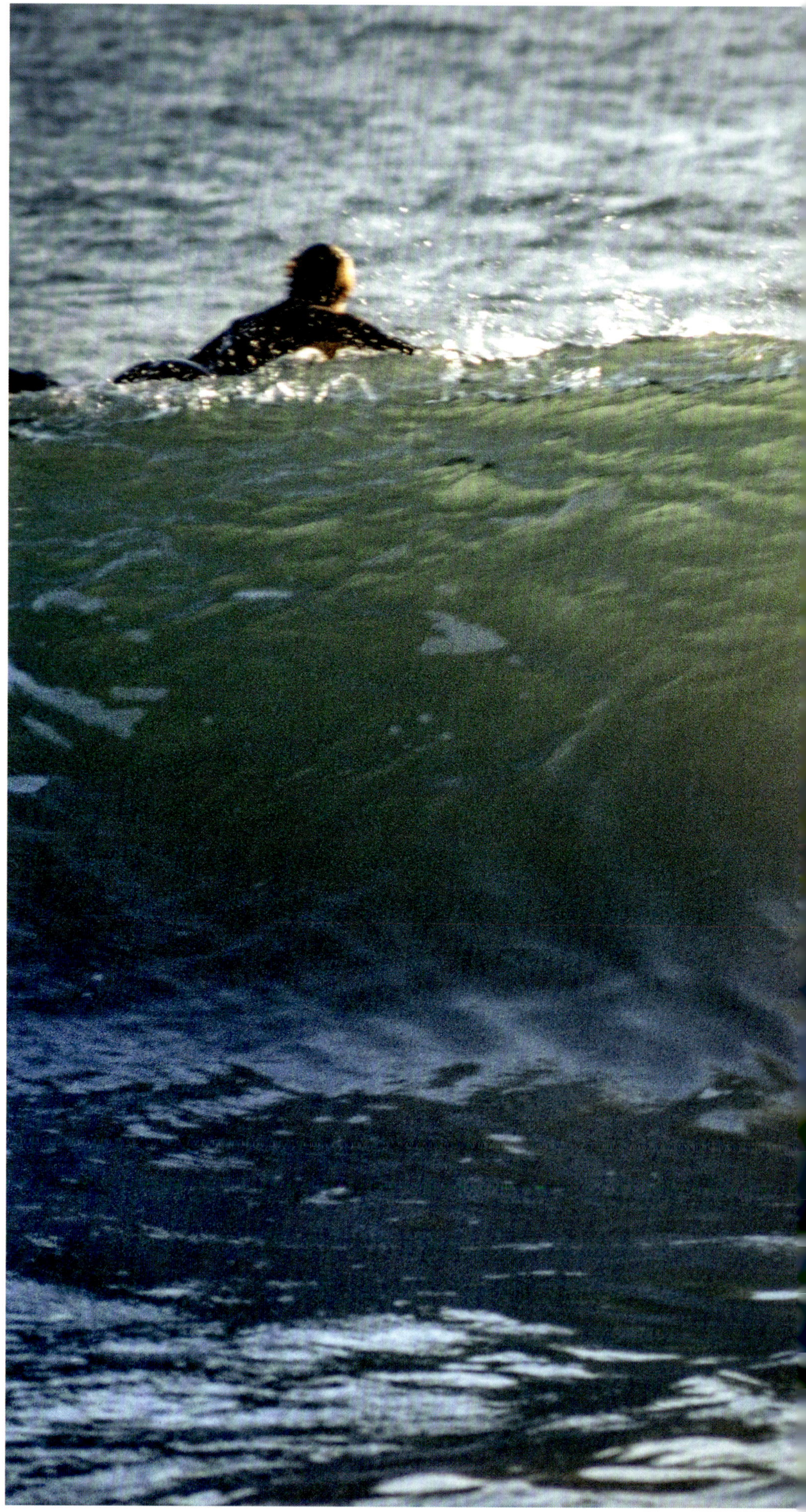

Spread
Breaking just yards away from Pacific Coast Highway near Ventura's Point Mugu, Super Tubes is one of California's most unlikely "secret spots." It's literally just right off the road, in plain sight of every passing car. The well-kept "secret," however, is the complex combination of swell size, swell direction, tide, and sand flow necessary to make this hollow tube clear the rocks and peel down the line. This photo was shot on the first day I actually saw Super Tubes break. Whenever it did appear, regular Mike "Mahay" Gabriele would be on it, flashing peace signs in the tube.

Pages 96–97
Steve Morris on one of the biggest waves ever photographed at Super Tubes. At this size, you have a chance for one bottom turn before the whole thing goes square.

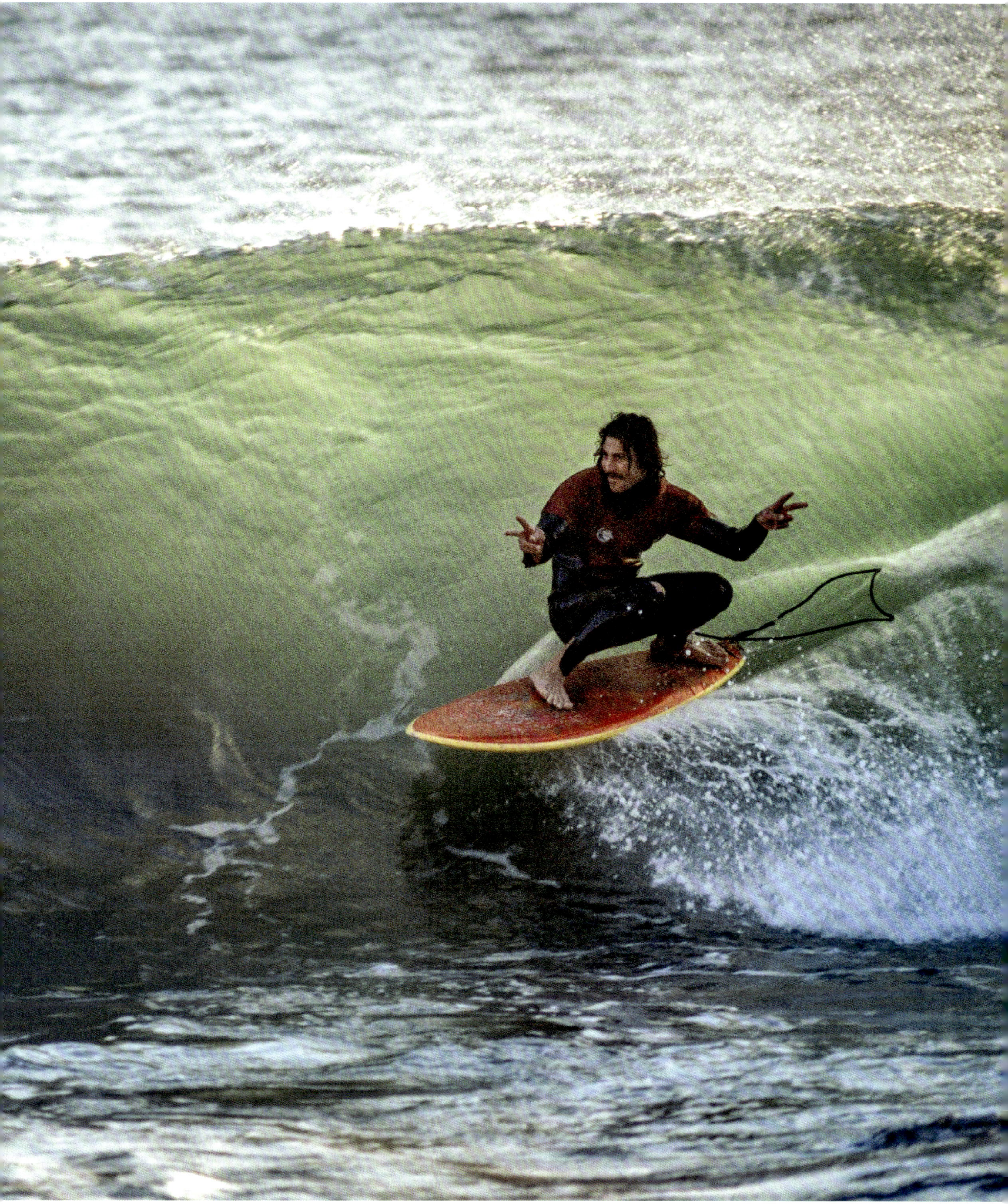

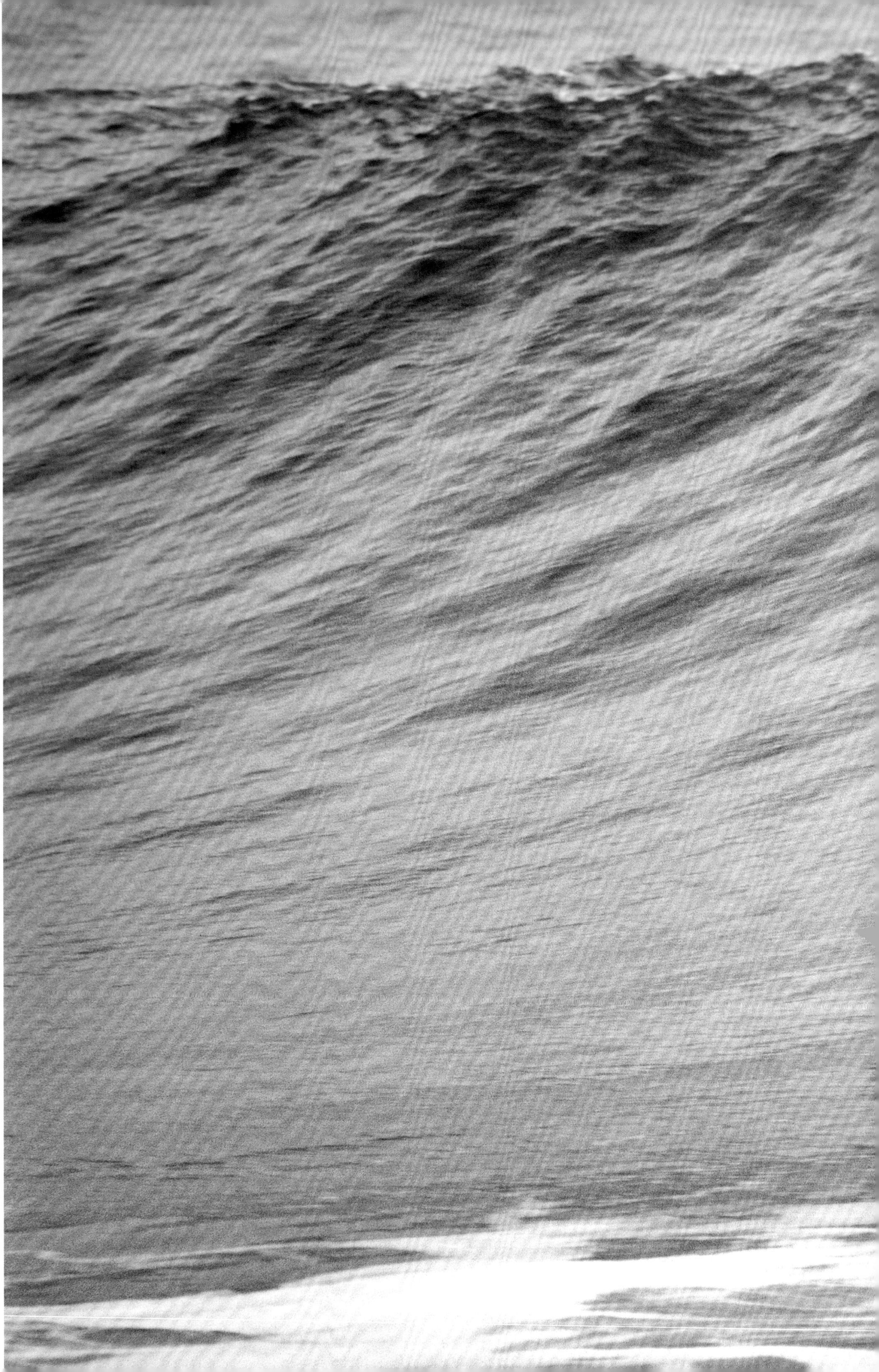

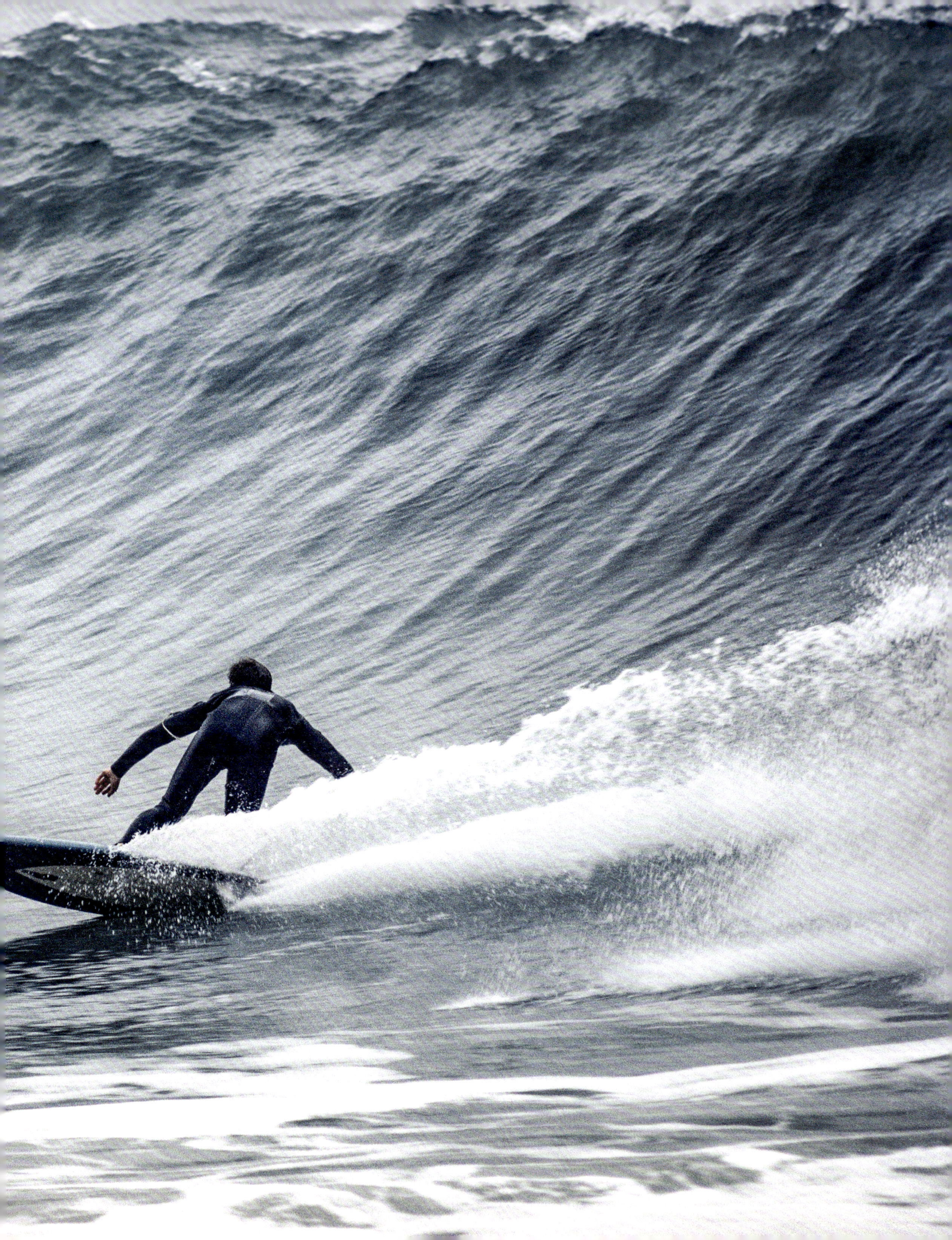

Stuff of Legend

I witnessed a lot of amazing rides during my time in California, but nothing to top Willy Morris's during a giant day at Super Tubes. In early 1981, we experienced a three-day swell event, coupled with minus tides in the afternoon, that made a run down to Super Tubes an easy call. Rounding Point Mugu, we could already see waves breaking off the rocks, with a handful of surfers sitting farther out than ever before. The highway shoulder was lined with cars and spectators, including plenty of surfers who obviously had second thoughts about jumping off the rocks and into the surging lineup. I perched myself halfway down the highway riprap and started shooting, capturing far more super wipeouts than super tubes, losing light quickly as the late afternoon progressed.

I had a partially used roll of black-and-white Kodak Plus-X film in my bag that offered one more stop of light sensitivity, with an ASA (ISO) of 125, and had just loaded that roll into the camera when Willy took off on a big set wave. He bottom turned smoothly, but then, halfway through his top turn, the wave began to hollow out and he free-fell into the tube. I was shooting with my motor drive set at three frames per second, standard for the time. Willy quickly found himself too deep as the wave swept down the coast. The odds of coming out seemed so unlikely—impossible, actually—that I stopped shooting and turned to chat with a spectator who'd joined me on the rocks. I'd just put my camera down when cars up on the highway started honking and flashing their lights. What? Then the guy next to me said, "I think he's still in there."

I quickly grabbed my camera, pointed it back at the wave, refocused, and pressed hard on the motor drive with just enough time to fire off a few shots before Willy flew out of the tube at full speed, arms held high in triumph way inside the cove. The length of the ride, let alone the time he'd spent behind the curtain, was hard to believe, and up on the highway the gallery erupted, honking horns and hooting, the flashing headlights creating a stadium-like atmosphere. Willy eventually climbed up the rocks and made his way back to the car, smiling and accepting congratulations the entire way. It was like no other surfing scene I'd seen before or since. Willy's ride became the stuff of legend that afternoon, but for me; that gap between image twenty-two and image twenty-three on the contact sheet haunts me to this day.

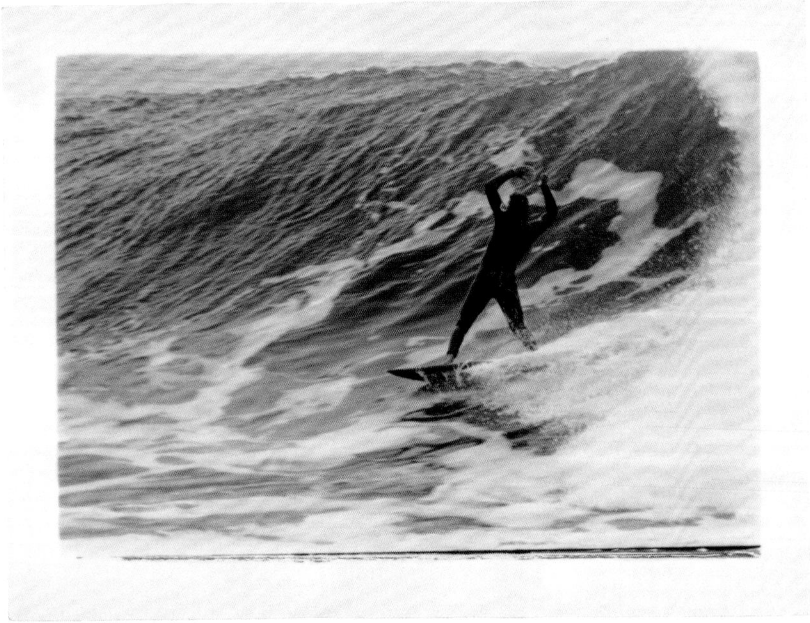

Pages 100–101

Only a few days after shooting serious Super Tubes, I saw real Sandspit come alive for the very first time. Peeling down a broad sandbar that regularly builds up along the mouth of Santa Barbara Harbor, Sandspit is one of those rarely breaking wonders that begins to work only on the very biggest of swells, and here it was in all its glory. When Tommy finally showed up after school, all the pieces of an epic session were in place.

Pages 102–103, left to right

Tommy Curren. Tommy Curren. Tommy, jogging up to the takeoff spot. Davey Smith's "bat turn" in the middle of the harbor.

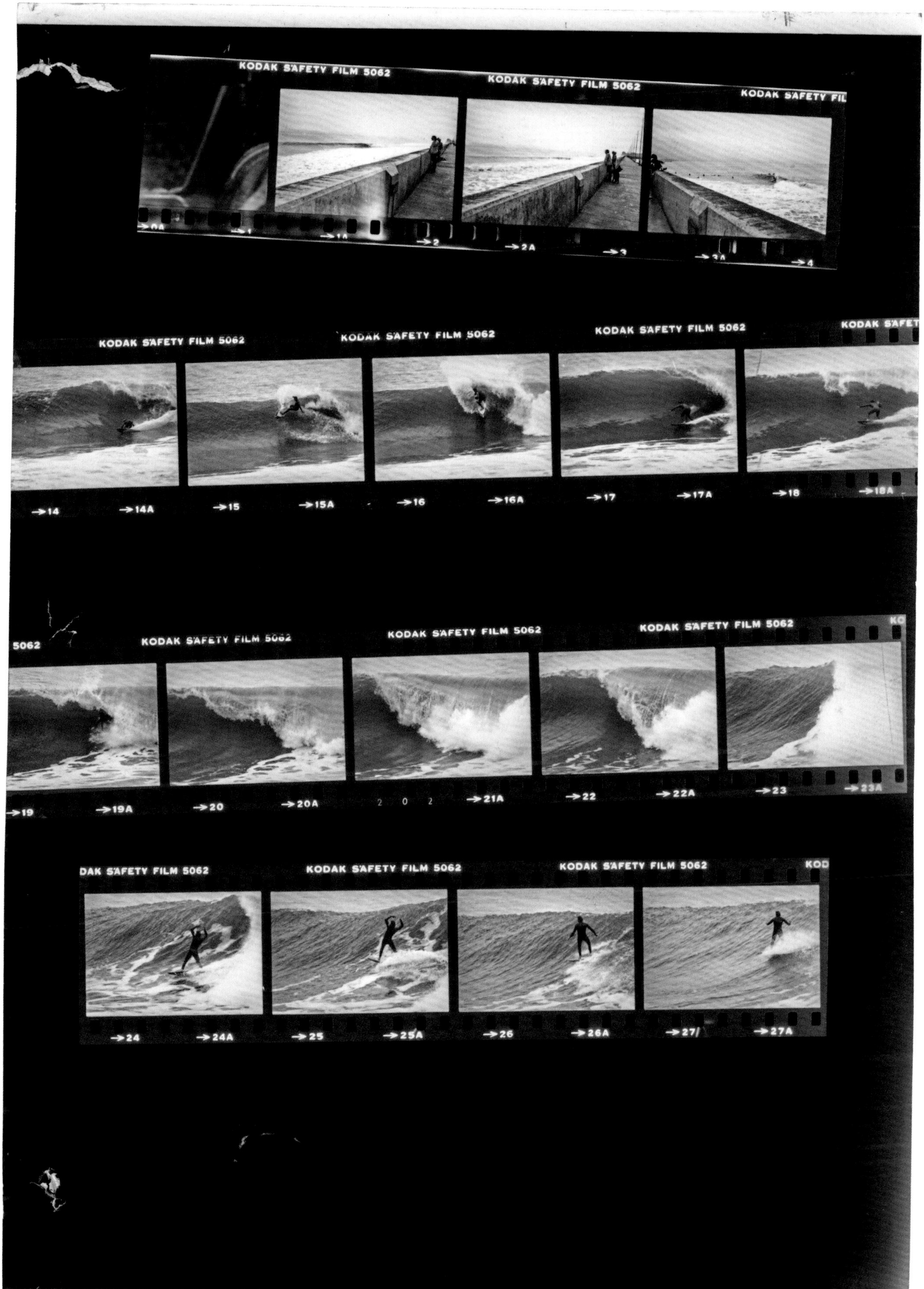
KODAK SAFETY FILM 5062
→0A →1 →1A →2 →2A →3 →3A →4
→14 →14A →15 →15A →16 →16A →17 →17A →18 →18A
→19 →19A →20 →20A →21A →22 →22A →23 →23A
→24 →24A →25 →25A →26 →26A →27 →27A

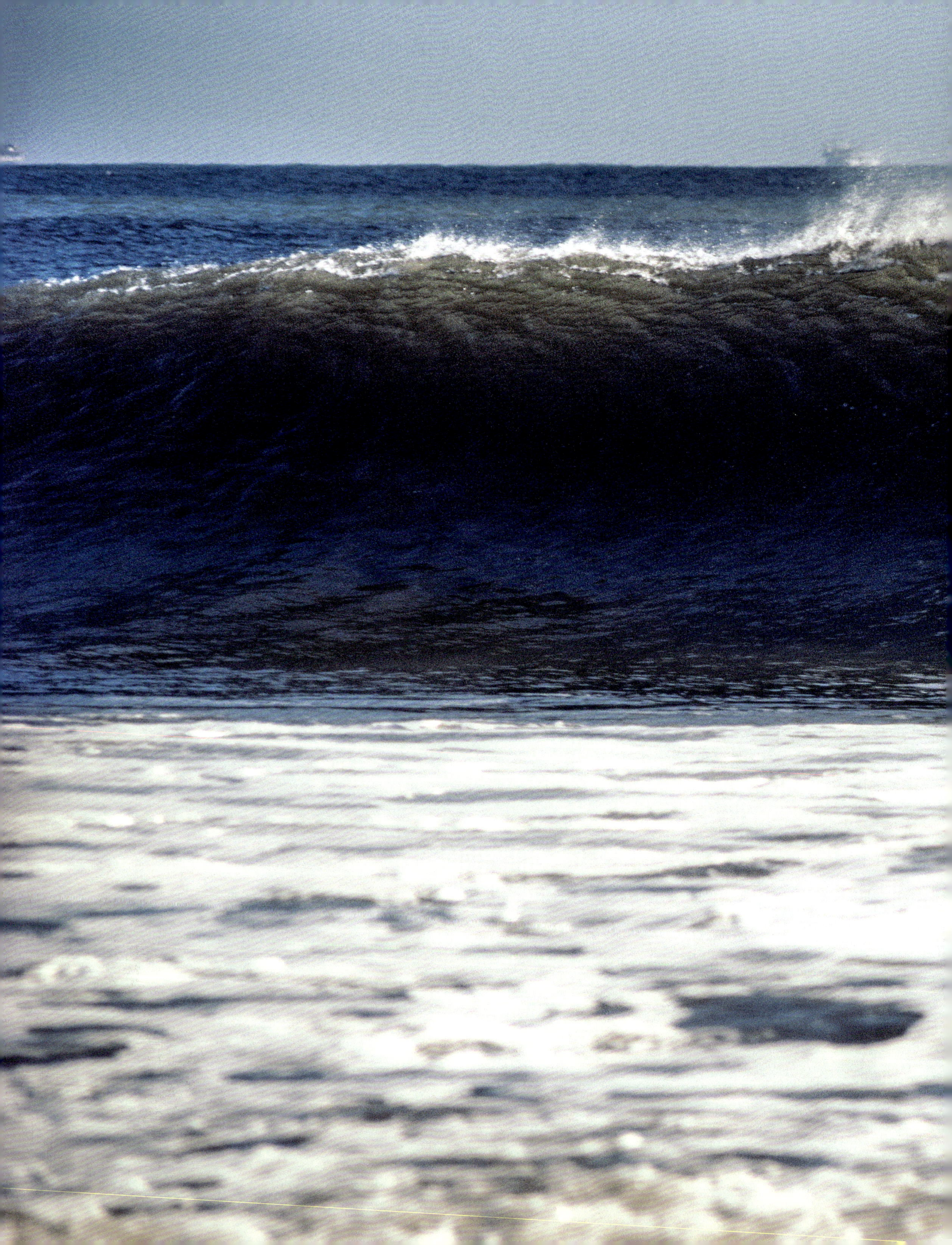

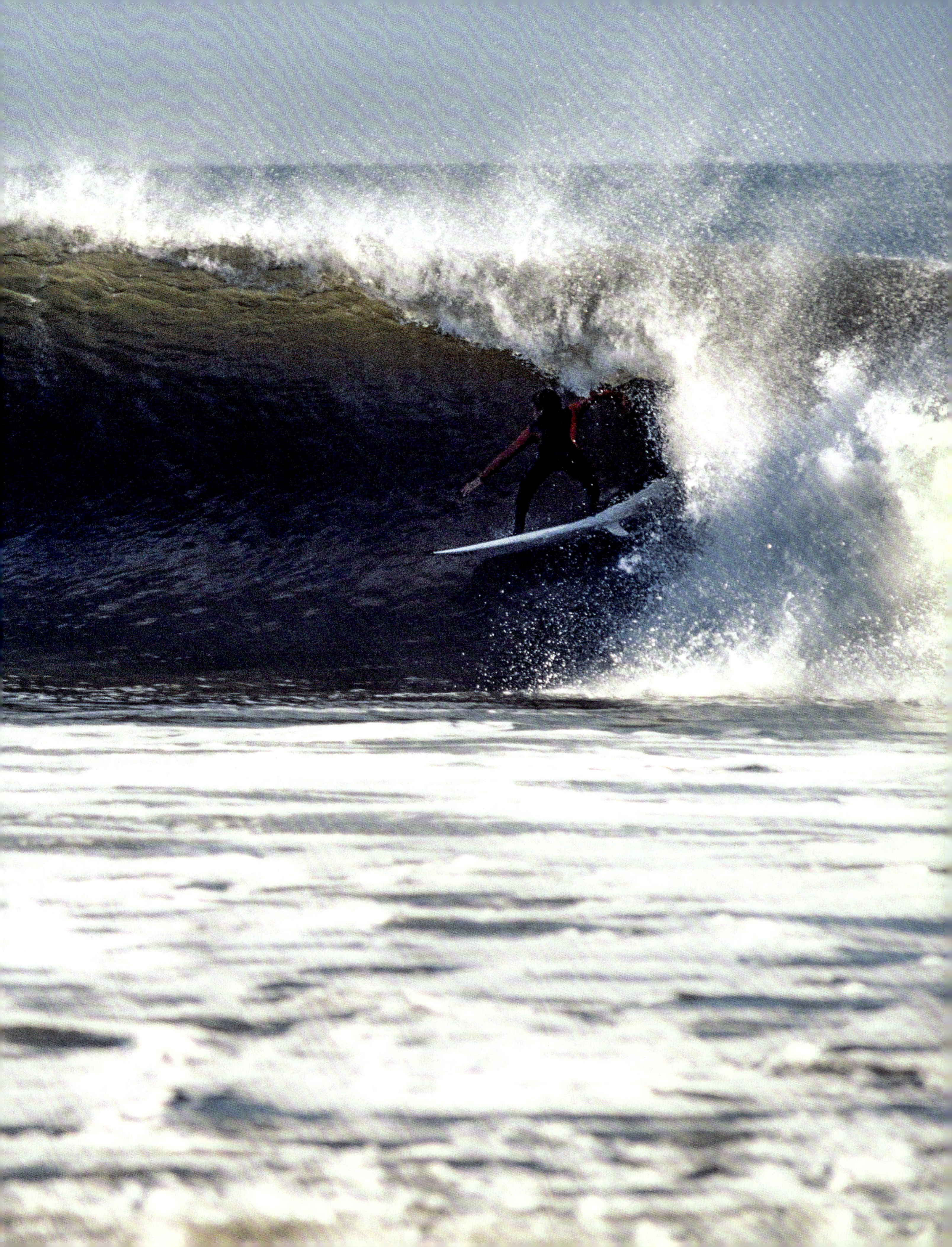

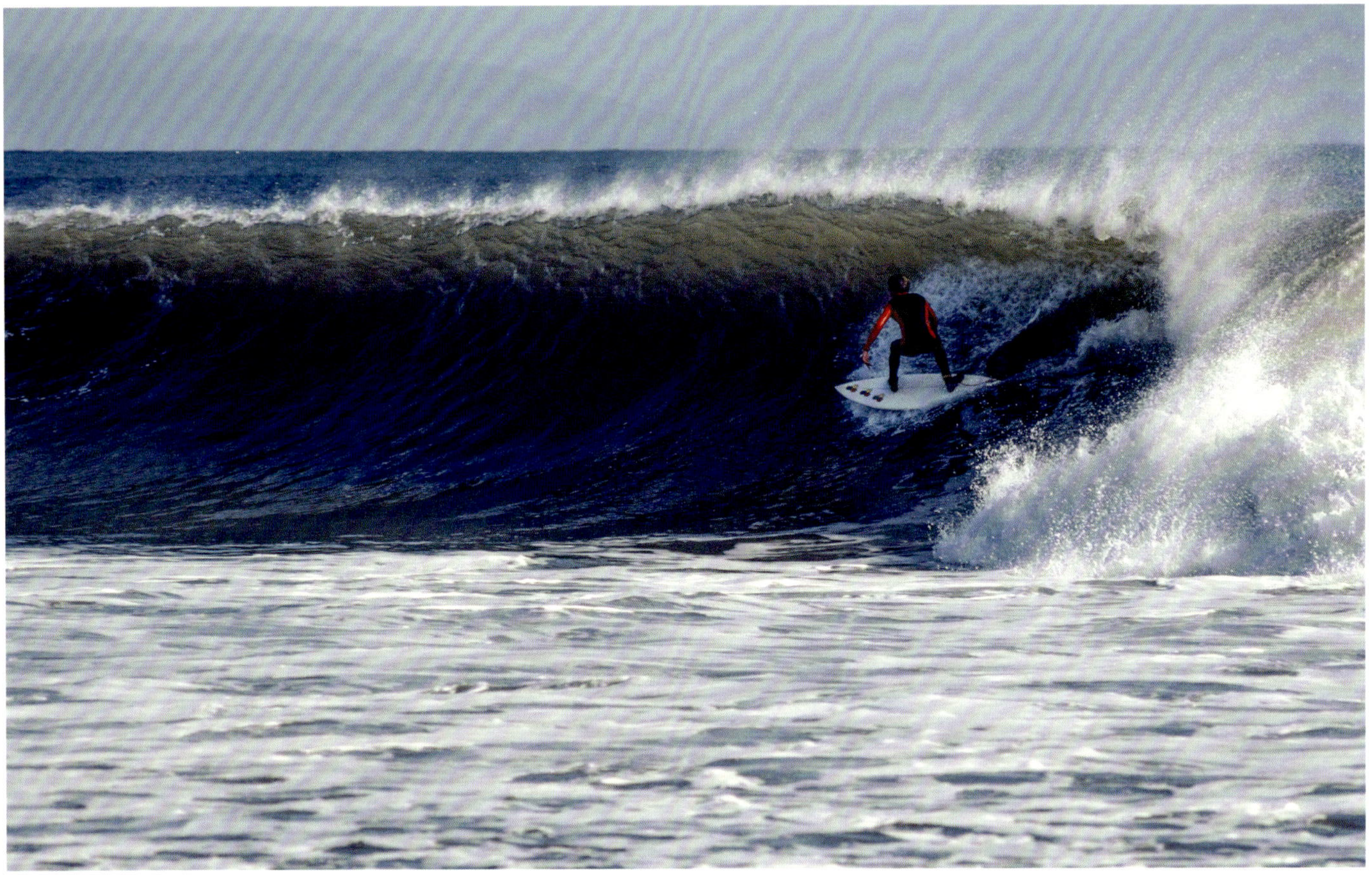

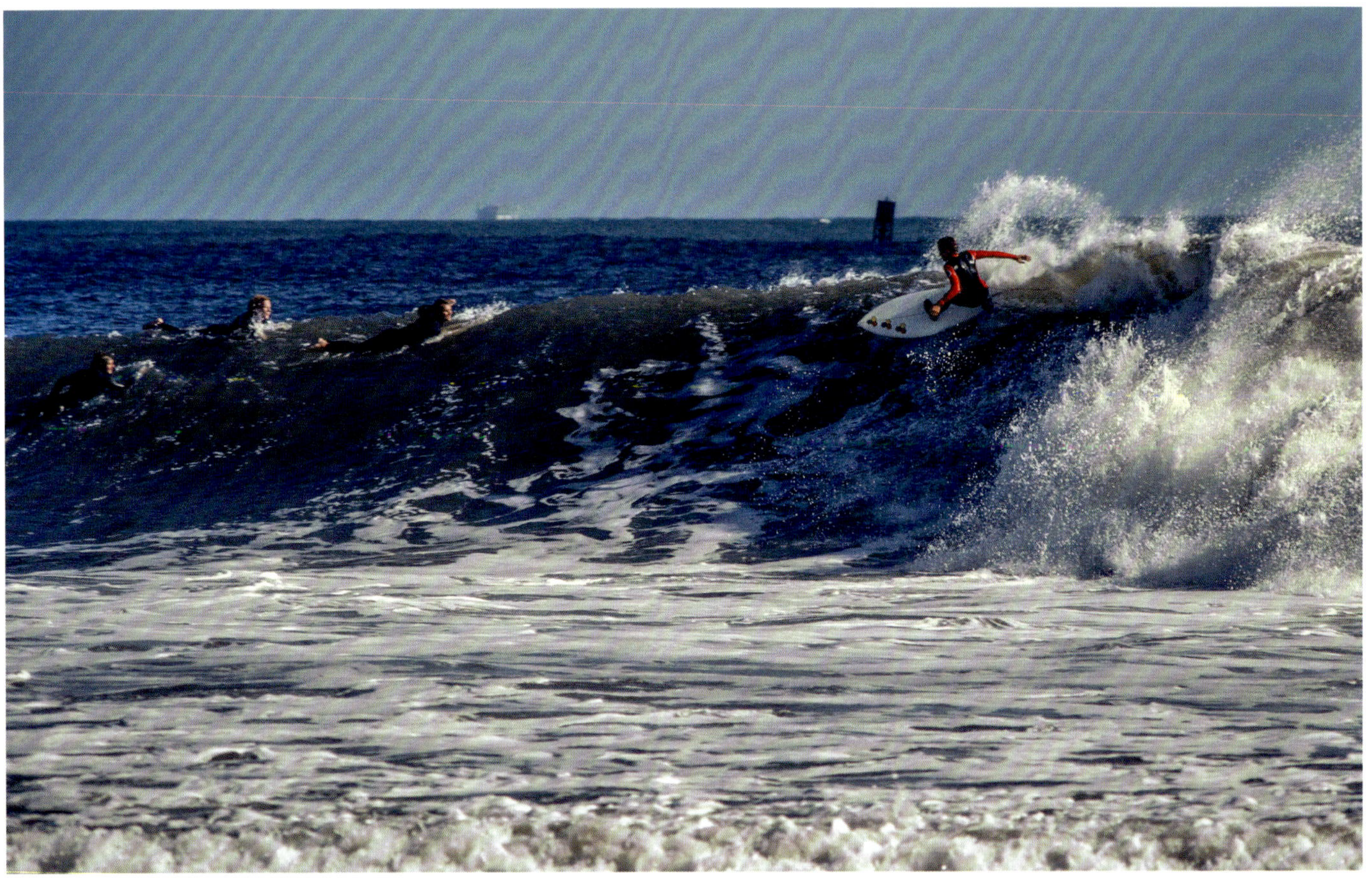

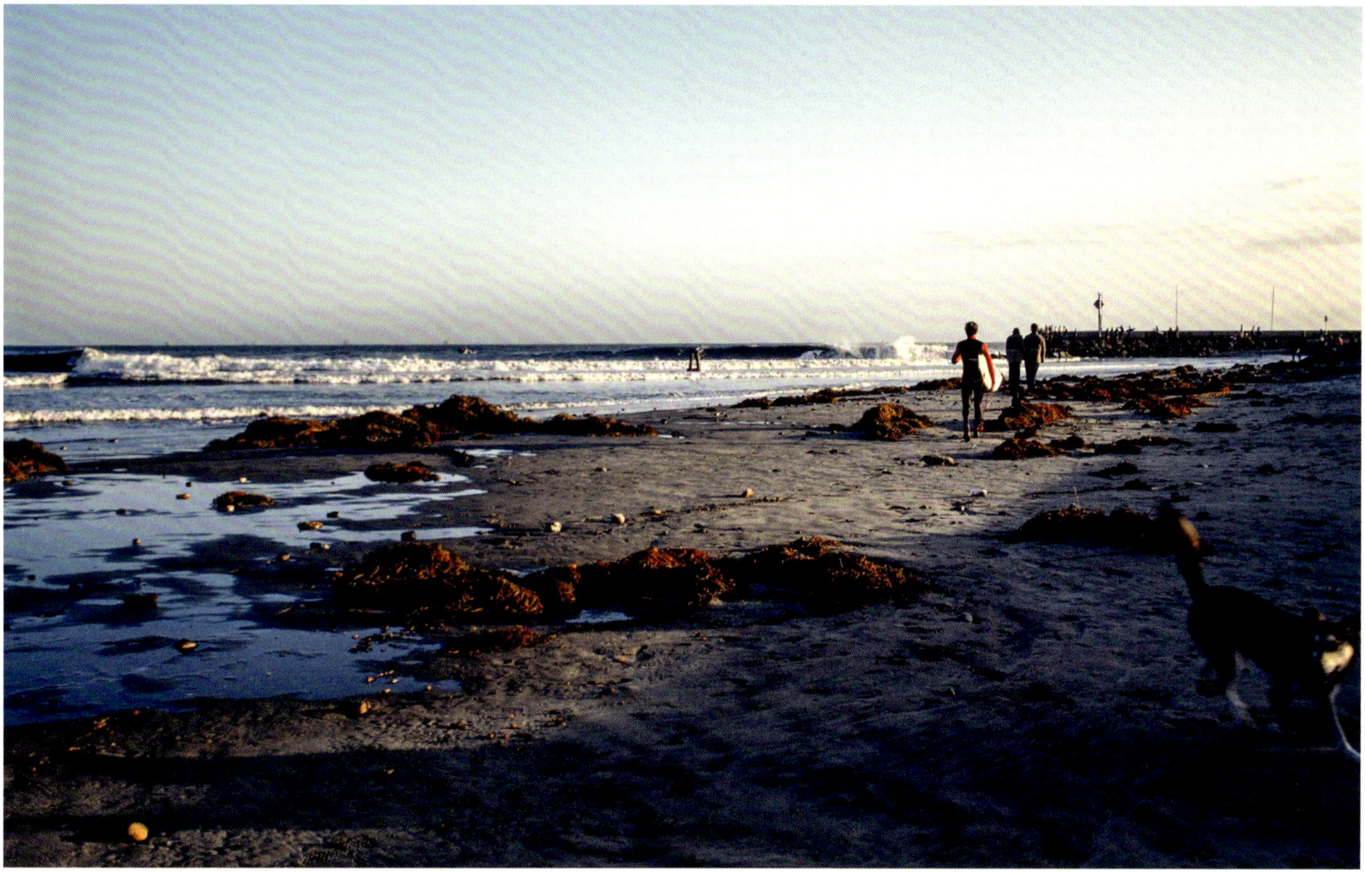

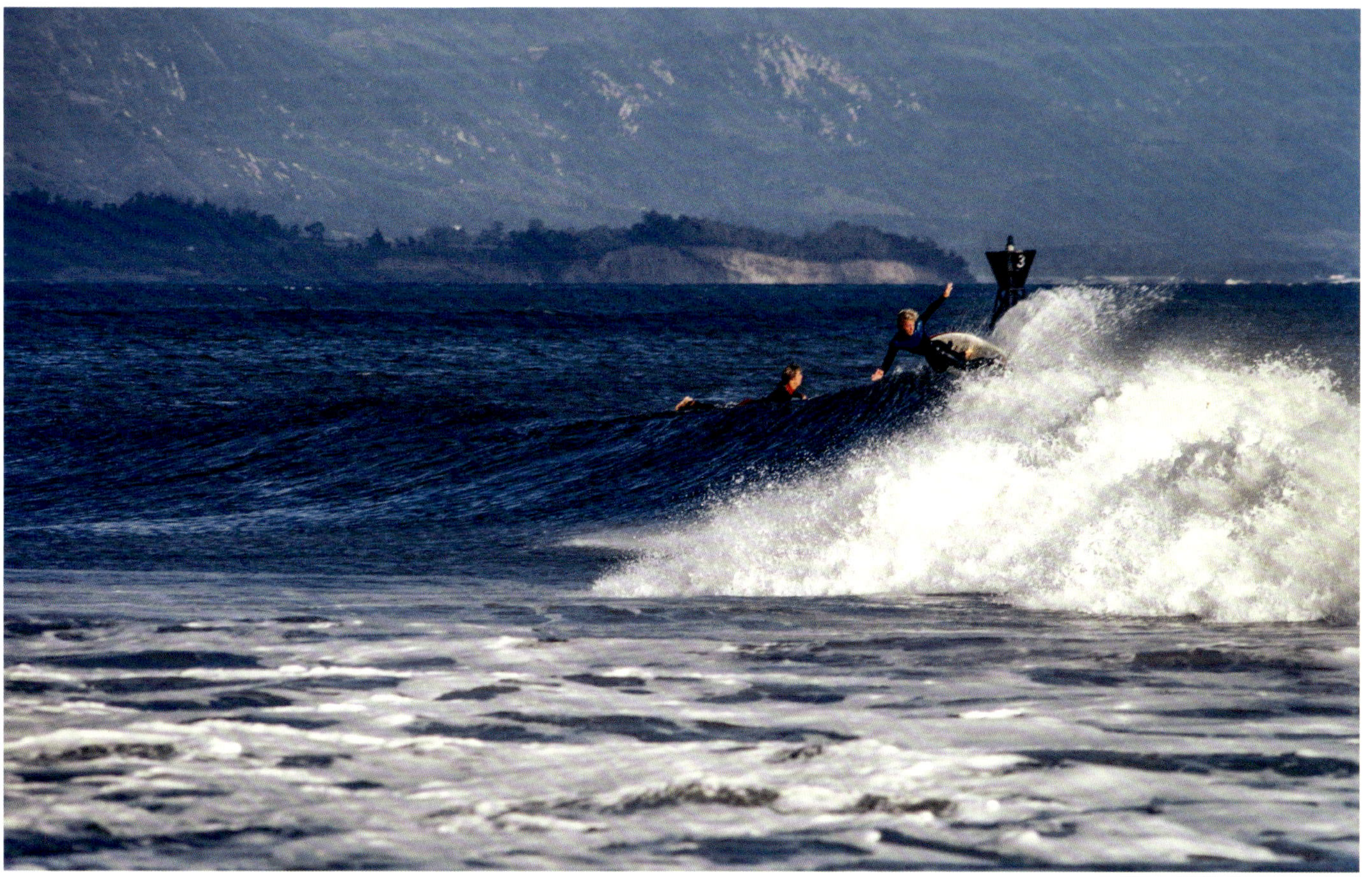

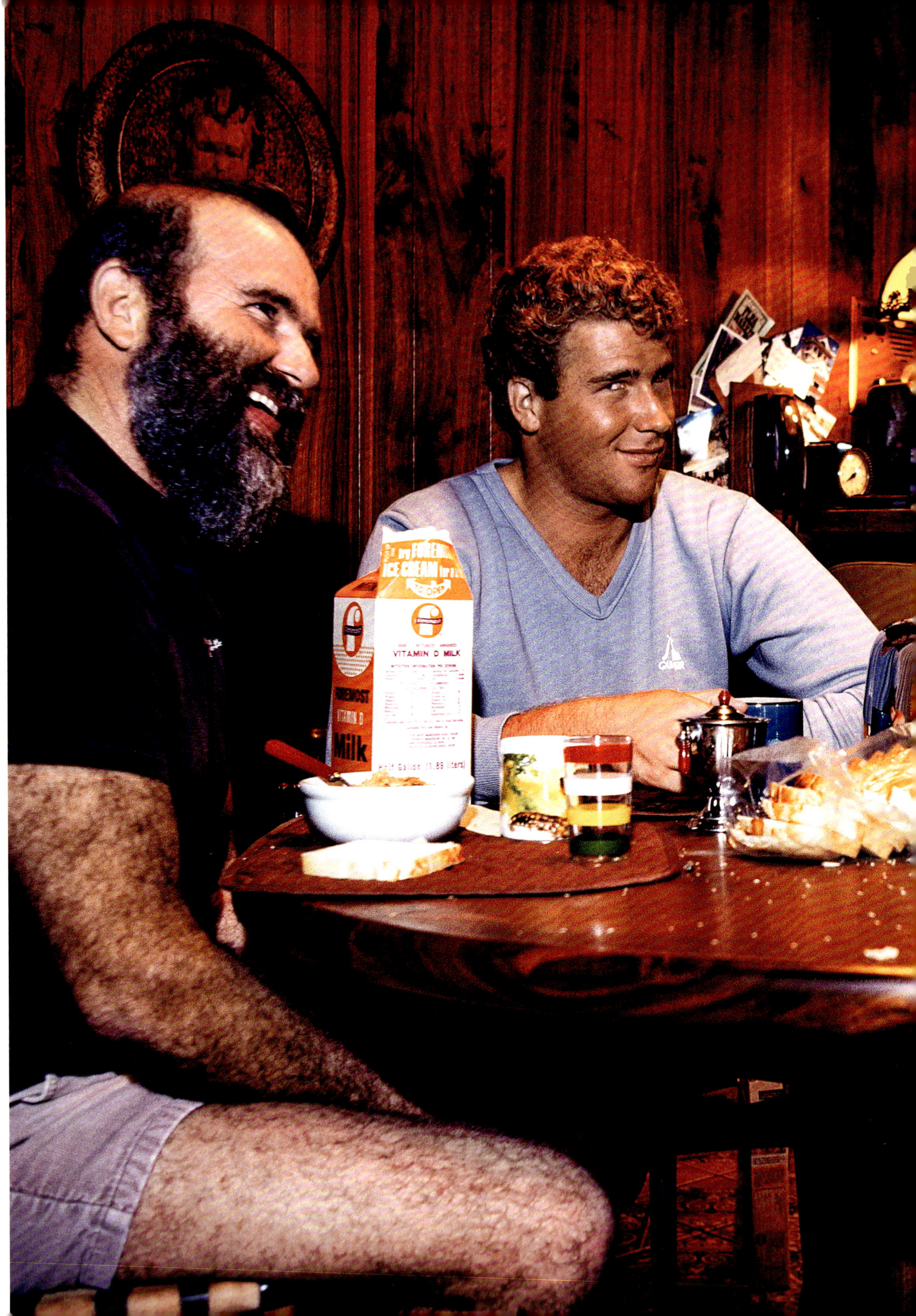
ICE CREAM
VITAMIN D MILK
Milk
Half Gallon (1.89 liters)

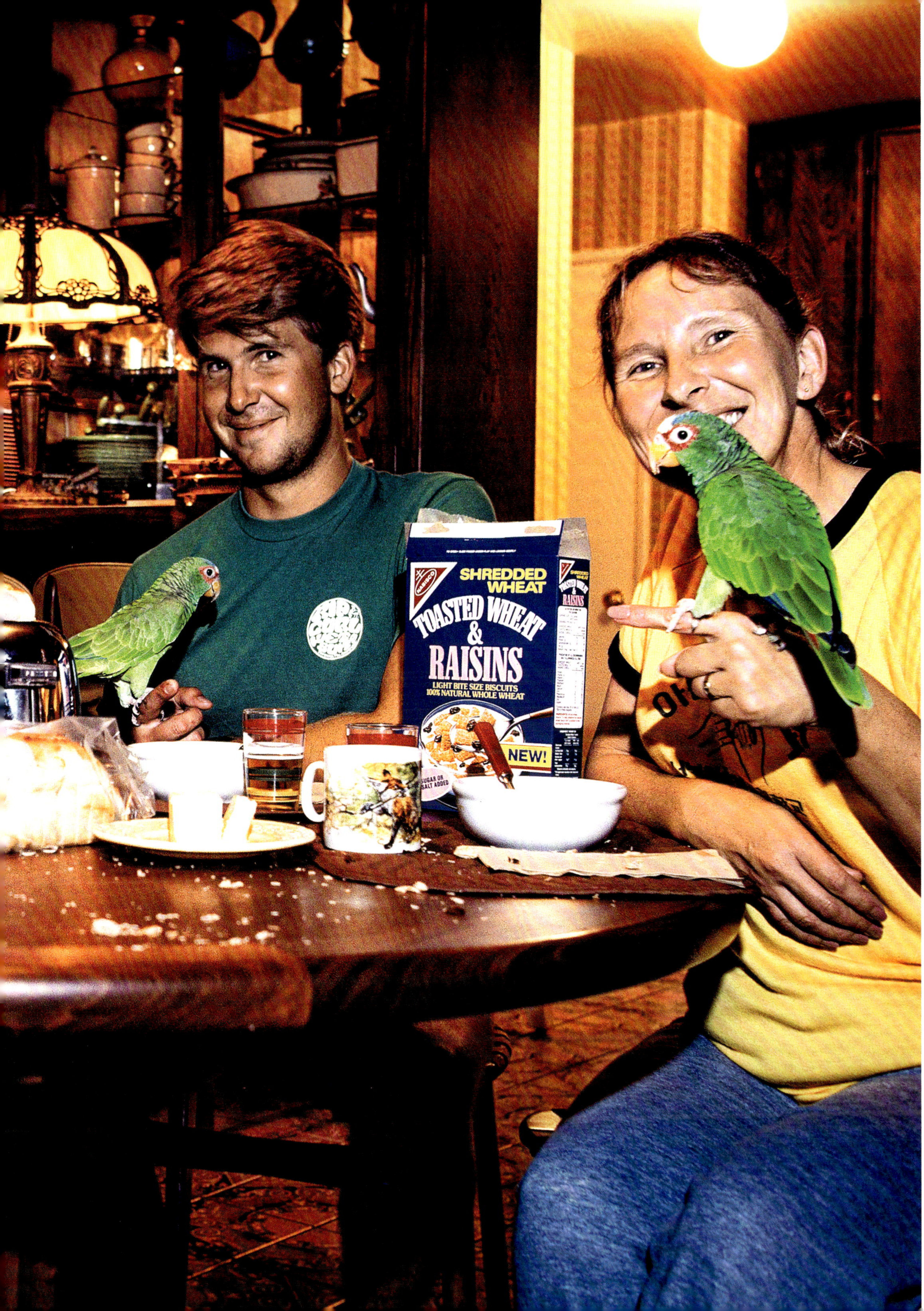
NABISCO
SHREDDED WHEAT
TOASTED WHEAT
&
RAISINS
LIGHT BITE SIZE BISCUITS
100% NATURAL WHOLE WHEAT
NEW!

Previous

Meet the Morris family: *(left to right)* dad Lee, Willy, Steve, and mom Sandra *(always "Mrs. Morris" to me)*.

Below

Steve Morris *(left)* and Willy Morris *(right)*, surfing Ventura's beaches, early morning, before the inevitable sea breeze kicks in.

Willy & Steve

Luckily, when I first started shooting with Steve and Willy Morris, they were amateurs like Tommy, before they were in major demand by the surf magazines. This gave me time to improve my shooting and acquire better equipment. In the beginning, my only lens was a 300 millimeter, which combined with a lot of enthusiasm; at most surf spots, those two things did not get you anywhere close enough to the action for what the surf magazines wanted. It would be through shooting with Willy and Steve and their close friend Dino Bortoli that I'd learn how to make it all work with the equipment that I had.

I can't count the miles I spent hunting waves with the Morris brothers. I learned more about swell direction, tides, wind condition, where to be, and when to be there from Willy and Steve than from everyone else combined.

A typical day would find me meeting Steve and Willy down at the Ventura beachbreaks, taking advantage of the morning light until the inevitable sea breeze kicked in around 11 a.m., spoiling the surf. A quick stop to refuel at Carl's Jr., then we'd be off to Rincon or Malibu, sometimes both, depending on the time of year and conditions, chasing the afternoon light at the wind-sheltered pointbreaks. I ended up missing some school, but I didn't miss many good days of surf.

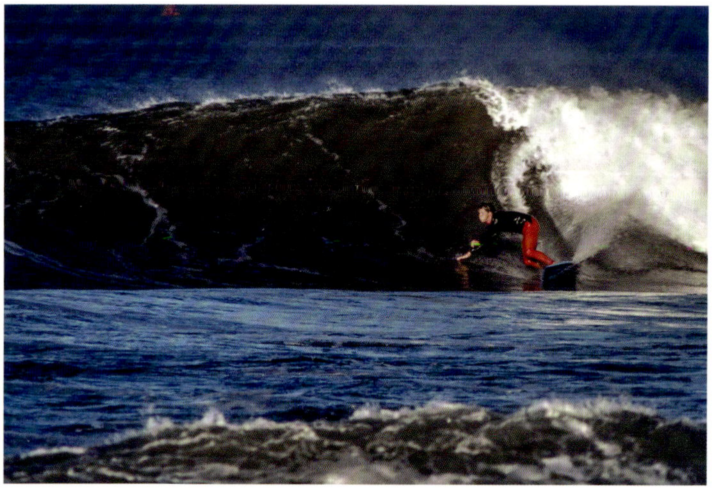

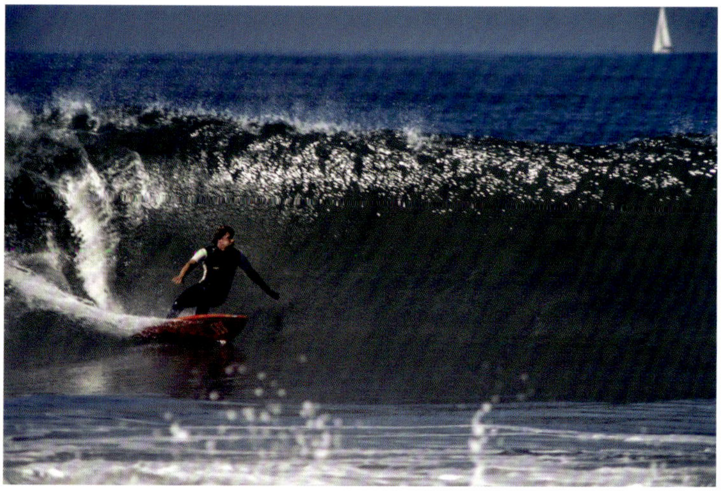

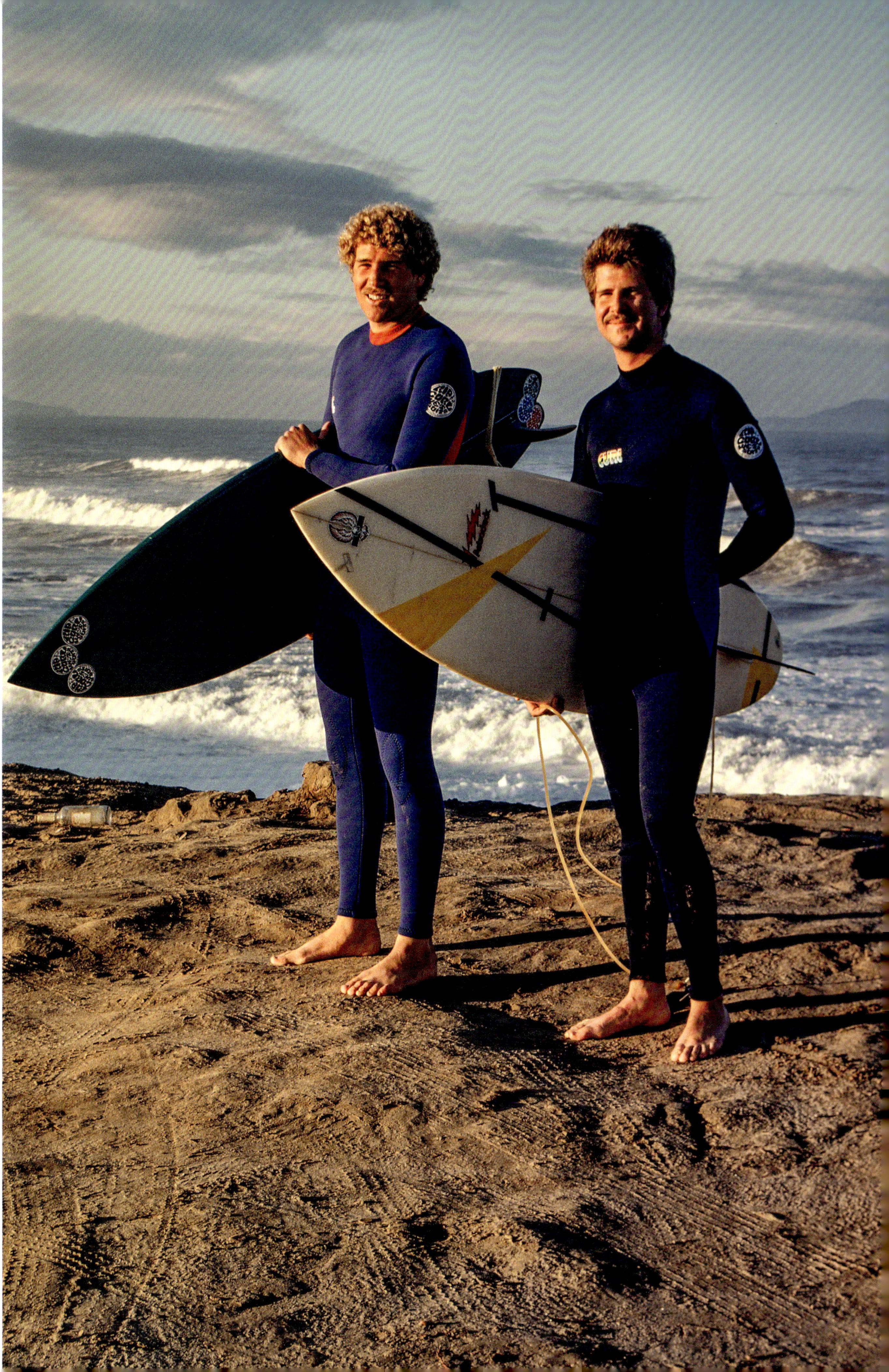

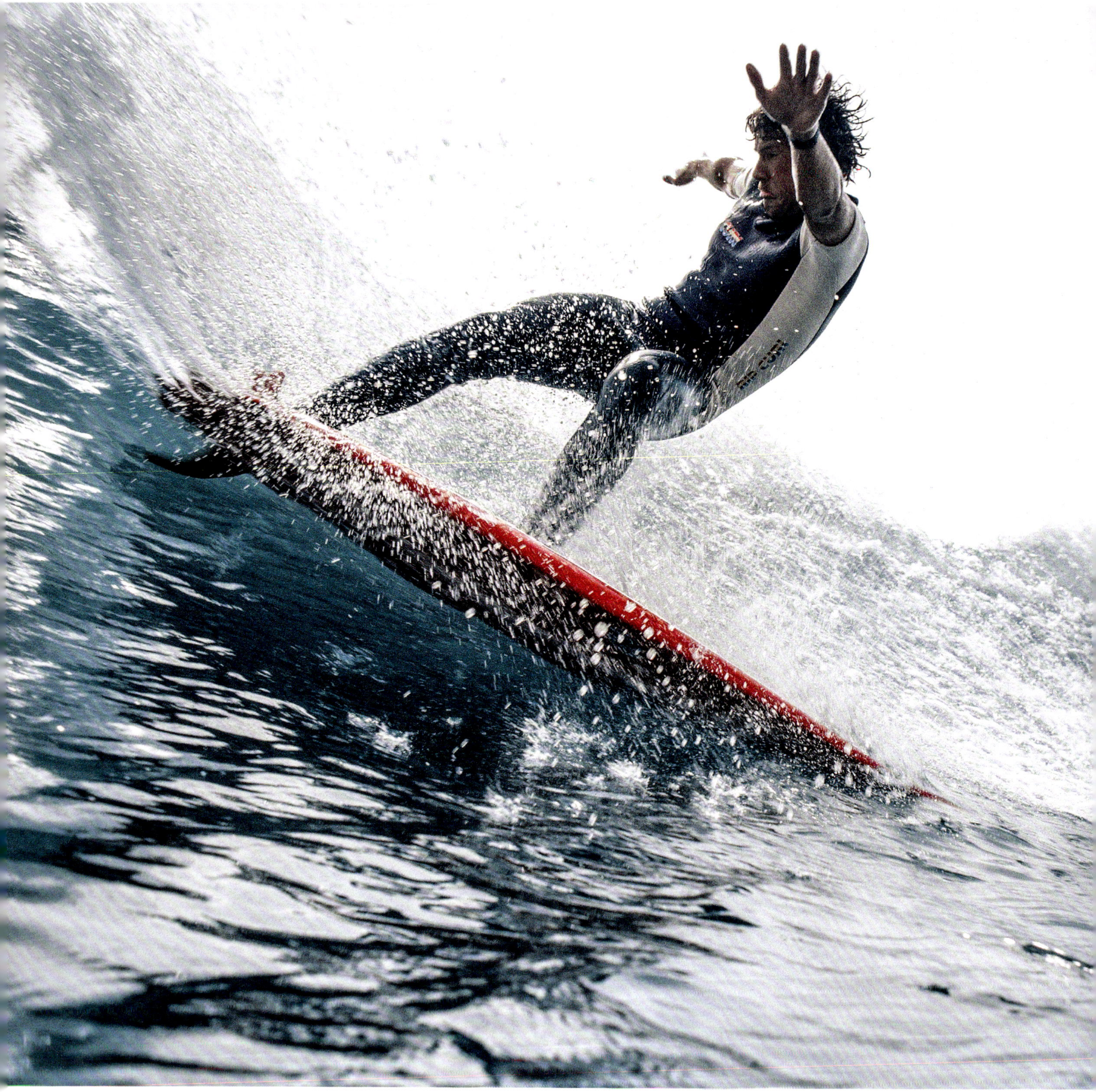

When shooting Willy from the water, you always wanted to avoid his spray, which hit you like rock salt blasted from a shotgun. This image first appeared in *Surfer* magazine's inaugural "Hot 100" article.

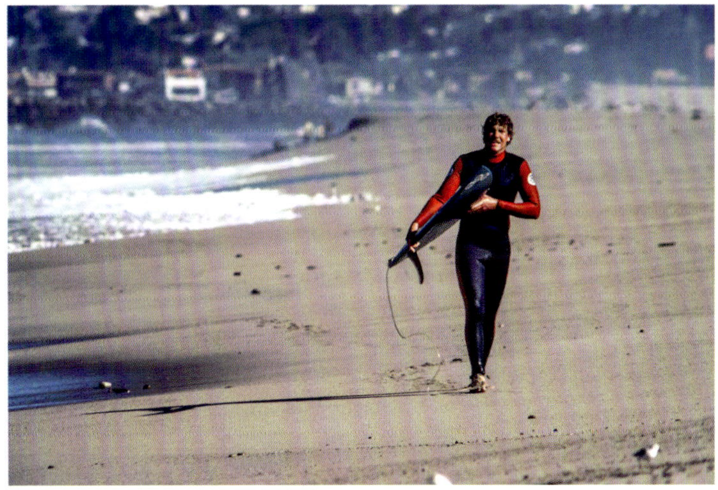

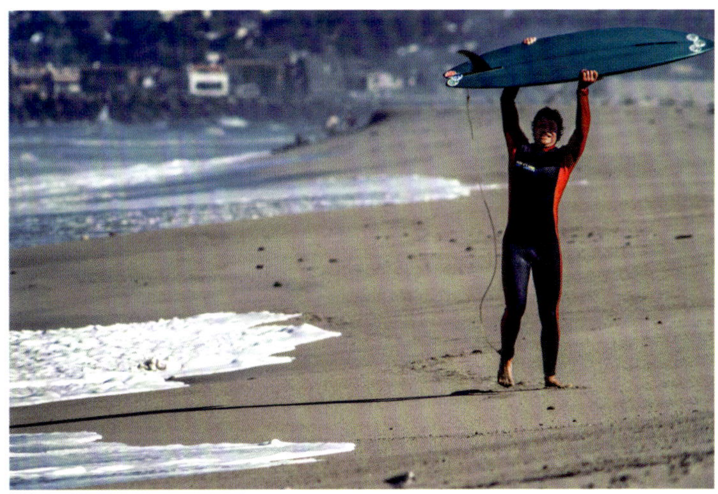

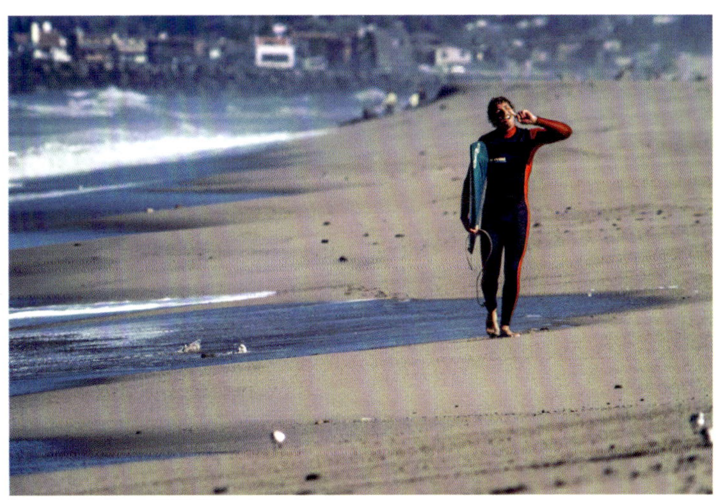

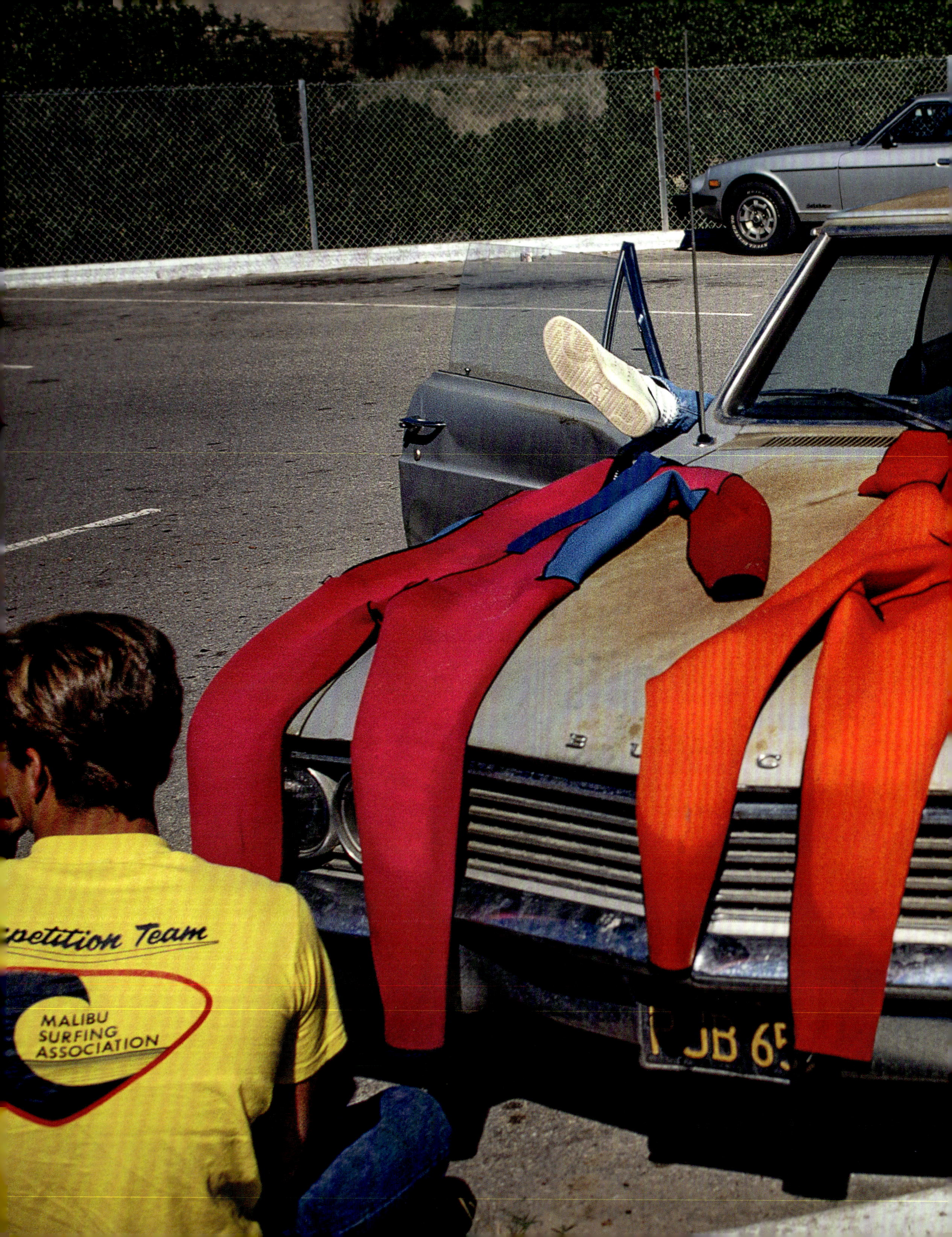
petition Team
MALIBU
SURFING
ASSOCIATION

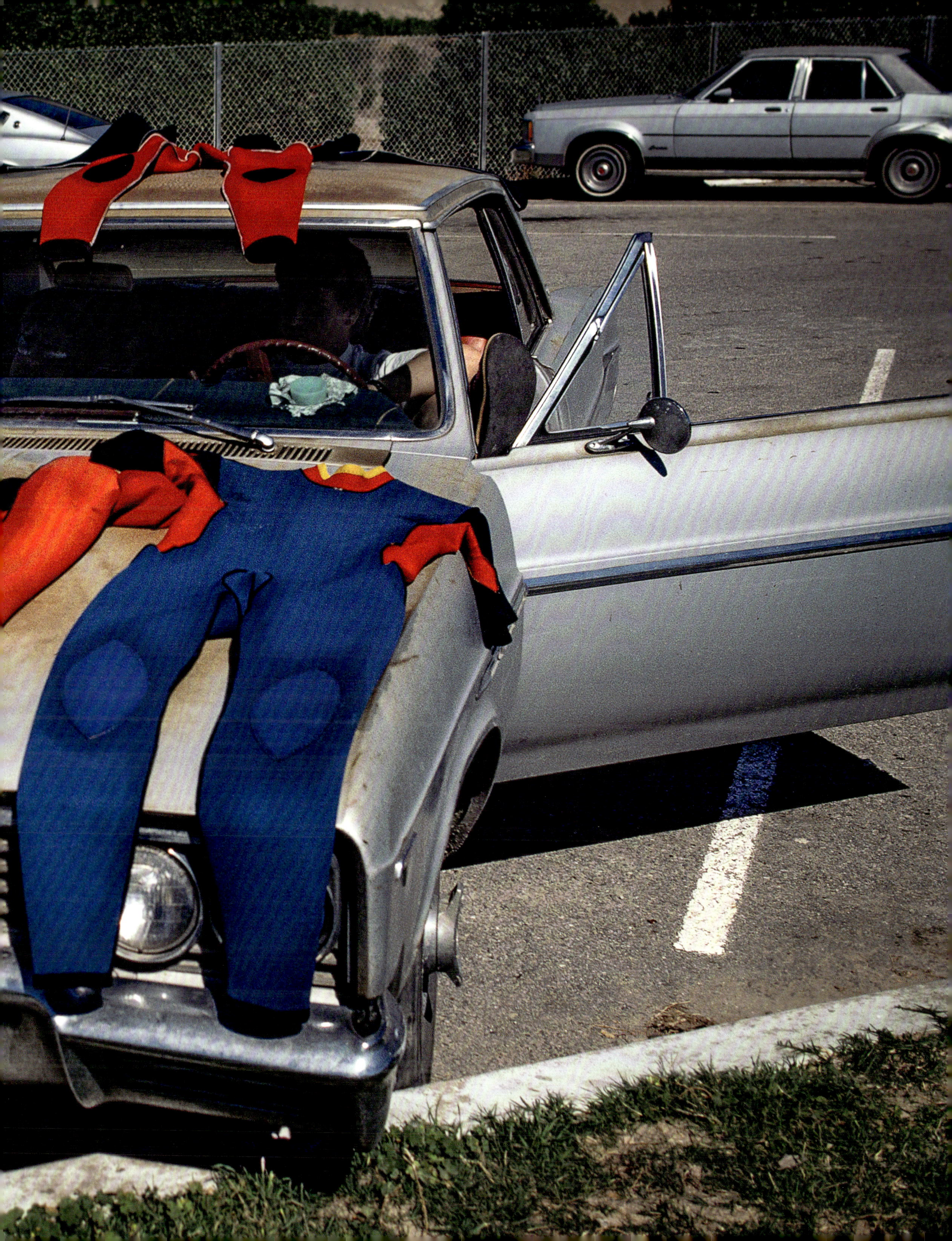

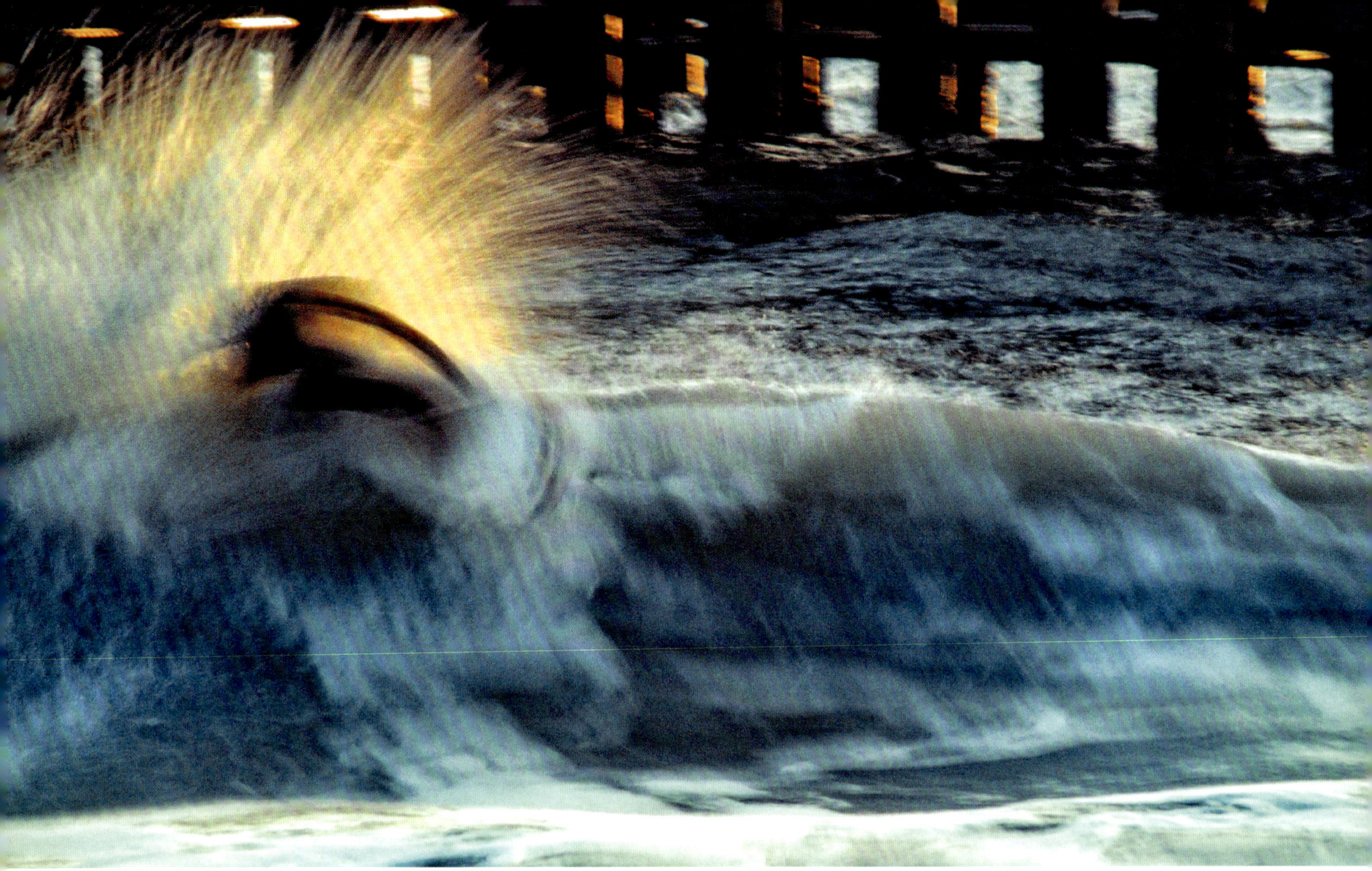

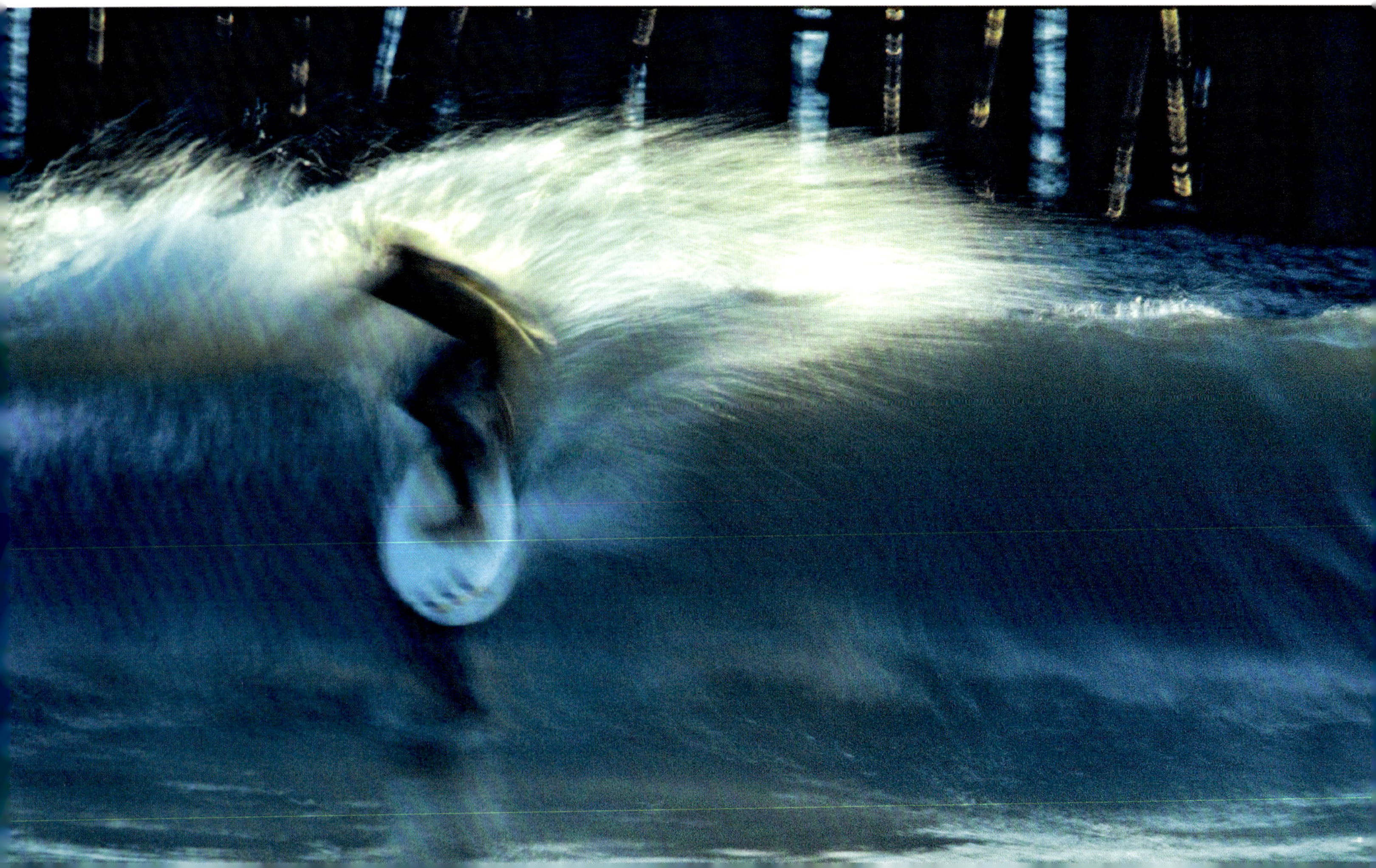

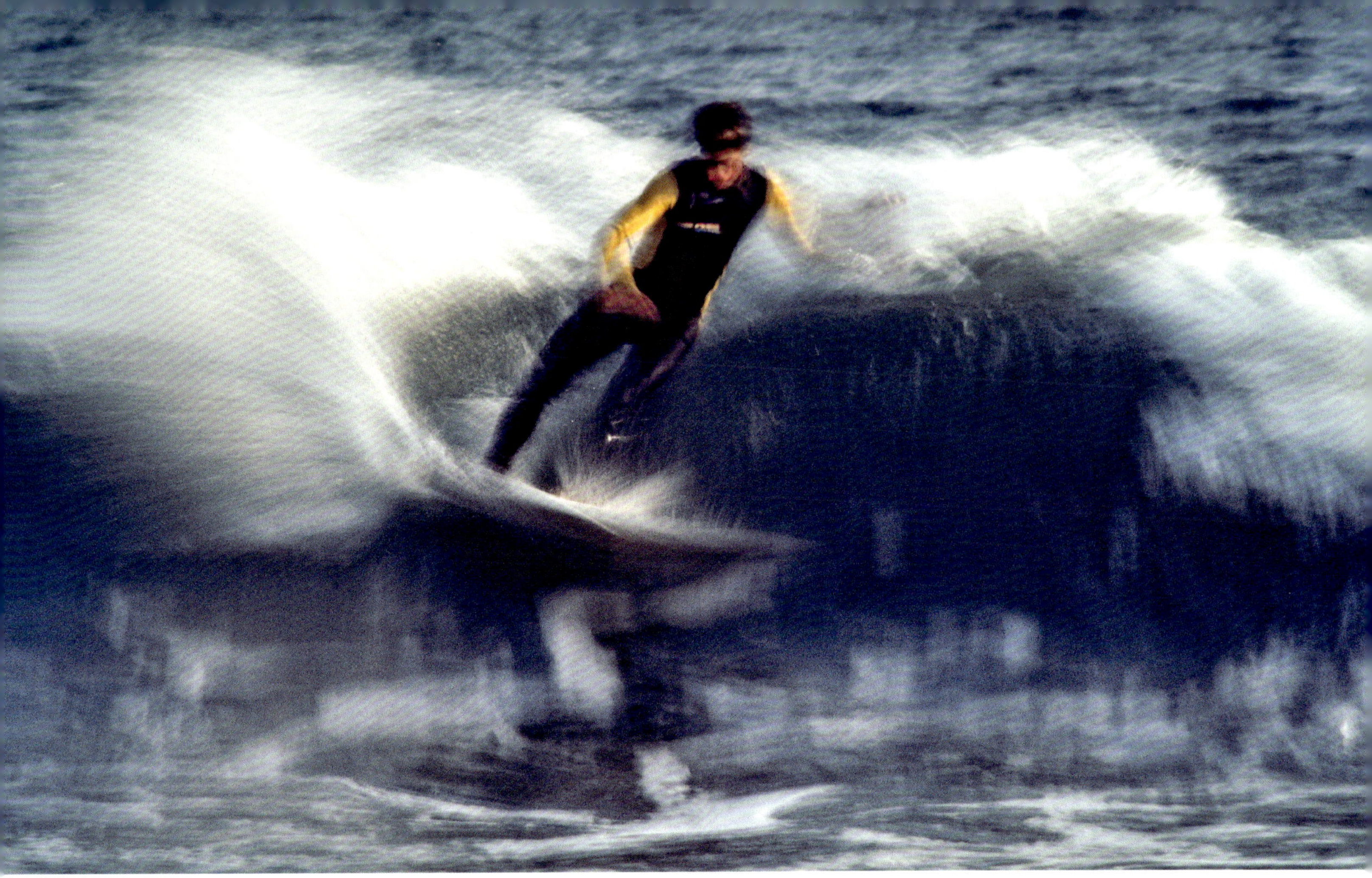

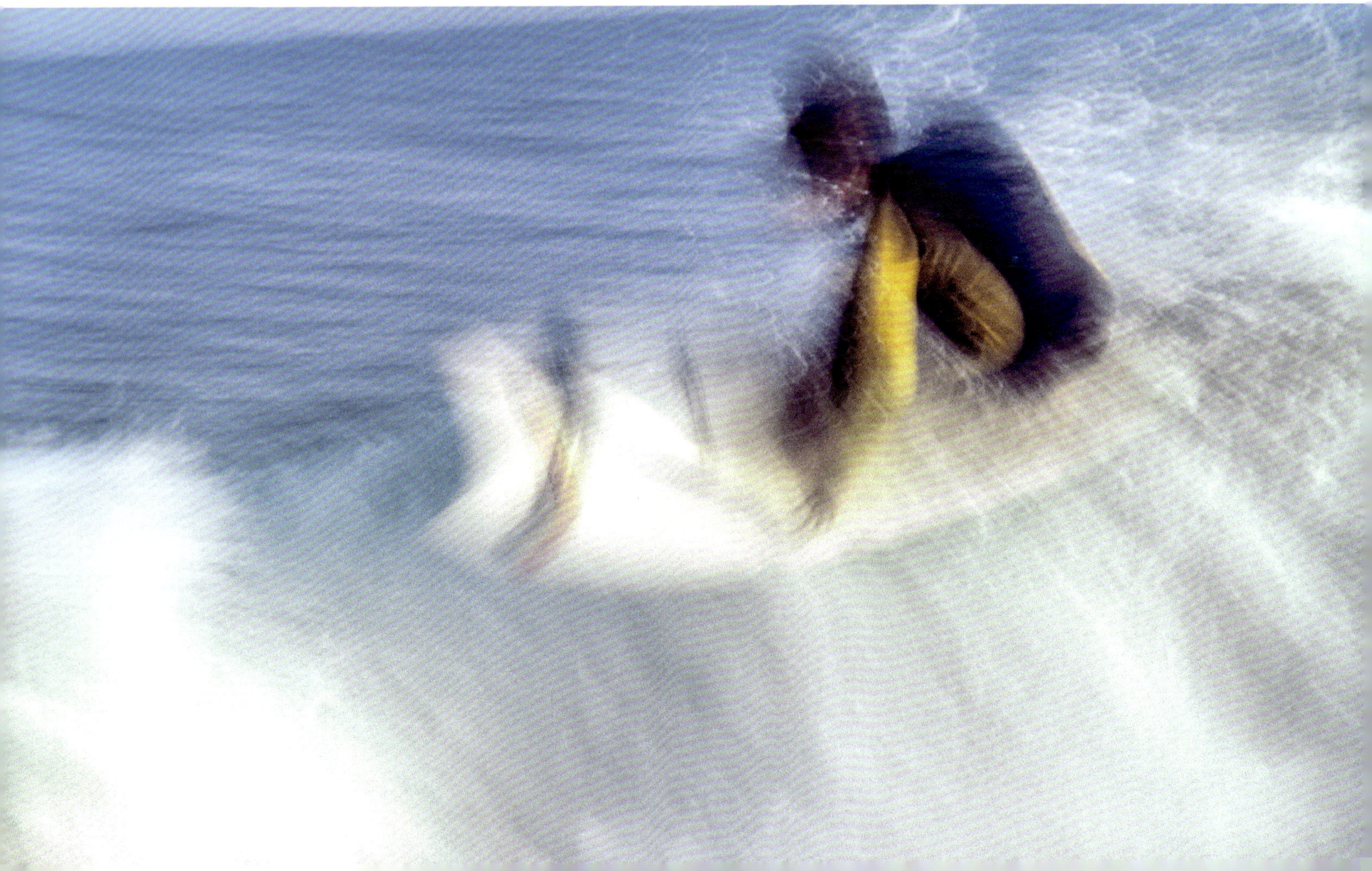

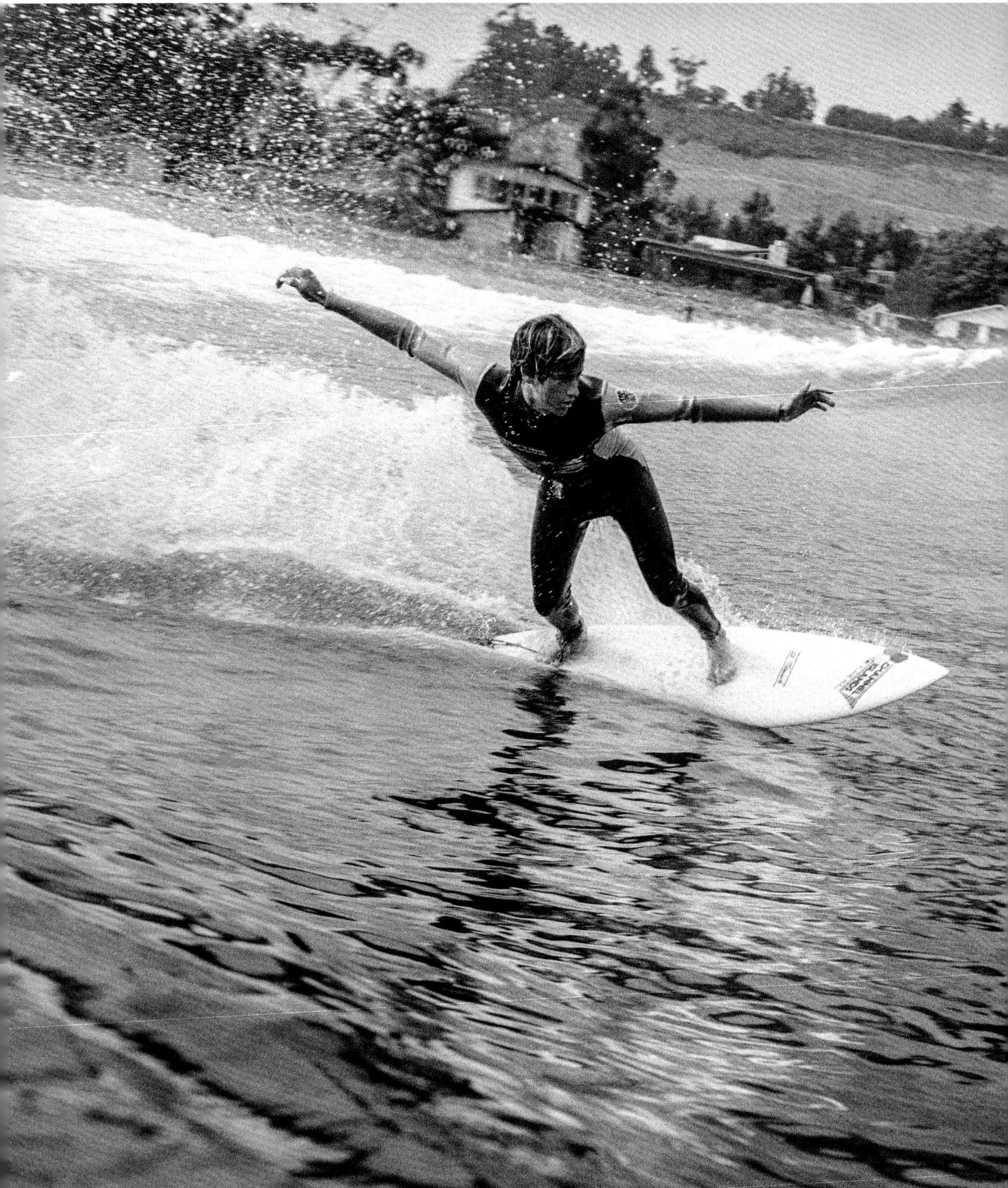

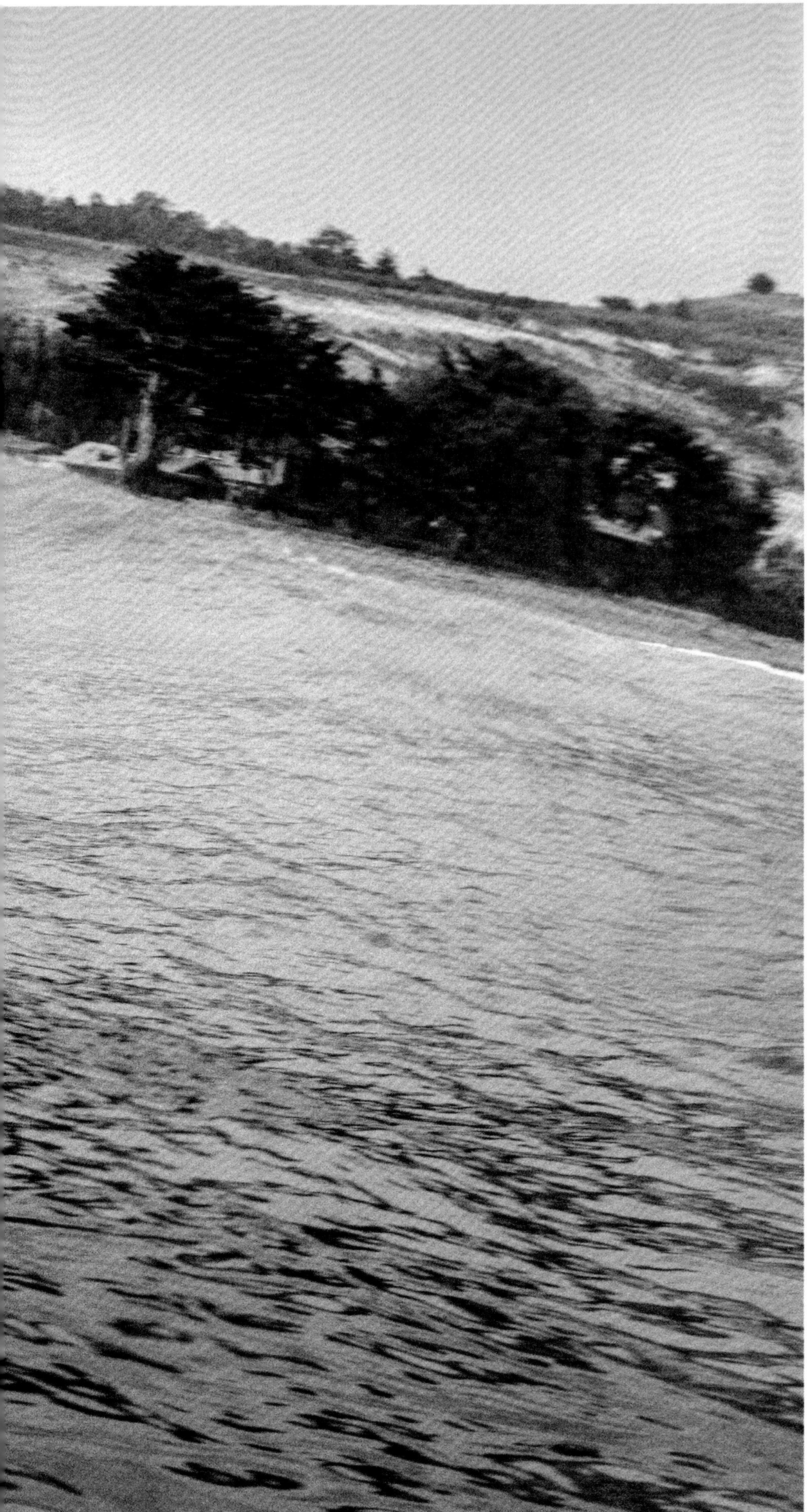

Pages 110–111

Waiting for low tide in Steve Morris's first car, the "Gray Ghost" 1967 Buick Skylark. Purchased for $200, it had a huge trunk that easily swallowed up to three 6'8" Kennedy single-fins, and a massive silver hood that was perfect for drying wetsuits. Dino Bortoli in the cool Malibu Surfing Association yellow tee, Steve and little brother Willy kicked back inside the cab.

Previous

While developing my own approach to shooting action, I was heavily influenced by the work of legendary photographer Ernst Haas, who in the 1950s experimented with slow shutter speeds while shooting rodeo and bullfighting images. I made do with Tommy Curren, surfing on a small day at Oil Piers.

Spread

I always loved shooting from the water at Rincon, especially when everything came together like in this shot of Tommy, capturing a quiet moment in his otherwise radical repertoire.

Overleaf

Shaun Tomson, Rincon. I was always amazed by Shaun's ability to leverage his tall frame to create power, the centrifugal force created as he whipped his board into a tight arc being the hallmark of his surfing. Impressive to watch, but intimidating, too, when performed a few inches from my water housing.

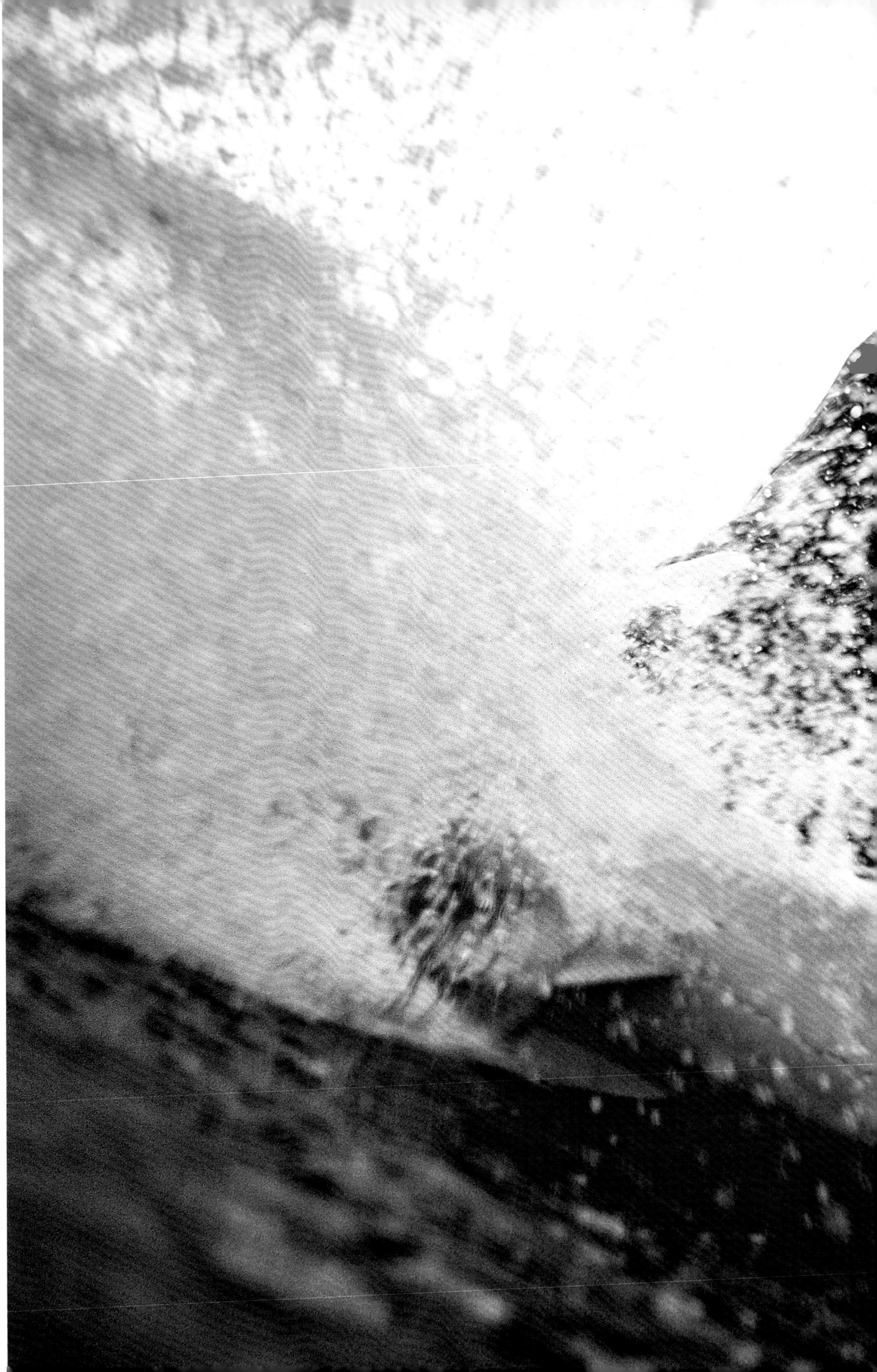

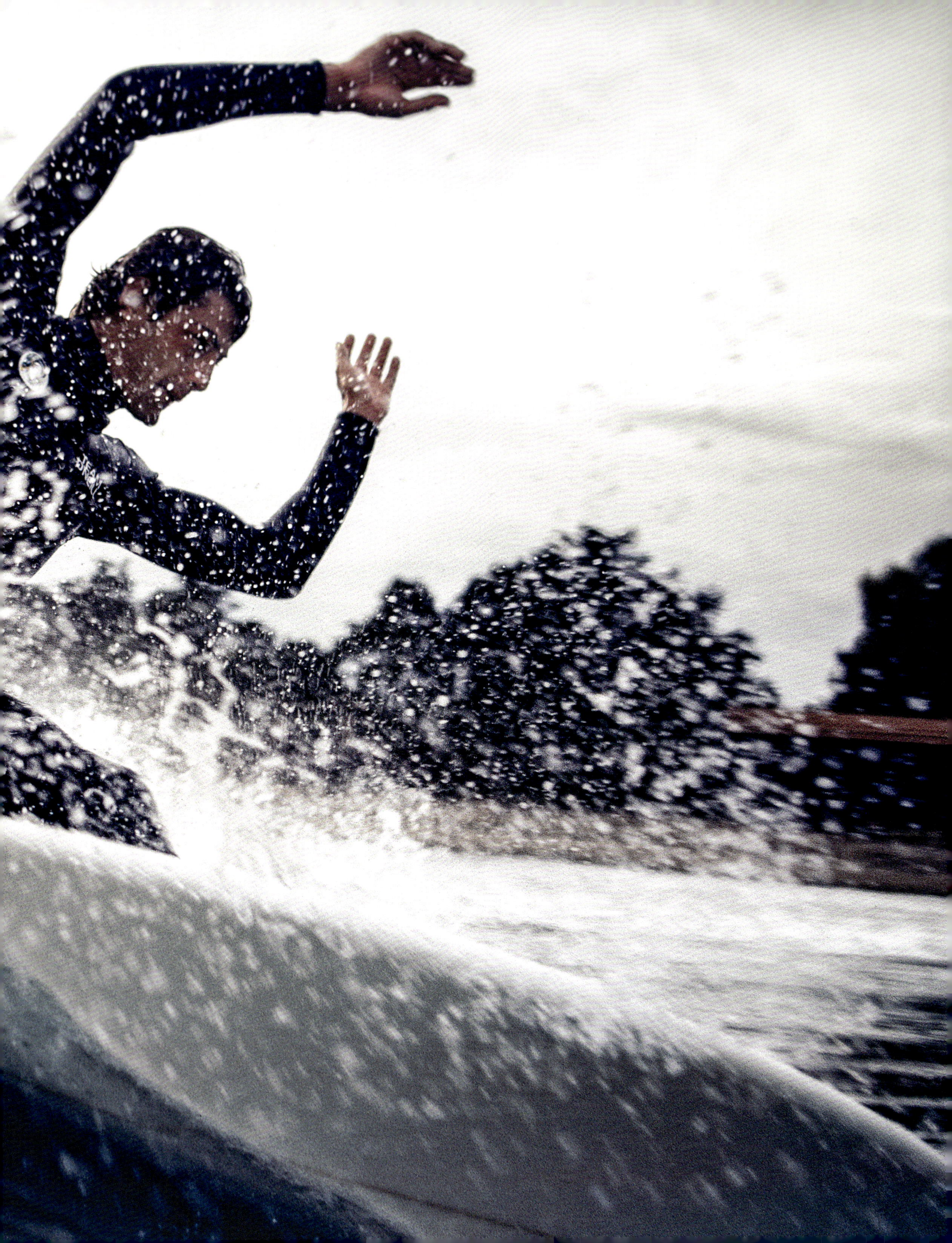

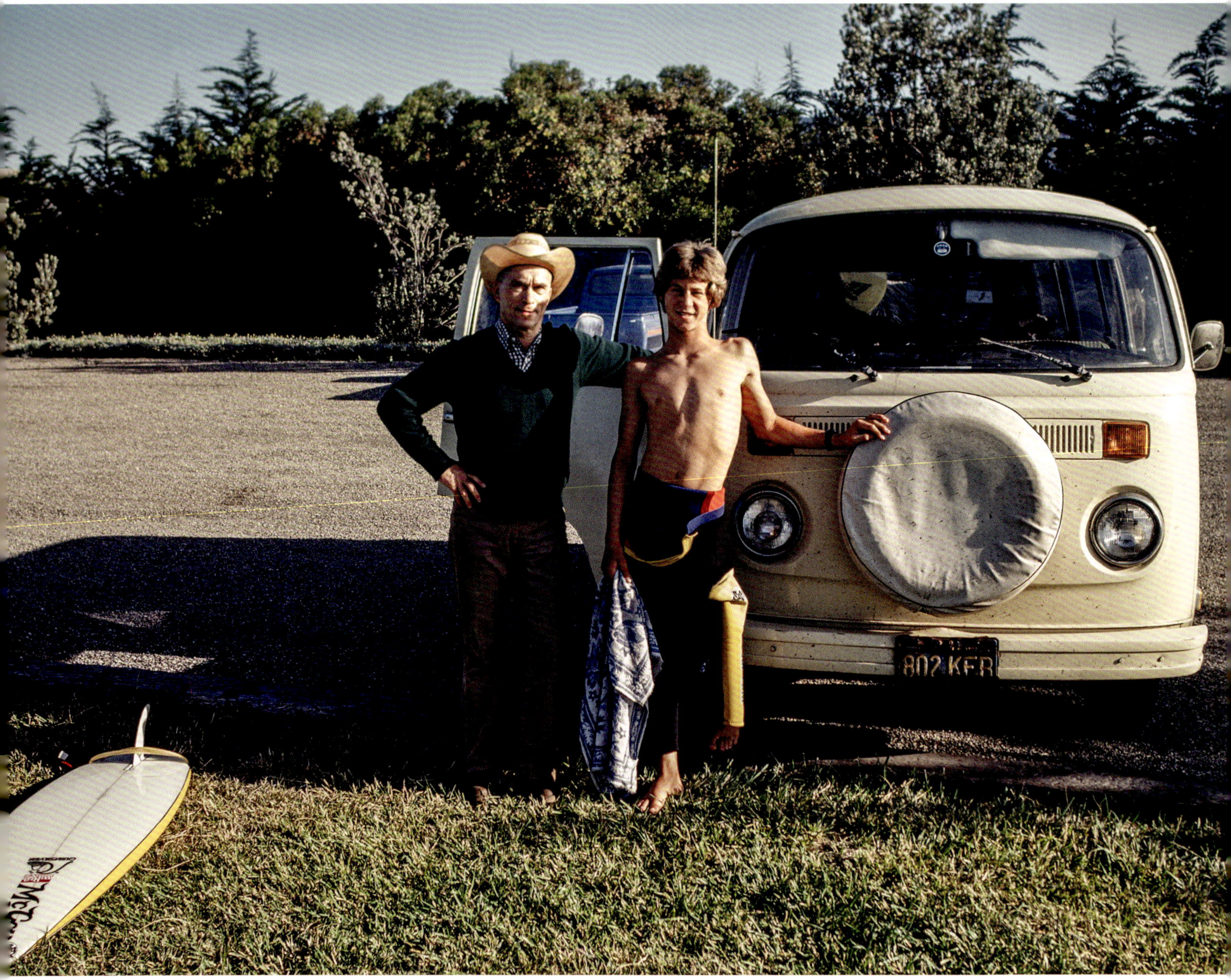

No Cameras Allowed

Like so many other surfers, I'd always dreamed of getting past the gate at Hollister Ranch, the fabled, and very private, stretch of coast northwest of Santa Barbara, home to some of the best waves in the world. I finally got my first chance with an invitation from South Bay surfer Jeff Novak, whose dad owned a ranch parcel, and who basically smuggled us in for a very enjoyable day of waves. Relatively small surf, but definitely good enough for me to relax the accepted "no cameras allowed" protocol.

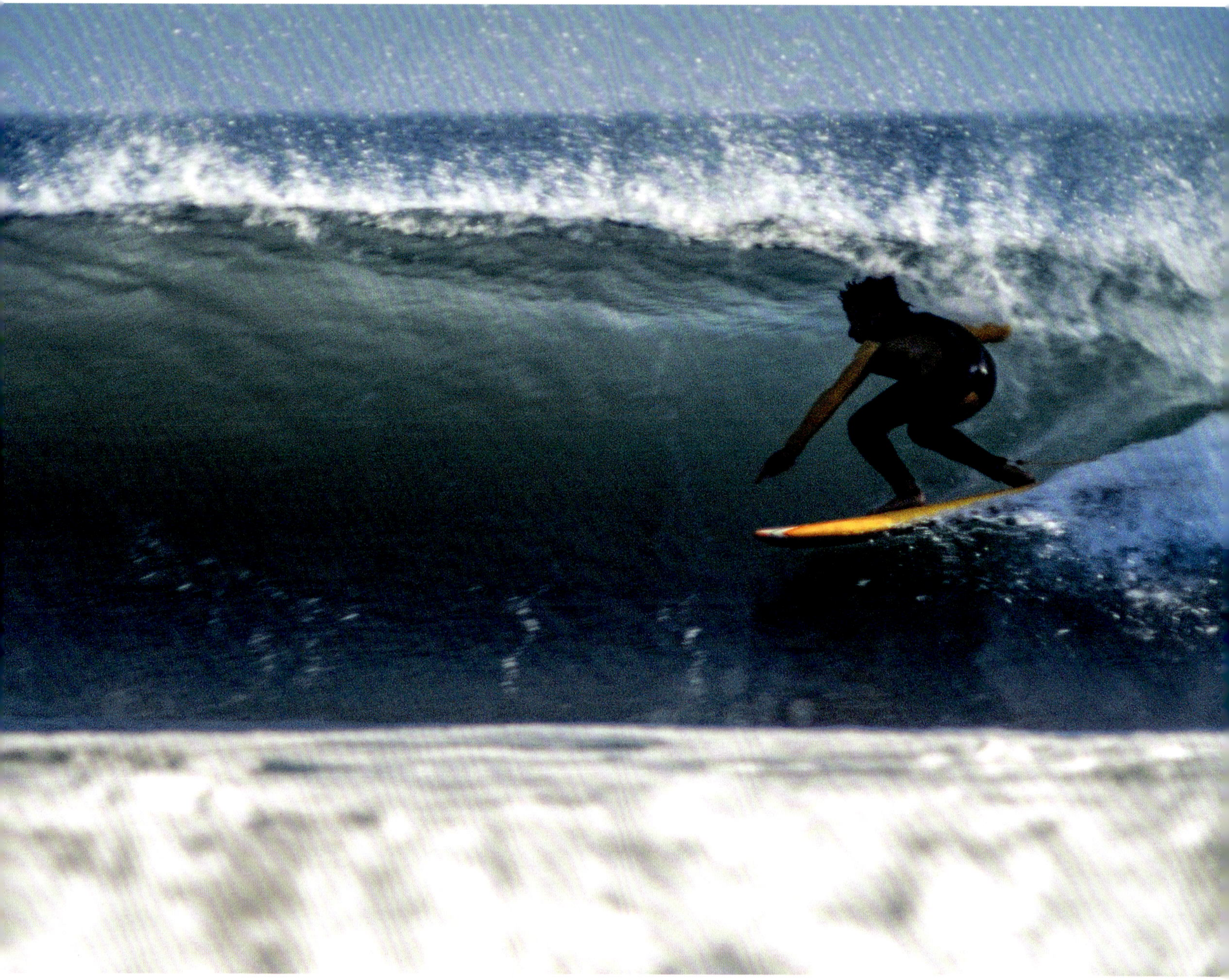

Jeff Novak and his father, Ranch parking lot. Jeff driving a perfect line through late afternoon Rights and Lefts.

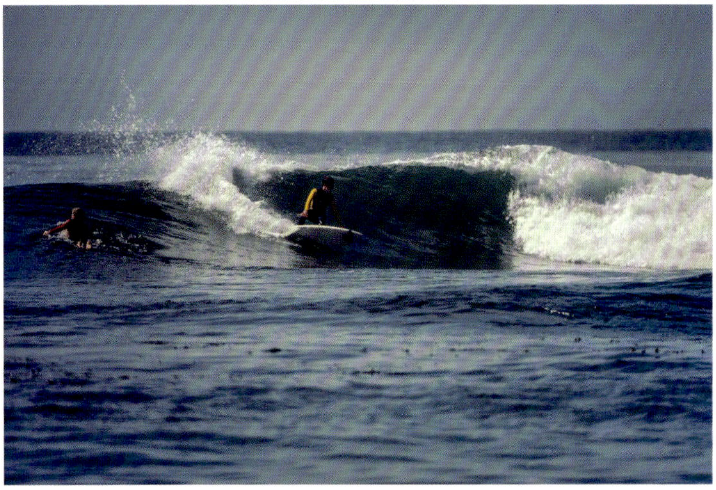

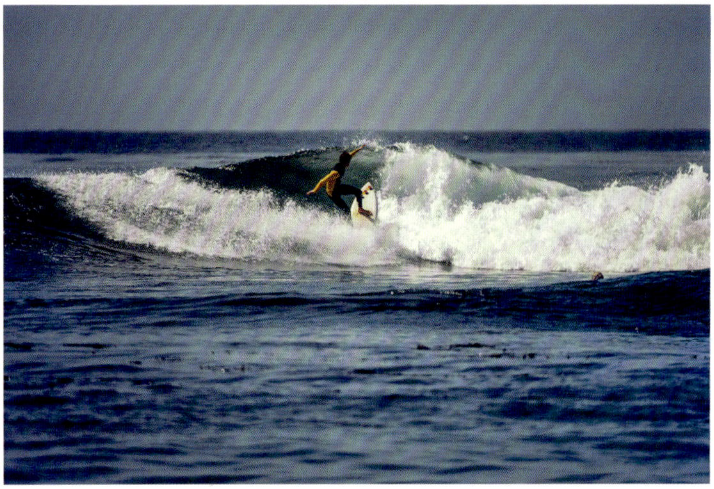

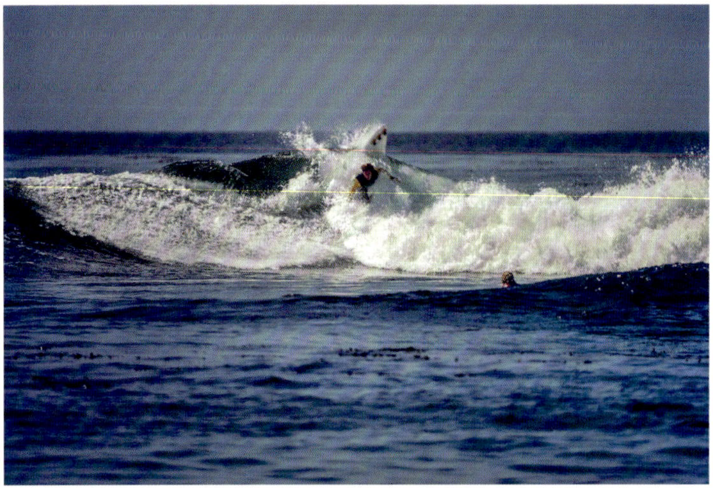

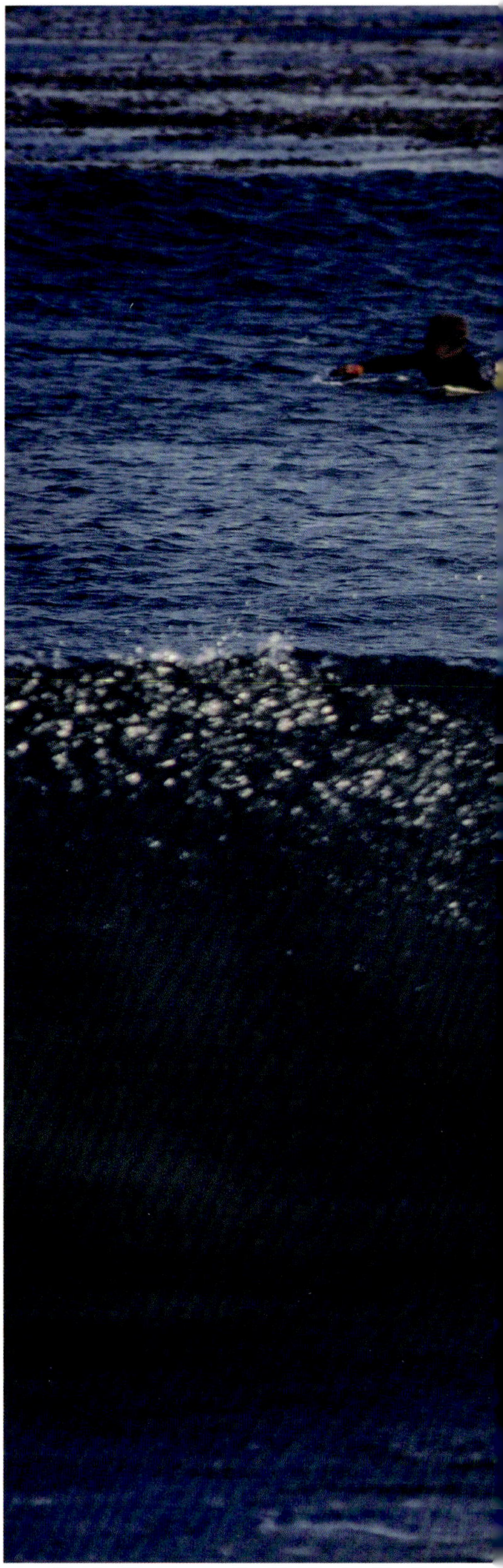

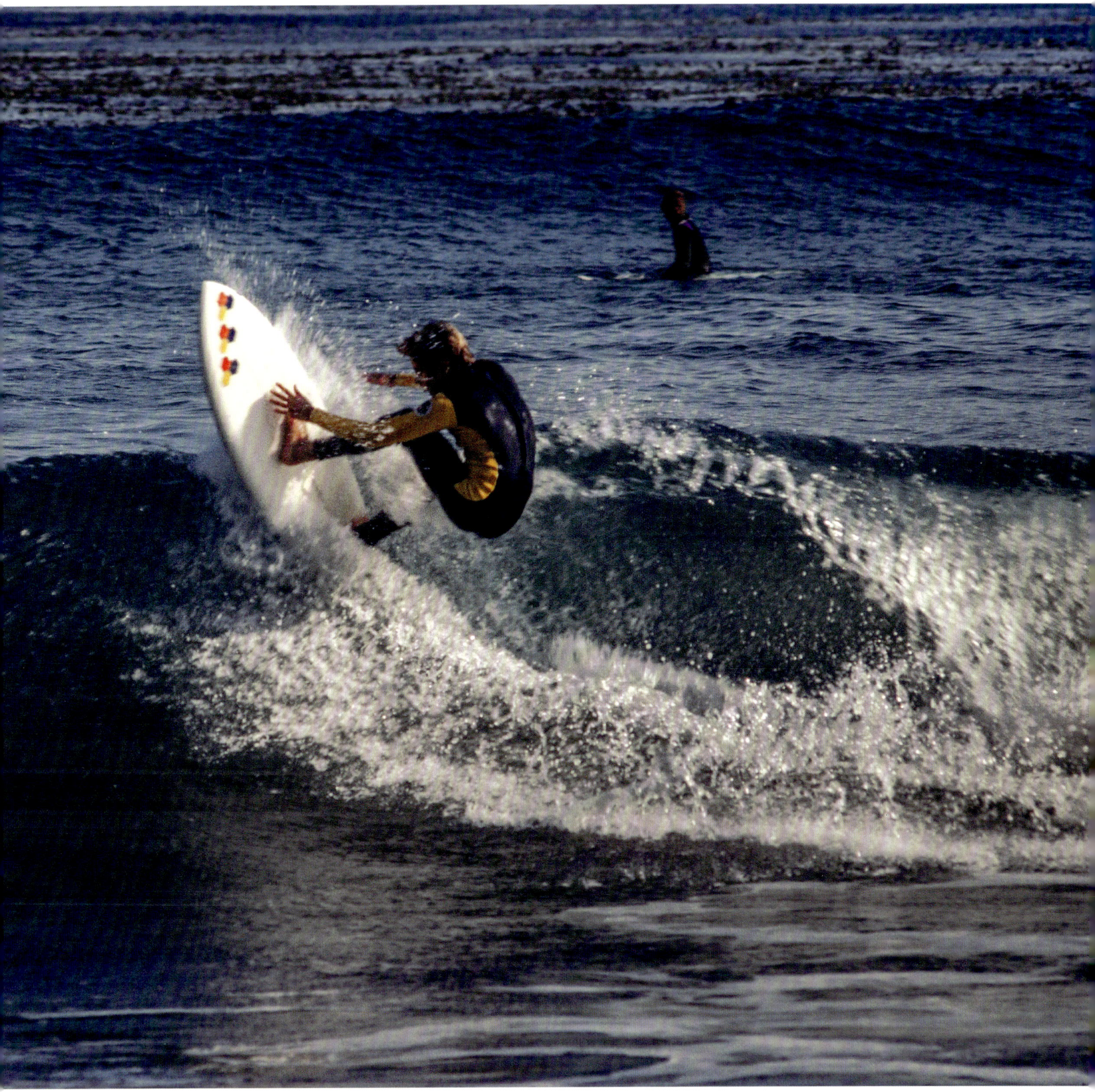

Looking back, I am glad to have broken protocol and have shot these rare early images of Tommy surfing at The Ranch. *(Left)* Arcing his tri-plane hull twin through a very roundhouse cutback at early morning St. Augustine; and then later *(above)*, a late evening "smack" off-the-top at Rights and Lefts.

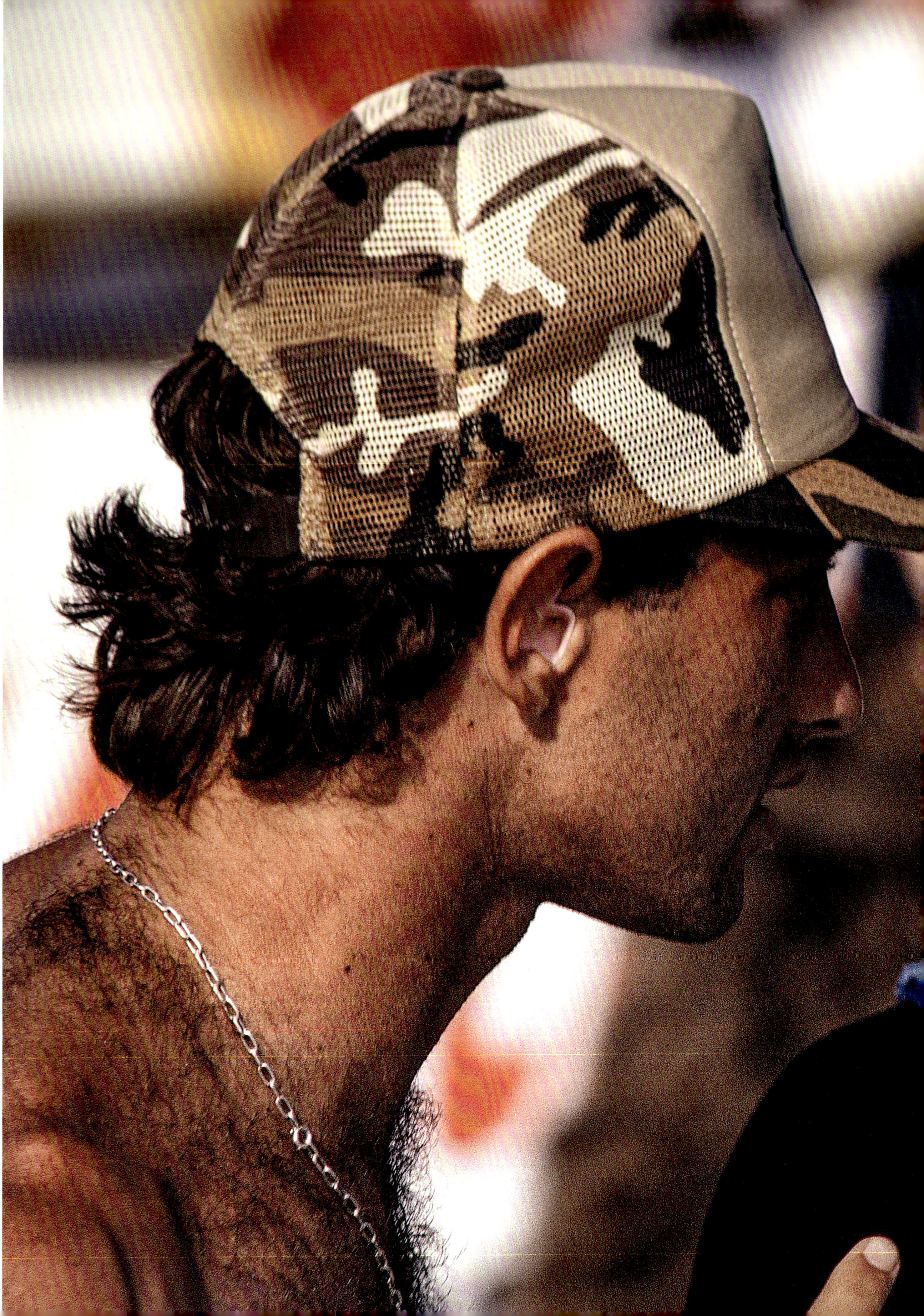

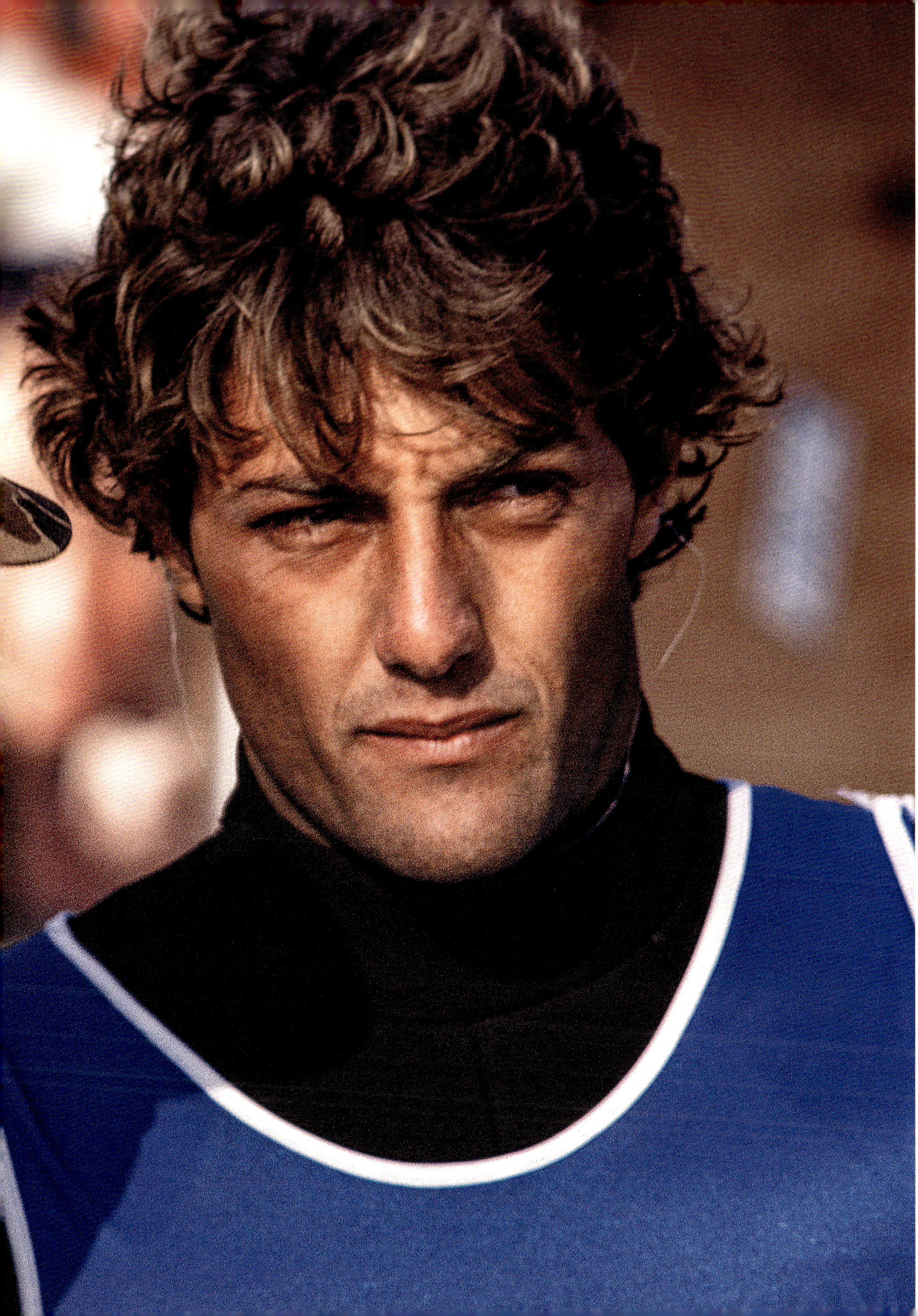

Previous

In the summer of '81, the Malibu Pro came back to town, this time held at its famous namesake. Unfortunately, the waves were so small that I found myself turning my camera to some of the more notable characters on hand rather than the action. Shaun, receiving pre-heat input from his younger brother, Paul. In two feet or twenty, Shaun was deadly serious about his contest performances.

Top

Al Merrick, deep in consultation with innovative Australian surfer/shaper Simon Anderson, designer of the modern thruster surfboard. With the help of his young CI team, Al would soon go on to refine Anderson's brainchild, helping it become the world's most widely ridden design.

Bottom

What would a day at the beach in Malibu be like without '60s legend Johnny Fain, one of that spot's only true locals? Never got a chance to ask him about the hat.

Facing

I turned to see Wayne "Rabbit" Bartholomew, Quiksilver's top sponsored pro, busily gnawing the logo off of a rival company's surf trunks, which surfers were required to wear in competition. If Shaun was serious about pro surfing, Rabbit was off the scale.

Pages 126–127

While La Jolla's Mark Brolaski looks on in amusement, 1976 world champion Peter "P. T." Townend reenacts a scene from the disastrous 1978 Hollywood surf film *Big Wednesday*, long before it became a cult classic.

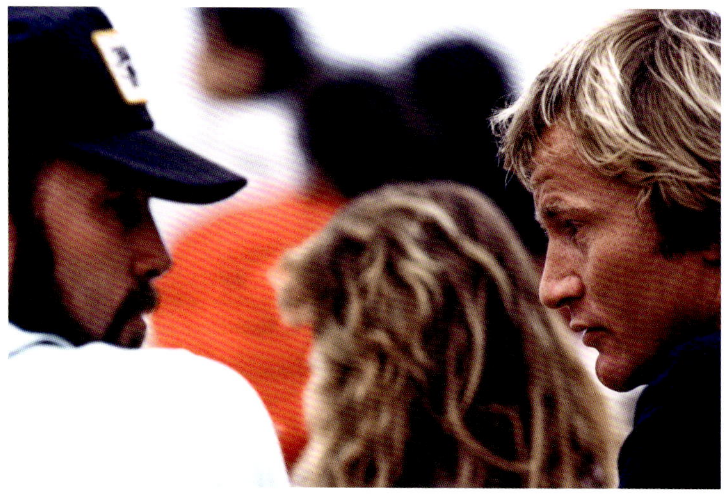

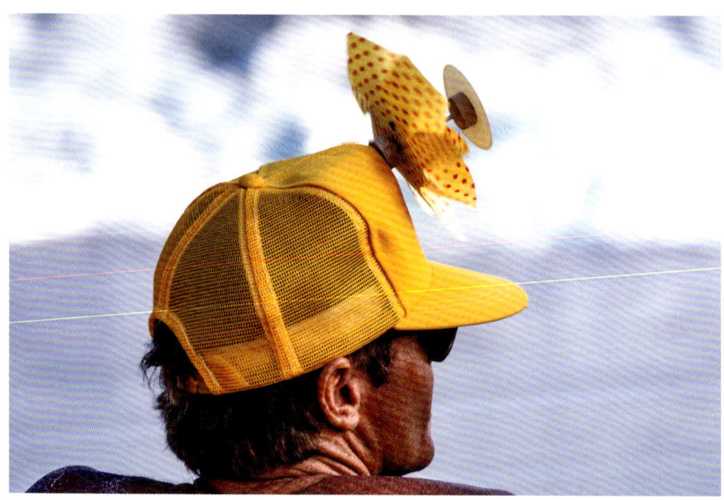

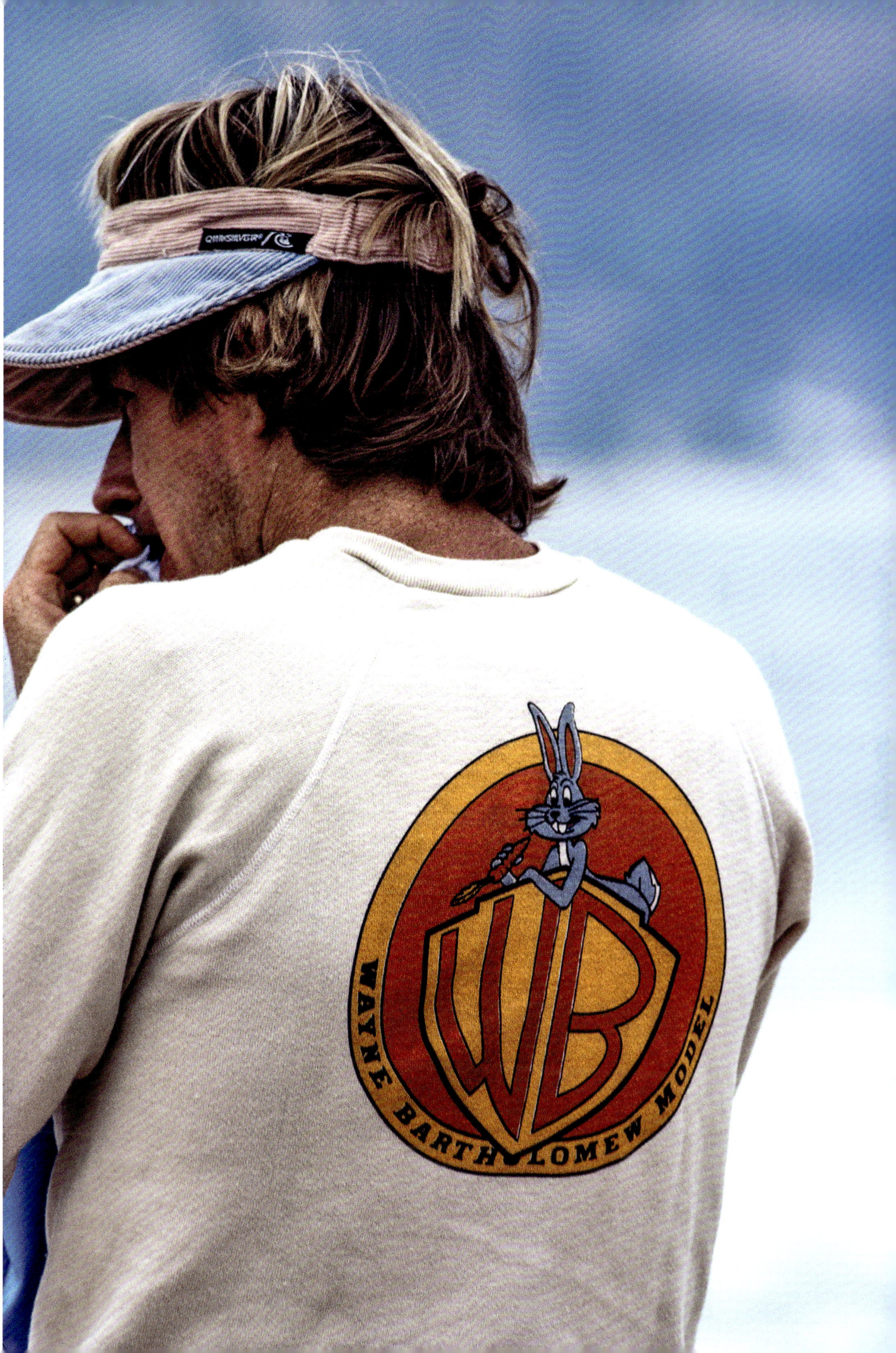
WB
WAYNE BARTH LOMEW MODEL

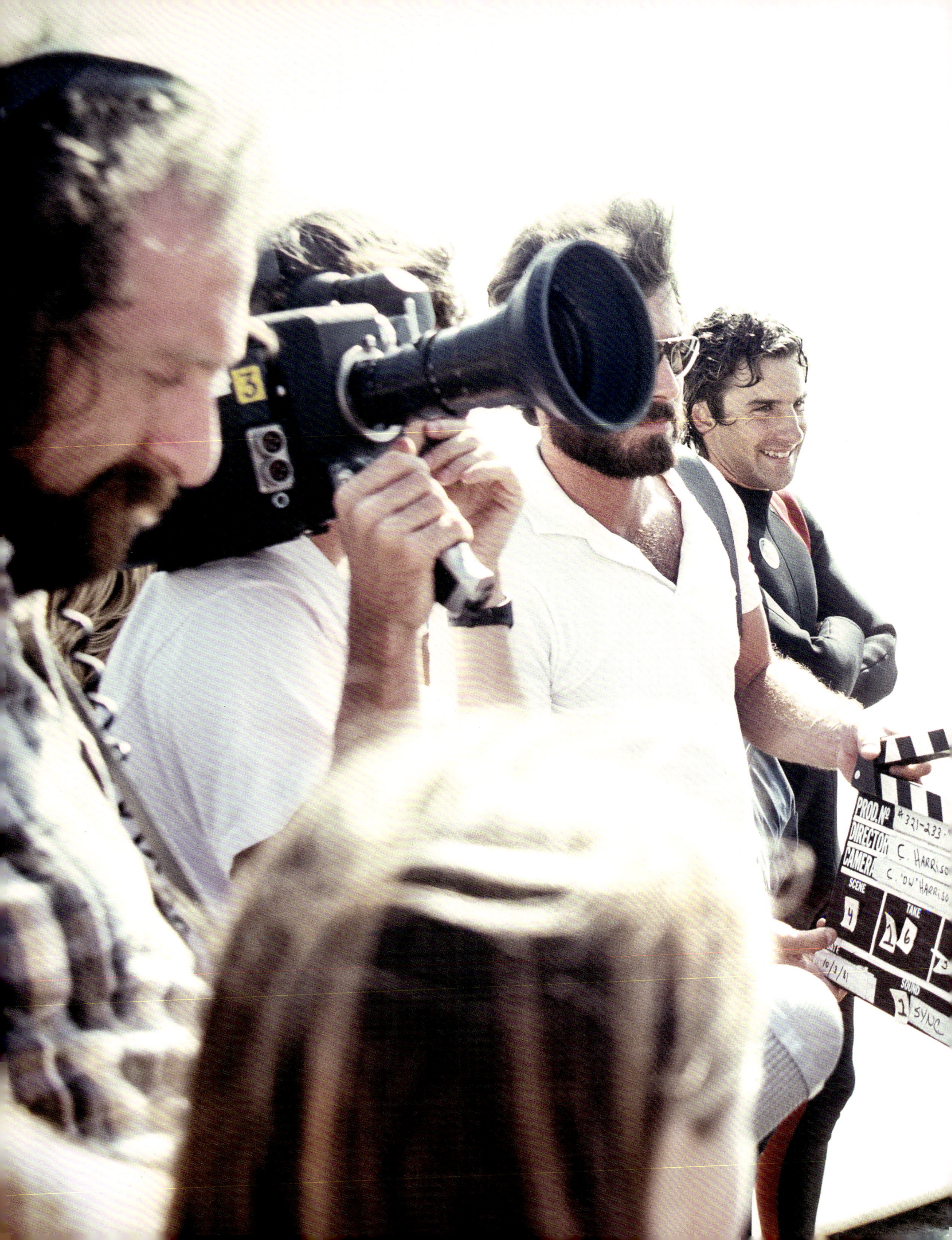
PROD.Nº
DIRECTOR
CAMERA
SCENE
TAKE
SOUND
SYNC

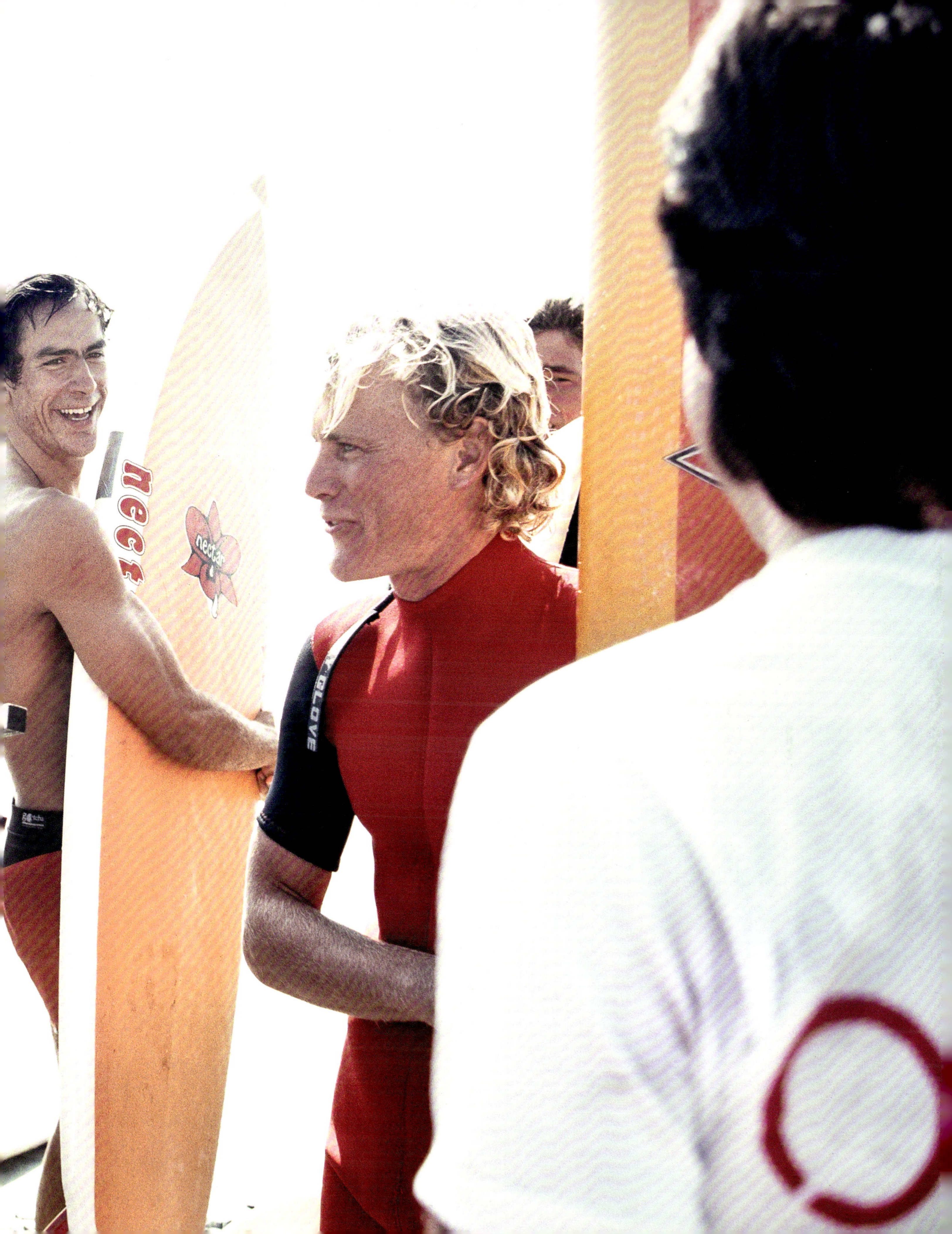
nectar
GLOVE

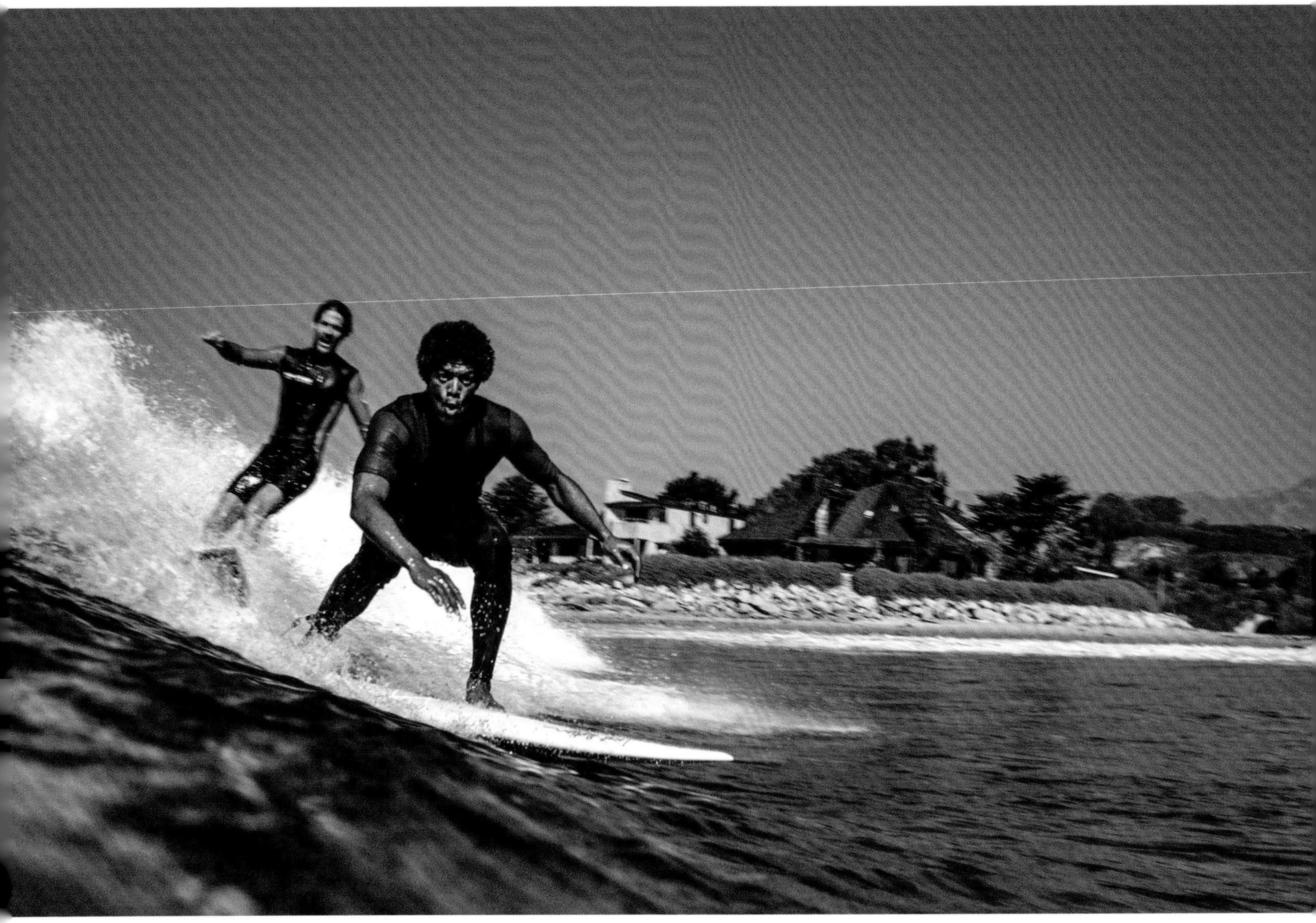

The magic of shooting from the water at Rincon was that you'd never know who might surf past. In this case, it was Montgomery "Buttons" Kaluhiokalani, the incredibly talented Hawaiian who was visiting California with his mentor, Ben Aipa, and whom I'd seen only in magazines and movies. You get a photo of Buttons, you put it in your book.

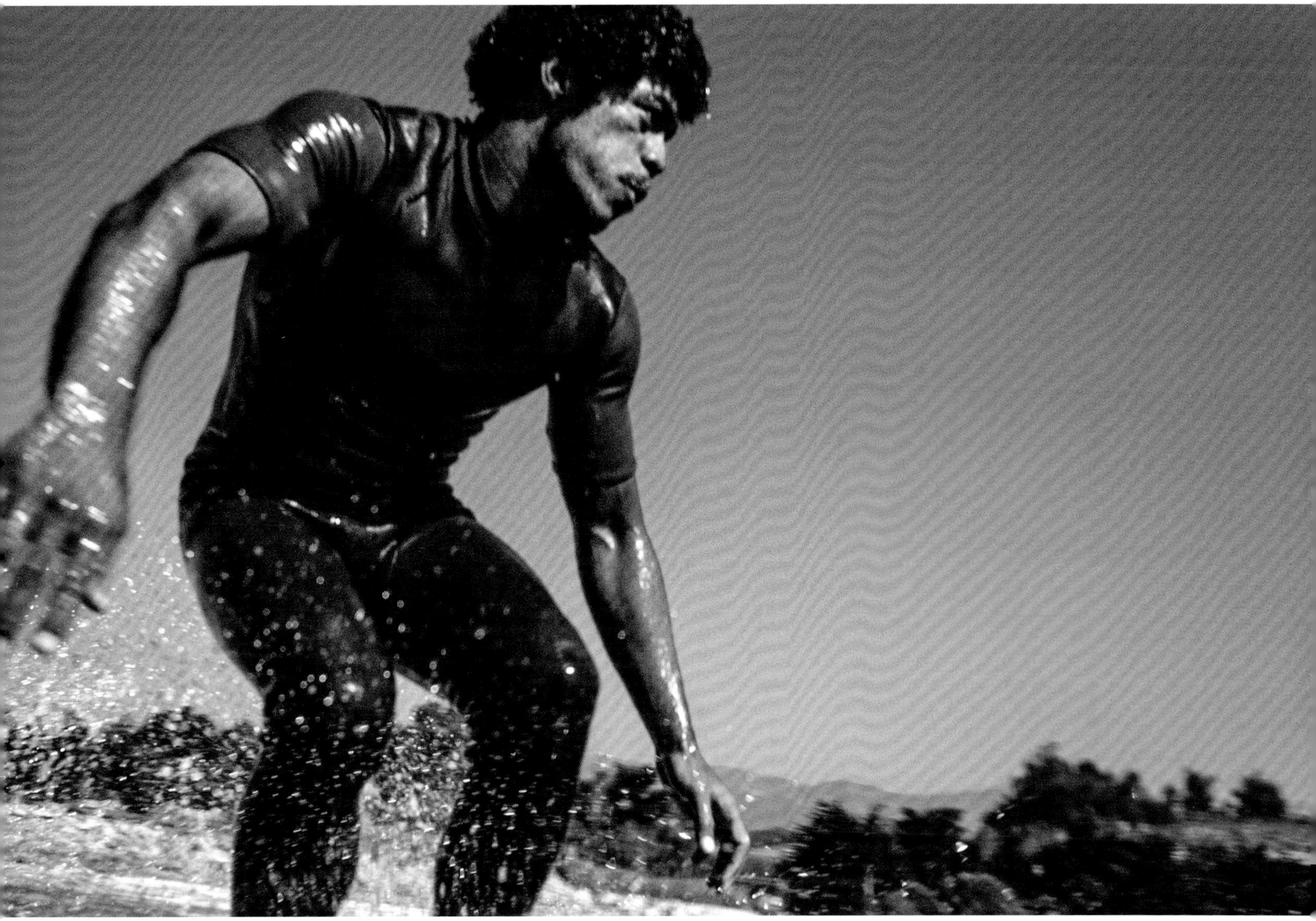

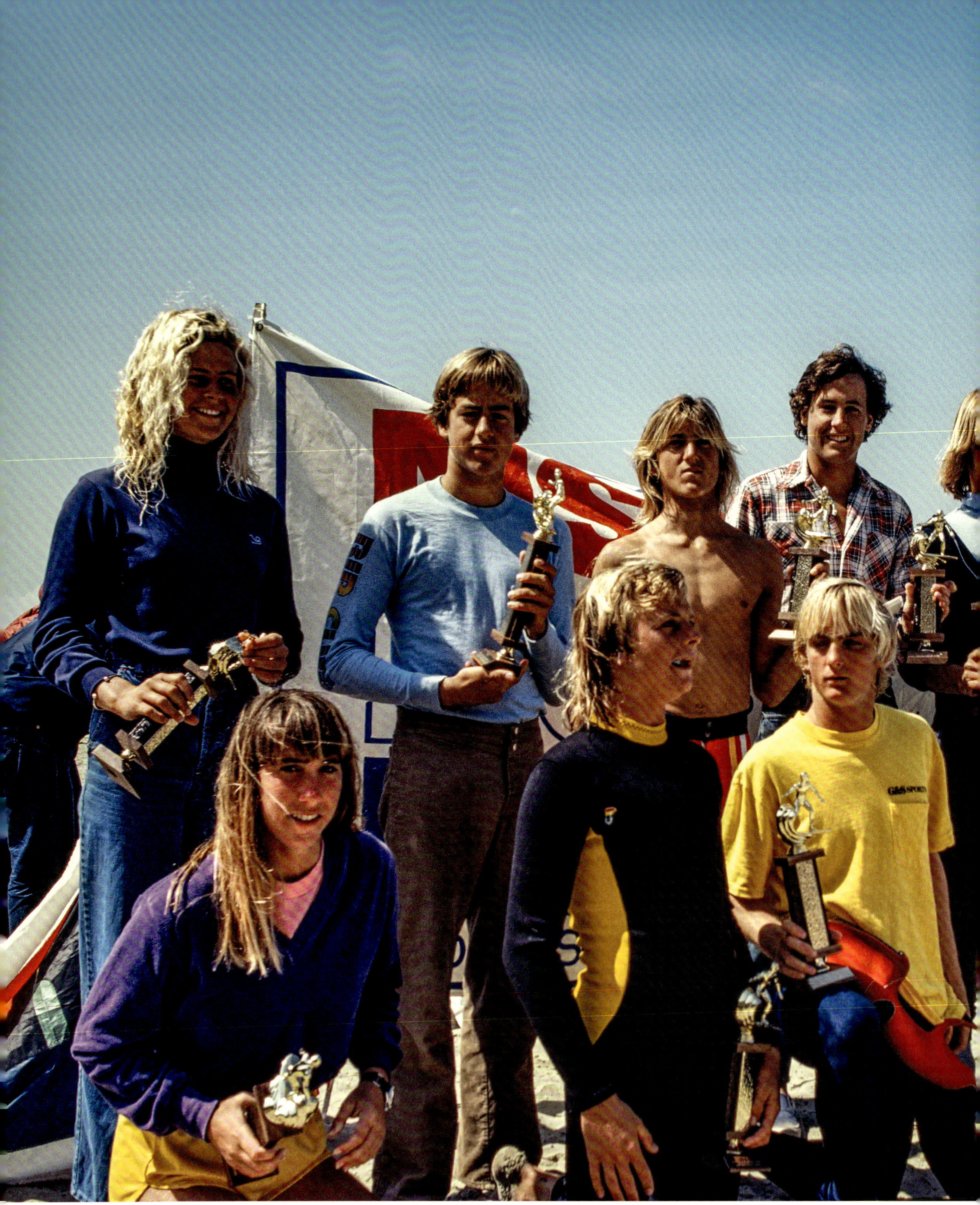

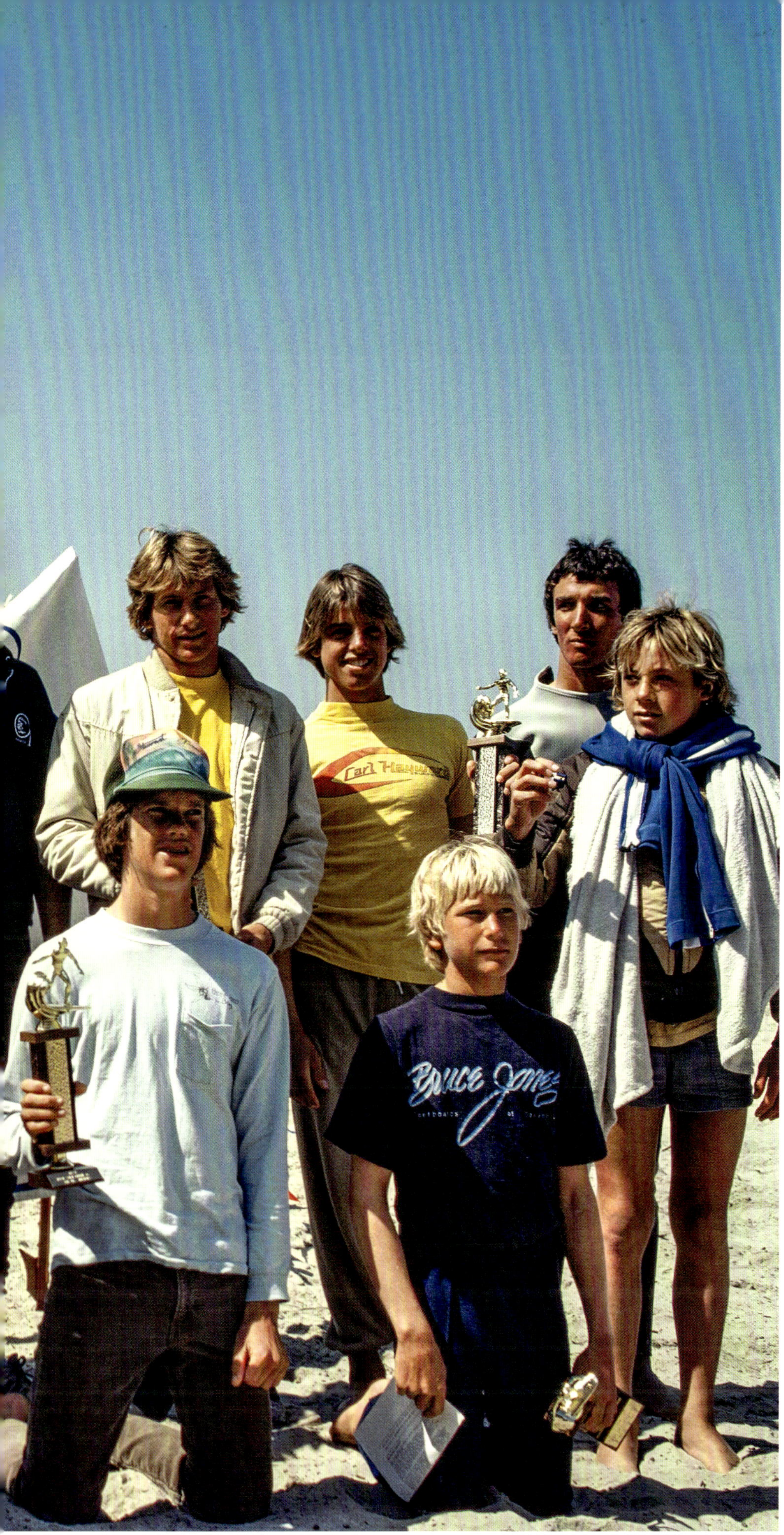

This shot, taken at the 1981 National Scholastic Surfing Association finals at Salt Creek in Orange County, features one of the heaviest collections of soon-to-be-famous young surfers ever assembled, with nine out of the fourteen pictured going on to successful professional careers. The list includes Kim Mearig, Tom Curren, Todd Martin, Mike Lambresi, and Scott Farnsworth *(back row, left to right)*, as well as Alisa Schwarzstein, Jimmy Hogan, Mike Parsons, and Gary Clisby *(front row, kneeling, left to right)*.

Spread

Tommy contemplates his latest shape out in the alley behind the old Channel Islands factory on Anacapa Street. It seems that every surfboard factory has a particular outside wall used for taking photos of surfboards. I was recently contacted by the present owner of this board, Warren "Waz" Boyes, a Western Australian surfer who still rides it today. Airbrush art by Bernie Tsao.

Pages 134–135

By the winter of '81, Tommy and I were pretty mobile, heading north or south every weekend, depending on the swell. Wherever we ended up, however, Tommy had an uncanny gift of making something out of nothing. Here, he surfs a small but high-risk day at Super Tubes. You can't let a little sand in the foreground fool you: inches under Tommy's board, it is all rock.

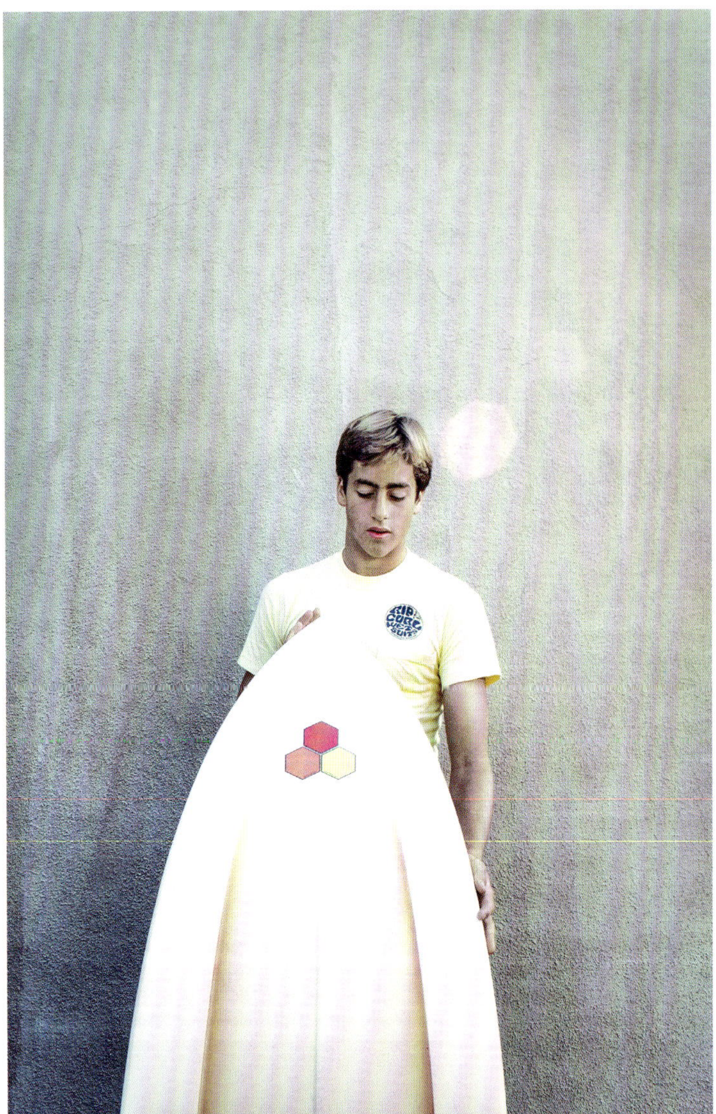

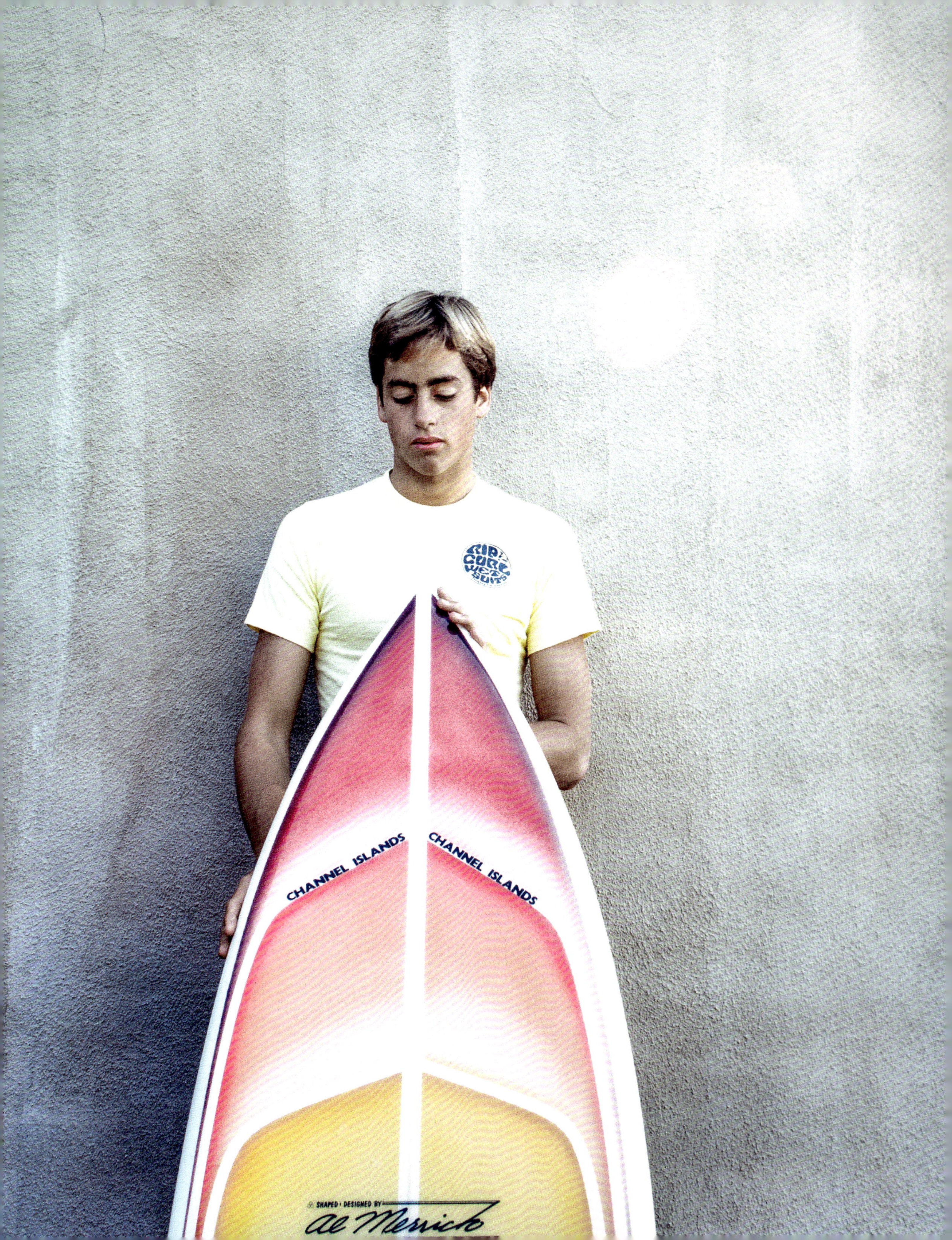
CHANNEL ISLANDS
CHANNEL ISLANDS
SHAPED • DESIGNED BY
Al Merrick

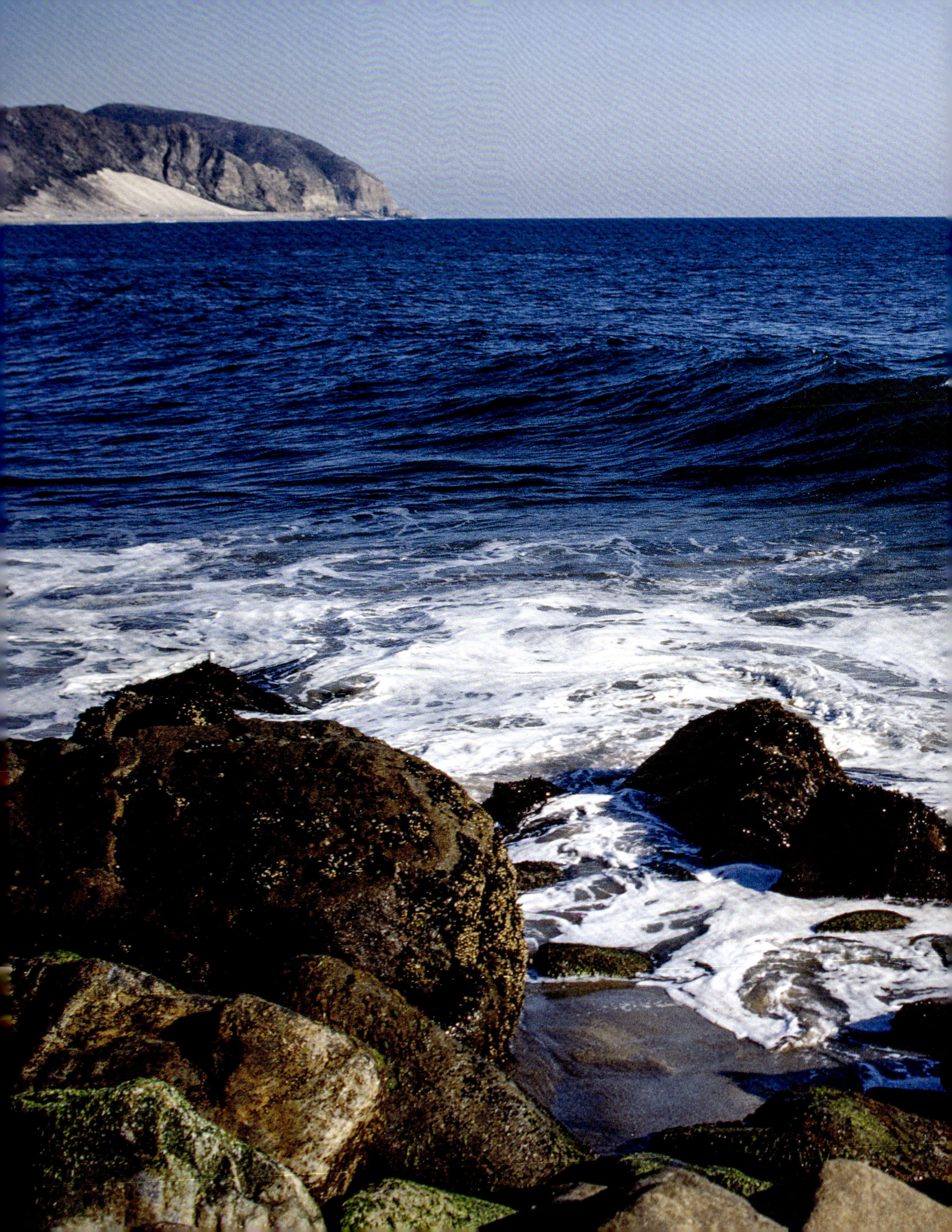

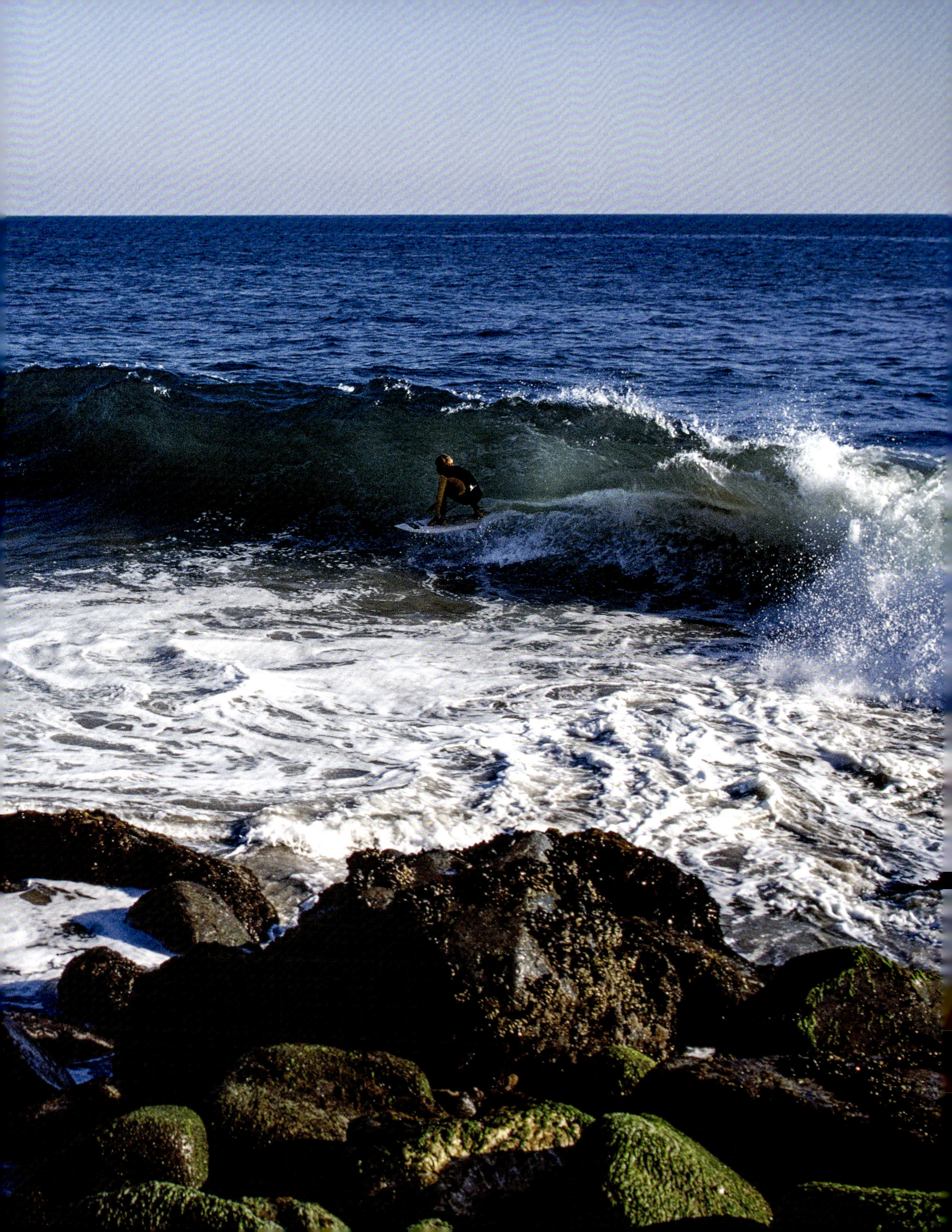

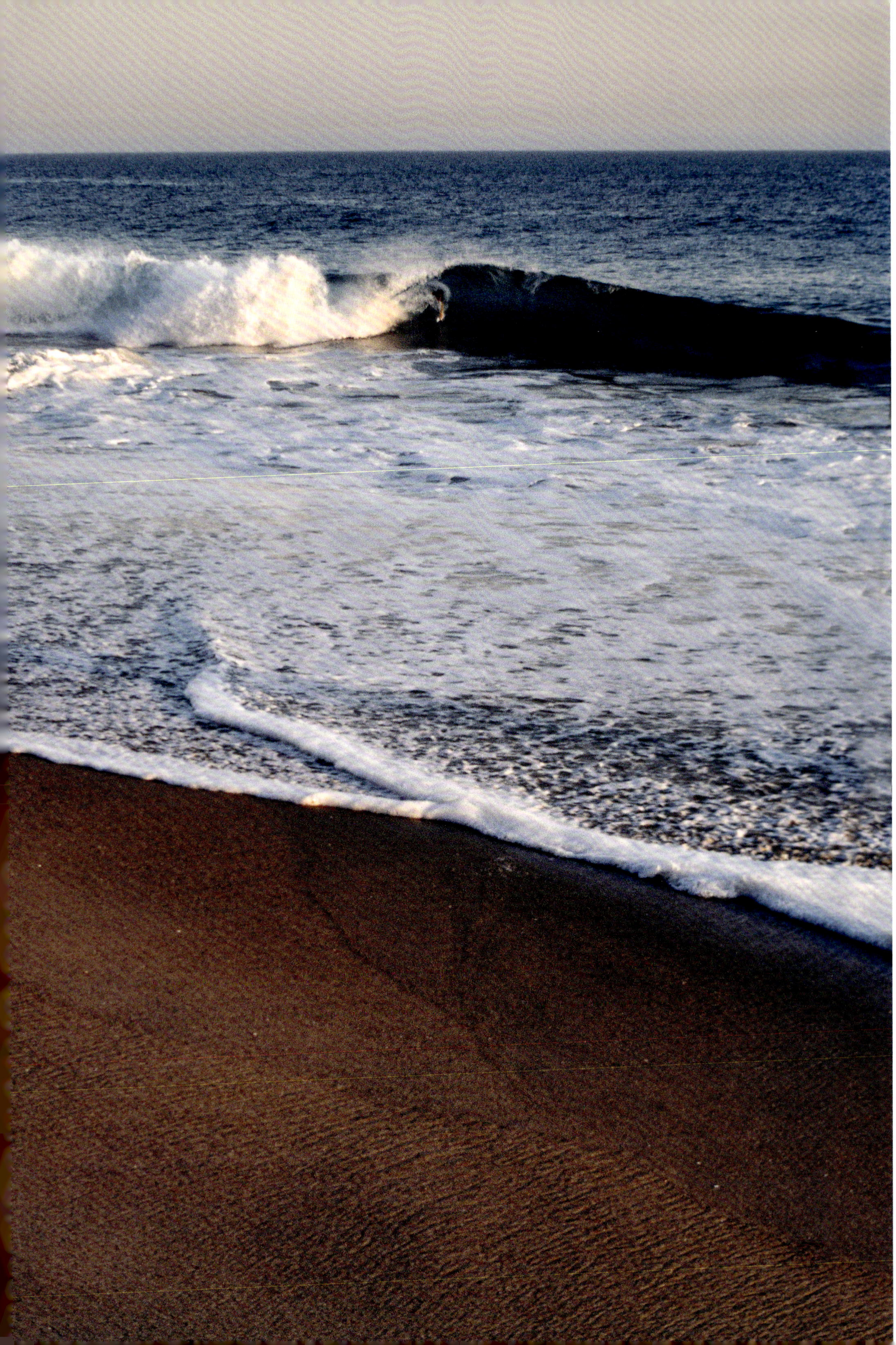

Pull Over, Pull Over

Tommy loved to bodysurf and was always telling me to pull over when he saw some random little wave that he wanted to swim out to. We'd be on our way to a real surf spot, or heading back home after a long day, sunburned and hungry, when suddenly he'd yell, "Pull over, pull over, I can bodysurf that wave!" I never wanted to stop, but who was I to argue? He would usually get only one or two waves, just enough to satisfy the urge, and then we'd be on our way. Just killing time, I snapped this photo at a nondescript stretch of beach between Point Mugu and Leo Carrillo State Beach; the historical value of recording Tommy's soul-deep love of surfing when I shot this image never crossed my mind.

Overleaf

Tommy, scraping the coping in the shorebreak at Ventura's Emma Wood State Beach. Years later, this funky little wave would help foster the talents of a future Channel Islands team rider named Dane Reynolds.

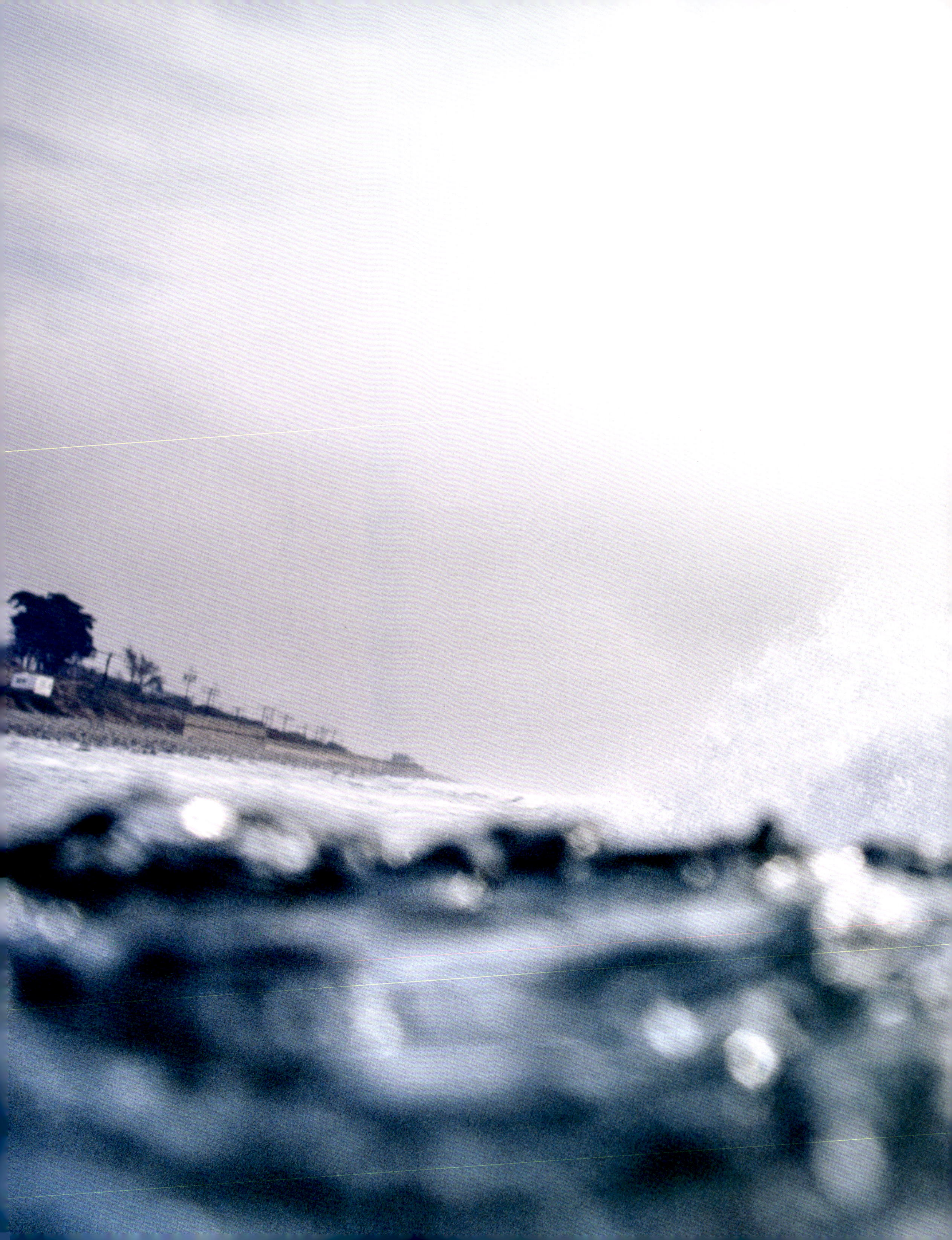

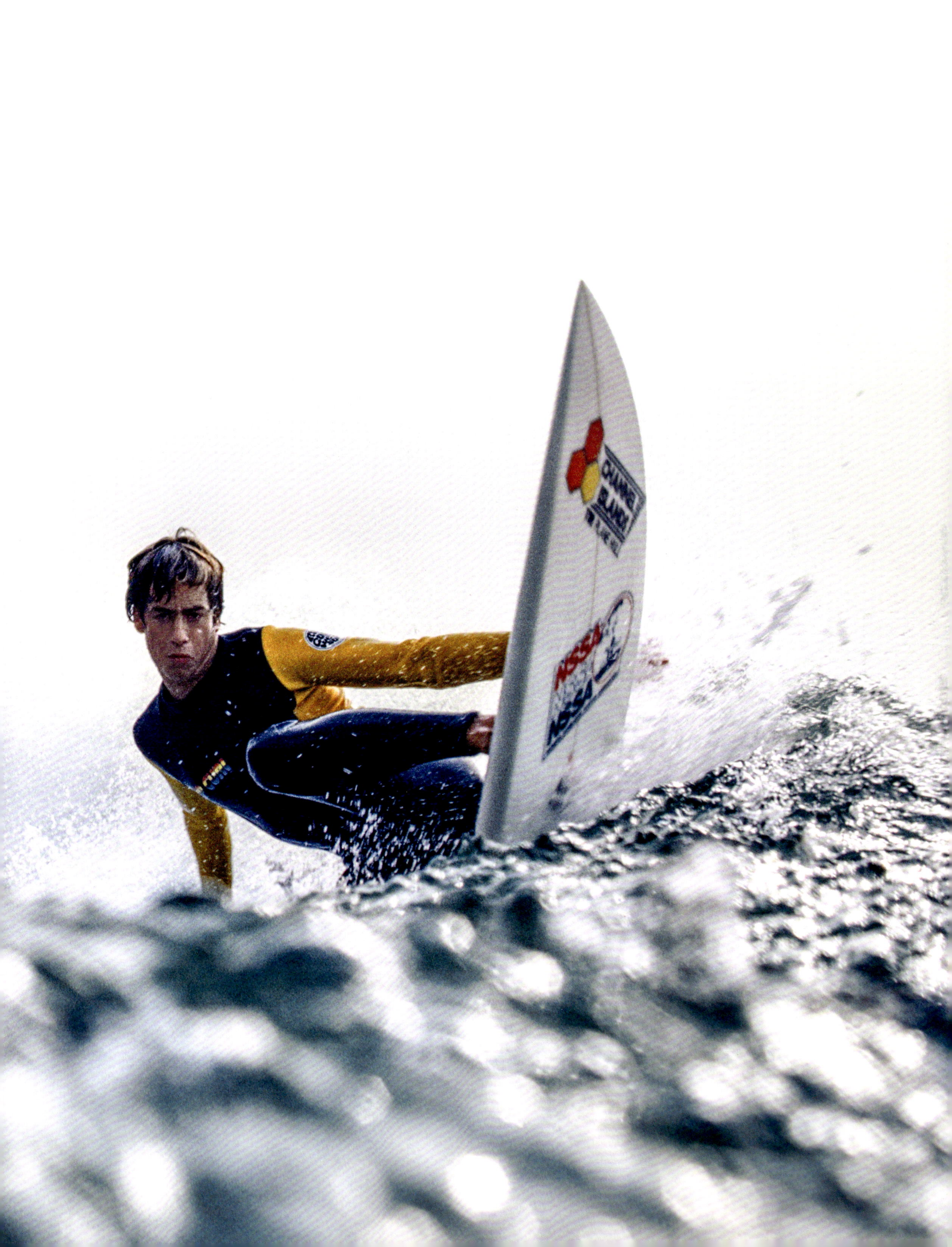
CHANNEL ISLANDS
NSSA
NSSA

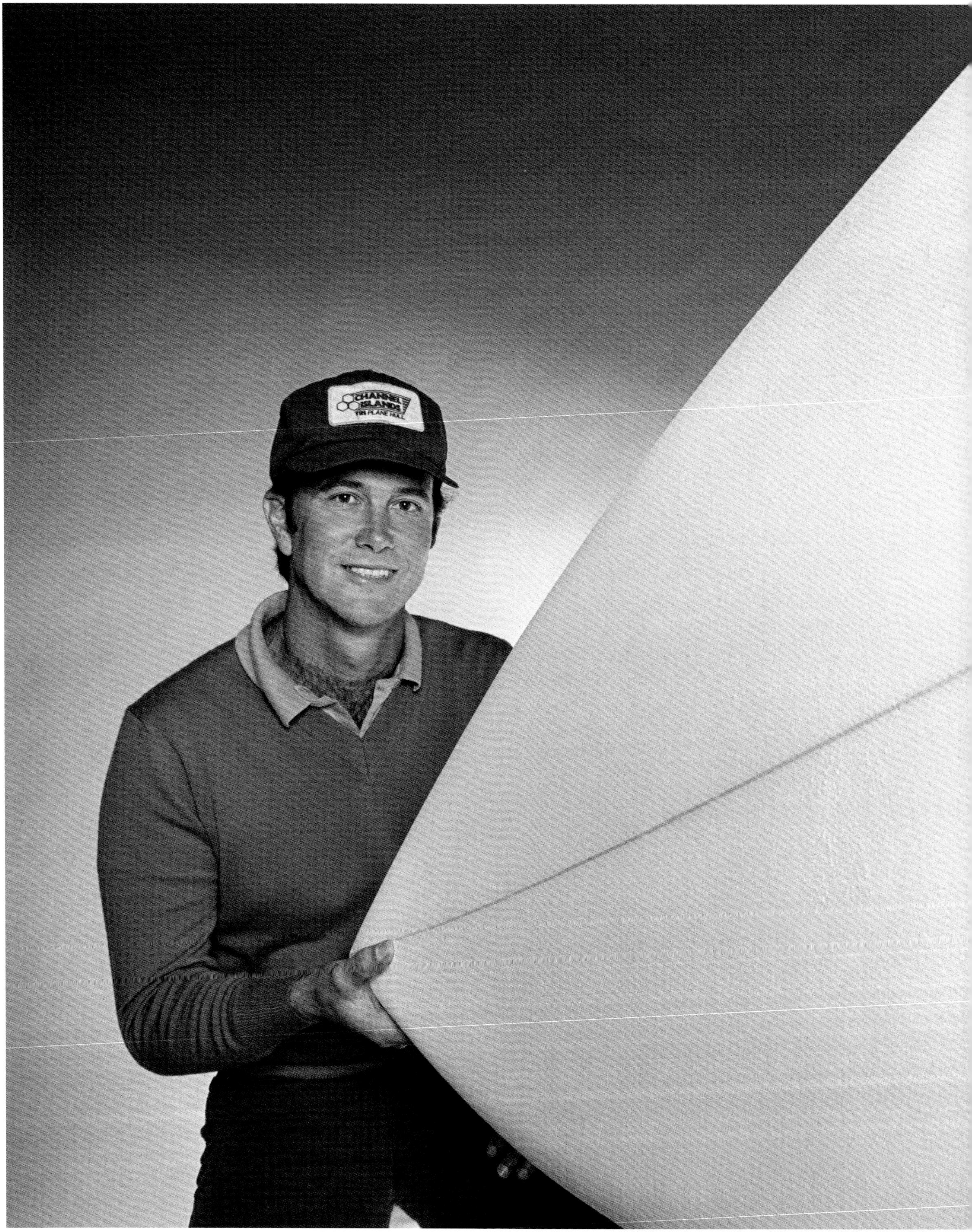
CHANNEL ISLANDS
TRI PLANE HULL

Schoolwork

Much of my schoolwork at Brooks required producing a steady stream of portrait subjects, so naturally I started pulling new surfing friends like Al Merrick, Tommy Curren, Kim Mearig, and Davey Smith into the studio. No one was safe from becoming part of a class assignment as I worked to perfect various lighting techniques and composition, and we always had a lot of fun. But it was also interesting to see who among this group was most comfortable in front of the camera; none of them had yet spent much time there, and certainly not in such a formalized setting. The gregarious Davey Smith won that heat.

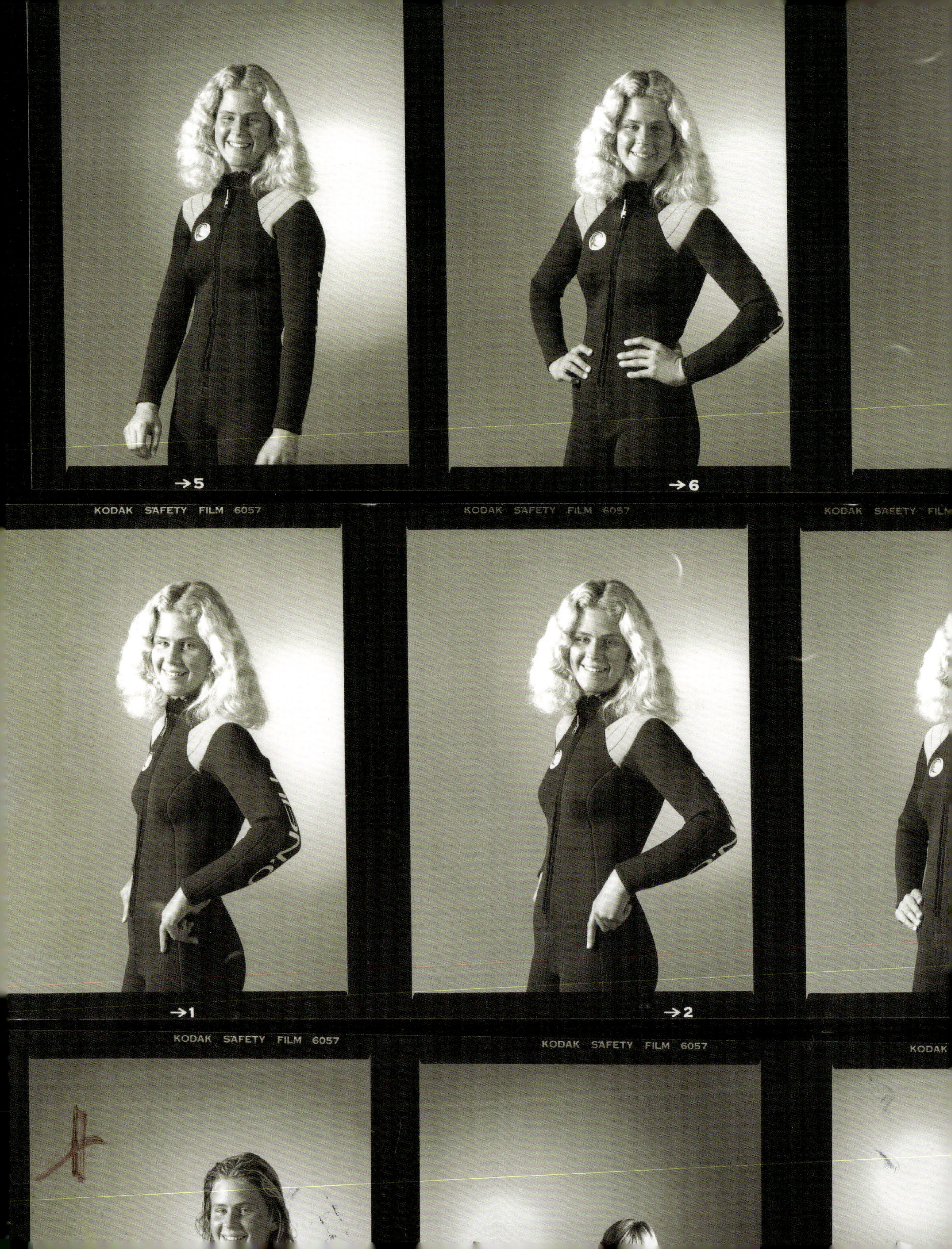
→5
→6
KODAK SAFETY FILM 6057
KODAK SAFETY FILM 6057
KODAK SAFETY FILM 6057
O'NEILL
→1
→2
KODAK SAFETY FILM 6057
KODAK SAFETY FILM 6057
KODAK

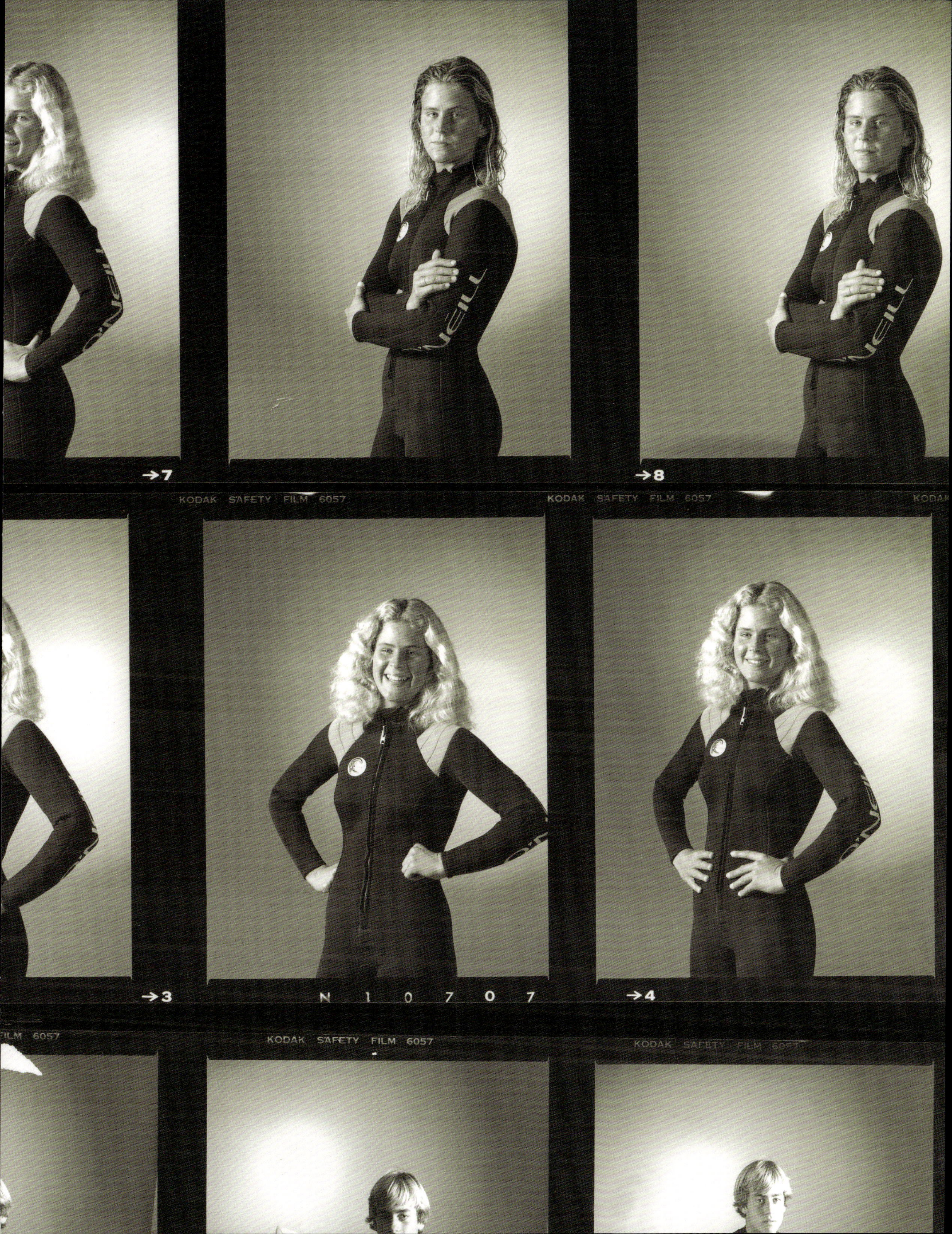
→7
→8
KODAK SAFETY FILM 6057
KODAK SAFETY FILM 6057
→3
N 10707
→4
KODAK SAFETY FILM 6057
KODAK SAFETY FILM 6057

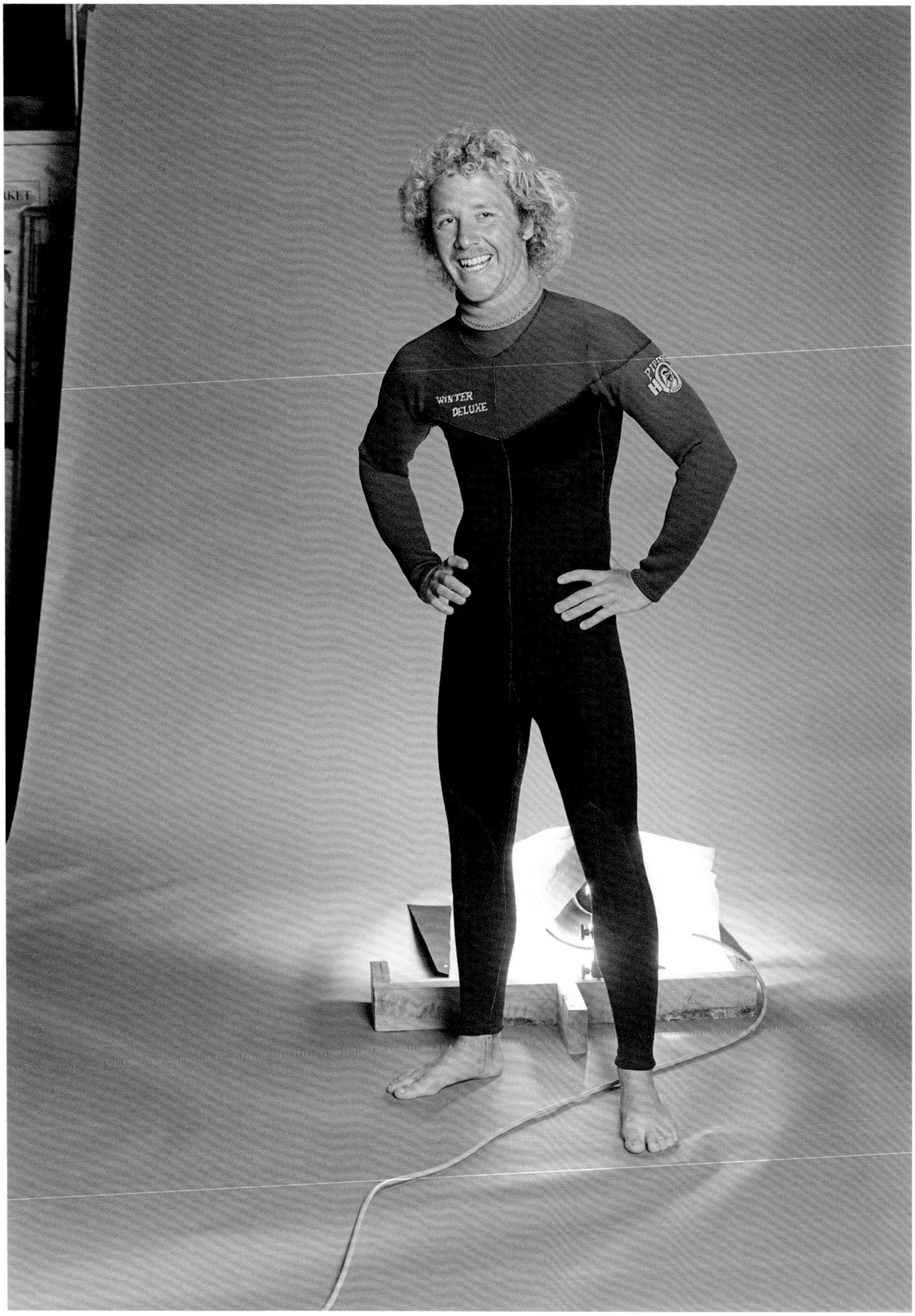
WINTER
DELUXE

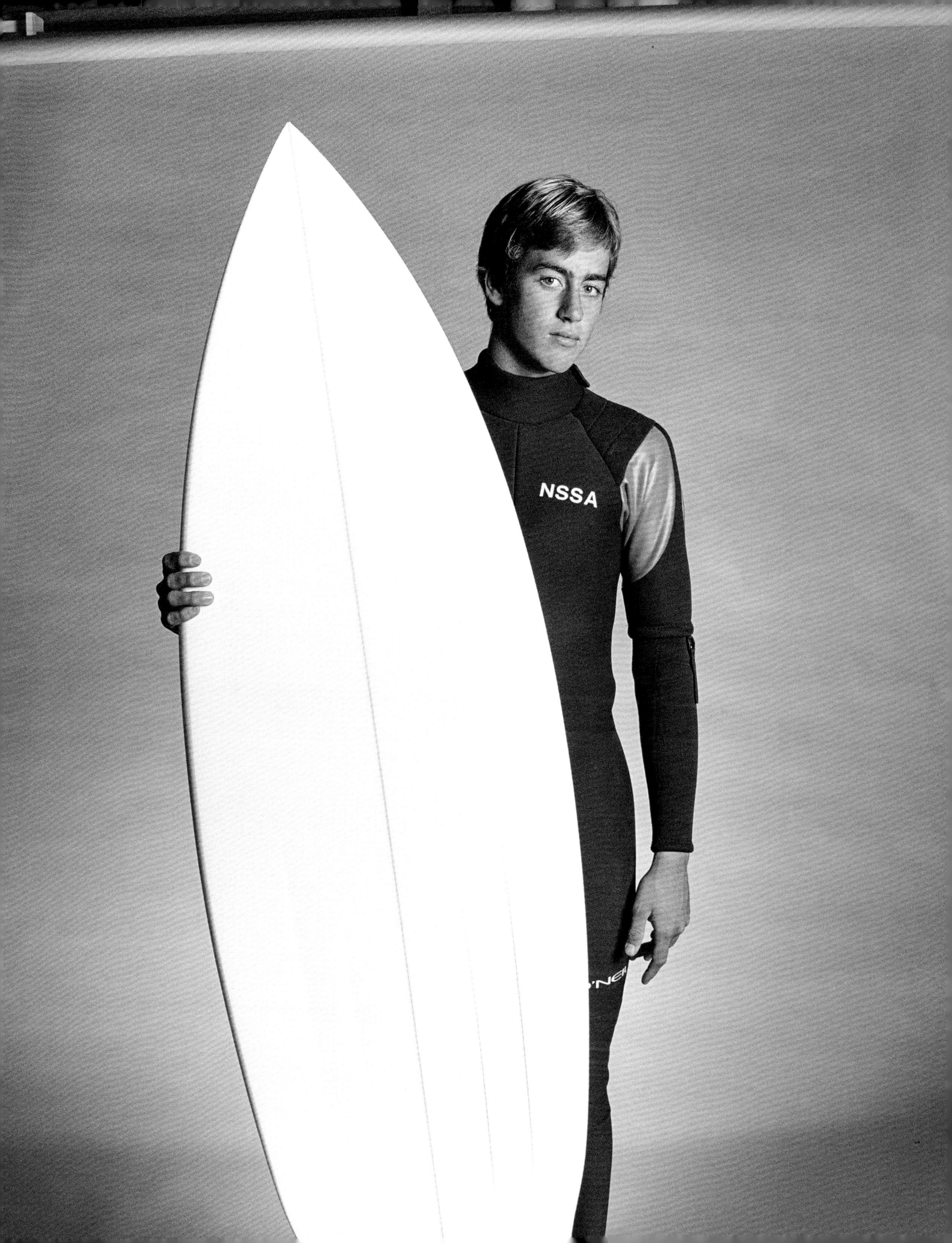
NSSA

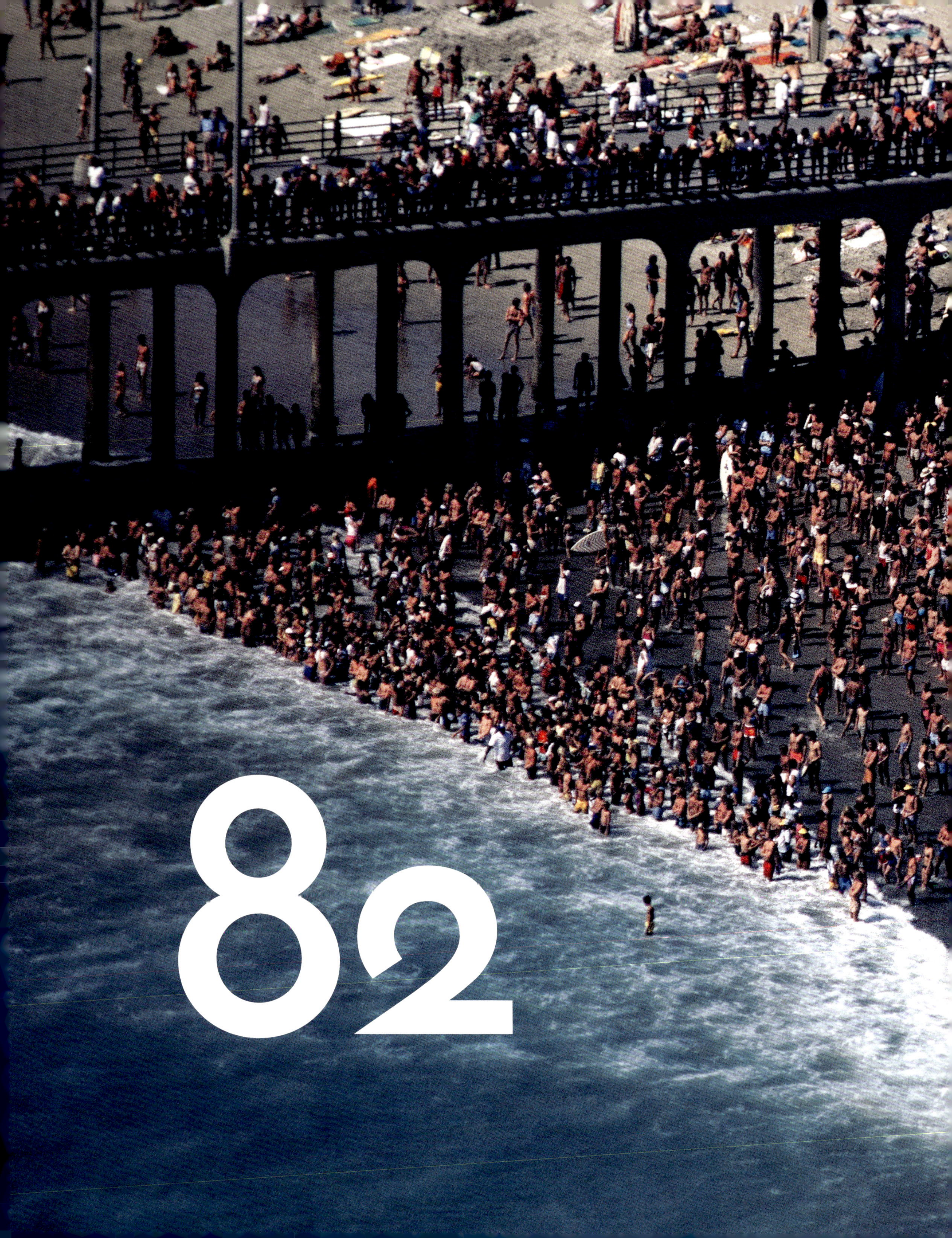
82

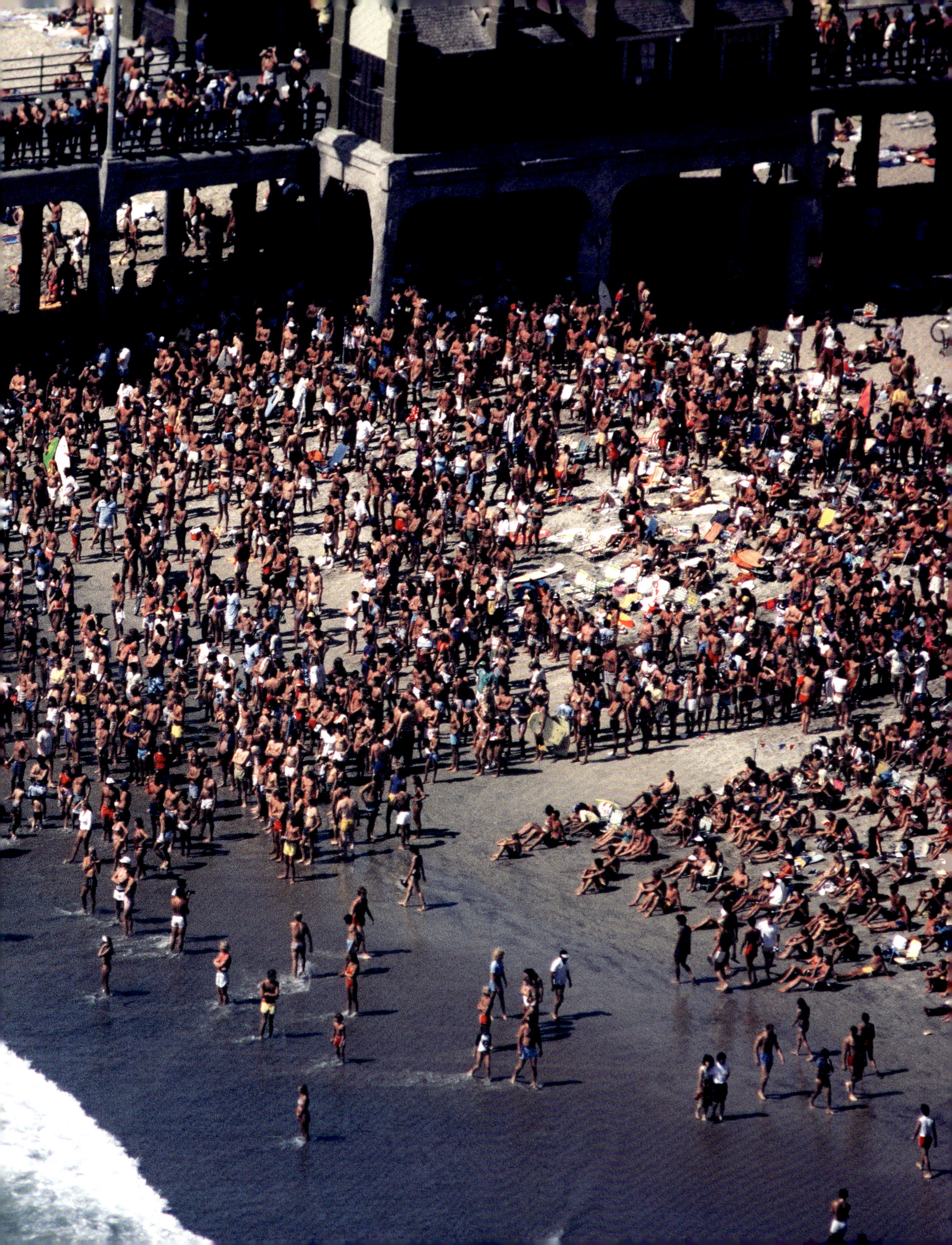

1982

That Yellow-Sleeved Wetsuit

The year 1982 started off with fairly lackluster surf in the 805 area code. With no real groundswell to speak of, you had to hope that the prevailing northwest winds that funneled between the offshore Channel Islands and the Santa Barbara mainland every afternoon would generate enough short-period windswell for a decent surf.

This lack of good waves never slowed us down. Every afternoon after school, I would pull up at the Currens' decidedly rustic compound, nestled between the Southern Pacific railroad tracks and the old Wilderness Surfboards shop off Milpas Street, and see Tommy's yellow-sleeved Rip Curl wetsuit hanging on the fence by the gate, where he had left it the night before.

Tommy started off the year wearing the same wetsuit he'd been wearing since mid-'81. He would not give it up. Not for the National Scholastic Surfing Association, which insisted that team members like Tommy wear their sponsor's suits; not for his mother, Jeanine, who insisted he should; not even when offered other potential endorsement deals. That yellow-sleeved wetsuit hanging on the fence was it.

For reasons I can't explain now, my car had no surf racks, so boards were thrown into the trunk, tied down with bungee cord, and padded by a towel or a wetsuit, because when crossing the railroad tracks the lid of the trunk would always bounce up and down, creating pressure dings. Slowing down wasn't an option; it wasn't a long drive to Rincon, but on these after-school afternoons in winter, we always seemed to be racing against the sun.

We weren't headed for Rincon's fabled point, which lay dormant without significant swell, but the flat stretch of beach at the top of the point, known as Backside Rincon. The waves here were generally awful, but we hardly noticed. I happily spent my time swimming through the less-than-desirable windswell with my camera in its waterproof housing, practicing the art of shooting surfing from the water. It's where I learned about aperture settings, how to shoot into the low afternoon sun, lining up, positioning. A lot of film was wasted on those crummy afternoons, with no chance of any of the photos taken ever being published, but that didn't matter. If nothing else, we were making memories.

Drop-offs afterward at the Curren compound were basically pickups in reverse. Jeanine, Tommy's mom, was always outside at the gate, greeting us with a smile, along with Tommy's little sister, Anna, and little brother, Joe, running in circles with their dog, Willy. Tommy would hop out of the car, grab his board, and then throw that wetsuit over the fence as he walked through the gate, where it would stay until the next day, when the morning sun would rise and warm it up.

The winter days were short. The sun always seemed to be setting. We never had enough time, but we always knew there would be tomorrow. And, in 1982, our tomorrows almost always brought us something new; change was drastic and coming fast. Tommy would give up his amateur status to turn professional, eventually signing record-breaking rookie contracts with companies like Ocean Pacific and Rip Curl, then going on to win his first international pro-tour event, the Marui World Surfing Pro in Chiba, Japan. He'd also graduate from high school and meet his first wife, Marie.

But 1982 wasn't all Tommy. Al Merrick, over the past three years a guiding force in Tommy's ascension, both personally and professionally, began meticulously refining the newly introduced three-fin thruster design into what would eventually become a surfboard-industry standard. Top surfers from beyond the region flocked to Santa Barbara, looking for a piece of the magic coming from Al's Anacapa Street shaping room. This was the year Channel Islands began its transition from a respected local label to a world-renowned brand.

Change came fast for me, too. Suddenly, or so it seemed, everything I had been shooting for the past few years was in high demand. The surf magazines needed more images of Tommy, Willy, Sam and Matt, Davey Smith, and Kim Mearig, and actually handed me assignments: "Jimmy, we need a portrait of Al with his new thruster design," or "Jimmy, we need a shot of Mrs. Curren."

It was all becoming very exciting—not just being around it, but being a part of it all. Yet as exciting as it all would become, sometimes, when reflecting back on 1982, it's that last simple time before the whirlwind that I miss the most. When it was all ahead of us. When we were young, innocent, and working without a script. When I would drive away from the Curren compound and see that yellow-sleeved wetsuit in my rearview mirror, hanging there, waiting for tomorrow and the next day's sun.

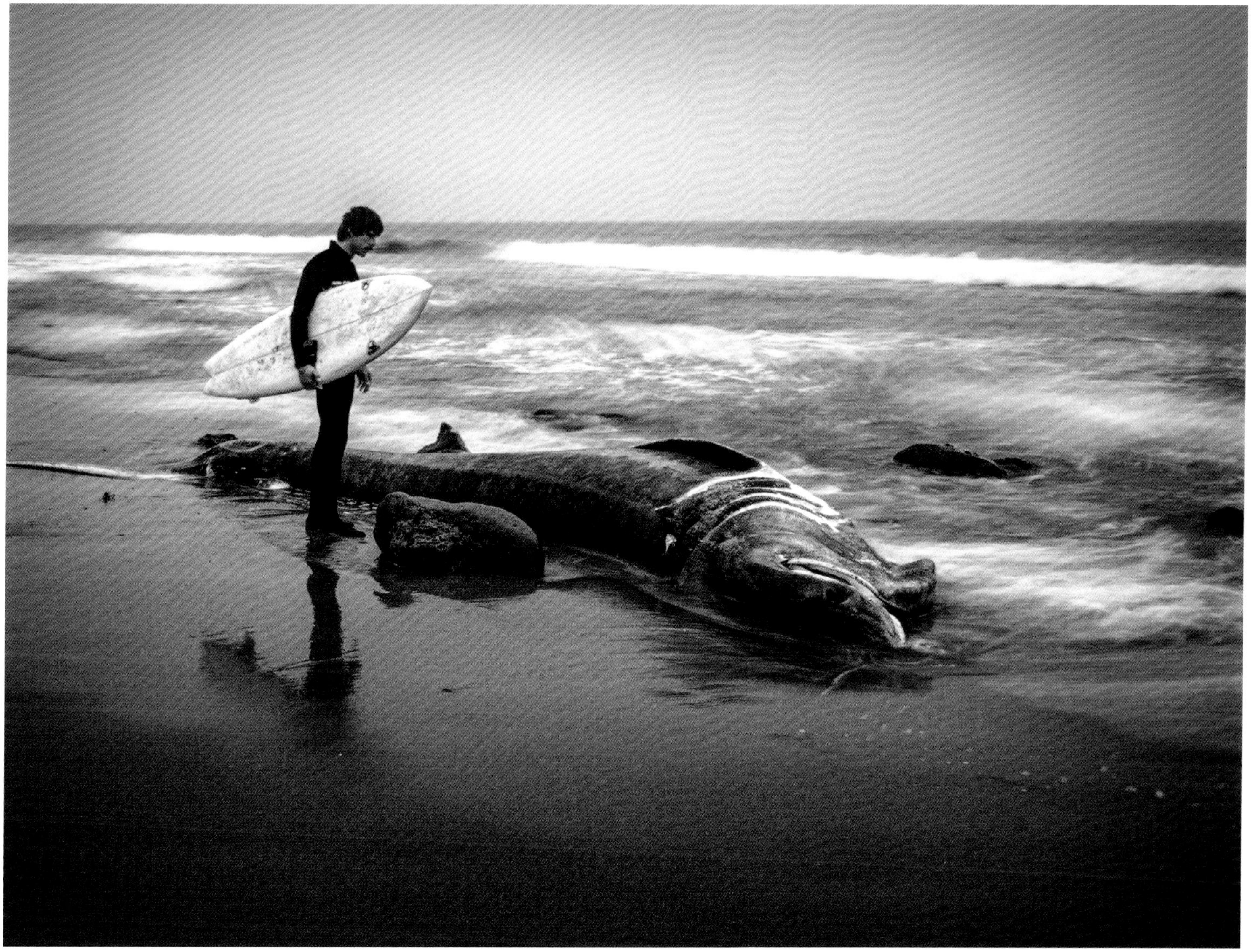

Carpinteria surf/shaper and Rincon master Matt Moore pauses to consider the fate of an 18-foot basking shark whose carcass washed ashore one dreary morning. Cetorhinus maximus is a filter feeder, posing no threat to surfers and water photographers, but this was still a reminder that there are some big fish out there.

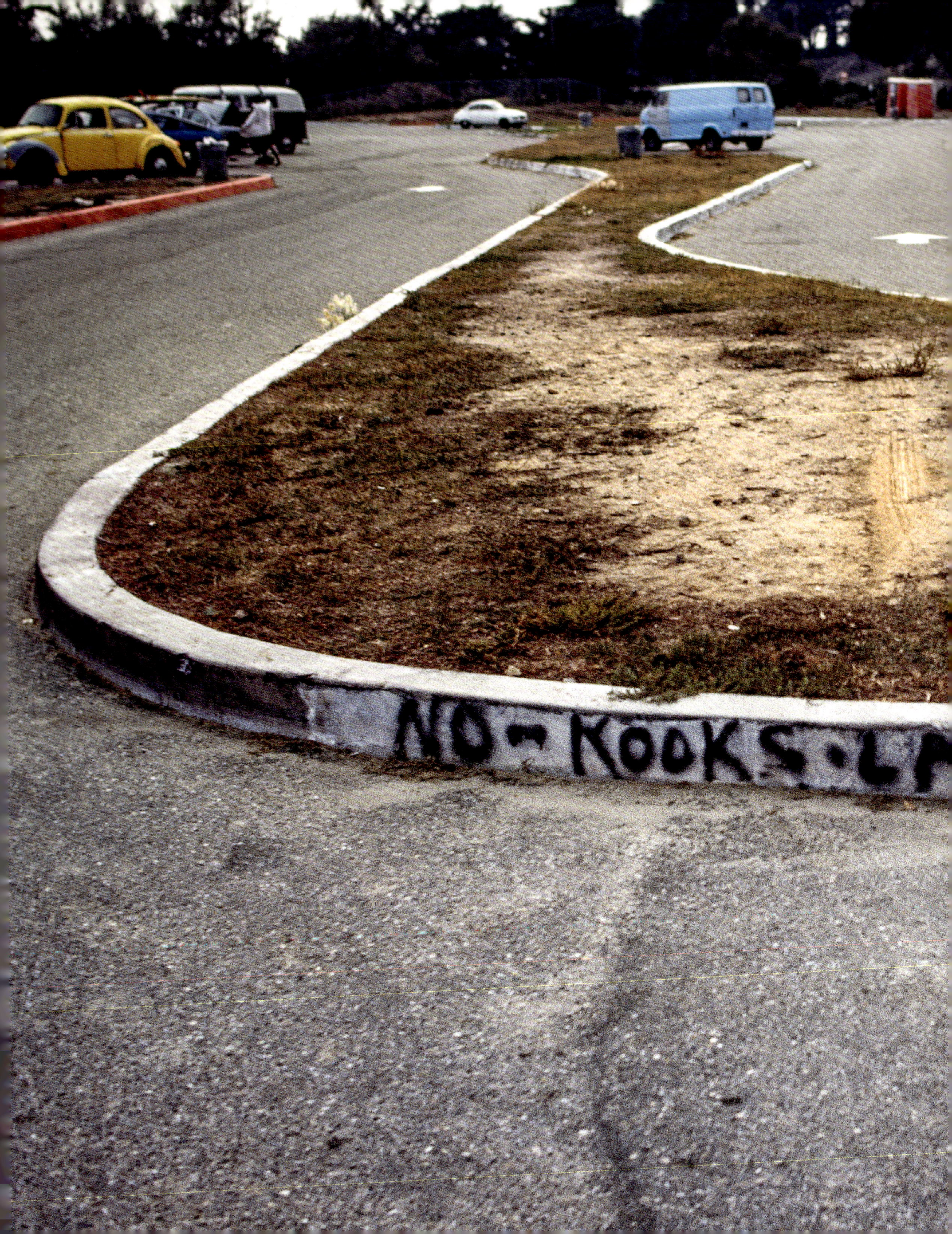
NO - KOOKS

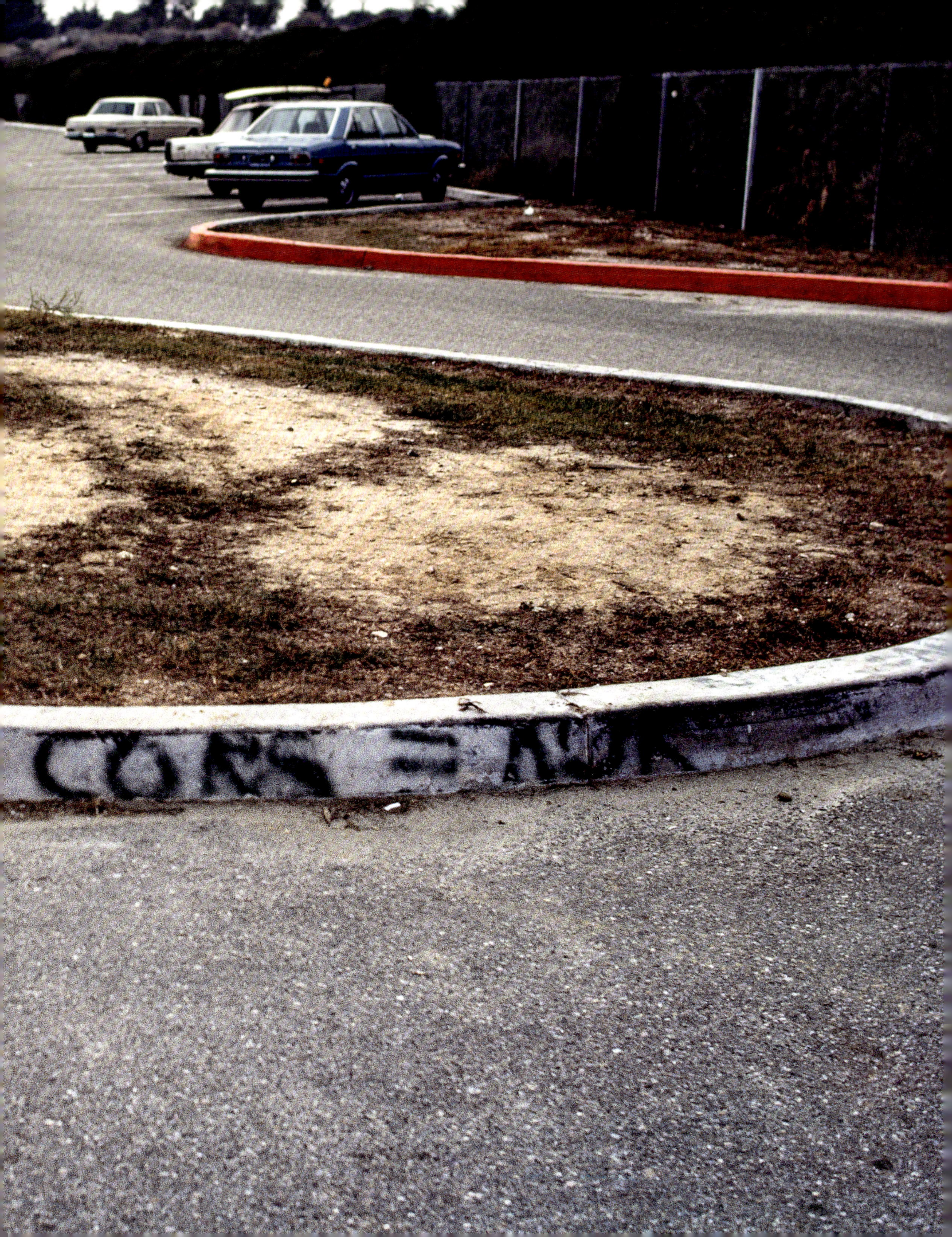

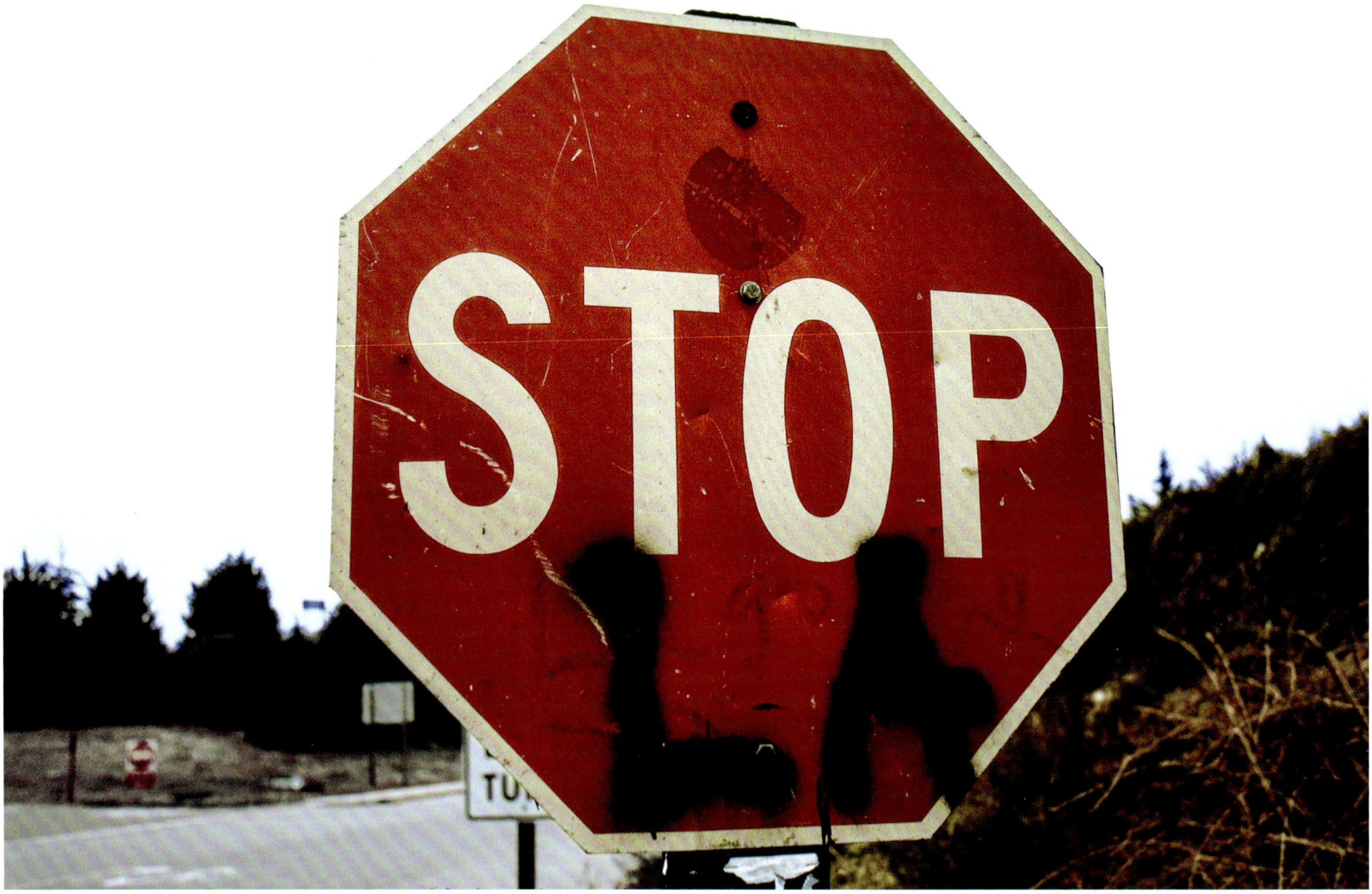

Previous

Life in the Rincon parking told a story all its own, complete with heroes and villains. The tire tracks on the island belonged to Al Merrick's yellow Toyota pickup, its owner, by general consent, given executive parking privileges even on the most crowded days. And the villains? Anyone driving up from the dreaded 310 area code.

This page and facing

Seeing as how during anything even resembling a swell, the Rincon parking lot would be full to overflowing, I can't help but marvel at the futile efforts of these self-appointed "protectors of the point." This stenciled warning stands out, however, if for no reason other than the effort made and the attention to detail in its execution.

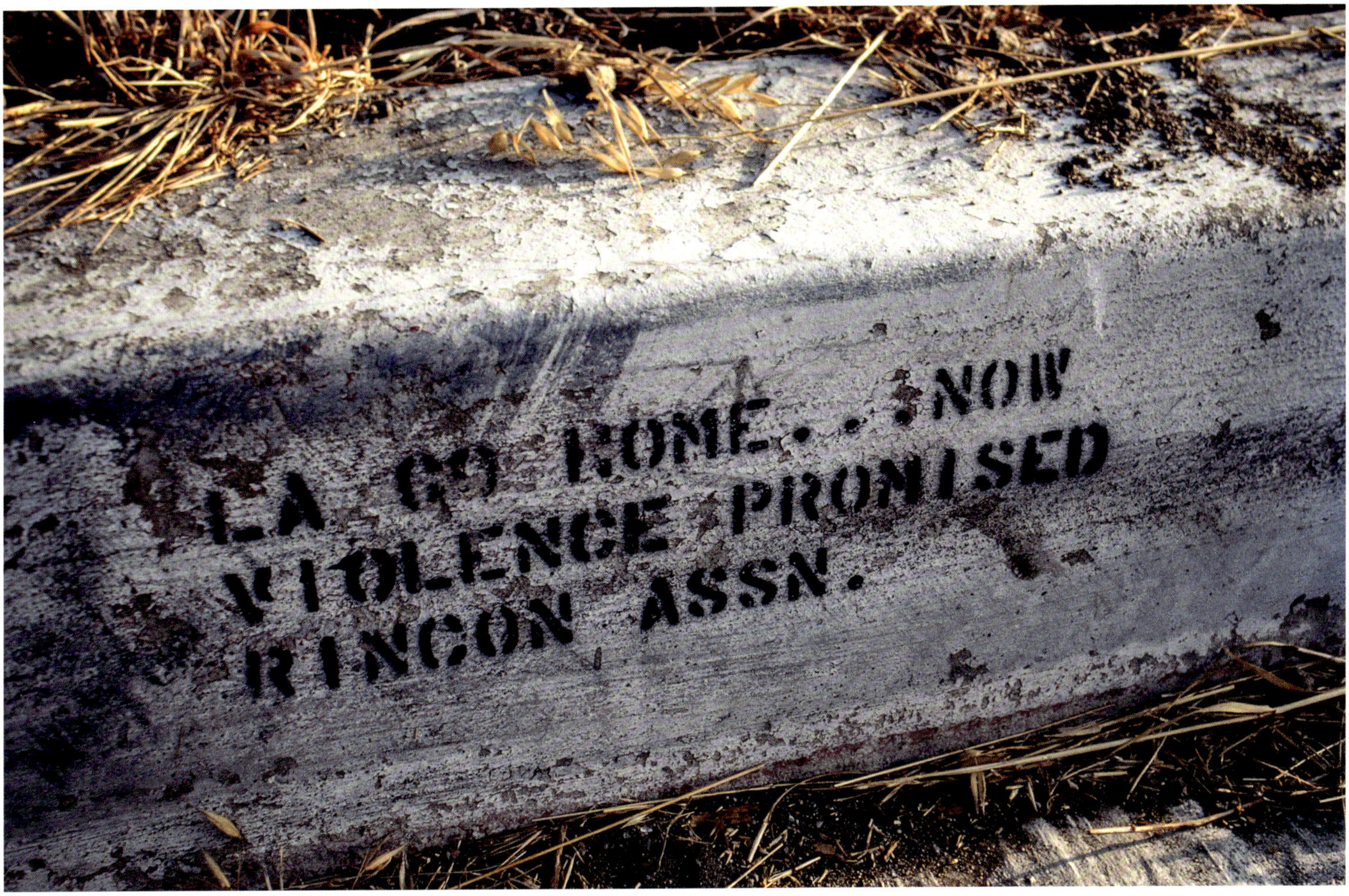
LA GO HOME...NOW
VIOLENCE PROMISED
RINCON ASSN.

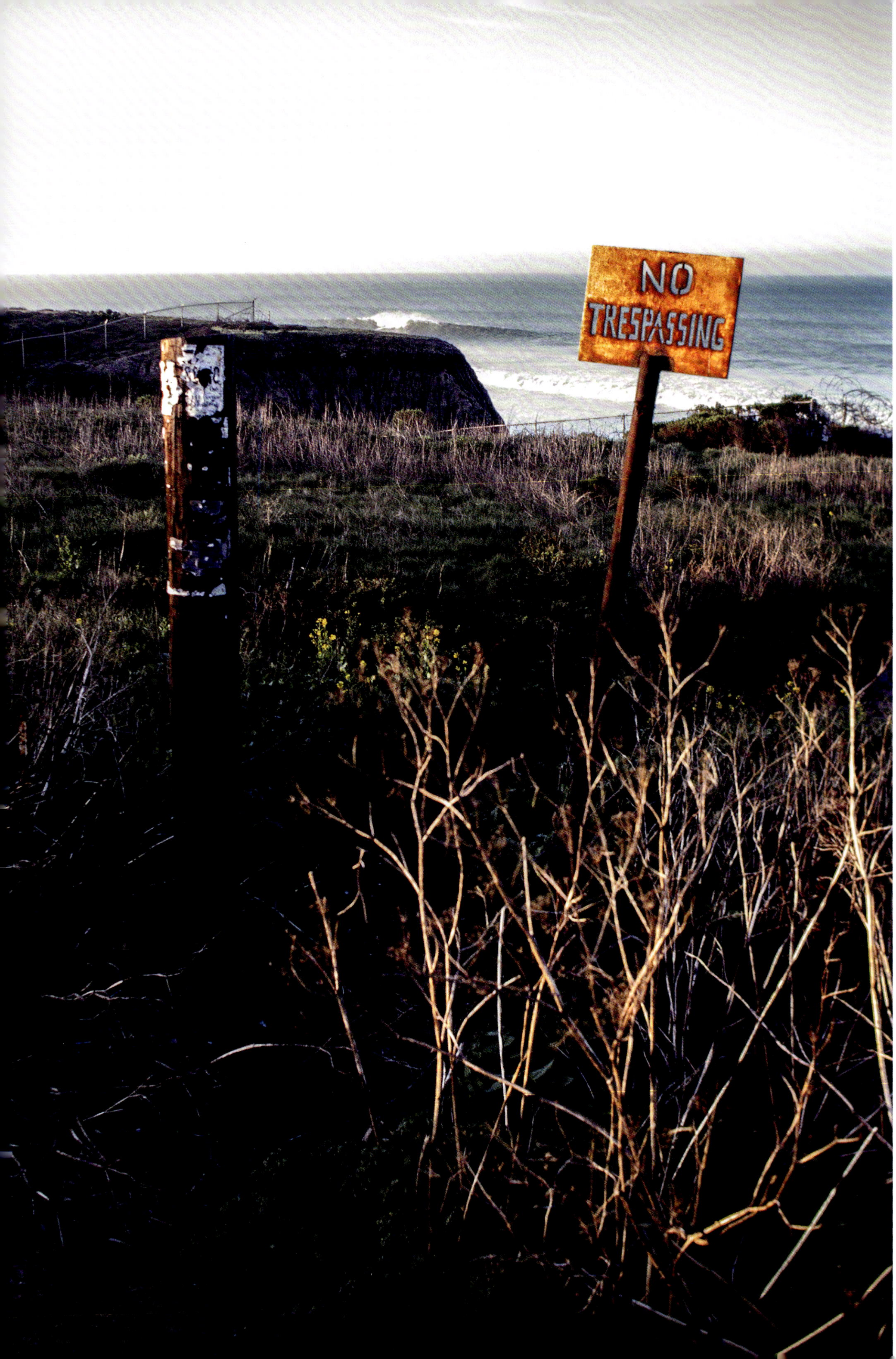
NO
TRESPASSING

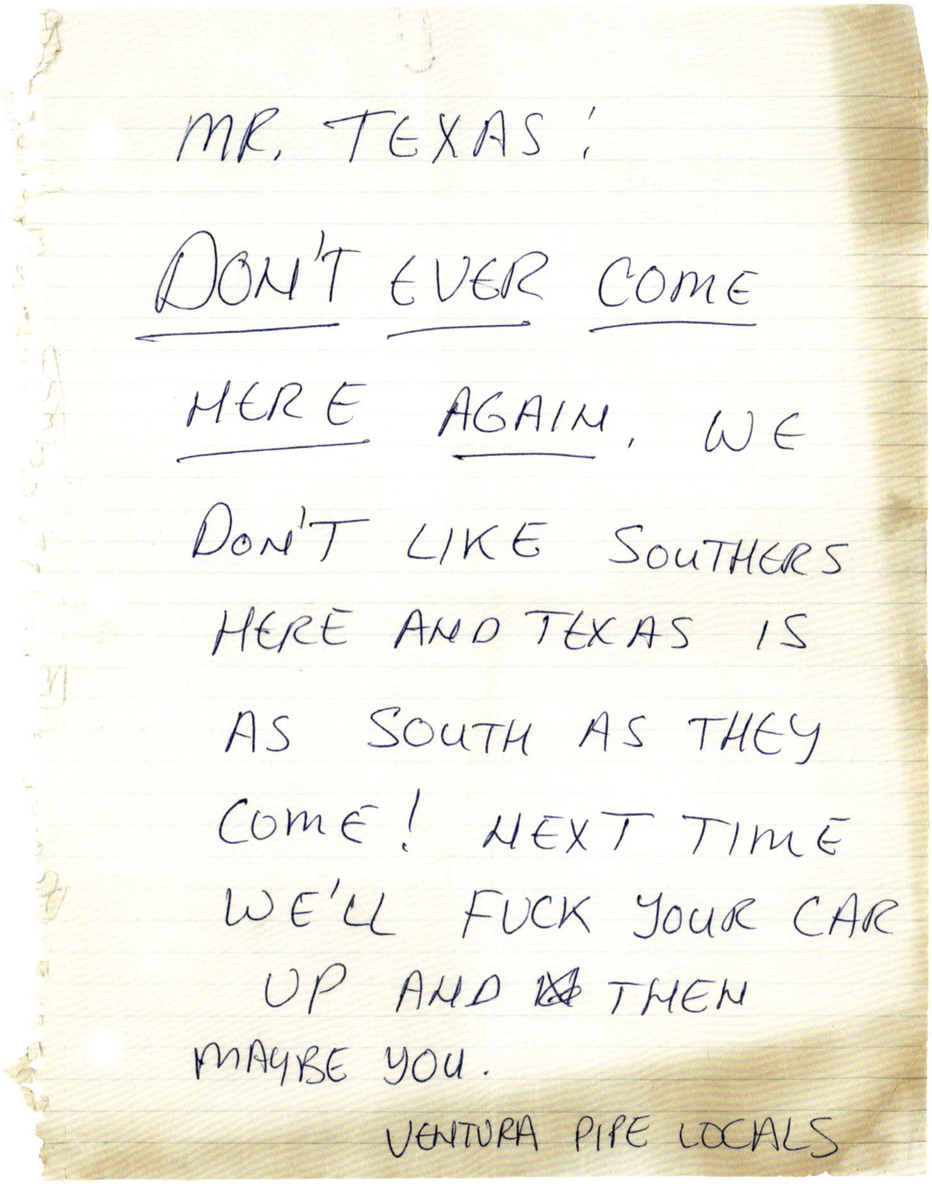

MR. TEXAS:

DON'T EVER COME HERE AGAIN, WE DON'T LIKE SOUTHERS HERE AND TEXAS IS AS SOUTH AS THEY COME! NEXT TIME WE'LL FUCK YOUR CAR UP AND THEN MAYBE YOU.

VENTURA PIPE LOCALS

Opposite
What's not evident in this picture is the cut barbed-wire entrance and well-worn trail leading to this otherwise very hard-to-reach surf spot north of Point Conception.

Above
Long before C Street's gentrification. In the early '80s, nothing was paved; there was only a dead-end dirt parking lot, distant strains of Jerry Garcia, and the roar of the Hells Angels' bikes at the Ventura County Fairgrounds. If you wanted to shoot, you dealt with it. Having Texas plates didn't help.

Overleaf
A bold declaration of brand allegiance on the overpass of a Ventura Freeway off-ramp. Though only fifteen miles south of Rincon, Ventura was nowhere near Channel Islands country. *(Years later, I would become good friends with the artist/surfer, Brad Johnson. Medium: charcoal on concrete.)*

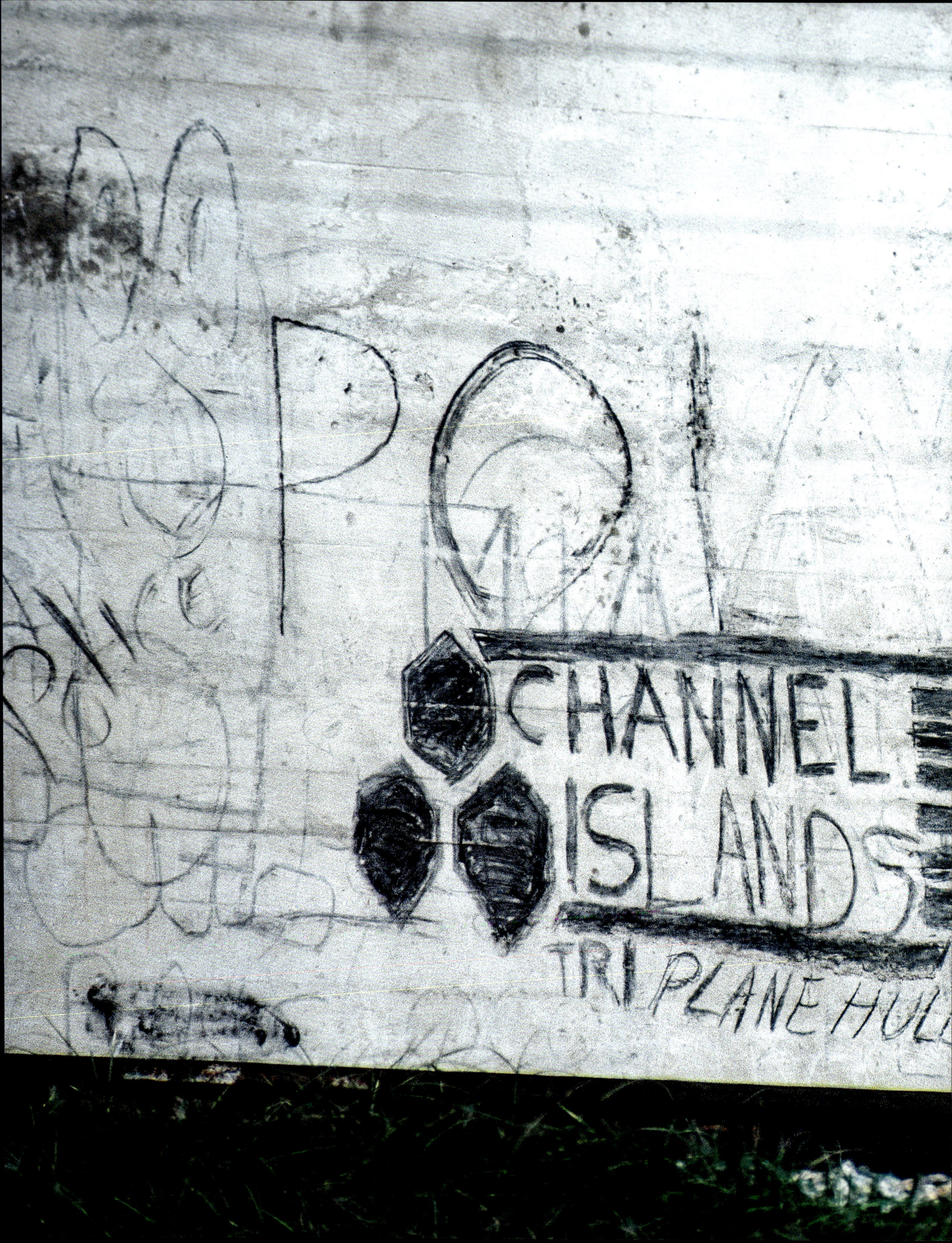
CHANNEL
ISLANDS
TRI PLANE HUL

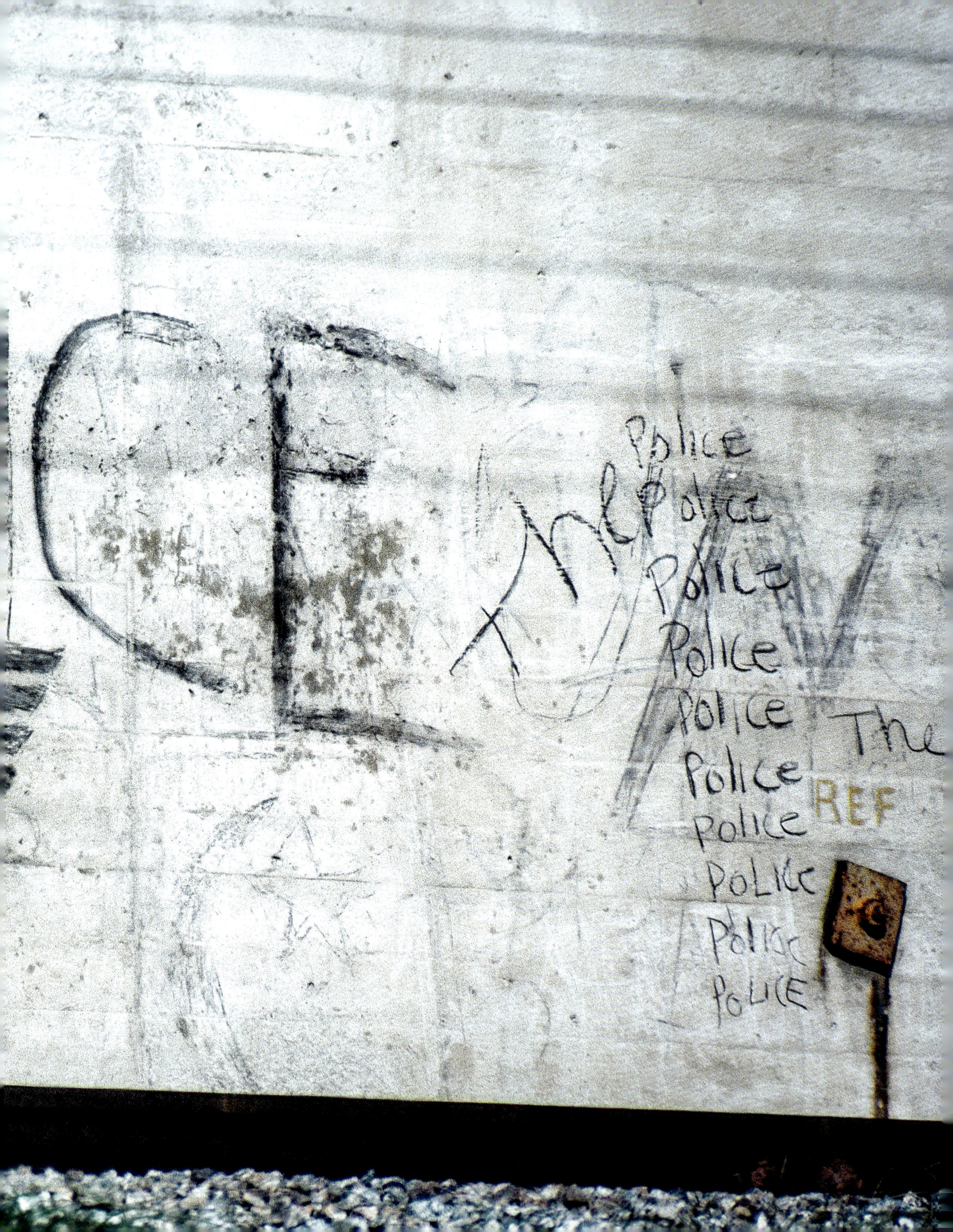
The
Police
Police
Police
Police
Police
Police
Police
POLICE
Police
POLICE
The
REF

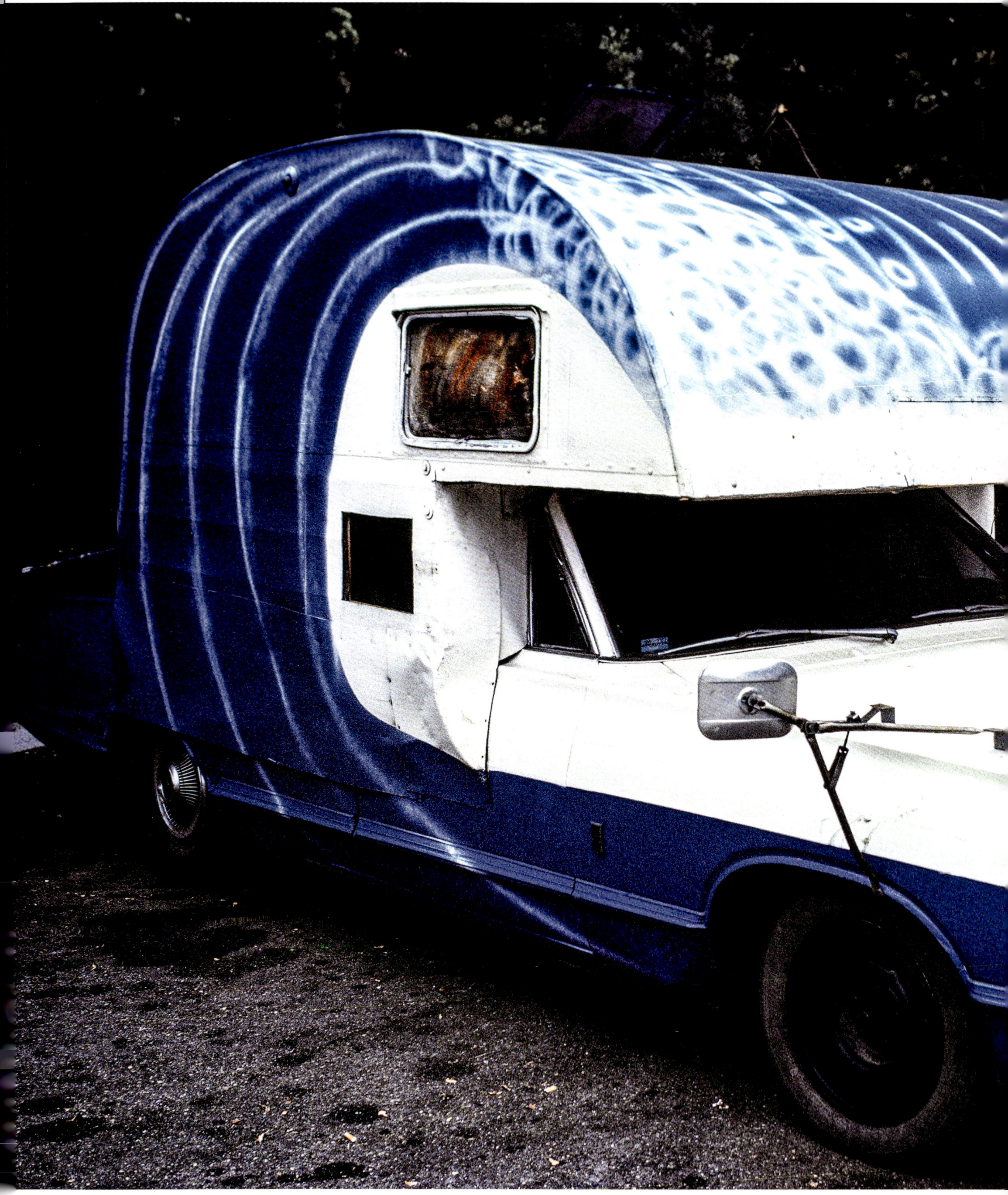

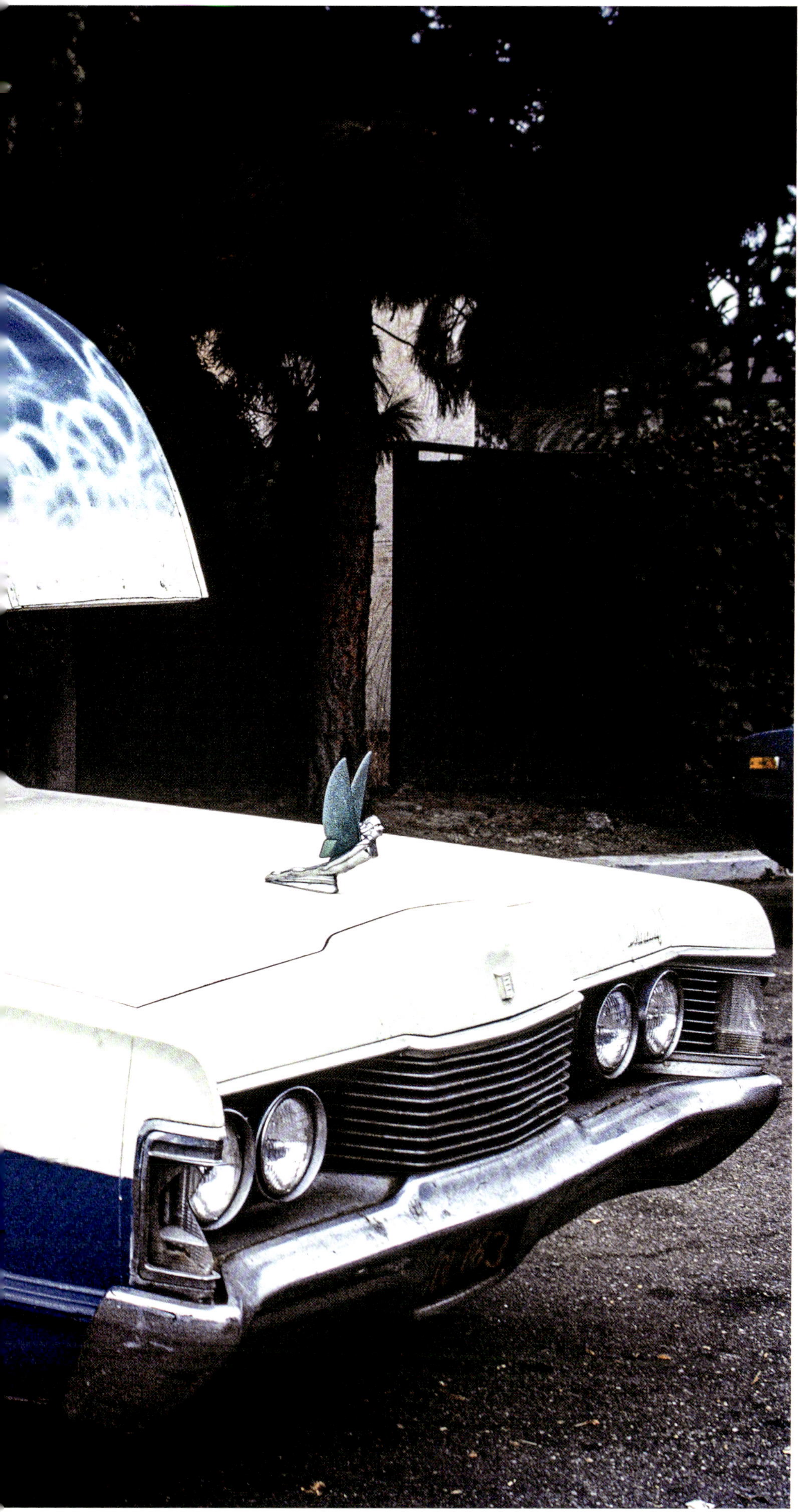

Spread

"Van life" is nothing new. Back in the day, virtually every surf-spot parking lot had at least one free-spirit-in-residence who'd creatively cut themselves loose from more material considerations in order to remain close to the source. For the owners of this pre-Sprinter creation, parked near the trail leading down to Hammonds Reef, I always wondered if their nights were filled with dreams of perfect tubes or of nightmares of going over the falls.

Overleaf

Contrary to his reputation for deliberately eluding photographers, which developed later in his career, in the early days Tommy worked hard to "get the shot" as much as I did. On this day, however, after we'd linked up in a few great tubes, he asked if I would go in and shoot from the beach. Apparently I was causing the tube to close down at the end of the ride. I went in and sat on the beach and just watched him surf, without shooting anymore. I knew I had what I came for. This image first appeared in *Surfer* magazine's inaugural "Hot 100" feature.

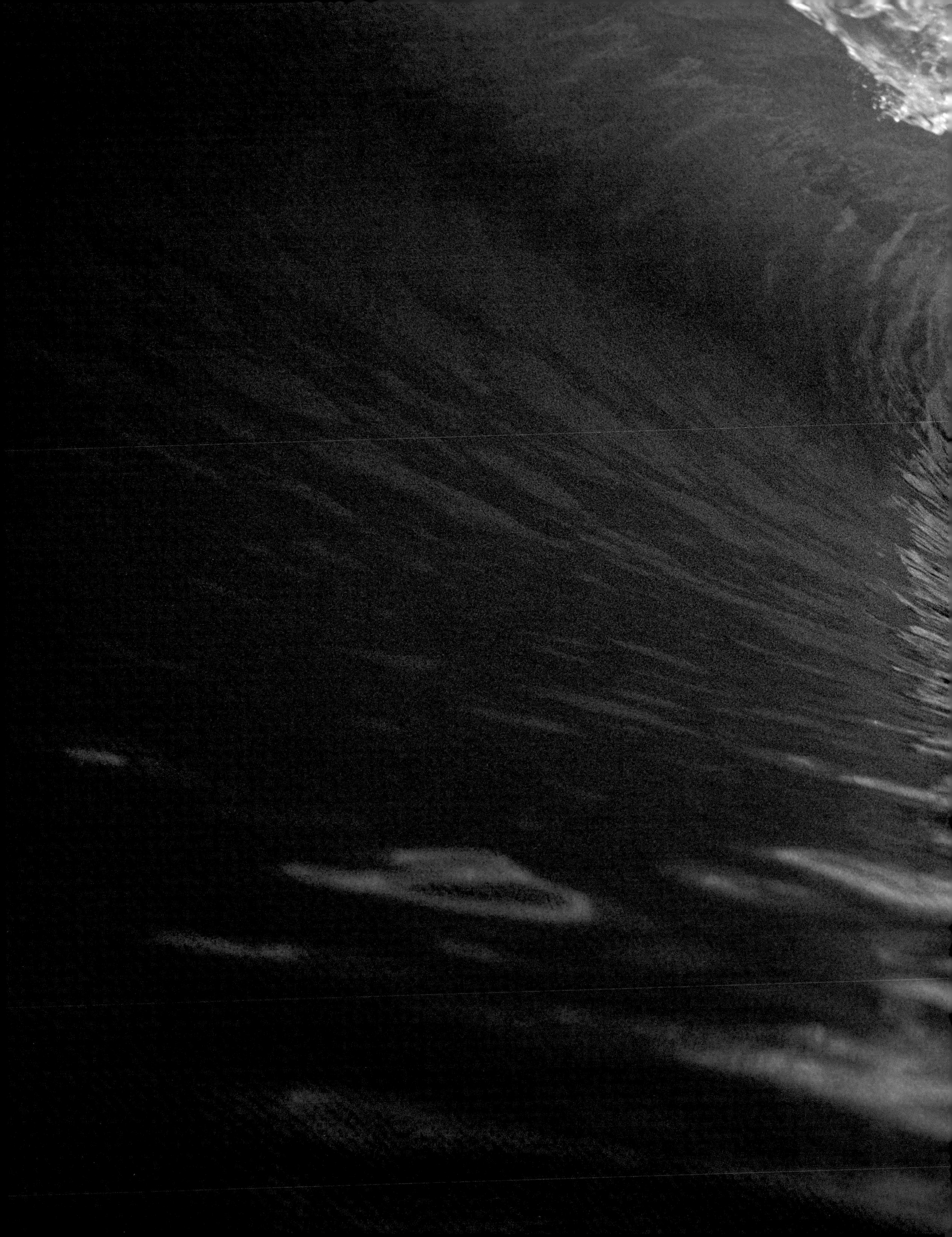

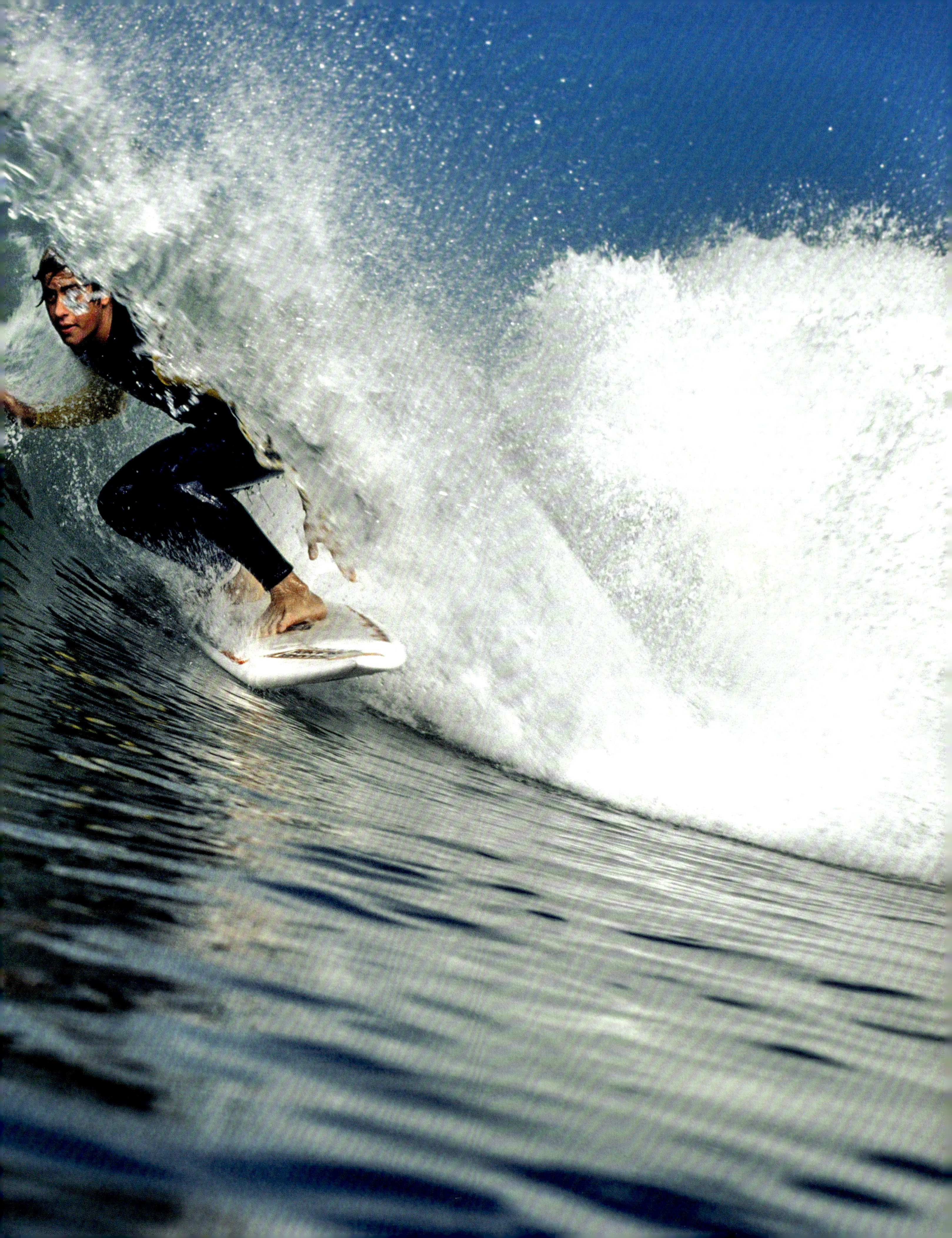

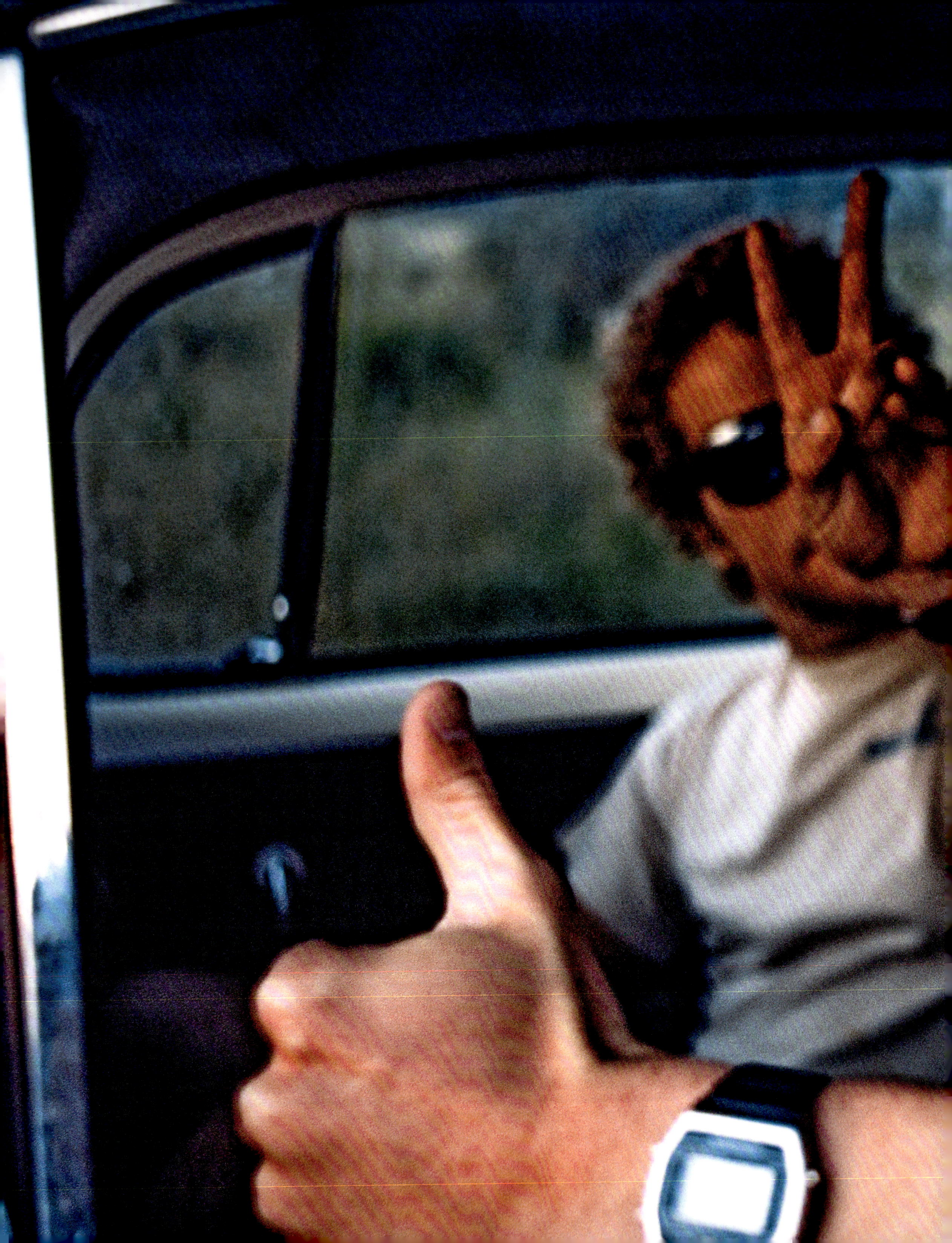

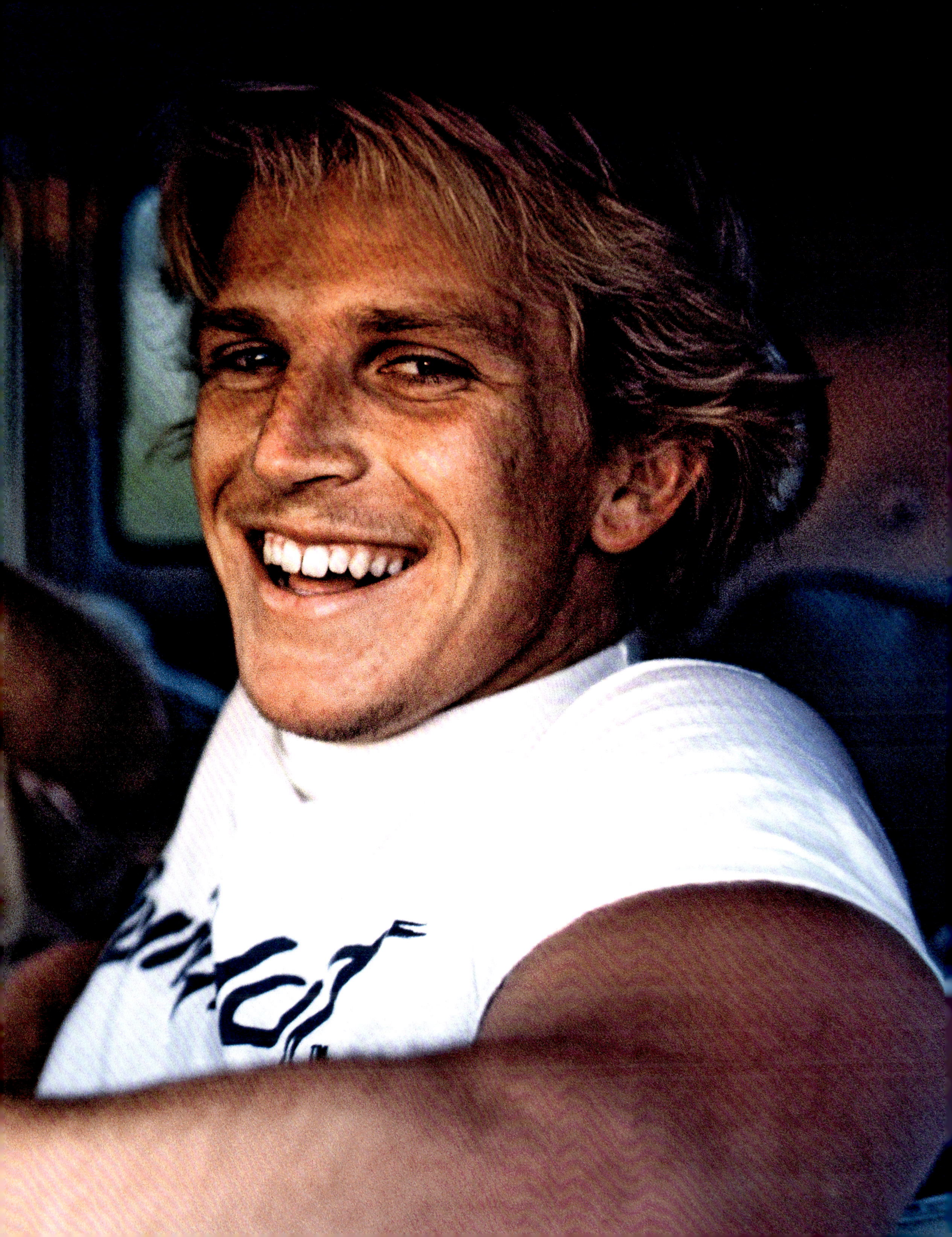

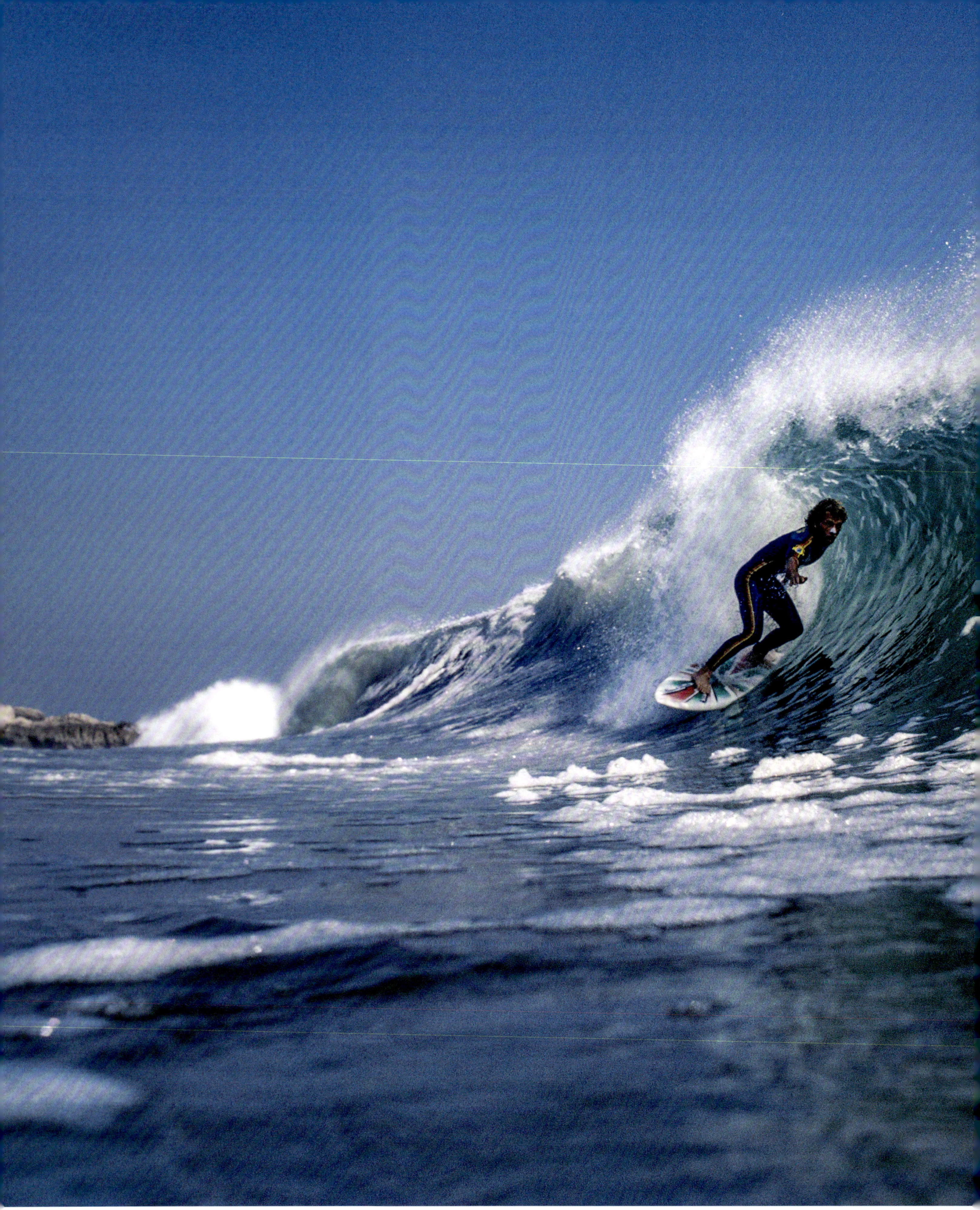

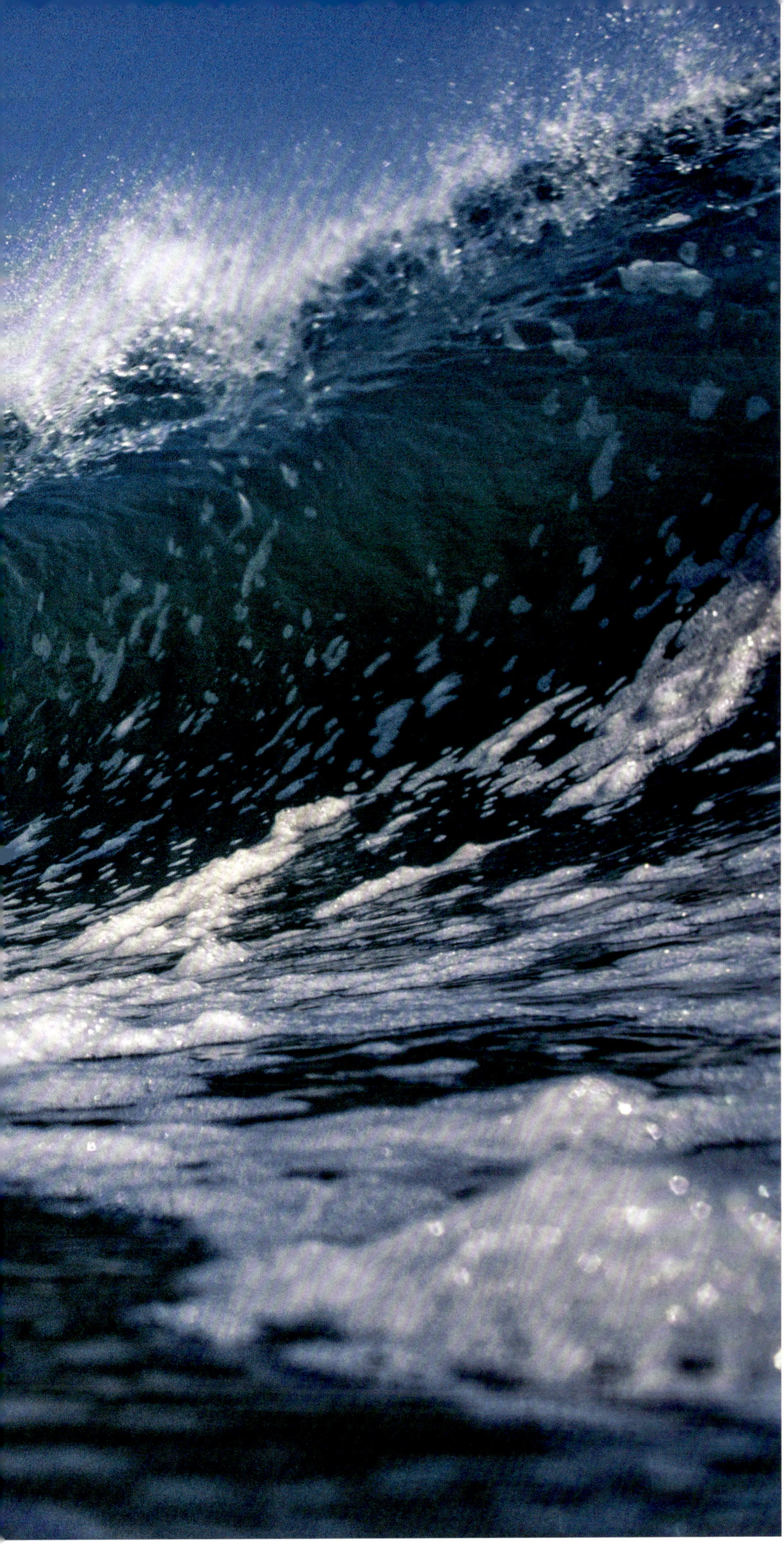

Previous

New Jersey transplant Steve Dwyer *(in the driver's seat)* and Davey Smith *(sitting shotgun)*, stoked to be heading out on a strike mission to a secret south-swell spot in North Los Angeles County.

Spread

Davey Smith, setting up for the barrel at a wave we dubbed "Death Tubes" not due to any particular danger—it broke over a shallow, flat sandbar—but because of the high surfboard mortality rate involved in shooting from the water.

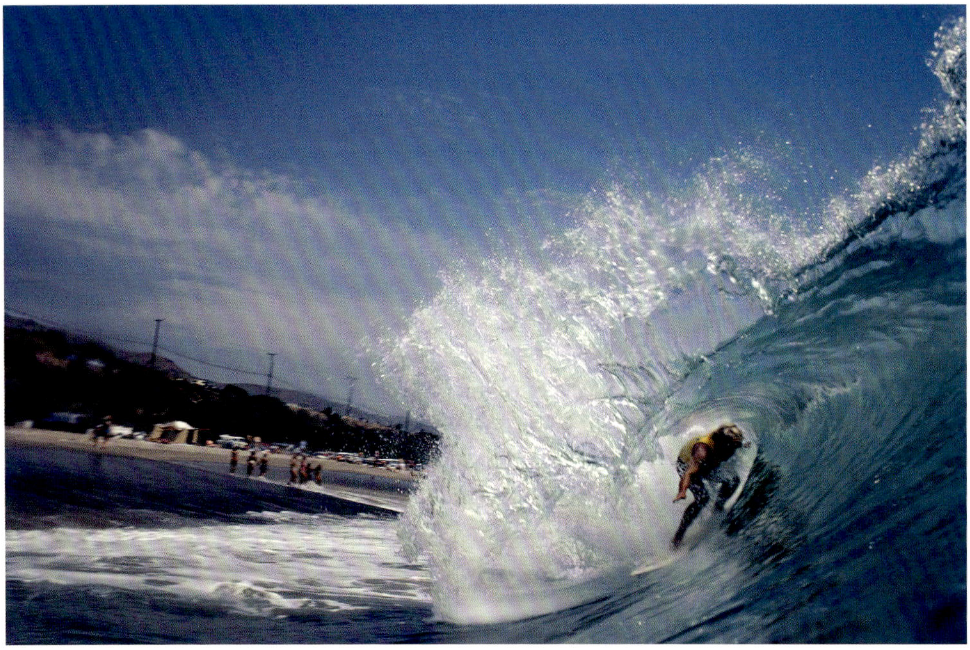

Beach Party

Even though I was too young to have seen them in a theater, as a young surfer growing up in Texas I made sure never to miss any of the American International Beach Party movies whenever they showed on TV. Yes, they were super corny, and the surfing sequences of Frankie Avalon and Annette Funicello up against a green screen were ridiculous, but none of that mattered so long as I got at least a glimpse of the California beach lifestyle that I longed to be a part of.

Fast-forward a decade, and Davey Smith and I are huddled on the beach at Death Tubes following a chilly crack-of-dawn photo session, both feeling drowsy as the rising sun warmed. The rhythmic hammering at a construction site over at the point added a hypnotic effect, and, wrapped in our towels, we were both soon asleep. An hour later, we woke up in 1962. Or so it seemed. While we slept, an entire movie set had been staged and a scene was being filmed on the beach around us, complete with a cool beach shack, brightly colored prop longboards, and a crowd of swinging guys and girls with boss '60s hairstyles and bathing suits dancing away on the sand. It was *Beach Party* come to life. What I didn't know then was that the original movie had been filmed at this very spot, and that when planning its reenactment for the upcoming film *Airplane II: The Sequel*, starring Robert Hayes, producers pushed for authenticity—including the casting of Funicello for the scene we had woken up in the middle of. Strangely, nobody paid us any attention, so we gathered up our gear and snuck back to the 1980s.

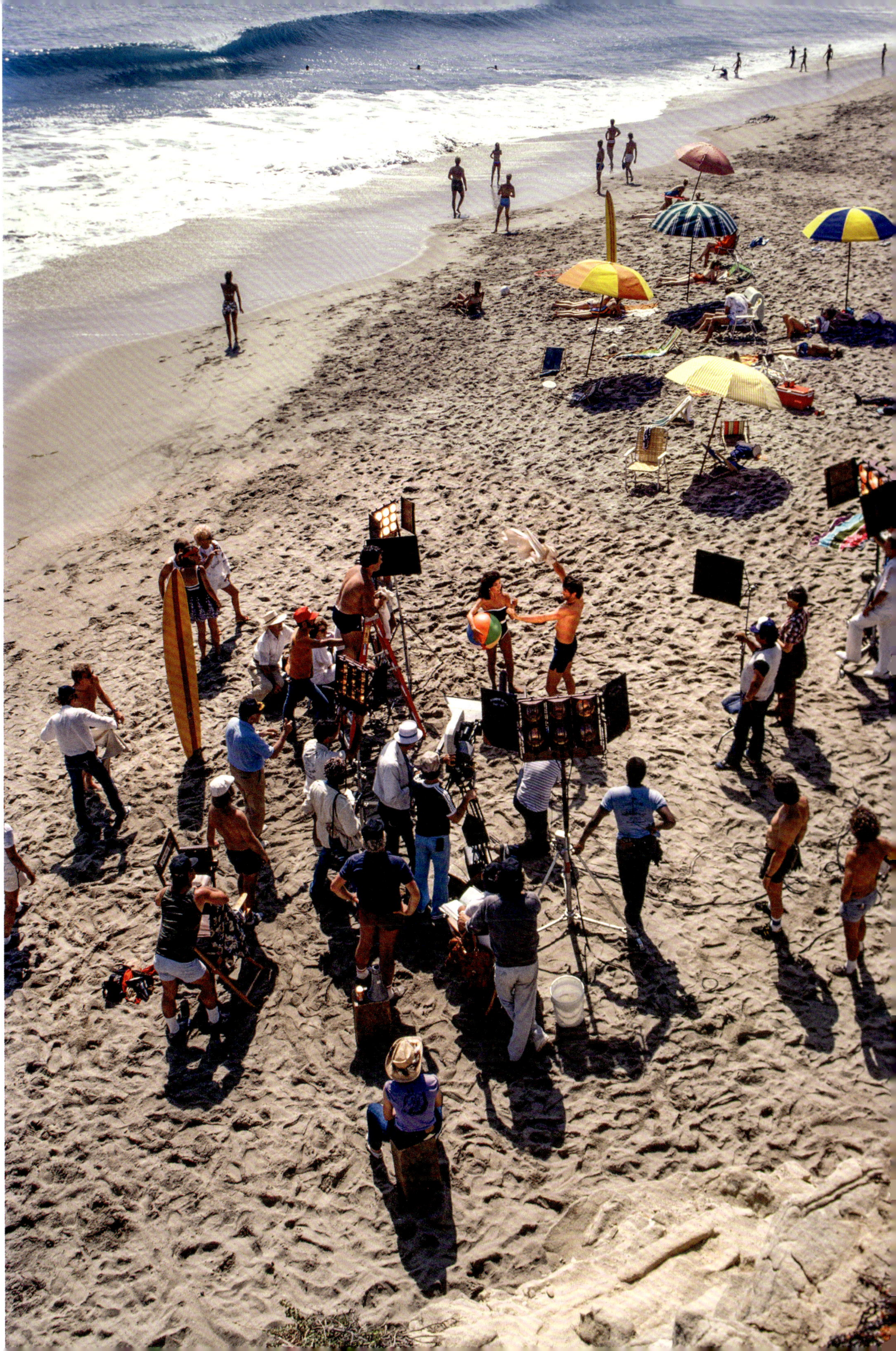

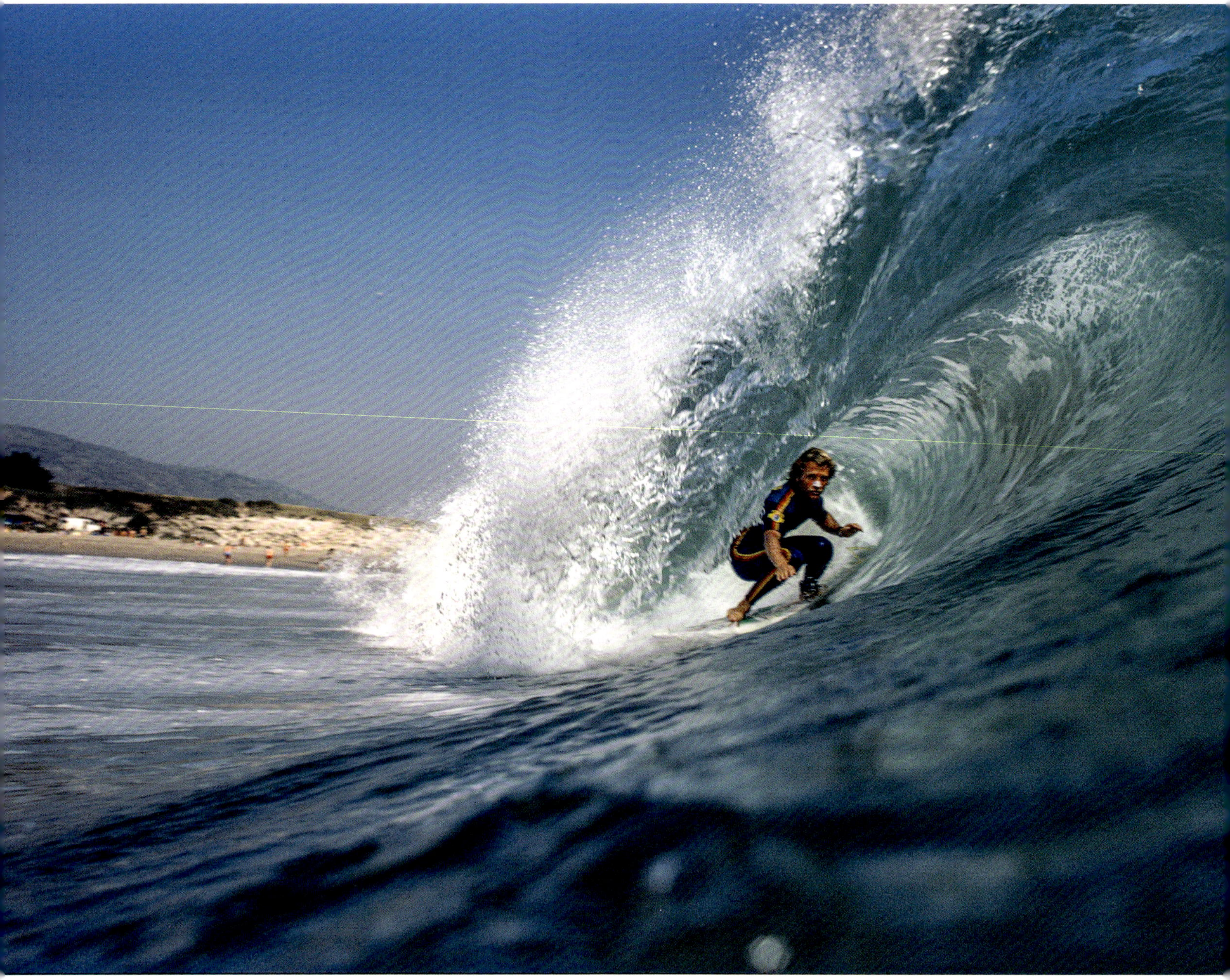

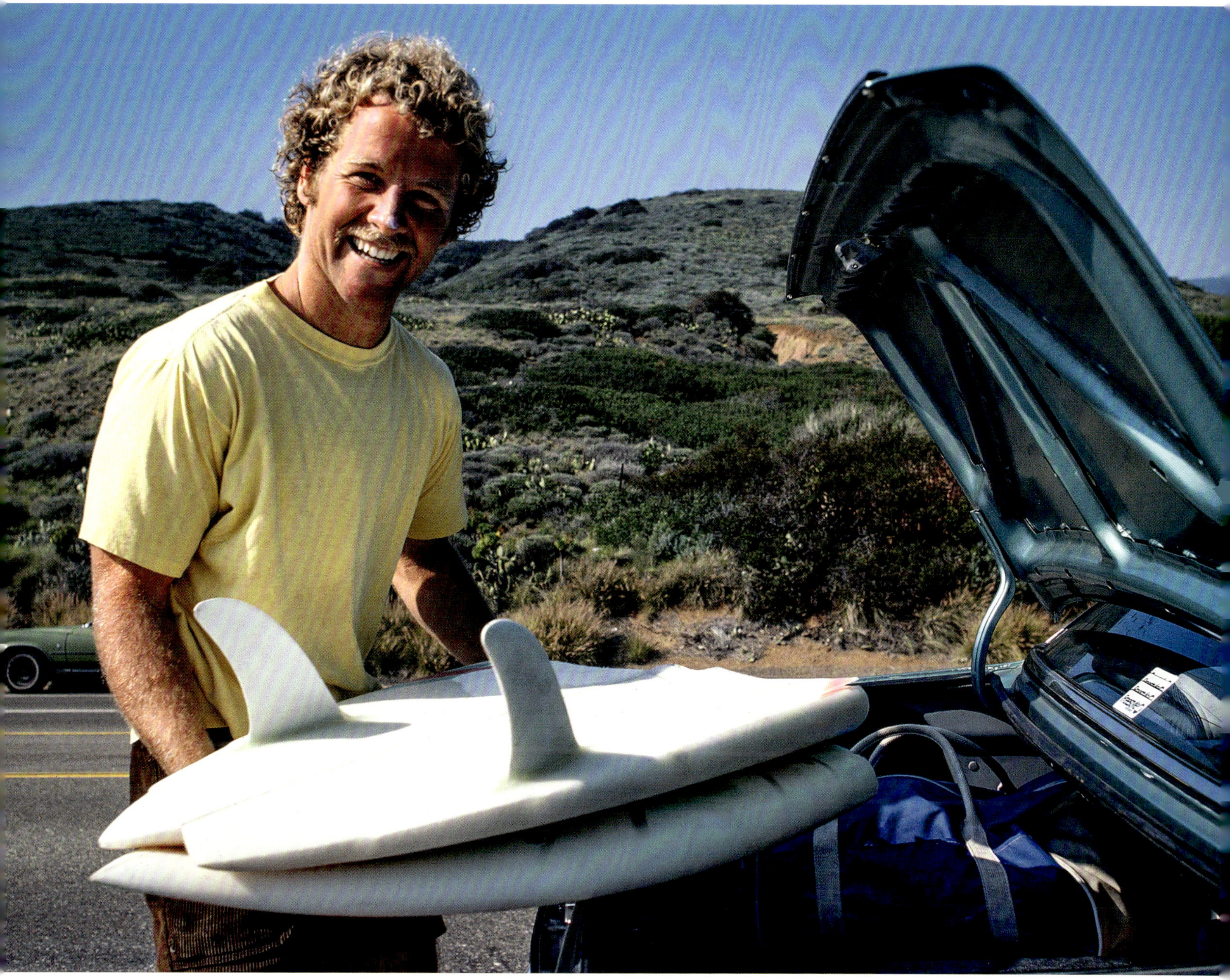

Costly cause and effect at Death Tubes. Many years later, we would learn this spot is actually called "Heavens" by the area's locals. In the early '80s, you did not keep a backup surfboard in your car. Inevitably, when this wave snapped your one board in half, it was time to call it a day, throw the pieces into the trunk, and head back to Santa Barbara to order a brand-new one from Al. All you could hope for was that you'd captured enough publishable images to pay for the shattered foam and fiberglass.

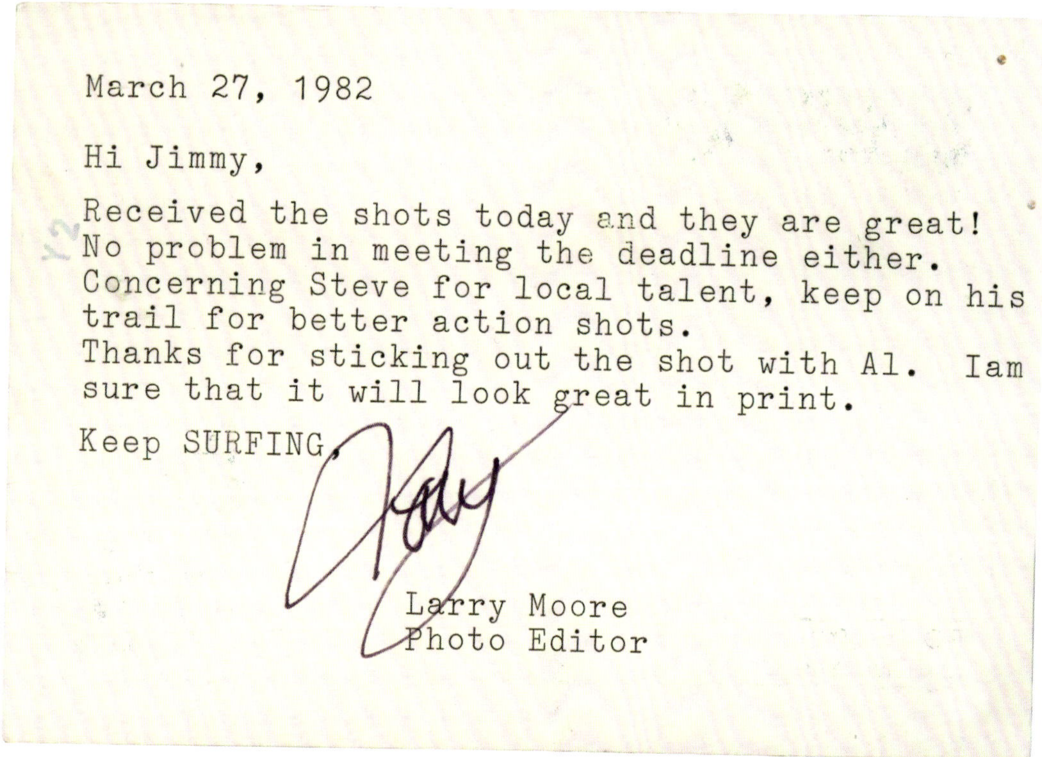

March 27, 1982

Hi Jimmy,

Received the shots today and they are great!
No problem in meeting the deadline either.
Concerning Steve for local talent, keep on his trail for better action shots.
Thanks for sticking out the shot with Al. Iam sure that it will look great in print.

Keep SURFING,

Larry Moore
Photo Editor

Reshoot

Surfing magazine requested images of Al with the two hottest boards for 1982: the tri-plane-hull twin-fin and the squashtail thruster. I shot the first one on Stearns Wharf, overlooking the harbor, but was ultimately asked to do a reshoot in Al's shaping room. This led to a bit of awkwardness because Al had an unwritten rule never to have glassed boards in his shaping room. The shoot ended up going well, the resulting image used for an article showcasing five prominent California shapers and their top team rider. This particular photo marked a pivotal point in the career trajectories of both Al and Tommy, but it also had unintentional influences. Other shapers, upon finding out that I had taken this photo *(pages 172–173)*, would tell me they set their shaping rooms up to emulate Al's, specifically being sure to line up their tools as seen here. They were no doubt disappointed when I would tell them that I had lined the tools up that way for the shoot in order to direct the eye to the standing board.

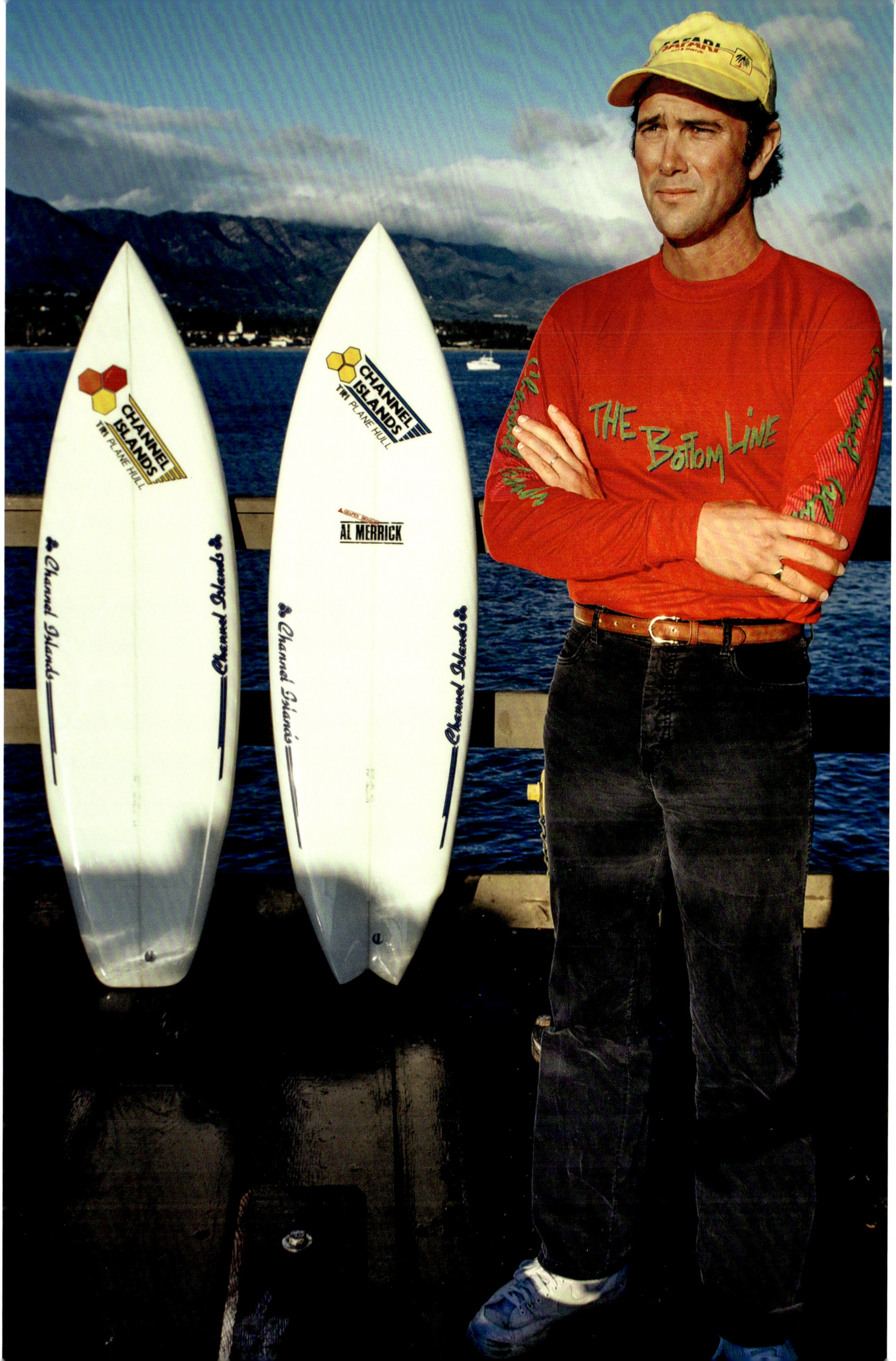
SAFARI
CHANNEL ISLANDS
TRI PLANE HULL
Channel Islands
CHANNEL ISLANDS
TRI PLANE HULL
AL MERRICK
Channel Islands

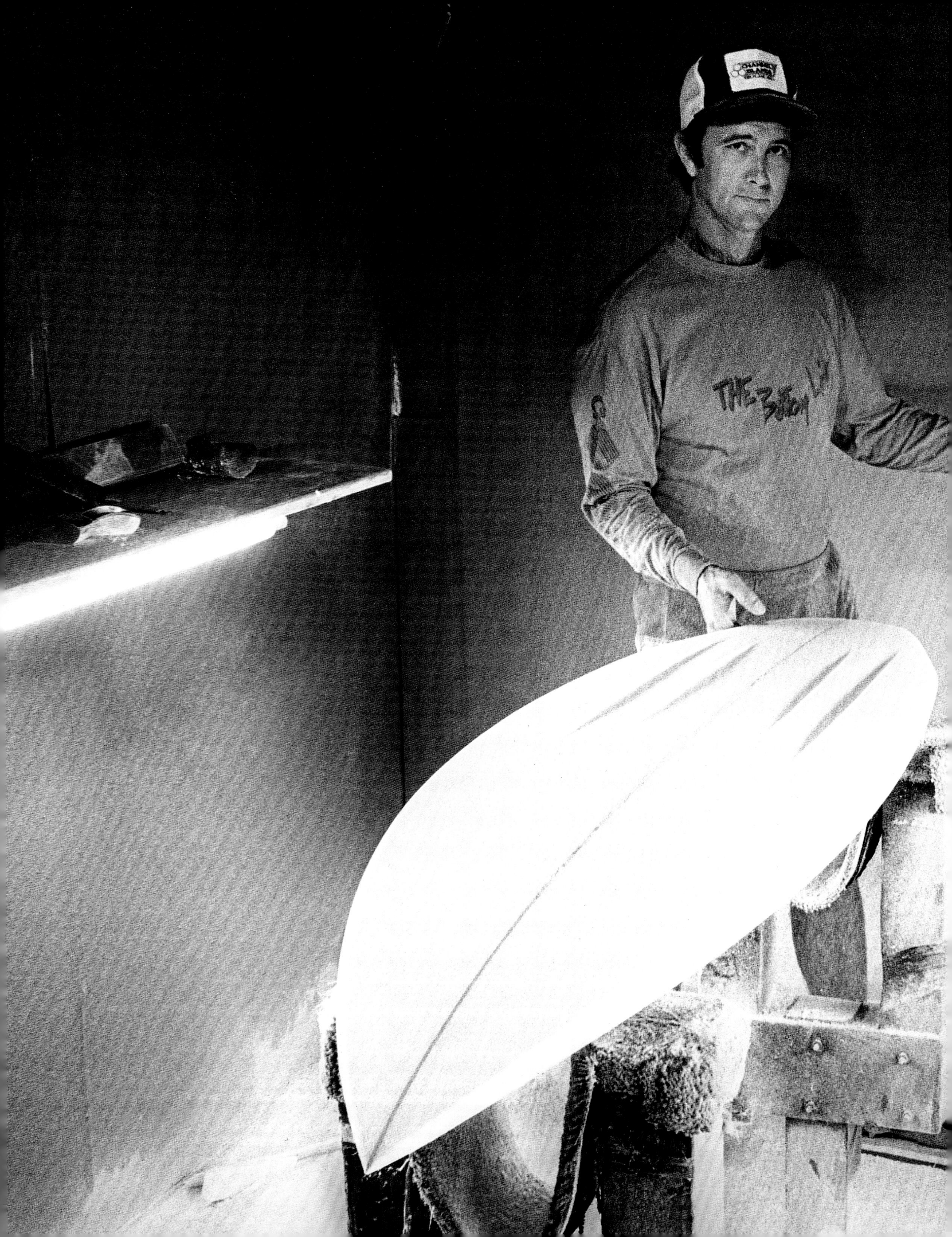
THE Bottom

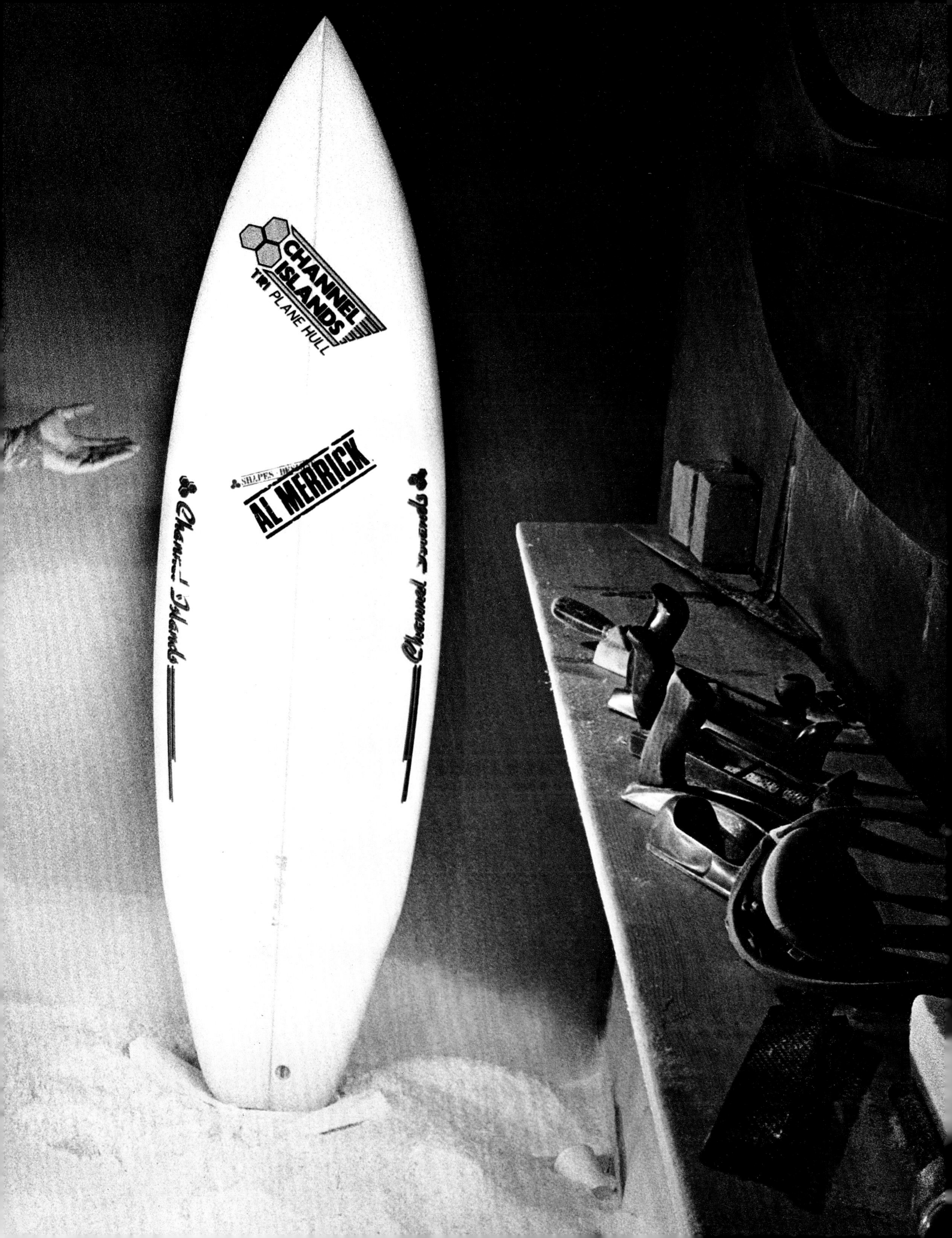
CHANNEL ISLANDS
TRI PLANE HULL
AL MERRICK
Channel Islands
Channel Islands

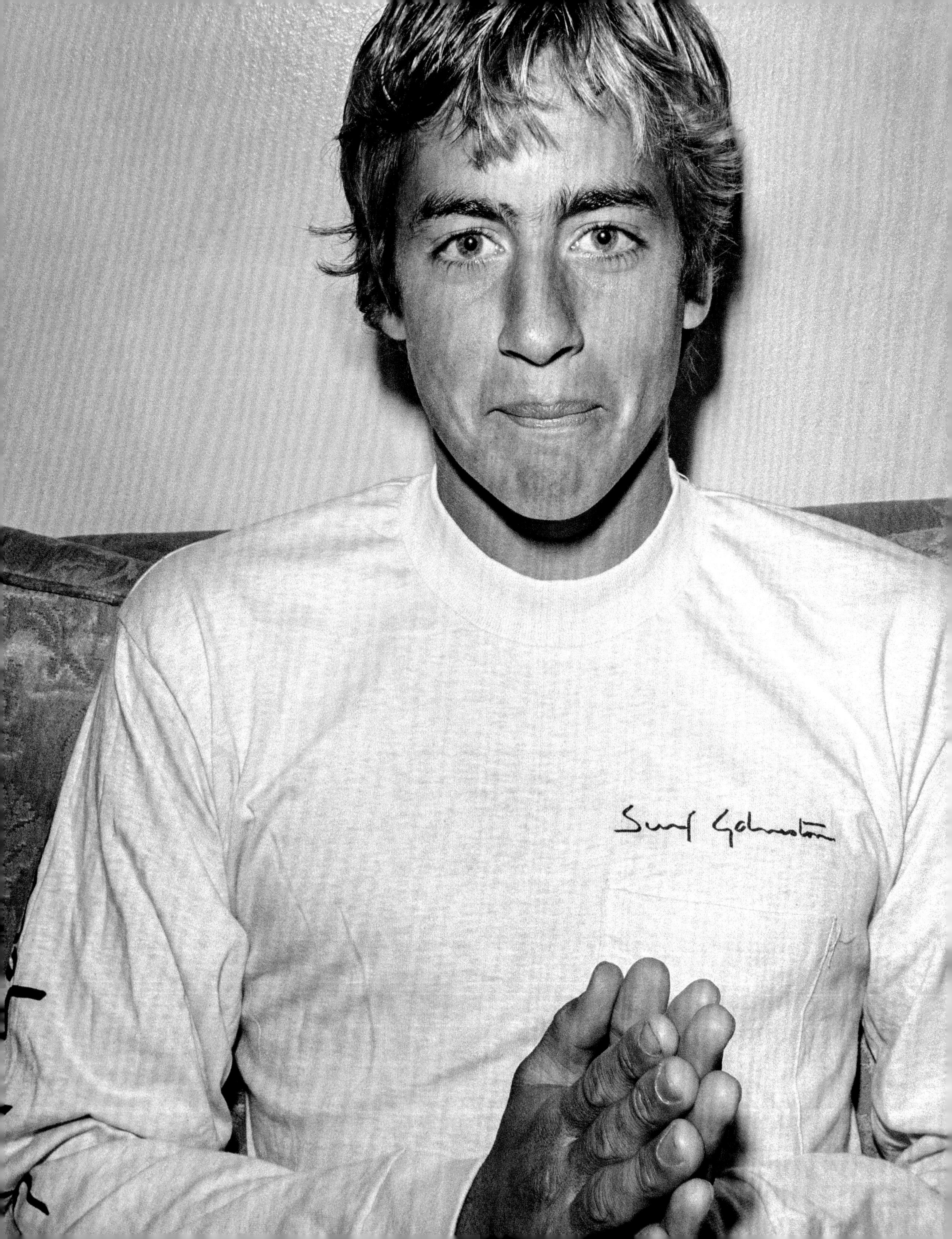

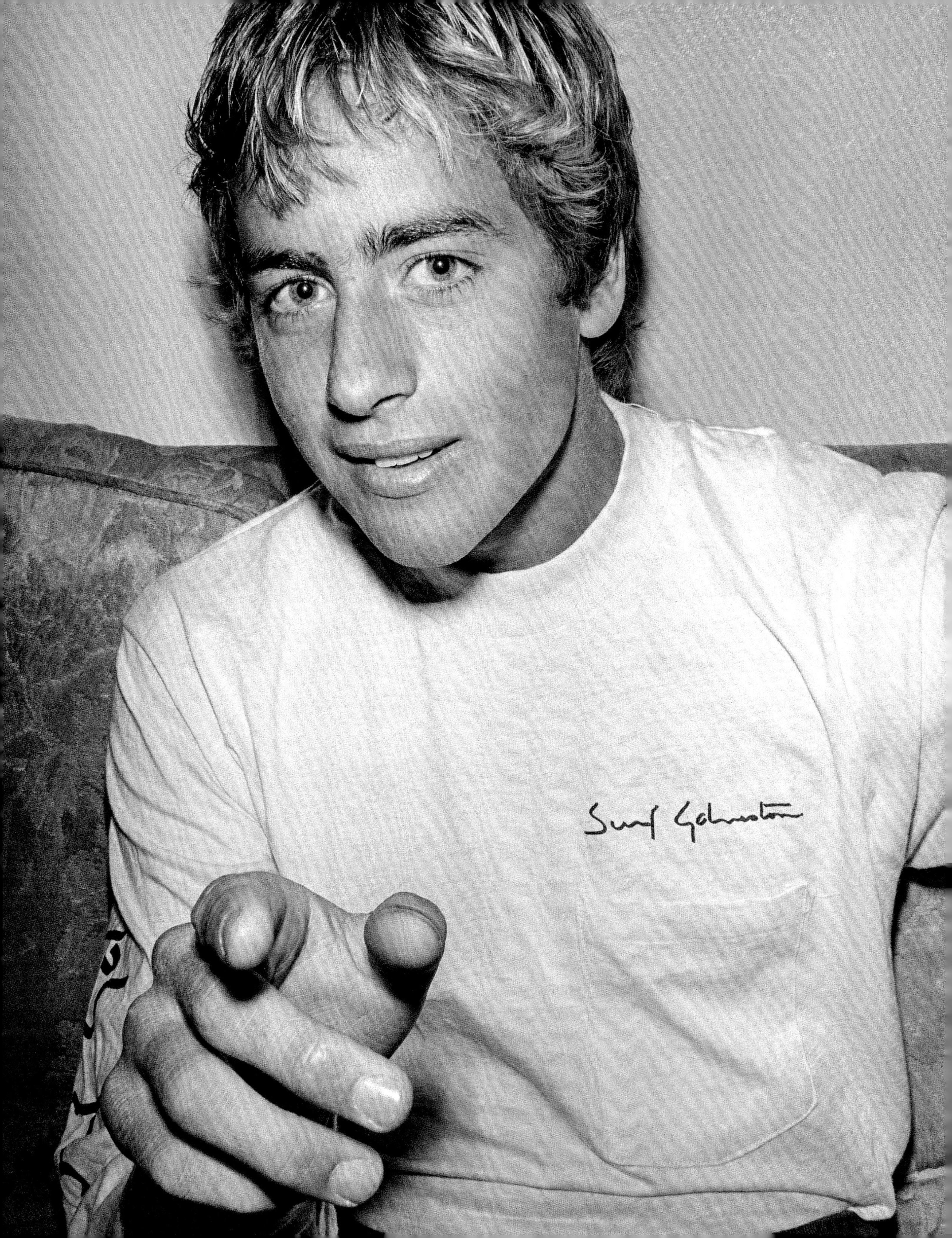

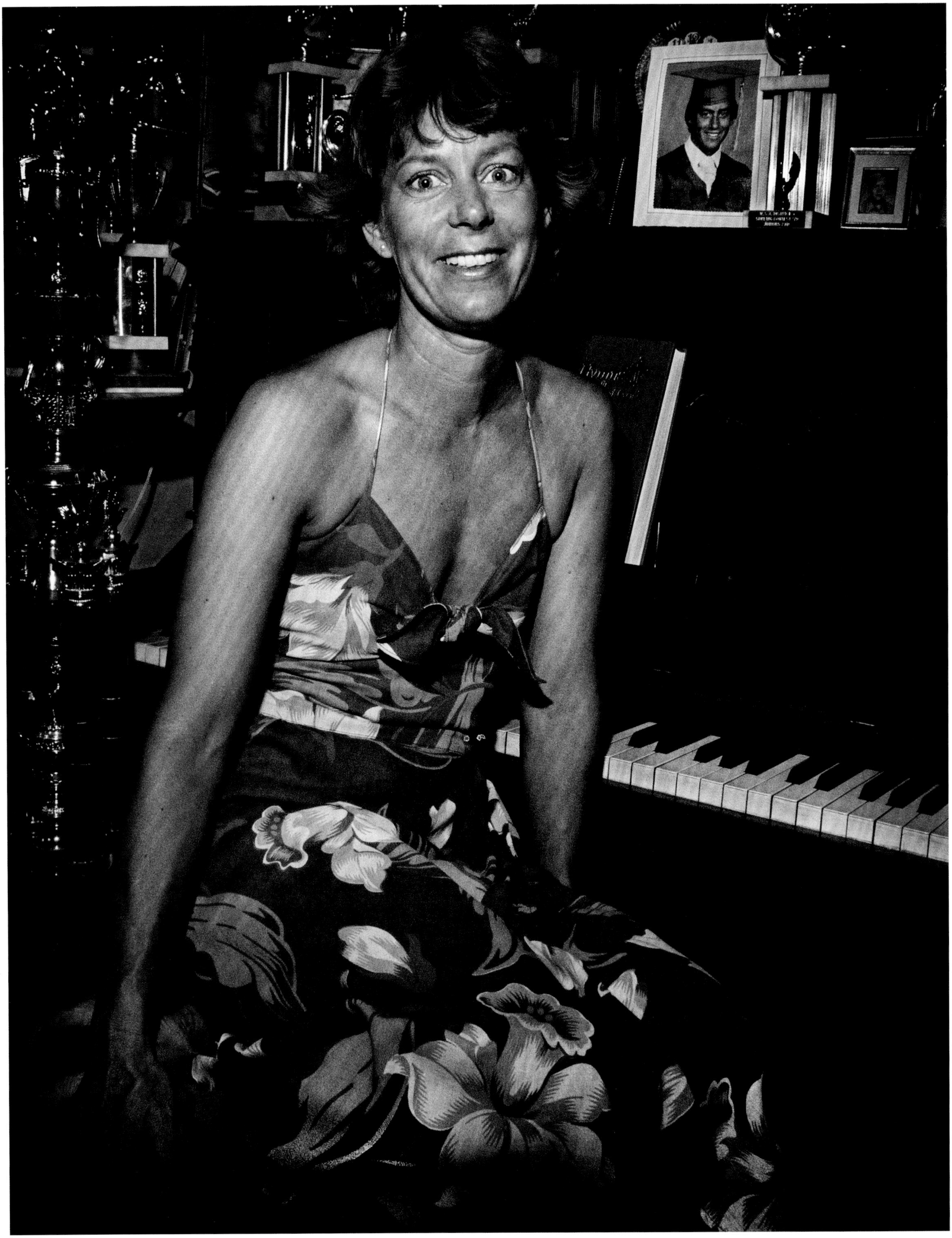

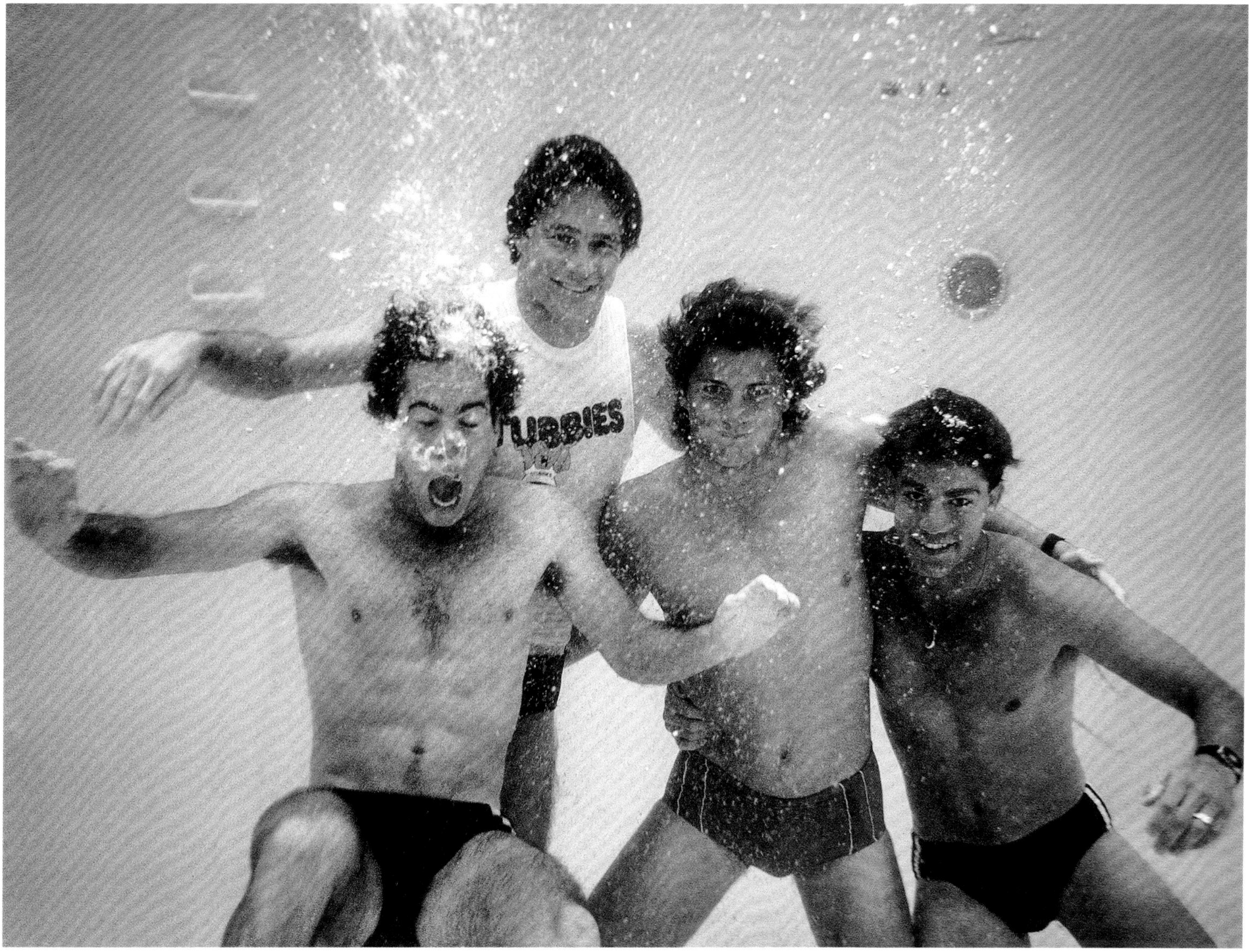

Pages 174–175
Headshots of Tommy for a magazine feature. I had just returned from Texas, bringing this "Surf Galveston" T-shirt as a gift, and Tommy insisted on wearing it for the photo shoot.

Opposite
Tommy's mom, Jeanine. This was shot for an interview in *Surfing* magazine. Mrs. Curren set the standard for devoted surf parenting, and Tommy would not be Tommy if not for Jeanine's unflagging energy and commitment to his career.

Above
Few knew that there were actually four George brothers: Greg, Matt, Sam, and Mike. When these four got together, mayhem quickly escalated. For use in a *Surfer* article, this image was shot in Mike's Brentwood apartment pool.

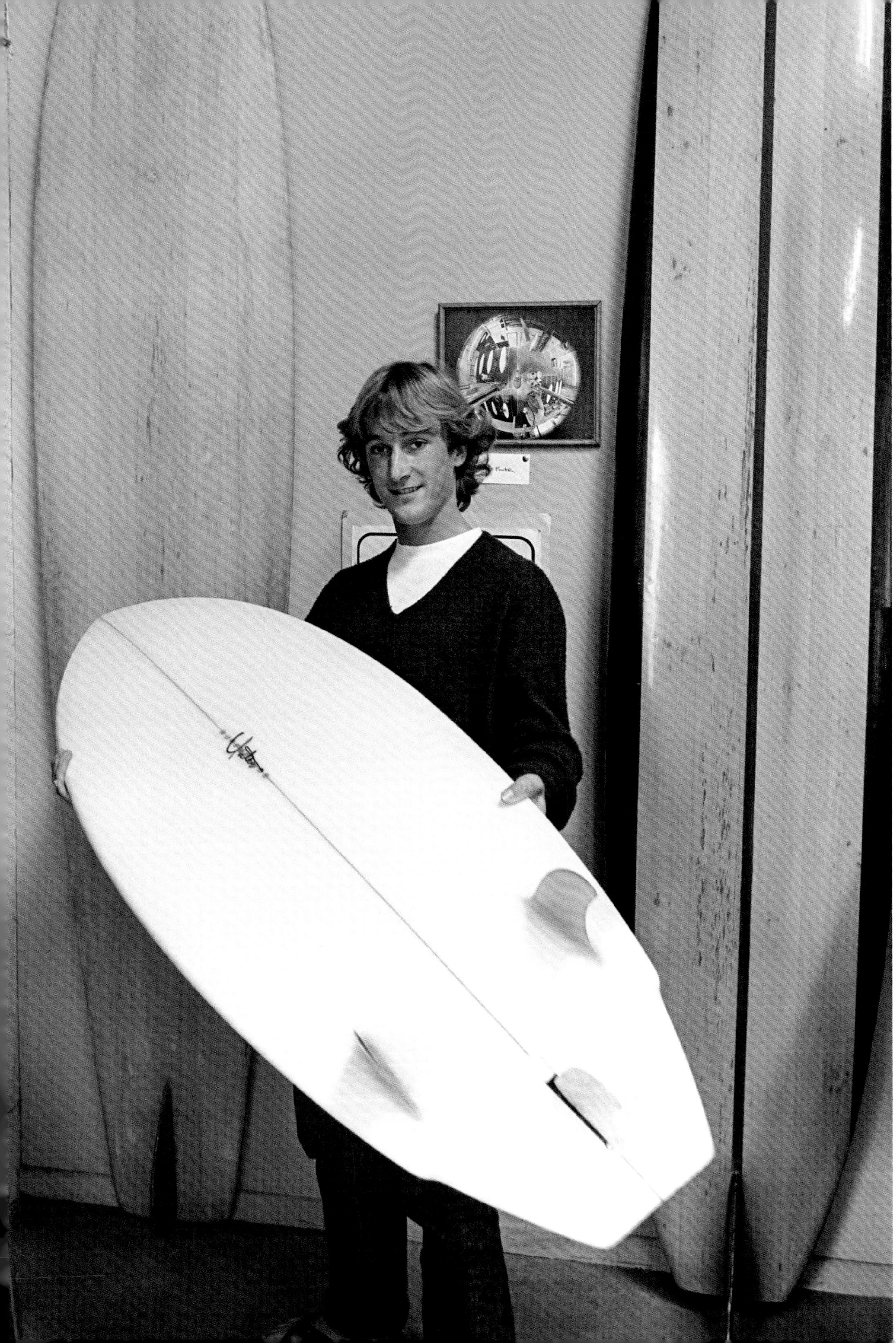

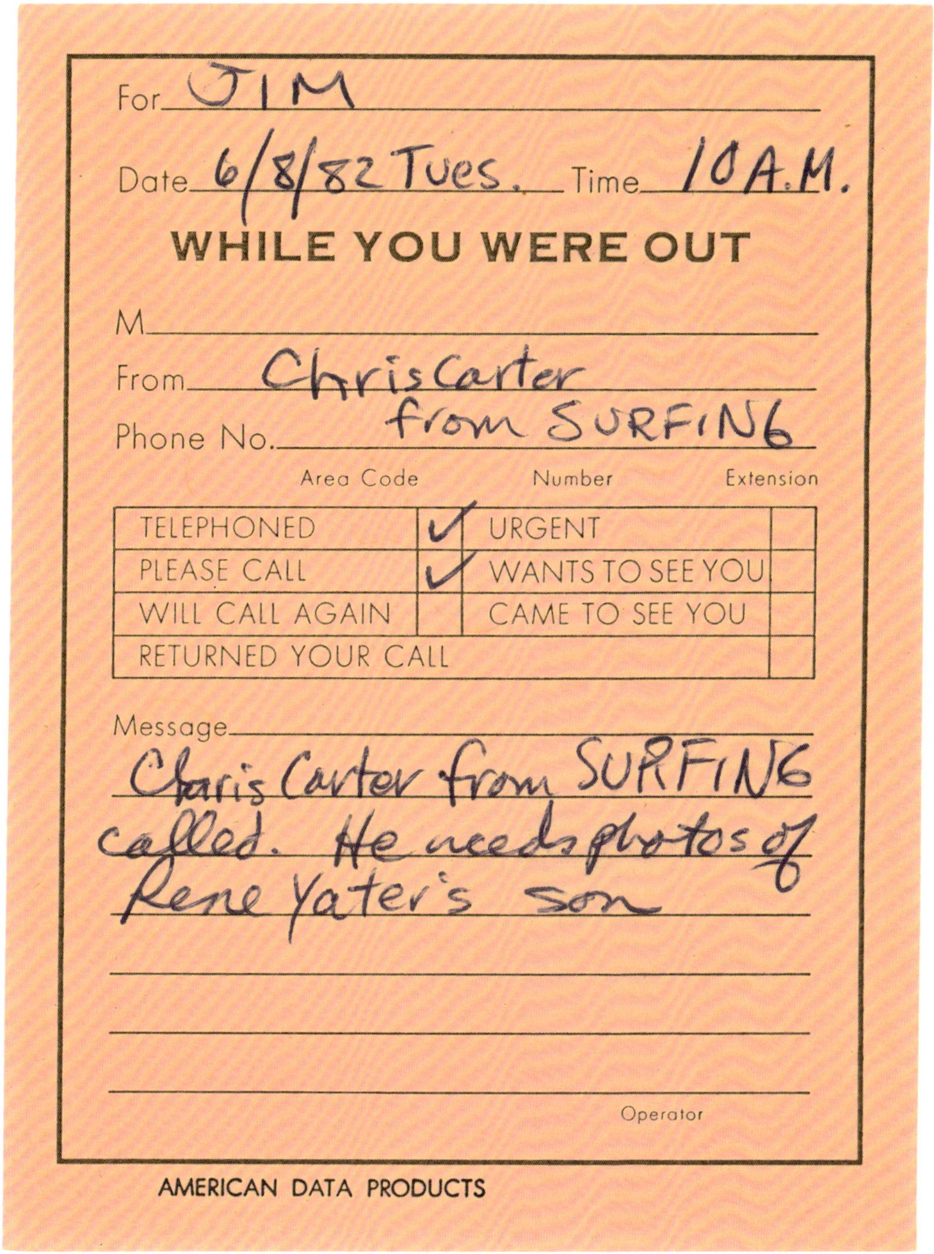

For JIM

Date 6/8/82 Tues. Time 10 A.M.

WHILE YOU WERE OUT

M

From Chris Carter

Phone No. from SURFING

Area Code Number Extension

TELEPHONED	✓	URGENT	
PLEASE CALL	✓	WANTS TO SEE YOU	
WILL CALL AGAIN		CAME TO SEE YOU	
RETURNED YOUR CALL			

Message

Chris Carter from SURFING called. He needs photos of Rene Yater's son

Operator

AMERICAN DATA PRODUCTS

Opposite

While Tom Curren became an archetype for the growing pro movement, Lauran Yater, son of legendary Santa Barbara shaper Reynolds "Renny" Yater, personified the region's soulful, anti-commercial aesthetic: no sponsors, only clean lines on local waves, riding self-shaped boards.

Above

"WHILE YOU WERE OUT" request from *Surfing* magazine's then–senior editor, Chris Carter, who would later go on to create the science-fiction drama television series *The X-Files*.

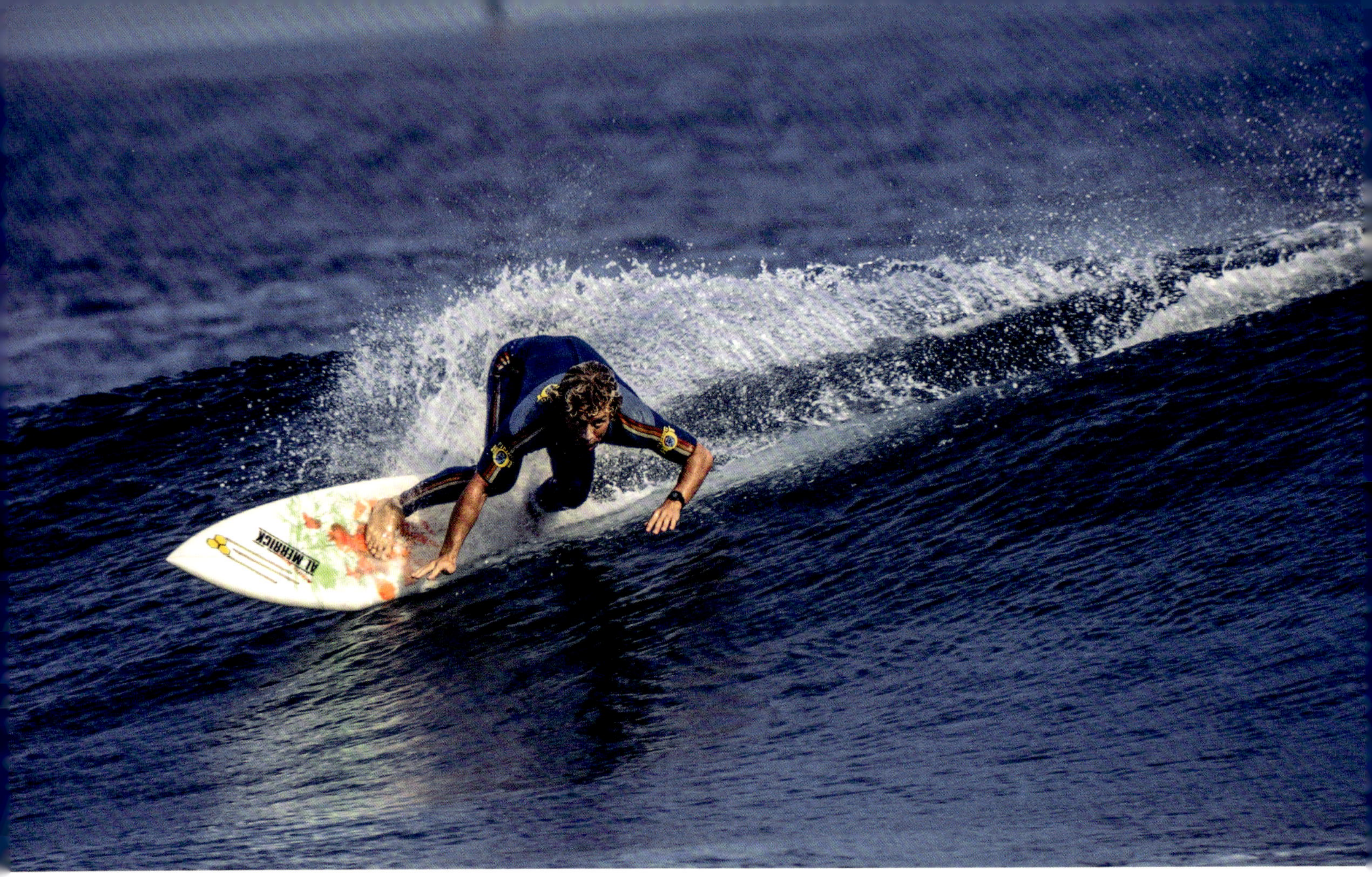
AL MERRICK

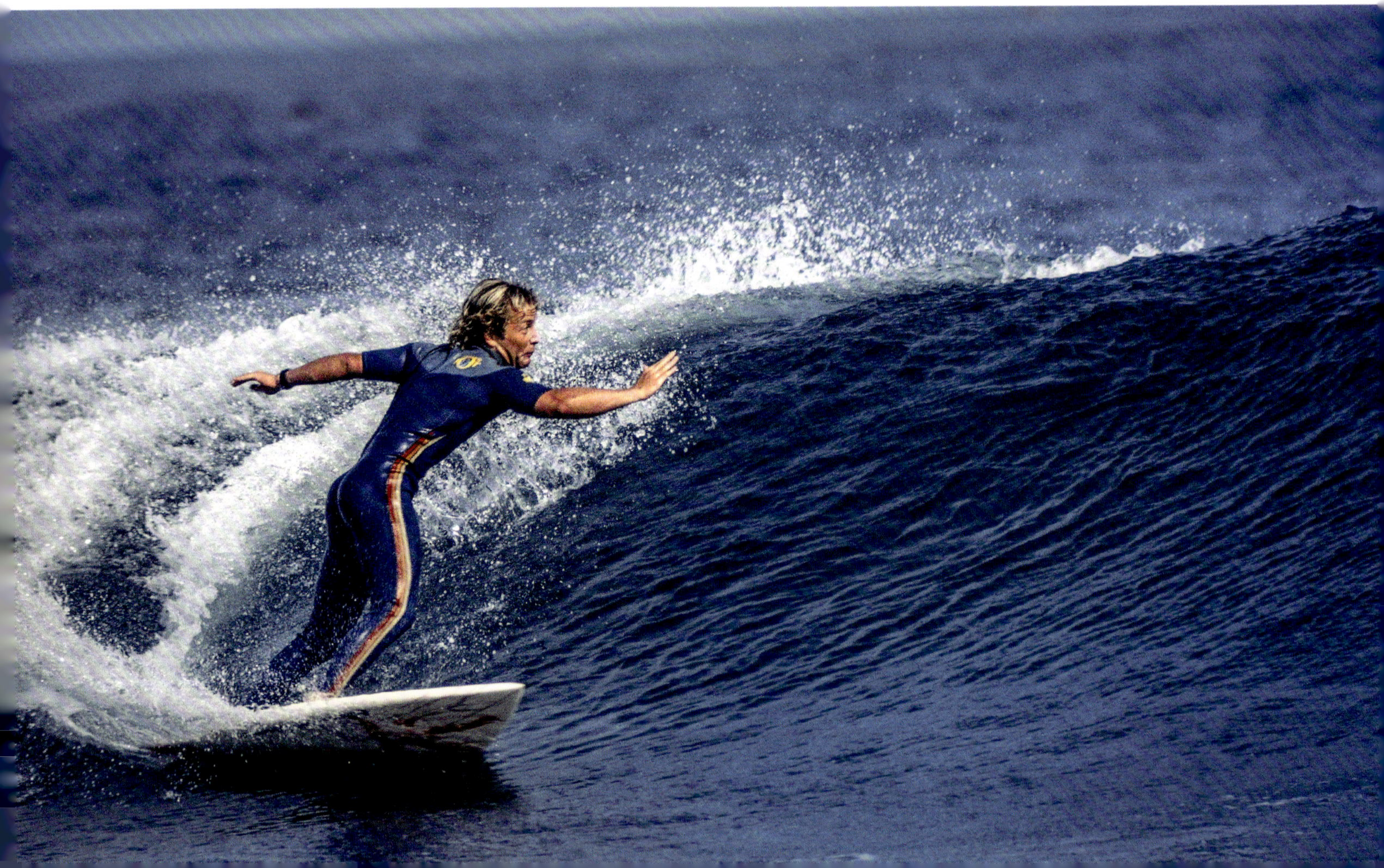

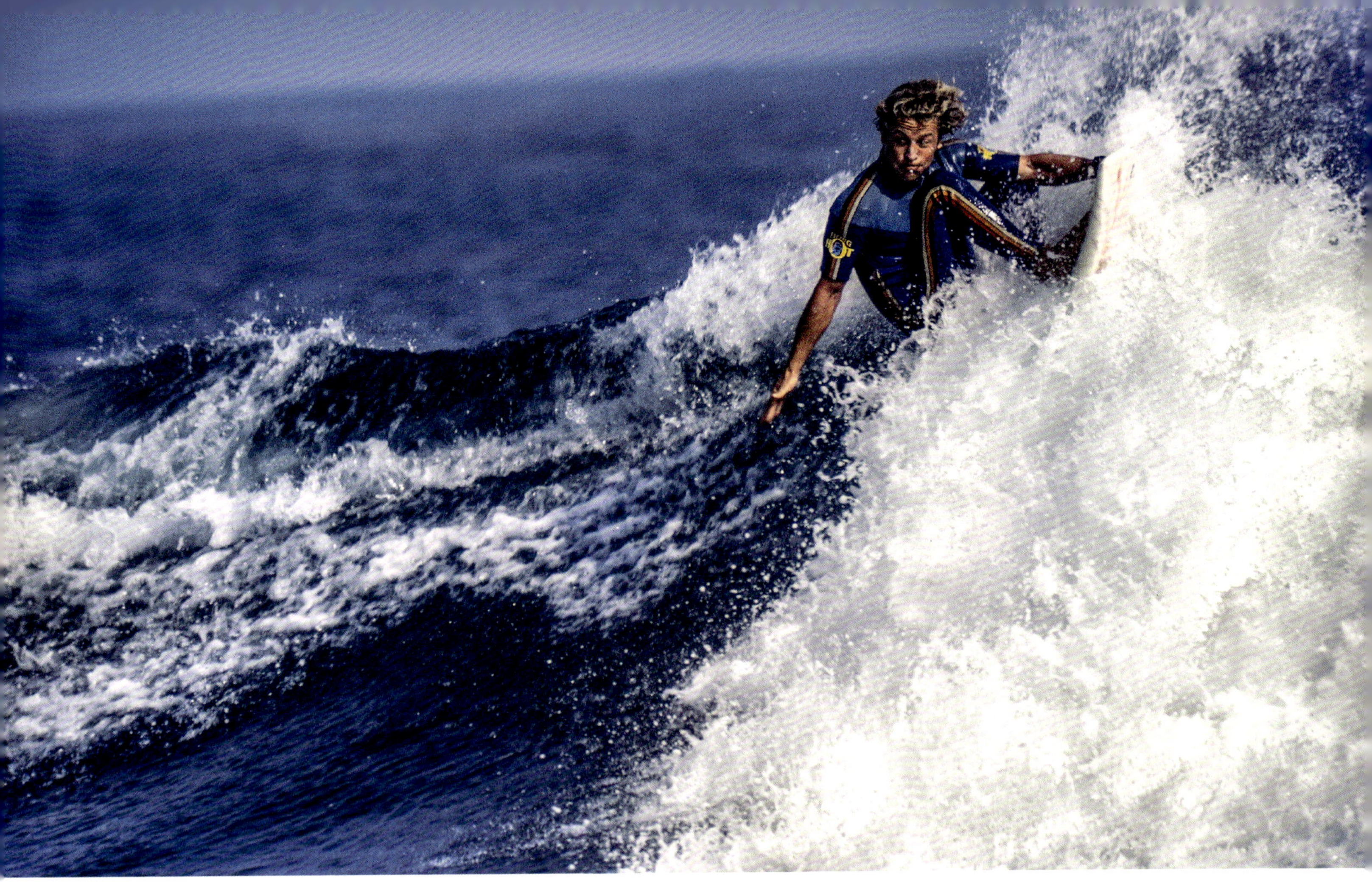

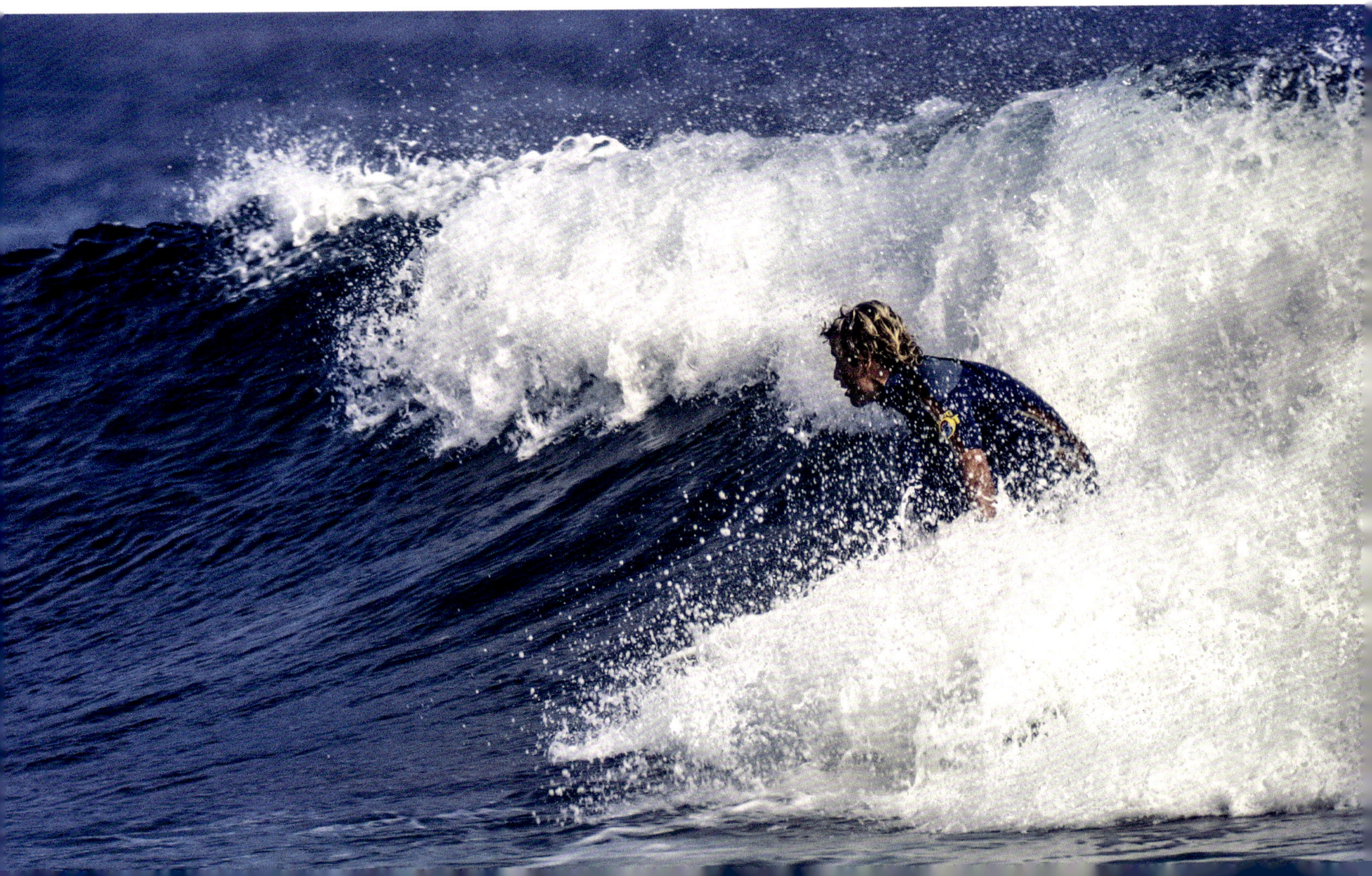

Previous

Davey Smith at Secos. Davey's backside cutbacks always brought to mind a Porsche 917 powering through a tight corner at Le Mans. You could almost hear the engine's whine as he downshifted through the gears without any loss of speed.

Spread

Secos, with its prime south-swell window and perfect-afternoon-quality lighting, was our go-to summer photo studio, and the number of published photos taken here made the one-hour drive south from Santa Barbara well worth it. This is one of the first images of Tommy riding a three-fin thruster, having only recently made the transition from his beloved twin-fins.

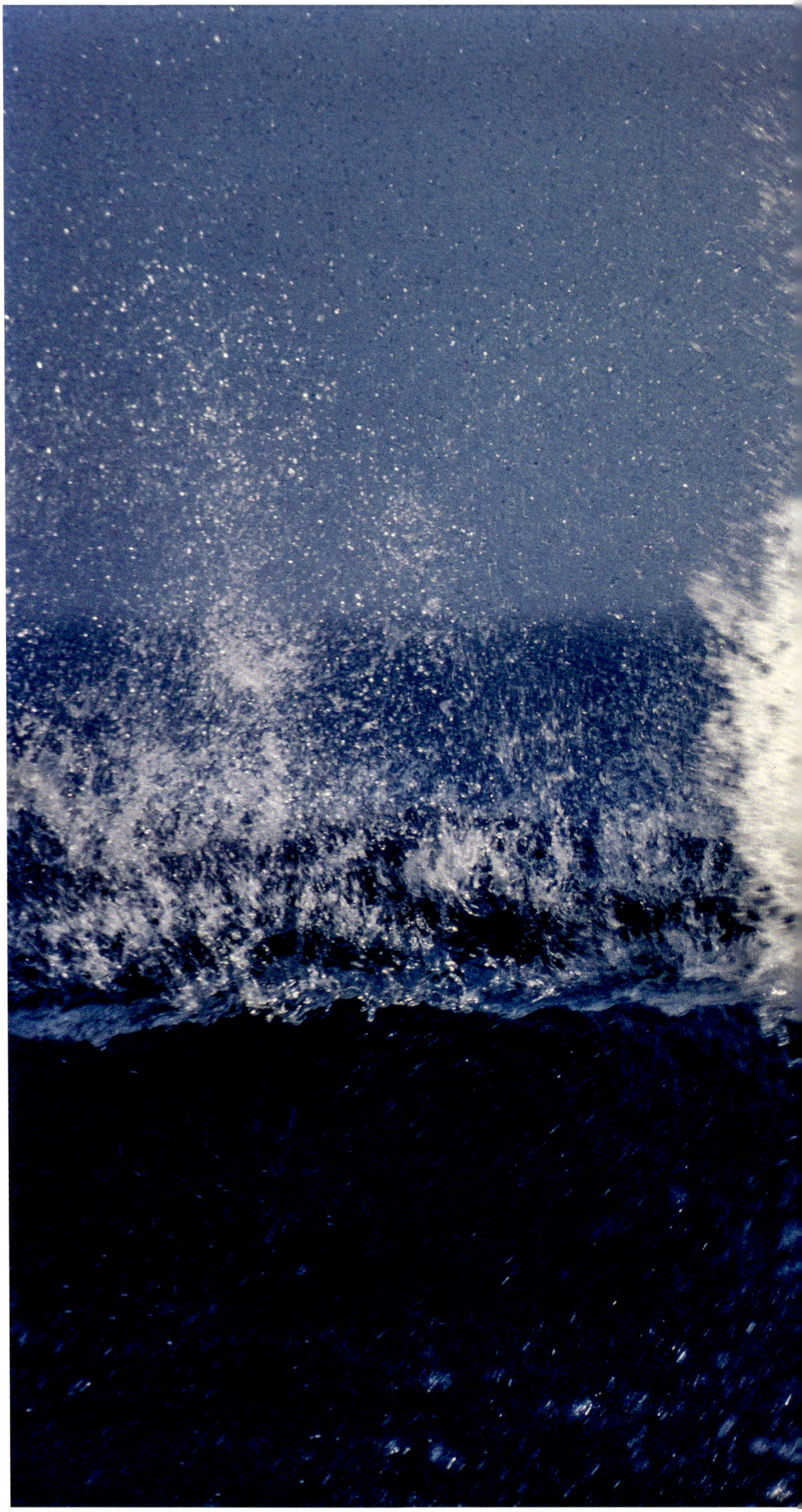

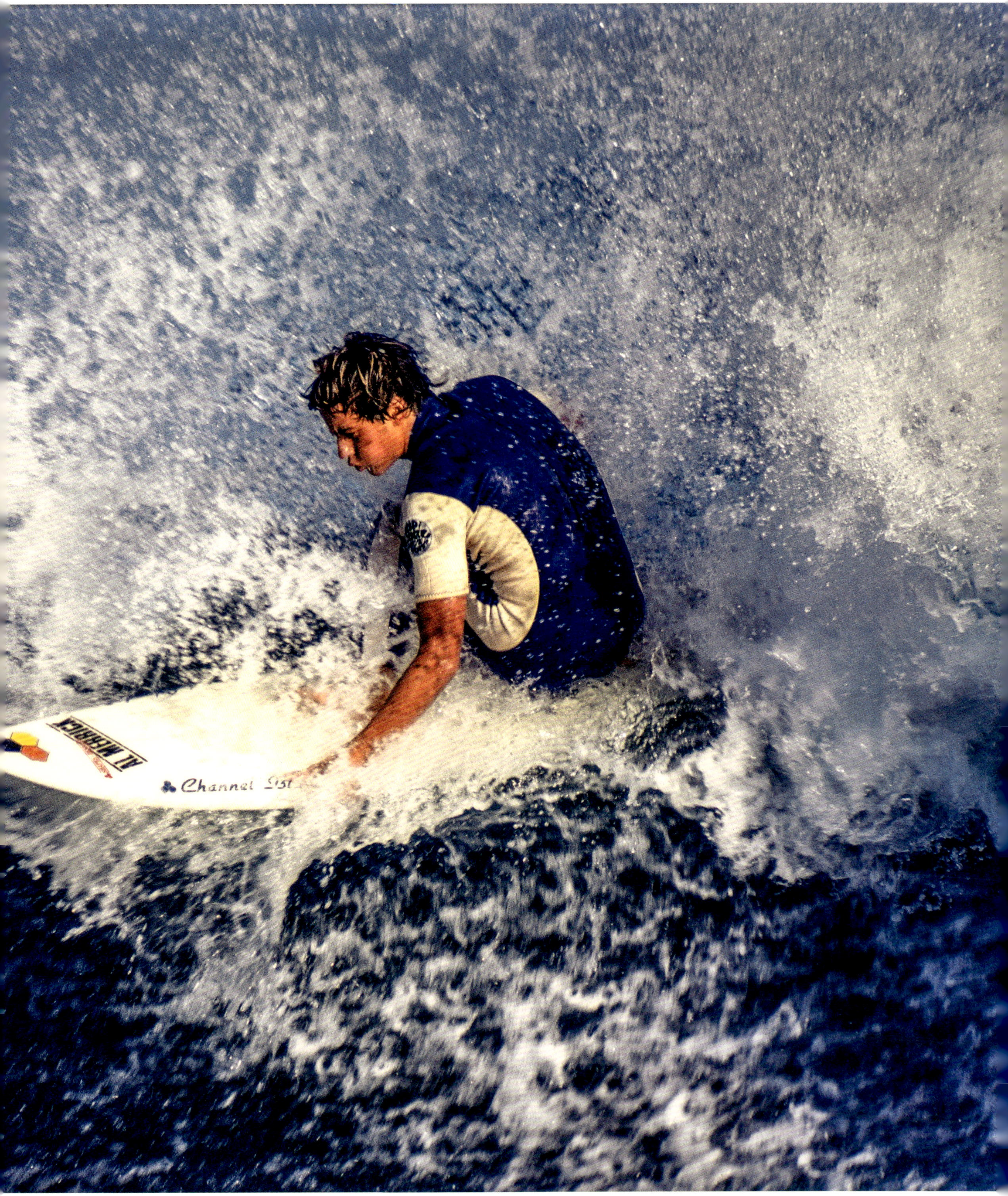
AL MERRICK

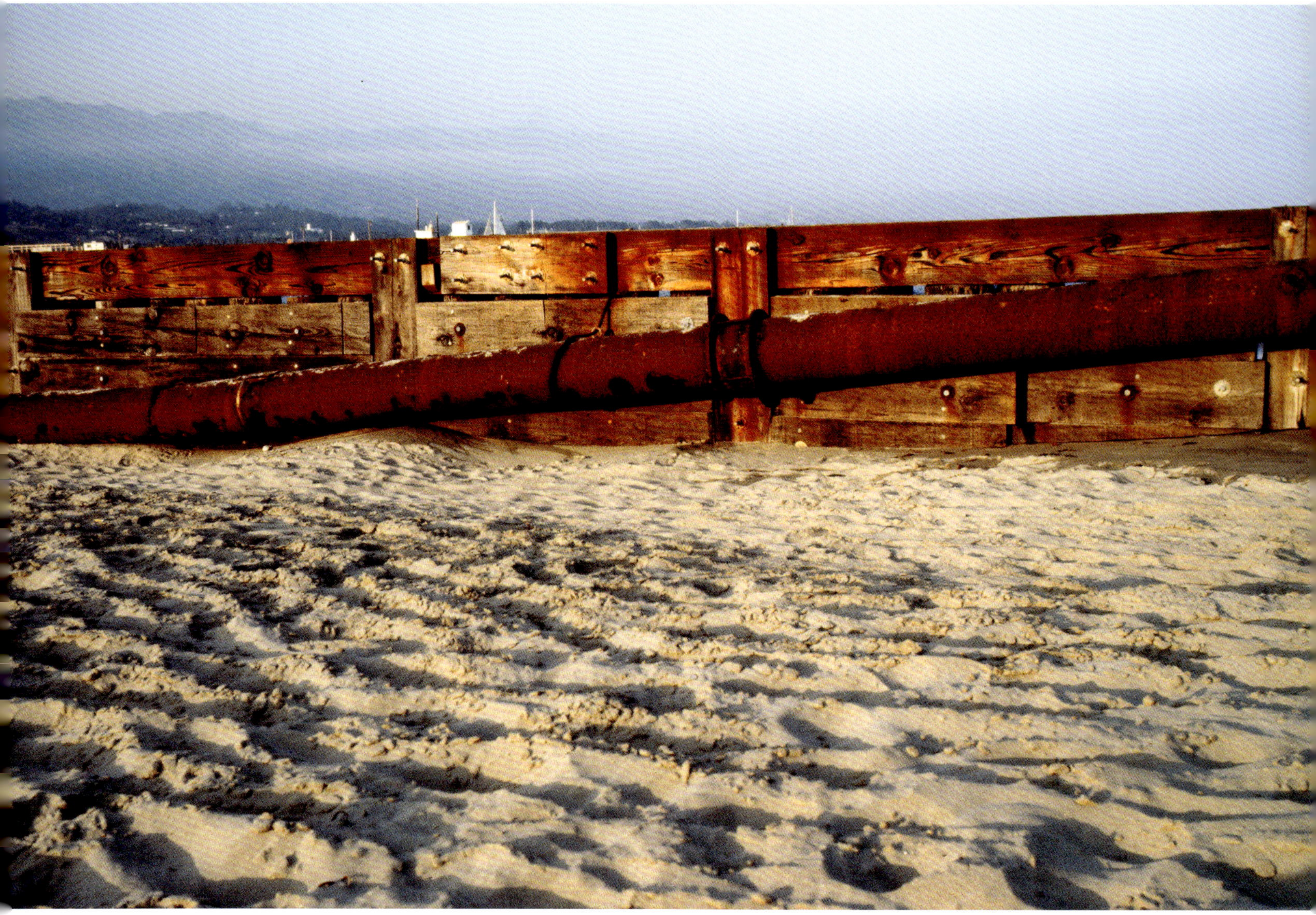

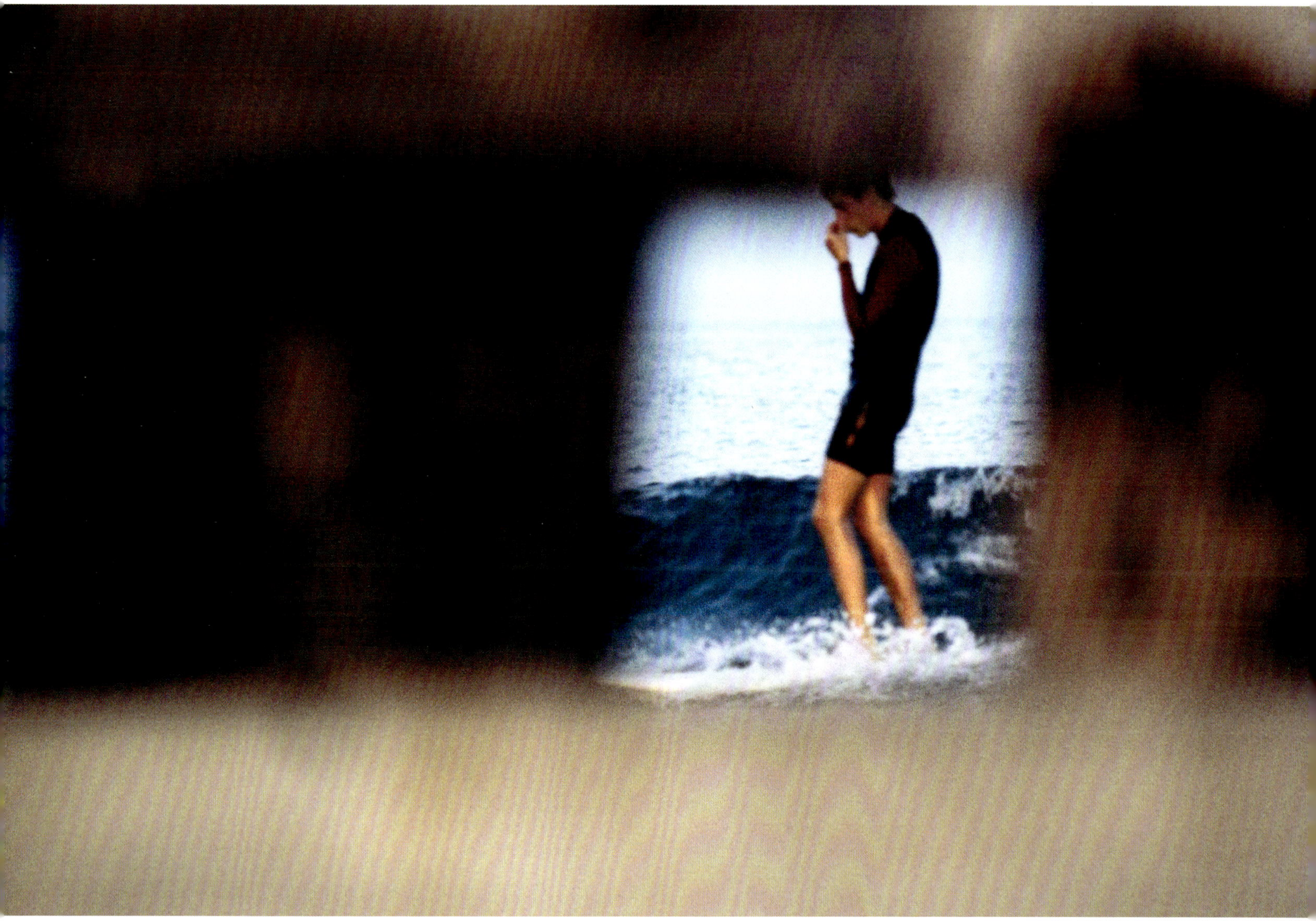

Riding out the flat Santa Barbara summers meant for some creative diversions, like riding ripples along the harbor dredge pipe inside Sandspit. Tommy, pictured here riding one of his dad Pat's eleven-foot elephant guns.

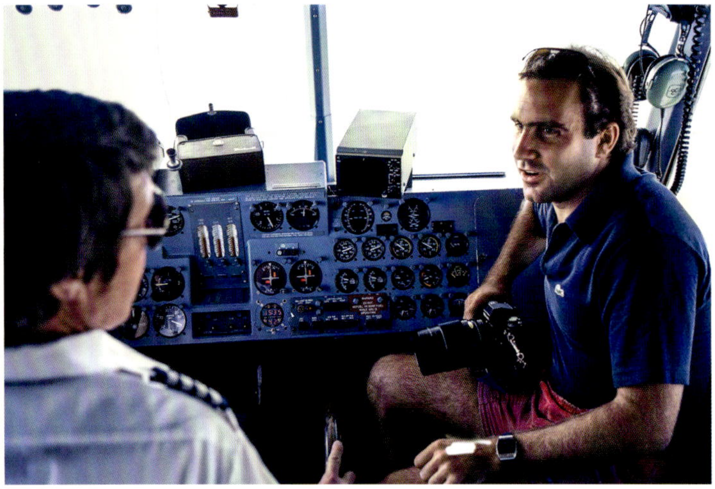

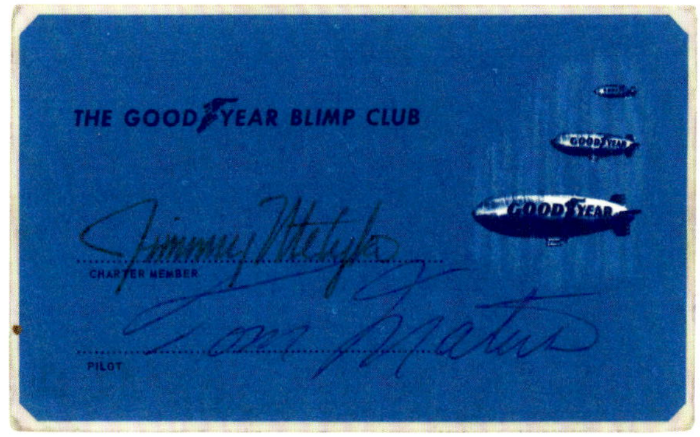

View From The Blimp

When, to help cover finals day at the inaugural Op Pro in Huntington Beach, *Surfing* magazine photo editor Larry Moore secured me a spot on the Goodyear Blimp, I knew it was going to be a thrill. What I didn't know was just how much of a thrill it would turn out to be. We motored down from the blimp's hangar in Long Beach and circled the contest site for most of the day. I was the only surfer among the media on board, which probably explained why I was the only one who hooted when Cheyne Horan pulled off a last-minute backside 360 to win the event.

We were about halfway back to Long Beach when the pilot suddenly got up, announcing that he needed to use the toilet. "Who wants to fly the blimp?" he asked. Everybody froze, myself included. But I was closest, so he sat me down at the controls. "Can he crash this thing?" asked one of the TV cameramen, more than a little nervous. "This isn't a thing, it's the Blimp," said the pilot. "And yes." Then he ducked into the bathroom.

Two pedals on the floor controlled the blimp's right-and-left orientation. Next to the seat, on the right, was a vertical steering wheel, which controlled the blimp's fore-and-aft pitch. Simple—and it was smooth sailing for about a minute, until the blimp's nose began to rise. I slowly spun the wheel forward. Nothing. I spun the wheel harder. Finally, the nose began to tilt back down, but then it kept going down, past horizontal, and we were headed for the deck. Flashes of the Hindenburg disaster instantly came to mind as I spun the wheel again, desperately bringing the nose back up. At the same time, I'd somehow jammed my foot against the right rudder pedal, so as well as going up and down like a rocking horse, we were spinning like a top. I'd never been so relieved as when that pilot finished his business and took back the controls. "What have you been doing with my blimp?" he asked with a mischievous smile. Wiping my brow, I expressed concern that footage of the Goodyear Blimp weaving drunkenly over Long Beach would be sure to make the evening news. "No chance," he said. "We've got every local TV channel's cameramen on board with us."
Many years later, I showed these images to a young photographer. "Cool," he said. "I didn't know you had drones back then."
"Yeah," I said. "They just weren't as easy to fly."

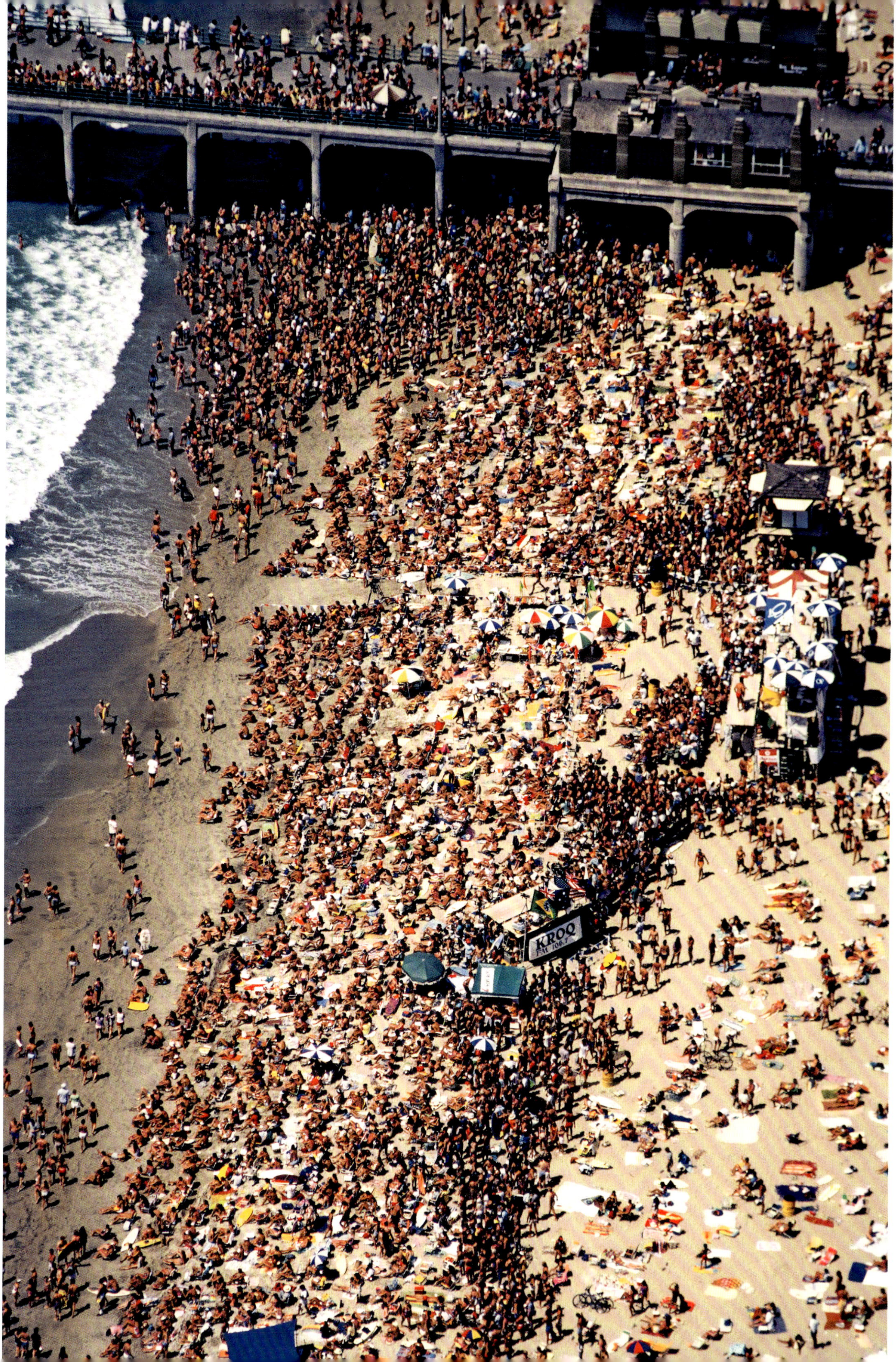
KROQ
FM 106.7

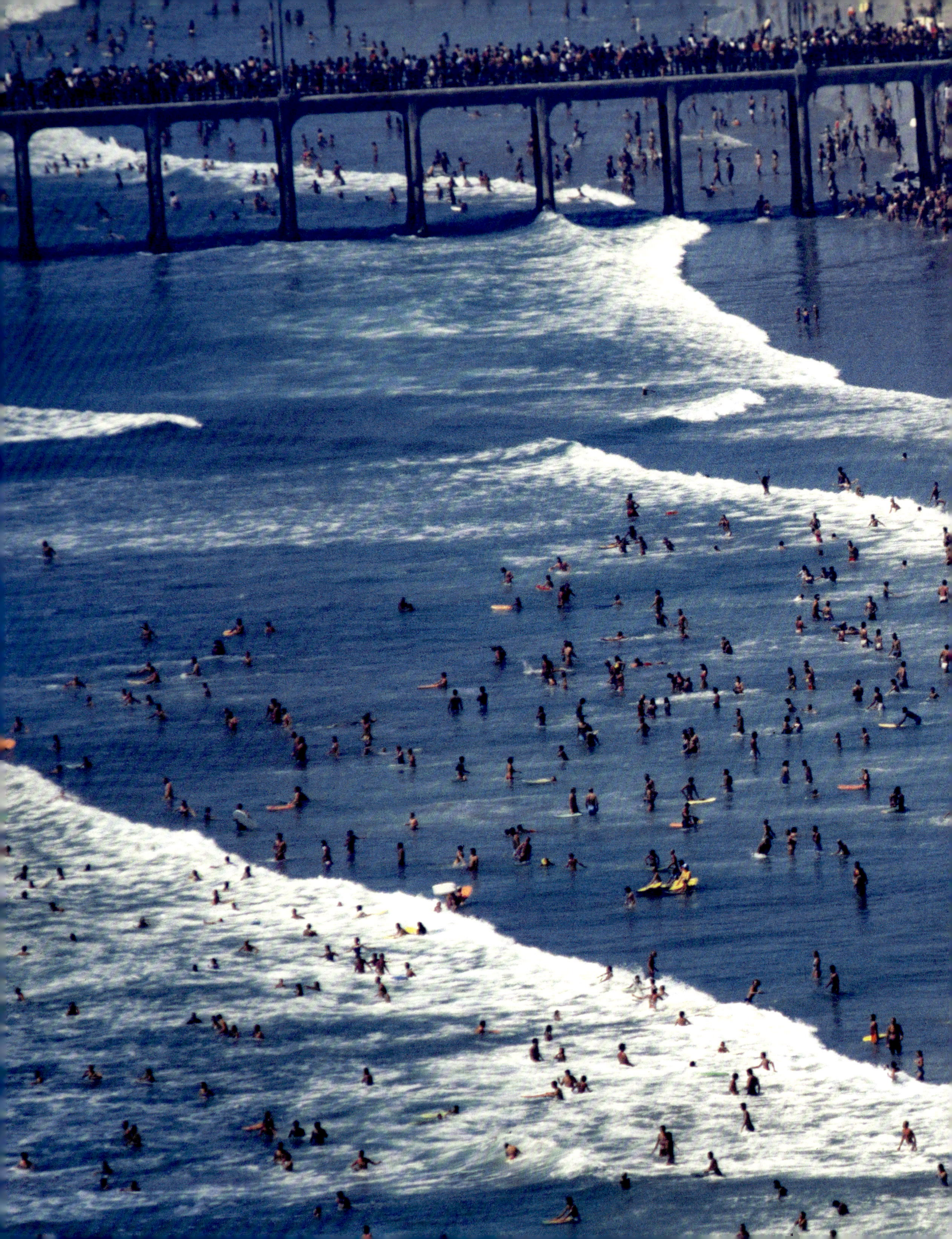

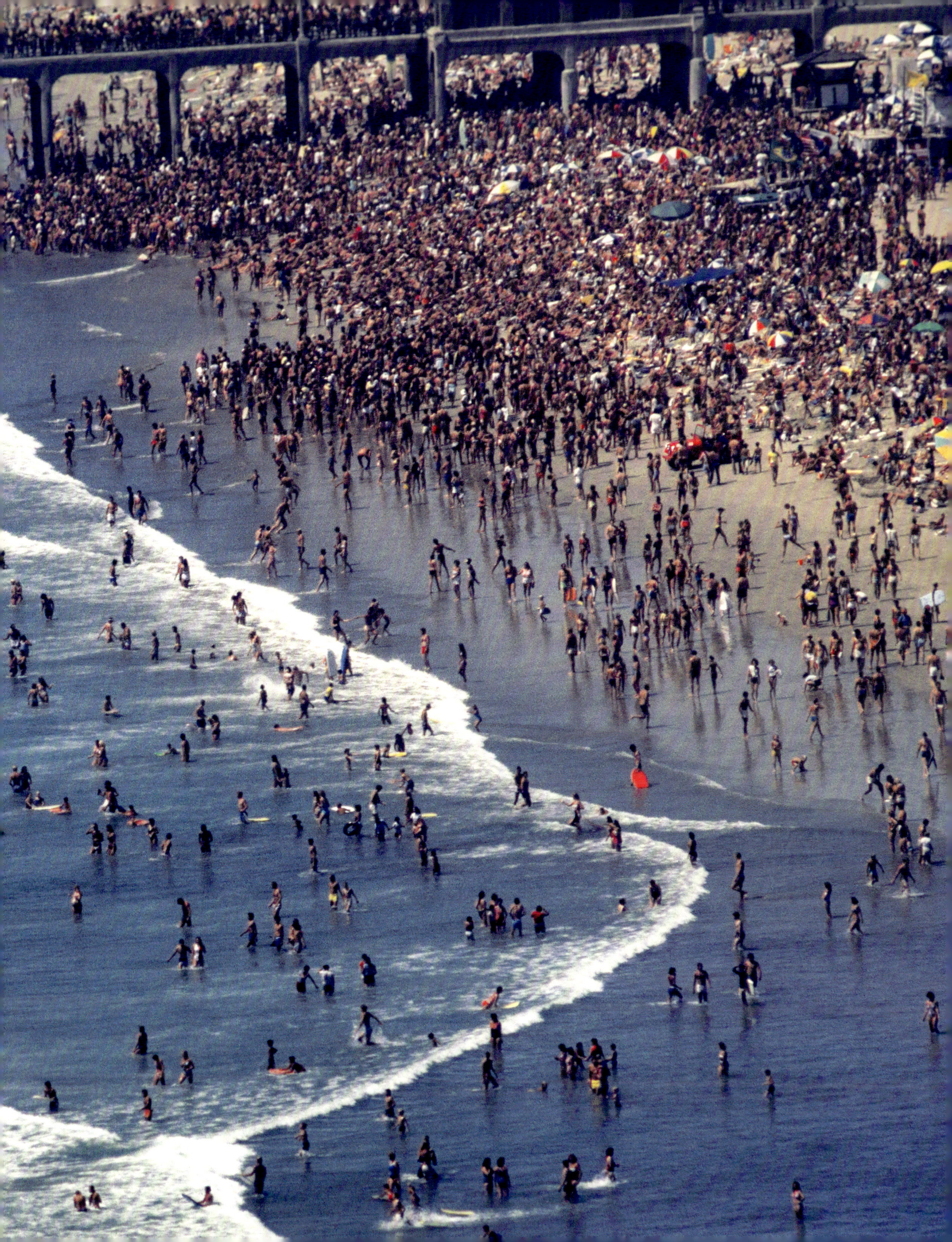

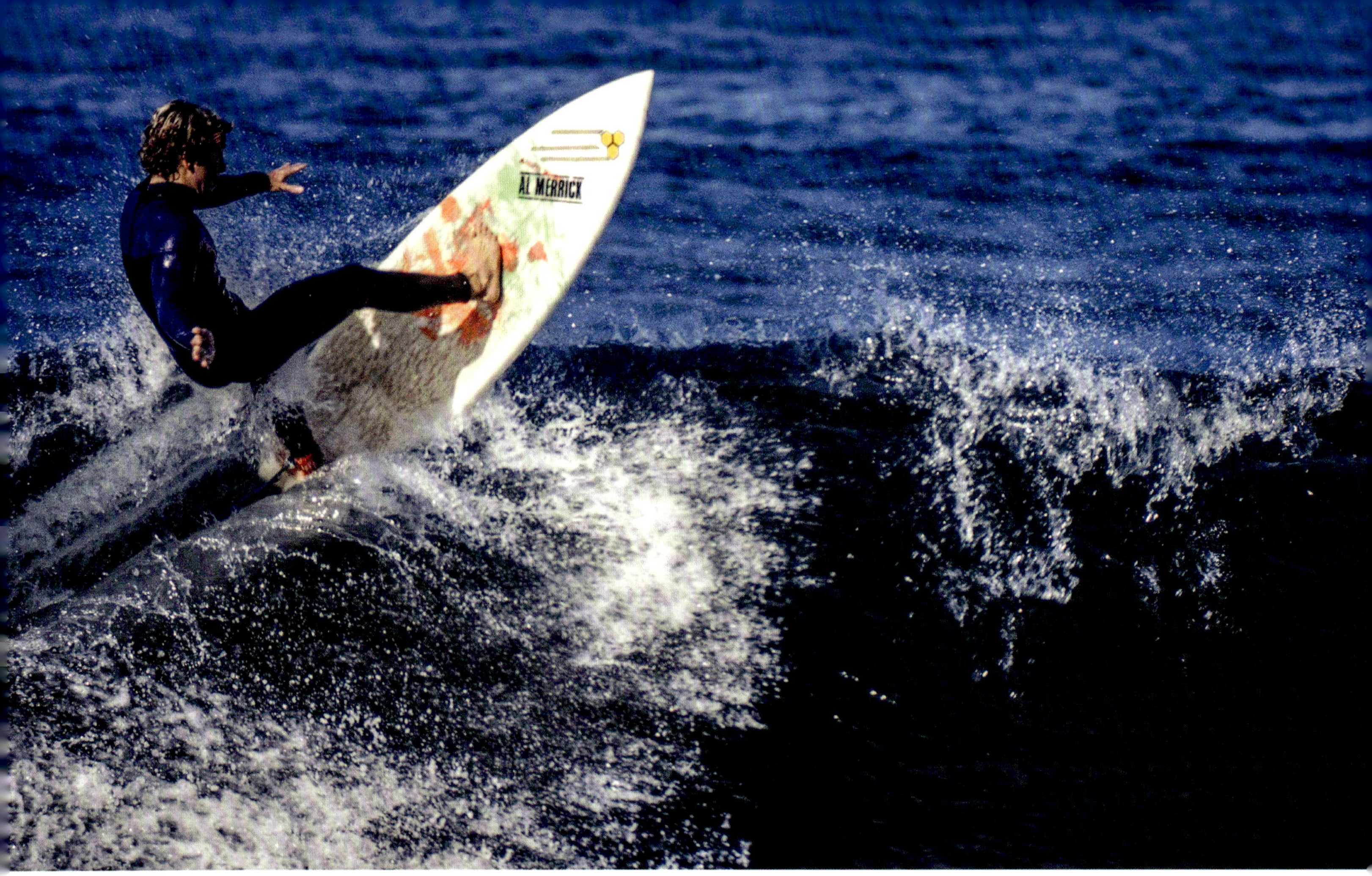
AL MERRICK

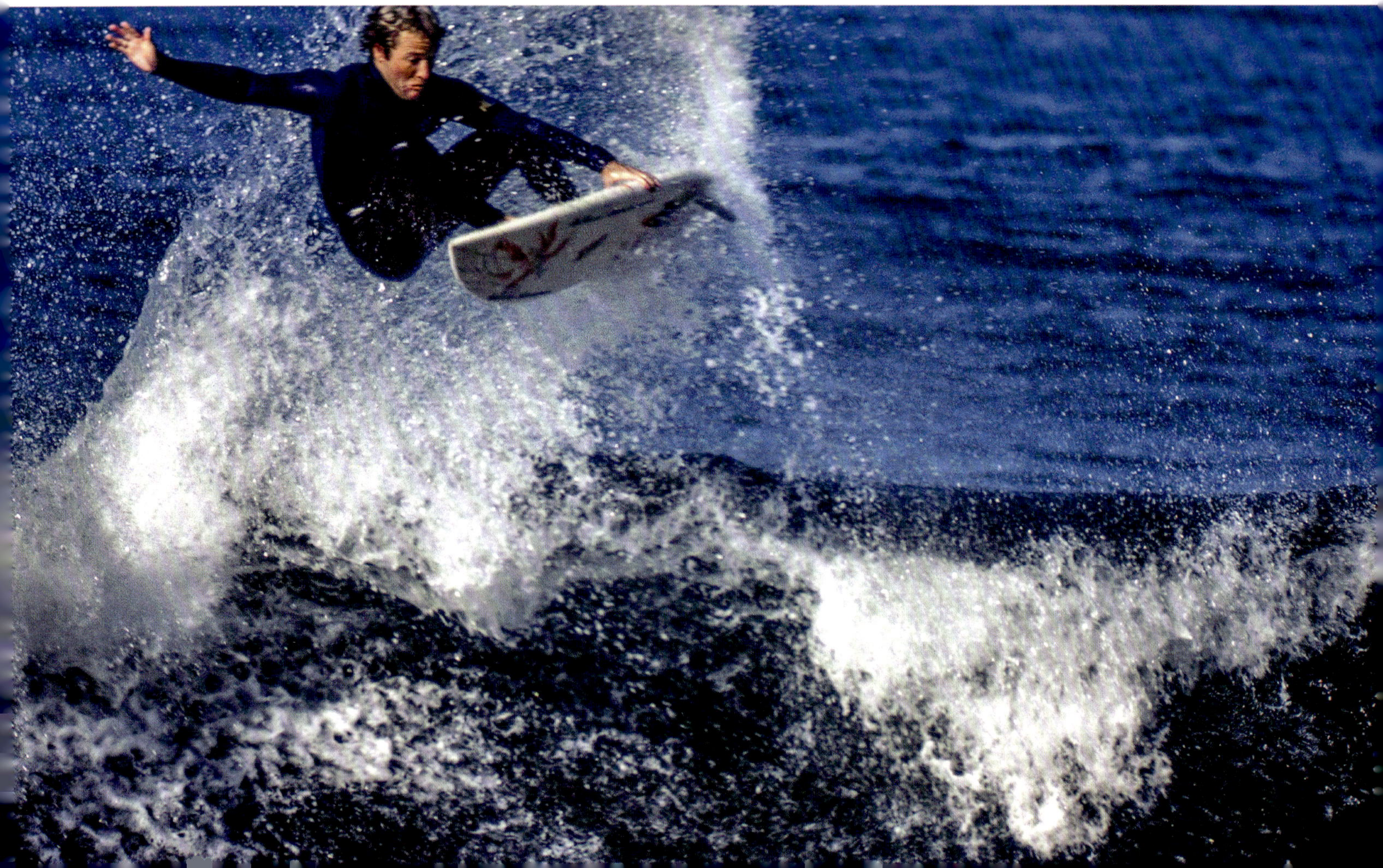

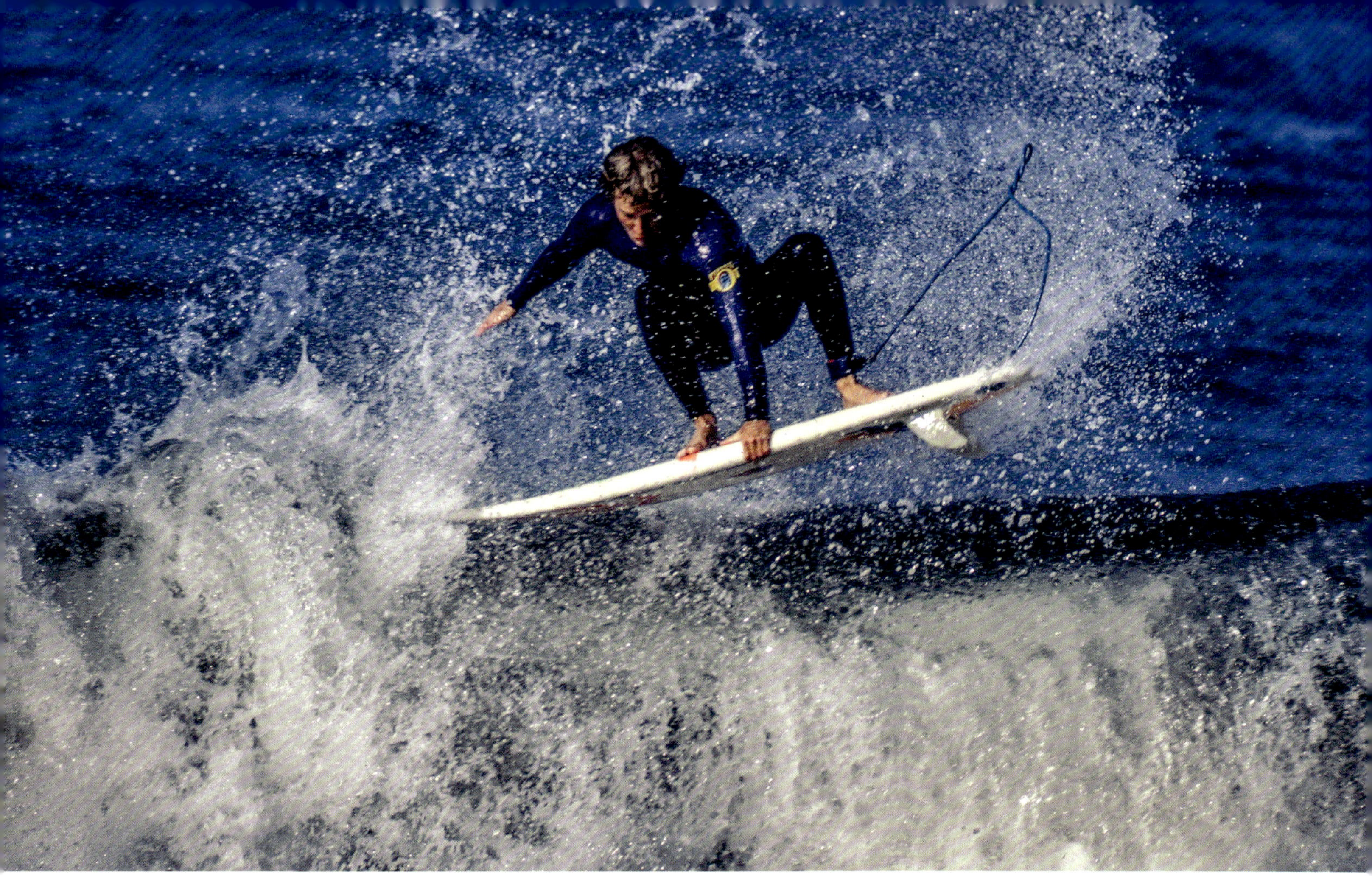

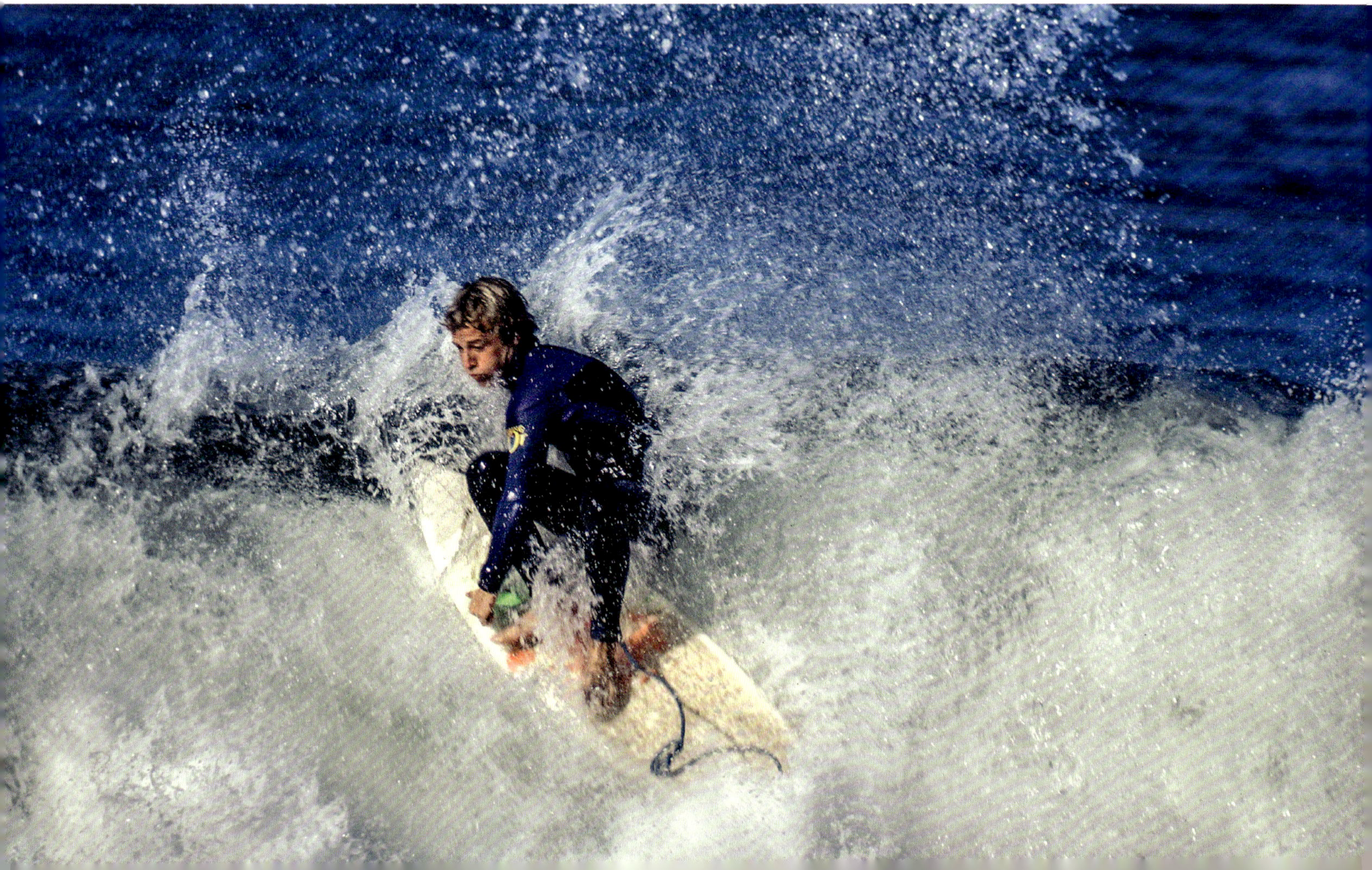

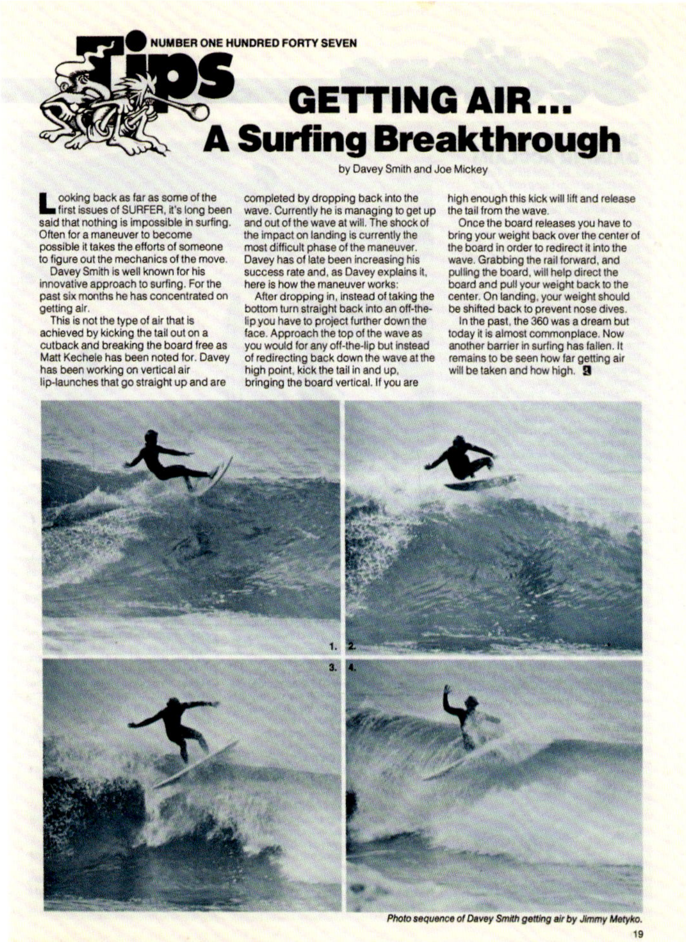

Tips NUMBER ONE HUNDRED FORTY SEVEN

GETTING AIR... A Surfing Breakthrough

by Davey Smith and Joe Mickey

Looking back as far as some of the first issues of SURFER, it's long been said that nothing is impossible in surfing. Often for a maneuver to become possible it takes the efforts of someone to figure out the mechanics of the move.

Davey Smith is well known for his innovative approach to surfing. For the past six months he has concentrated on getting air.

This is not the type of air that is achieved by kicking the tail out on a cutback and breaking the board free as Matt Kechele has been noted for. Davey has been working on vertical air lip-launches that go straight up and are completed by dropping back into the wave. Currently he is managing to get up and out of the wave at will. The shock of the impact on landing is currently the most difficult phase of the maneuver. Davey has of late been increasing his success rate and, as Davey explains it, here is how the maneuver works:

After dropping in, instead of taking the bottom turn straight back into an off-the-lip you have to project further down the face. Approach the top of the wave as you would for any off-the-lip but instead of redirecting back down the wave at the high point, kick the tail in and up, bringing the board vertical. If you are high enough this kick will lift and release the tail from the wave.

Once the board releases you have to bring your weight back over the center of the board in order to redirect it into the wave. Grabbing the rail forward, and pulling the board, will help direct the board and pull your weight back to the center. On landing, your weight should be shifted back to prevent nose dives.

In the past, the 360 was a dream but today it is almost commonplace. Now another barrier in surfing has fallen. It remains to be seen how far getting air will be taken and how high.

1. 2. 3. 4.

Photo sequence of Davey Smith getting air by Jimmy Metyko.

19

A Surfing Breakthrough

Capturing the first successfully completed aerial on film didn't happen by chance. Beginning in early 1982, Davey Smith and I made this our mission. We would sit in the car before a surf session, talking strategy: him working out how to land one, me working out how to shoot it. It was extremely hard to manually follow-focus his first aerial attempts, and while through plenty of trial and error Davey eventually upped his success rate, we still didn't have the photographic proof we needed. Which, in our case, meant a completed sequence.

Davey's first aerial was in 1975 at Rocky Point on the North Shore of Hawaii, photographed by legendary surf photographer Bob Barbour, since we had seen images of surfers flying up and out of waves. Guys like Santa Cruz's Kevin Reed and Hawaii's phenomenal Larry Bertlemann getting their fins free above the lip would appear in the surf magazines, and by 1981 talented East Coast surfer Matt Kechele was having success getting his board off and on the wave face. But a true completed aerial had never "made the mag." And back then, if it didn't appear in the magazines, it never happened. Finally, during September's Hurricane Olivia swell, it all came together at Emma Wood. The resulting sequence was featured in *Surfer* magazine's "Tips" section, Vol. 24, No. 2, touted as "a surfing breakthrough." It gave Davey a little something to smile about, especially as he'd recently achieved a breakthrough of a different kind: the first ankle broken in an aerial attempt.

Previous and this page

Davey Smith pulling the first aerial spin.

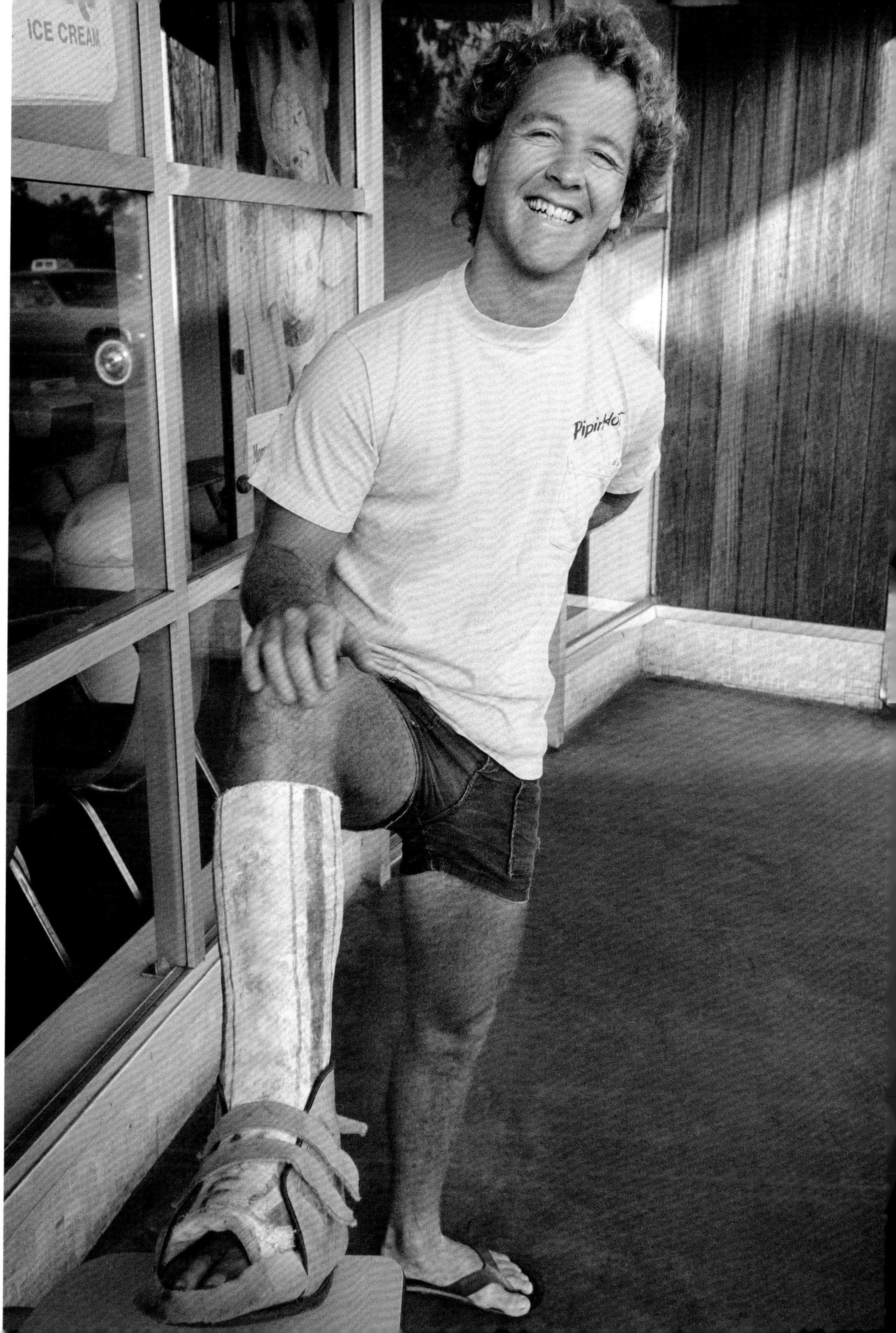
ICE CREAM

I first met Jamie Brisick when Jeff Novak and Steve Brisick started to bring Steve's younger brother with them to shoot. The mischievous kid ripped. Fourteen-year-old Jamie on a Geoff McCoy Lazor Zap single-fin: this was shot just months before Jamie followed his Woodland Hills/Malibu role model Willy Morris to the Channel Islands stable.

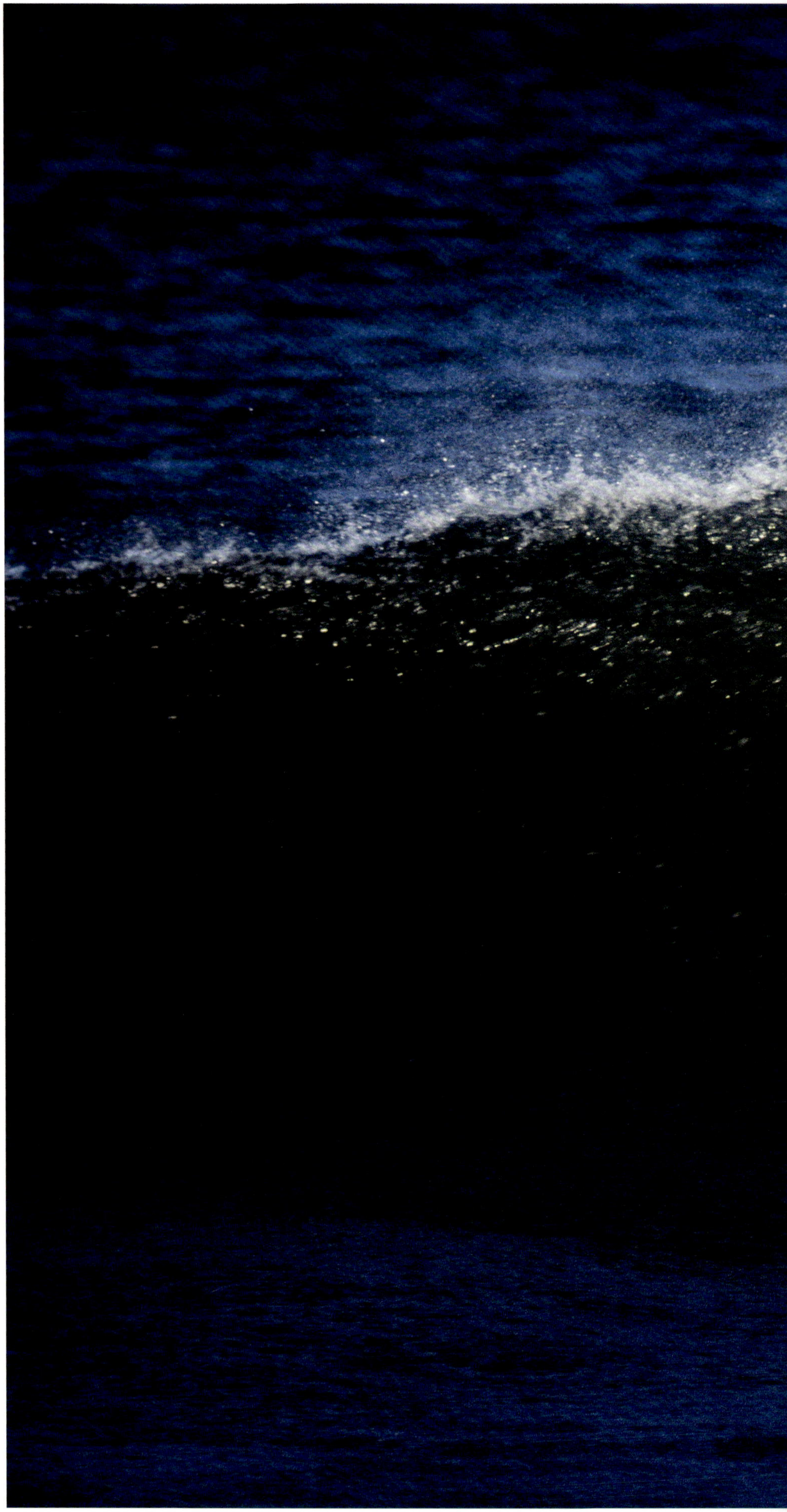

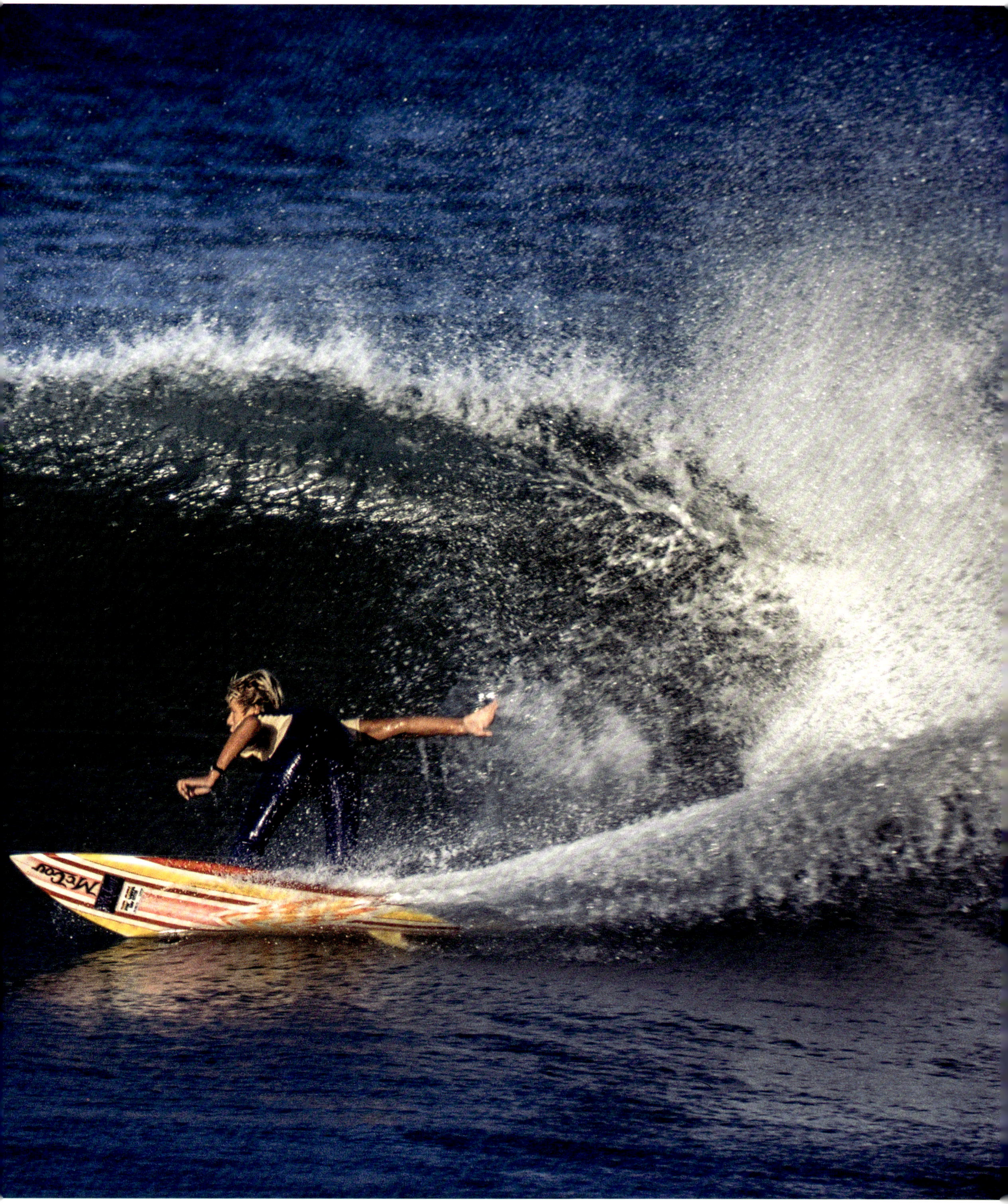
McCoy

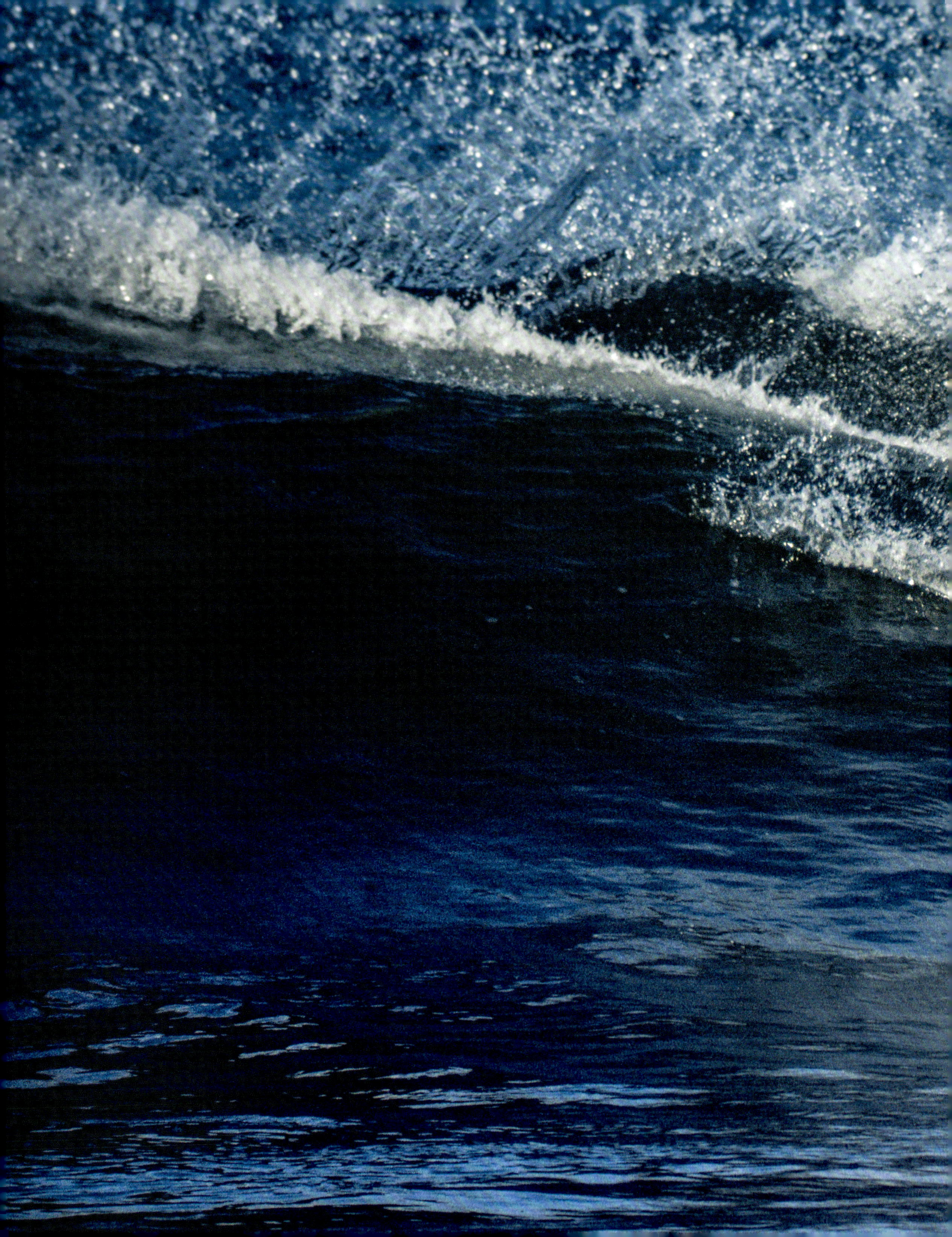

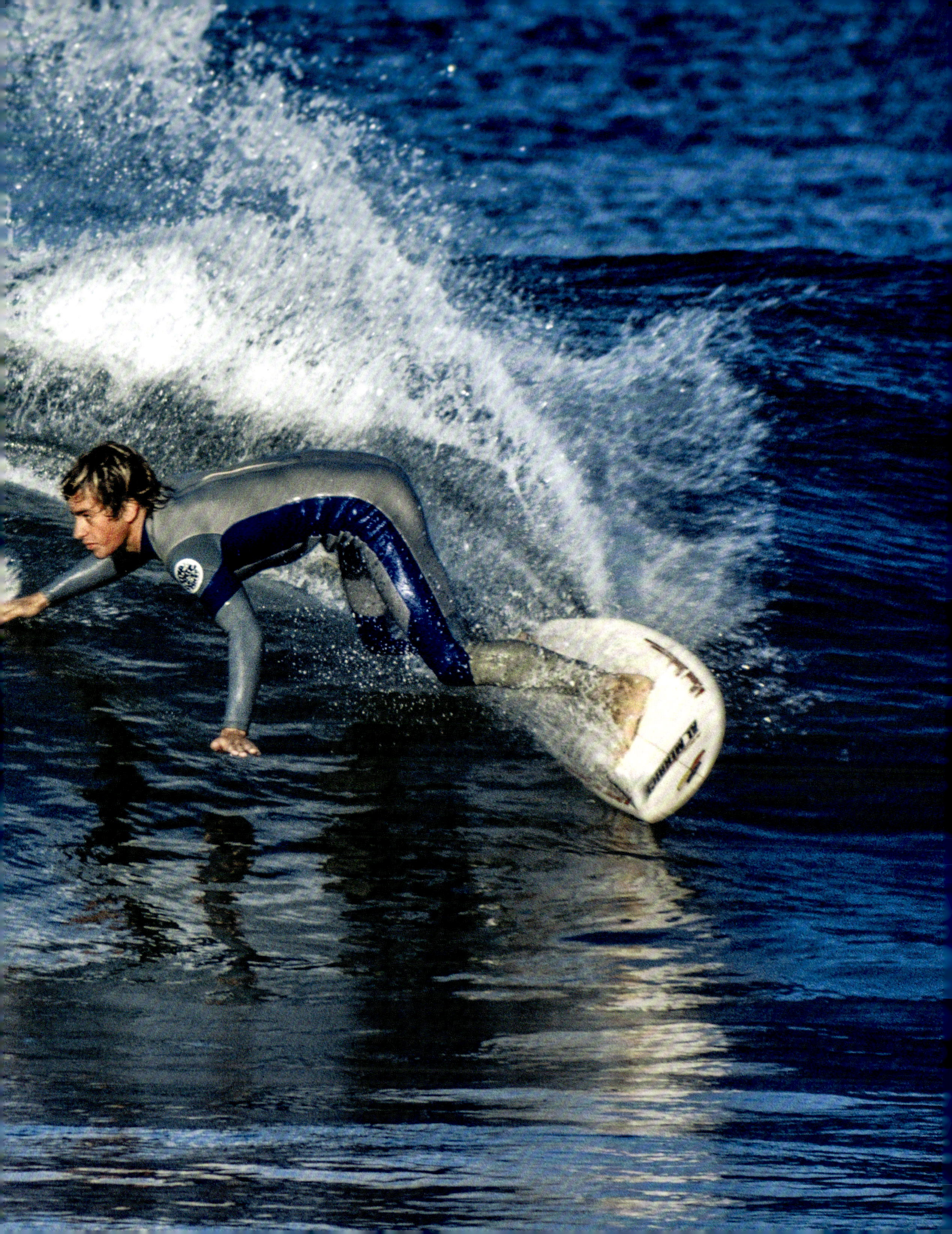

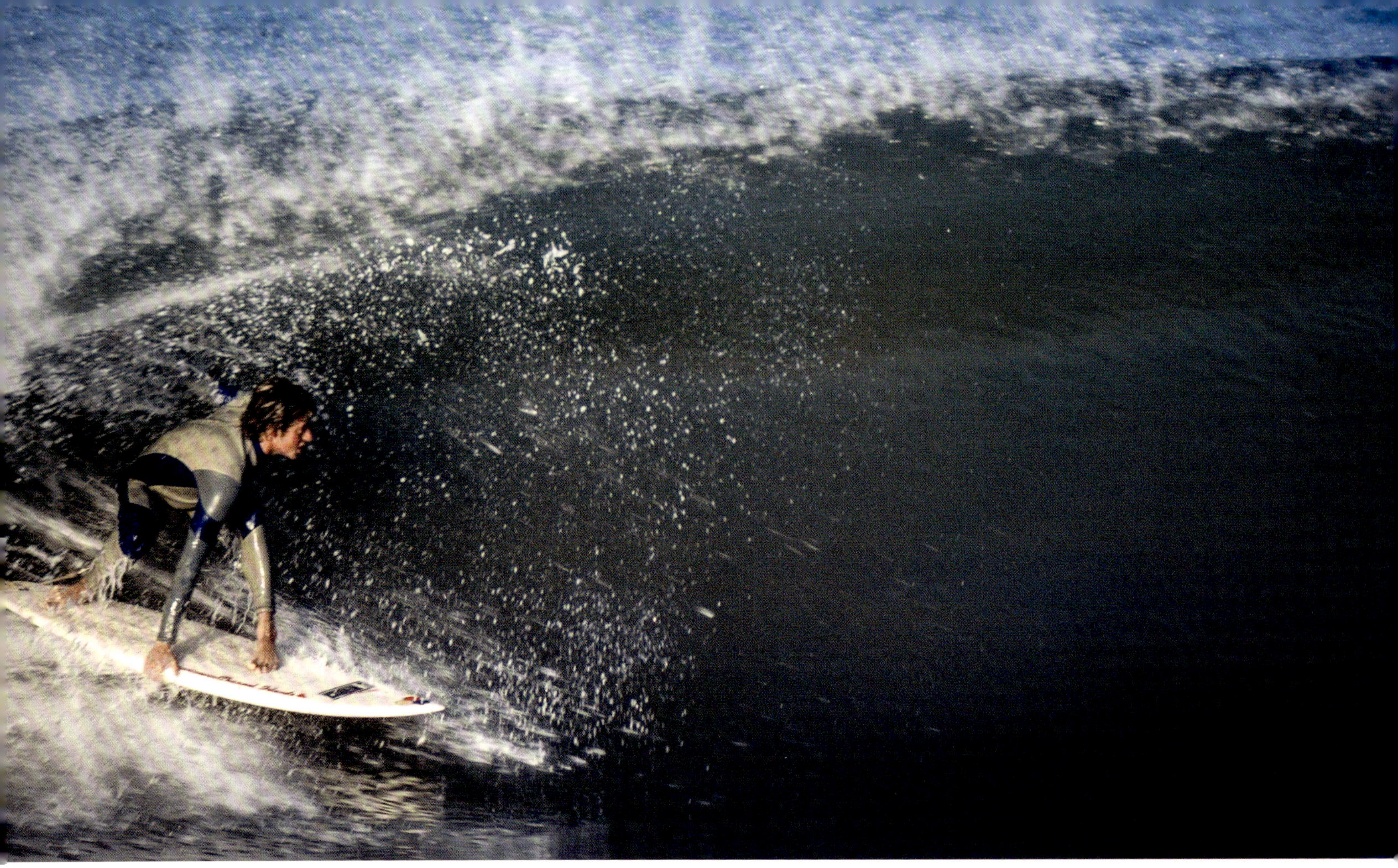

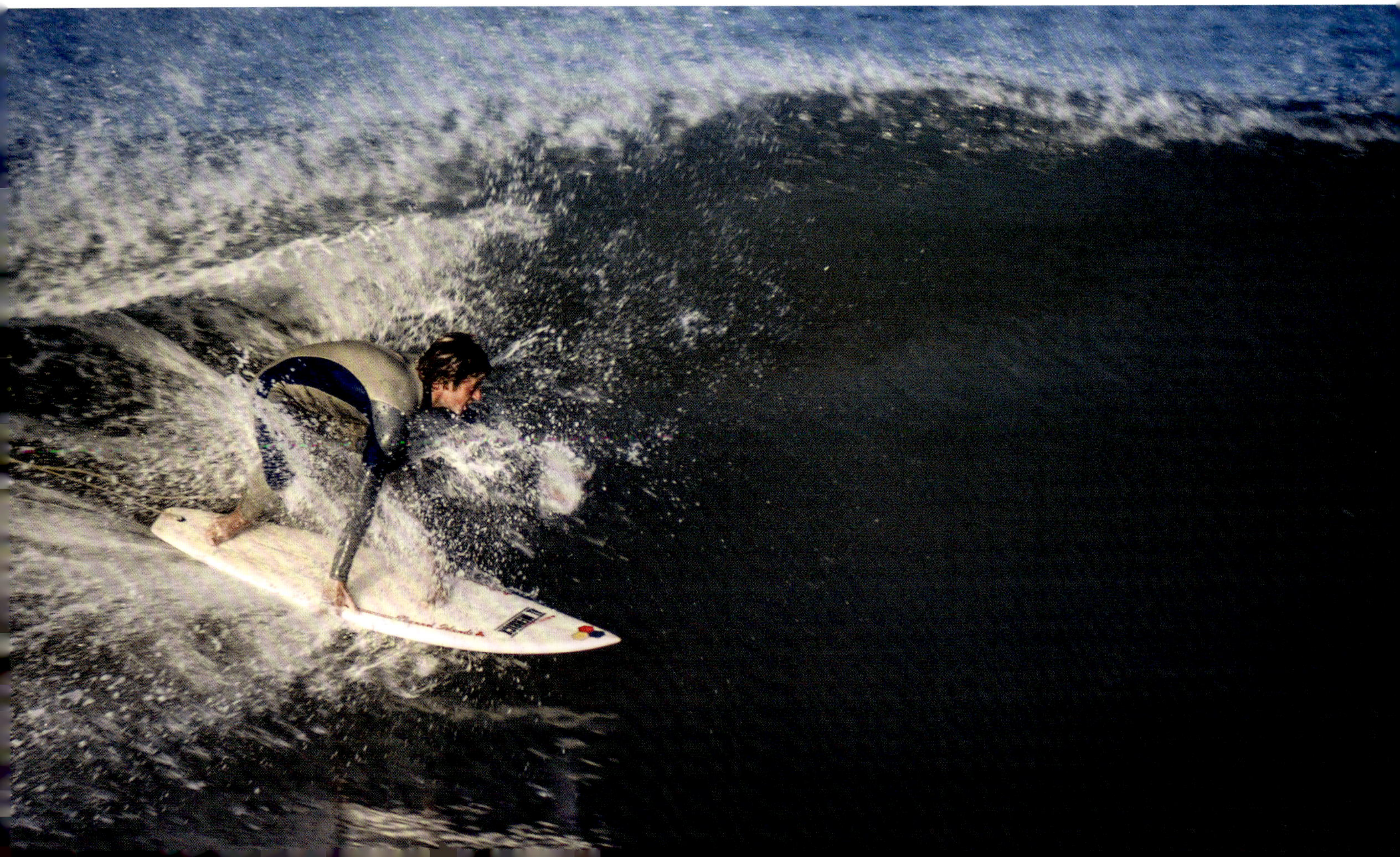

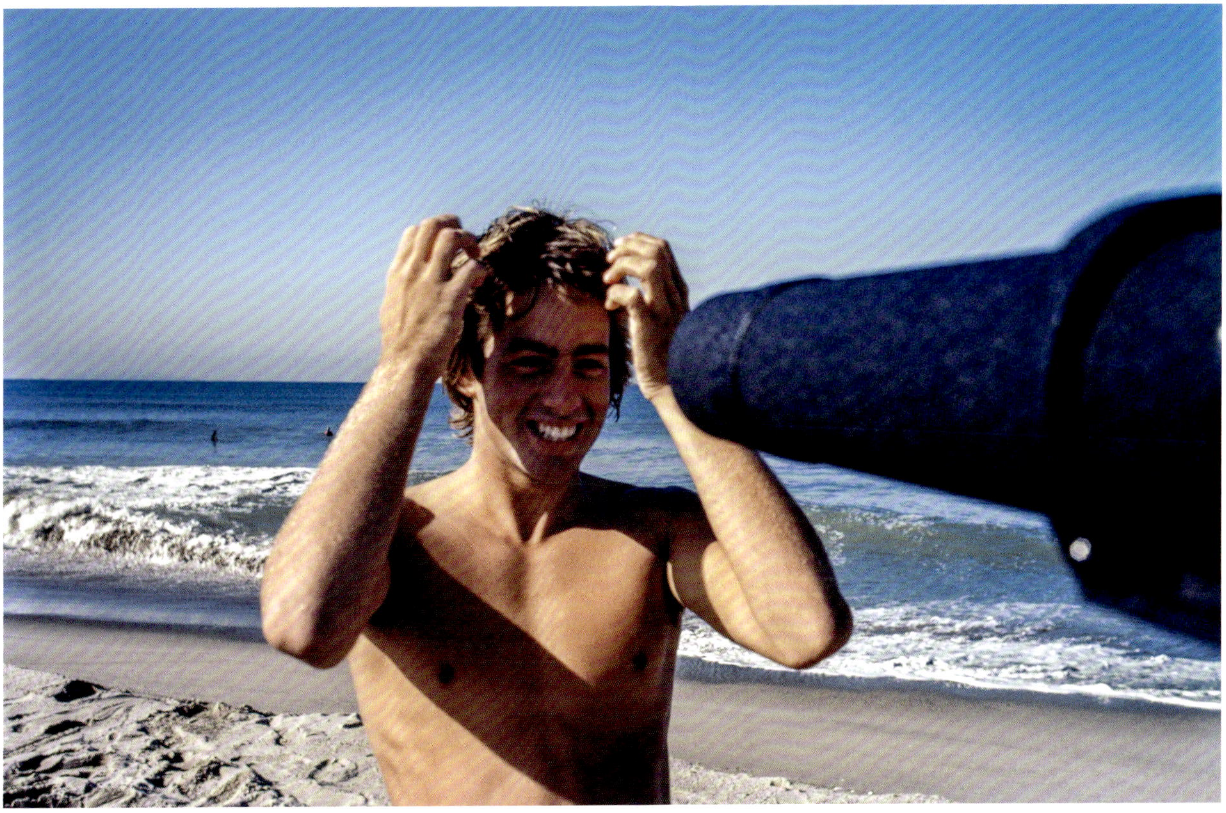

Dawn Patrol

The international operator asked, "Will you accept a long-distance collect call from a Mr. Tommy Curren?" From an airport somewhere in France, Tommy told me he'd be arriving back home the next morning and wanted to do a Ventura dawn-patrol surf session before leaving for Japan the following day. Typical Tommy, for whom surf sessions on the way to or from the airport were a regular occurrence, regardless of flight schedules. Who was I to say no, let alone bring up anything about jet lag? Turned out that I got more A-plus images from the few hours we spent at Santa Clara Rivermouth that morning than ever before, including an eventual *Surfer* cover shot. Less than twenty-four hours later, Tommy would fly to Japan, where he would go on to win the Marui Pro at Chiba, his first world-tour victory. Again, typical Tommy.

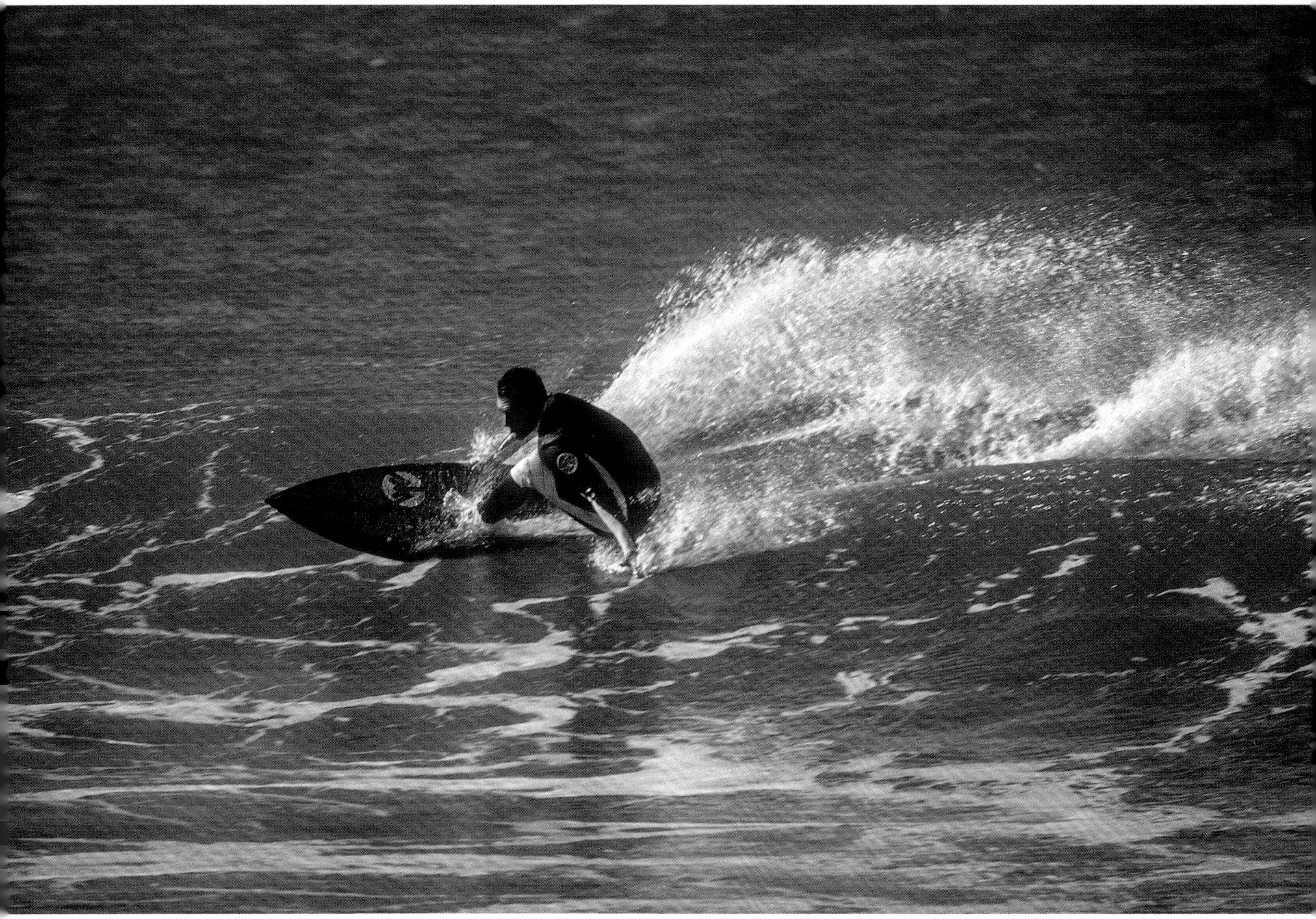

Meeting Jay

When shooting from the beach, I usually kept a gallon of water with me; it gets pretty hot behind the tripod. One day at Malibu, Jay Adams, whom I'd never met, got out of the water, walked right over, and, without a word, grabbed my water bottle. Now, I knew Adams had a pretty heavy reputation at the time, but I had to say something. "Hey, I have the flu," I stammered. With the bottle poised at his lips, he just looked me up and down and said, "I don't give a fuck."

So went my first meeting with Jay.

Anyone who skateboarded—from clay wheels to urethane and into the Dogtown era—knew of Jay. He wasn't that little blond kid anymore, but, along with fellow Z-Boys teammate Tony Alva, someone I spent countless hours in the 1970s trying to emulate on concrete.

Later, we met up several times to shoot in Ventura. He admired Davey Smith's surfing and knew I was shooting all the aerials.

The last time I saw him, he was leaving the beach. He turned to me and said, "You're cool, Metyko."

"Glad you think so, Jay," I said. "Because I've always been kinda scared of you."

He just laughed. This was only a few months before he'd be convicted of assault, eventually spending six months in prison.

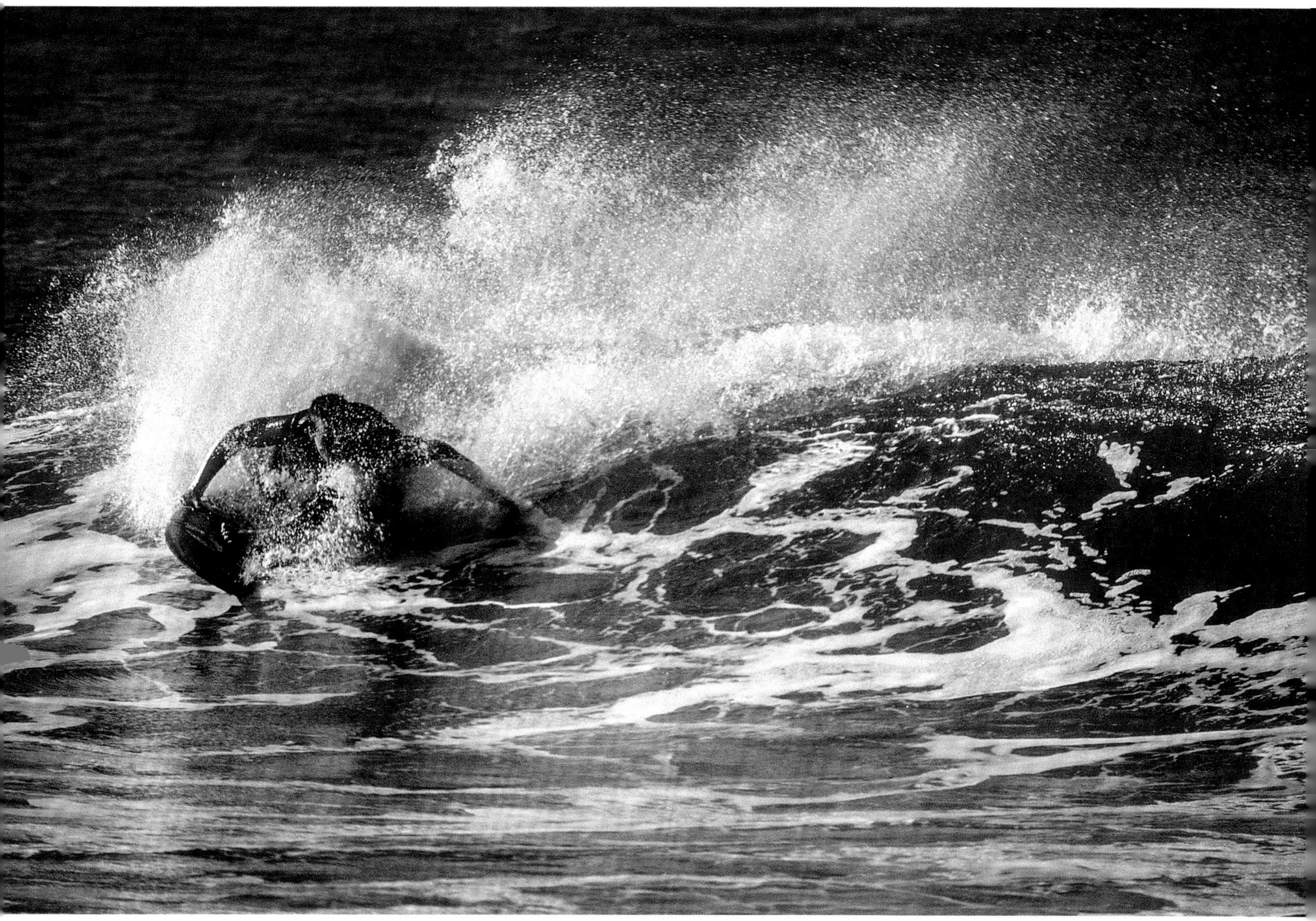

Overleaf

Shooting from the water at super-crowded Third Point Malibu was...well, pointless, unless Willy Morris was out laying down his trademark power turns. Then there were absolutely no "drop-ins" to worry about.

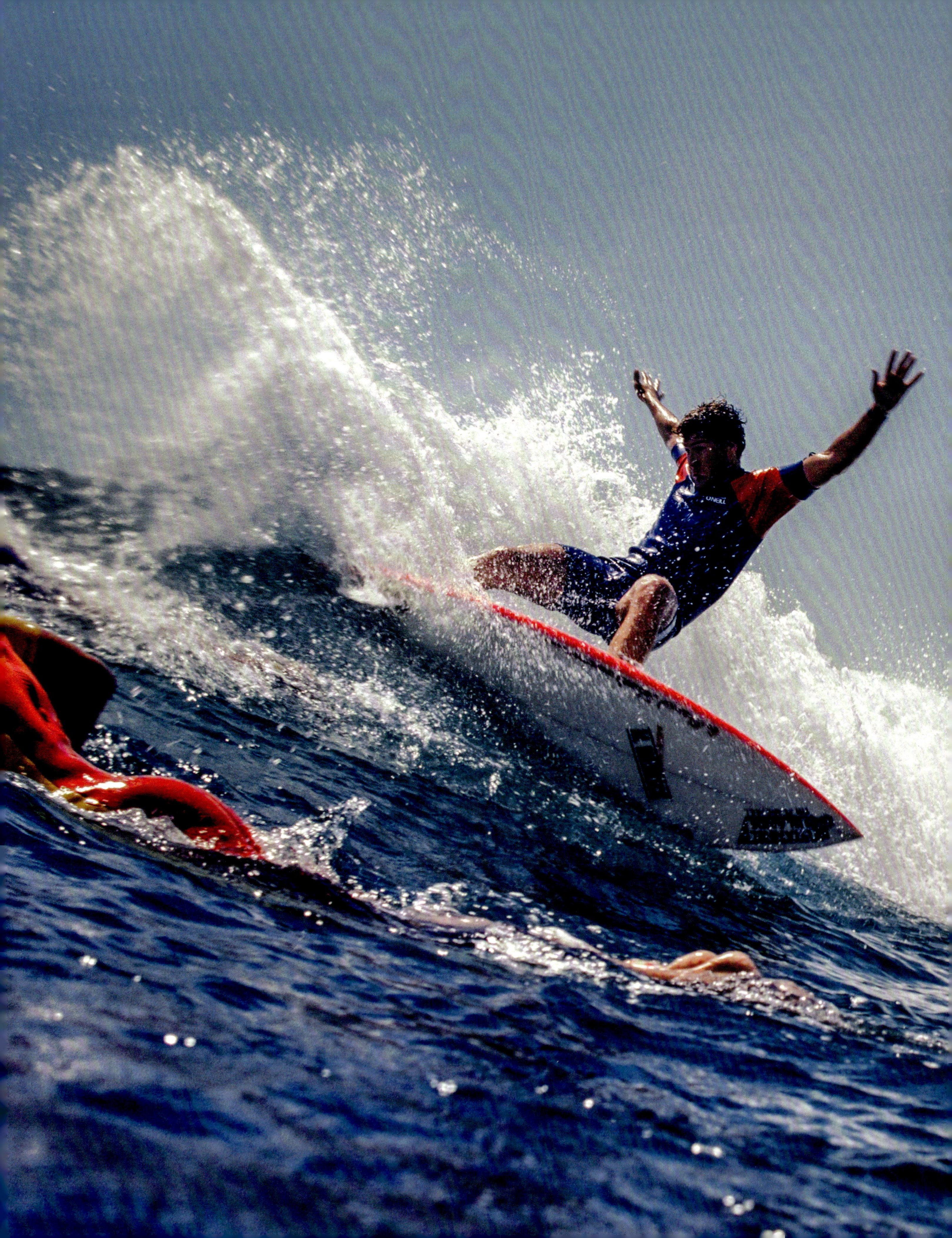

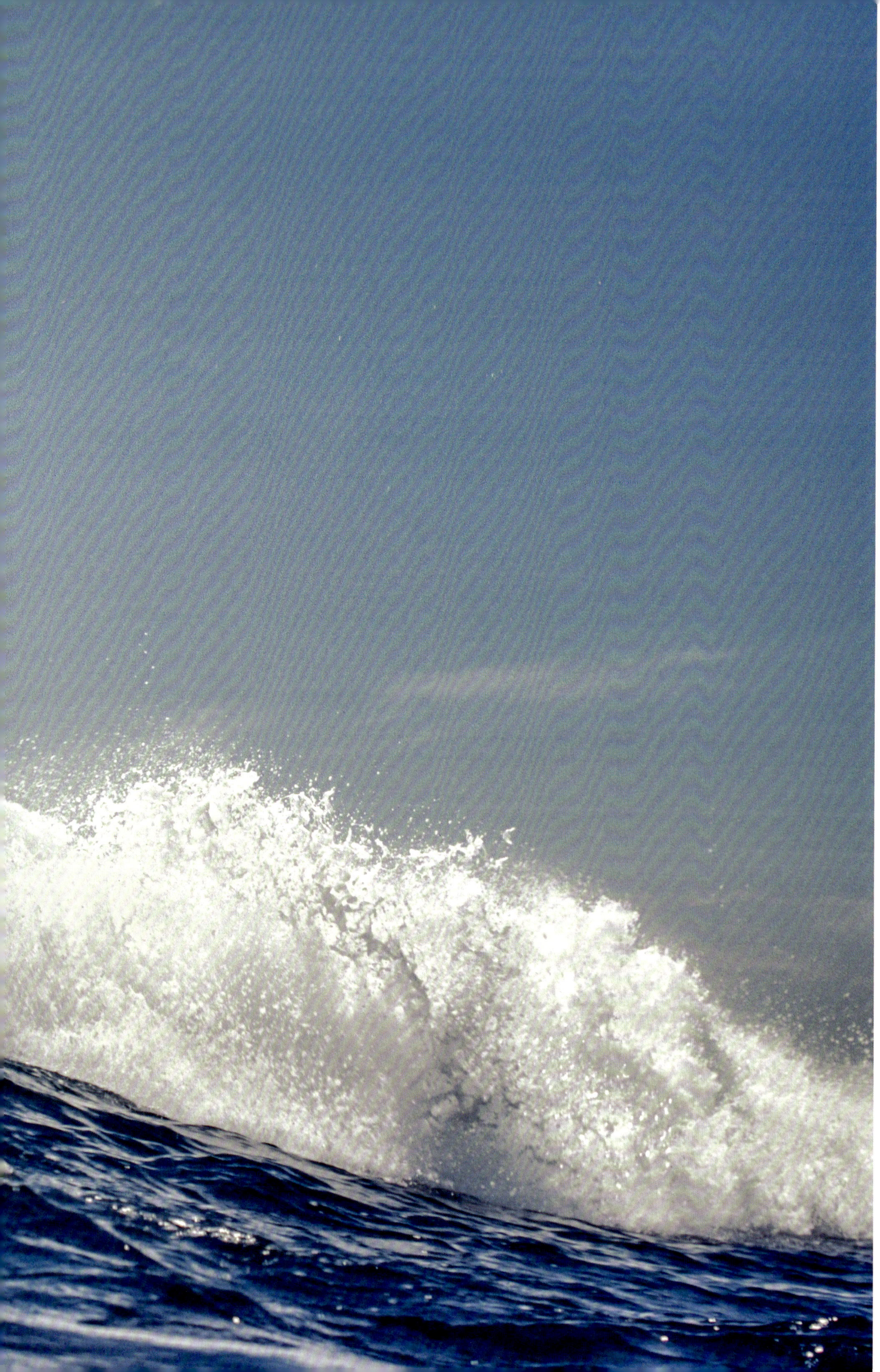

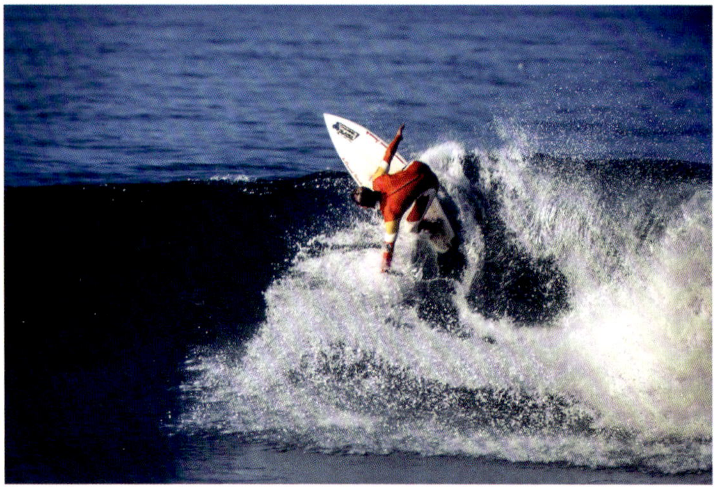

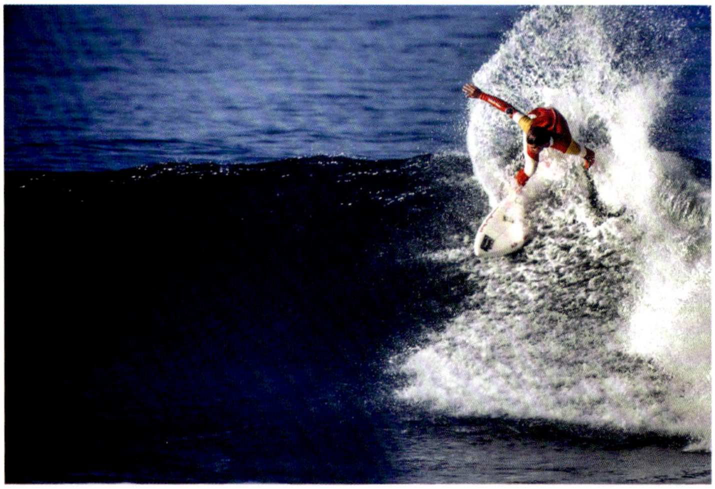

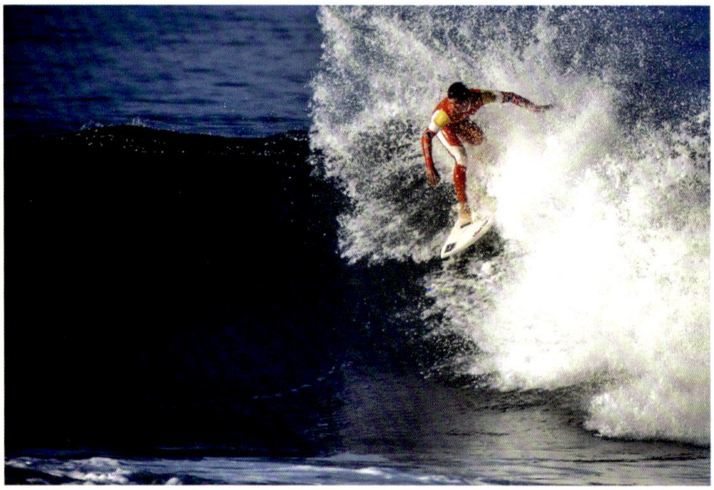

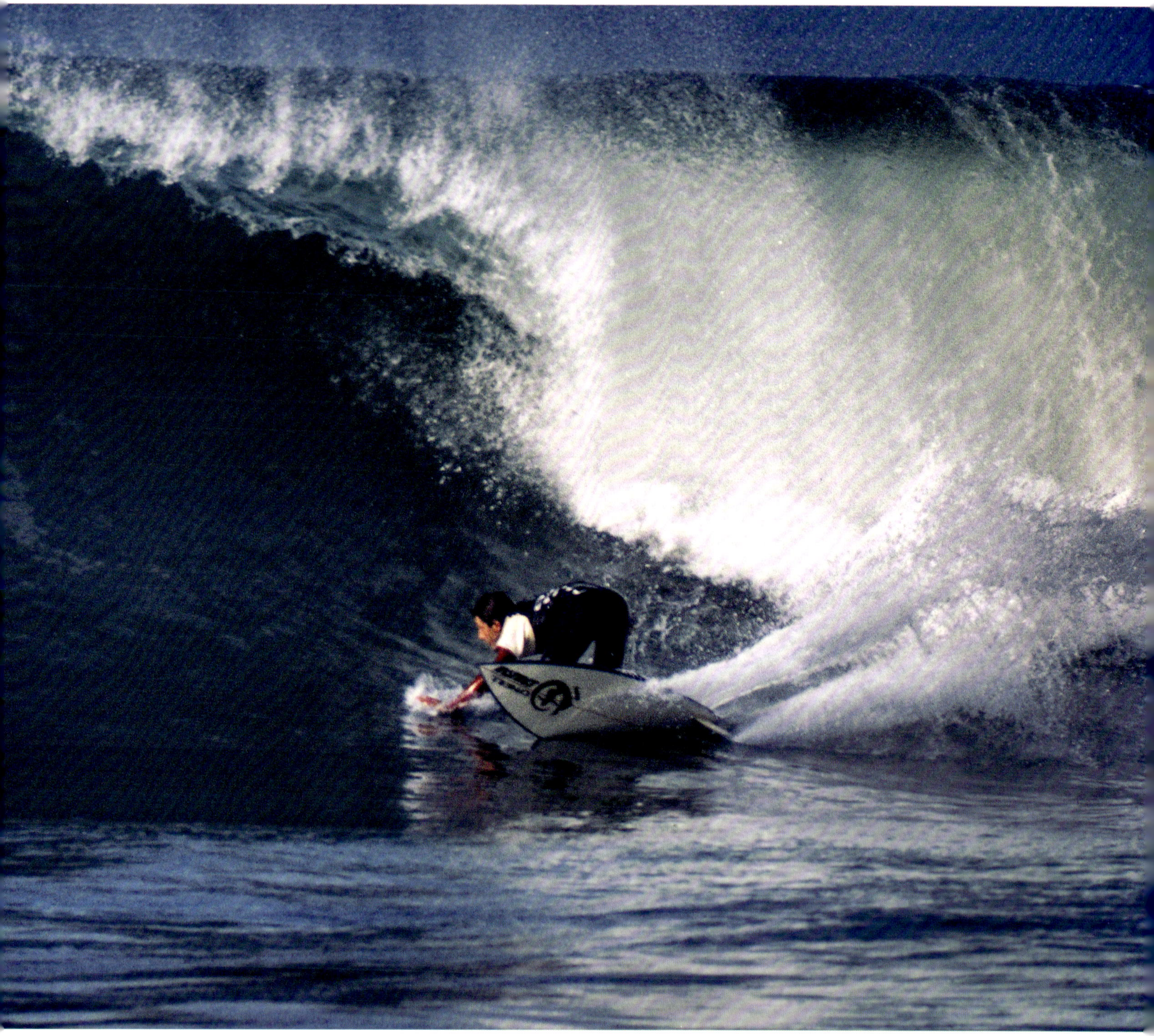

Opposite
Dino Bortoli, a good friend of the Morris brothers, was just one of the many good surfers who came out of the inland San Fernando Valley. Must've had something to do with easy freeway access.

Above
When I first moved to Santa Barbara, I was hoping just to see Shaun Tomson surfing Rincon. I never could have imagined that I'd one day be driving around with him looking for waves, and then be the only camera on the beach watching him put on some of the best surfing I would ever personally witness. On this particular morning at Oxnard Shores, Shaun put to rest the idea that twin-fins were strictly a small-wave design.

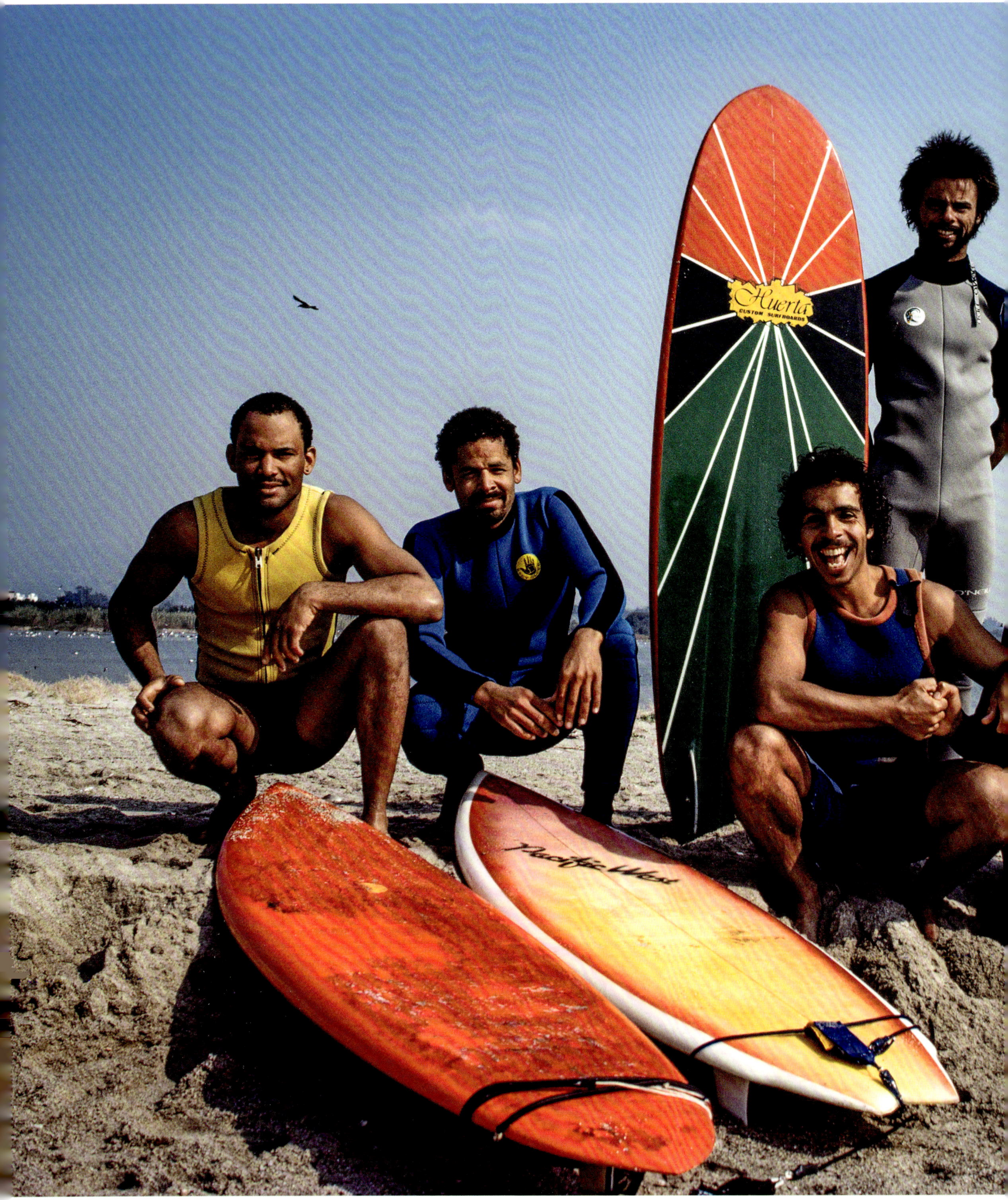
Huerta
CUSTOM SURFBOARDS
Pacific West

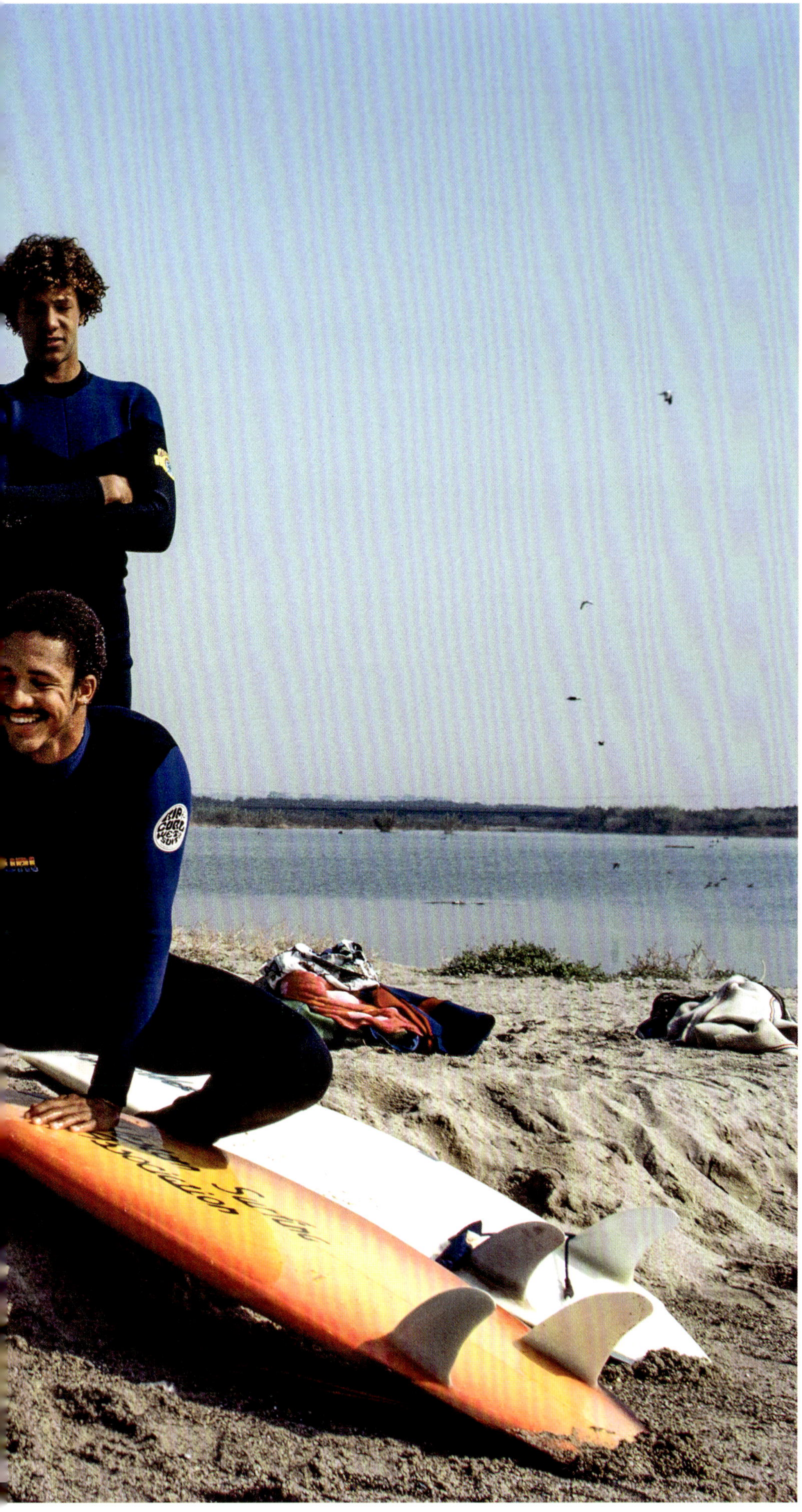

Spread

One morning in Ventura, Sam George and I stumbled into a session with members of the Black Surfing Association (BSA). Apparently, they were scheduled to be photographed for a *Surfer* magazine feature. When the photographer pulled a no-show, Sam, who knew a few of the crew, provided an introduction, and I ended up shooting the entire article, including this portrait featuring three groundbreaking surfers: Western Surfing Association director David Lansdowne *(second from left)*, BSA founder Tony Corley *(center)*, and top California amateur competitor Solo Scott *(standing, on right)*.

Pages 208–211

Though often overshadowed by the meteoric rise of CI teammate Tom Curren, Kim Mearig's ascension from shy, talented young amateur standout to eventual world champion was no less remarkable, especially considering how little industry support existed for women's surfing at the time. Her graceful style on a wave and sweet smile on shore masked a fierceness reserved for her toughest competitors—and anyone else who told her she couldn't.

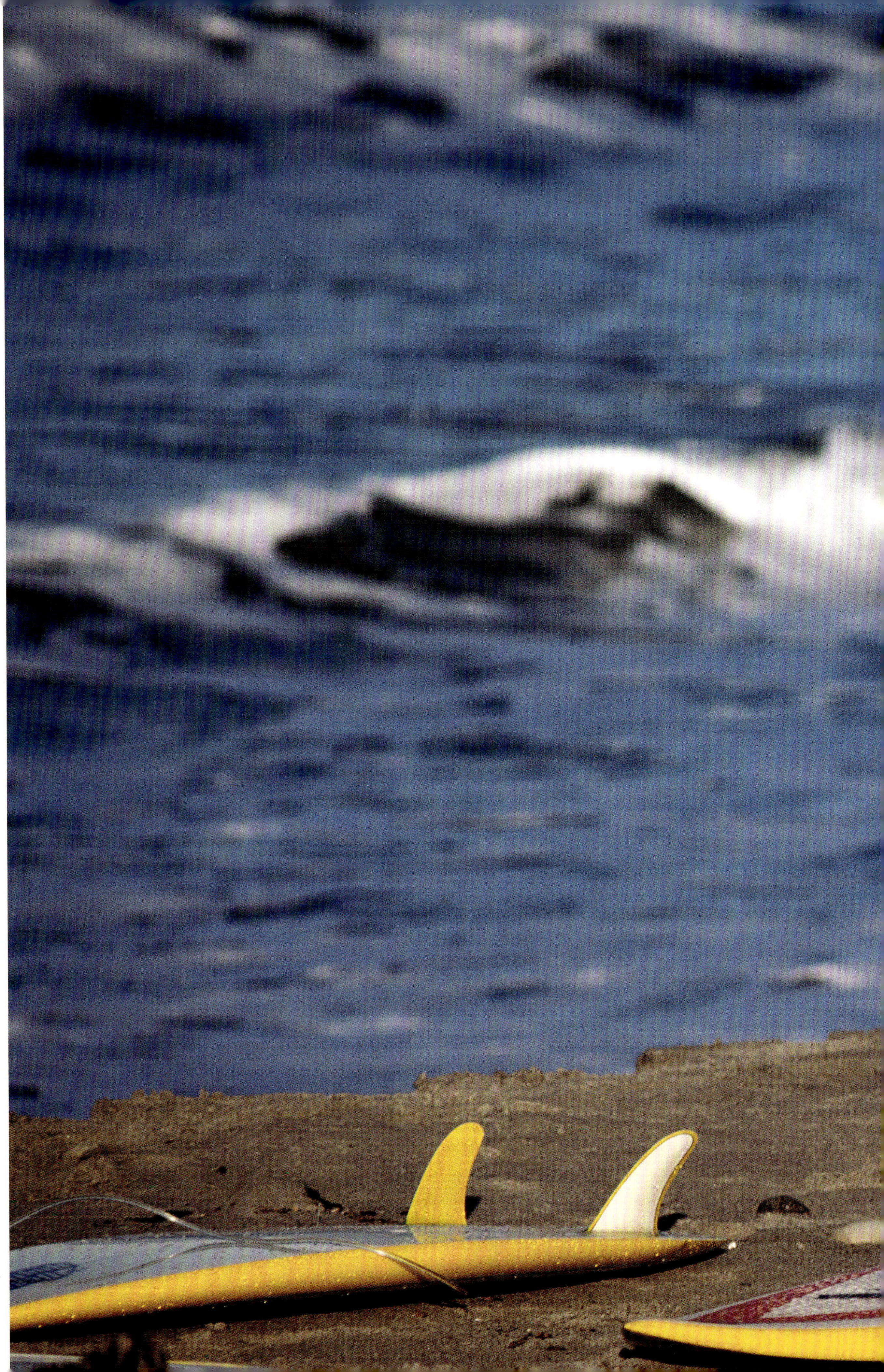

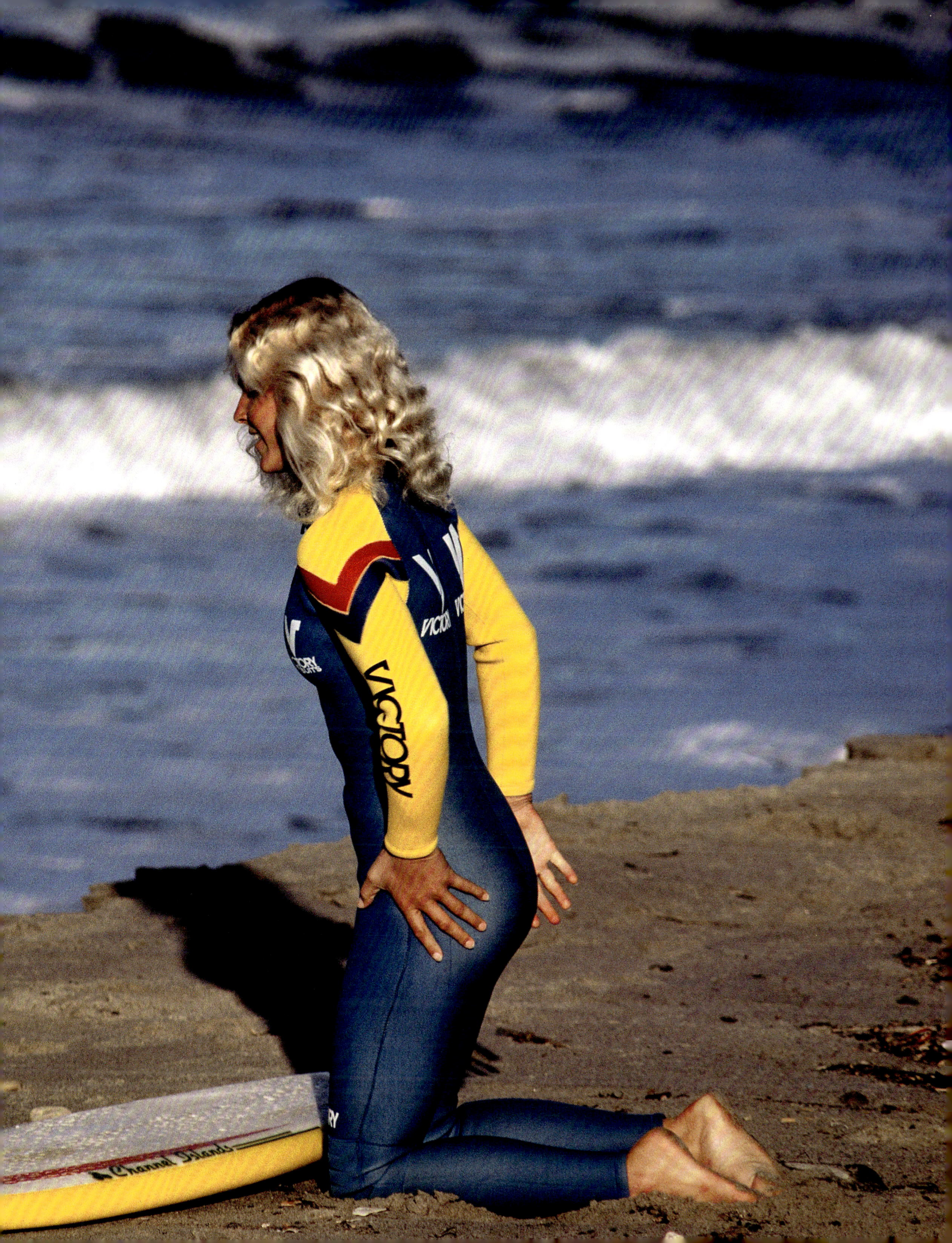
VICTORY
Channel Islands

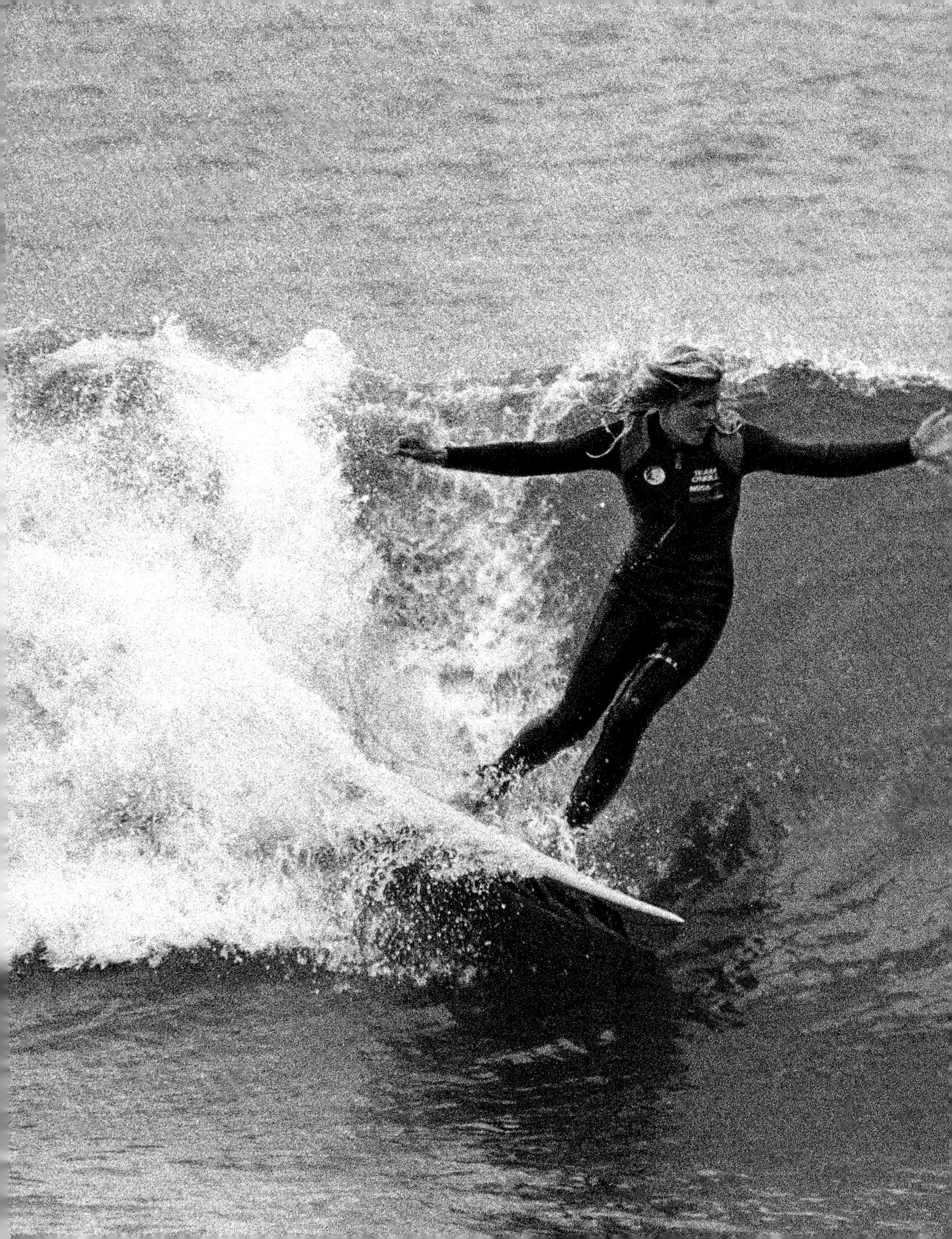

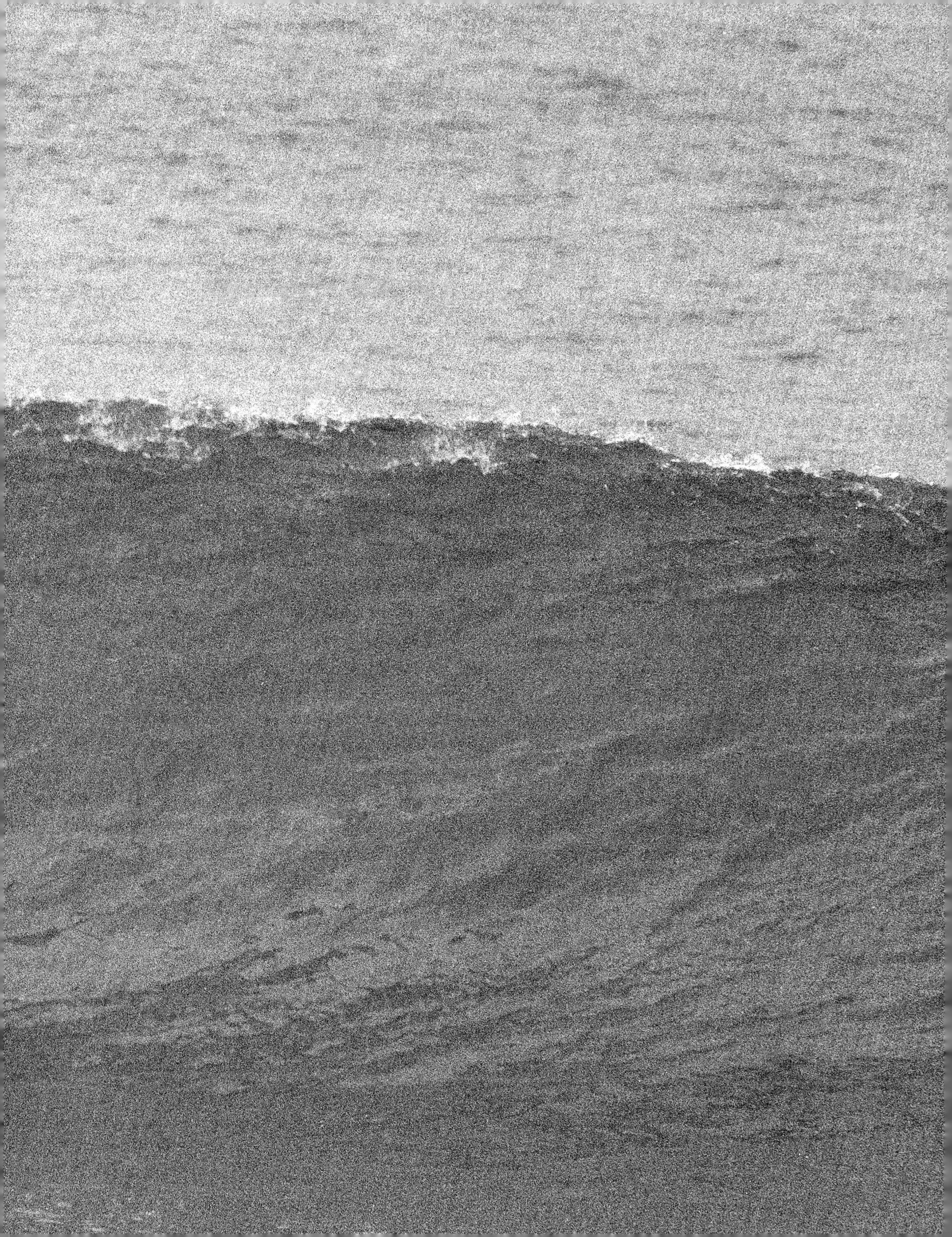

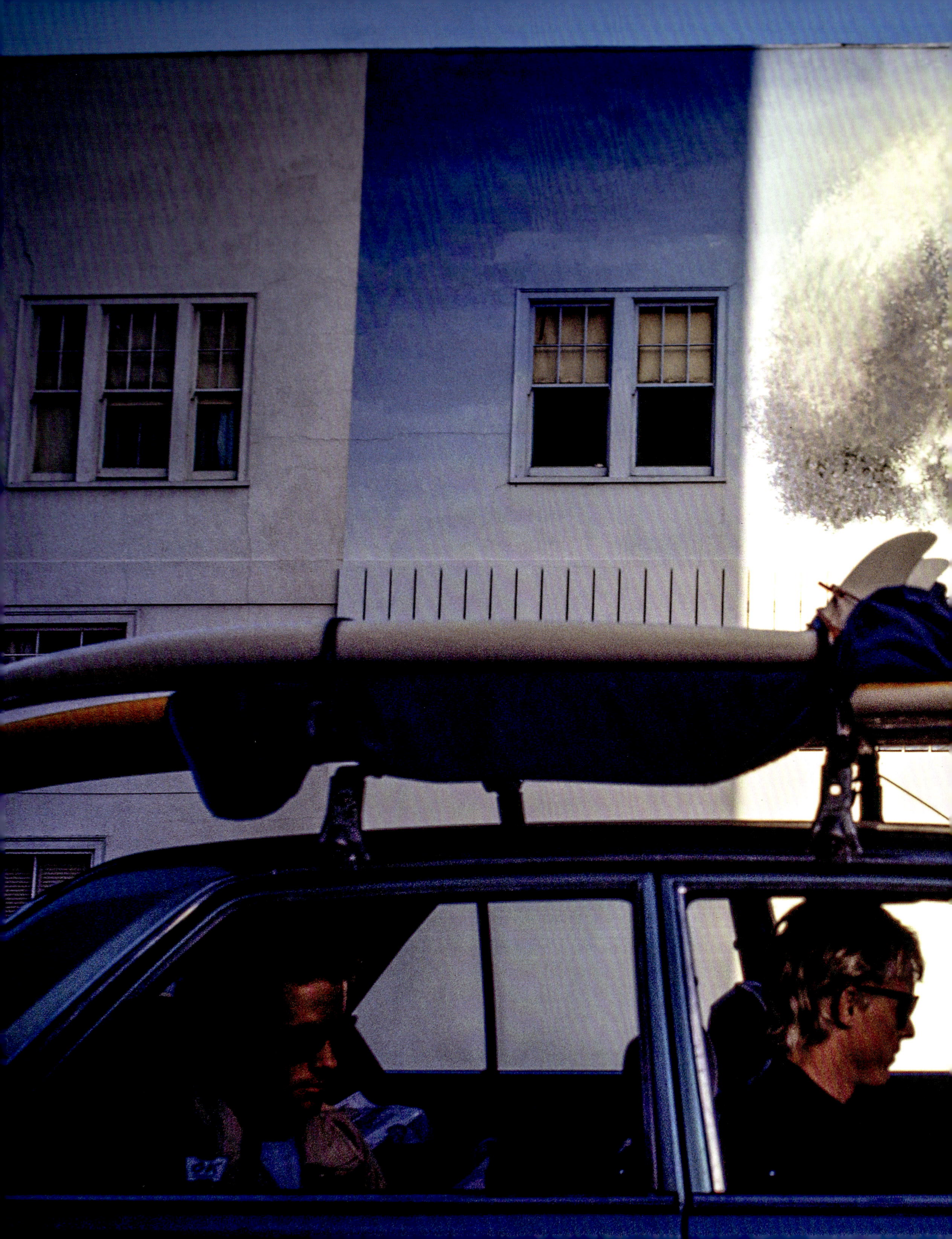

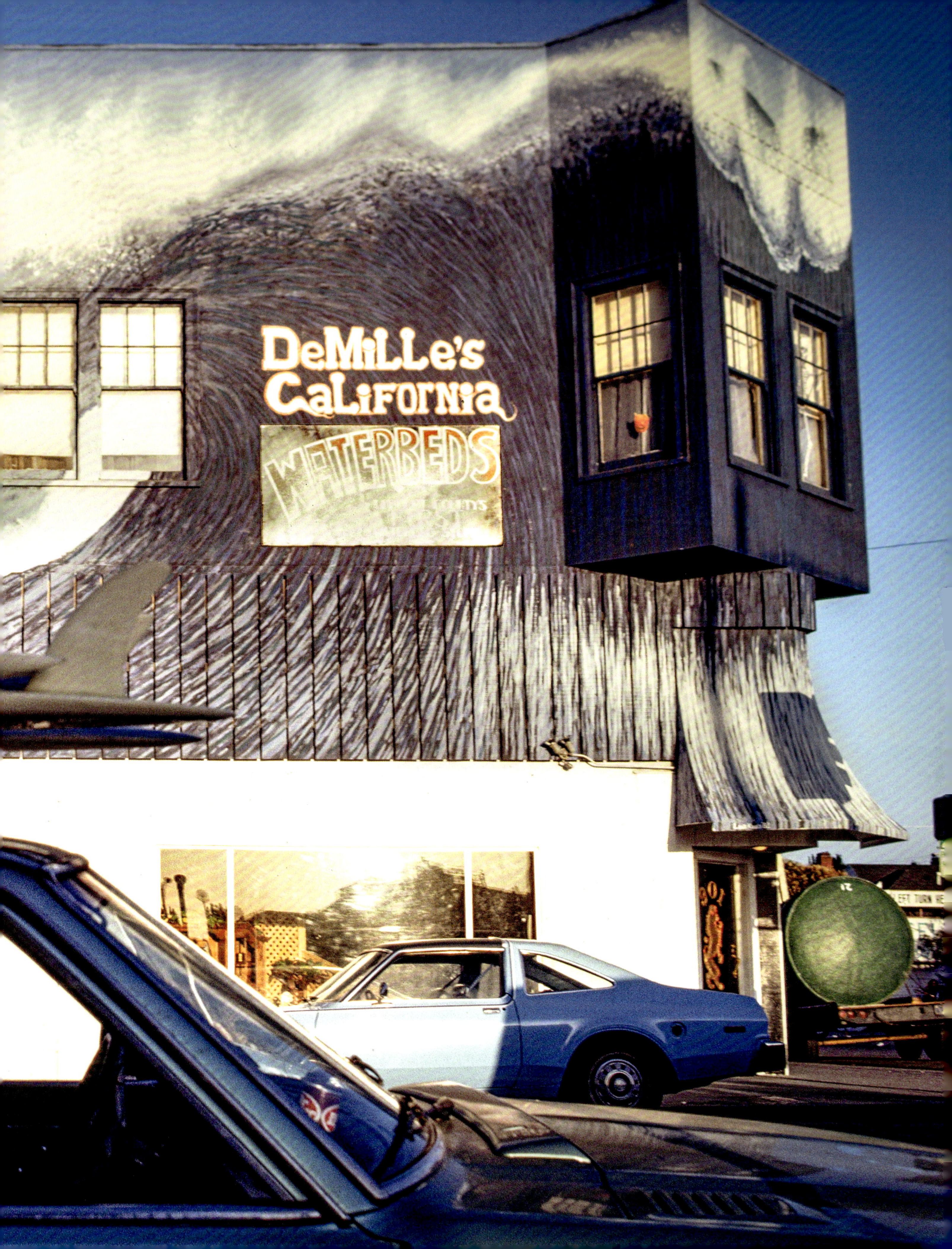
DeMiLLe's
CaLiFoRNia
WATERBEDS

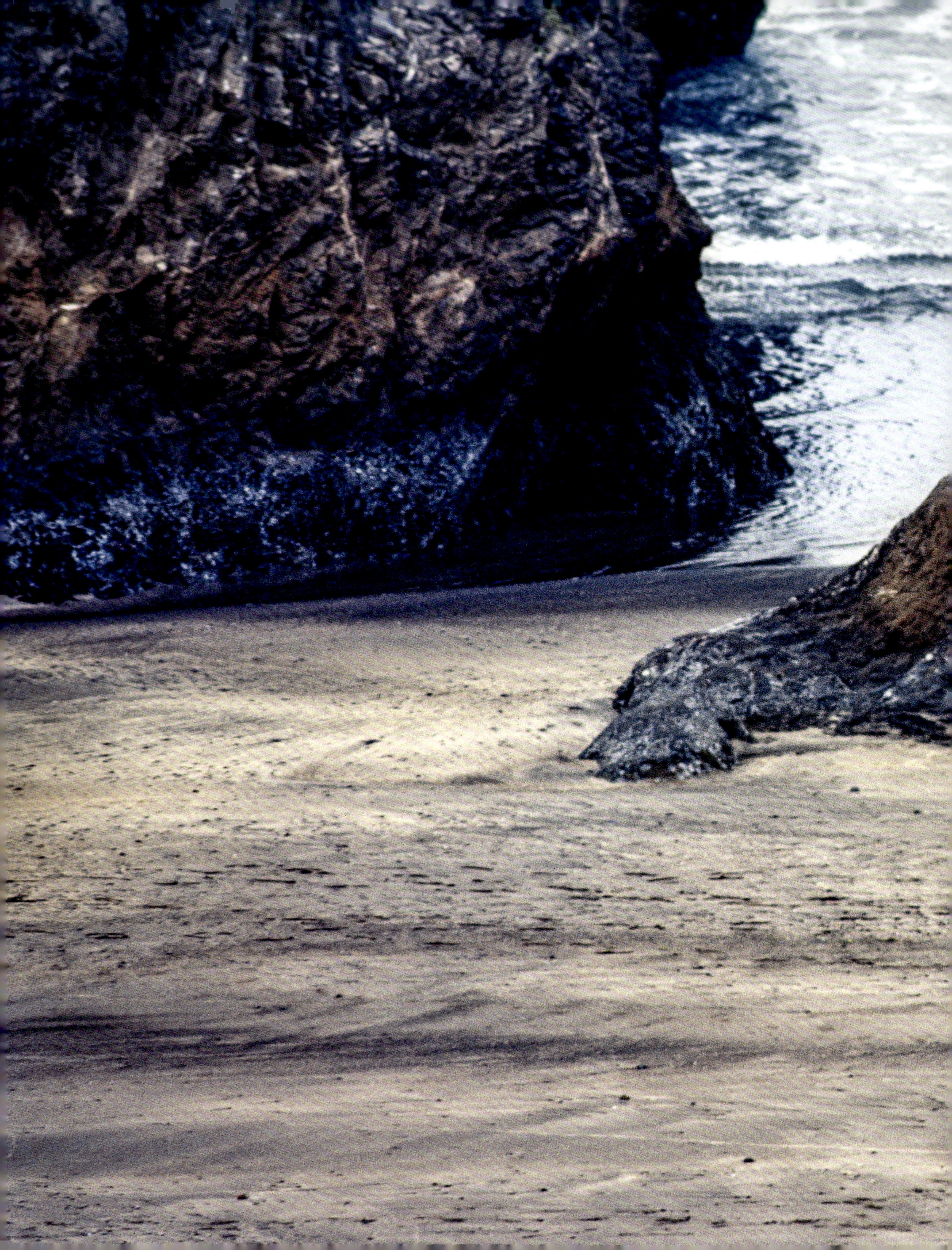

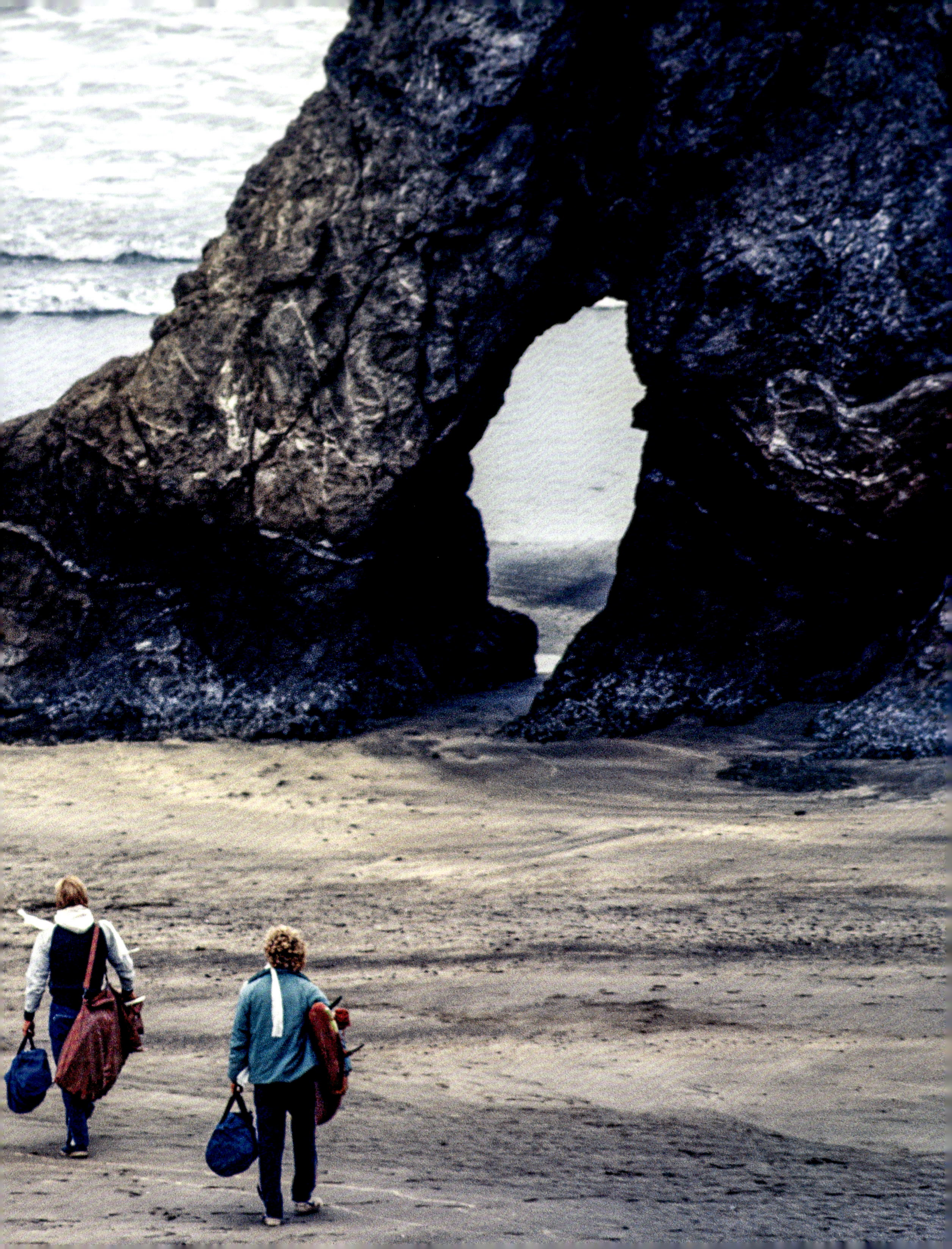

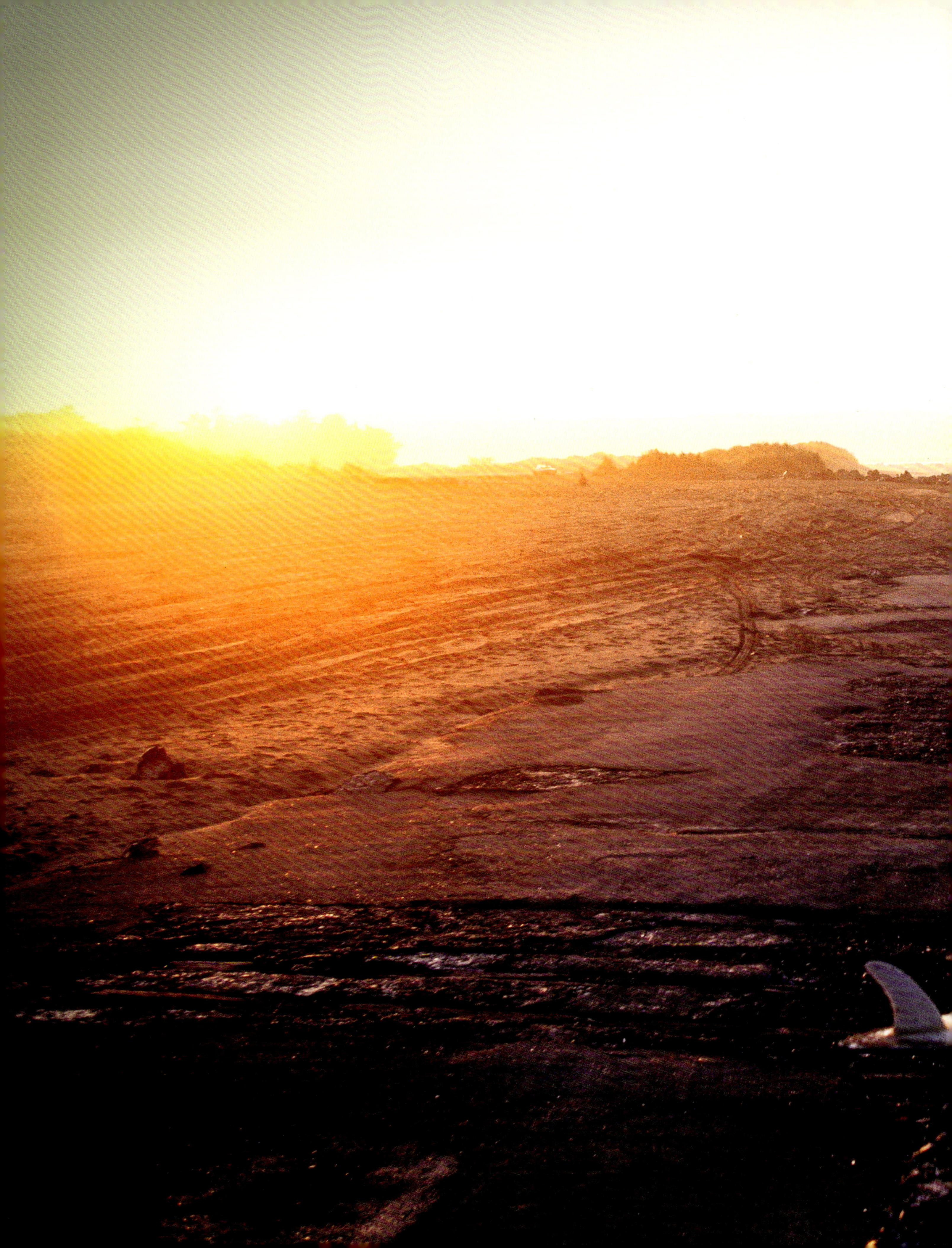

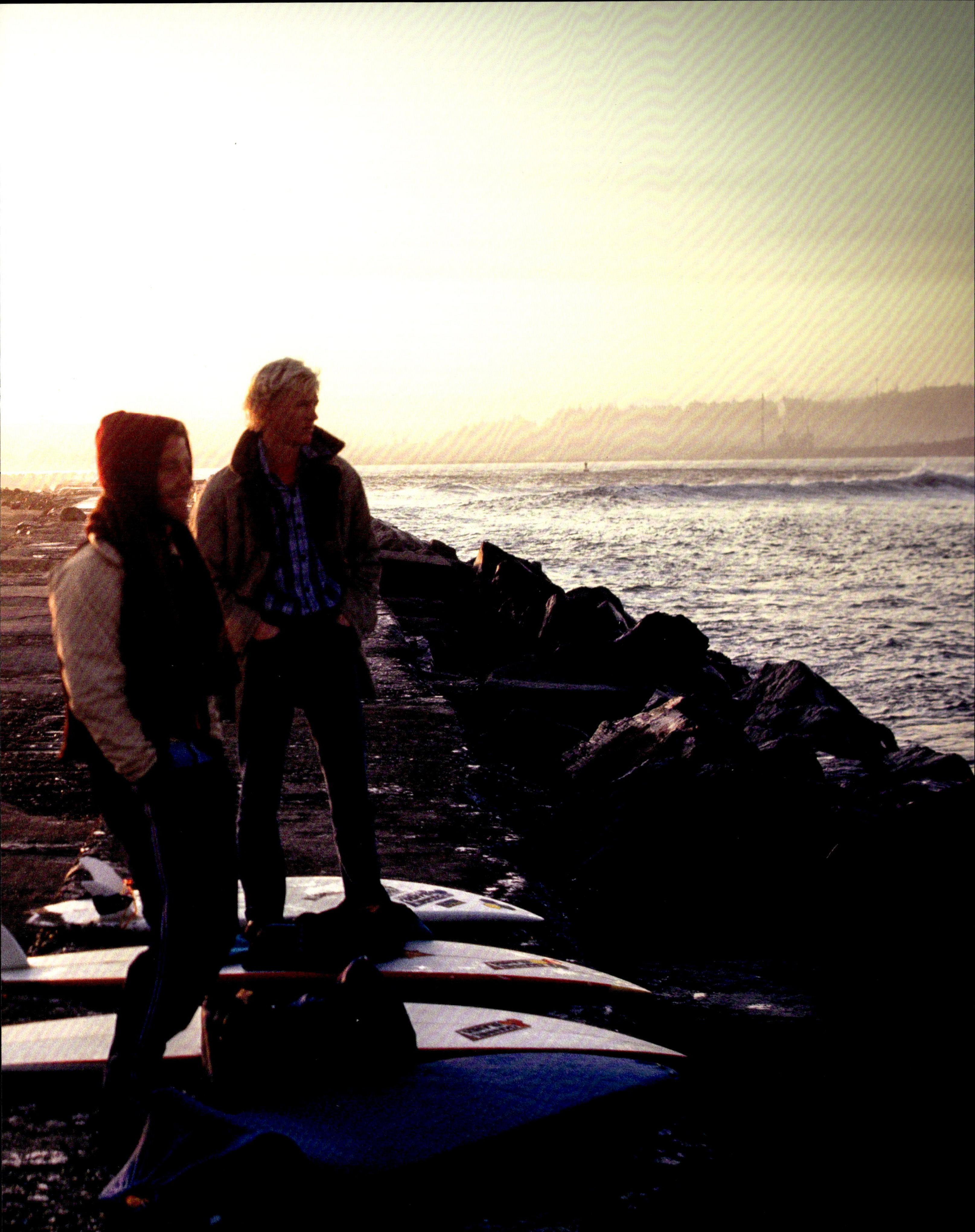

Pages 212–217
Three distinct phases of a fruitless search for surf, way north of the Golden Gate Bridge.

North of Golden Gate

Long before any reliable surf forecasting, a trip up to Northern California didn't require much planning other than coordinating your buddies' schedules; the waves were always big up there, especially in wintertime. Or so it seemed to us Down Southers, shadowed, as we were, in the lee of Point Conception. The truth is, the waves do occasionally go flat north of Point Conception, north of Point Reyes, even north of Cape Mendocino, our distant destination on a weeklong road trip up Highway 1 and into the redwoods. So picture three surfers—Davey Smith, Steve Dwyer, and Steve Hanson—one photographer, and a lot of neoprene crammed into a small sedan, going down every winding road, checking every beach, following every lead to every secret spot we'd ever heard of, only to find the surf as flat as a flapjack.

Sure, optimism remained high for about three days of this. But after the umpteenth time of being almost run off dusty logging roads by barreling eighteen-wheelers loaded with freshly cut California redwood, after climbing over that last dune, or sneaking into that last hidden cove, or detouring fifty miles around that locked ranch gate and finding nothing to surf, things start to get a little tense. By the fourth day, you can start to distinguish each other's particular body odors; by the fifth day, you find yourself hoarding the toilet paper; by the sixth day, you can drive a hundred miles without anyone speaking. And by the seventh day, after the long drive home—when, dropping everybody off, you say, "Hey, yeah, that was fun," but really mean, "I never, ever want to see you again"—you eventually find yourself standing in a hot shower, rinsing off the road grime and the disappointment, yet knowing that maybe not now, not even tomorrow, but someday soon, you and those three guys will be laughing and joking about your disastrous trip north and looking forward to the next one.

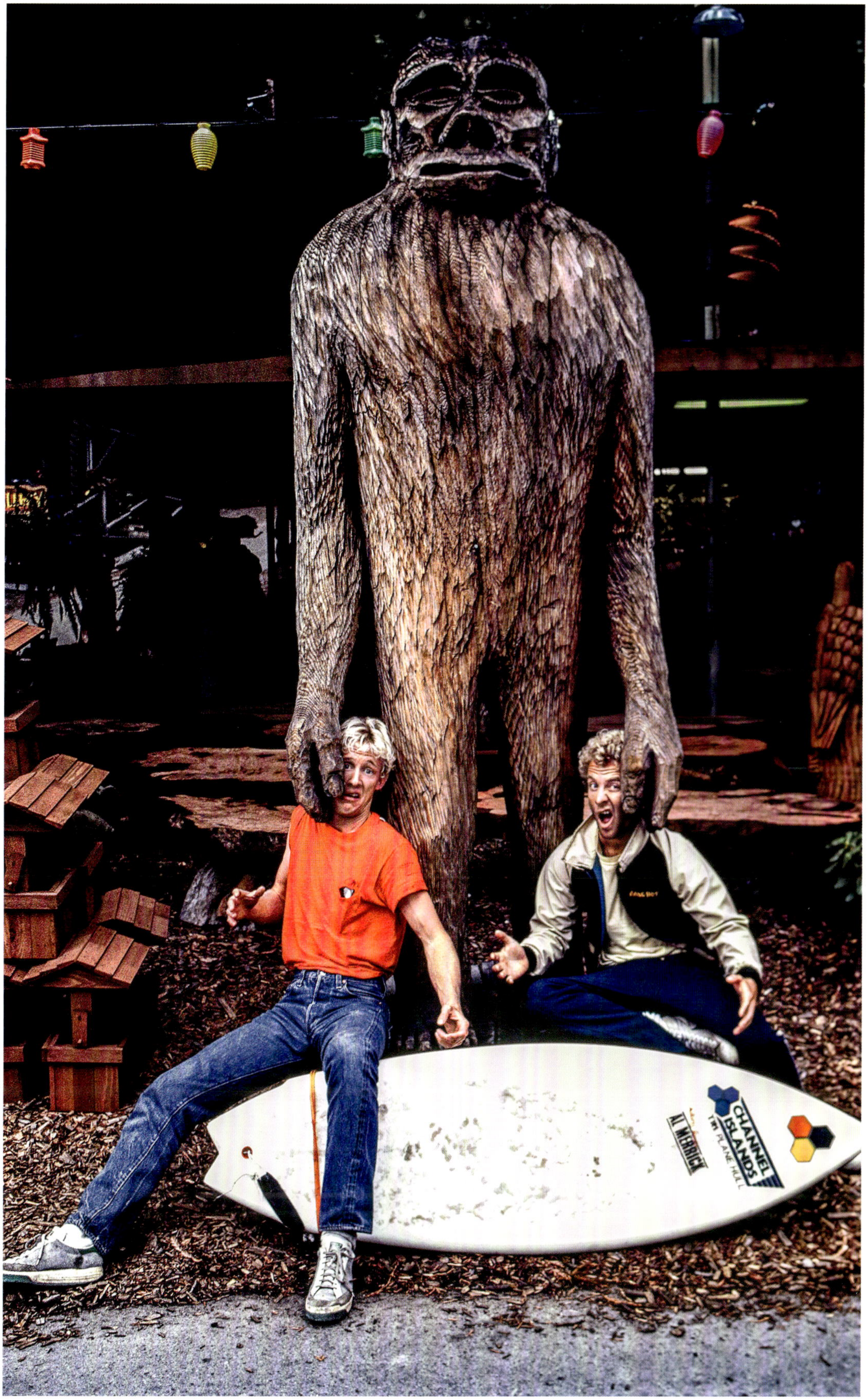
CHANNEL ISLANDS
PLANE HULL
AL MERRICK

Year's end at Jalama Beach County Park: John Schuyler, Davey Smith, and a friend visiting from Japan, making the long walk back to the campground.

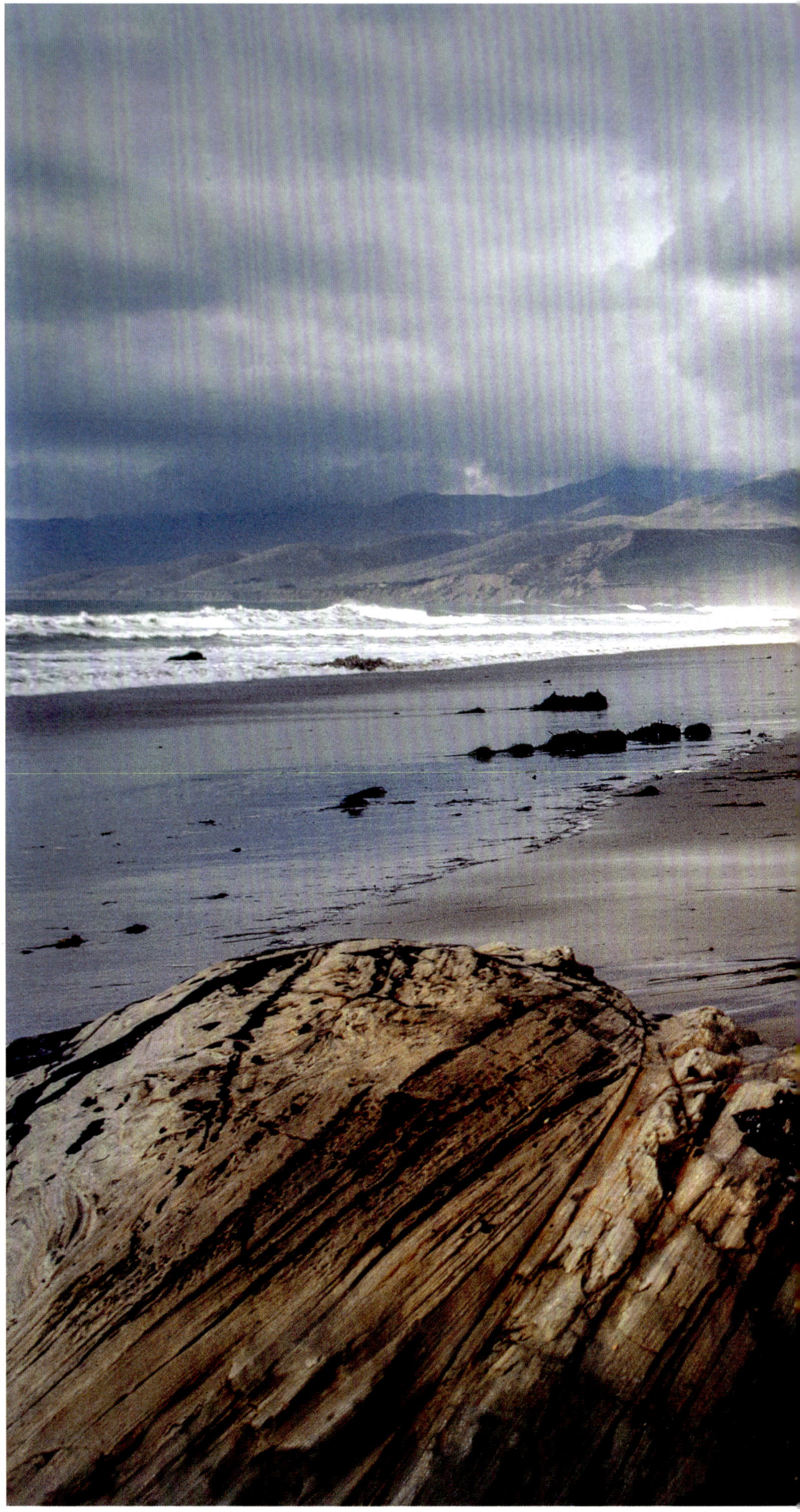

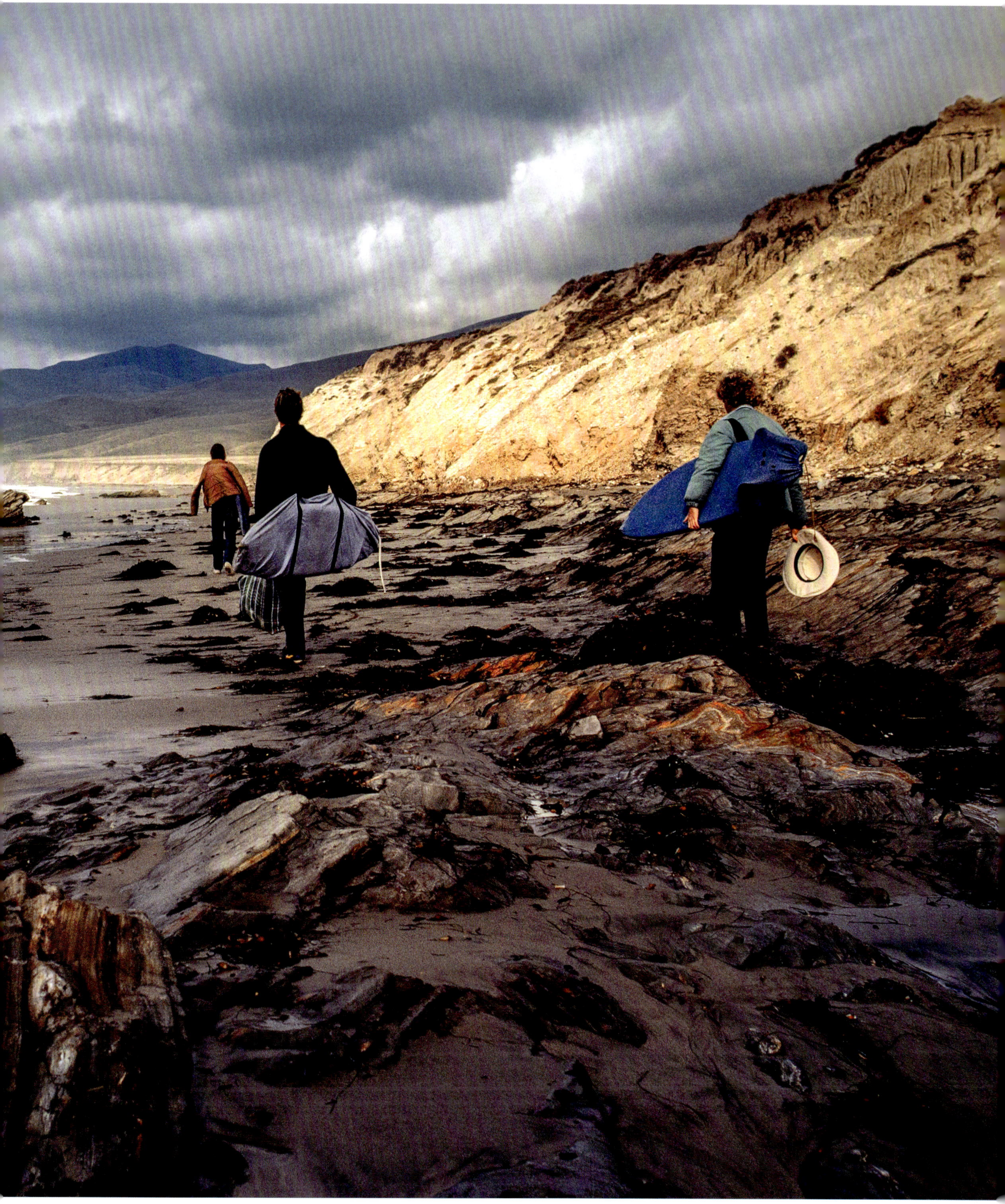

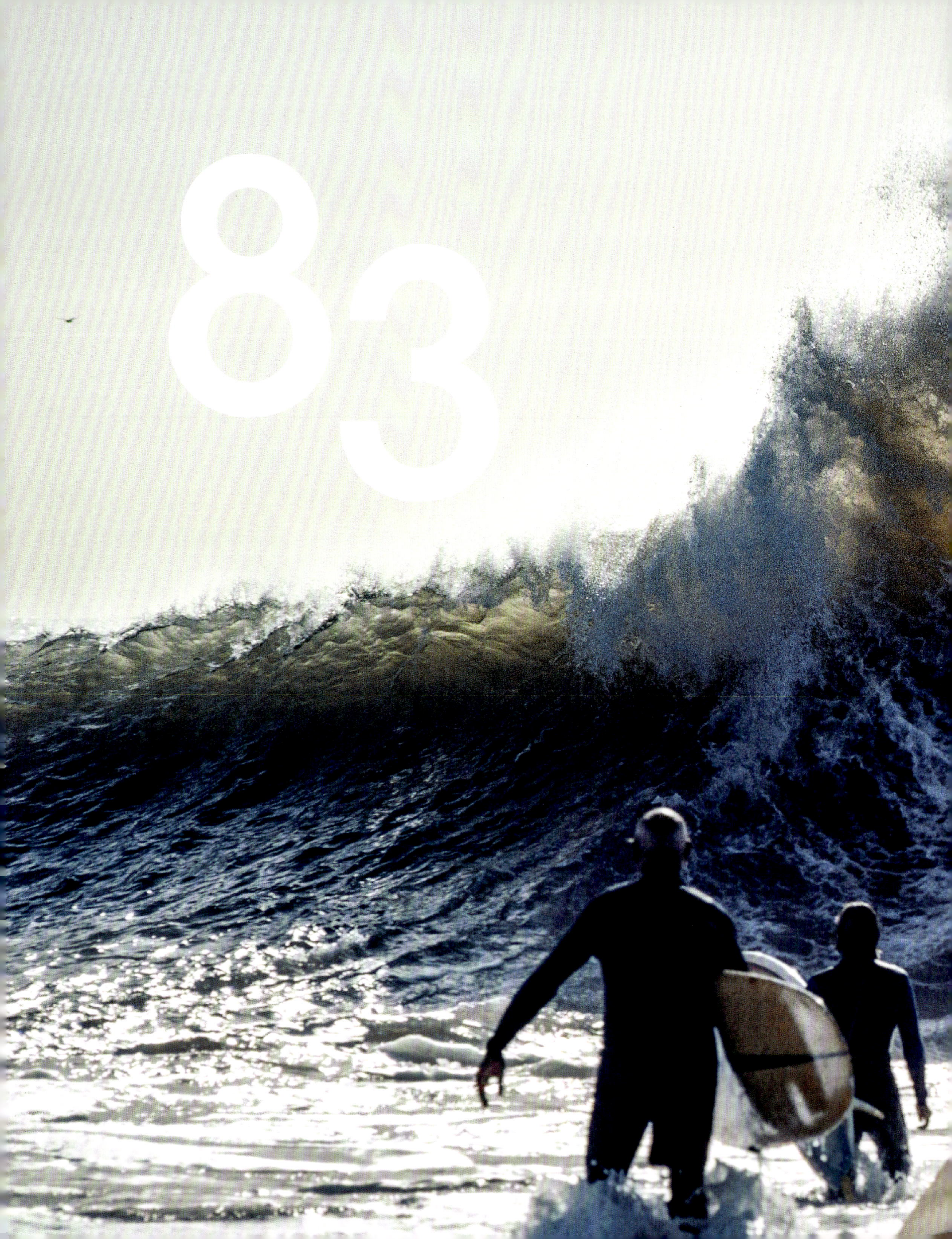
83

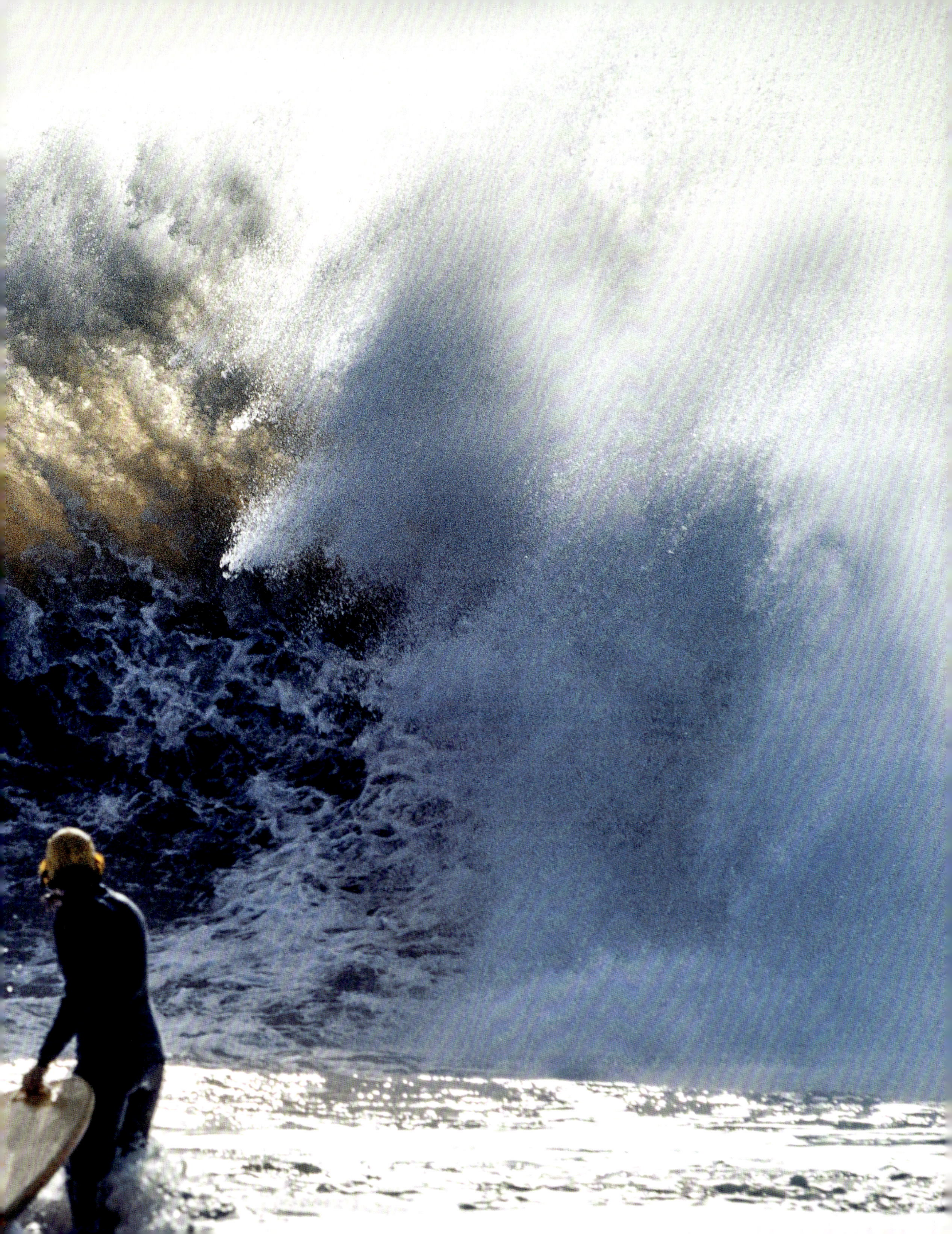

1983

The El Niño Year

By the end of 1982, I felt that I'd seen and photographed the very best that the Santa Barbara and Ventura surf spots had to offer—so many great days at Rincon, Sandspit, Santa Clara Rivermouth, and Super Tubes. Still, you couldn't spend much time around local surfers without someone inevitably comparing any exceptional day of big waves to the "Epic Swell of '69." In January of that year, a massive North Pacific low-pressure system, one of the largest ever recorded, generated monster swells that, after smashing the northern shores of the Hawaiian Islands, headed straight for the California coast. The churning storm surf arrived on our shores during one particular three-day period, groomed to heavy perfection by their distance from the storm's center and the seasonably fine weather conditions. The result, in Santa Barbara's case, was some of the biggest waves ever surfed in the region, including one memorable day of glassy, ruler-edged, triple-overhead Rincon. That day became the stuff of legend, as did the stories passed down by older locals telling of surf breaking out past the kelp beds and on offshore reefs seen neither before nor since. "You'll probably never see surf like that in your lifetime," they'd tell us. "Or at least when you're still young enough to paddle out."

As the old saying goes, we really missed it. The older guys had their Epic Swell of '69, and the rest of us would just have to make do with our "average" best days. How could we have imagined what Mother Nature had in store for surfers along the coast of California in January 1983—especially in Santa Barbara?

At the time, very few people outside a relatively small circle of meteorologists had ever heard of the weather phenomenon known as El Niño, the moniker describing the sporadic warming of surface sea temperatures in the Eastern Pacific that changes the position of the jet stream, the high-altitude winds that steer storm systems. In more technical terms, "During El Niño events, the jet stream over the Pacific becomes less wavy and splits into a strengthening subtropical jet stream near the equator and a weak polar jet stream, resulting in a greater number of storms."

We didn't know any of this. All we understood was that when we looked at the available Pacific Coast weather maps (this was long before accurate surf forecasting came on the scene), the big storms barreling down out of the North Pacific looked like 747s lined up to land at LAX, bringing with them wind, rain, and waves—lots of them. Too many, and too big, in some cases. This wasn't like 1969, when the big day arrived with clean weather and conditions. Rather, it was a relentless onslaught of angry surf. While it broke outside the kelp beds and on reefs that nobody had ever seen, as it did back then, it also swamped boats, stripped away sandy beaches, washed through beachfront homes, and even shut down Santa Barbara Harbor, trapping its fishing fleet at their moorings for weeks at a time.

At its peak, El Niño was hardly a surfer's friend. I distinctly remember one rainy, south-wind day when I met with Sam, Willy, his brother Steve, and Shaun Tomson in the empty Rincon parking lot, desperate to eke out some kind of session between storm fronts. The waves were the biggest any of us had ever seen there, with giant sets clearly visible over the tops of trees that ordinarily blocked the view of the surf. When we got down to the point, the lonely parking lot made sense. Blown ragged by the southeast wind and stained chocolate brown by Rincon Creek's runoff, the waves were ugly and uninviting, the point's various lineups understandably empty. The foursome decided to paddle out anyway. I didn't even pull out my camera, but just stood and watched as Shaun and Willy, who chose to fight their way out through the Rivermouth section, got caught inside by a huge set. Back then, none of us were allowed to accurately estimate the size of these waves; by surfing's collective decree, no surf outside of Hawaii could be considered to be bigger than fifteen feet. But Shaun later told us that one gnarly double-up that sucked him over the falls while he was paddling out resulted in a wipeout as bad as anything he'd experienced at Sunset Beach in Hawaii. Willy never did get out, while Sam and Steve, who cautiously chose to paddle out at the top of the cove, both took tremendous beatings attempting to ride in conditions that were truly out of control. The photos I would later take chronicling the devastation unleashed on Santa Barbara Harbor made this clear.

But the 1983 El Niño wasn't all chaos and destruction. As Sam would later write, "It wasn't just the giant 'Big Wednesdays,' but the run of smaller but consistent Tuesdays and Thursdays that made that season so special." All this surf offered the perfect opportunity for Tommy and the growing stable of Channel Islands team riders to have freshly shaped Al Merrick prototypes, glassed overnight at Haakenson Fiberglass to be immediately surfed the next day, providing almost instant feedback on performance. The result was both rapid refinement of Al's board designs and rapid improvement of everyone's surfing skills—especially Tommy, who was preparing for his first full year on the tour.

At the same time, I was in my final year at Brooks and had been hoping to graduate in the summer of 1983. Classes included instruction in industrial applications and infrared and ultraviolet wavelength photography—all cool stuff, but having nothing to do with surf photography. This being the case, during the first three months of 1983 I probably spent more time shooting surfing than attending school. While this became a problem, I did have one teacher who supported my extracurricular efforts, assuring me that what I was doing out in the real world was just as important as anything I'd learn in class. Yet by mid-March it had become clear that I'd been missing too much class, and that if I didn't want to flunk out I'd have to repeat all the previous semester's courses—meaning I wouldn't be graduating until the end of 1983. But it also meant that, unlike many of my more studious classmates, my eventual graduation portfolio show would largely consist of actual published images that I shot while cutting school.

Thanks, El Niño.

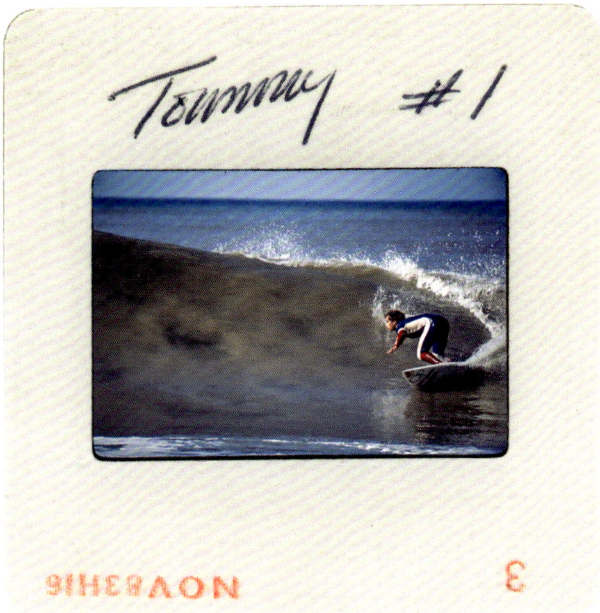
Tommy #1
3

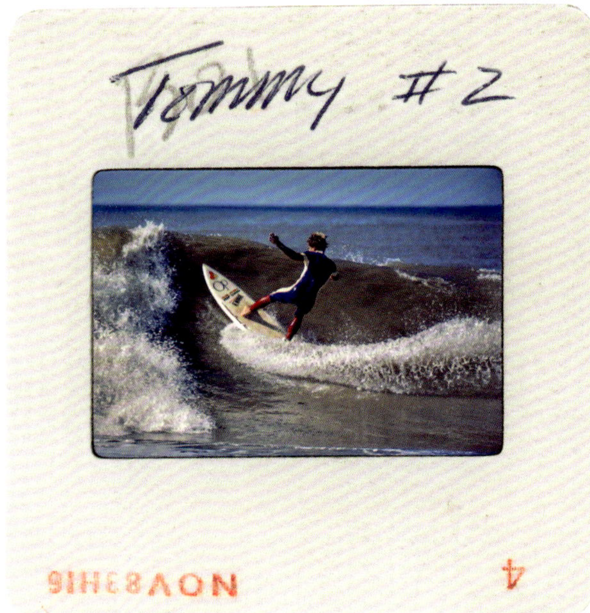
Tommy #2
4

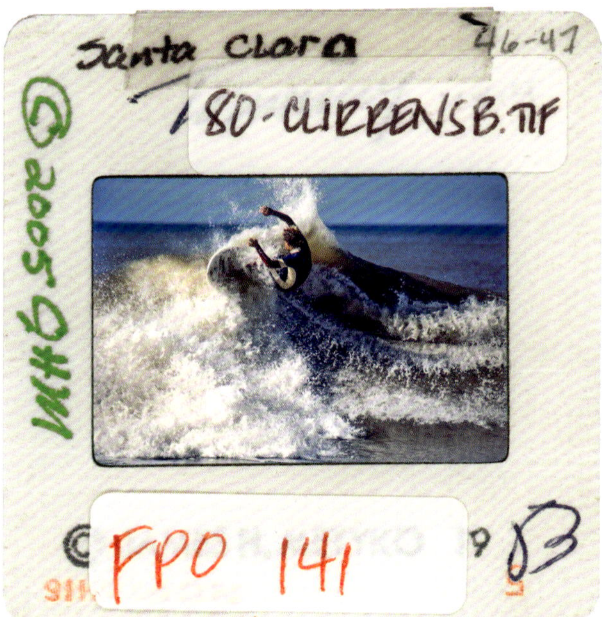
Santa Clara
46-47
180-CURRENSB.TIF
FPO 141

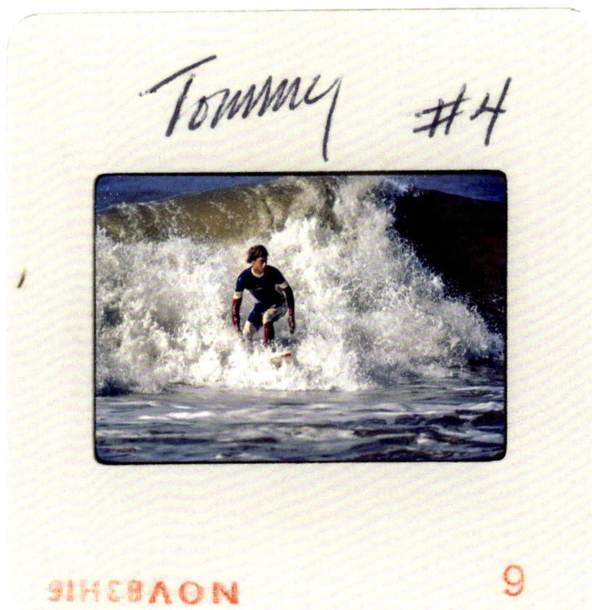
Tommy #4
6

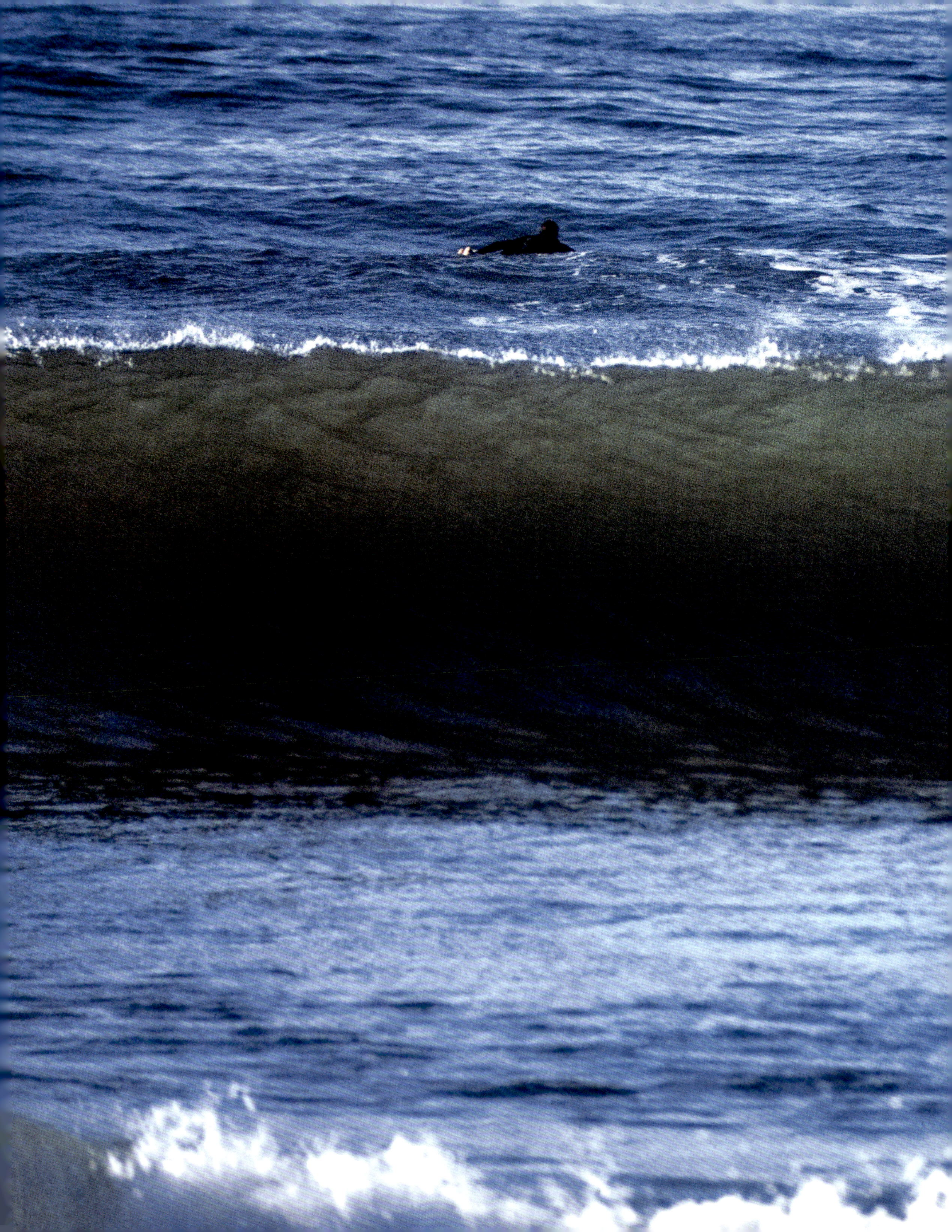

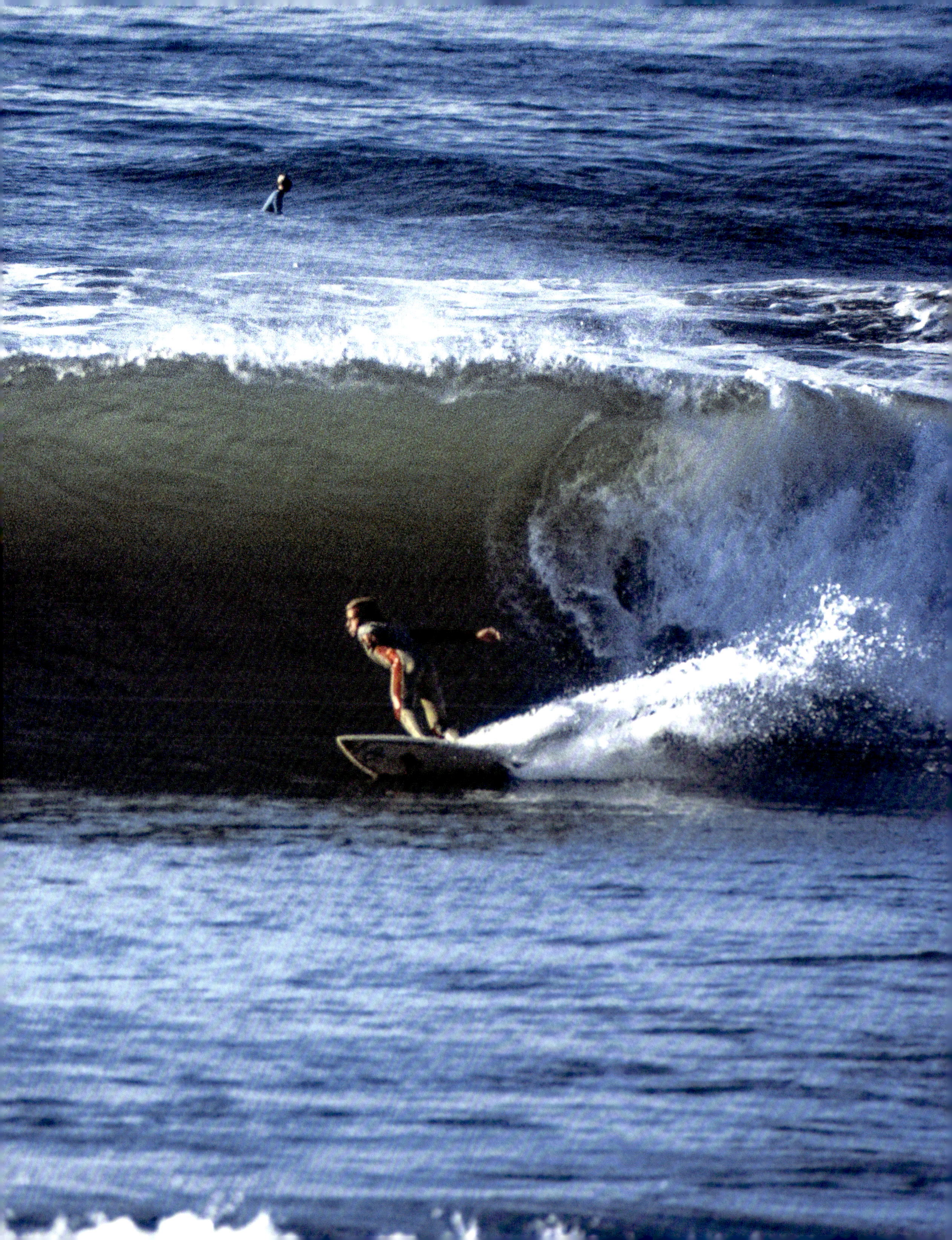

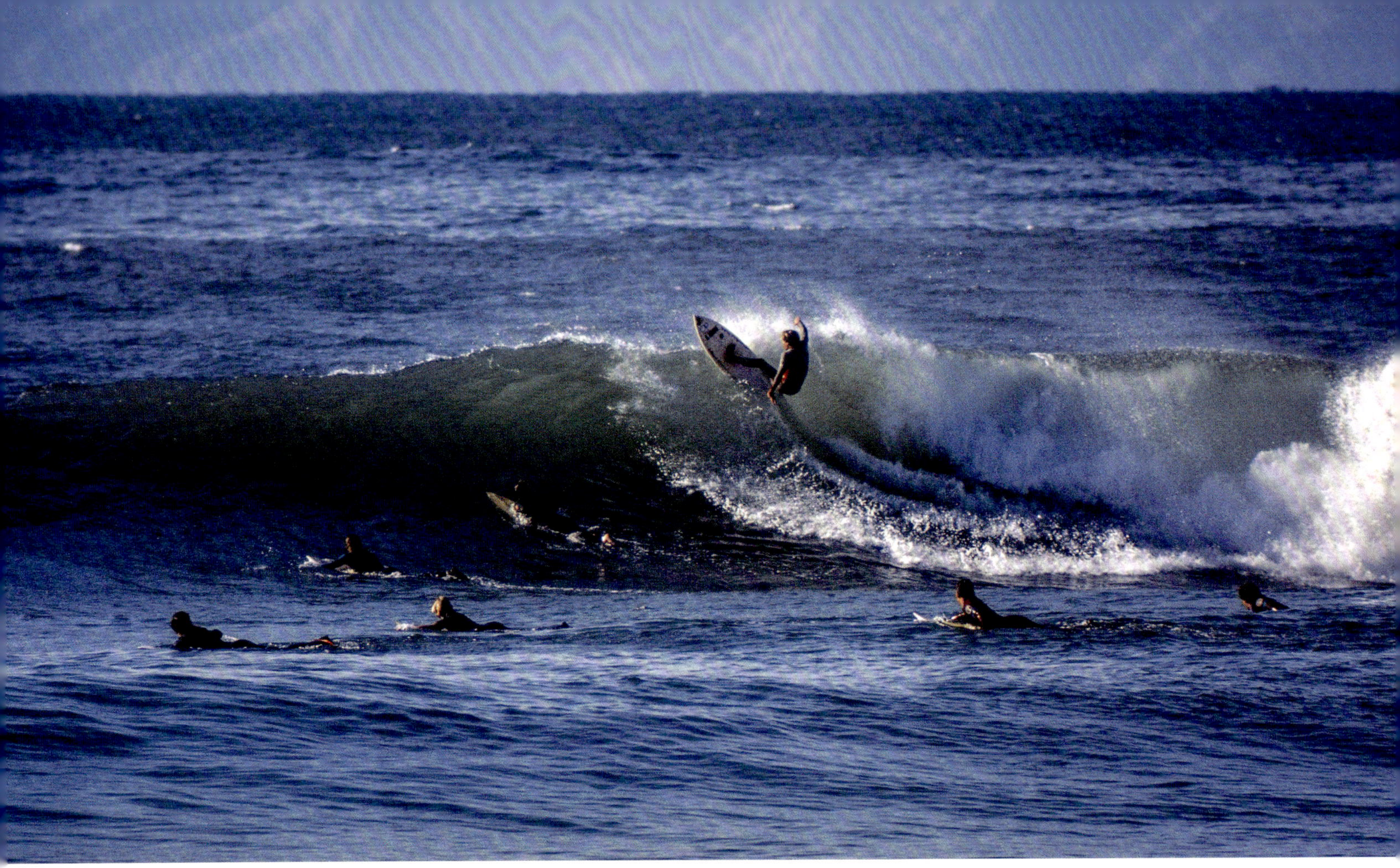

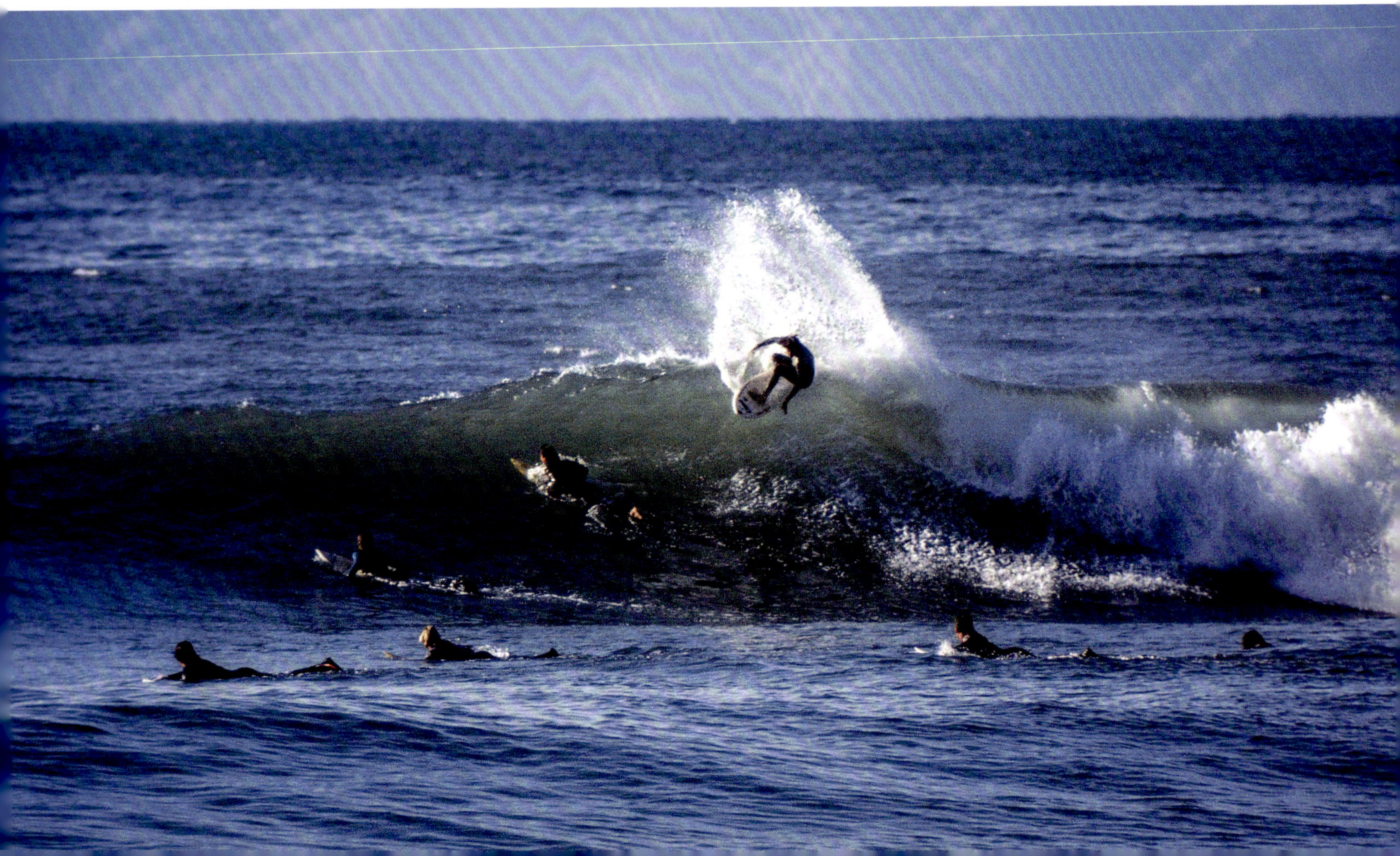

Previous and opposite

Occasionally, Rincon receives giant windswells generated by intense low-pressure systems spinning not in the Aleutians, but closer to home, off the coast of Northern California. These are not the perfect, ruler-edged lines more commonly associated with the "Queen of the Coast." Yet with the right tide and local wind conditions, these rough-margin waves clean right up as they move into the cove, offering entirely different performance options. Shot from up on the highway, Tommy is seen dancing through a perfect Rincon windswell day.

This page

Tommy went through so many boards that he never had enough sponsor laminates. He got really good with that Magic Marker.

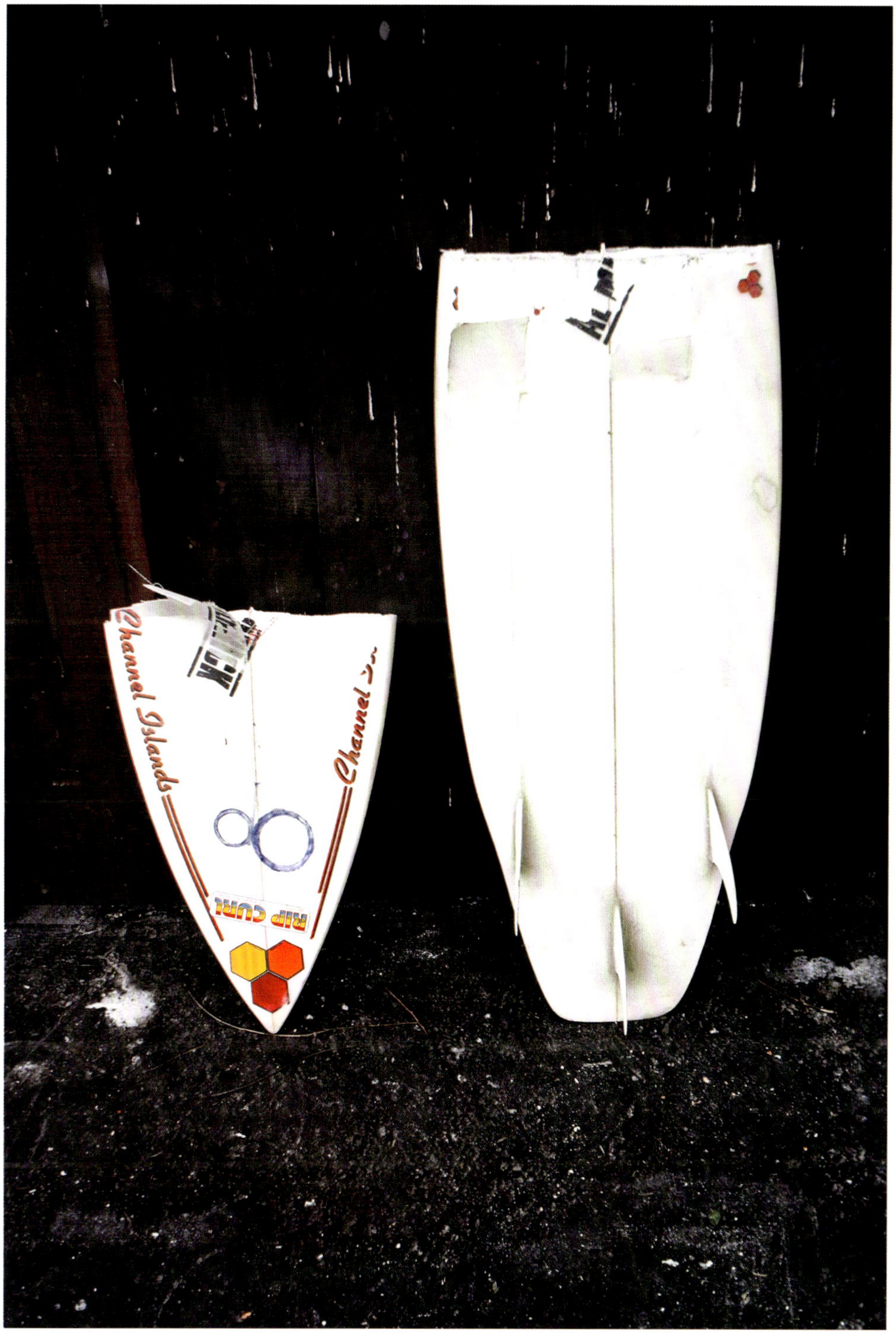

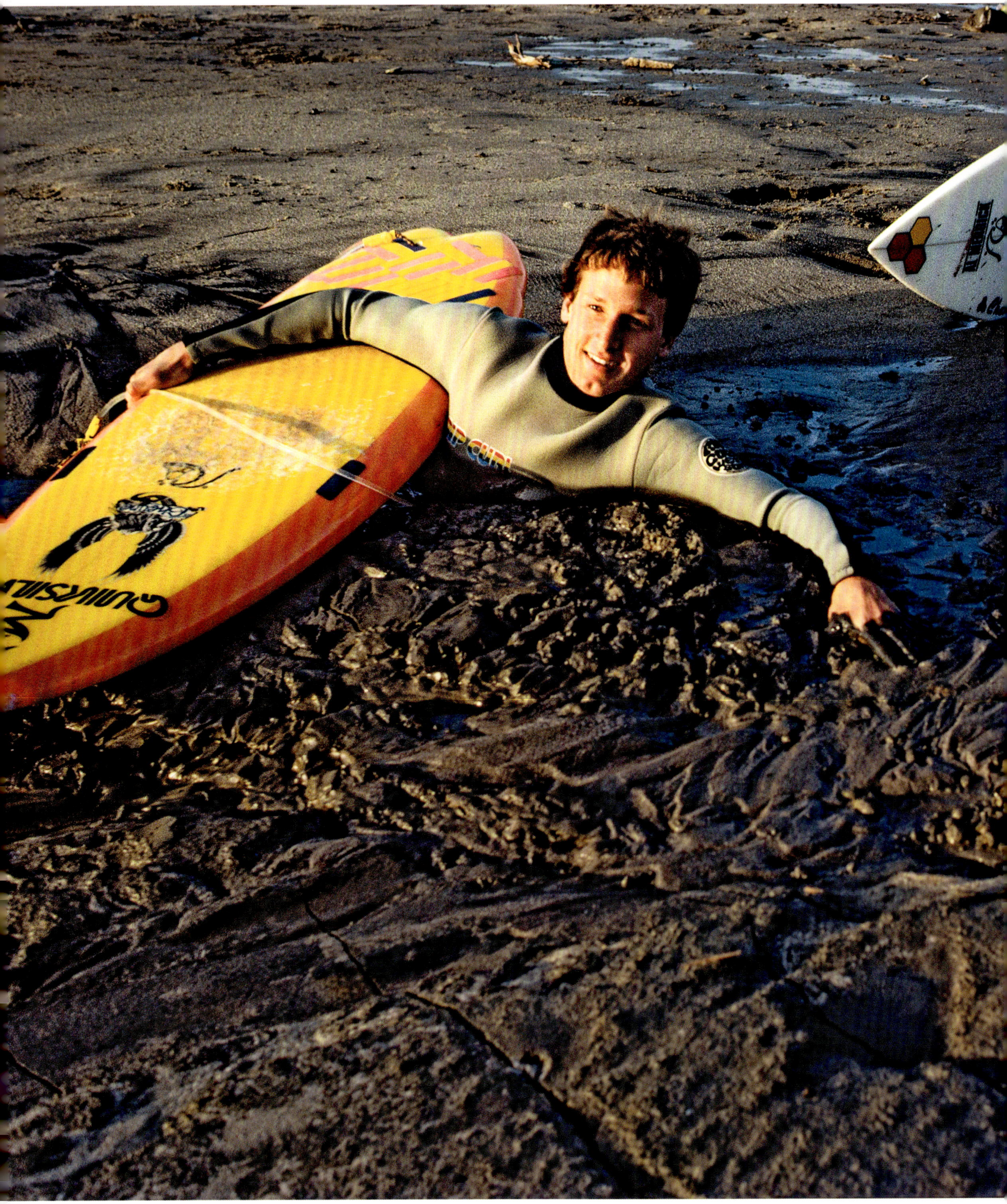

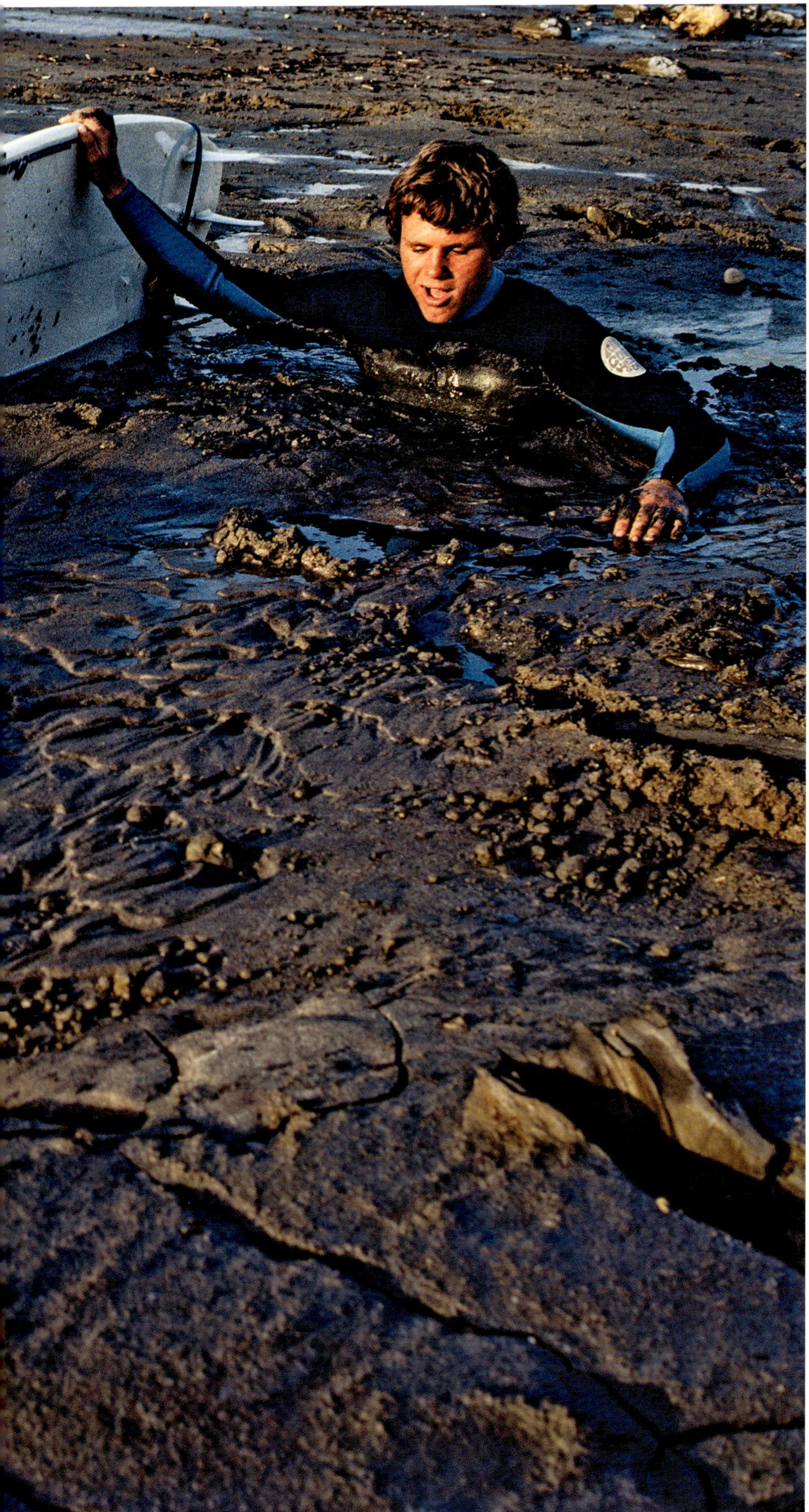

Spread

Two of Santa Barbara's brightest young talents, Tim Smalley and Dana McCorkle were also two very committed practical jokers, as evidenced by this very obviously staged shot of them sunk up to their necks in the Ventura Harbor dredge sludge that piled up on the beach during wintertime operations. But in fact a number of people that season found themselves in the very same position, when tricked into walking across the viscous mud by its layer of sun-dried crust.

Overleaf

Nineteen eighty-three was a banner year for the seldom-breaking points west of Santa Barbara, the most lusted-after being El Capitan, which when it's working is one of the world's most perfect pointbreaks. I shot this from the highway, looking down at the very inside section—which gives anyone who's ever surfed there some idea of how big the swell was. The cabin is the park ranger's home, and I could only imagine what it would've been like to grow up there.

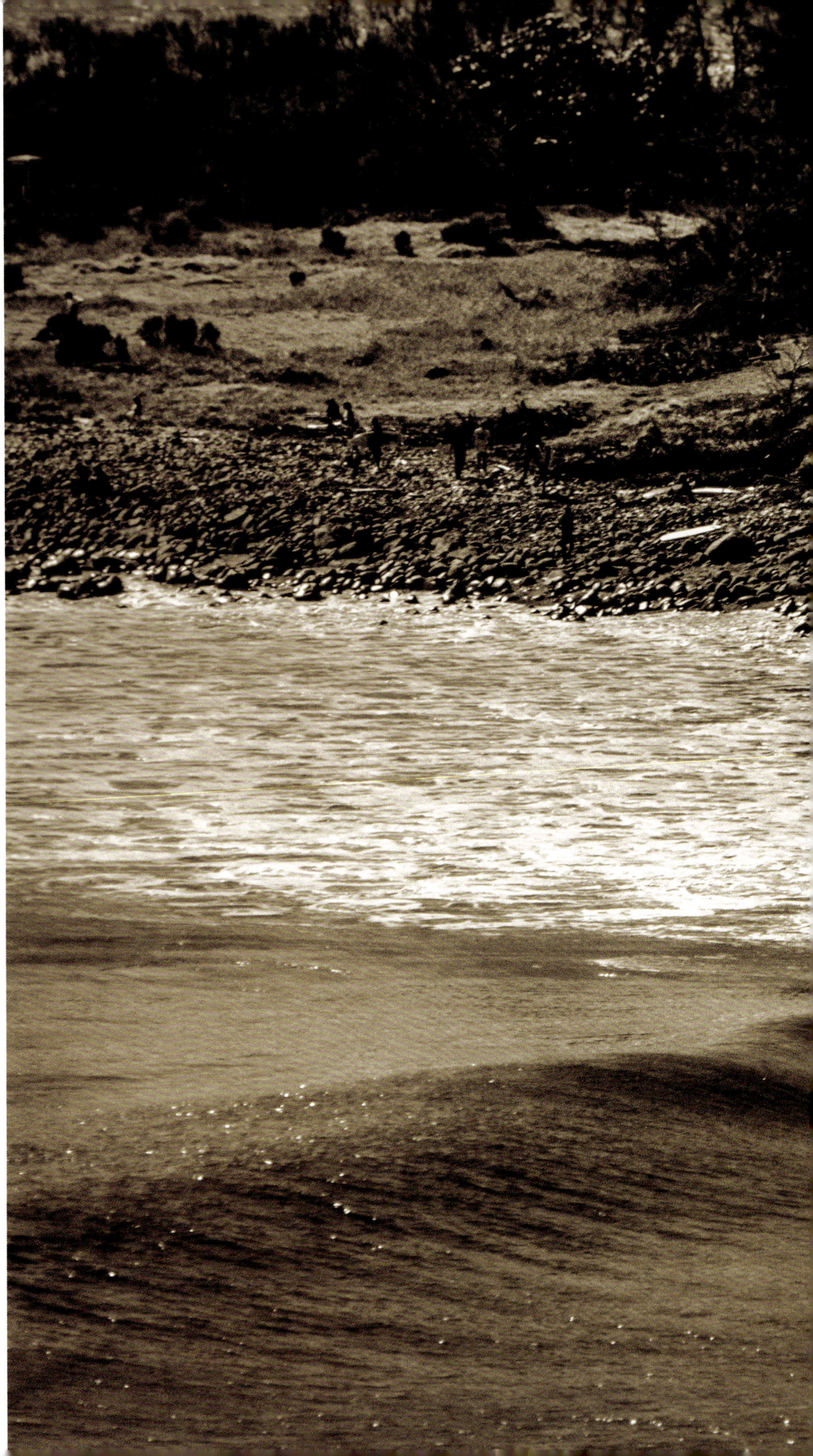

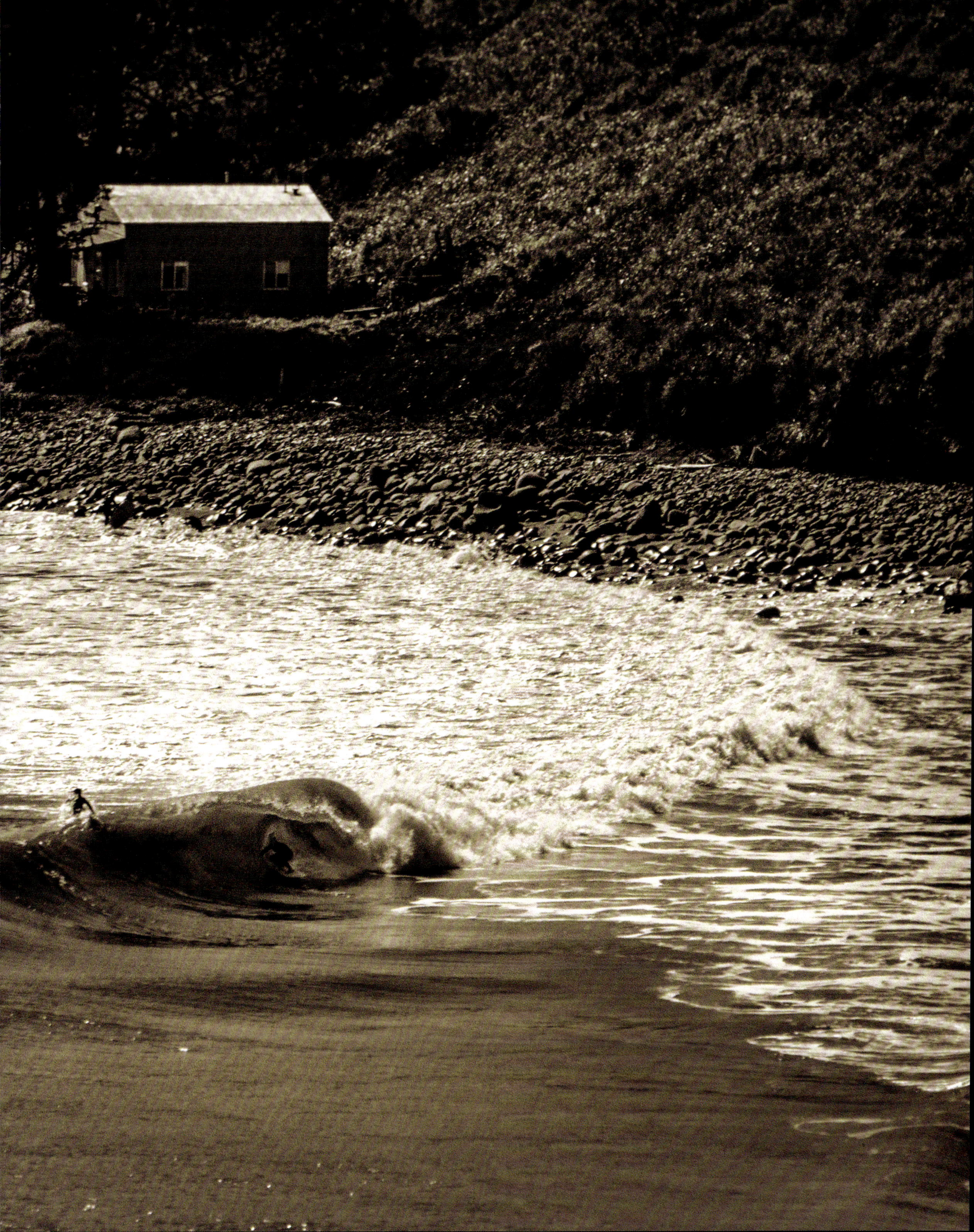

Seen here coming in from an evening Rincon session, surfer/filmmaker/writer Paul Gross was a one-man George Greenough Society, single-handedly championing the flexible kneeboard designs on which in these very waters the eccentric Santa Barbara innovator spearheaded the late-'60s "Shortboard Revolution."

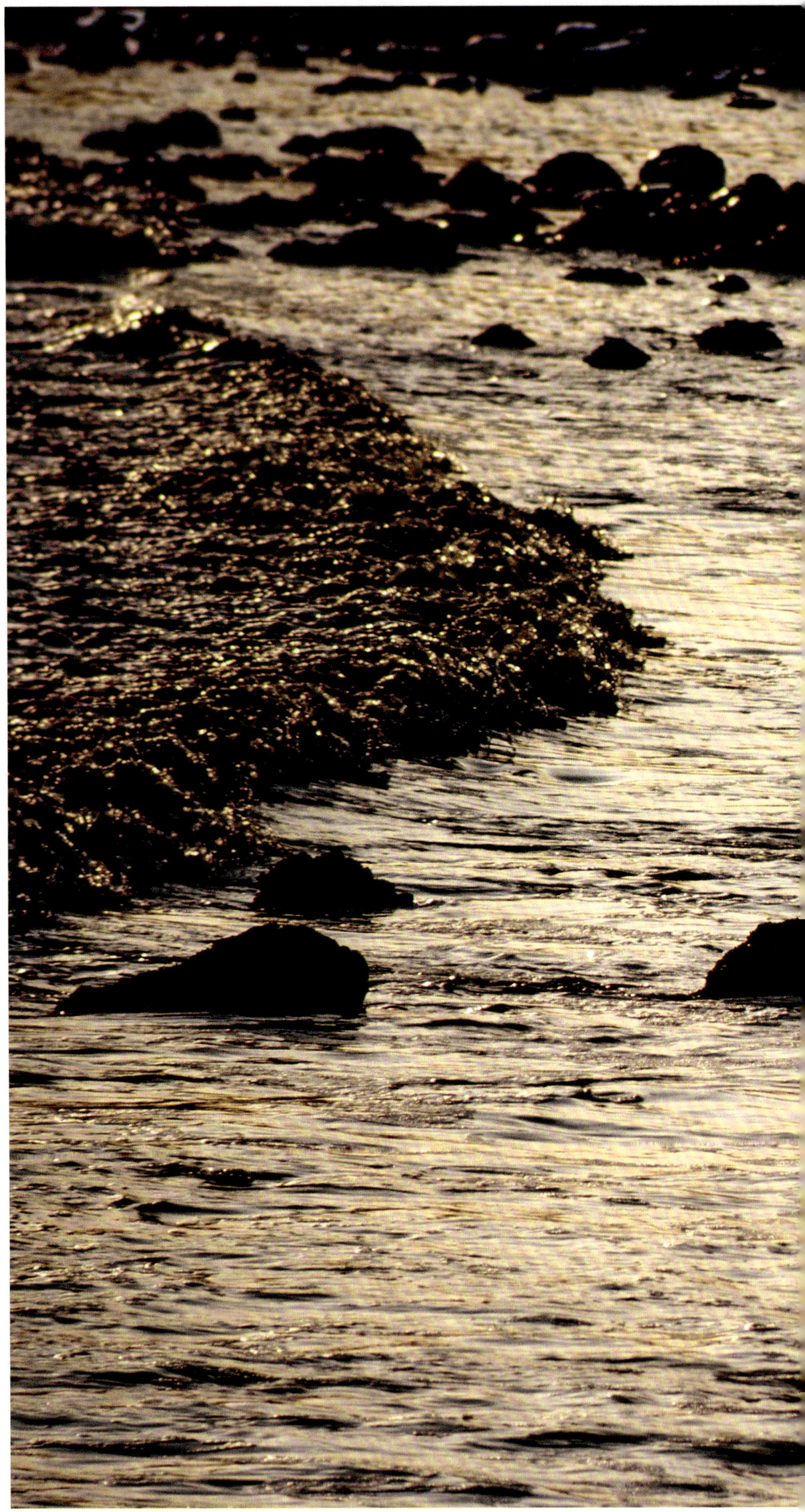

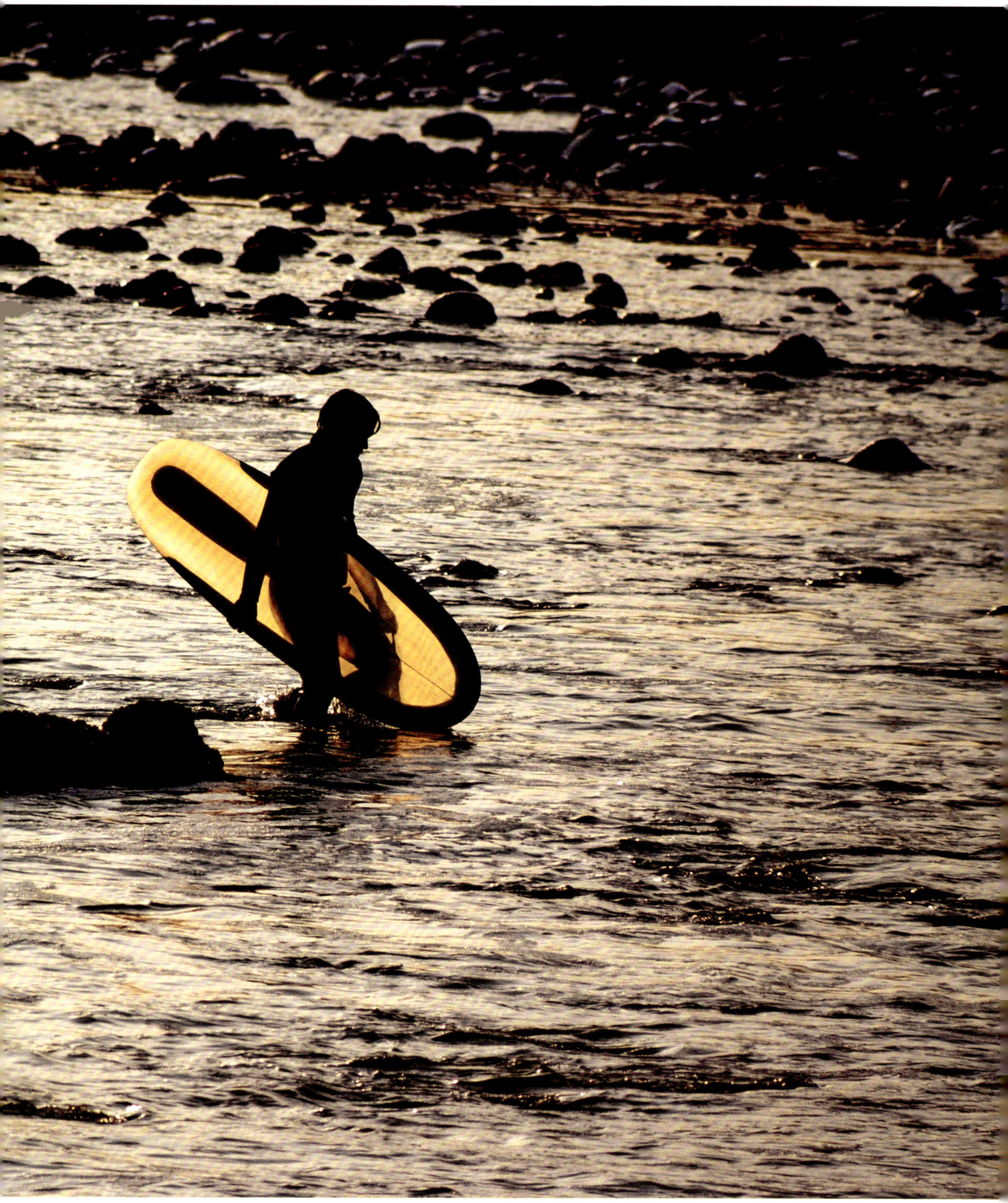

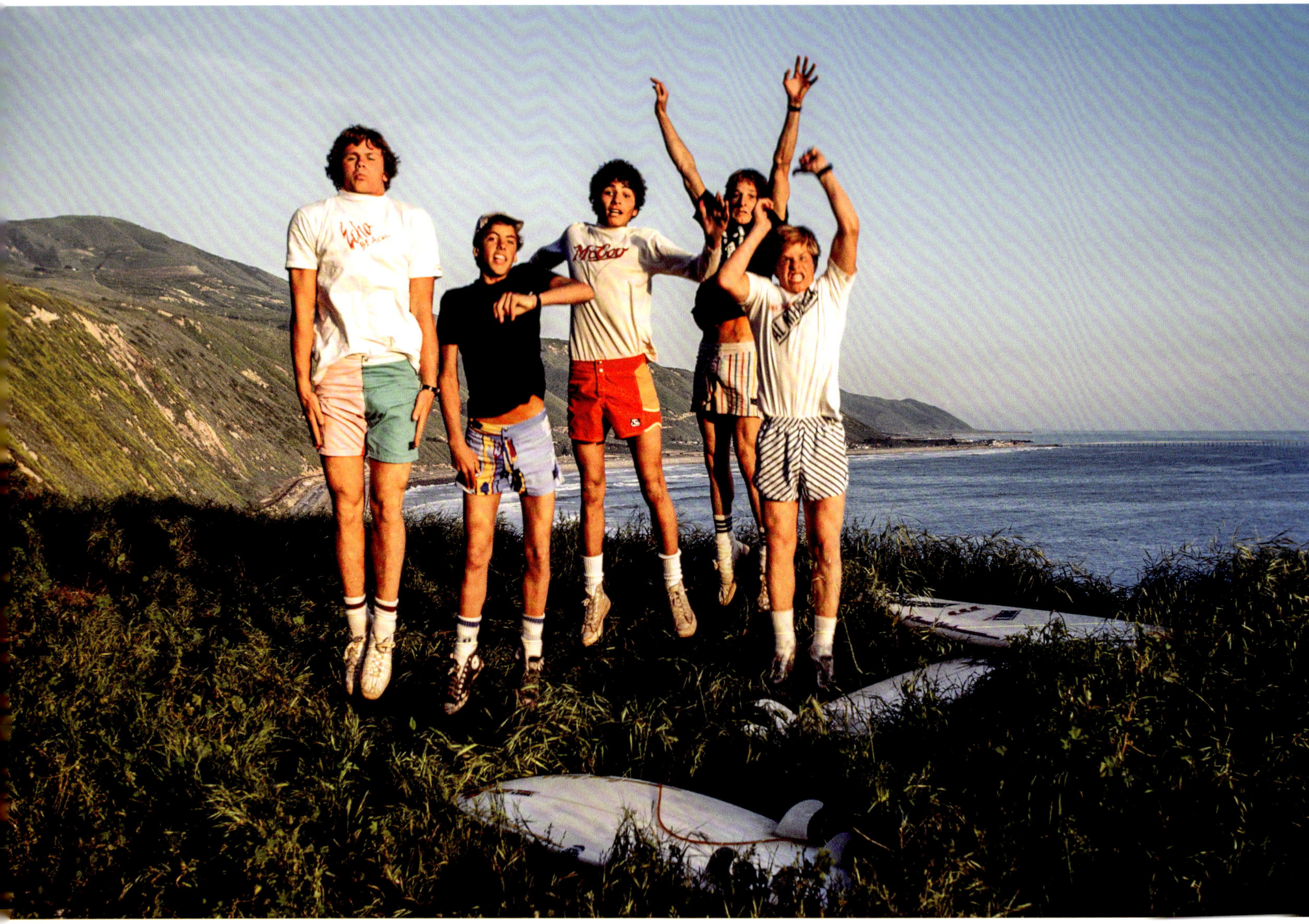

The Hammonds Kids, a collective name given to dozens of Santa Barbara high schoolers populating Hammonds Reef after school and on the weekends in the early '80s—an extremely fortunate pack of talent who came of age right during the whole Tommy/Al Merrick/El Niño confluence, ranging from amateur competitive surfers to sons of fishermen, future world-class shapers, and future A-list actors. *(Left to right)* Dana McCorkle, Matt Mondragon, Gabriel Novoa, Tim Smalley, and Josh Klein.

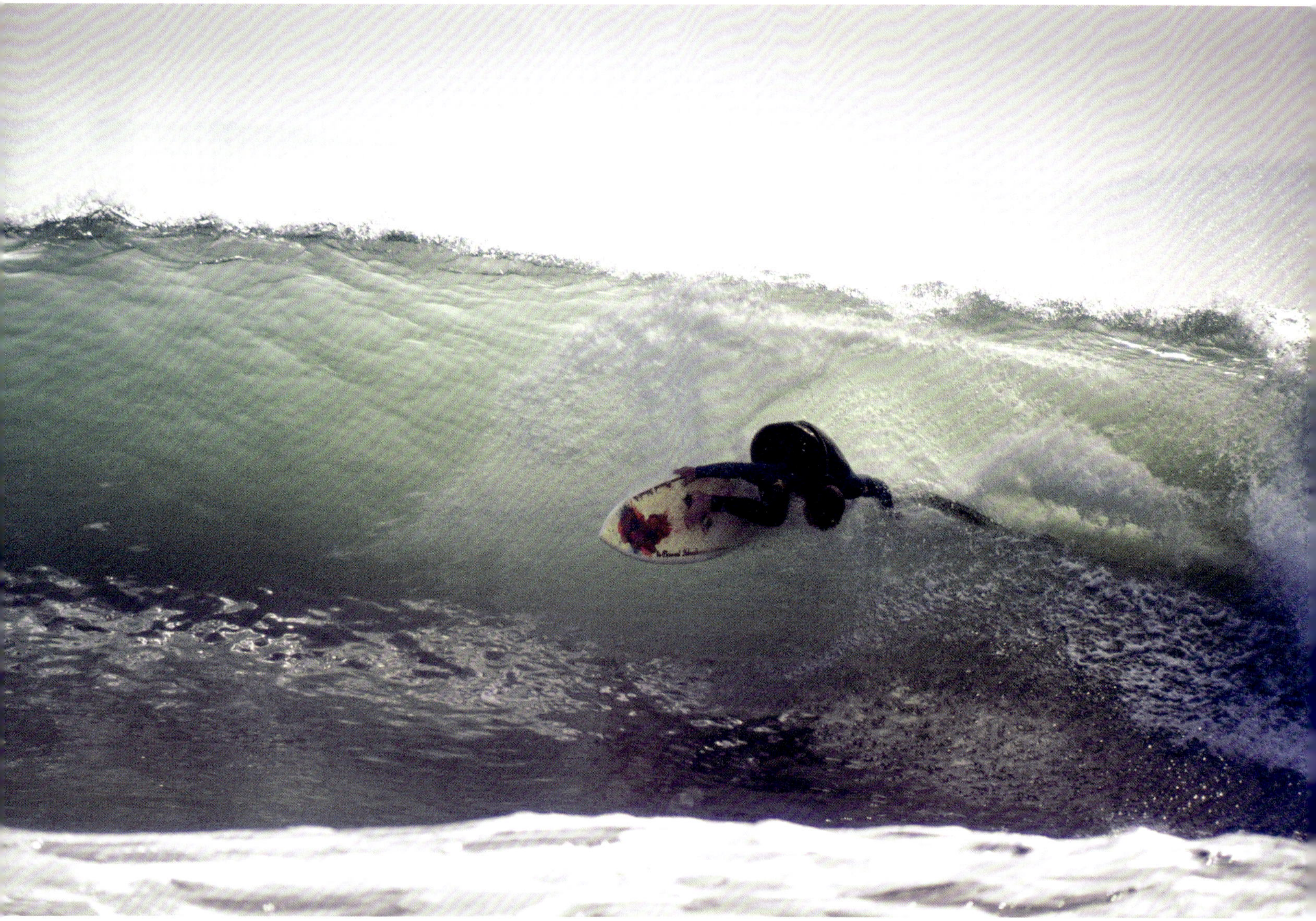

Davey Smith hated surfing crowded Rincon and would sometime drive right by just so he could look in his rearview mirror and see it as a left pointbreak. Whenever he did go out, he ripped the place backside, setting the pace for future Santa Barbara goofyfooters like Bobby Martinez.

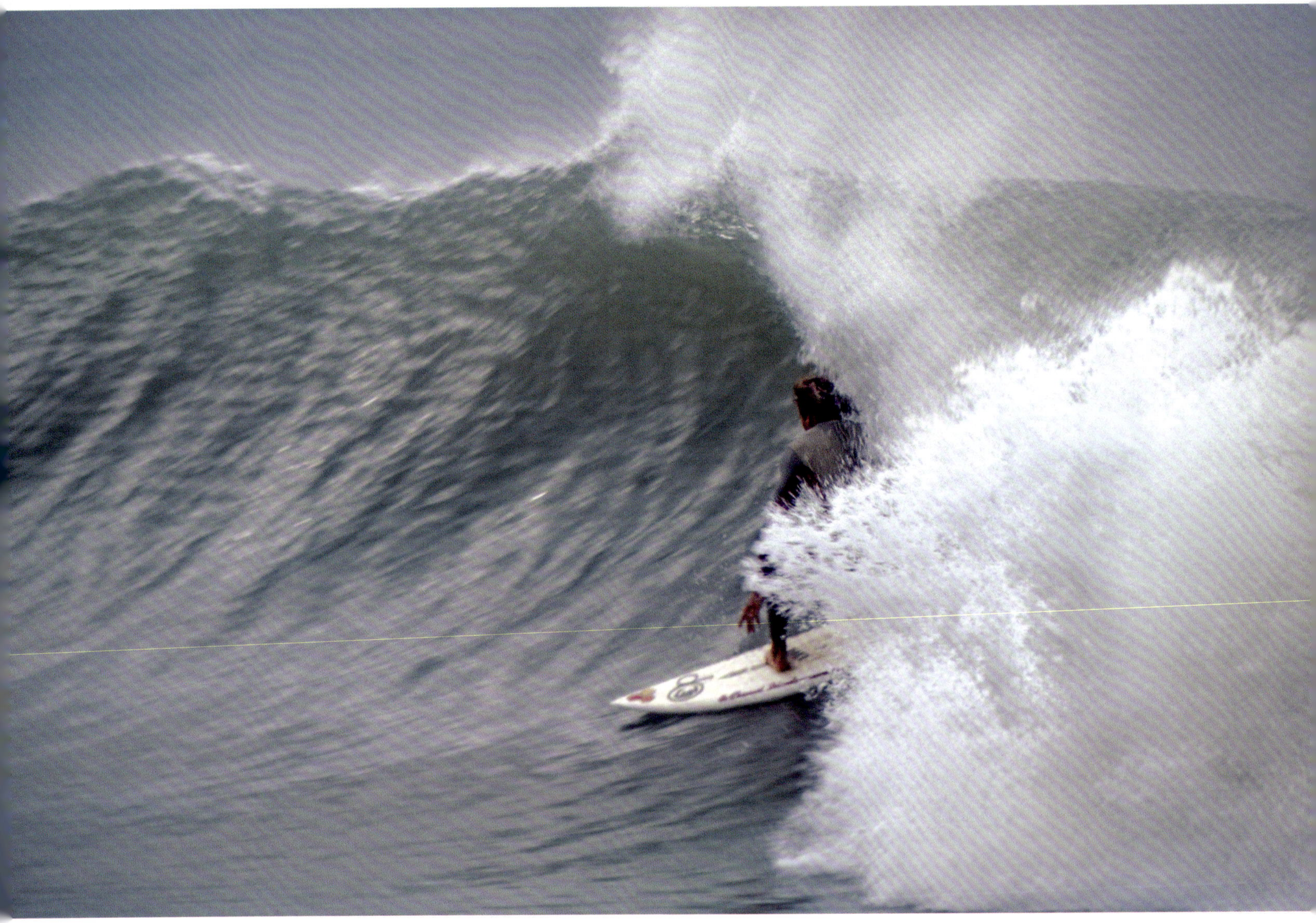

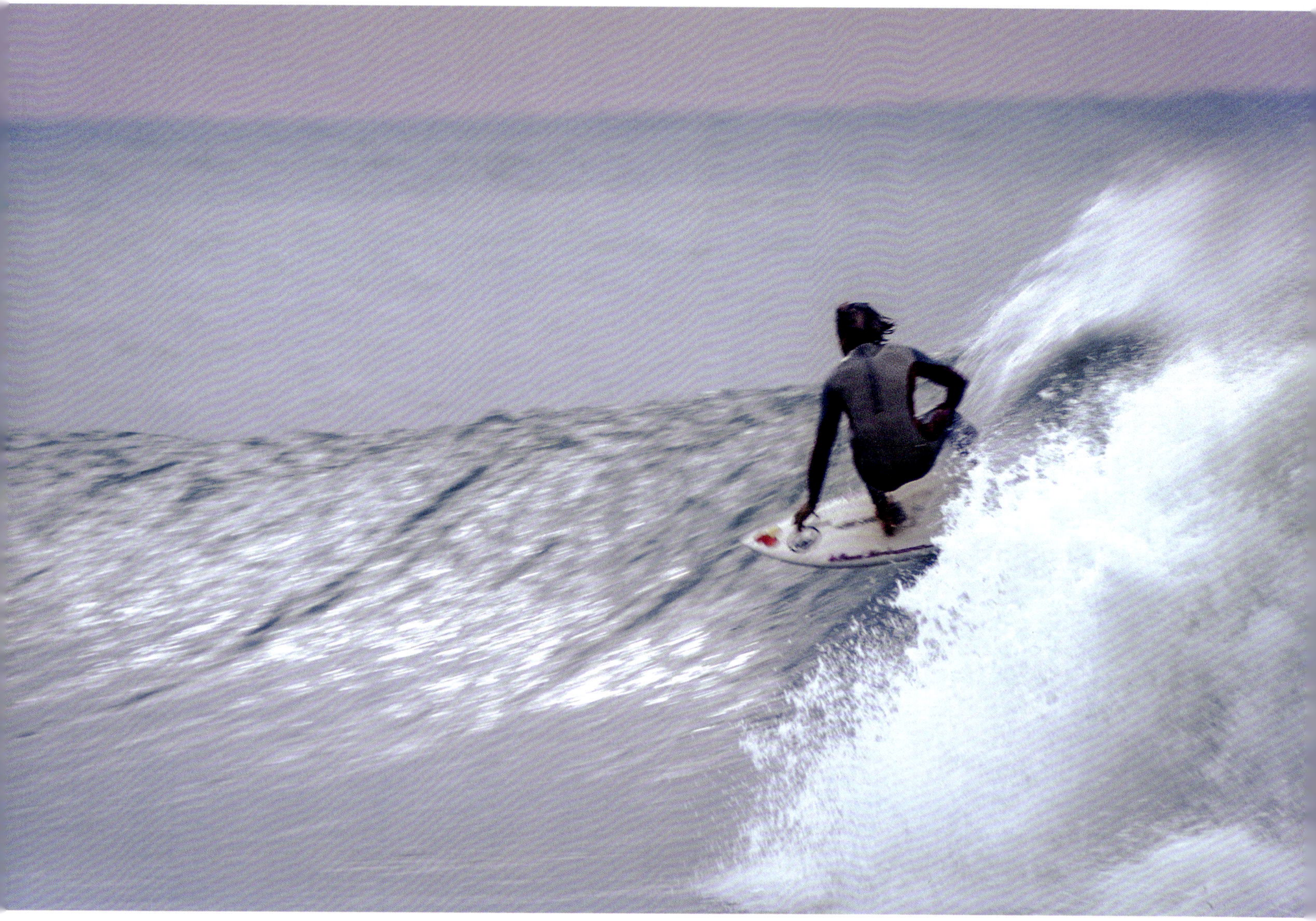

Tommy, speed-blurring into the barrel at all-time Pitas Point in Ventura. On this rainy, otherwise junky morning of surf, Sam and I, at Tommy's behest, had cleverly ditched a well-known surf filmmaker who had wanted to shoot Tommy for his upcoming movie. Luring the poor guy back to chopped-up Rincon, we instead backtracked to Pitas, where we found the wind had switched offshore, the waves had turned on, and only Sam and Tommy were there to ride them. Tommy had said he just wanted to go surfing, without having to worry about being filmed. By this point in our relationship, I was guessing my camera didn't count.

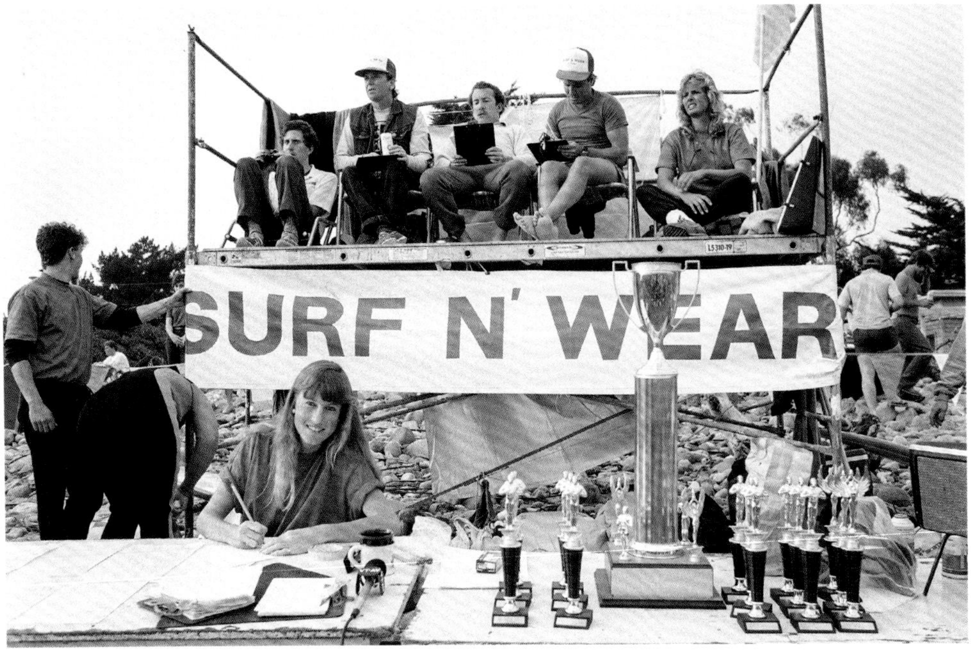

The Rincon Classic

Dubbed "The Best Little Pro/Am Surf Contest in California," the Rincon Classic has remained the region's premier "locals only" event for more than forty years. First run in 1979, the Classic was conceived by Santa Barbara surf shop owners Jeff White and Roger Nance of Surf N Wear as a way to bring a disparate collection of area surfers together as a community, and for seventeen consecutive years they were successful beyond anyone's expectations. Chris Keet and the Surf Happens crew restarted the engine in 2001 and have continued to foster the event's legacy to this day.

Above

While judges look on from their so-called tower, head tabulator *(and popular Surf N Wear shop employee)* Lauren Wilmot does the math.

Facing

Part of the Rincon Classic's charm is how world champions get an opportunity to relive their roles as local heroes, to the obvious delight of everyone involved. Kim Mearig and young Sarah Aresco, sharing the vibe.

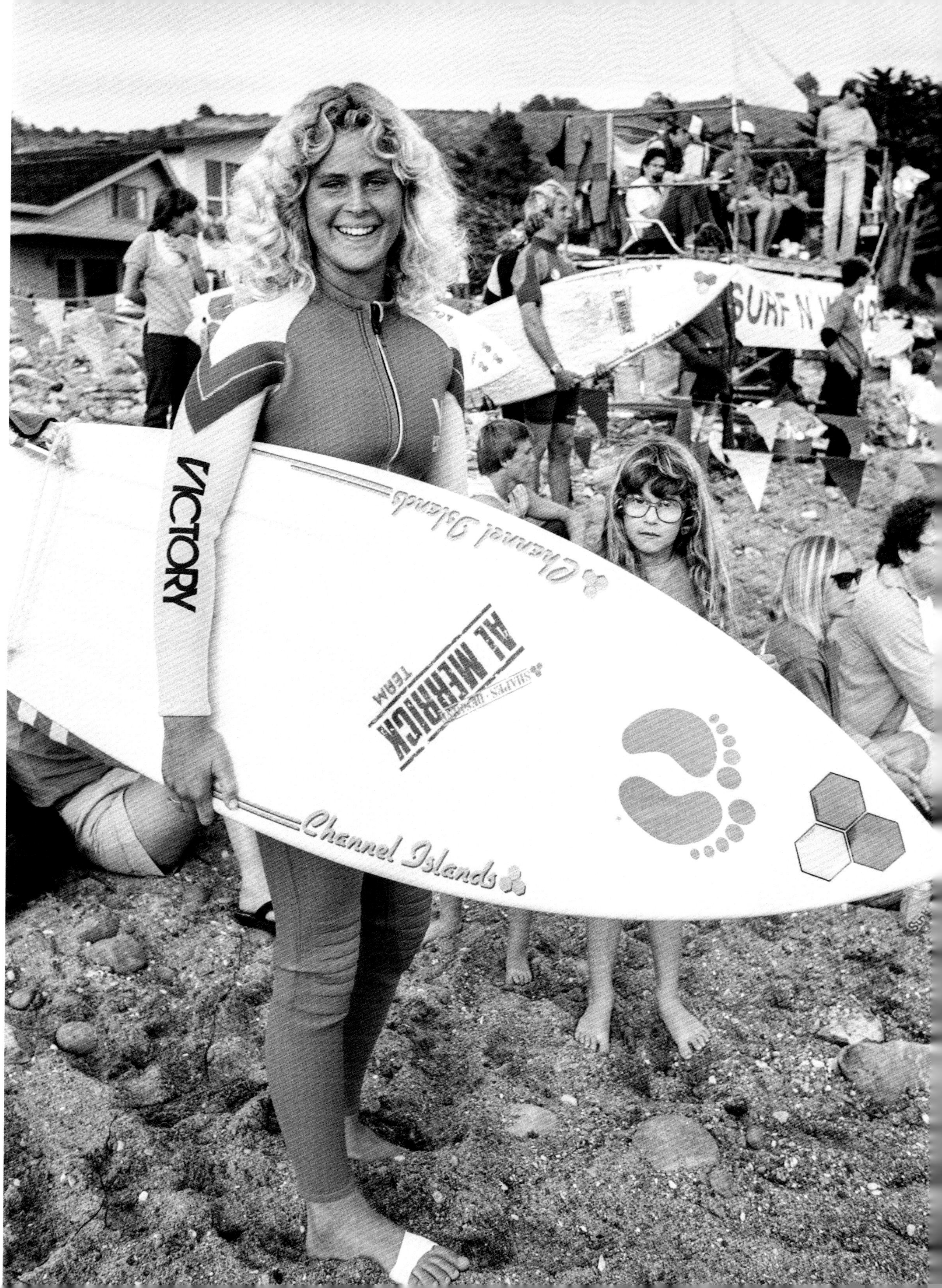
VICTORY
Channel Islands
AL MERRICK
TEAM
Channel Islands

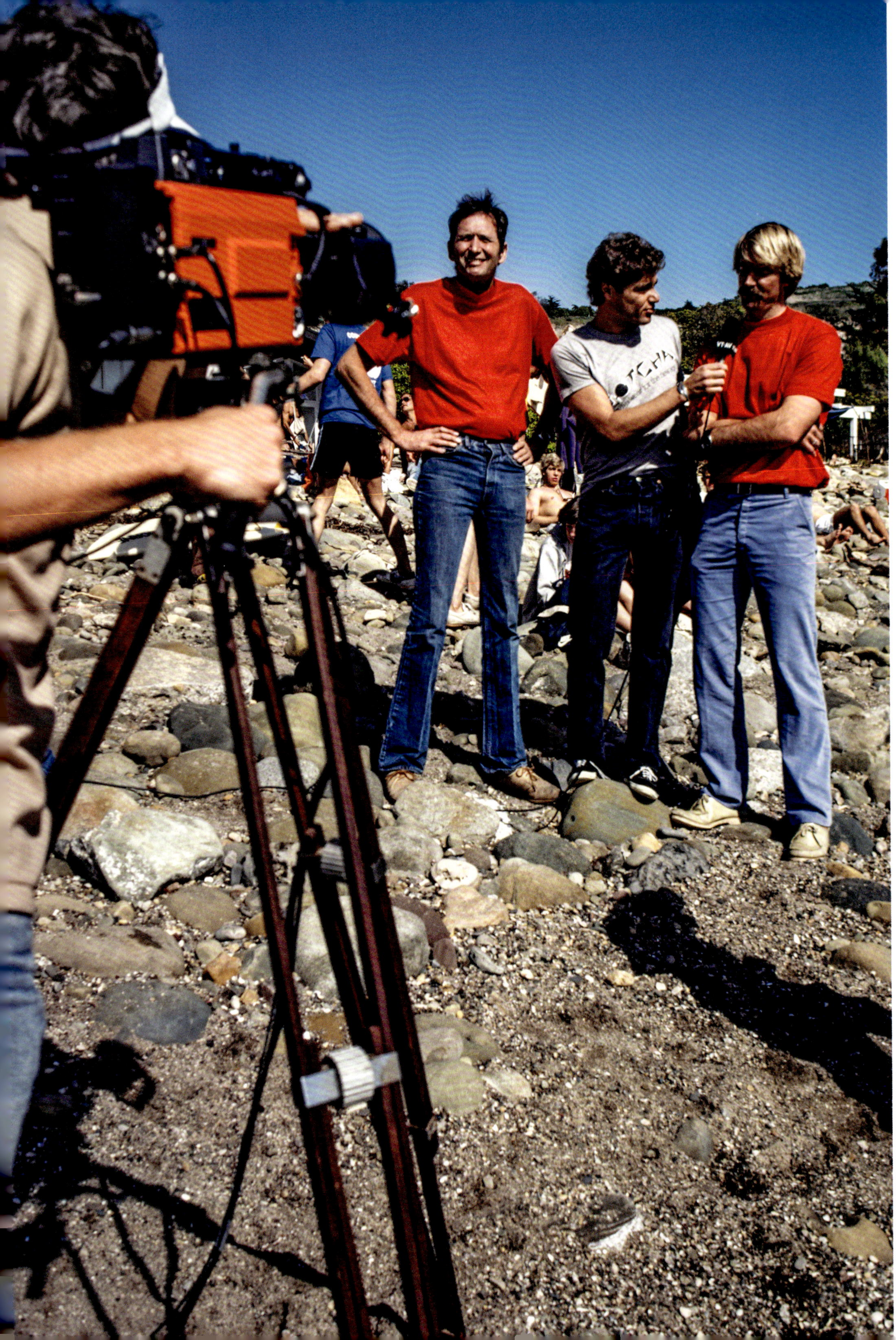

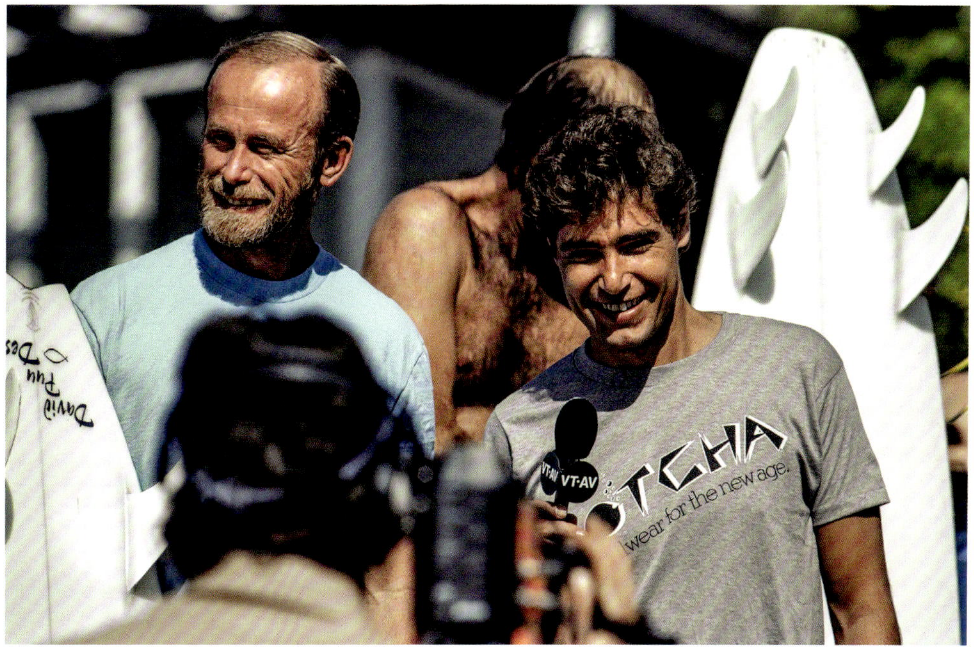

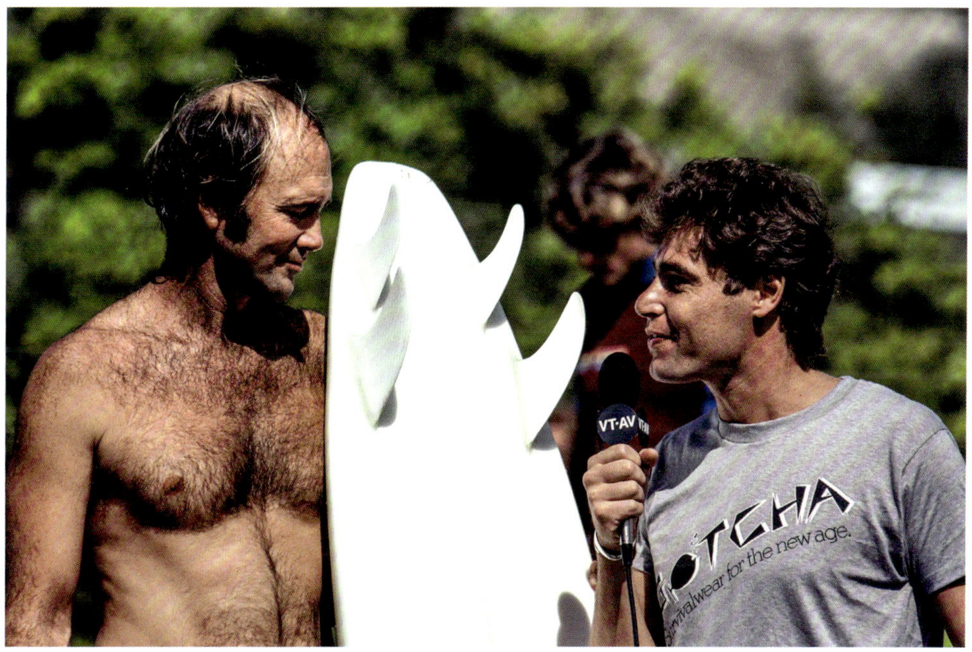

This year for the Rincon Classic, Michael Tomson, Shaun's cousin *(and founder of Gotcha Sportswear)*, was on hand to man the mic for lead sponsor Gotcha's film on the event, handling interview duties with local notables like Jeff White and Roger Nance *(left)*, venerable fiberglasser Bob Haakenson *(top)*, and Al Merrick *(bottom)*.

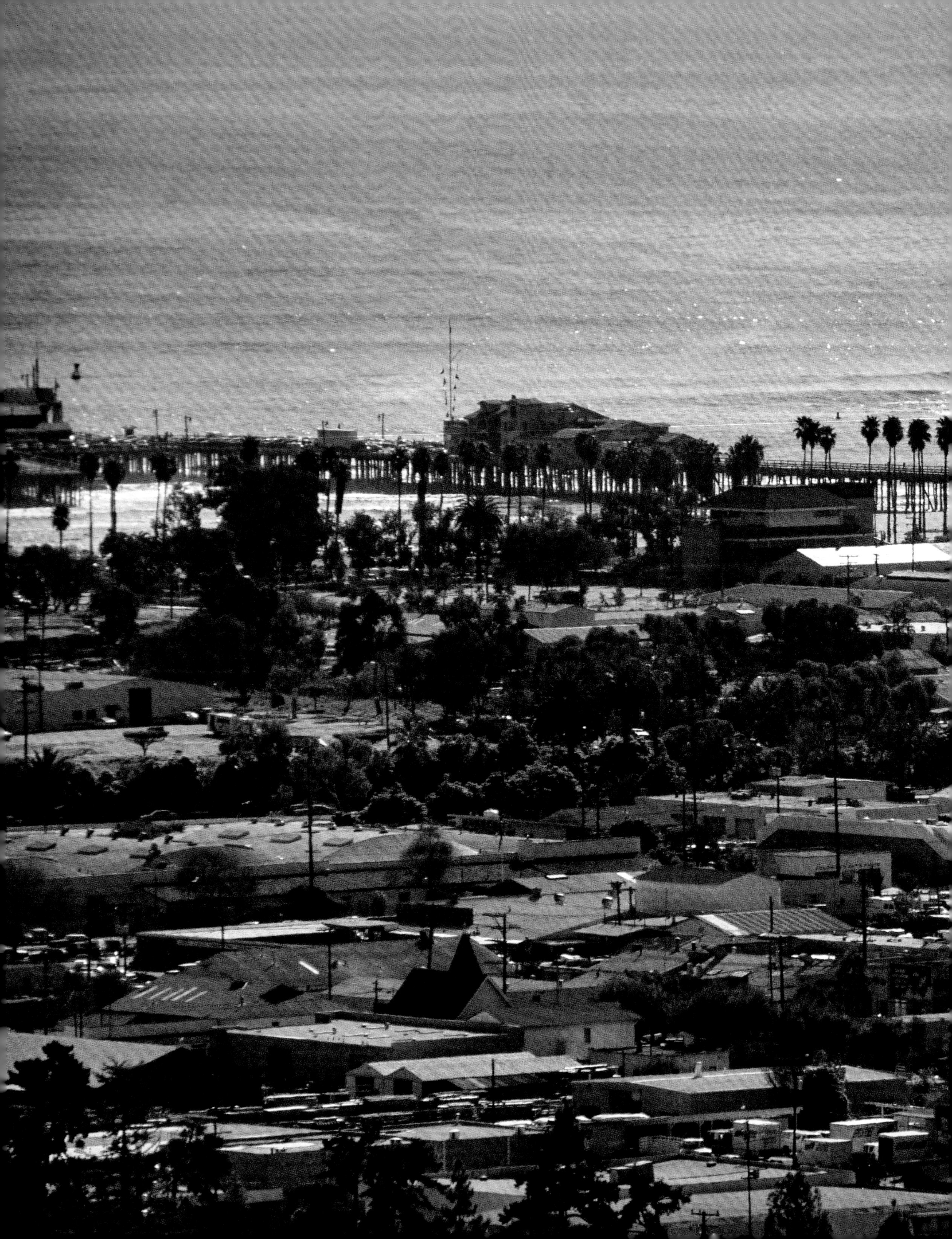

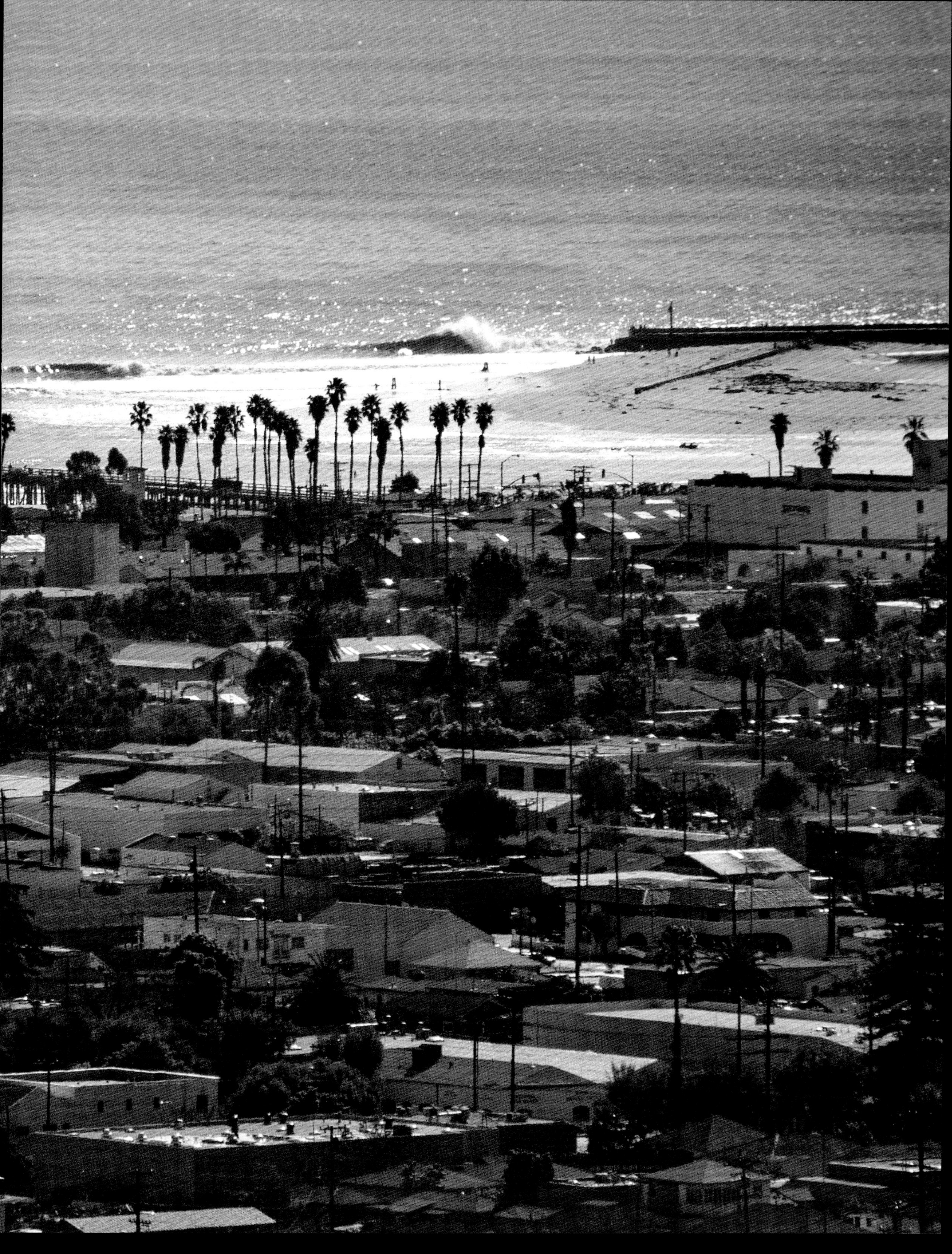

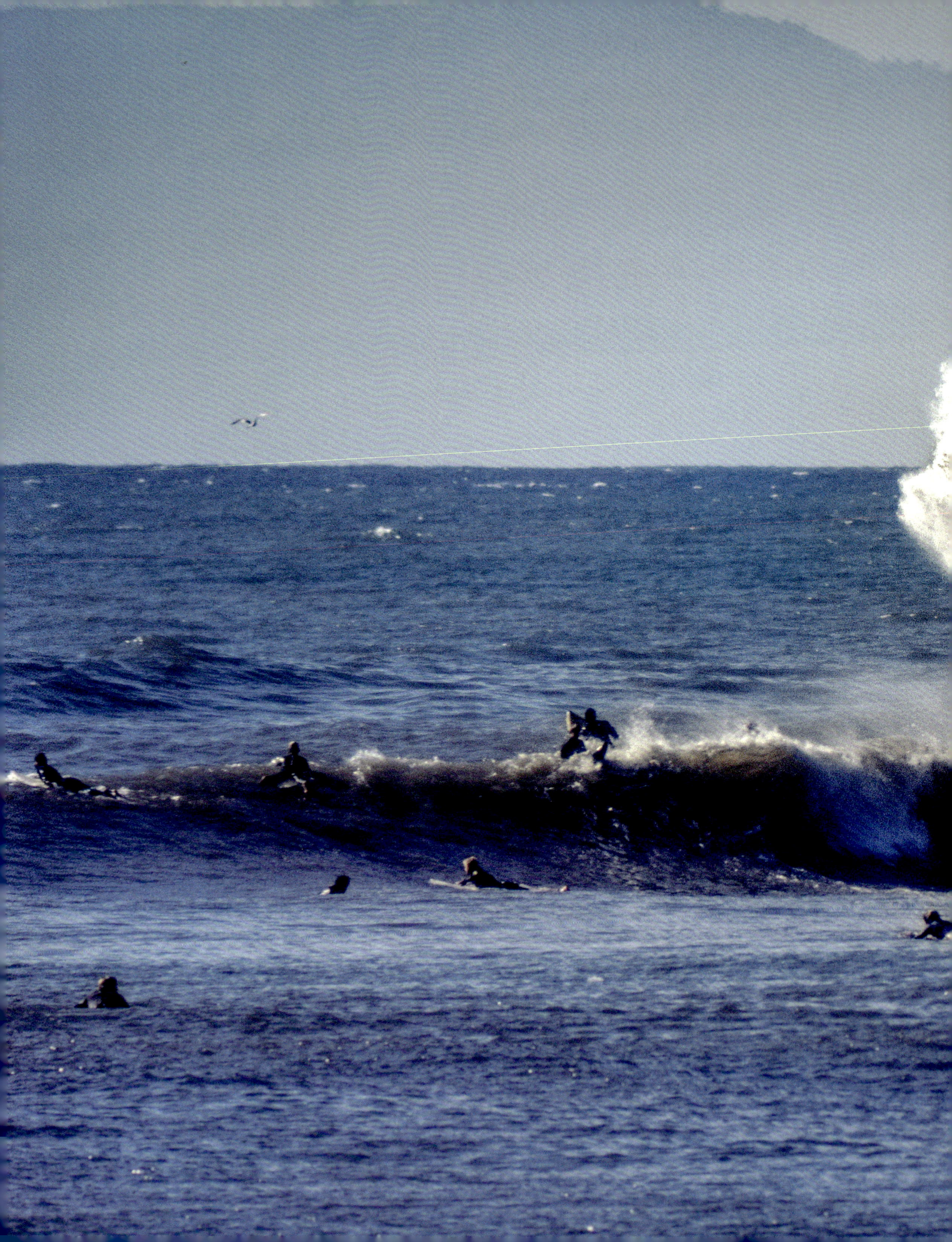

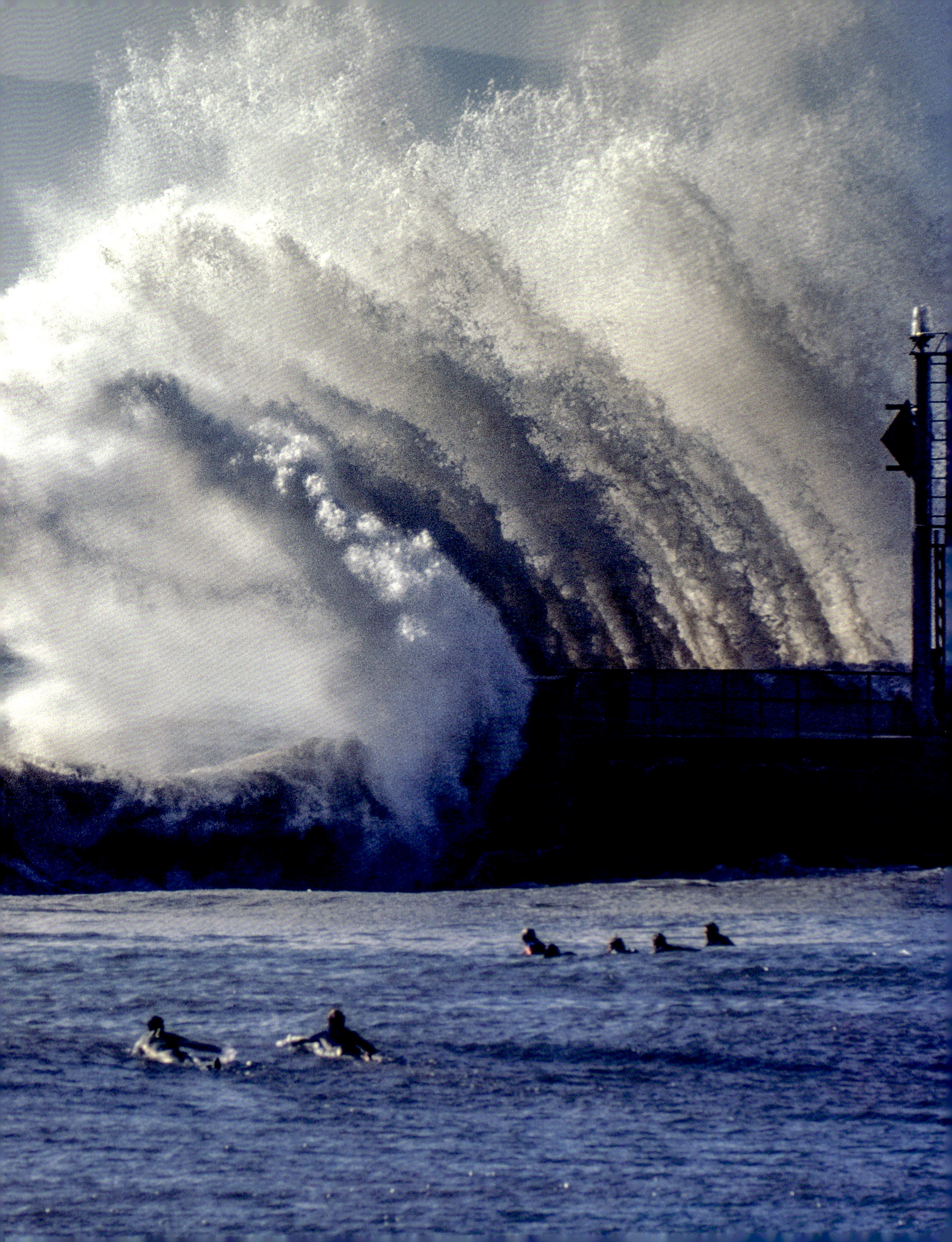

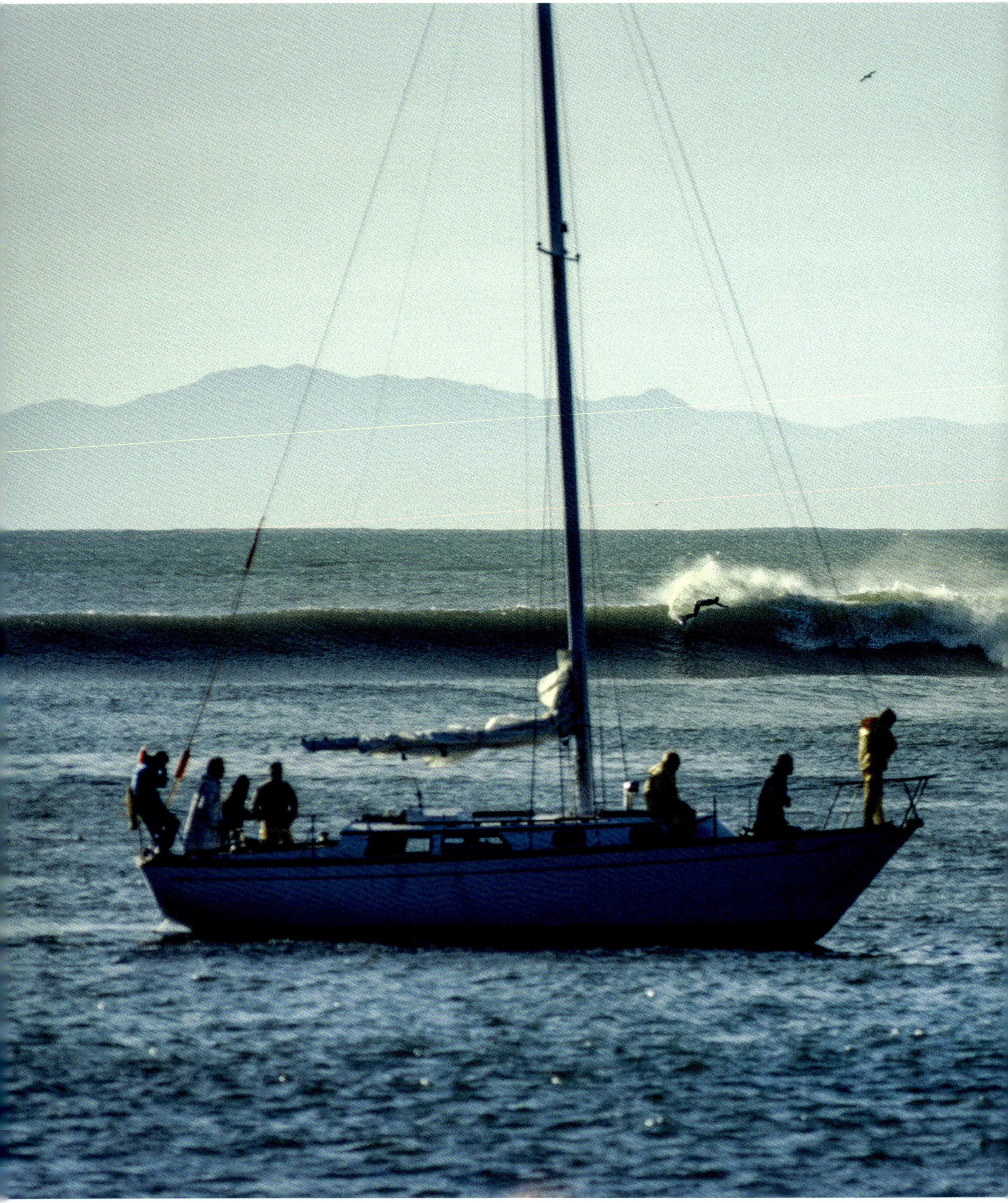

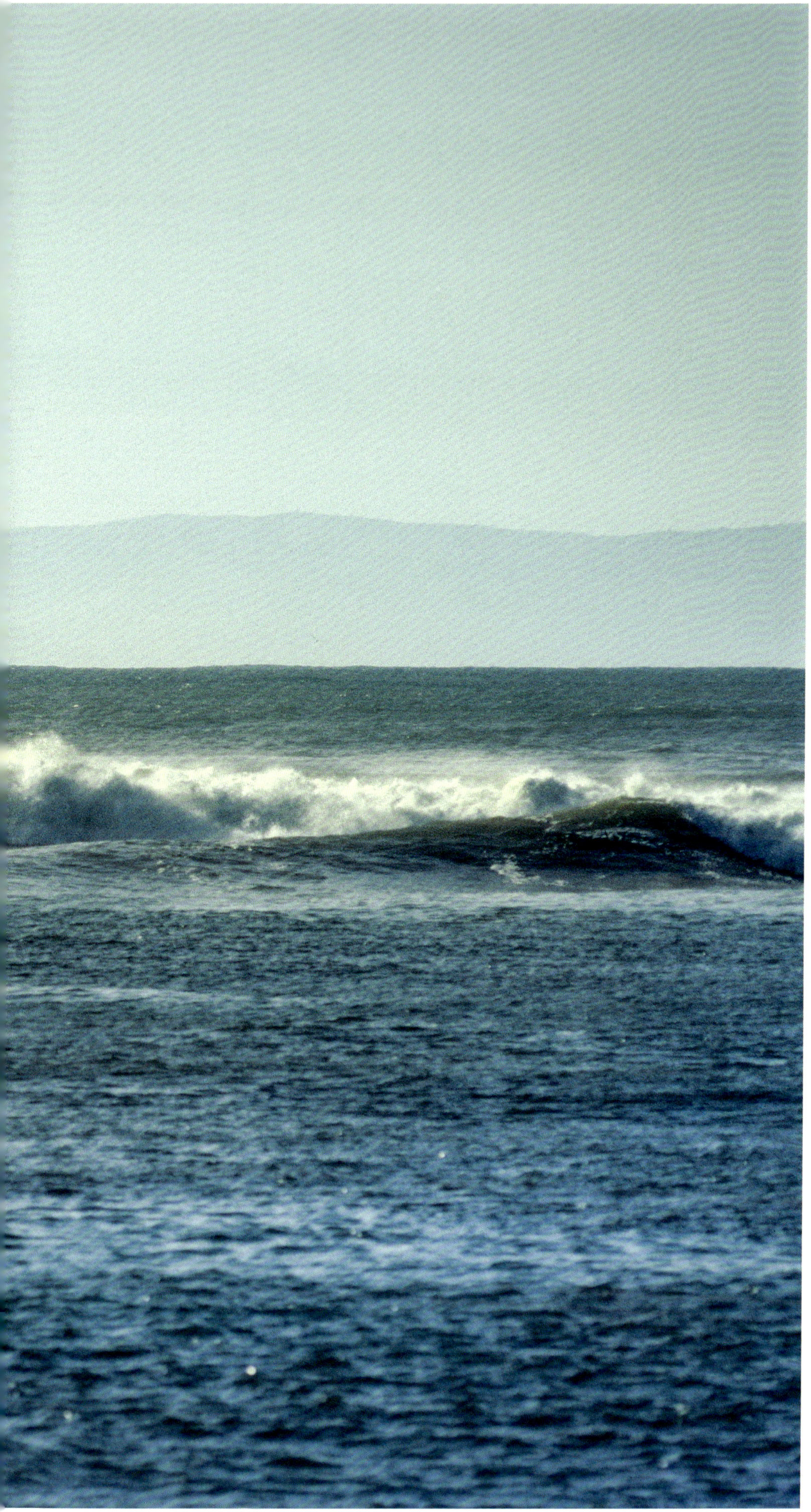

Pages 244–245

When I first moved to Santa Barbara, the best advice I received about the Sandspit was, "It's too inconsistent to wait for. Go about your life, and when it happens, it will happen." Sandspit broke so many times during the El Niño year of 1983 that surfers who'd ordinarily never miss a chance to surf there must've taken that advice too, as during less-than-epic swells there were plenty of uncrowded days. This is the view from a Brooks Institute parking lot, shot between classes.

Previous and this page

The wave at Sandspit does a lot of work before finding a surfer to ride it. First it must make its way around geographically prominent Point Conception to the northwest. Next it has to sneak past San Miguel, Santa Rosa, and Santa Cruz islands, which wait just offshore to block its path. Then it has to hit Santa Barbara Harbor's west-to-east-oriented breakwall at just the right angle, rippling along its length rather than colliding head on. Finally, if it survives the crazy, unpredictable backwash off the breakwall's tip, it rolls onto the exquisitely shaped sandbar that has earned the devotion of several generations of local surfers, none of whose names it will ever know.

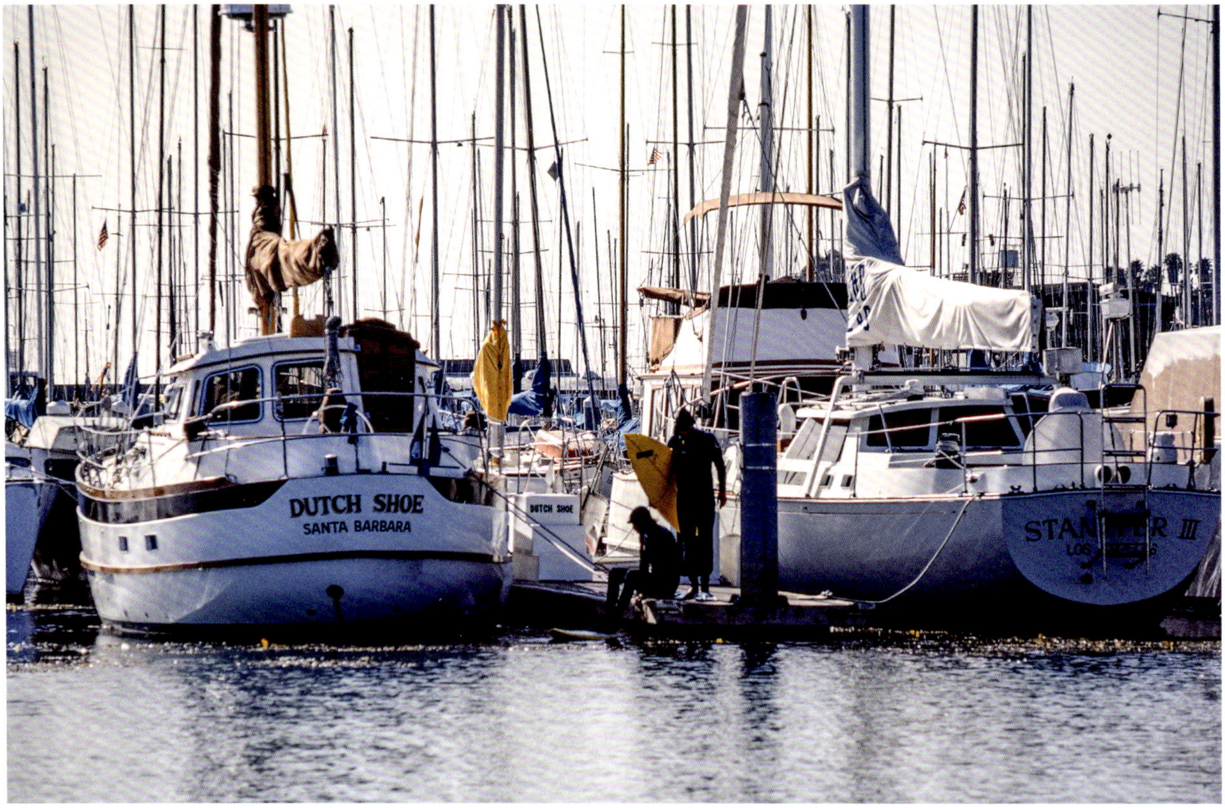

The Harbor

At one point in the winter season, Sandspit had been breaking for two weeks straight—more than at any other time in living memory. And just like that, Santa Barbara Harbor, home to working-class abalone, urchin, and swordfish fleets, transformed into a surf town, especially for the lucky "live-aboards" who operated out of their rented slips. For those two weeks, at least, these fortunate few could eat, sleep, and surf without ever leaving the harbor, as did this pair of temporary locals, who paddled out with the tide, then later drifted back in on it, with at least a portion of their enviable reputations intact.

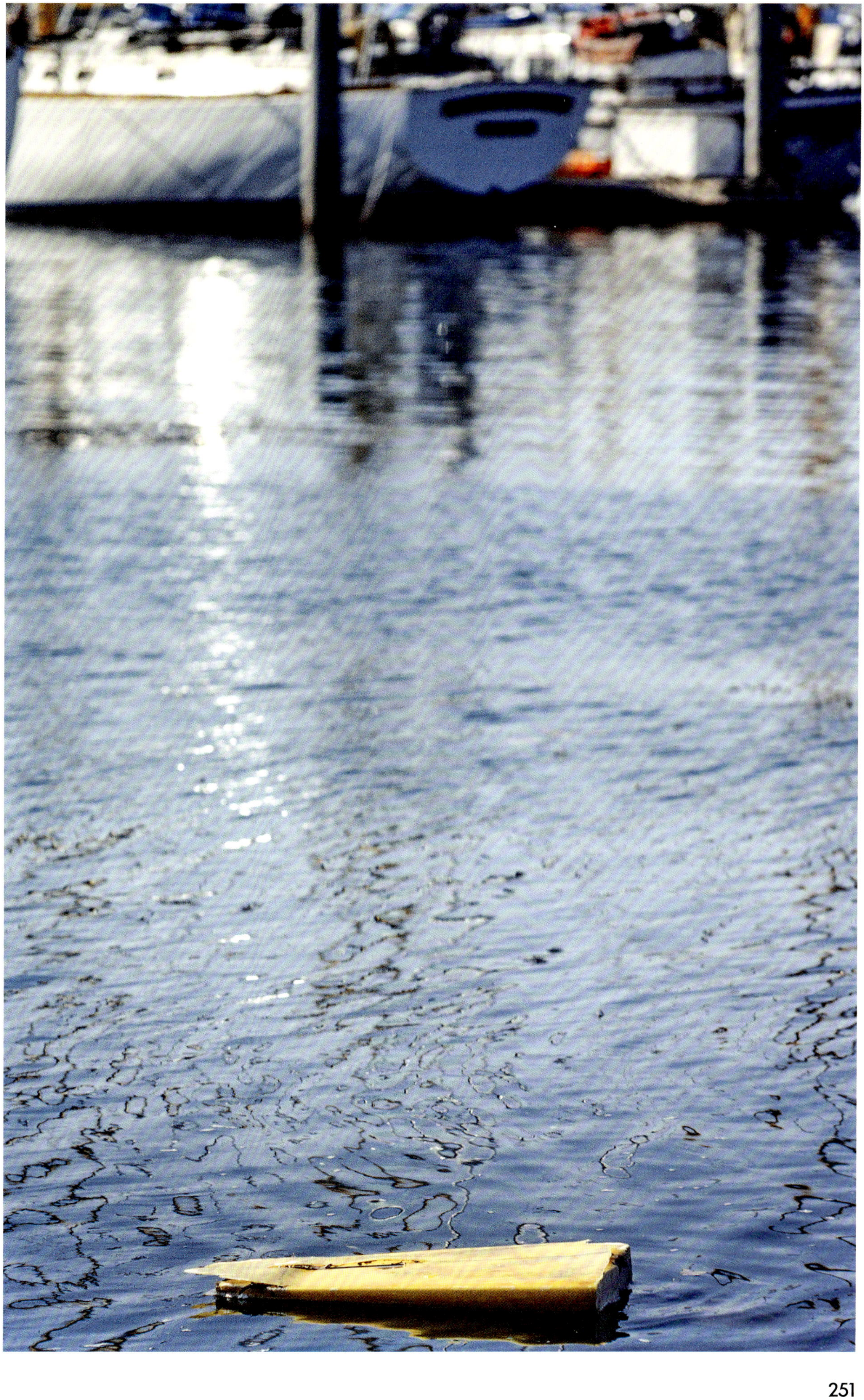

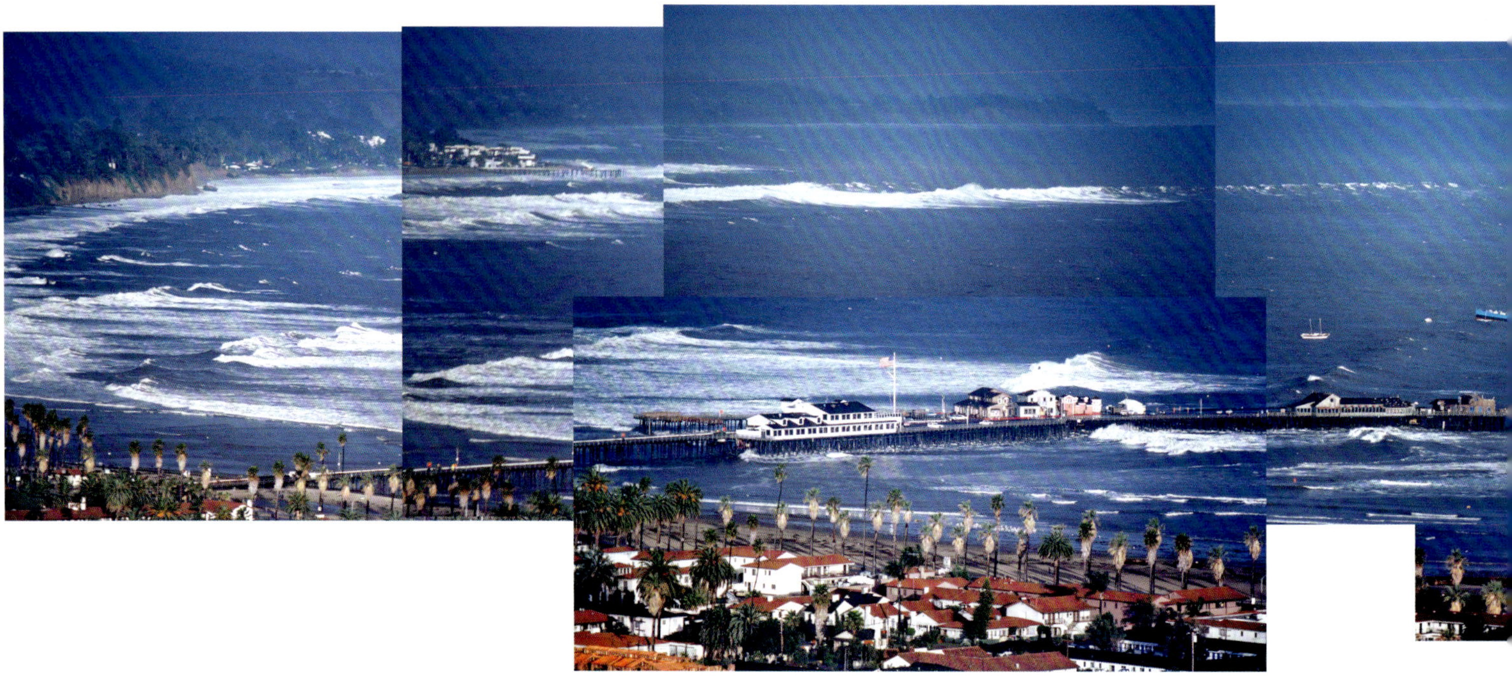

Hundred-Year Storm

In February 1983, the Santa Barbara area was lashed by a relentless series of winter storms, effectively steered by the El Niño–influenced North Pacific jet stream to deliver a powerful three-punch combination of wind, rain, and waves to the region's shoreline. One in particular, officially categorized as a "hundred-year storm," inflicted millions of dollars of damage to Santa Barbara's wharf and harbor area, thrashing buildings, boats, and beaches alike and shutting down the harbor for a full six weeks. Pictured above is a montage assembled from images taken between storm fronts on what is perhaps the biggest day of surf ever seen along this coast. Shot from atop the highest point on the mesa, it captures the entire Santa Barbara waterfront, from the harbor down to the Coral Casino/Hammonds Reef area, with Summerland and Carpinteria in the distance. Long-period swells can be seen sweeping past the harbor, its channel now filled in with sand, and lifting the bow of a commercial vessel well above the relative fifteen-foot height of the Stearns Wharf upper deck, putting the swell's height at an estimated twenty feet. In the distance, waves are also shown breaking hundreds of yards out past the normal configuration of Hammonds Reef. Although the wreckage was terrible to see, I was glad to have been there to record this historic event.

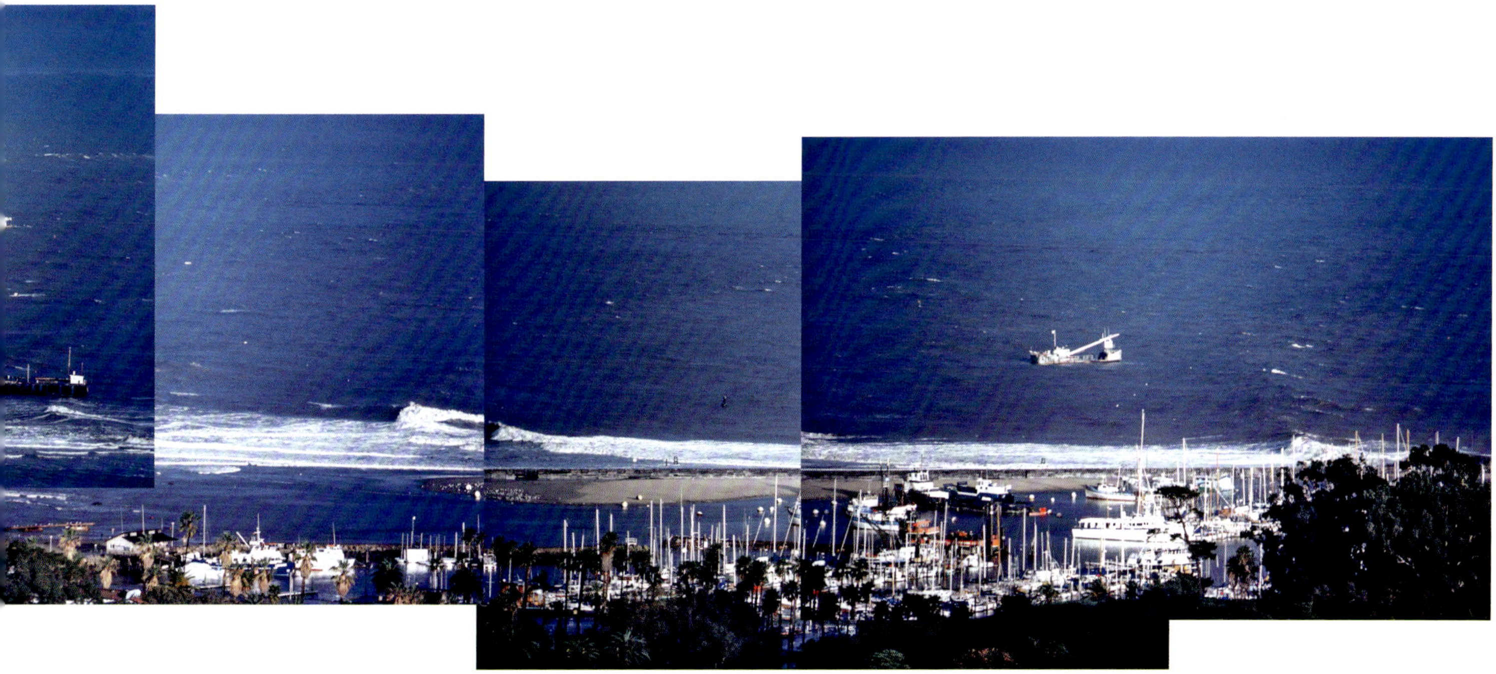

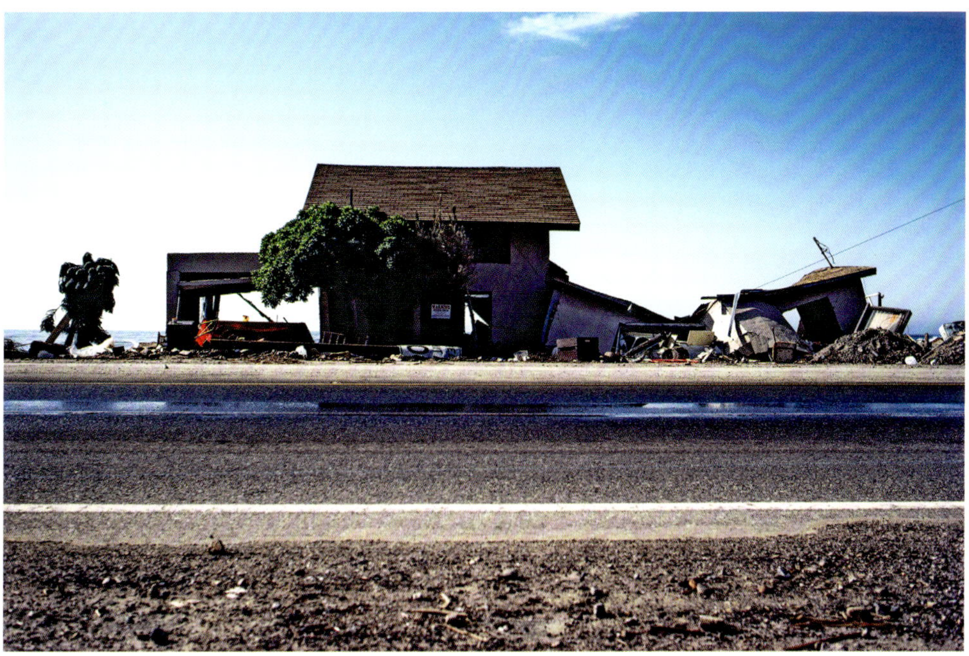

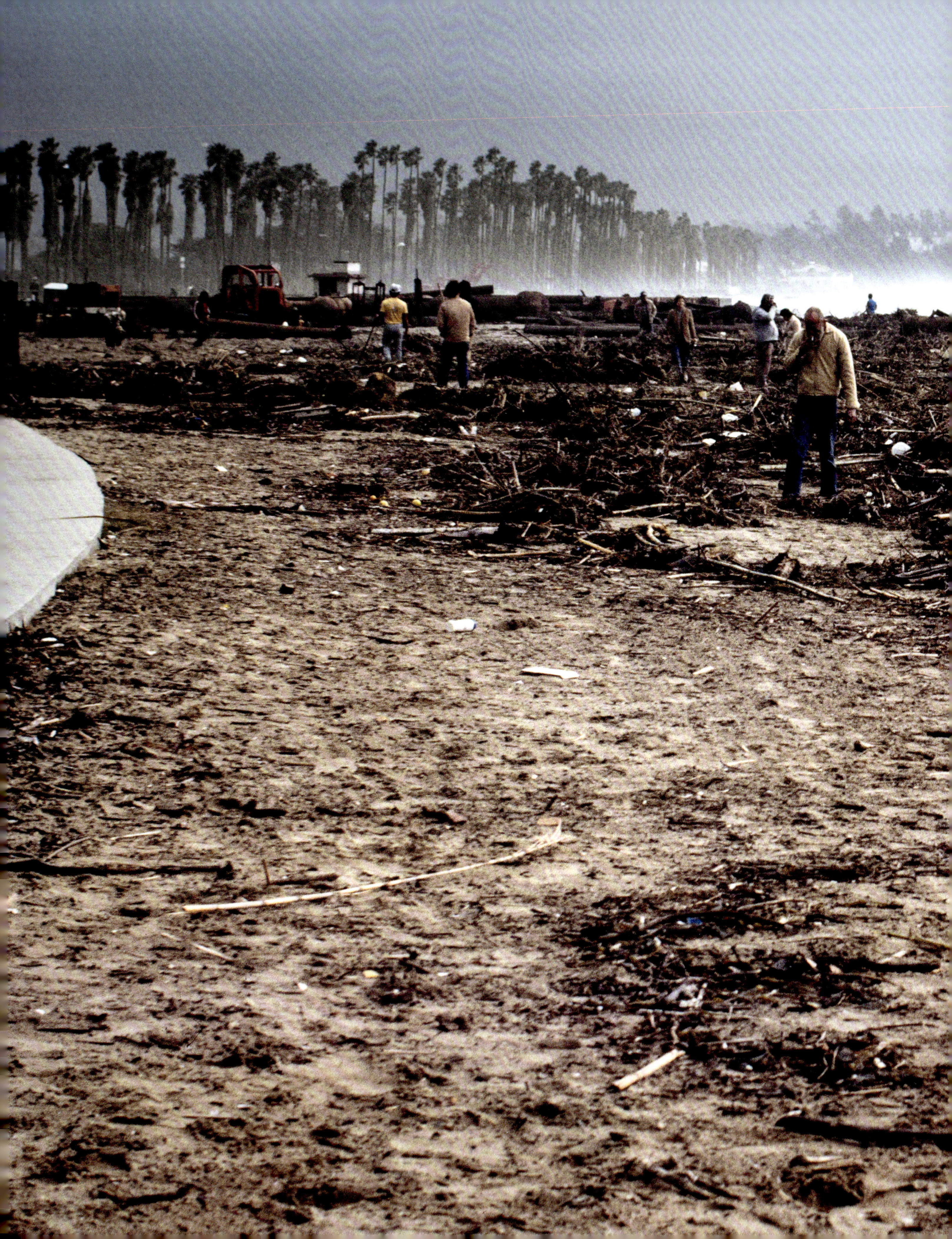

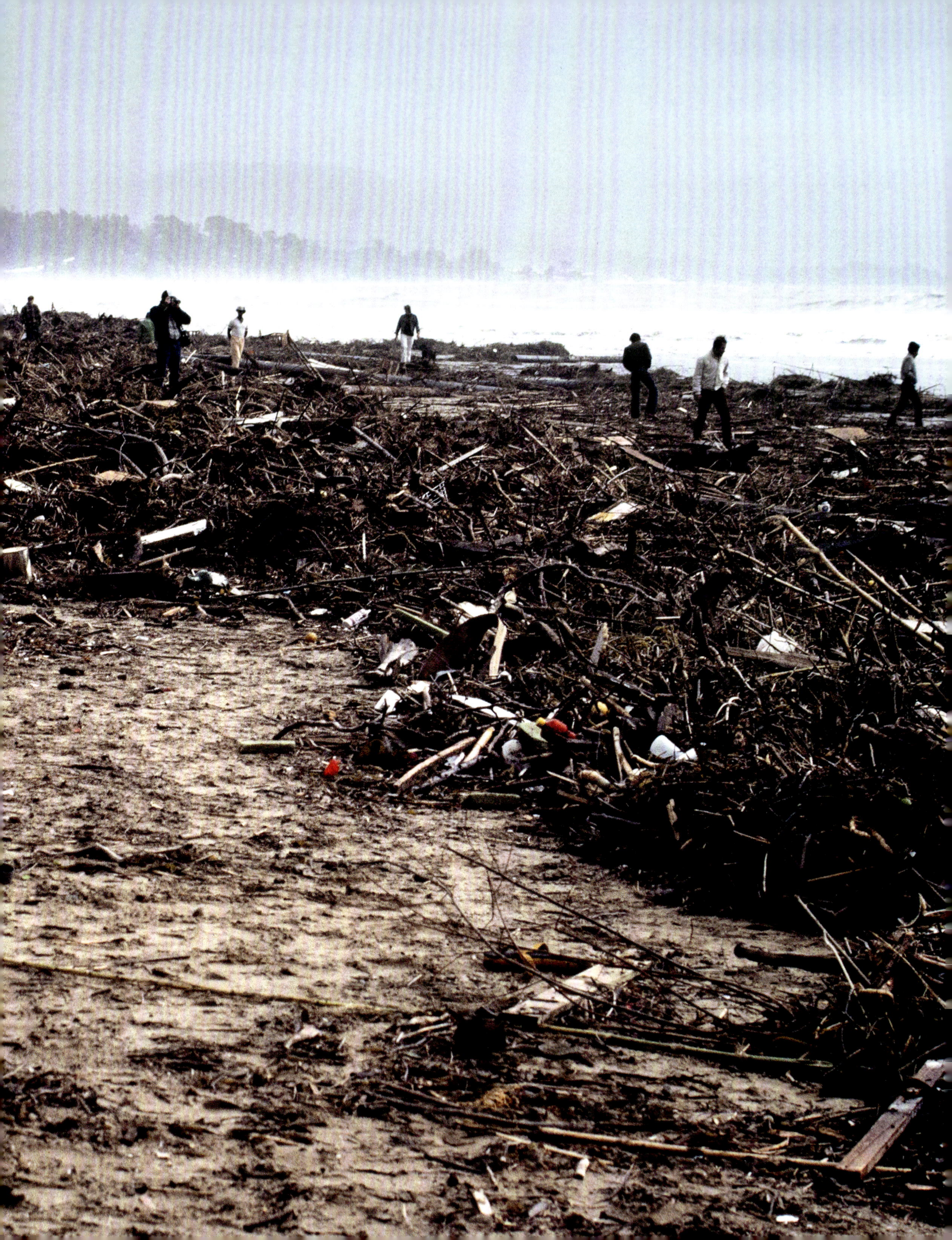

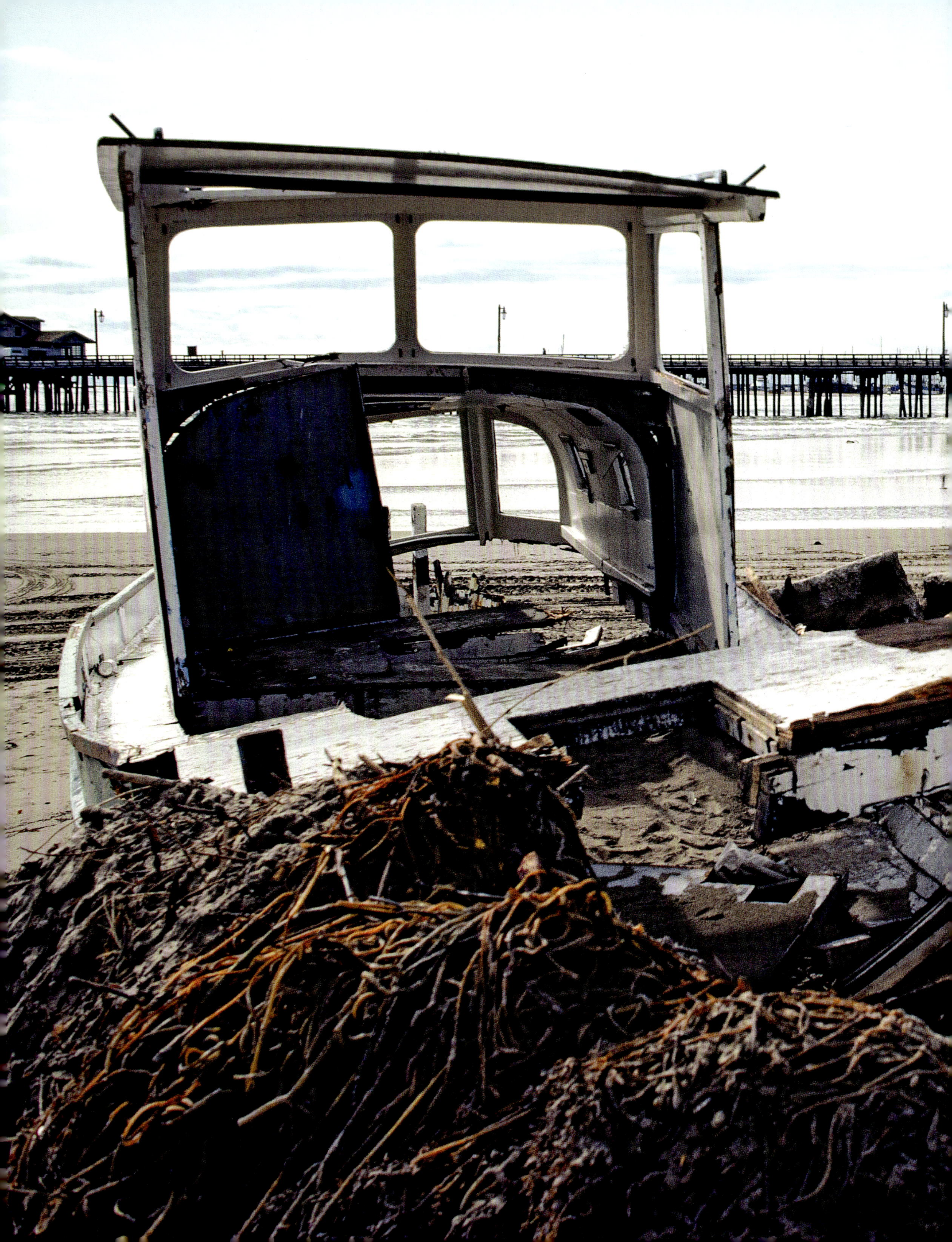

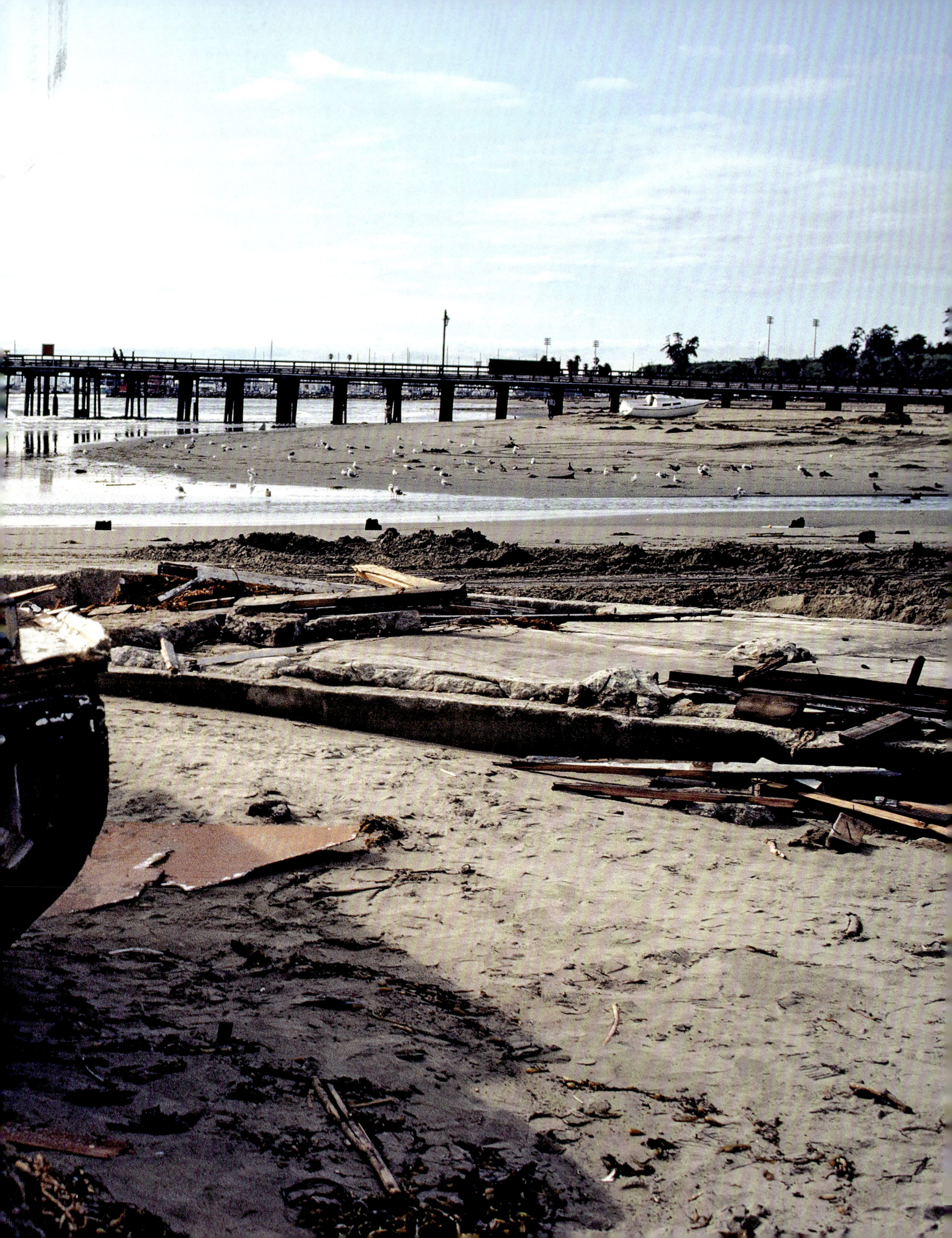

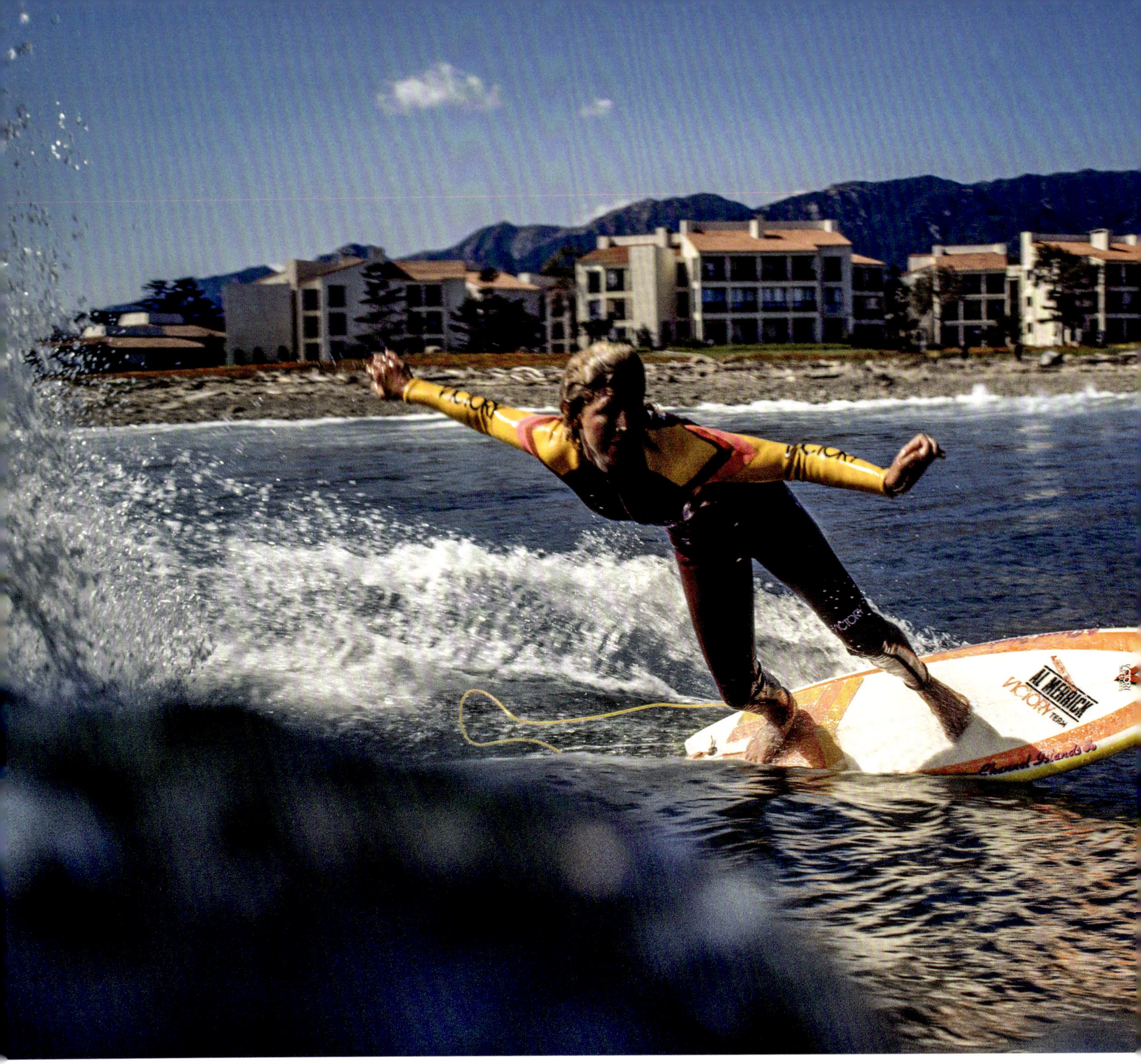

In Between Storms

During a break between storms, I headed down to Hammonds Reef, walking along the railway tracks then cutting through the eucalyptus grove and out onto the lovely meadow that was once the site of the palatial Hammonds Estate. It started as a warm, sunny day with light offshore winds—too nice to last, I felt, considering all that Santa Barbara had been through lately, so I quickly rigged my water housing and swam out just in time for the next good set. Kim Mearig zoomed by, and I fired off a shot looking down on her bottom turn. Dana McCorkle was on the next wave and barreled all the way across the reef, and I had him perfectly in frame. We shared high fives as they paddled back out, but, before they reached the lineup, the wind turned onshore. The next storm was arriving.

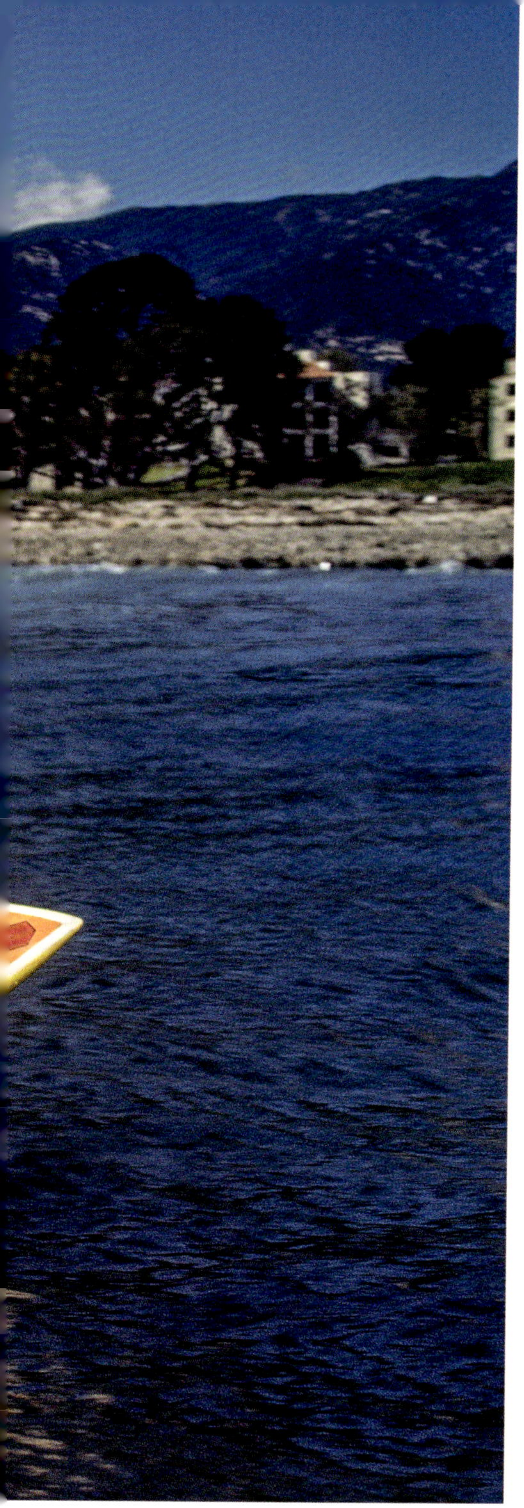

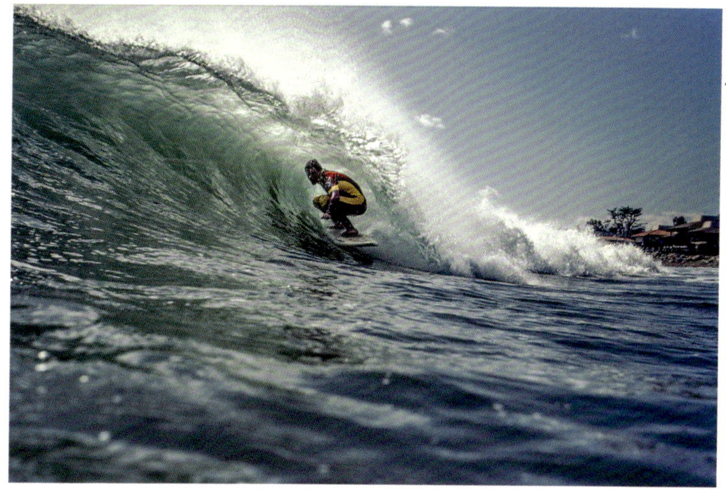

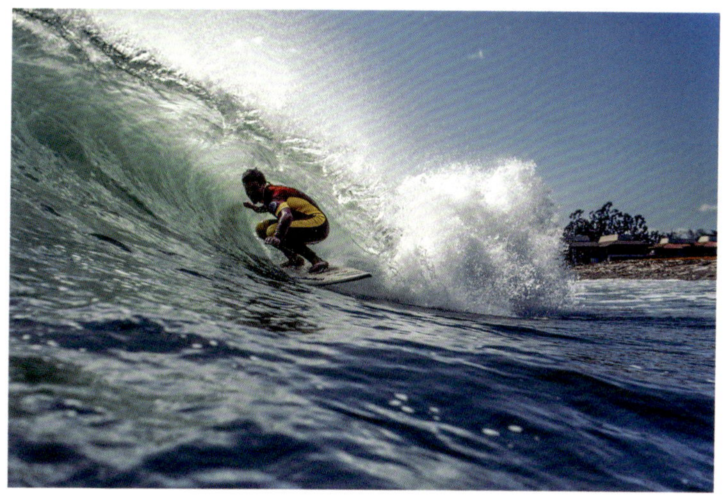

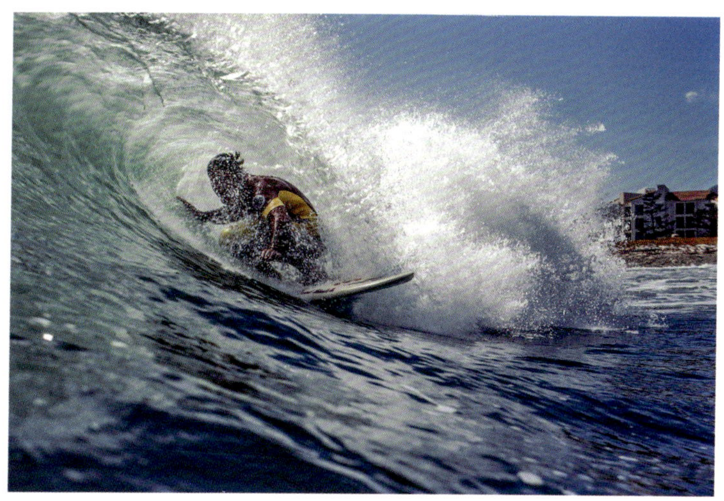

We were all hanging out in the new Channel Islands surf shop, relocated to Lower State Street, when a flatbed truck passed by and turned down East Yanonali Street. Barely balanced on the bed, hanging over both sides, was what looked like one of those giant fake plaster fish they mount above the entrances of coastal seaside seafood restaurants. It wasn't. Great white sharks loomed large in our imaginations—especially for a water photographer—and visions of those jaws rocketing up out of the murky depths to tear into our soft underbellies were steeped in dread. This was years before great whites became a protected species—before we collectively understood that the only thing scarier than a great white shark would be an ocean without them. Back then, however, they were still our monsters, and to see one for the very first time—even a dead one being driven down to Castagnola Brothers Seafoods for processing—confirmed our worst fears.

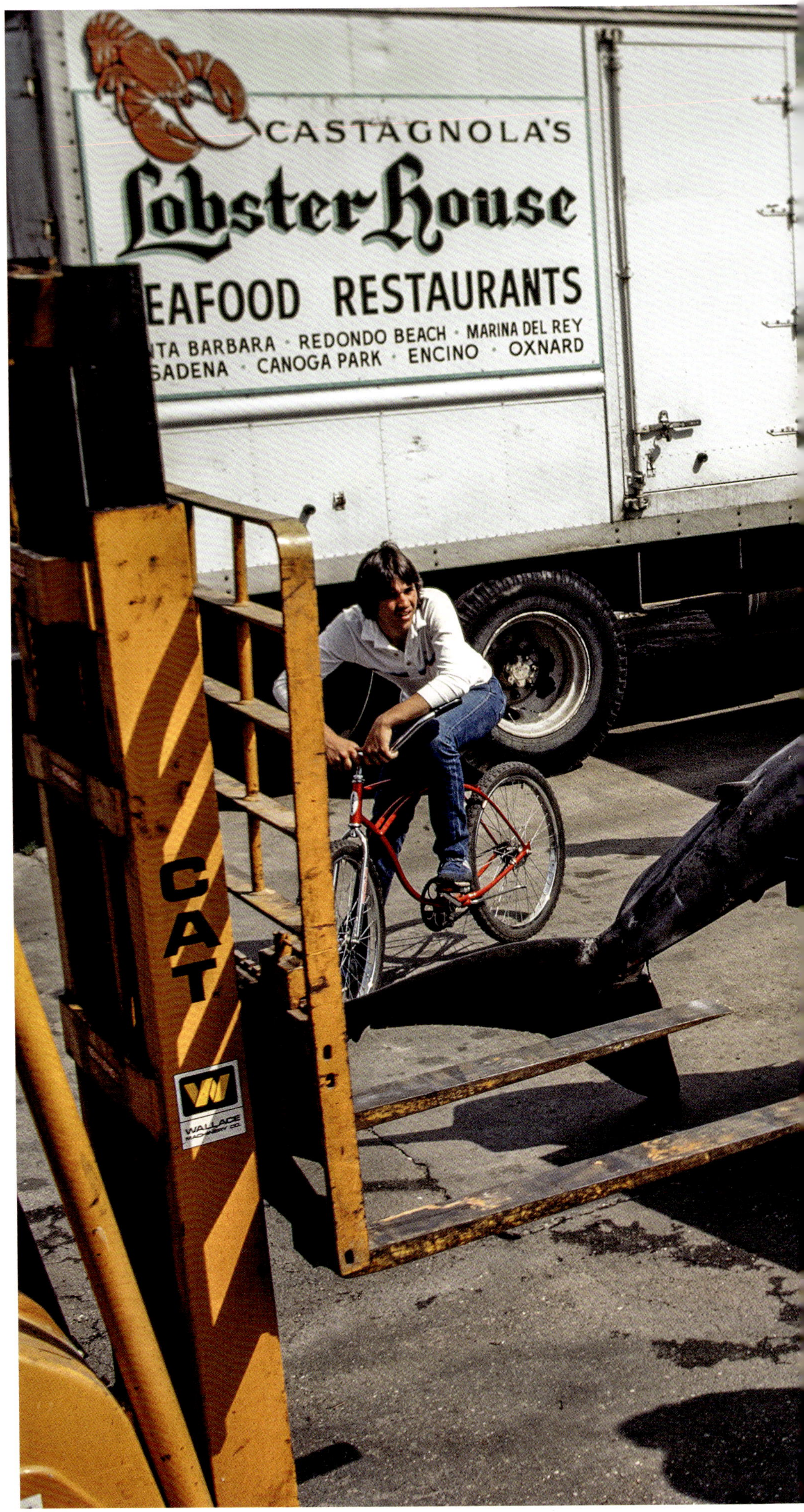

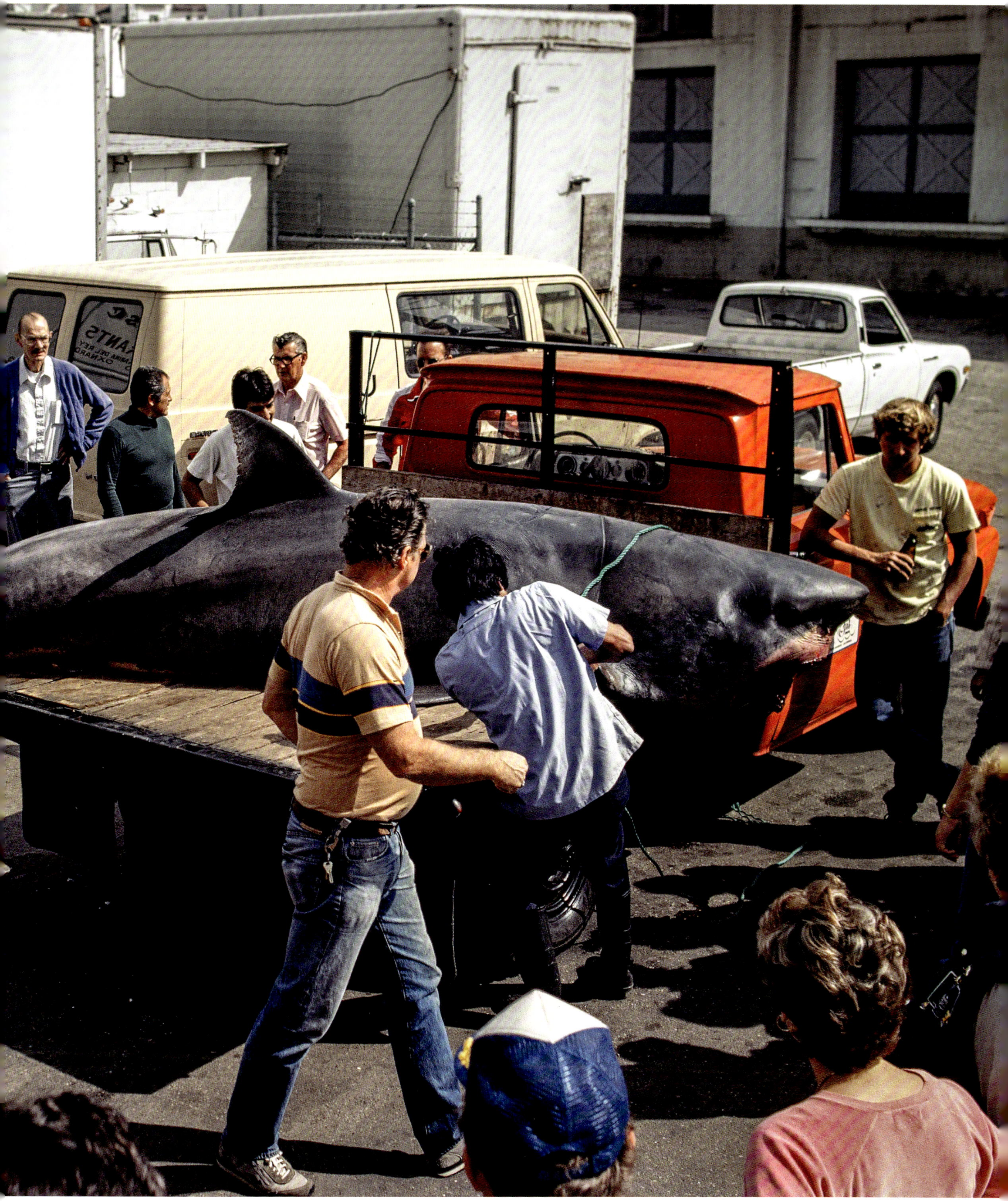

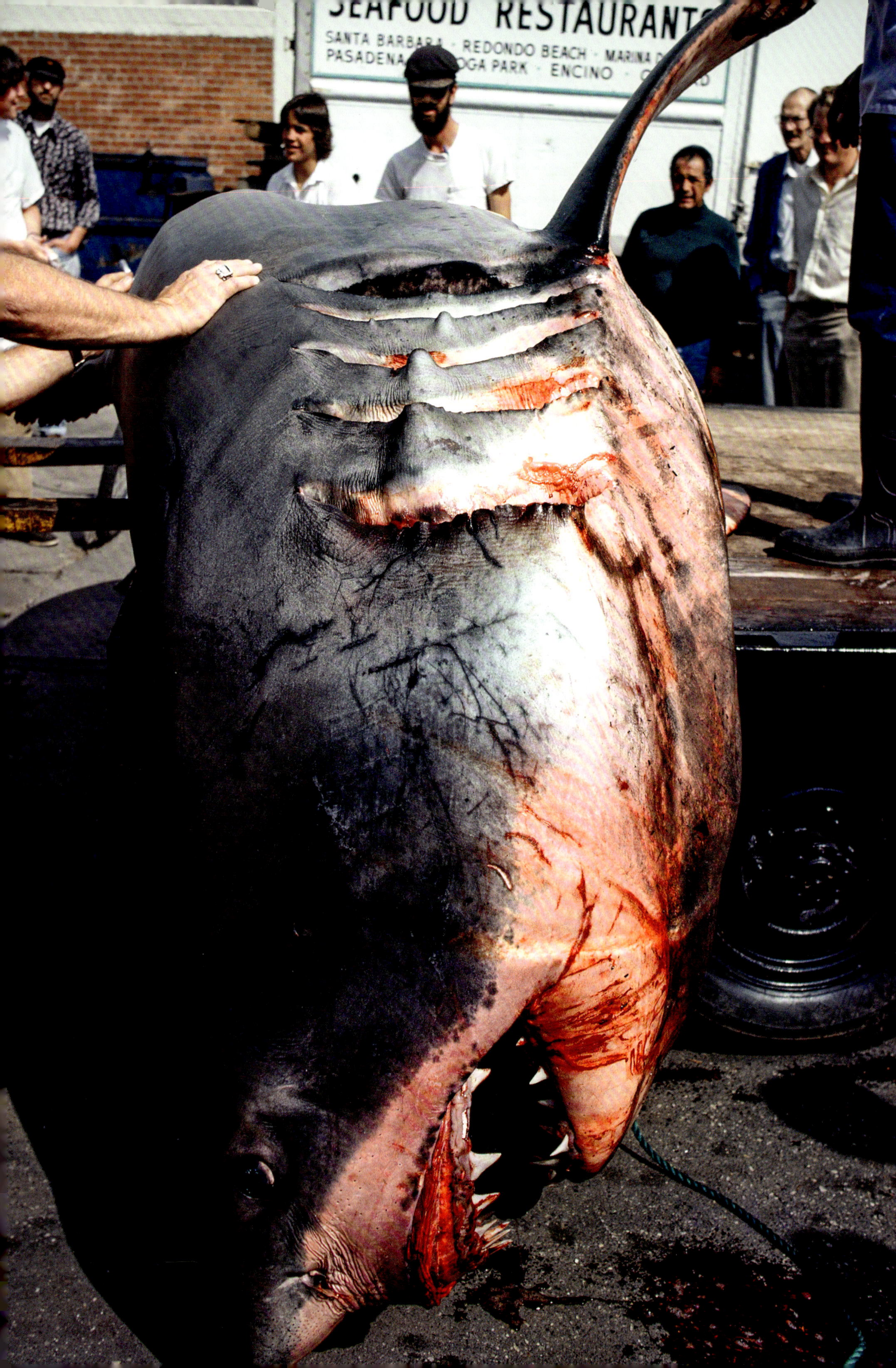
SEAFOOD RESTAURANT
SANTA BARBARA · REDONDO BEACH
PASADENA
ENCINO

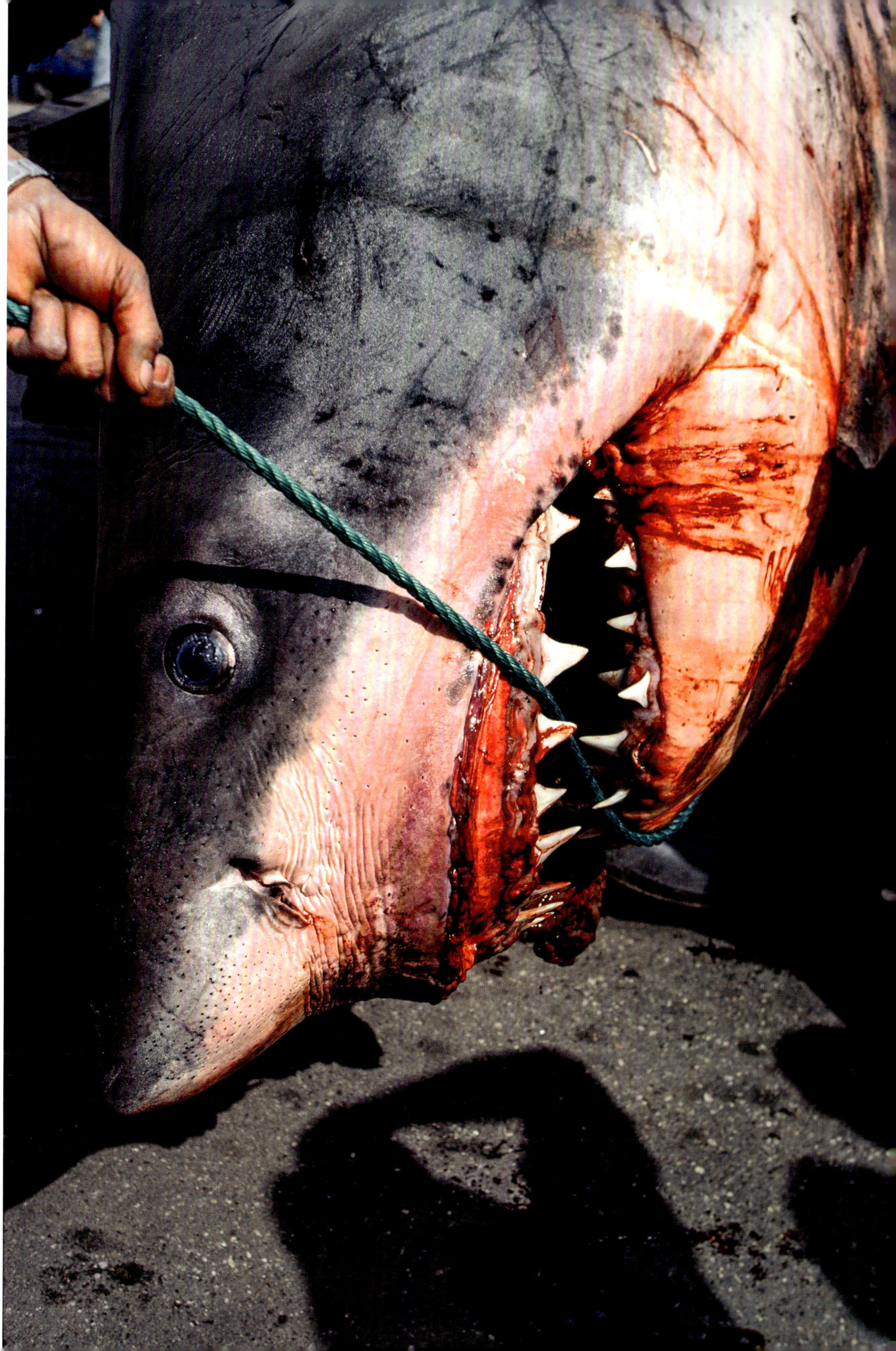

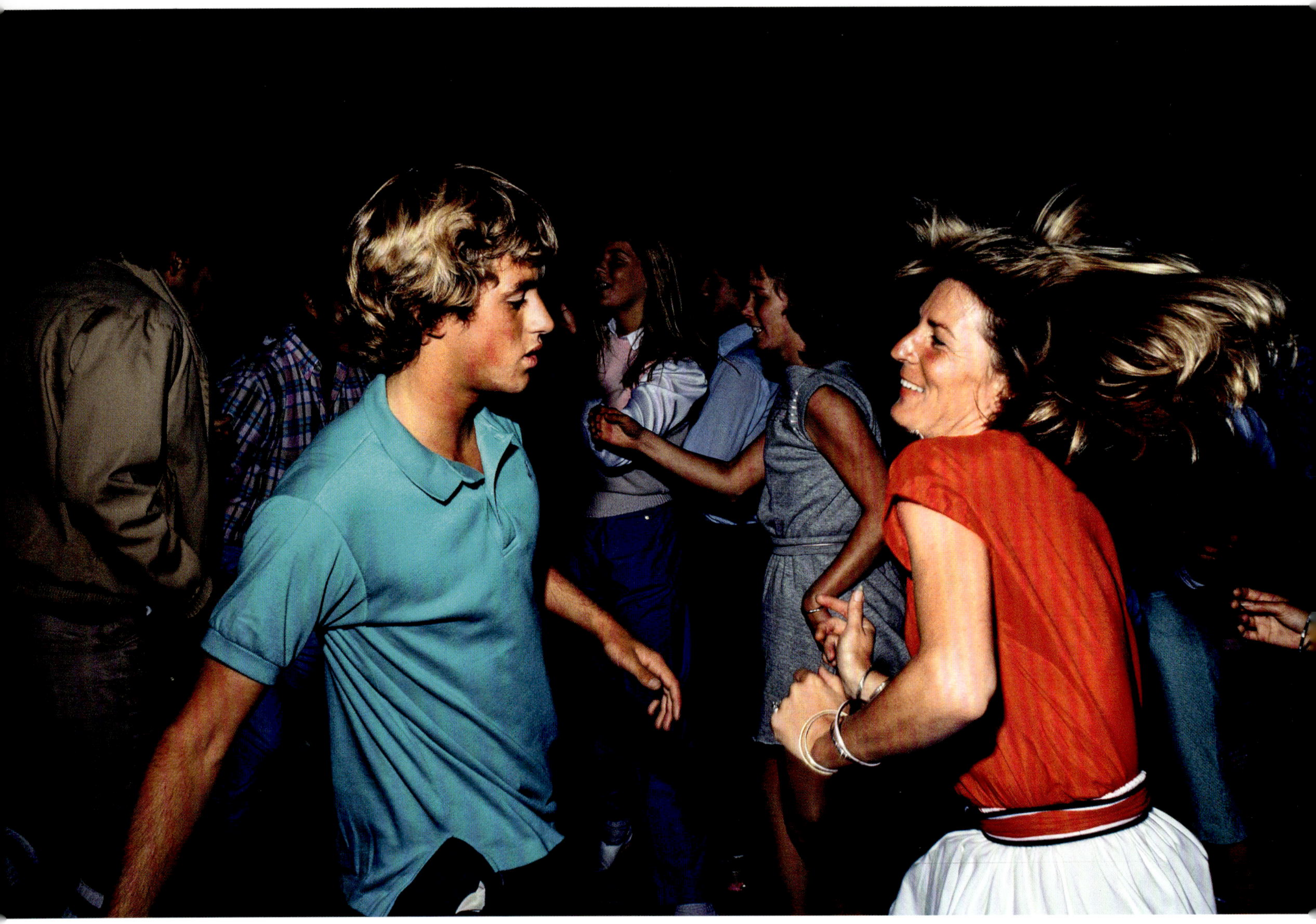

Backyard BBQ

Al and Terry Merrick's backyard barbecues became the main social events for the extended family of friends associated with the Channel Islands shop. It was also a chance to see what a lot of us looked like actually wearing clothes and not just wetsuits. Some even put on shoes. But with Al happily grilling white sea bass and tri-tip, Terry playing the consummate host, little kids and dogs running around, and the rest of us laughing, dancing, eating, and watching surf slideshows, these evenings became more than just a good time. At the end of the night we'd all head home, laughed out, bellies full, leftovers in hand, feeling less like the eclectic bunch of characters we were and more like a tight, supportive surf community. Which, of course, was Al and Terry's plan all along.

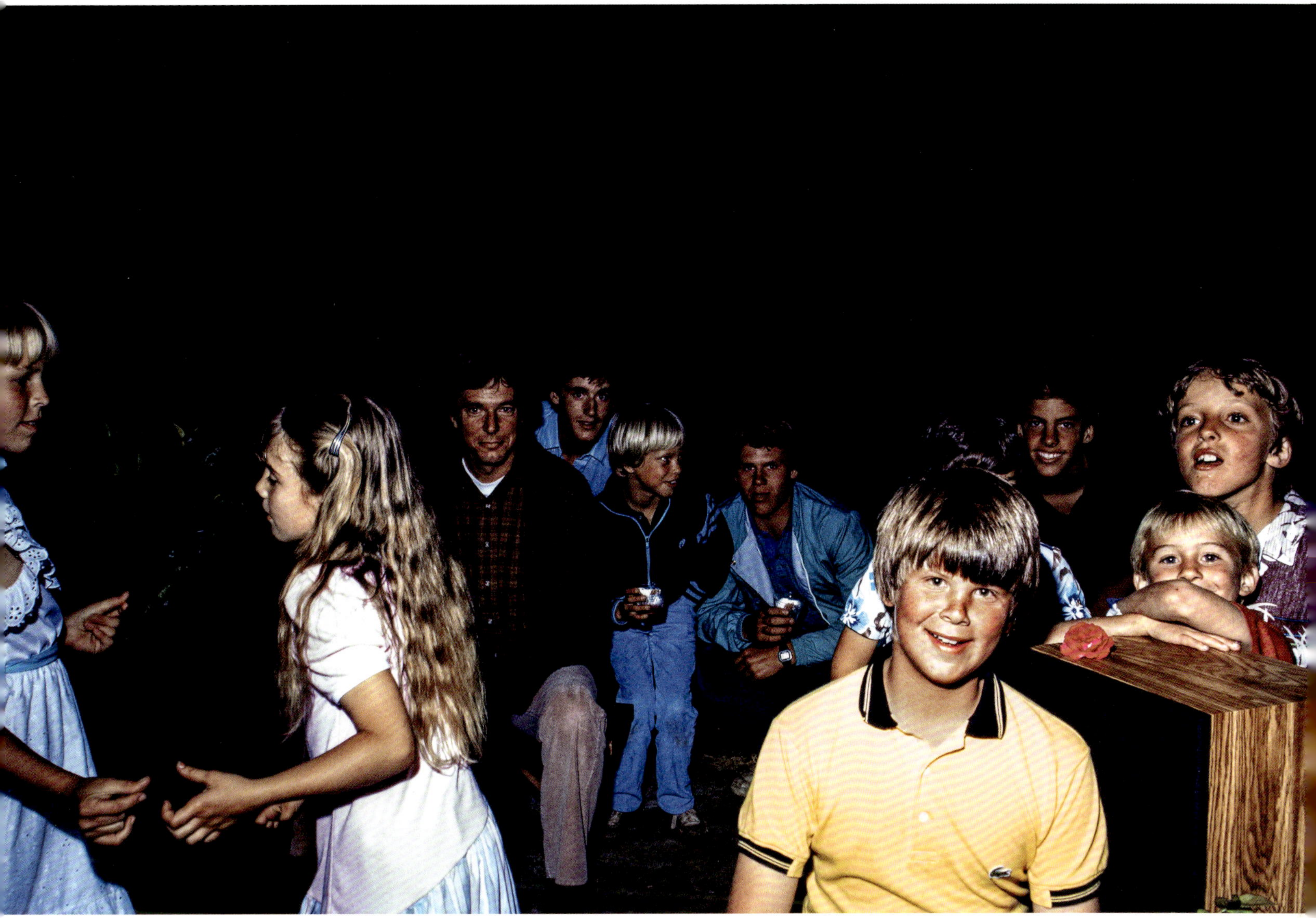

Terry Merrick *(left)*, demonstratively proving that moms can dance. The kids are alright. *(Right to left)* Gretchen Severson, Heidi Merrick, Dave Brown, Kevin Eagan, Chris Brown, Dana McCorkle, Matt Mondragon, Joe Curren, Shane Robinson, and Britt Merrick.

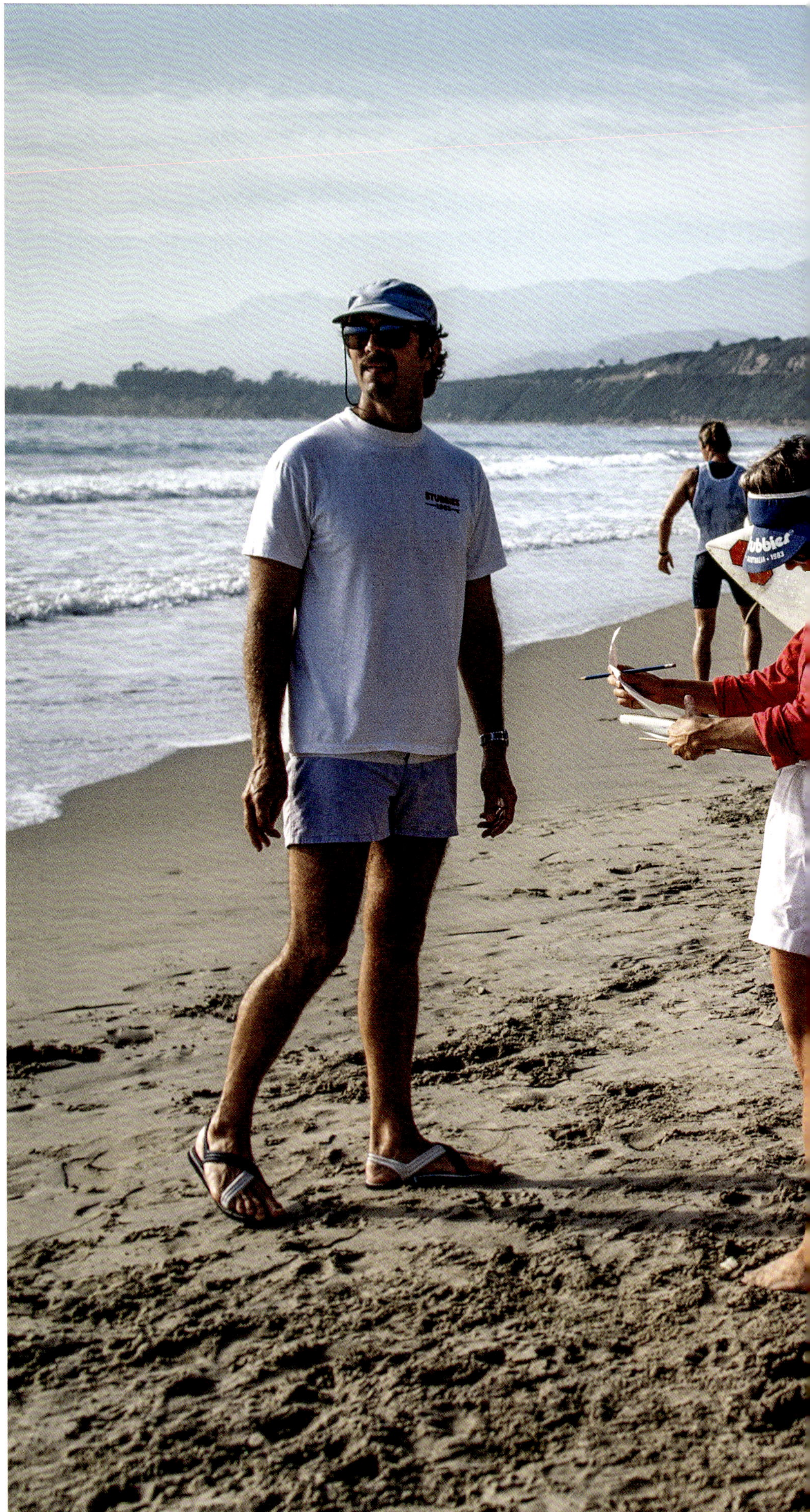

Spread

Despite how it might've looked in the surf magazines, Al Merrick's focus wasn't entirely on champions like Curren, Tomson, and Mearig. Mentoring all members of his Channel Islands team was of equal importance to Al, as evidenced by his innovative team practices, where he helped hone the next wave's competitive skills. Al, seen here with Jeanine Curren, conducting mock heats at Backside Rincon.

Pages 268–269

Kim Mearig, shot shortly after signing with Ocean Pacific sportswear. By the end of '83 she had won the Op Pro, *Surfer* magazine's annual Reader Poll, and the Association of Surfing Professionals (ASP) women's world title. Not a bad year for a shy Santa Barbara surfer just barely out of her teens.

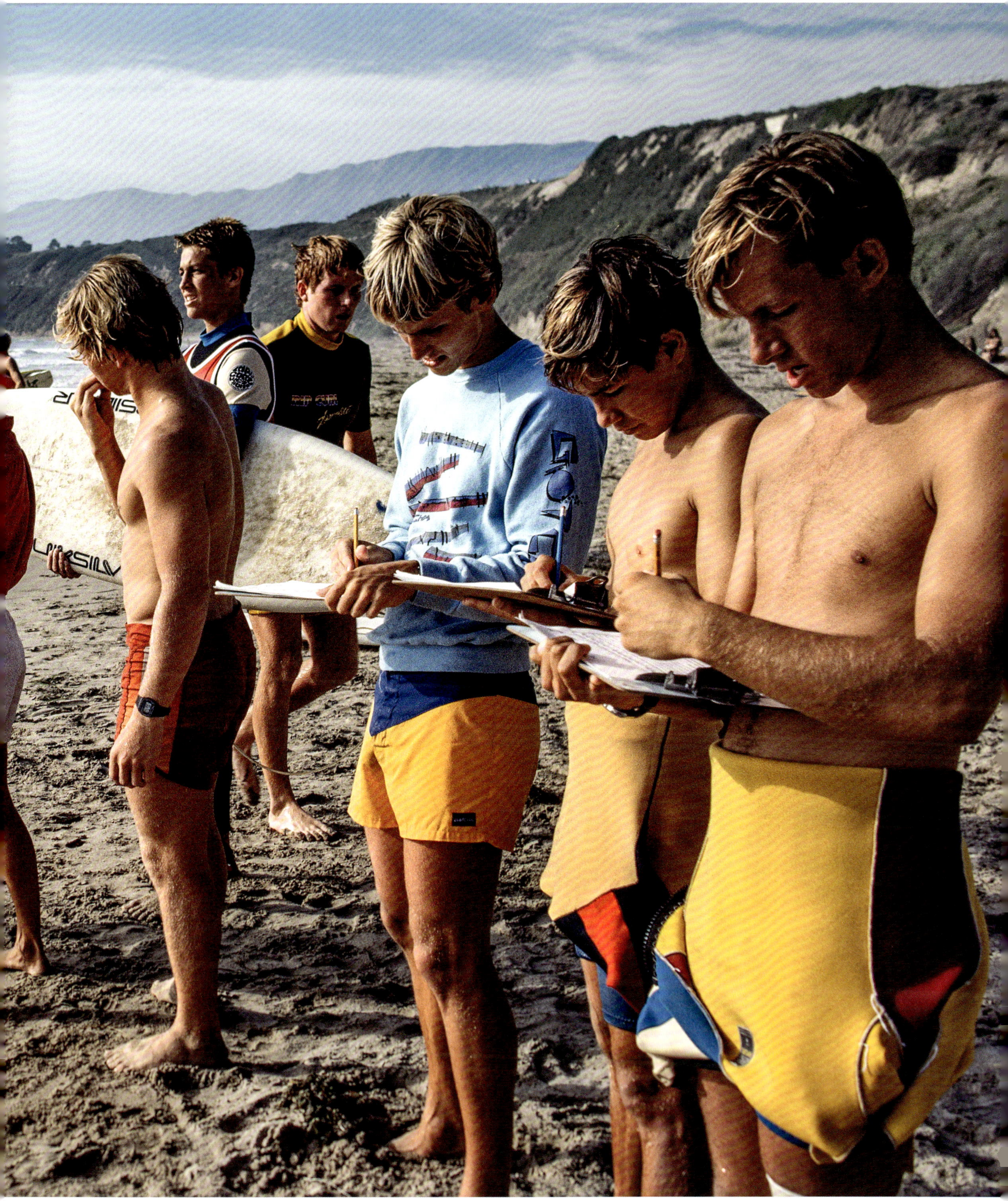

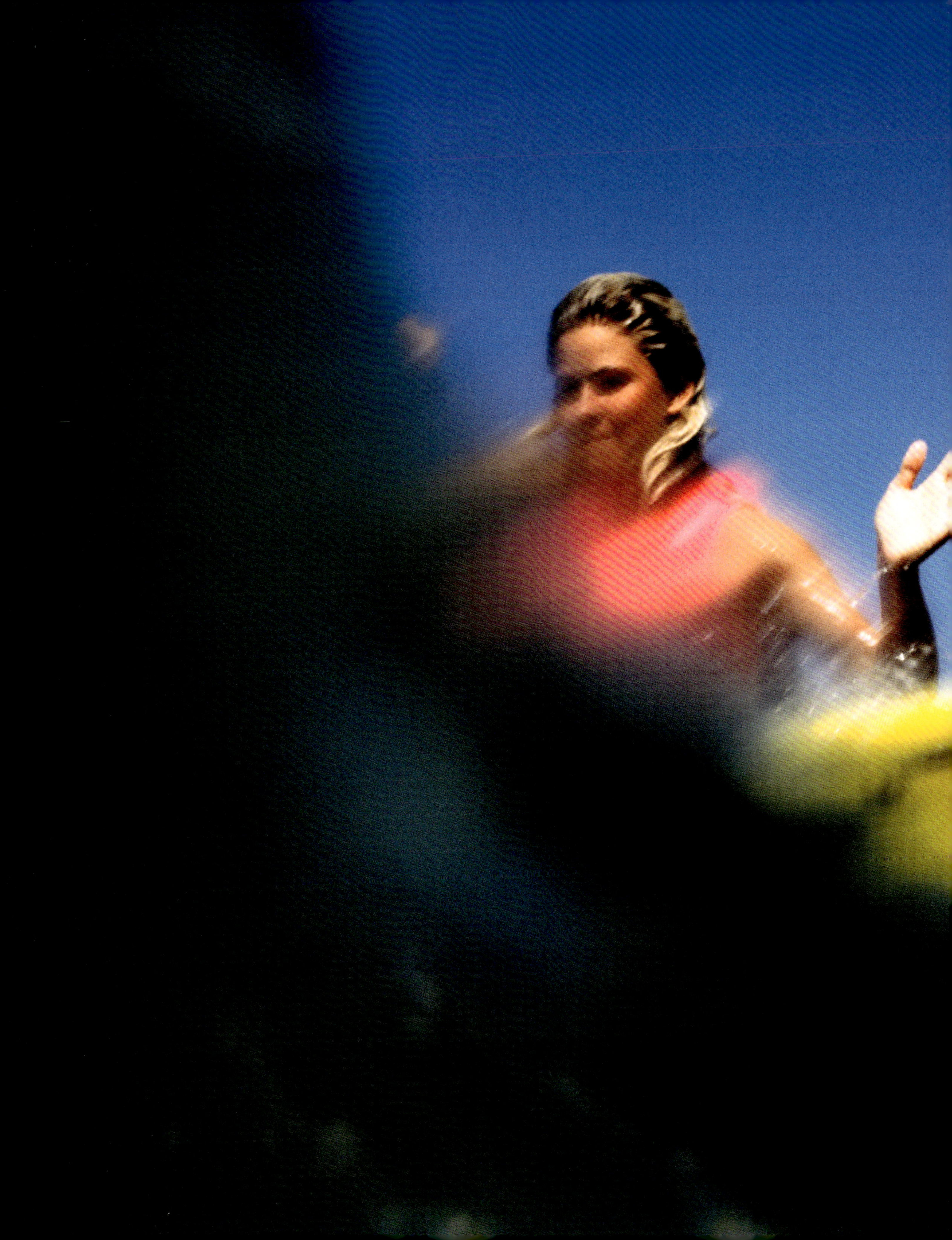

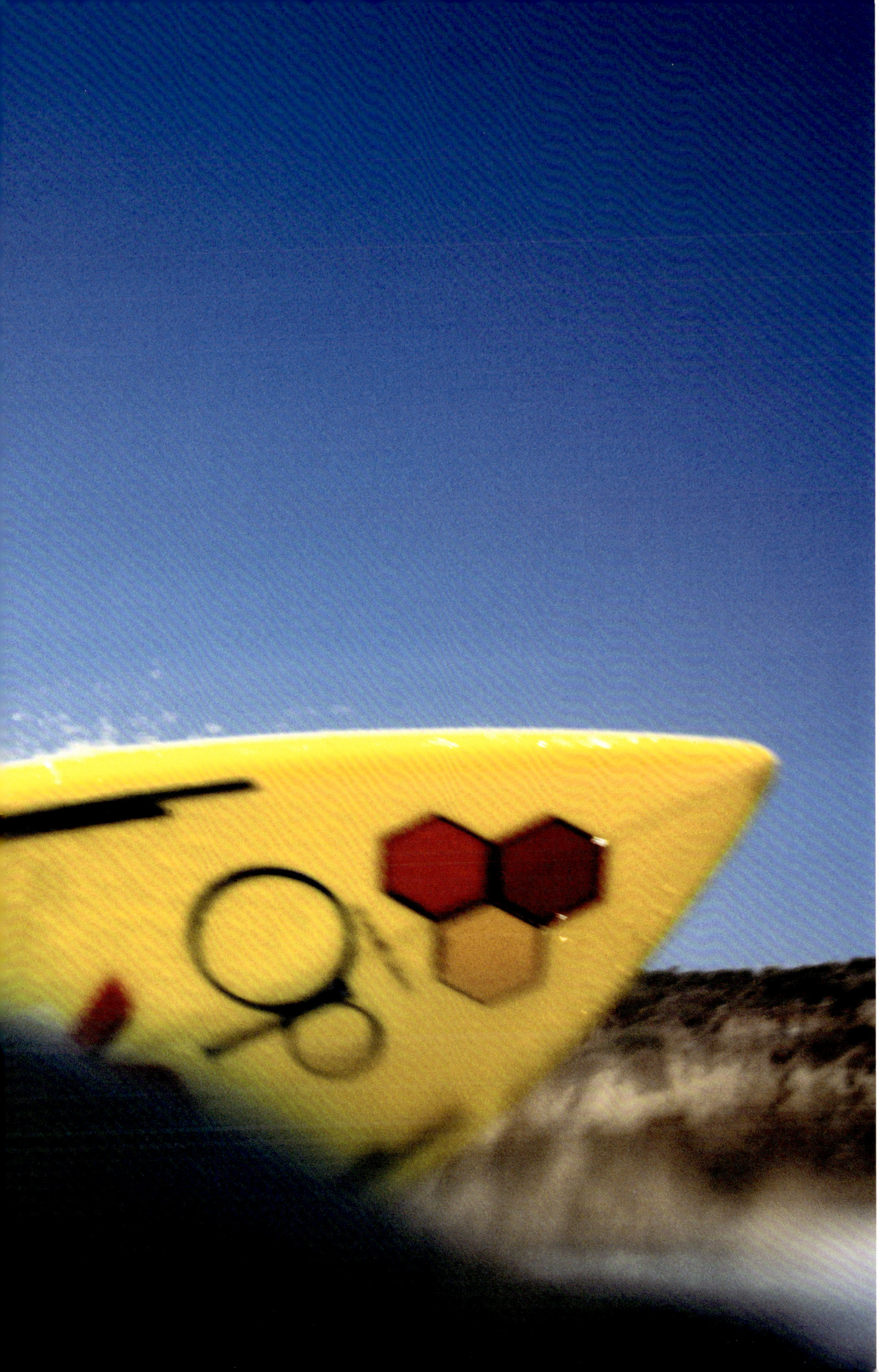

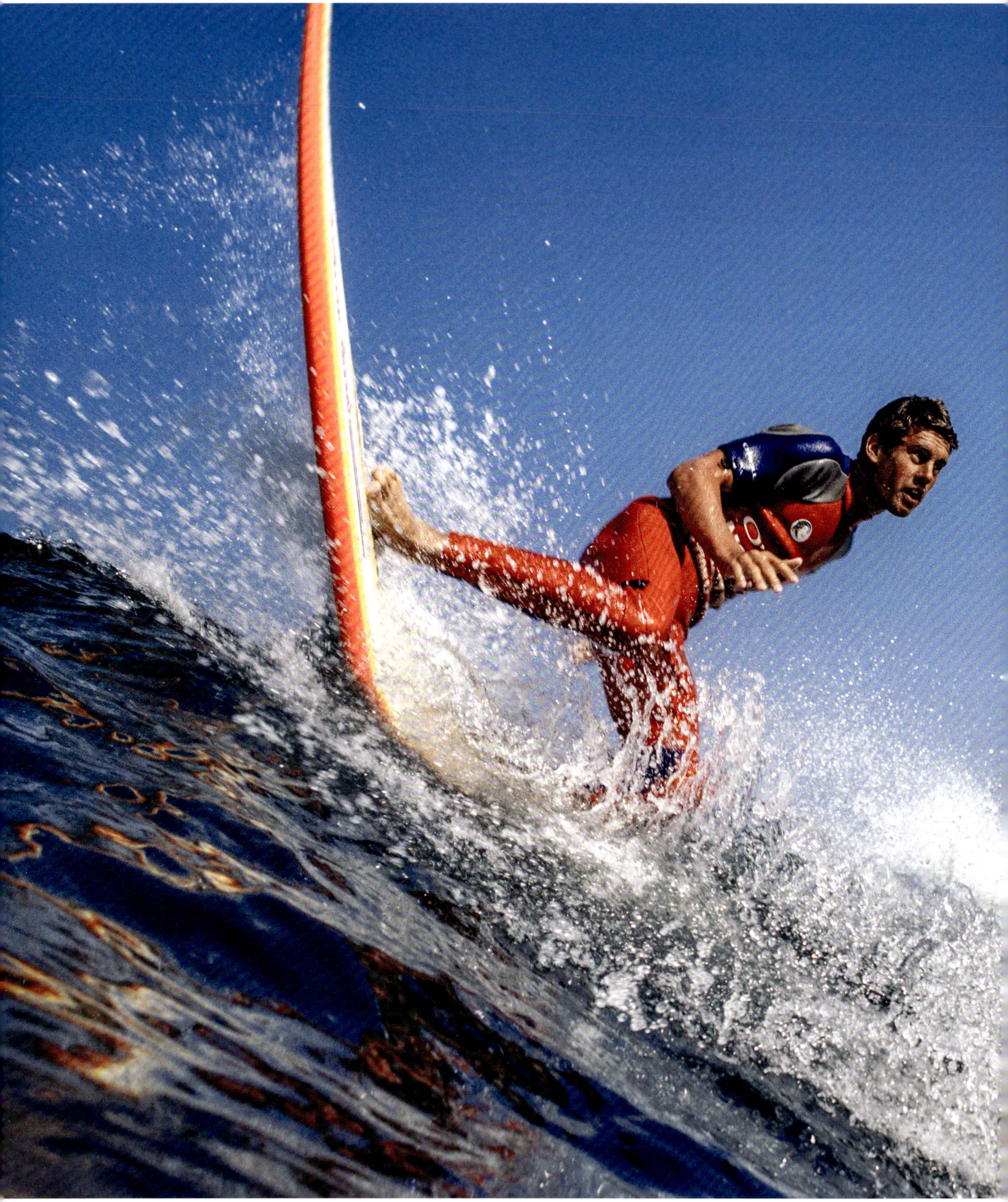

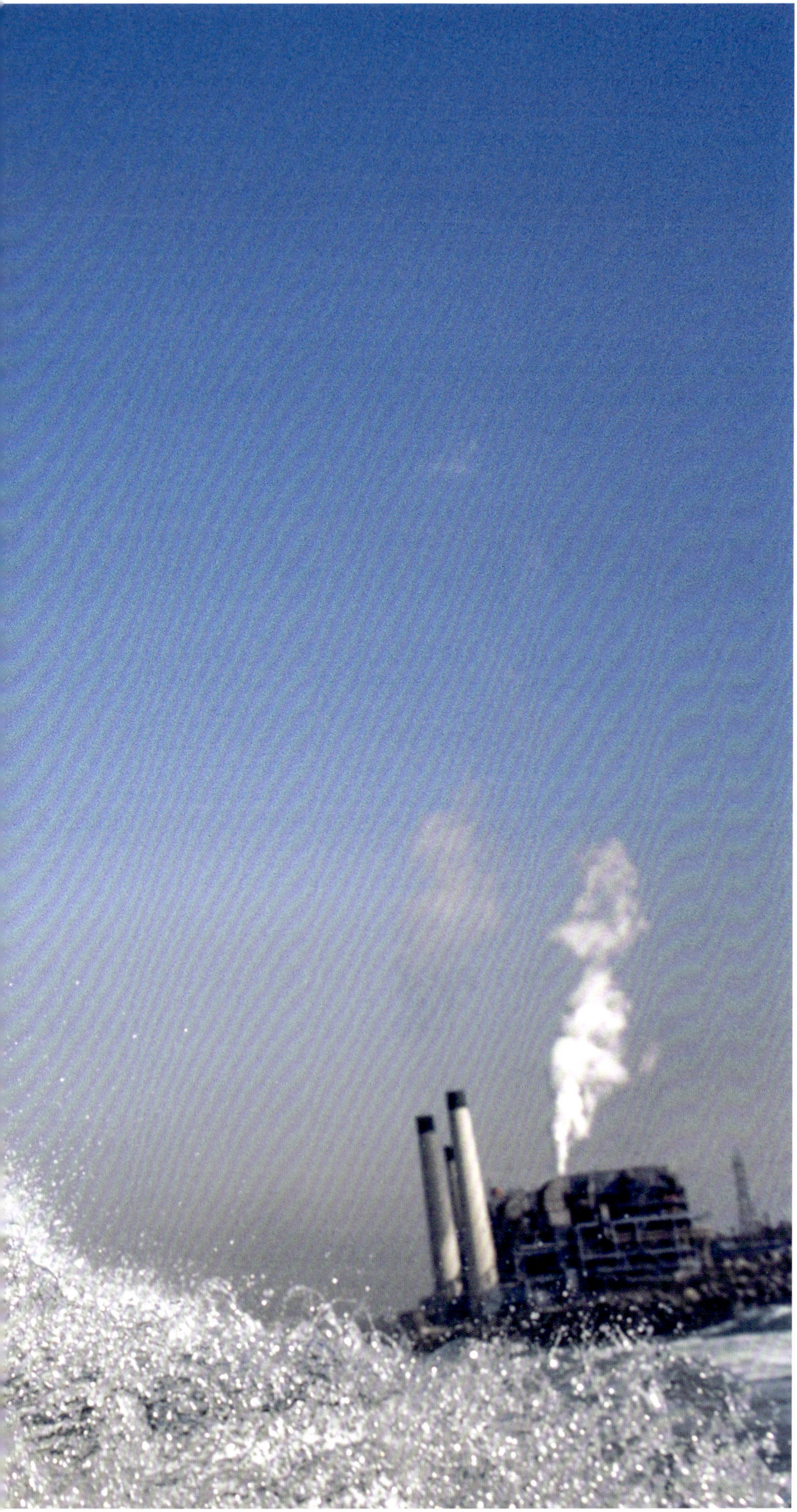

Spread

Ted Robinson was a top amateur turned pro from Manhattan Beach who followed Willy Morris's lead by dropping his local shaper and traveling north to Santa Barbara to be part of the Al Merrick/Channel Islands juggernaut. His home break at the foot of Rosecrans Avenue was as far south as I could drive in the morning and still catch quality morning light.

Overleaf

One morning, Sam and I gambled on an early morning run to Malibu and were rewarded with clean conditions at the Drainpipe section of Zuma Beach.

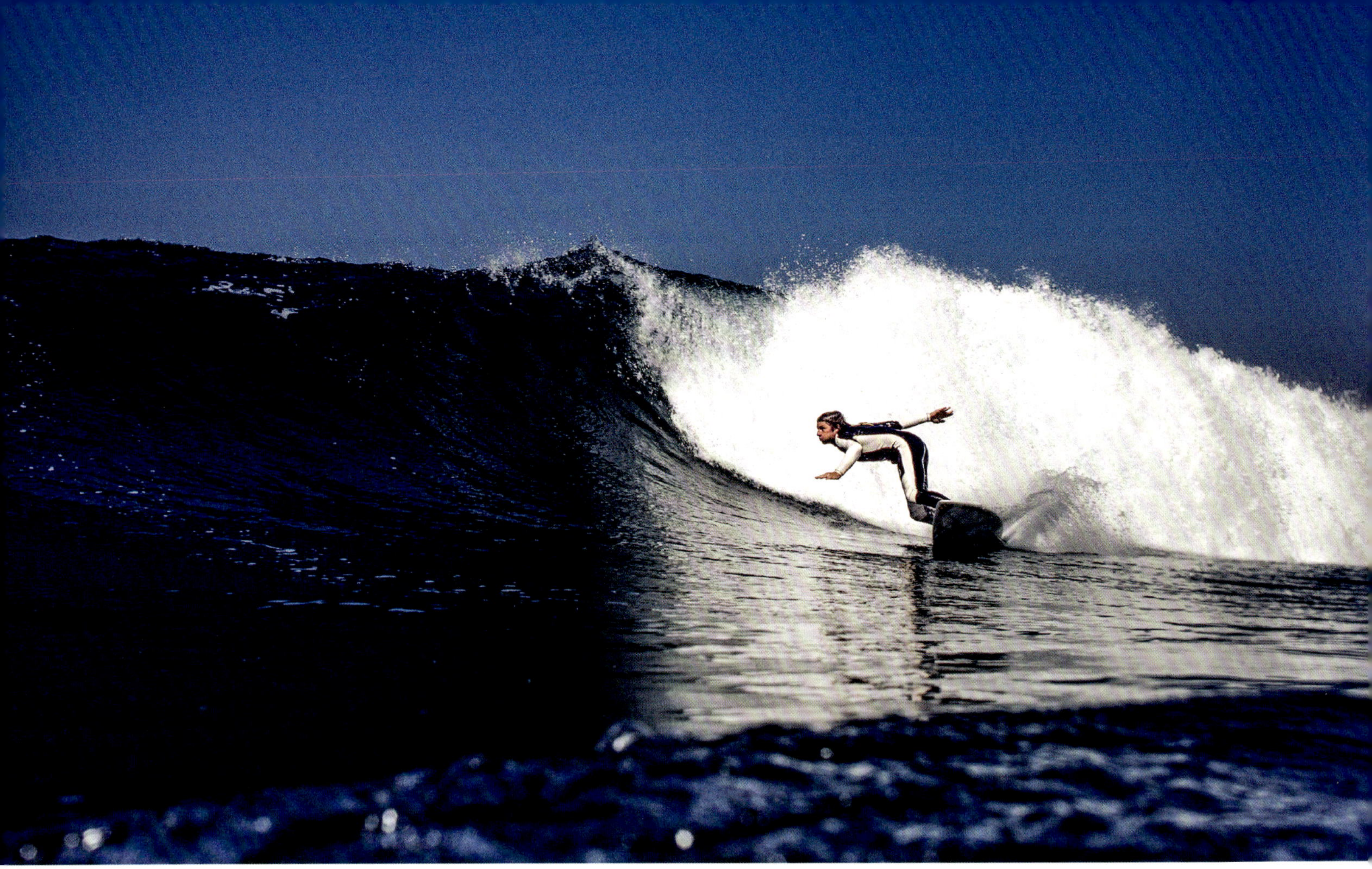

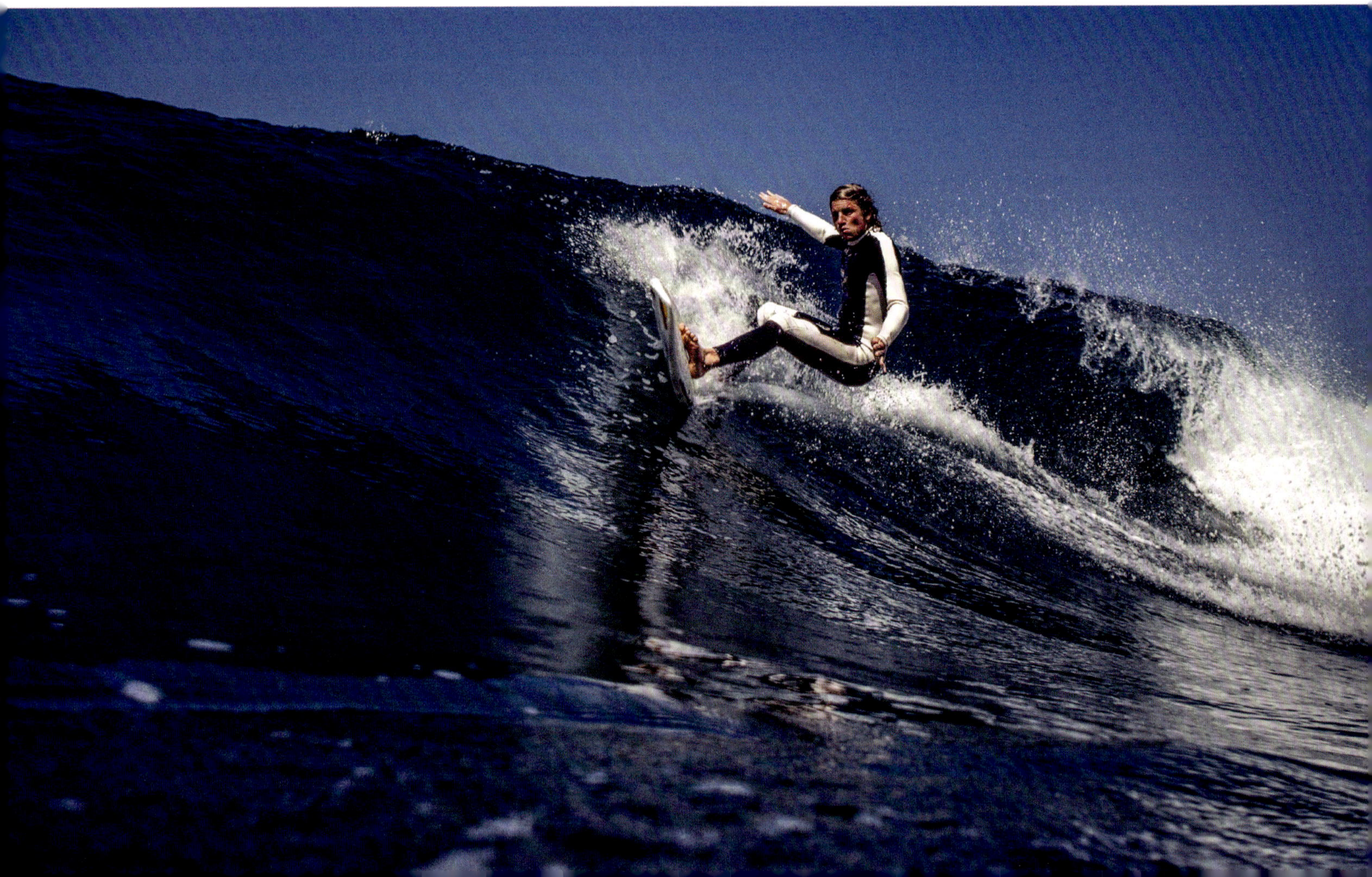

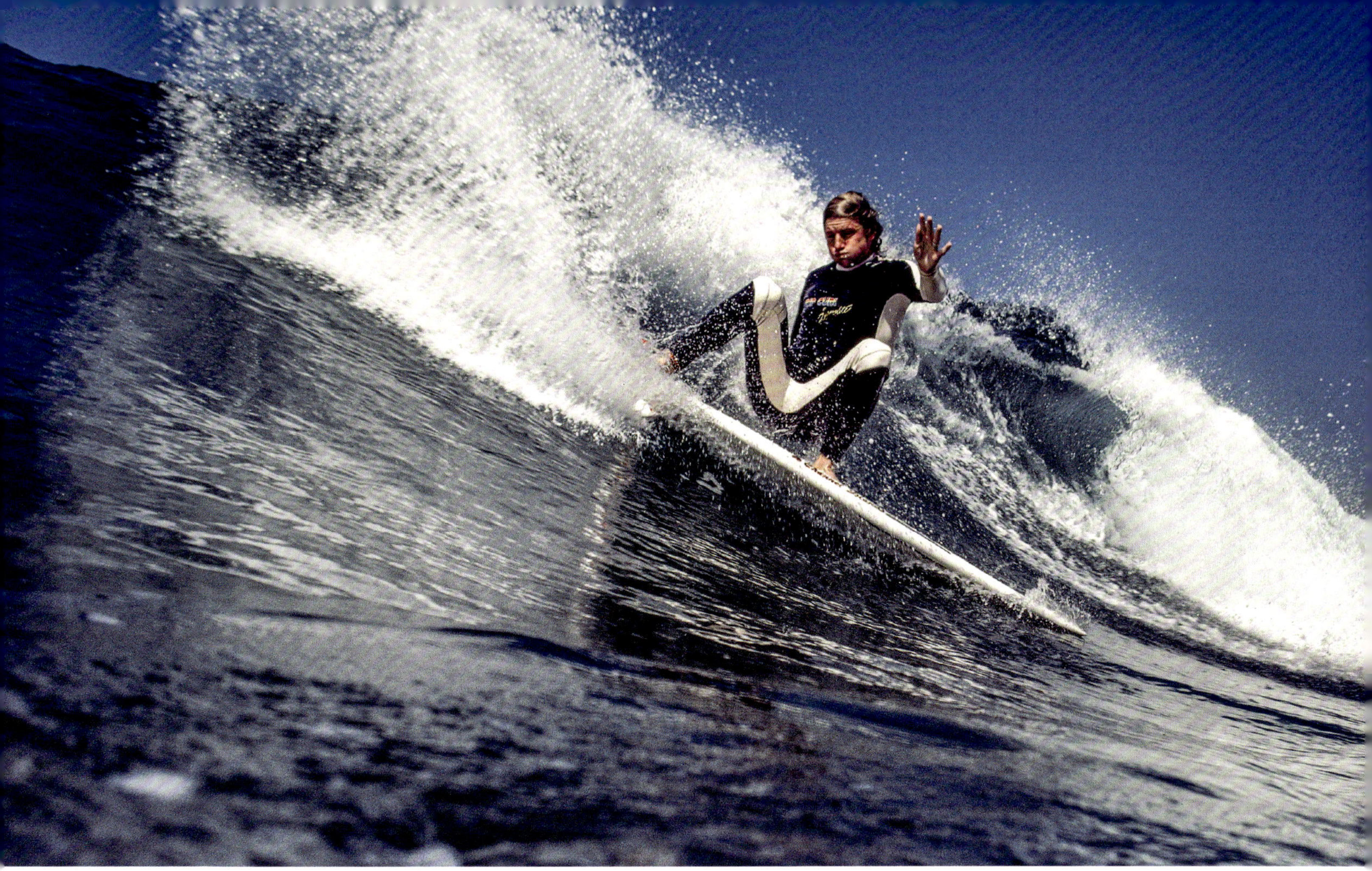

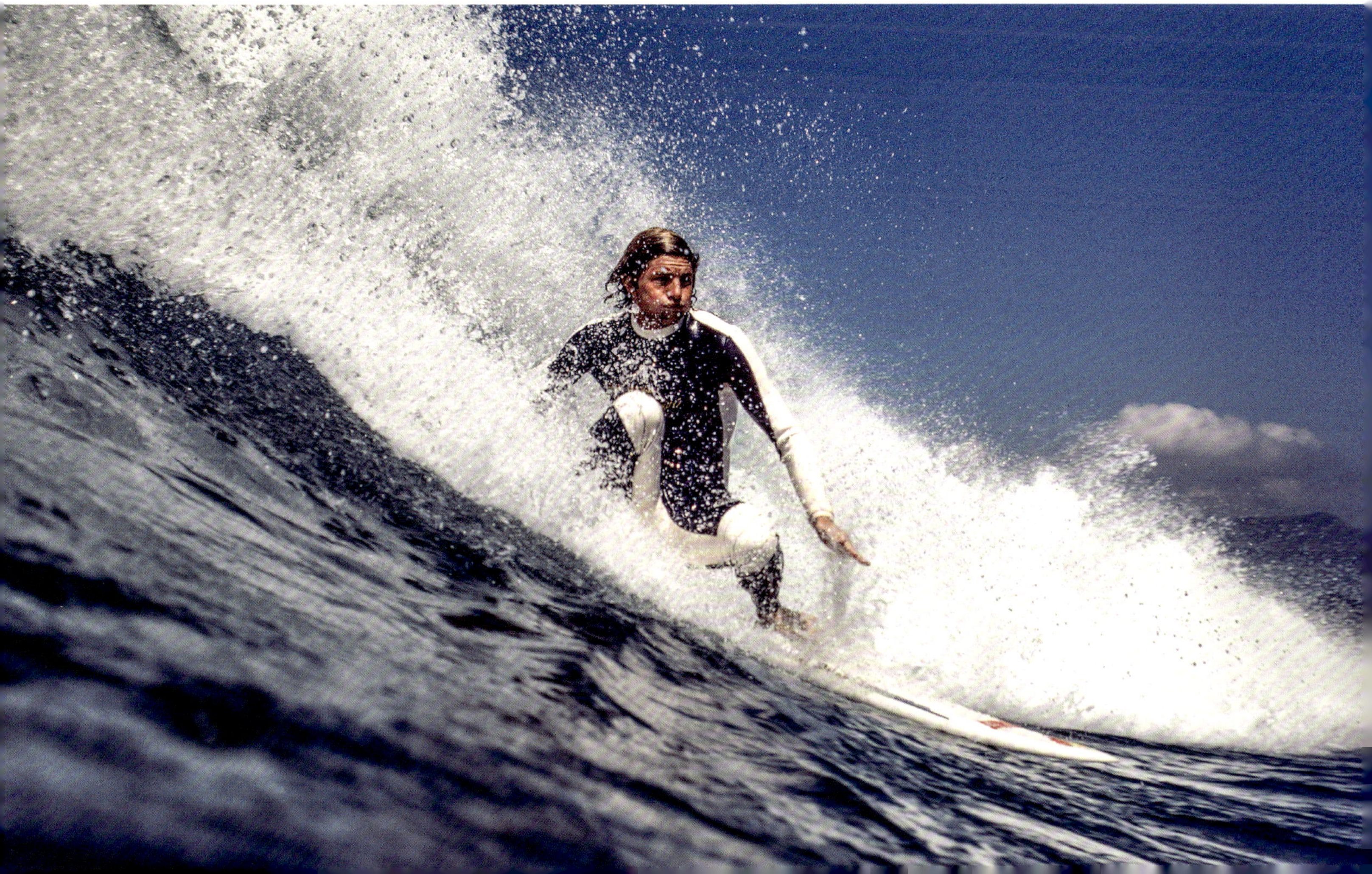

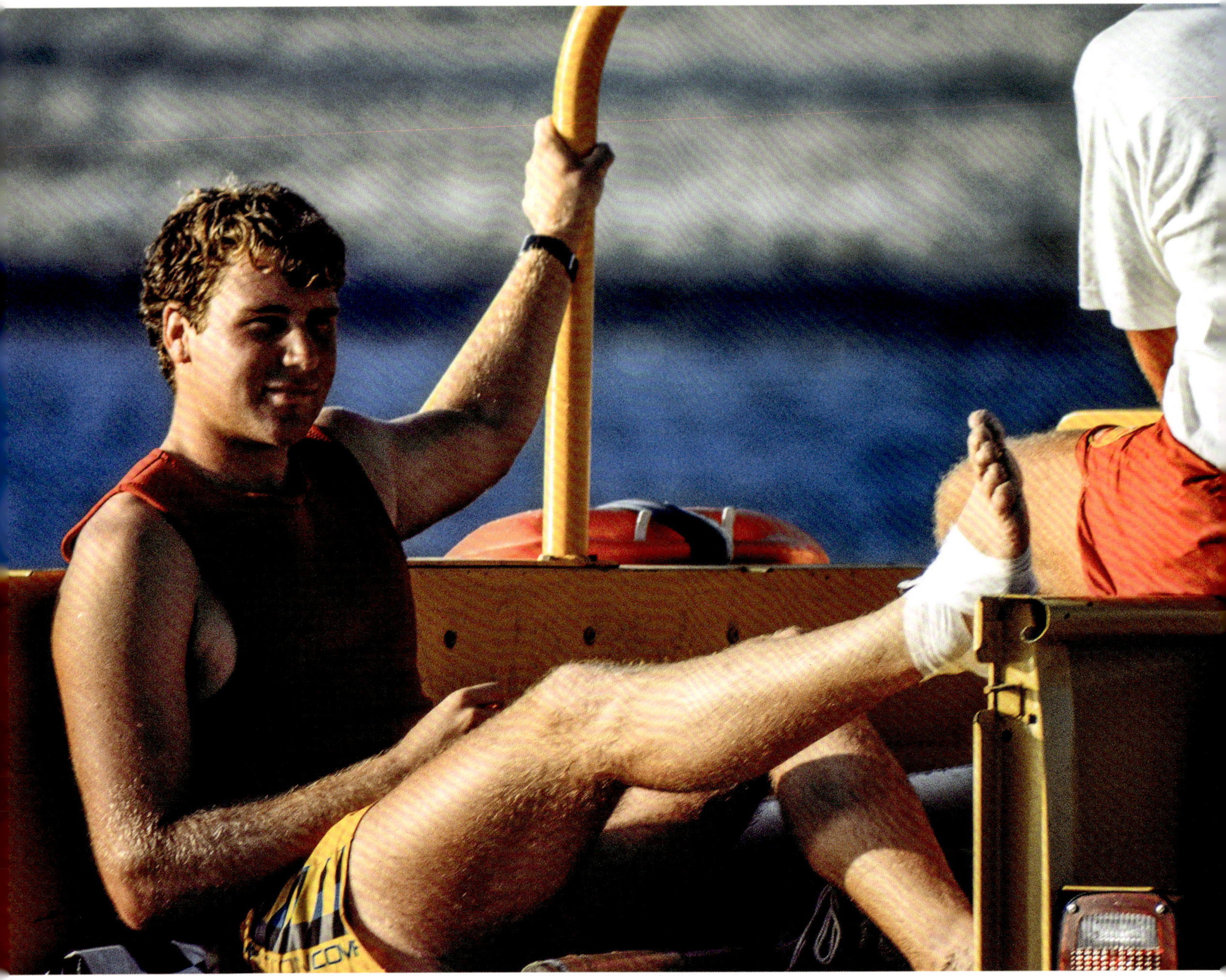

Malibu Royalty

Willy Morris, romping through First Point Malibu's Kiddie Bowl section. Willy landed hard, caught an edge, and sliced his ankle pretty badly with a fin. He was quickly patched up by head lifeguard John Baker, who then gave the slightly embarrassed Willy a quick ride back to the parking lot. In those days, nobody got a ride in the lifeguard truck unless there was an ambulance waiting or you were Malibu royalty. By 1983, Willy was certainly that.

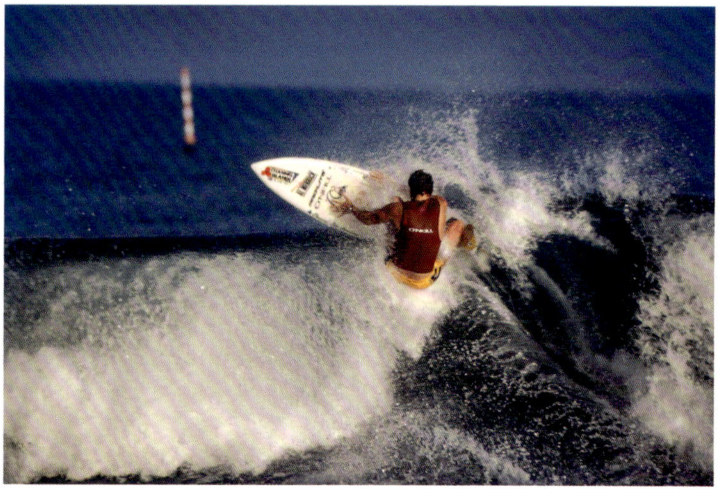

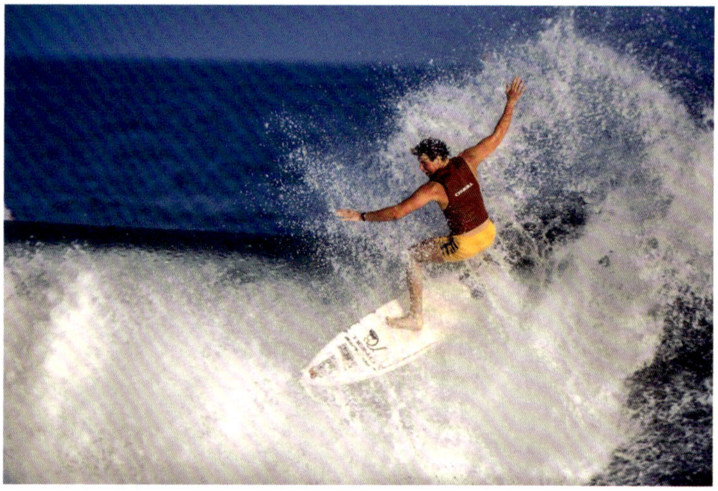

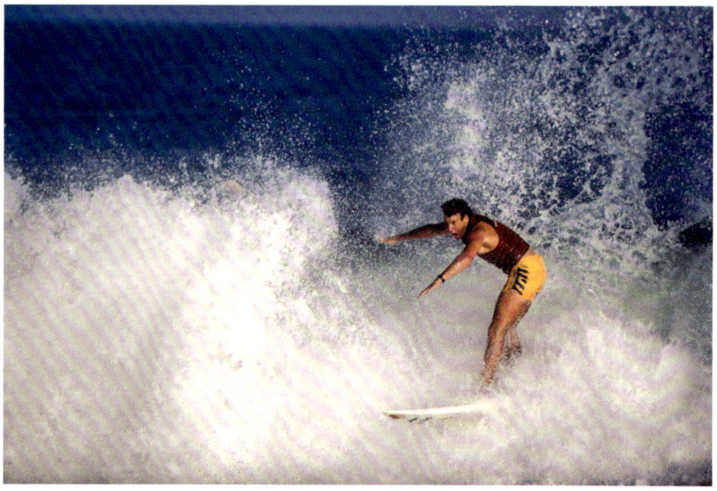

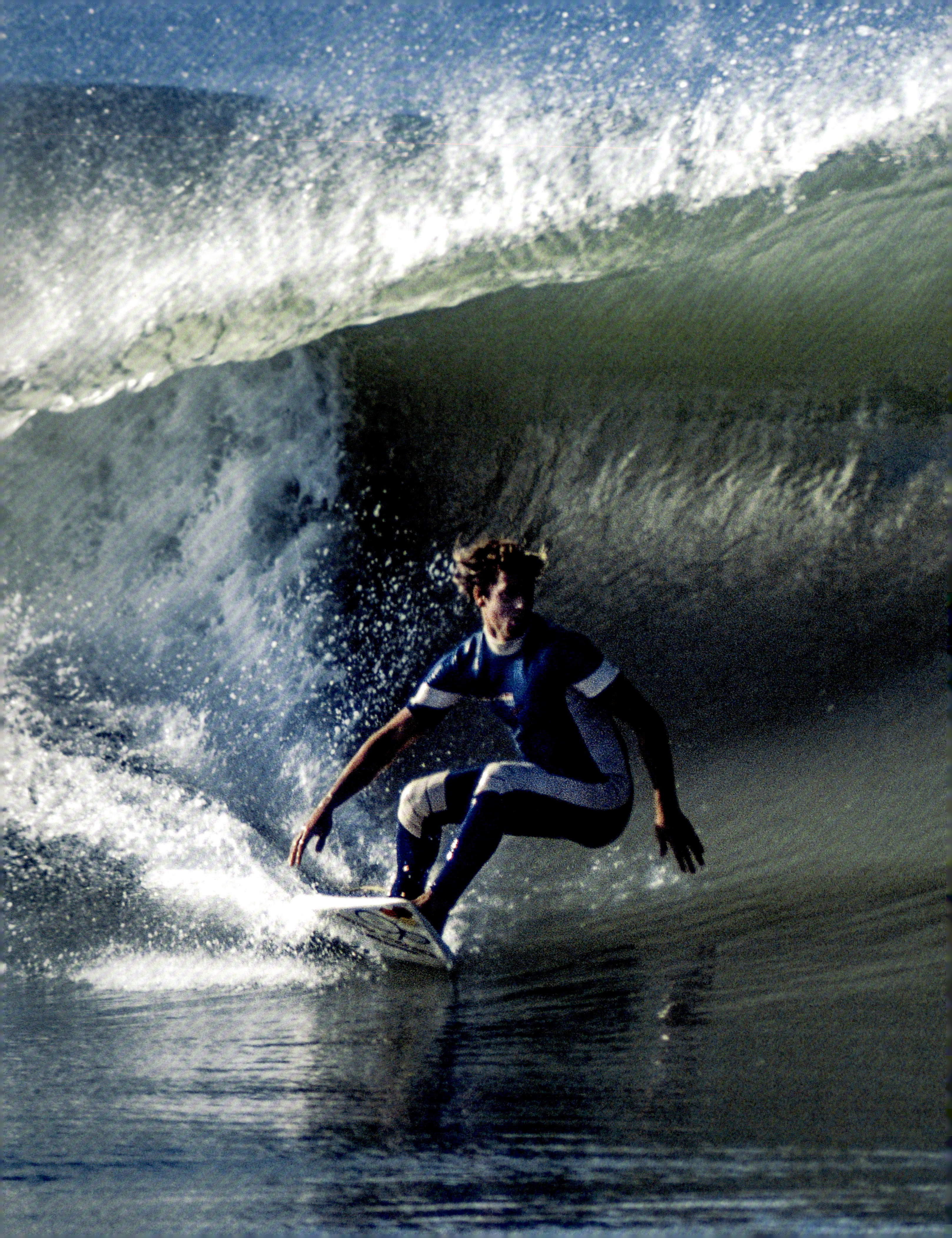

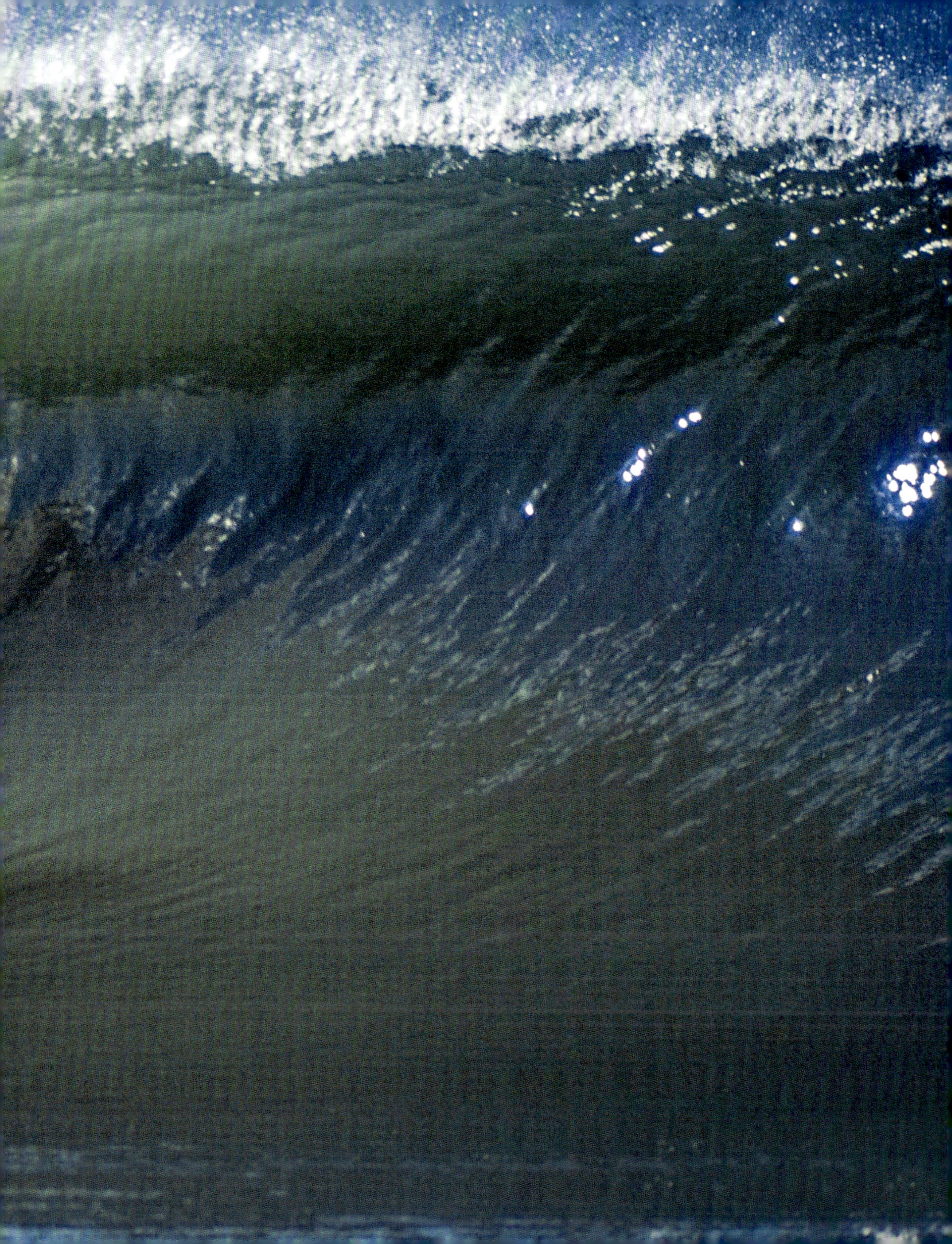

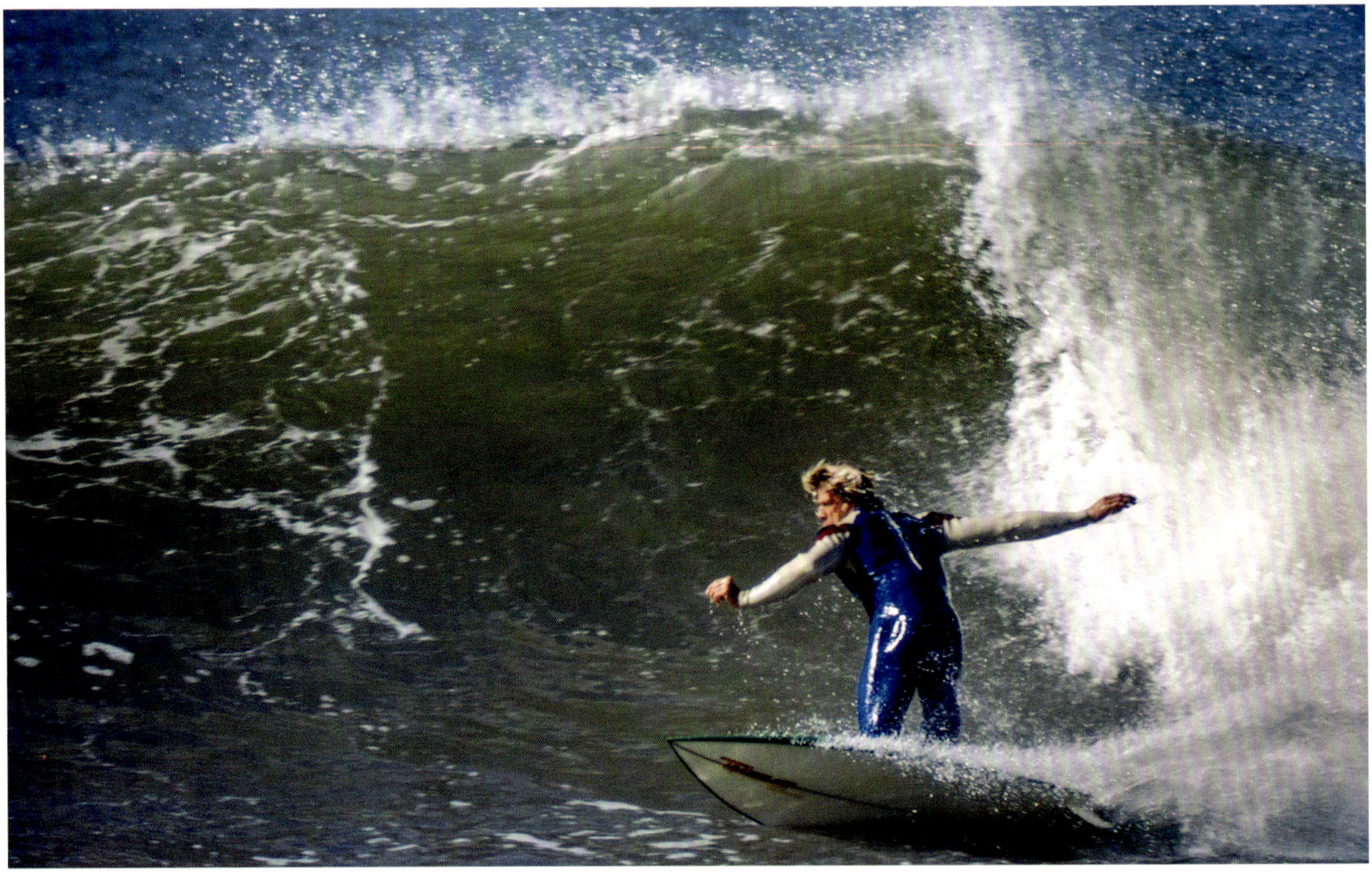

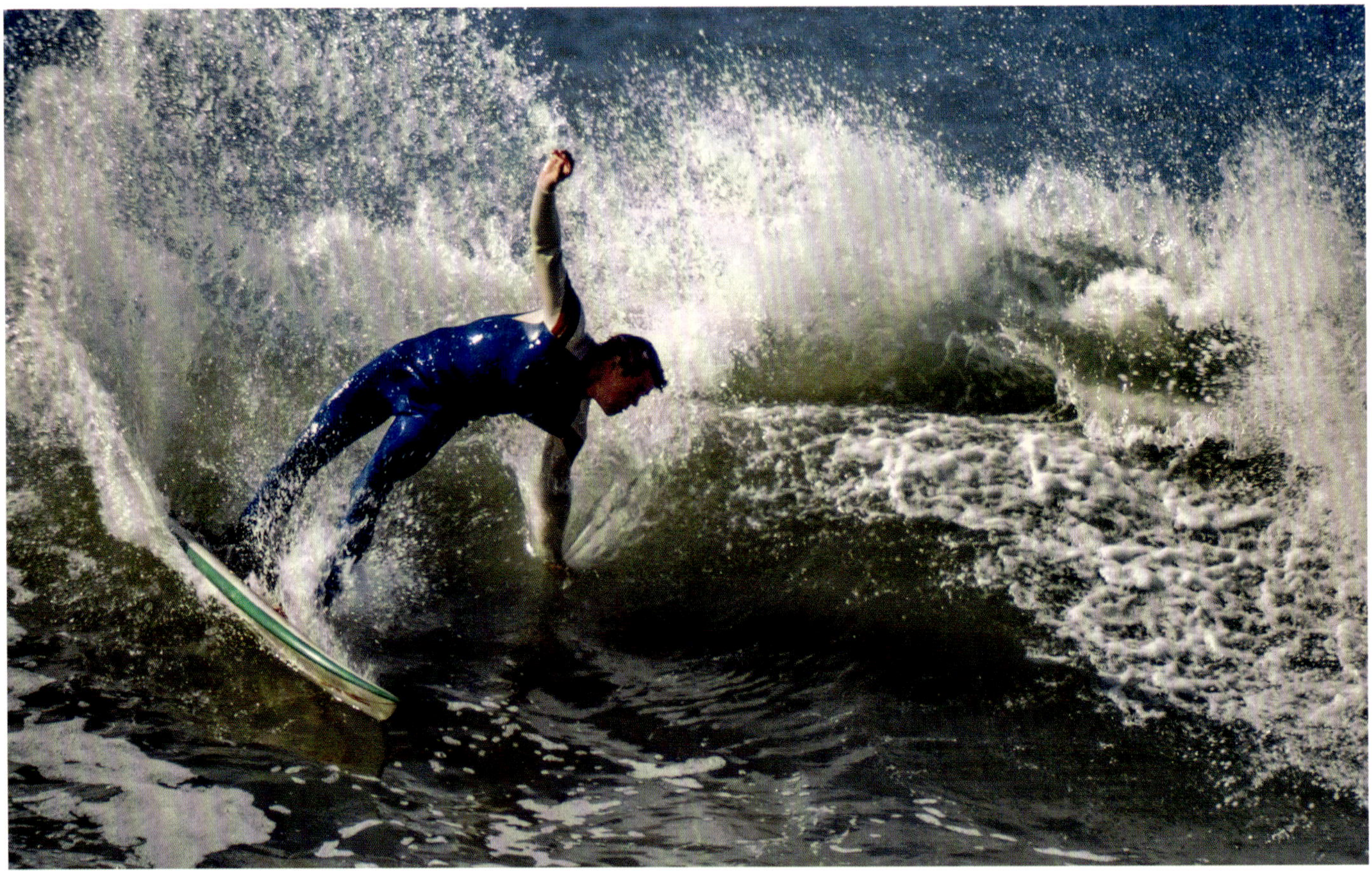

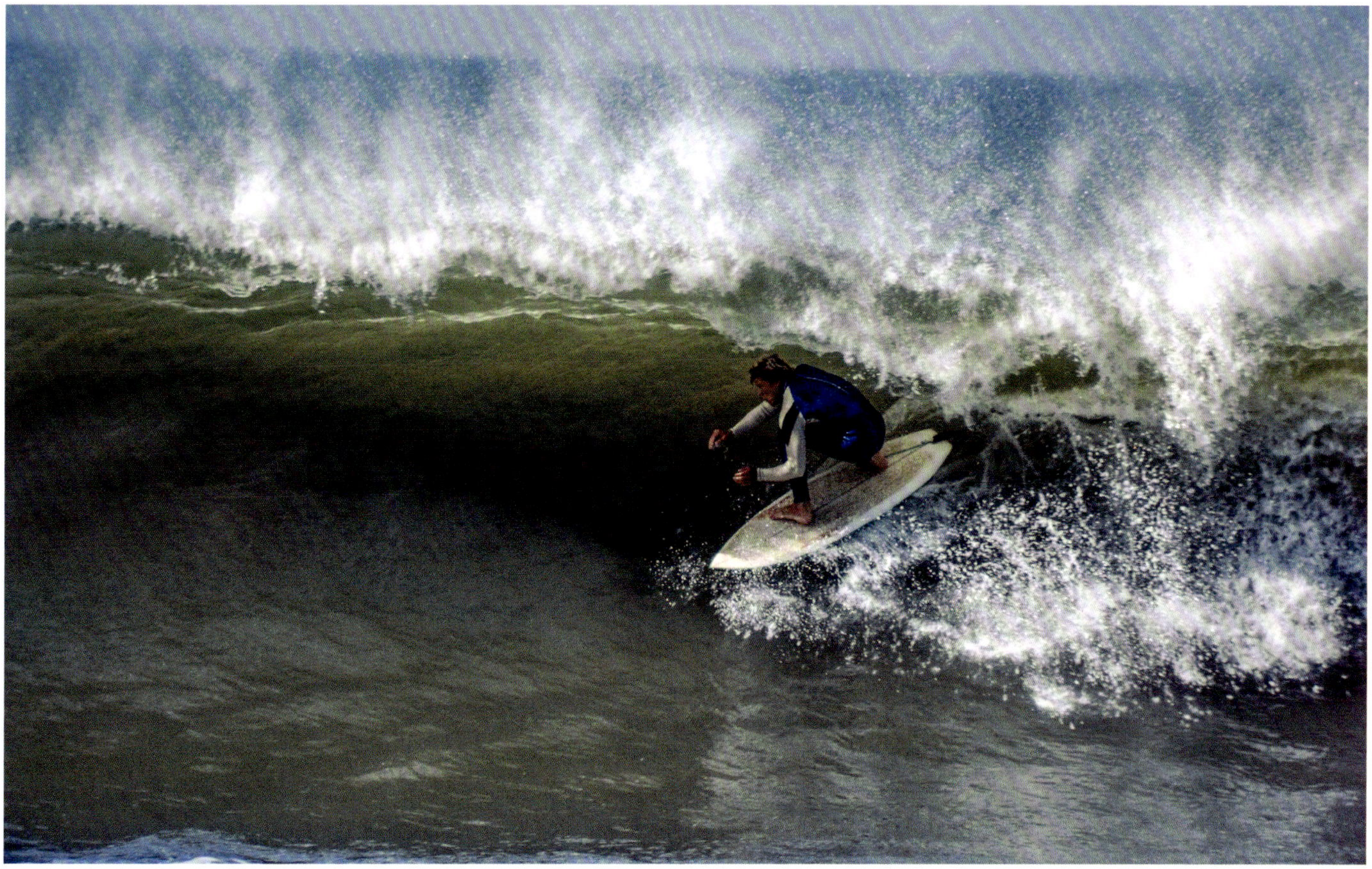

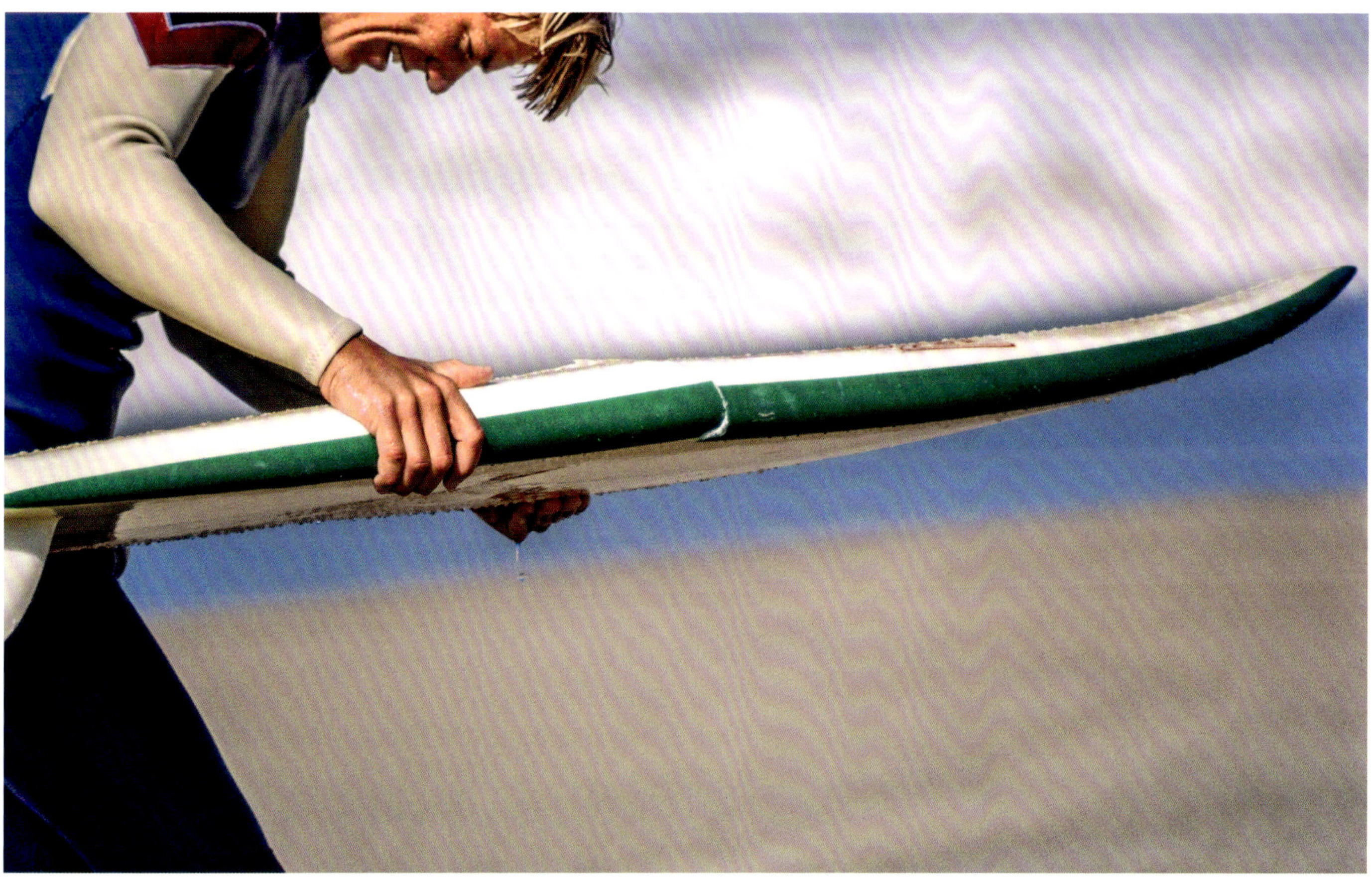

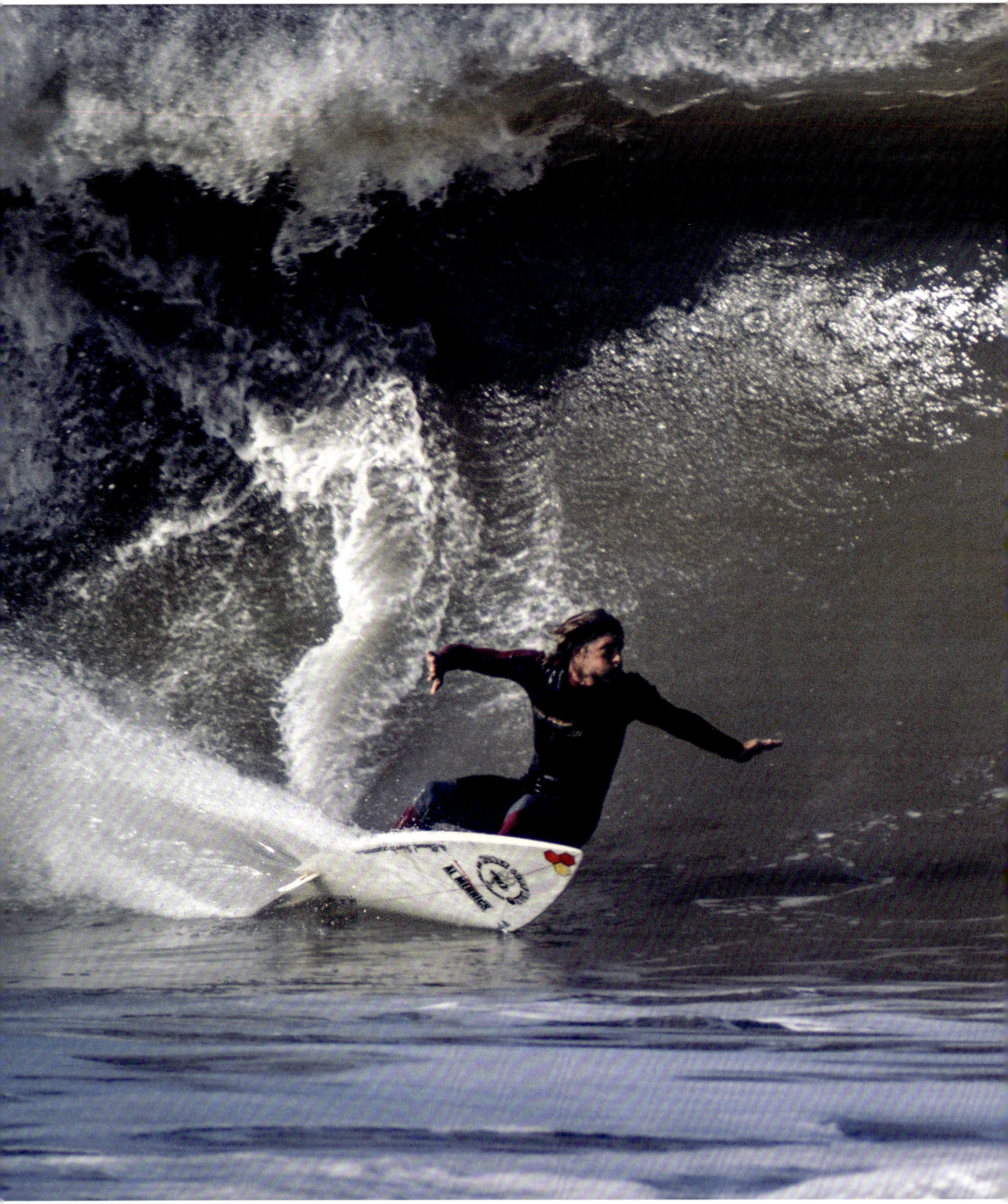

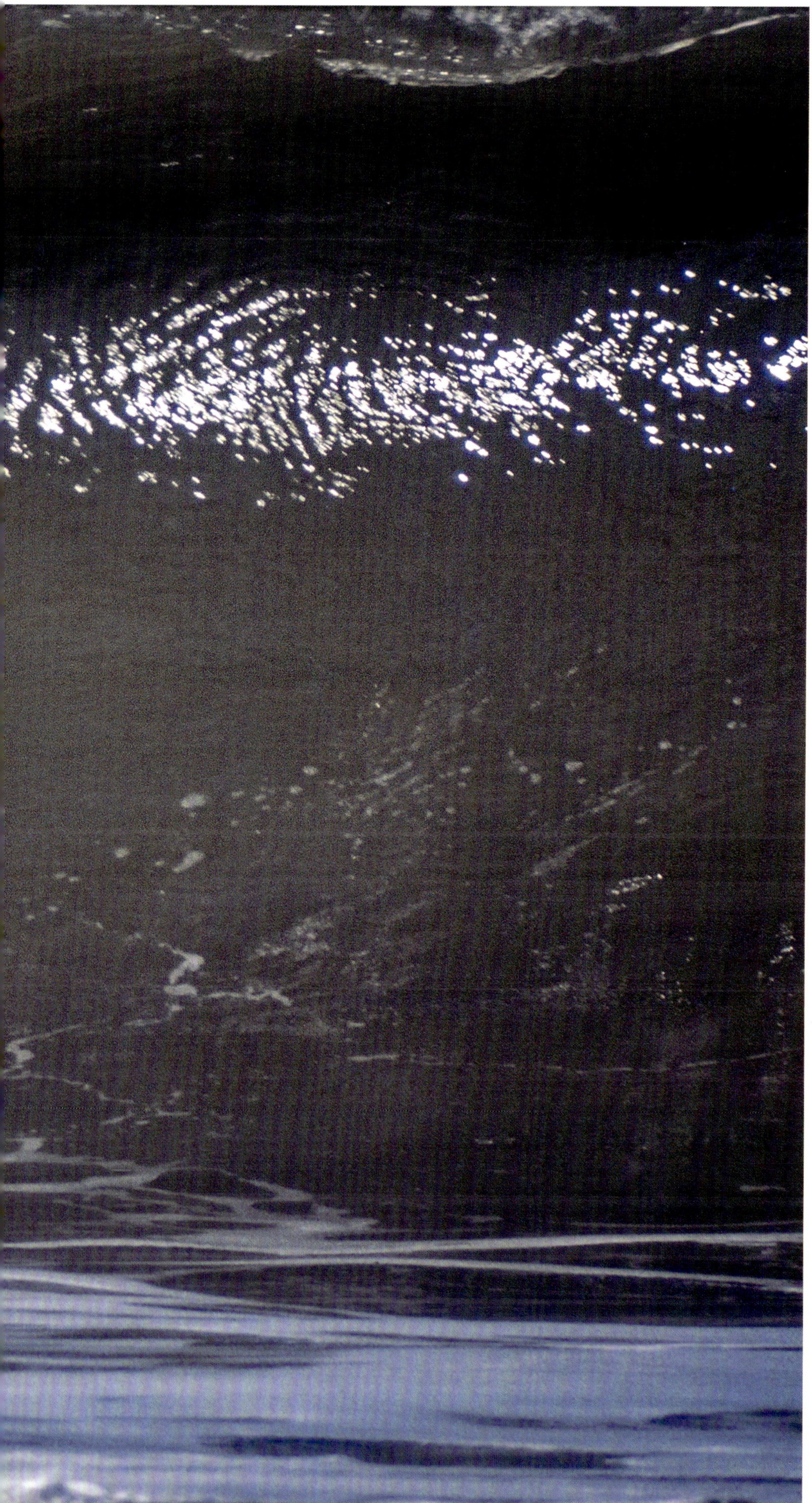

Pages 276–277
I had grown up staring at published photos of Oxnard and Ventura's beachbreaks, captured on their very best days by hometown photog Craig Fineman and featuring hot local surfers like Russ Short and the Campbell brothers in what looked like the most perfect waves I'd ever seen. I took one of my own on this particular morning at Santa Clara Rivermouth, with Tom Curren doing the honors.

Pages 278–279
Davey Miller was one of Ventura's best, certainly the most dominant of its young surfers. Standing well over six feet, Davey had a unique style that may have lent itself to more-powerful waves, but didn't stop him from bending his tall frame through some tight turns in smaller surf. These photos were shot a year before he would land on Oahu's North Shore and successfully campaign the Banzai Pipeline.

Spread
On the biggest day I'd ever seen surfed at Santa Clara Rivermouth, Sam maintained impeccable positioning and form, going all out on a brand-new Merrick thruster. He pulled into the tube on this wave and snapped it. Paddled back out on his backup and broke that one on the next wave.

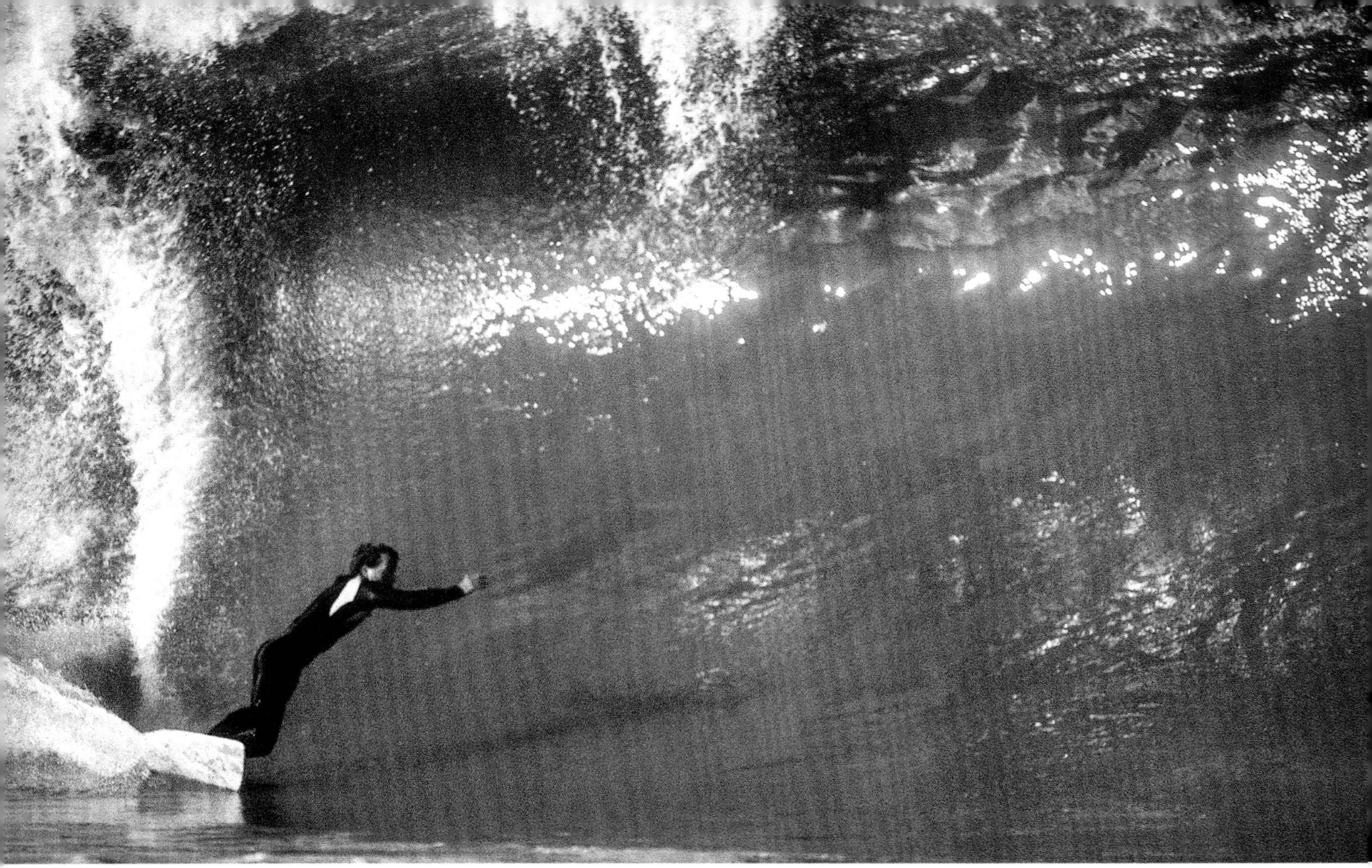

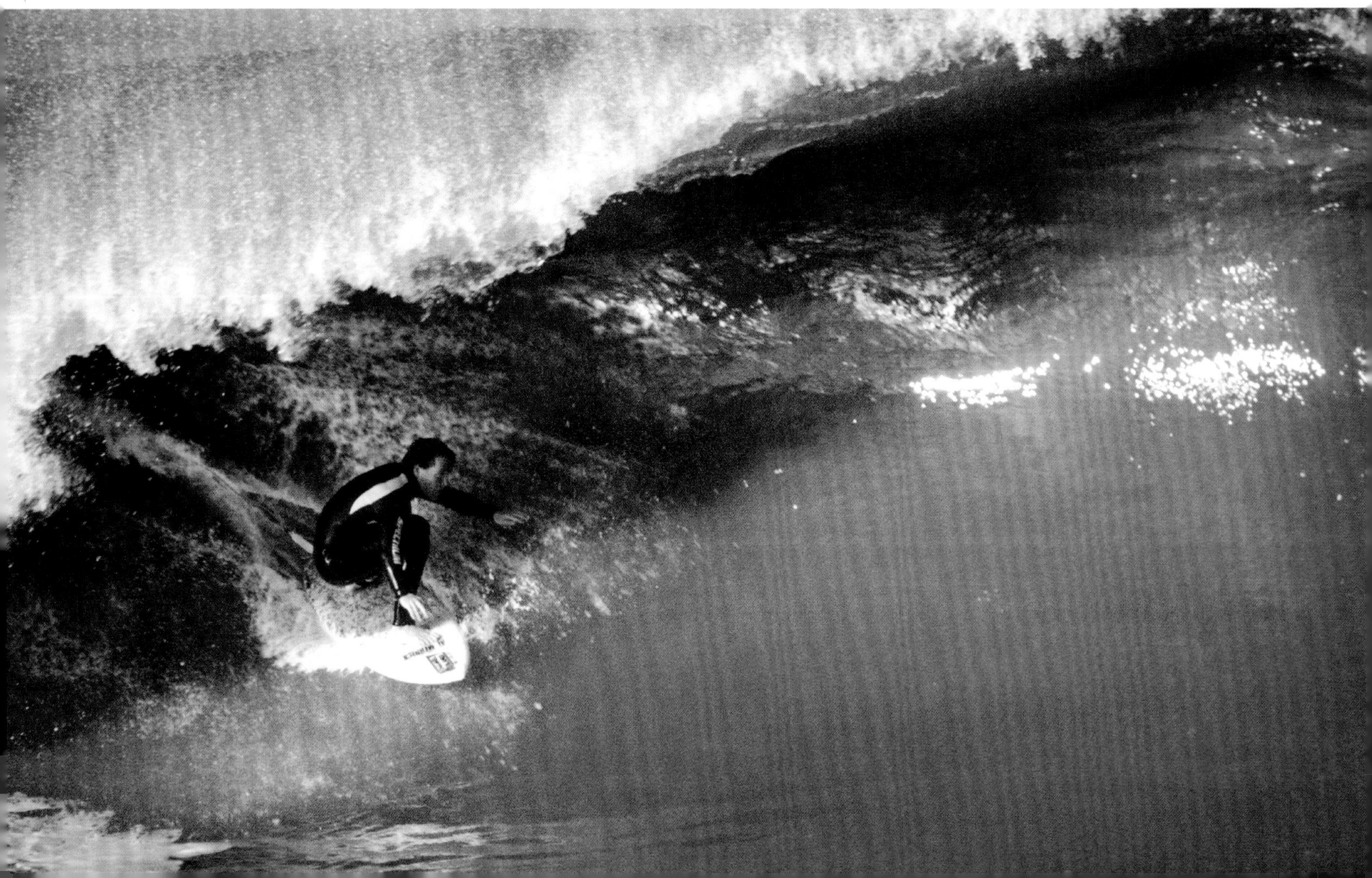

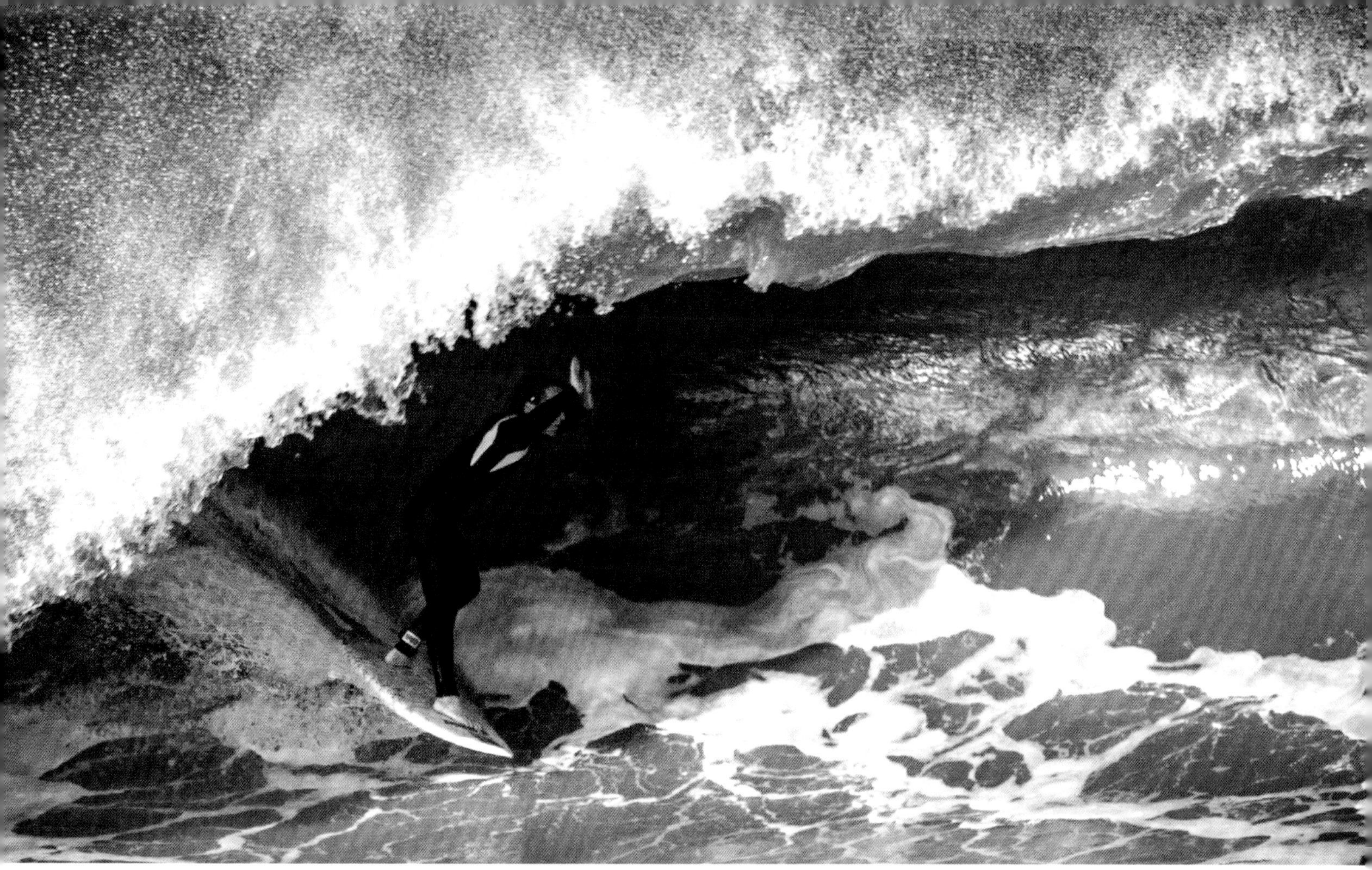

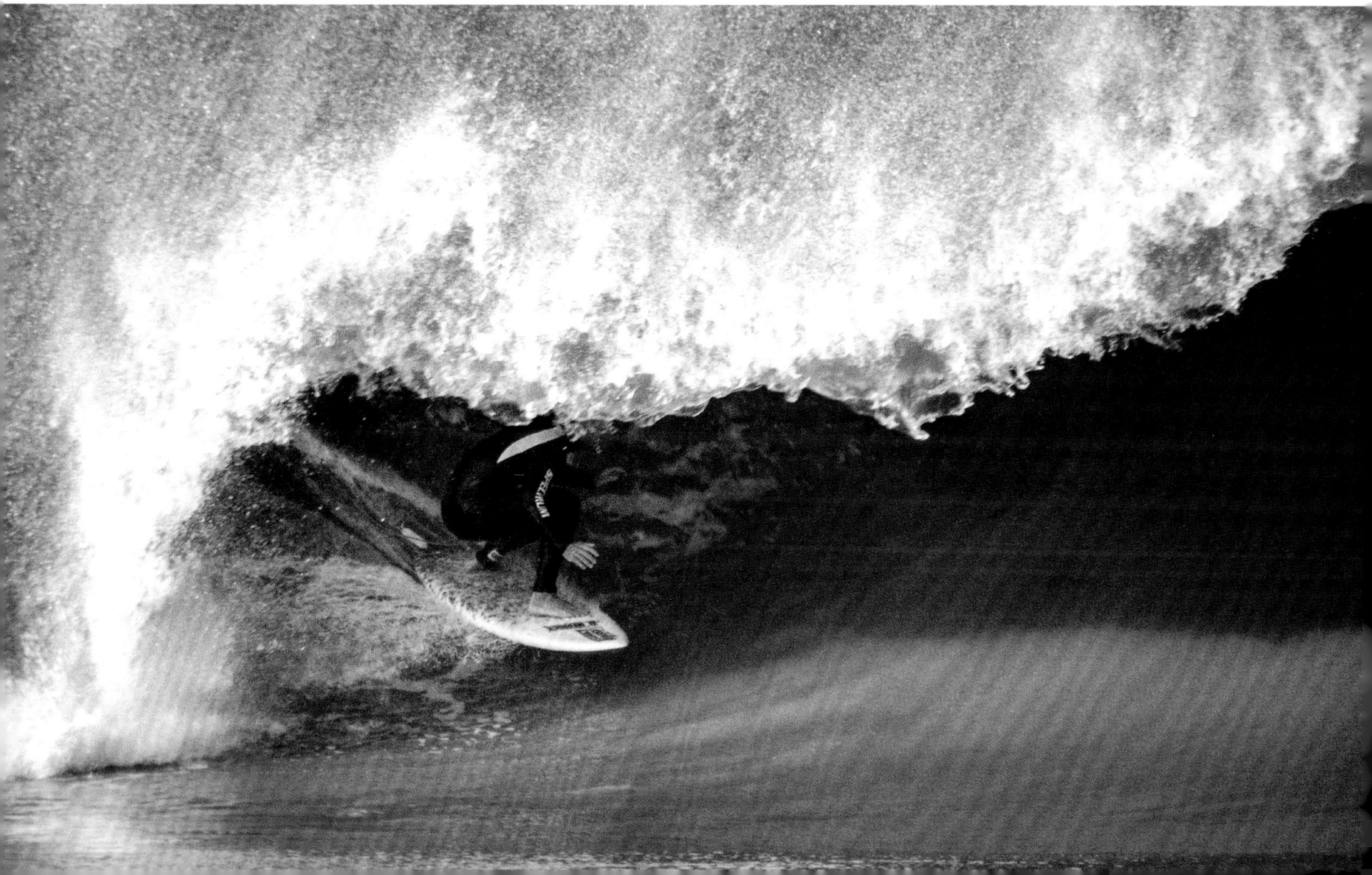

Pages 282–283
As much attention as Davey Smith received for his pioneering aerial surfing, all he really cared about was finding big, round lefts—the bigger and rounder, the better. Davey's shown here pulling into a serious section on the same five-and-a-half-foot four-fin that he'd boost aerials with in Emma Wood shorebreak.

Below
For civilian Ventura beachgoers, the brown freshwater runoff spoiled an otherwise pretty ocean view. For the area's surfers, however, post-storm river-borne sediment meant epic sandbars and ruler-edged walls. Goleta's David Pu'u, taking advantage of both.

Facing
Sam George, holding two halves of what only minutes before was an impressive pair of custom Merricks, wondering how he would break the news to Al.

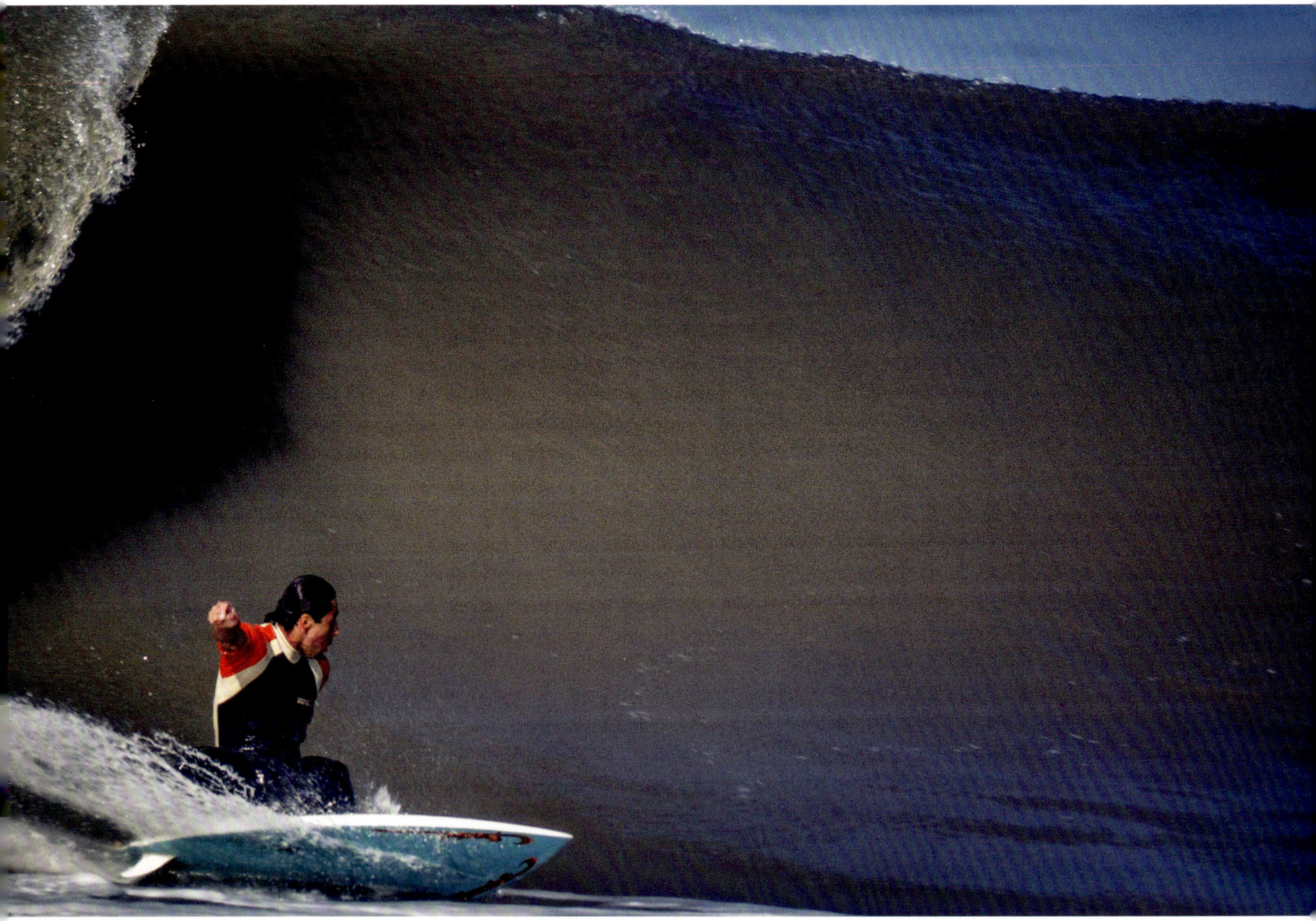

Overleaf

Ray Call was an underground Ventura hero, earning his reputation on those bigger days when his uninterrupted flow in heavy positions brought to mind legendary Hawaiian goofyfoot Gerry Lopez, complete with the Pipeline Master's signature sensitive hand-drag.

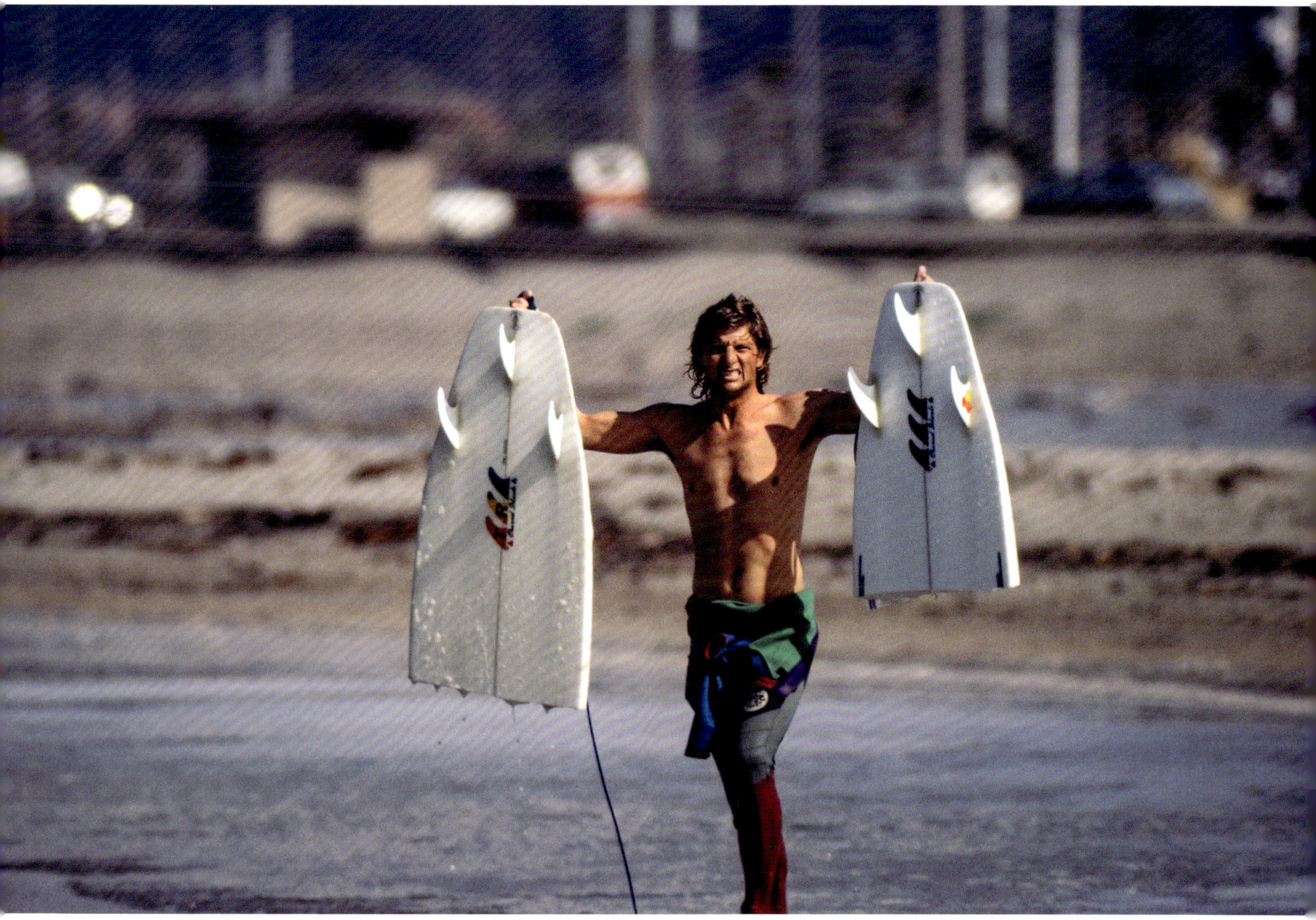

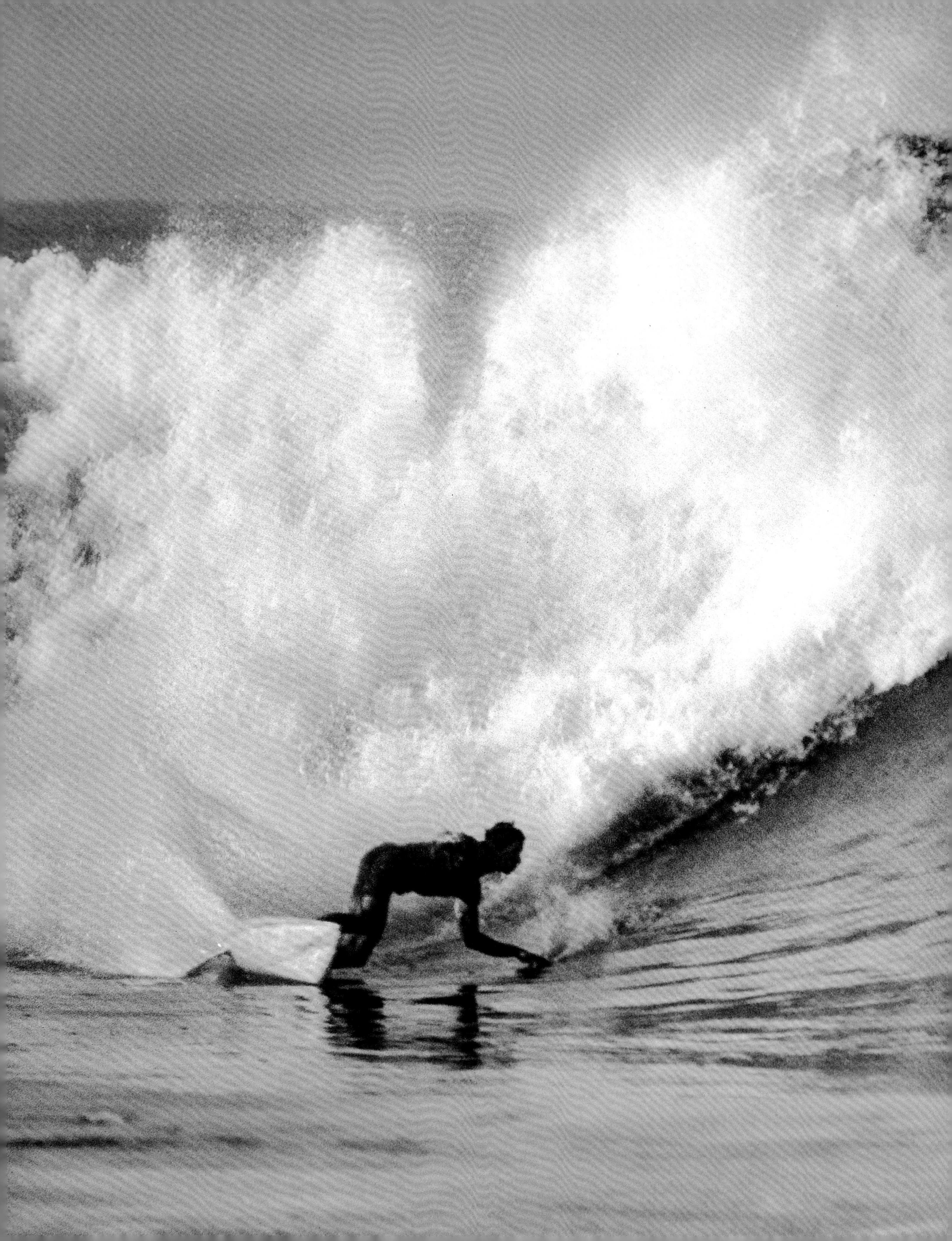

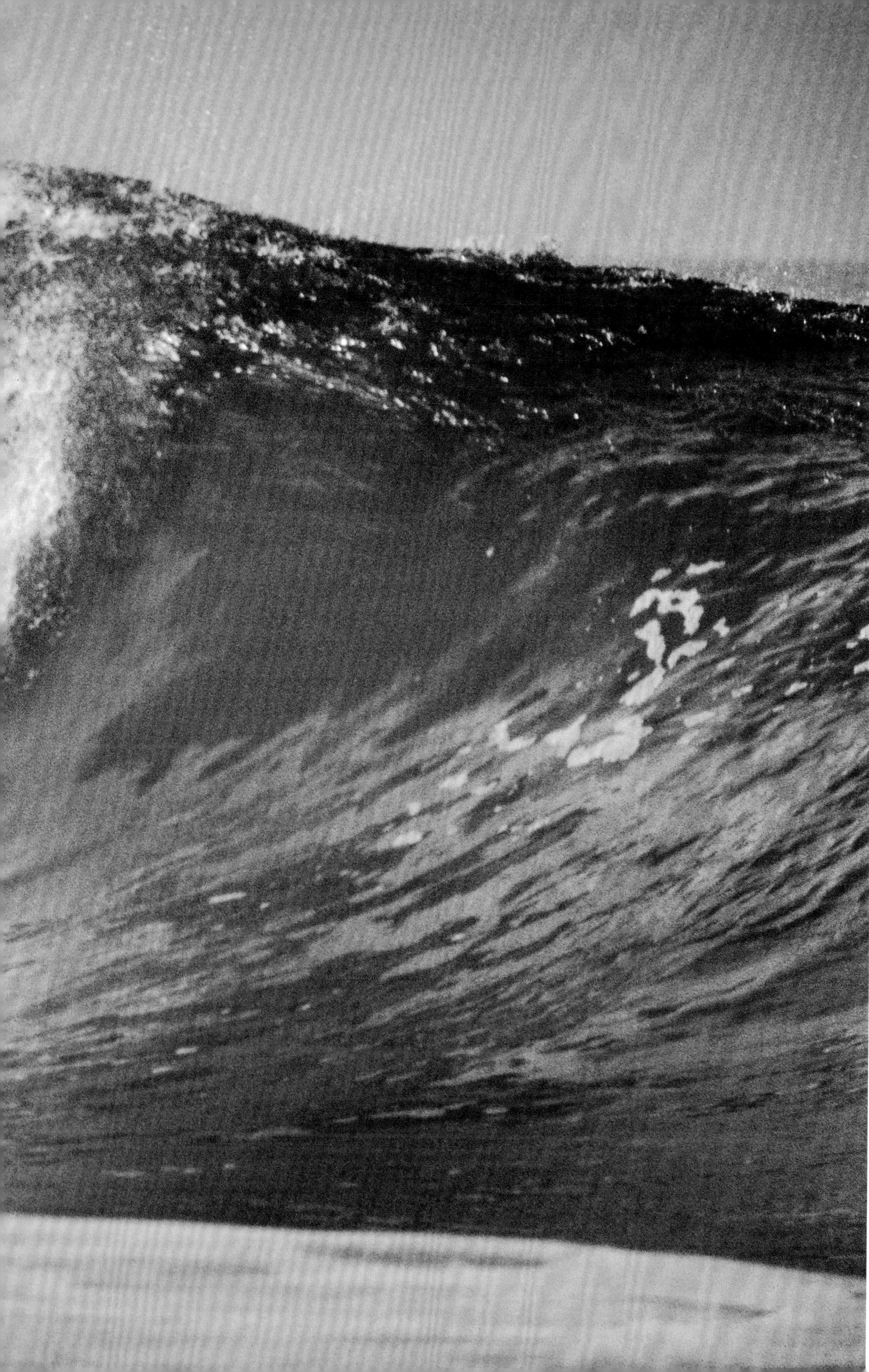

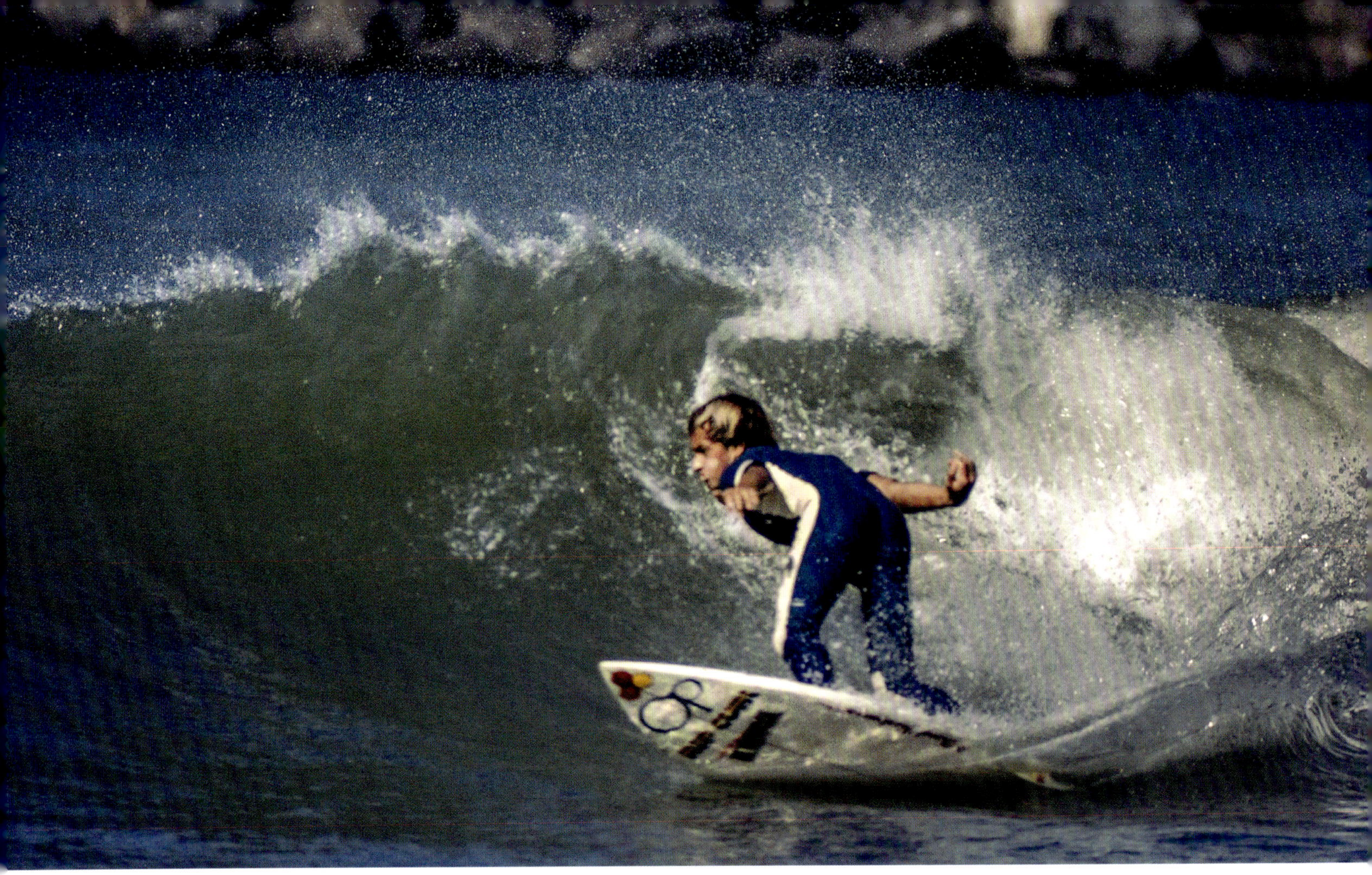

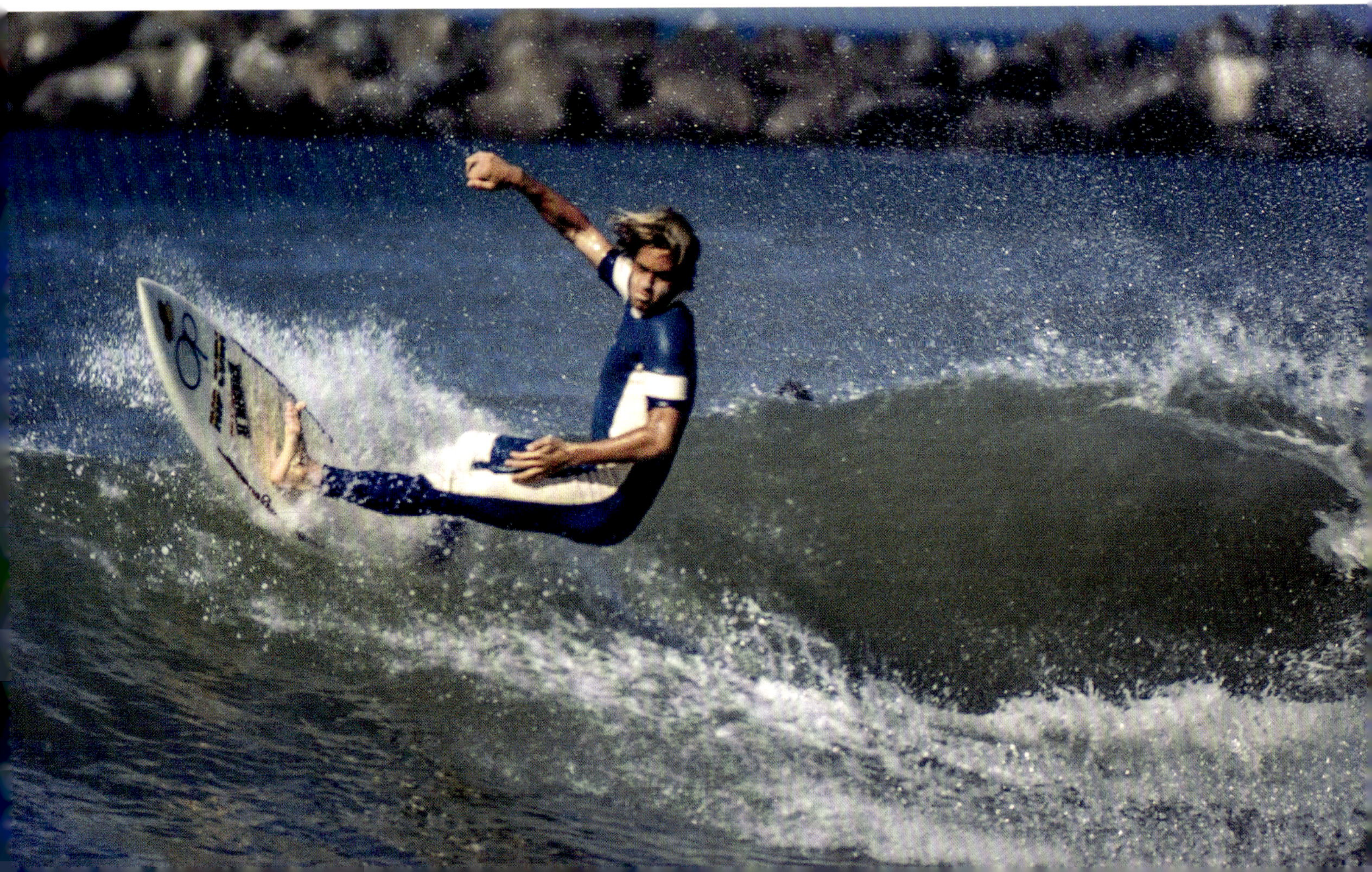

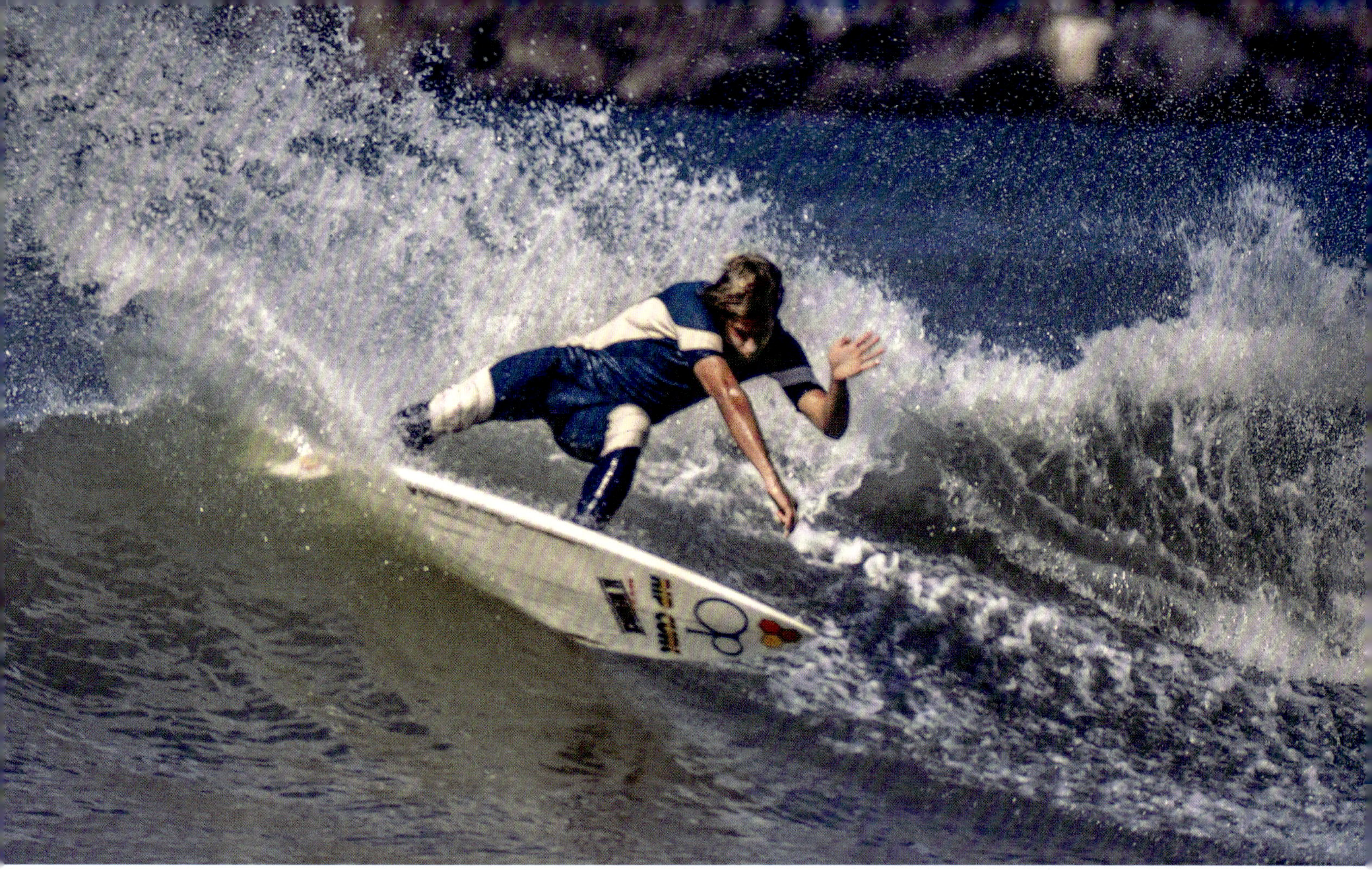

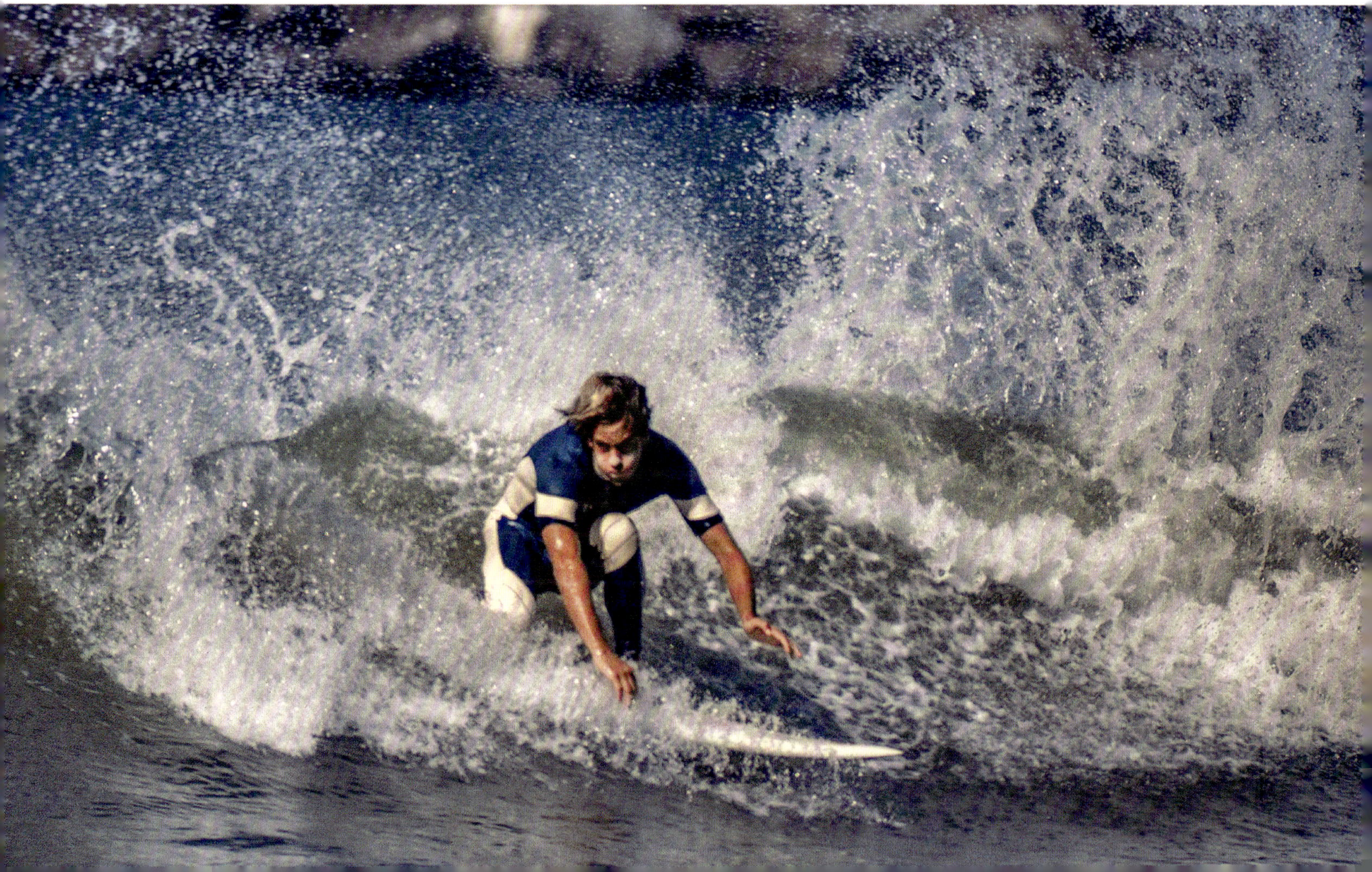

Previous

Tommy, stoked to be back in home waters after a few months on the pro tour. I remember being startled by how much he'd upped his performance level, realizing, as he slashed through this turn, that I was probably witnessing the best two-foot-wave surfing being done in the world at that moment.

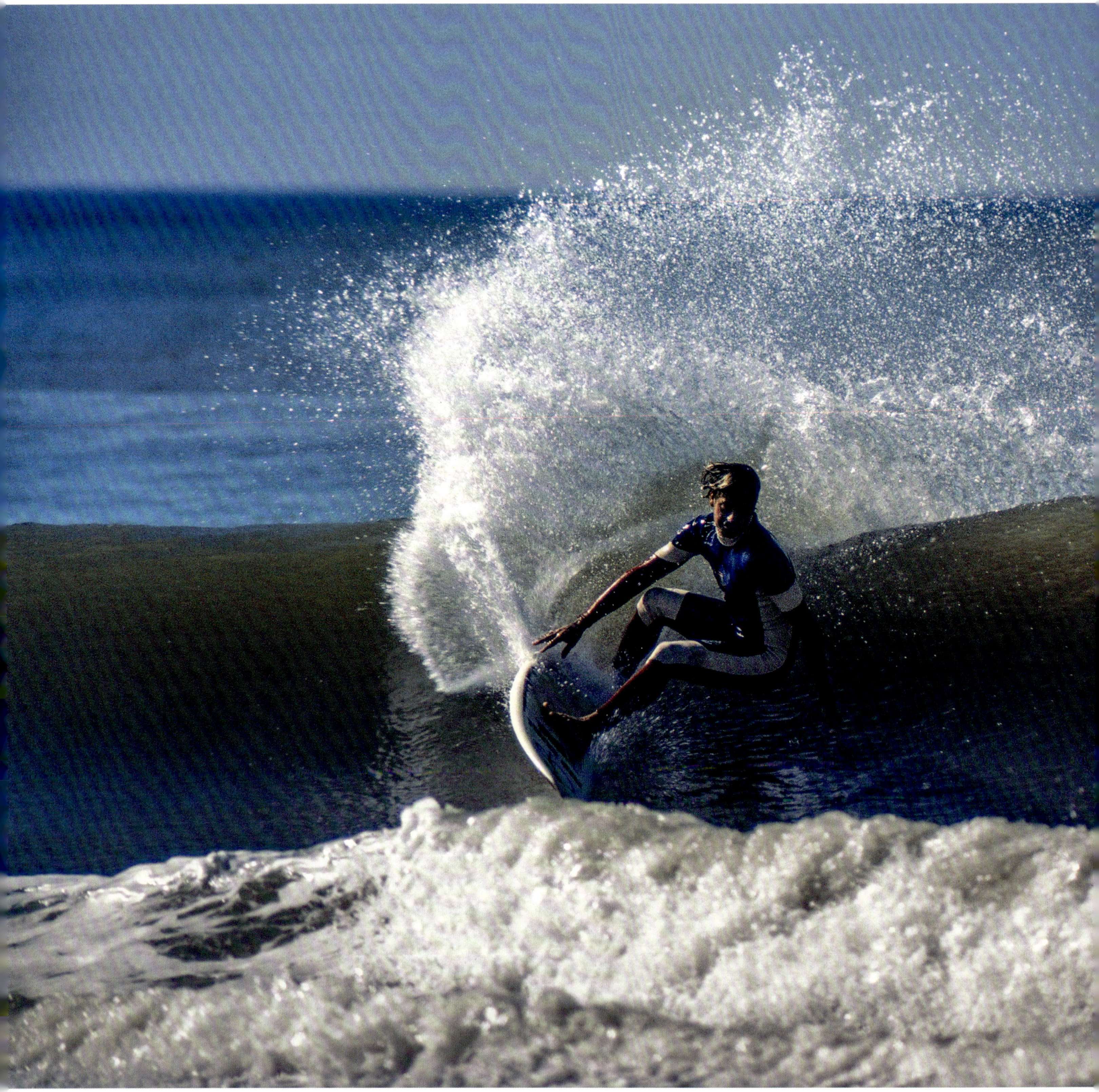

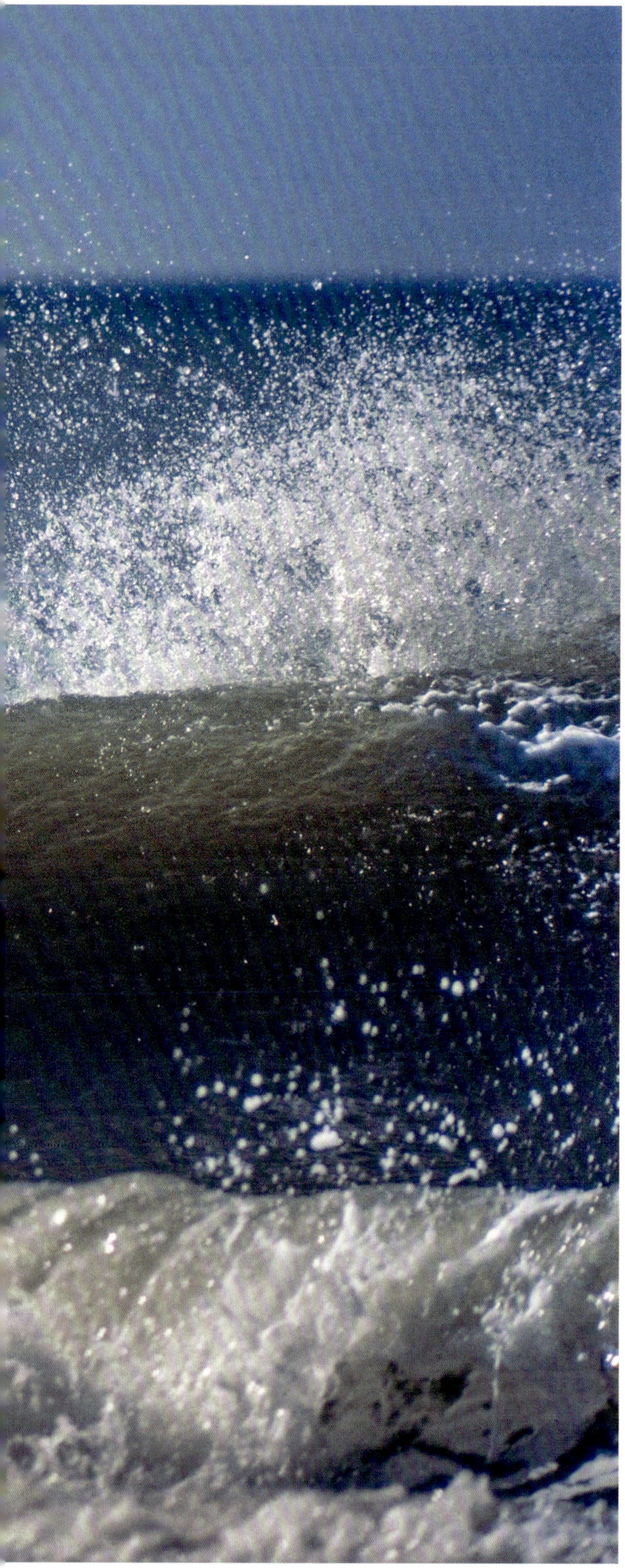

Got Some Good Ones

By 1983, Tommy Curren and I had spent a lot of time together—years, in fact—chasing waves and good lighting, shooting photos from land and in the water, composing tube shots and formal portraits. And never once in all that time did he ask to see a photo I'd taken of him. I really don't think he was that interested, personally. Oh, he'd be stoked for me when, getting a good batch of slides back, I'd assure him that we'd connected for a few guaranteed "mag shots." Then his eyes would really light up. "Got some good ones, huh?" he'd ask, but the excitement was all for me, supporting my efforts, not his own. This was one of Tom's most endearing qualities, that of being genuinely interested in other people's passions, seemingly more so than in his own. Which is probably why he never asked to see this cutback shot, one of my better ones, when I got it back from Kodak developing. But I'd bet he still remembers how happy I was that day.

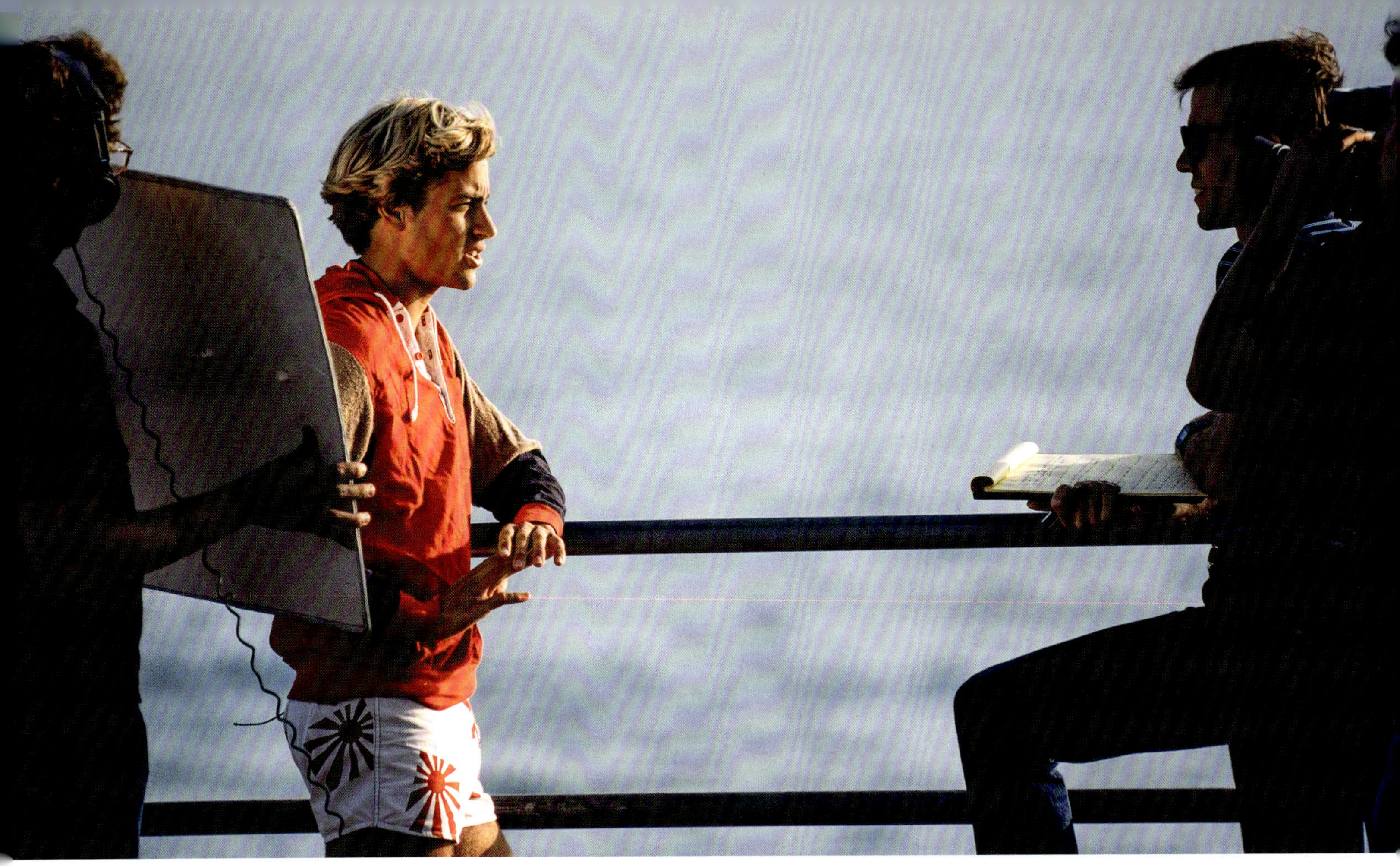

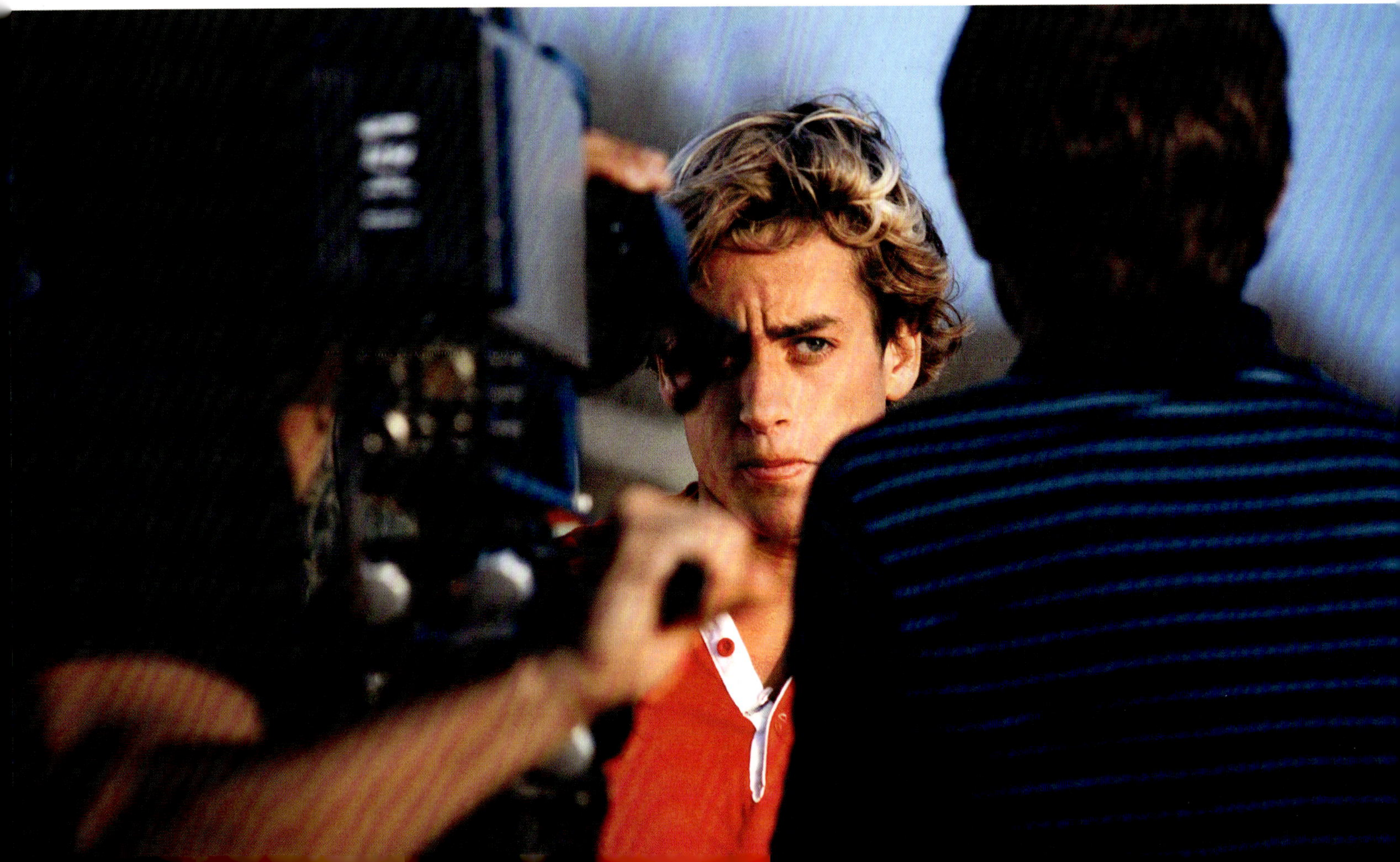

Spread

From that funny, slightly eccentric, preternaturally gifted kid I'd pick up from the Curren compound off Milpas Street, to the fully formed professional champion, how I found myself in position to photograph the entire Tommy Curren arc is still a wonder to me. Yet as my time in Santa Barbara drew to a close, there came a growing sense that after having Tommy in the front seat of my car for the past four years—functioning, essentially, as his personal surf photographer—I was now handing him off to the wider world, and I couldn't help but wonder how he'd handle the intense focus that was sure to come. His expression during this "Eye on LA" television interview spoke volumes.

Pages 294–297

These were taken on my last photo shoot with Tommy before moving back to Texas, fittingly at Santa Clara Rivermouth, where so many of our best images were captured. As he carved past me on this wave, I was instantly transported back to South Padre Island and the first time I saw Tommy surf, wishing then that I had a camera, knowing that I was watching a future world champion. Seeing him as I did now: an exceptional young man, an exceptionally talented surfer, moving effortlessly forward, his sights set firmly down the line.

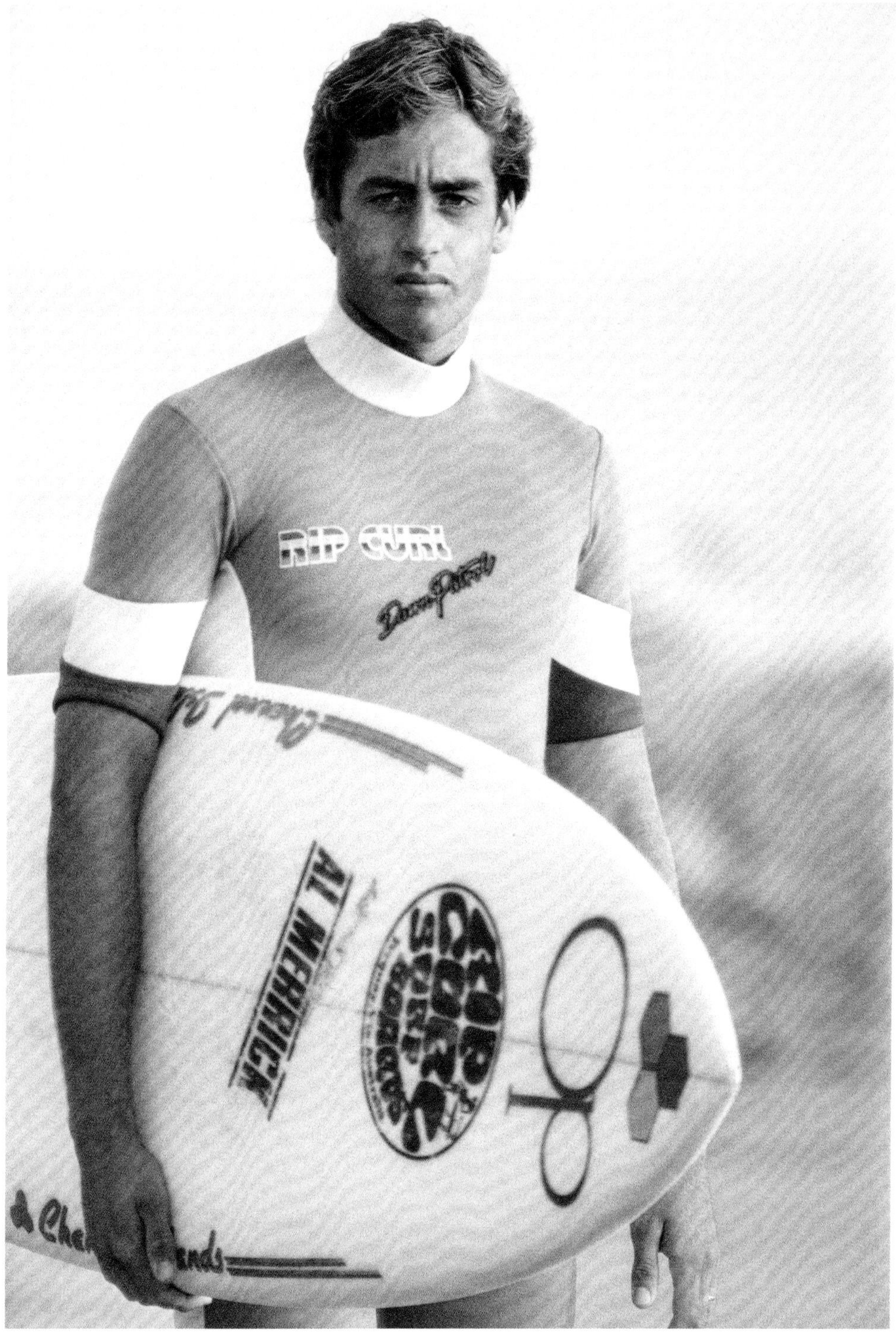

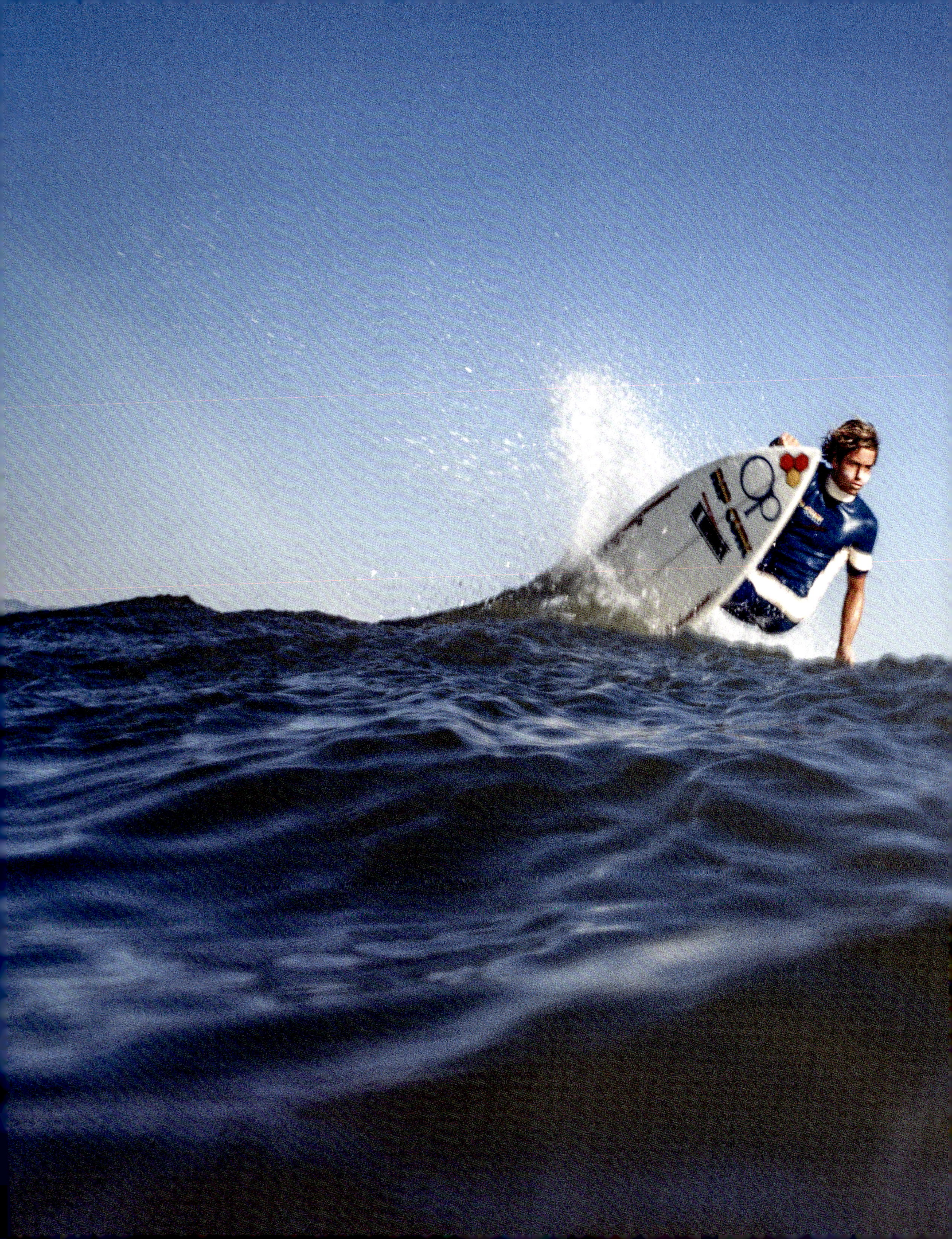

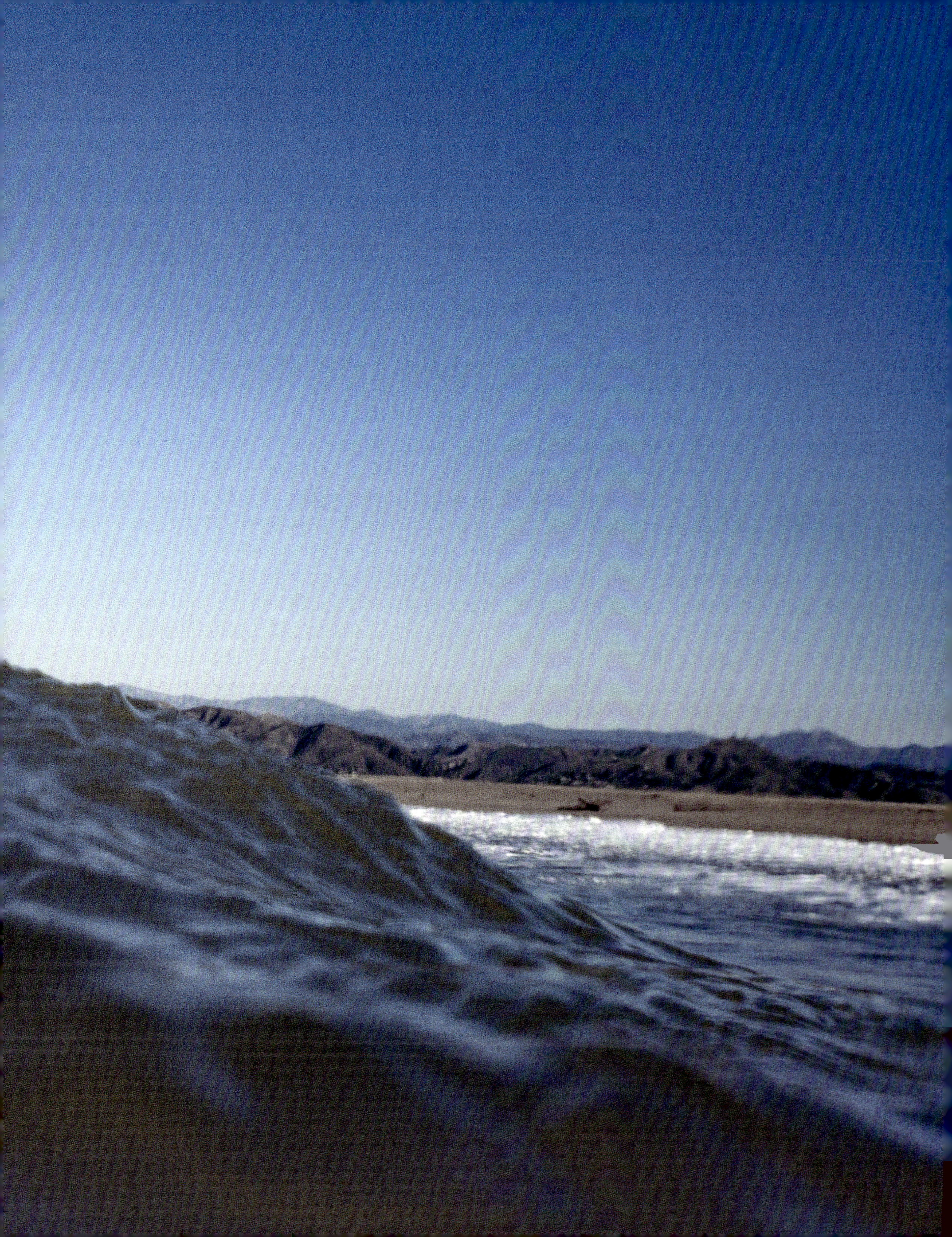

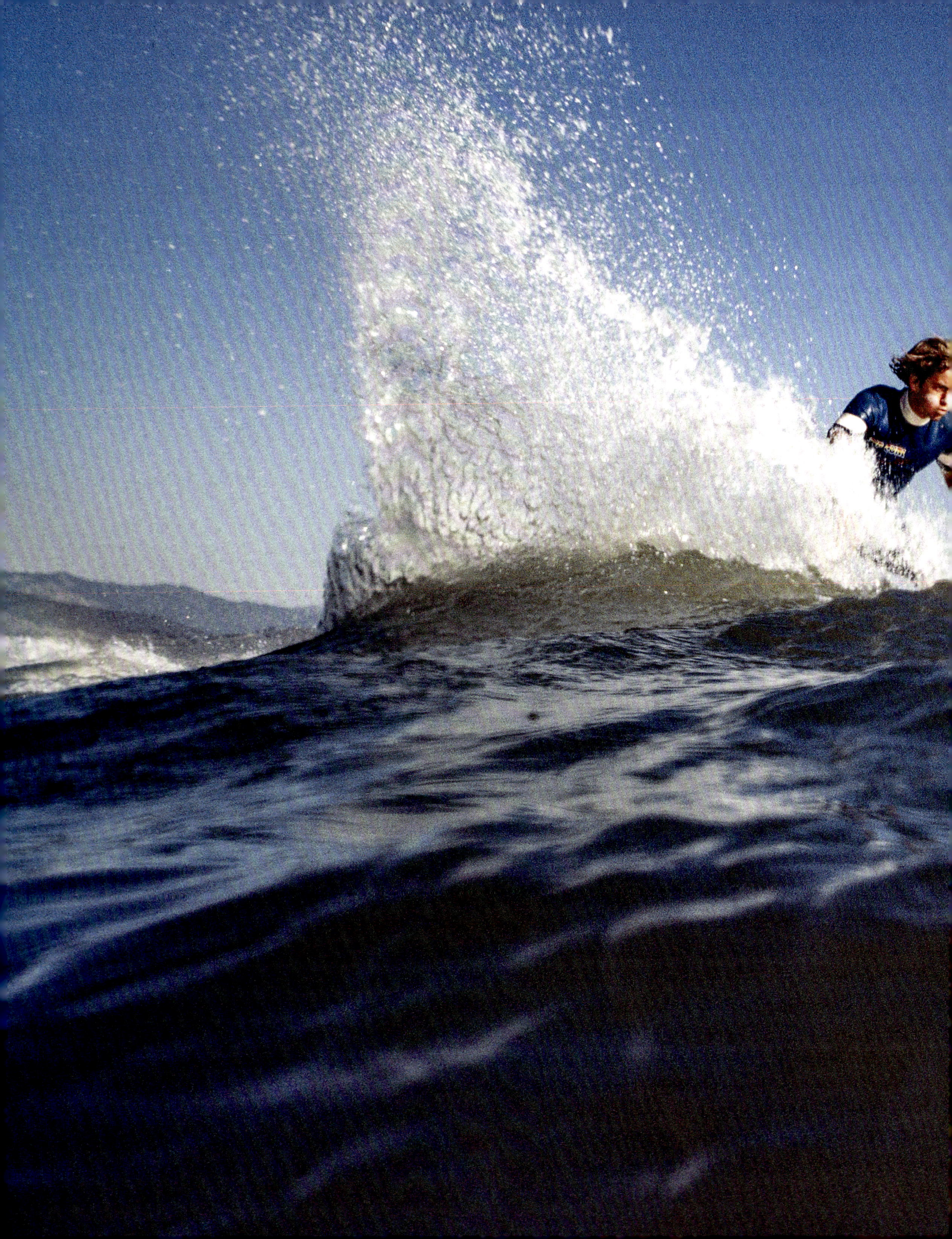

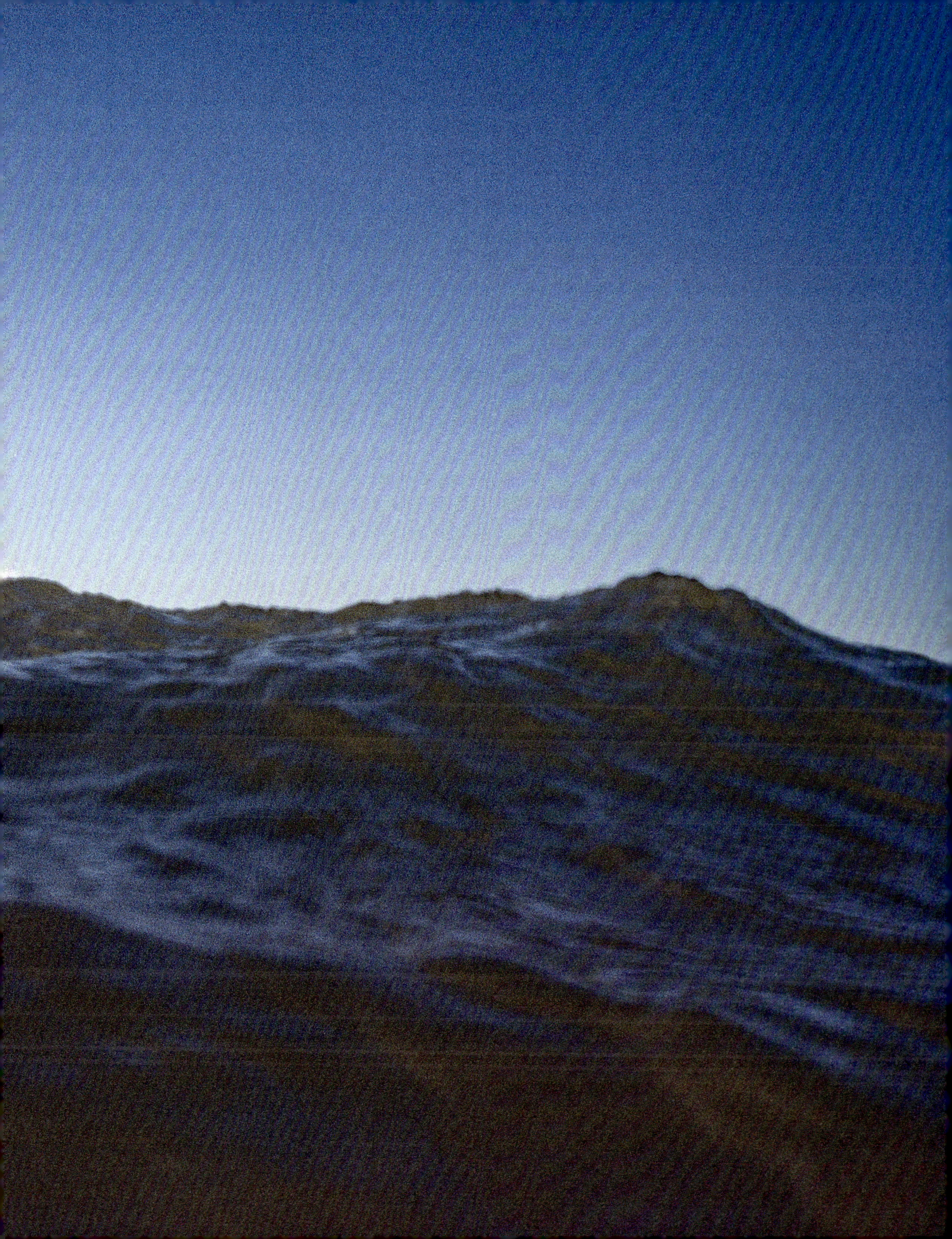

EPILOGUE

In 1987, *Surfer* magazine asked me to cover the US Surfing Championships, held again on Padre Island, Texas. Which is why, almost eight years after sitting on the beach and seeing Tommy Curren surf for the first time, I found myself on the same sand, witnessing another skinny fourteen-year-old surf circles around everyone else. Competing in the boys' division, amateur competitive surfing's version of the frosh-soph team, this young kid from Cocoa Beach, Florida, was displaying maturity beyond his years—poise, style, and crisp execution of maneuvers, combined with a physical awareness that exhibited none of the awkwardness of youth. It was obvious that this kid had the same indefinable "thing" that Tommy had at the same age, surfing these same waters. From the moment Kelly Slater kicked out of his first wave, I knew that I was watching a future world champion. Even then, I understood how it was all going to play out for him: the continued amateur success, a growing relationship with a renowned shaper, interest from the magazines, publicity, sponsors, a successful teenage professional debut, then off around the world chasing fame, fortune, and perfect waves. All this I knew because I had seen it happen before, from this very starting point, here on the Texas sand. Only this time it was all happening without me. Or so it seemed.

When finally graduating from Brooks Institute in 1983, I was faced with a big decision. Having made so many lifelong friends over the prior four years, as well as establishing myself as a legitimate surf photographer, I had every intention of basing myself in Santa Barbara while following the tour with my camera, hoping to see Tommy win his first world championship somewhere along the way. But shortly after graduation I was told that my father's cancer had taken a turn for the worse, and even though I had just begun living the life I'd always dreamed of, there really was no question about which direction I'd be heading. It was time to return home to Texas. Yet the transition from one path to another was so abrupt that, as time passed, I found myself wondering if the previous four years had ever happened at all, if everything I felt I'd been a part of—all the energy and innovation, fun and excitement, camaraderie and sense of common purpose—could really be reduced to just a few faded photos in old, dog-eared surf magazines.

In 1986, after Tommy won his first world title, I was able to make it to Santa Barbara for his victory party, celebrating along with the whole Channel Islands crew and all of Tommy's supporters at the greatest Merrick backyard barbeque ever. But for me it was as bittersweet as it was joyous, so strong was the feeling that even though I was among good friends, I was now watching all of this from the outside.

This feeling stuck with me right up until that day I sat on the beach at Padre Island, shooting photos of young Kelly Slater. Because it was then that I realized I wasn't watching something that was happening without me, but merely the next chapter of a story that, I was fortunate to have had a small role in actually help shape.

Thinking about the incredible time I'd spent in Santa Barbara, and of all the characters I'd shared it with—Al and Shaun, Sam and Matt, the Morris family, Davey and Kim, Dana and the Hammonds Kids, Jeanine and Terry, and, of course, Tommy—it was easy to see just how those years had helped mold this young champion I was now watching. From the Channel Islands surfboard he'd eventually ride, to the close relationship that would develop between him and Al Merrick, to the sandy footsteps of Tom Curren he'd follow in to a record eleven world championships and the more enduring title of "Greatest of All Time," Kelly's career would always reflect the influence of the era we helped define. As would the lives of the many young surfers, men and women, who'd follow, pursuing their dream of a surfing life.

Nineteen eighty to nineteen eighty-three in Santa Barbara truly was an amazing time in surf history, and I'm so grateful to have been a part of it all.

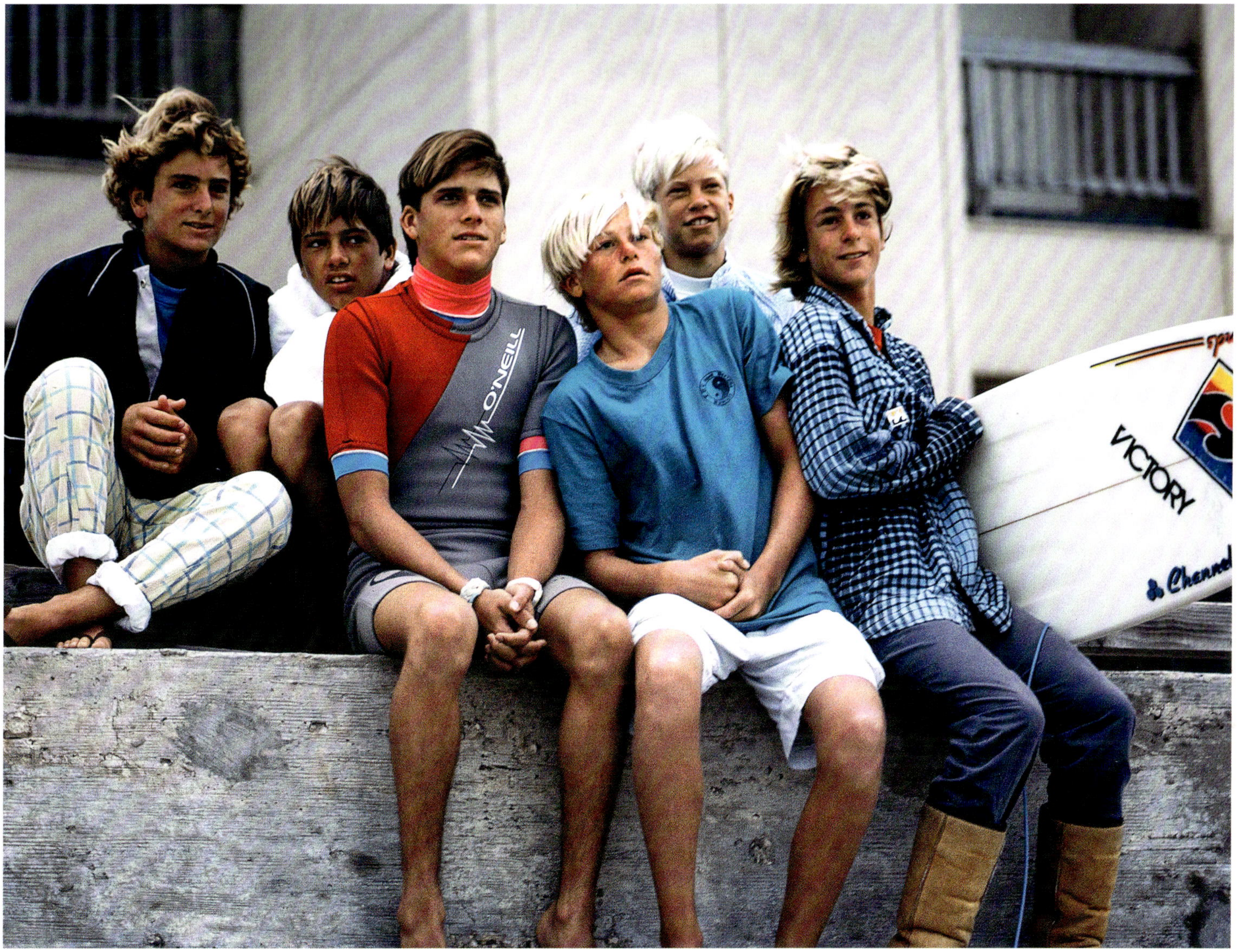

This page

Amateur competitive surfing's version of the frosh-soph team. *(Left to right)* Pete Rocky, Kelly Slater, Sean Slater, Strider Wasilewski, Chris Brown, and Jamie George at the 1987 US Surfing Championships (USSC) on North Padre Island, Texas.

Overleaf

Fourteen-year-old Kelly Slater at the 1987 USSC in Texas, showing off the abilities that eventually would win him that year's championships. *(Right)* Seen just eighteen months later, surfing his home break of Sebastian Inlet, Florida—taller, stronger, and now riding boards shaped by Al Merrick—Kelly showed similar form, with an even more powerful display of the prowess that would win him a record eleven world titles.

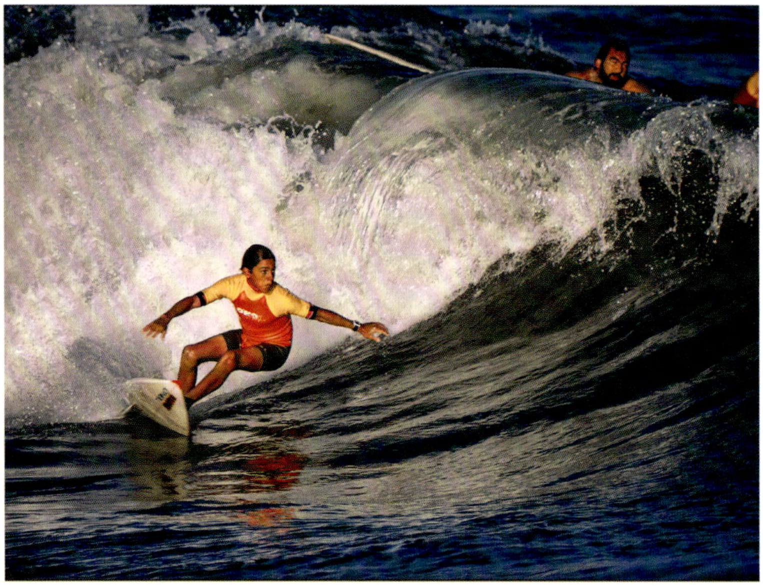

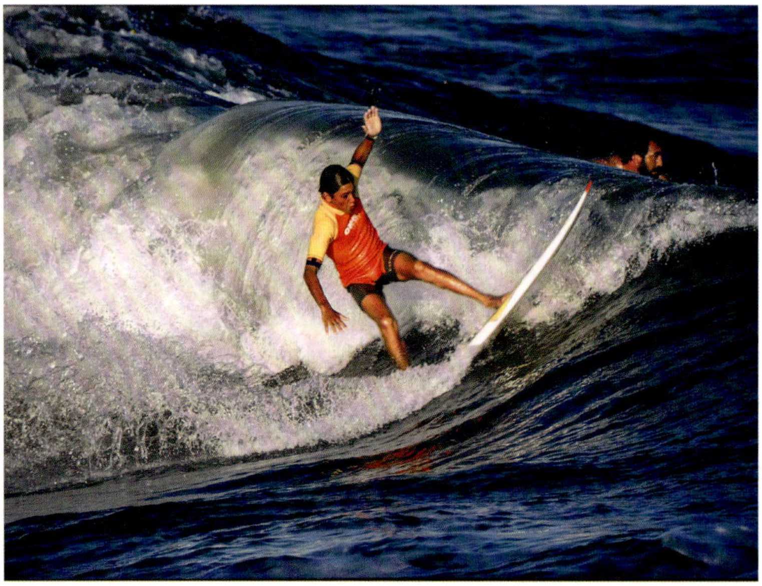

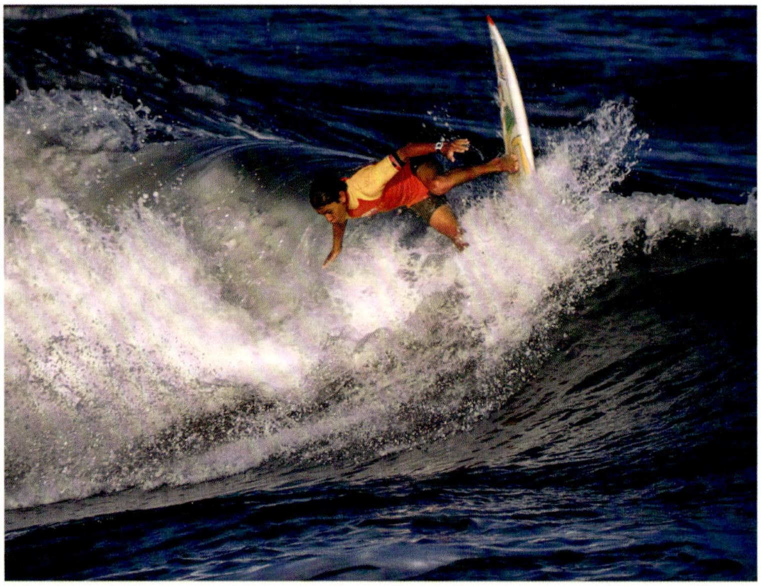

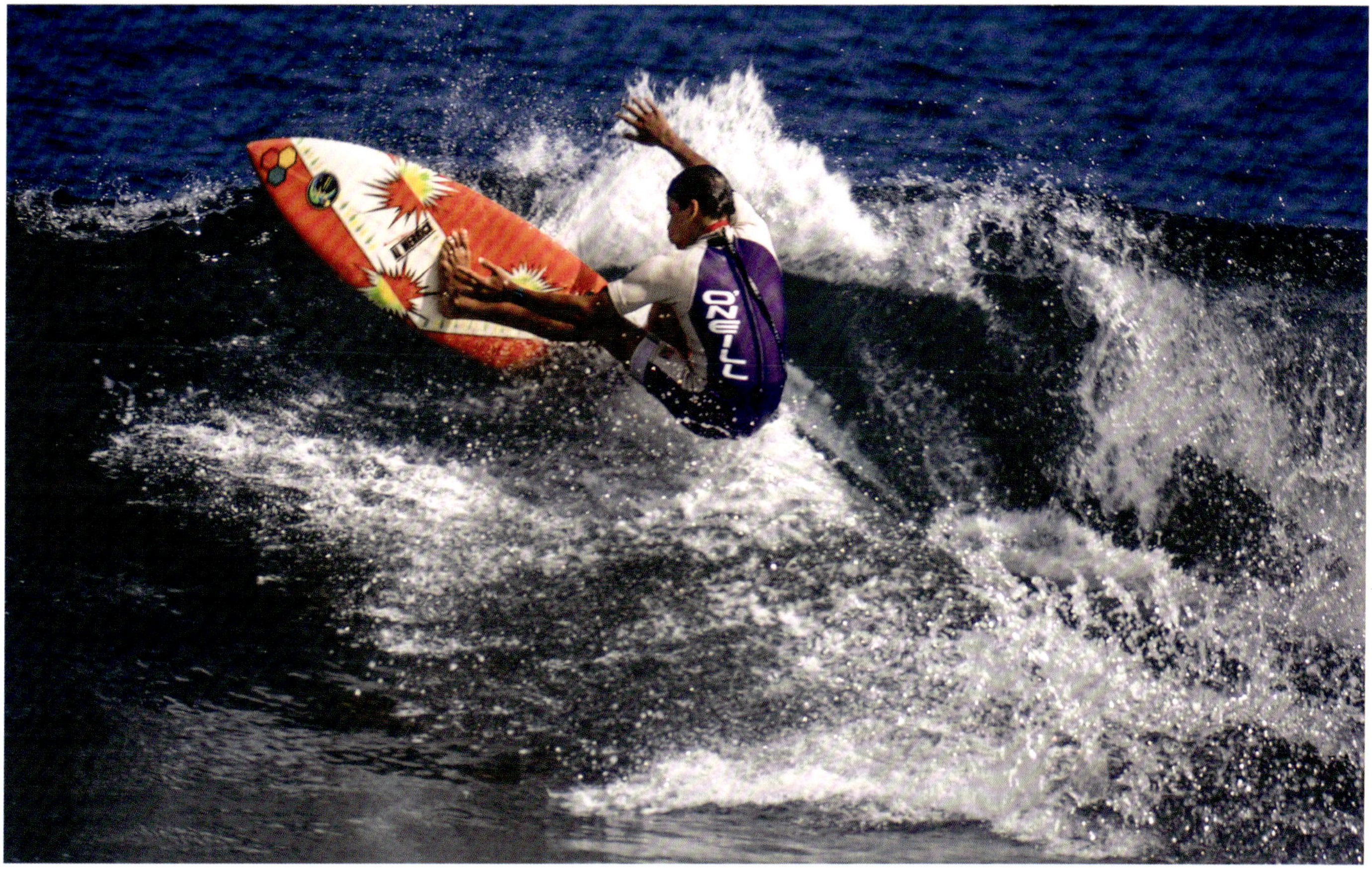
O'NEILL

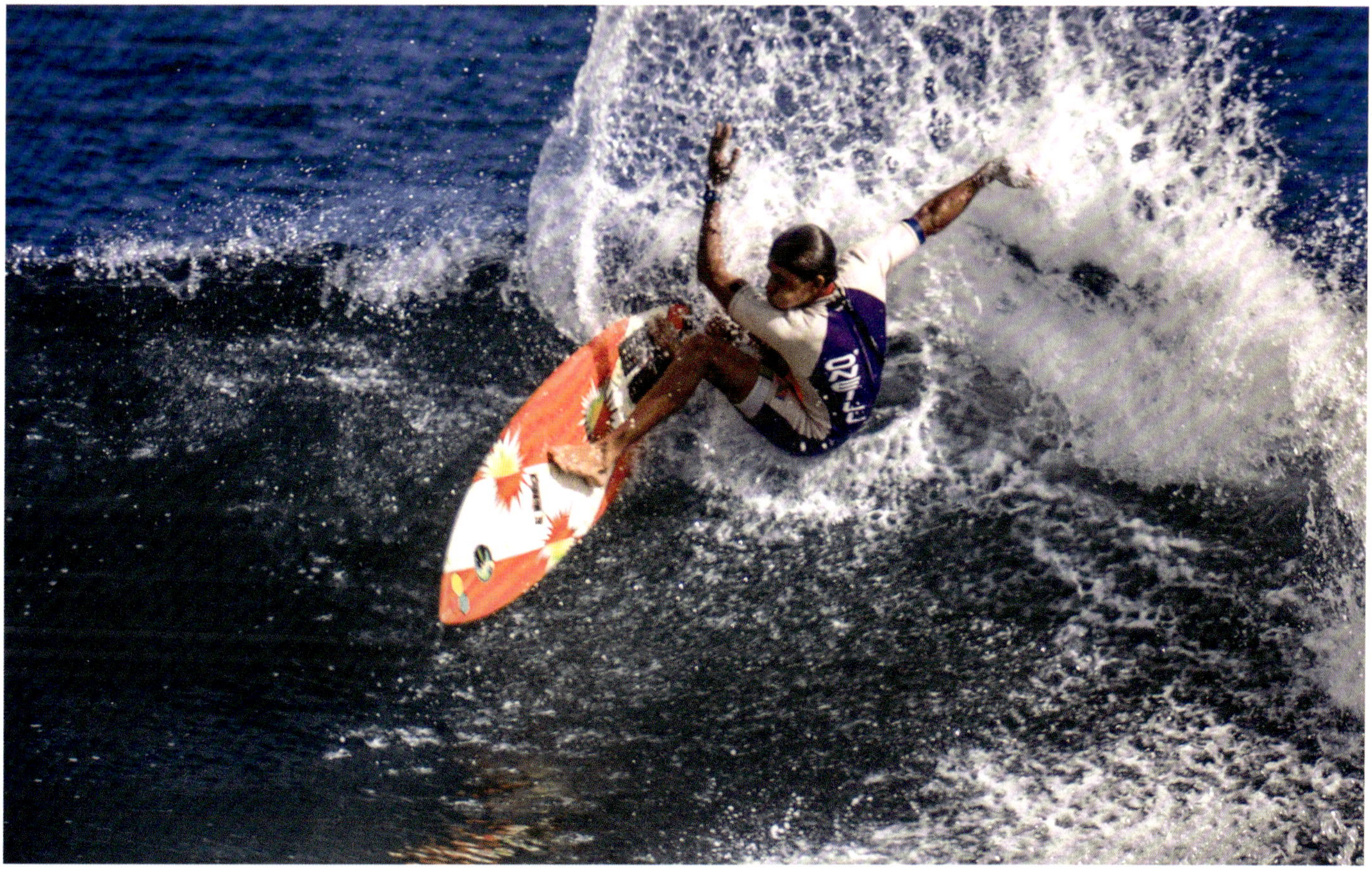
O'NEILL

Acknowledgments

To my wife, Minh Metyko, and my daughter, Melissa Metyko, for all their love and support through this project.

Special thanks to this project's brilliant creative team, for without their talent and patience it would not have been possible: Martynka Wawrzyniak, Sam George, Jamie Brisick, Jim Newitt, and Kim Stravers.

Grant Ellis, for his enduring skills, talent, and advice.

Paul Calderon, Robert Taylor, and Kerry Poole, for their support and digital services.

Scott Hulet, the Pezmans, and all at *The Surfer's Journal*, for their ongoing support and for allowing the use of some caption material previously appearing in *TSJ*.

The *Surfer* and *Surfing* magazines crew of the 1980s: Jeff Divine, Art Brewer (RIP), Larry "Flame" Moore (RIP), Jim Kempton, Paul Holmes, Dave Gilovich, Chris Carter, Steve Pezman, Bob Mignogna, and John Severson (RIP)—the inspiration to us all.

The Merrick family: Terry, Al, Britt, and Heidi.

The Curren family: Tommy, Makeira, Frank, and Pat; Jeanine, Joe, and Anna. Marie, Nathan, and Lee-Ann.

The Morris family: Sandra (RIP), Lee (RIP), Willy (RIP), Steve, Alexandra, Charlotte, and Jennifer Bass.

The Smith family: Theresa, Davey, Erin Nicole, and Brandon.

The Tomson brothers: Shaun and Paul.

The George brothers: Sam, Matt, Michael (RIP), and Greg.

The Gruetzmacher family: Kim (Mearig) and Brian.

The Robinson family: Teresa "Risa," Shane, Jason, and Kim (especially Kim, for being from Texas and a lifelong friend).

The McCorkle family: Linda, Mike, and Dana.

Steve Brisick, for insisting that I dive into the archives and share these images.

The crew at Channel Islands Surfboards: Britt Merrick, Scott "Ando" Anderson, Devon Howard, Jonathan Regehr, Sean Lesh, Scott Martinson, Nathaniel Curran, Mike Walter, Evan Gambetta, and everyone else through the years, for their ongoing support and friendship.

The crew at Rip Curl: James Taylor, P. J. Connell, Brandon Smith, and, last but not least, Jake Howard.

I would also like to thank all who have offered help, support, advice, or encouragement, or just shared some of the memories along the way:

Don Balch, Jim Banks, Anna Bissell, Steve Bissell, Dino Bortoli, Tyler Breuer, Chris Bruno, Bob Canaday, Allen Carrasco, Tony Corley, Mattson Culbert, Tim Culbert, Don Craig, Wyatt Daily, Ashtyn Douglas-Rosa, Steve Dwyer, Eric Eliel, Greg Elliott, Beth Fisher, Brent Flaaten, James Fulbright, Jamie George, Mike Goldsby, Chuck Graham, Jamie Graupner, Bob Haakenson, Soren Hansen, Steve Hanson, Lisa Harrington-Kleyweg, Darrell Hawkins, Derek Hoffmann, Greg Huglin, Brad Johnson, Matt Kechele, Chris Keet, Dennis Kiggins, Kevin Kinnear, Josh "Bagel" Klassman, Josh Klein, Wade Koniakowsky, David Lansdowne, Donn Leva, Pat Leva, Allen Lizza, Karen McKay, Steve Mendelson, Matt Mondragon, Matty Morgan, Chip Mortan, Dale Mortan, Tom Mortan, Guy Motil, Heather (Moorehead) Mozart, Deano Mueller, Mike Muir, Nathan Myers, Grayson Nance, Roger Nance, Jeff Novak, Gabriel Novoa, Cheyne O'Farrell, Frank Padon (RIP), Matt Padon, Shawn Parkin, Courtney Parks, Rosemary Parks, Kirk Pearson, Nia Peeples, Joel Plessala, Reggie Pooley, Kirk Putnam, David Pu'u, Simone Reddingius, Jimmy Redmon, Phil Regan, Ted Robinson, Pete Rocky, George Salvador, Sunday (Bissell) Rylander, John Schuyler, Solo Scott, Chris Shannon, Kelly Slater, Sean Slater, Andy Smalley, Tim Smalley, Sarah Aresco Smith, Brendon Thomas, Steven Tiller, Michael Townsend, Kevin Voegtlin, Mary Volz, Clay Wagner, John Watkins, Susan Weber, Matt Wessen, John Witzig, Lauran Yater, and Caroline Zimmermann.

A special acknowledgment to all who appear or are mentioned in these pages, but are no longer with us. They are sorely missed:

Jay Adams, Ben Aipa, Art Brewer, Chris Brown, Dave Brown, Pat Curren, Lee Ellis, Johnny Fain, Stu Fredericks, Annette Funicello, Mike "Mahay" Gabriele, Michael George, Montgomery "Buttons" Kaluhiokalani, Glen Kennedy, Joe Mickey, Larry "Flame" Moore, Lee Morris, Sandra Morris, Willy Morris, Stanley Novak, Michael Tomson, and Jeff White. May you all rest in peace.

The Brooks Institute of Photography, and all my fellow "Brookies."

All the great surf photographers, before and after, who have dared to point a camera at the surf and our lifestyle.

My college roommates in Santa Barbara, Martin and Raymond Pulverman, for not making too big of an issue of it when I raided the refrigerator.

And last, but not least, my deepest appreciation to my fellow lovers of coffee-table-style photo books: Charles Miers, Martynka Wawrzyniak, and all the talented individuals at Rizzoli Books.

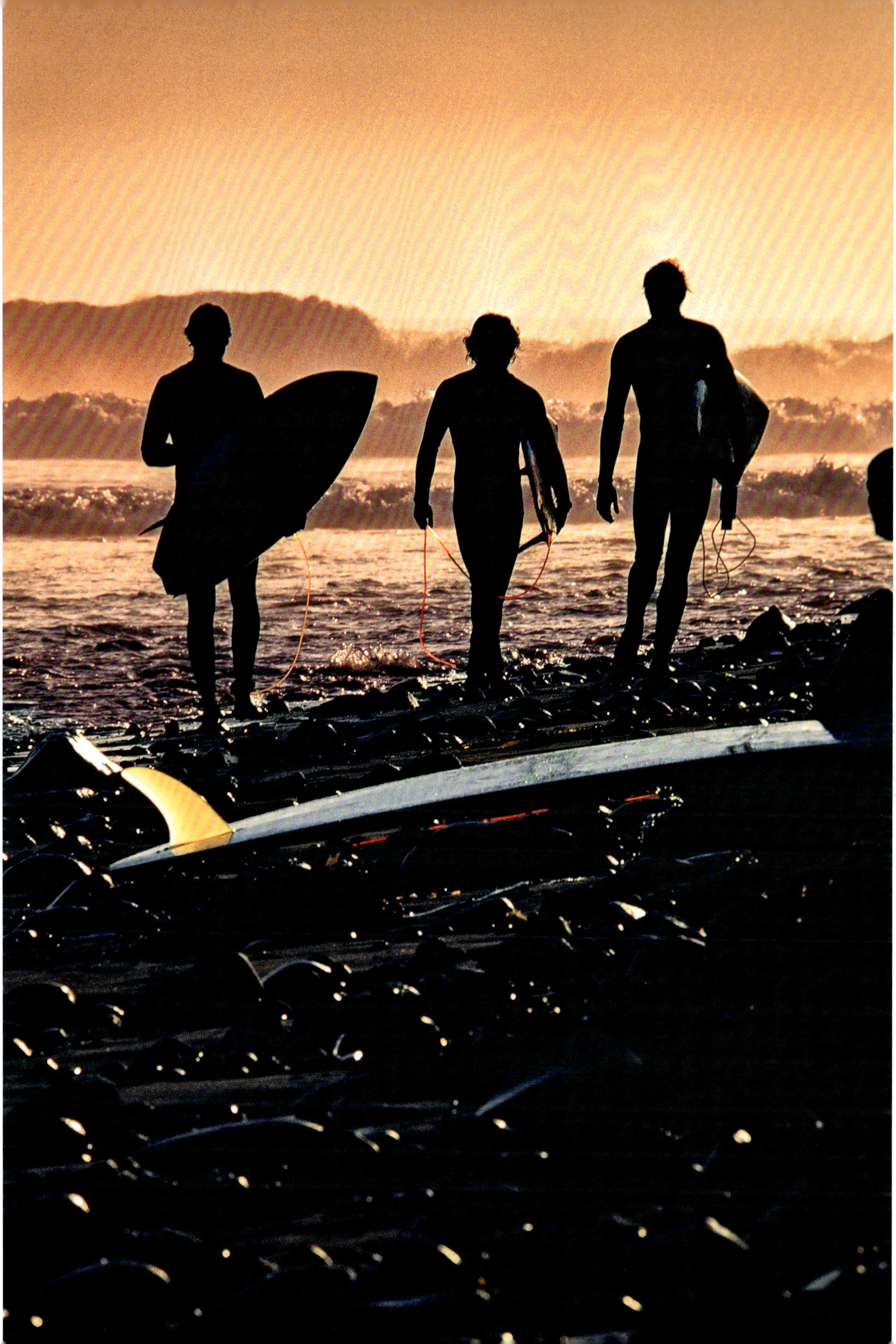

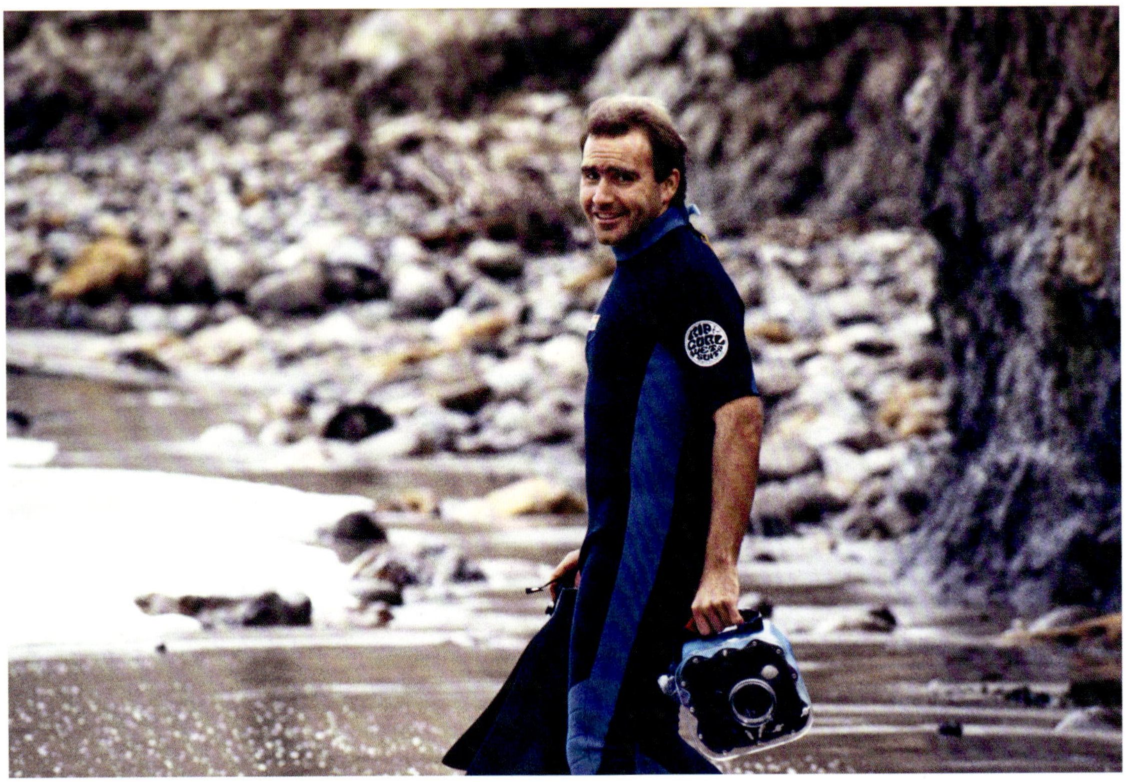

ALYO
5'10½"